HISTORICAL COMMENTARY ON THE AUGSBURG CONFESSION

HISTORICAL COMMENTARY ON THE AUGSBURG CONFESSION

WILHELM MAURER

Translated by H. George Anderson

FORTRESS PRESS   **PHILADELPHIA**

This translation is dedicated to
my wife, Jutta,
who helped at every stage
—H. George Anderson

Translated by H. George Anderson

Translated from the German *Historischer Kommentar zur Confessio Augustana.*
Band 1: *Einleitung und Ordnungsfragen,* Band 2: *Theologische und Ordnungs-*
fragen by Wilhelm Maurer, copyright © 1976 (Band 1), 1978 (Band 2),
Gütersloher Verlagshaus Gerd Mohn, Gütersloh, West Germany

Library of Congress Cataloging-in-Publication Data

Maurer, Wilhelm, 1900–
  Historical commentary on the Augsburg Confession.

  Translation of: Historischer Kommentar zur
Confessio Augustana.
  Includes index.
  1. Augsburg Confession. I. Title.
BX8069.M3513 1986   238'.41   86–45214
ISBN 0–8006–0781–3

8553C86   Printed in the United States of America   1–781

CONTENTS

Part 2
Theological Problems

ABBREVIATIONS OF SOURCES

A	Reworking of E by Melanchthon after March 27, 1530 (?); see pp. 17–19 below. Printed in Förstemann 1:68–84; Reu 79–91; Jacobs 75–86; and article by article in the apparatus of *BS* 83b–113 as "Torg."
A I	Copy by Chancellor Vogler of Ansbach from the German version of the CA (arts. 1–19), before June 16, 1530; see pp. 15 and 36 below. Noted in the apparatus for CA in *BS*.
B	Preliminary stage of Torg. Printed in Förstemann 1:84–87; Jacobs 86–88.
BC	Theodore G. Tappert, trans. and ed., *The Book of Concord* (Philadelphia: Fortress Press, 1959). Citations are printed with the page number followed by a period and then the section number; thus: 23.5.
BoA	Otto Clemen, ed., *Luthers Werke in Auswahl* (Berlin: Walter de Gruyter, vols. 1–4, 6th ed., 1966–68; vols. 5–8, 3d ed., 1962–66).
BS	*Die Bekenntnisschriften der evangelisch-lutherischen Kirche, Herausgegeben im Gedenkjahr der Augsburgischen Konfession 1930*, 4th rev. ed. (Göttingen: Vandenhoeck & Ruprecht, 1959). Citations from this work give the page number followed by a period and the line number on the page; thus: 34.9.
C	A broader and expanded preparatory work for the second part of the CA by Melanchthon, composed after May 2, 1530; see pp. 27–30 below. Printed in Förstemann 1:87–91; Jacobs 88–90; and in the apparatus of *BS* 120–24.
CA	Augsburg Confession (*Confessio Augustana*) submitted on June 25, 1530. Printed in *BS* 31–137; *BC* 23–96.
Conf. 28	Luther's personal confession of faith, printed as a supplement to *Confession Concerning Christ's Supper* (1528). See pp. 20–23 below. Printed in *WA* 26:499–509 (= *BoA* 3:507–15); *LW* 37:360–72.

CR	Karl Gottlieb Bretschneider and Heinrich Ernst Bindseil, eds., *Corpus Reformatorum, Philip Melanthonis opera quae supersunt omnia,* vols. 1–28 (Halle, later Braunschweig, 1834–60).
E	Series of articles by the Wittenberg theologians, a preliminary stage of the second part of the CA, apparently composed around March 15–16, 1530; see pp. 17–19 below. Printed in Förstemann 1:93–108; Jacobs 92–95.
Förstemann 1	Karl Eduard Förstemann, ed., *Urkundenbuch zu der Geschichte des Reichstages zu Augsburg im Jahre 1530,* vol. 1, *Von dem Ausgange des kaiserlichen Ausschreibens bis zu der Übergabe der Augsburgischen Confession* (Halle, 1833; reprinted, Osnabrück, 1966).
Fränk. Bek.	*Die Fränkischen Bekenntnisse: Ein Vorstufe der Augsburgischen Konfession.* Published by Landeskirchenrat der Evang.-Luth. Kirche in Bayern. Part 1, *Untersuchungen,* compiled by Wilhelm Ferdinand Schmidt; part 2, *Texte,* compiled by Karl Schornbaum (Munich, 1930).
Gussmann	Wilhelm Gussmann, ed., *Quellen und Forschungen zur Geschichte des Augsburgischen Glaubensbekenntnisses,* vol. 1, *Die Ratschläge der evangelischen Reichsstände zum Reichstag von Augsburg, 1530,* part 1, *Untersuchungen,* part 2, *Texte* (Leipzig and Berlin, 1911); vol. 2, *Johann Ecks 404 Artikel* . . . (Kassel, 1930).
H I	Hessian copy of A I; see p. 15 below and *BS* xvii.
Ja	Draft of the preface for the German CA, April 1530, now in the University Library at Jena; see pp. 40–42 below. Printed, among other places, in *BS* 35–39, and translated in Reu 91–95.
Jacobs	Henry Eyster Jacobs, *The Book of Concord,* 2 vols. (Philadelphia: General Council Pub. Board, 1908 [1883]). All citations are from vol. 2.
Kolde	Theodor Kolde, *Die älteste Redaktion der Augsburger Konfession* (Gütersloh, 1906).
LW	Jaroslav Pelikan and Helmut T. Lehman, eds., *Luther's Works,* 54 vols. (Philadelphia: Muhlenberg Press; St. Louis: Concordia Pub. House, 1955–).
Marb.	Marburg Articles, October 4, 1529; see pp. 9, 26–27 below. Printed in *WA* 30.3:160–71; *LW* 38:85–89; and article by article in the apparatus of *BS* 52–66.

Na
German translation of a preliminary stage of the CA, sent to Nürnberg on June 3, 1530; see pp. 13–14 below. Printed in Kolde; Reu 166–290; and article by article in the apparatus of *BS* 39–133.

Nb
First common formulation of the CA in German, sent to the Nürnberg Council on June 15, 1530; see p. 14 below. Printed in *Die Augsbergische Konfession in ihrer ersten Gestalt als gemeinsames Bekenntnis deutscher Reichsstände: Zum 25. Juni 1930 in Lichtdrucktafel hg. im Einverständnis mit der v. Scheurl'schen Familie* . . . , compiled by Johannes Ficker, Schriften der Gesellschaft der Freunde der Universität Halle-Wittenberg 2 (Halle, 1930). Cited in the apparatus of *BS* as N I.

Reu
Michael Reu, *The Augsburg Confession* (Chicago: Wartburg Pub. House, 1930). The book is in two parts, and all citations of this volume refer to the 2d part, "Collection of Sources."

Schwab.
Schwabach Articles (1529); see pp. 8–10, 23–26 below. Printed in *WA* 30.3: 86–91; Jacobs 69–74; Reu 40–44; and article by article in the apparatus of *BS*.

Sp.
German copy by Spalatin of the CA in process of composition from the period before June 15, 1530; see pp. 14, 35–36 below. Cited in the apparatus of *BS*.

StA
Robert Stupperich, ed., *Melanchthon Werke in Auswahl*, vols. 1– (Gütersloh, 1951–).

Torg.
Torgau Articles; see under A and E.

WA
D. Martin Luthers Werke: Kritische Gesamtausgabe, vols. 1– (Weimar, 1883–).

Wa
Fragment of a preface to the CA by Melanchthon, composed at the beginning of May 1530 (?); see pp. 41–44 below. Printed in Förstemann 1:109–12; *BS* 36–39; Reu 95–97.

WBr
Weimar Edition, Correspondence

PART ONE

INTRODUCTION AND QUESTIONS RELATING TO ORDERS

INTRODUCTION

1. COMMENTARY

This is a *historical* commentary on the Augsburg Confession. In its own way, it is a new undertaking that appears to jeopardize the rigid binding force of the Confession on later generations. The "Old Protestant" movement was not the only one that tried to use its expositions to reinforce the validity of the Confession and, by appealing to it, to defend and testify to evangelical truth. Recent expositors also—each from his own standpoint and historical situation—recognize this as their special task. That task remains.[1]

To fulfill that task today, however, requires historical consciousness. The living influence of the Lutheran confessions is indicated by the fact that they have entered the stream of tradition. Today their statements are heard in such a way that the voices of their earlier expositors and challengers chime in as well. That too must continue; those voices ought not be forgotten. They should not, however, drown out the original confession. The witness of Augsburg must ring out clearly; it must be heard in the way it was originally intended. And as every sound has its undertones and overtones, the voice of the Confession must also be heard in such a way that everything that provided it heights, depths, resonance, and body in 1530 still reechoes. Therefore historical commentary has its place along with the expositions of the dogmaticians.

Such a commentary faces a double task:

1. The present text of the CA must be understood in the context of its development. It had preliminary stages that, in the case of the first part (CA

---

1. The standard work of Edmund Schlink, *Theology of the Lutheran Confessions* (Philadelphia: Fortress Press, 1961), and the posthumous academic lectures by Friedrich Brunstäd, *Theologie der lutherischen Bekenntnisschriften* (Gütersloh, 1951), grew out of the experiences of the "church struggle." More historically oriented, noting the difference between Luther and Melanchthon, is Holsten Fagerberg, *A New Look at Lutheran Confessions (1529–1537)* (St. Louis: Concordia Pub. House, 1972). Cp. W. Maurer, "Erwägungen und Verhandlungen über die geistliche Jurisdiktion der Bischöfe vor und während die Augsburger Reichstags," *Zeitschrift der Savigny-Stiftung für Rechtsgeschichte* kanonist 55 (1969): 348–94; also in *Die Kirche und ihr Recht: Gesammelte Aufsätze zum evangelischen Kirchenrecht,* ed. Gerhard Müller and Gottfried Seebass, Jus ecclesiasticum 22 (Tübingen, 1976), 208–53.

1–21), represent independent confessions, each of which must be understood in the light of its own immediate purpose. In the early spring of 1528, Luther summarized his personal faith in the third part of his *Confession Concerning Christ's Supper.*[2] He wrote it expecting to die soon, and he claimed that it was a deliberate and irretractable statement. This personal confession forms the root of the CA. Also, as the articles were being worked out, Melanchthon occasionally referred to it.

At the beginning of July 1529, theologians and diplomats met in Wittenberg under the auspices of John the Steadfast to lay the groundwork for a Saxon confession. We do not have an official copy but have only differing drafts.[3]

In October 1529, the Saxons, together with the margrave of Ansbach and the Nürnberg Council, submitted it to the southern German cities at the conference in Schwabach, although that group did not adopt it. It thus bears the somewhat misleading name of the Schwabach Articles. From the earliest negotiations in the middle of May 1530, it was the direct precursor of the doctrinal articles of the CA.

It is less easy to recognize the predecessors of the second part of the CA (arts. 22–28). The so-called Torgau Articles were given that title in the early nineteenth century. They are actually a collection of opinions rendered by the Wittenberg theologians at various times and places on practical and juridical questions. Dating them properly and placing them in correct relation to the final versions of the CA pose special problems whose solutions are of decisive importance in the interpretation of individual articles.

2. A historical commentary, however, cannot be written on the basis of these predecessors alone. A word study, picking through individual phrases and sentences, cannot plumb the depths of confessional statements. Those statements are not the quick results of some facile theological formulation; they are the yield of a slow theological development. The cluster of theological problems addressed primarily in the first articles was, in substance, determined by Luther's personal Confession of 1528. But the theological content of those articles, as well as of the following seven "disputed articles," was hammered out in the writing of Luther and Melanchthon from as far back as 1522–23.[4]

Our task is not just to comb through these writings for set phrases that

2. *WA* 26:499–509; ET: *LW* 37:360–72.

3. W. Maurer, "Zur Entstehung und Textgeschichte der Schwabacher Artikel," in *Theologie in Geschichte und Kunst: Walter Elliger zum 65. Geburtstag* (Witten, 1968), 134–51; and idem, "Motive der evangelischen Bekenntnisbildung bei Luther und Melanchthon," in *Reformation und Humanismus: Robert Stupperich zum 65. Geburtstag* (Witten, 1969), 9–43.

4. This limit is set by Luther's return from the Wartburg and the consequent structuring of the evangelical territorial churches. For Melanchthon it began in 1524, when he started to collaborate on ecclesiastical structure.

either are used in the CA or remind us of terms that are. Our commentary has to pick up the underlying theological ideas as they developed in Reformation writings from Wittenberg in the 1520s. Often those by Melanchthon show different groupings and have a different stamp from Luther's. To the extent that our commentary brings out these differences, it offers a contribution to the often-discussed question of whether Luther or Melanchthon had a greater share in the CA. It is far more important, however, to compare the unfolding of basic Reformation ideas in their private writings with the brief formulations of the confessional articles and then to ask, To what extent do they reproduce those ideas adequately? What do the articles leave unsaid, either laid aside as less important or quite consciously suppressed? Does that curtail the thought, or introduce shifts in emphasis? Or are the articles intended as supplements that are to bring the Reformation content to full expression?

As our commentary draws upon the underlying Reformation ideas and gives them voice, they resound like deep undertones providing confessional statements with their full sonority. Admittedly, there is a danger of overinterpretation, but this danger is only taken seriously when one constantly reckons with the possibility that the articles contain abbreviations of substance. These may have been dictated by the situation in Augsburg, but they also may arise from theological differences among the Reformers. Both possibilities must be tested in the commentary, and possibly be presented side by side. Such a procedure demands a constantly critical participation from the reader, a continual readiness to draw new theological conclusions from the text of the Confession. Whoever does that will get good practice in Reformation theology. In the process you will be rewarded by perceiving at the center of this theology variety in unity and richness in economy. The Confession thus becomes a motivating force in your own theological thinking. You experience it—with all respect for its normative power, which lets you know you are one with the fathers—as an inexhaustibly bubbling spring from which you draw strength for your own perception and decision.

Thus this commentary should at the same time provide access to original Reformation theology. To that end it must at first limit itself to theological statements from the 1520s; they alone can supply the basis for the Confession of 1530. But the commentary is by no means obliged to remain within that boundary; the classical testimonies of the Reformation from the period following 1530, stamped especially by Melanchthon's influence, ought not remain unheard. At least the statements produced during the diet in contemporary writings and letters may, in fact must, be drawn upon. And ultimately the reaction the presentation of the Confession and the conclusion of the diet aroused in Wittenberg ought to be considered. Lecture notes and letters offer a rich resource for that task. And for the heart of the CA, Christology, and the doctrine of justification, Luther himself furnishes a probing and vivid commentary in his second series of lectures on Galatians in 1531. In that commentary he provides an ample substitute for the work on justification that he had planned at the Coburg during the diet; we will be able to use his preliminary studies for that work. These contributions from the post-CA period form the overtones our commentary must permit to resound in order to let the full voice of the Confession be heard.

2. FROM SPEYER TO THE CONVENING OF THE DIET AT AUGSBURG[5]

The Second Diet of Speyer had ended in an open breach; its final decree was issued on April 22. Two days earlier, on April 20, 1529, the evangelical princes and cities had adopted a protest against the repeal in practice of the articles on religion of 1526, and they had—in vain—tried to present their protest to King Ferdinand. On April 25, the "Protestants" agreed to send their protest, along with other actions concerning the diet, in the form of an appeal to the emperor.

The decree of the diet not only completely prohibited activity by the Anabaptists, resulting in their bloody annihilation in areas where it was enforced, it also demanded that the estates of the empire prosecute those who opposed the "blessed sacrament of the true body and blood of our Lord Jesus Christ" in doctrine and worship. Their preaching was forbidden; the medieval mass was to be fully restored.

The protest was published in almost identical form by Hesse and Saxony at the beginning of May—a procedure unusual in imperial law. The Protestants protected themselves against the decision of the diet in religious questions by saying that "in matters of God's honor and our soul's salvation every person must stand before God and give account for himself." They maintained that evangelical preaching was in accordance with Scripture and defended the legality of the reforms that had already been introduced, including the reform of the mass. They did not directly mention the conflict over the Lord's Supper but argued that open questions in regard to the sacraments must be dealt with by a future council. They thus took the Zwinglians under their wing and recognized their doctrine and practice of the Lord's Supper as Christian (in the eyes of imperial law).

Even before April 24, when the two parties that had opposed each other at the diet concluded a peace treaty that was brief in form and vague in content,

5. Hans von Schubert, *Bekenntnisbildung und Religionspolitik 1529–30* (1524–34) (Gotha, 1910); Ekkehart Fabian, *Die Abschiede der Bündnis- und Bekenntnistage protestierender Fürsten und Städte zwischen den Reichstagen zu Speyer und zu Augsburg 1529 bis 1530*, Schriften zur Kirchen- und Rechtsgeschichte 6 (Tübingen, 1960).

the protesting princes and the southern German imperial cities had, on April 22, agreed on a plan for a league. "With all faithful and good hearts" they would stand by one another in case of danger. That gave the isolated cities support and strengthened the financial and military capability of the princes. Nothing was said about the religious differences in the question of the Lord's Supper; on that point as well, Landgrave Philipp of Hesse was already trying to reach a theological settlement.[6]

Philipp Melanchthon, the leading representative of Wittenberg theology at Speyer, was hit hard by this political development. In the hope of a comprehensive agreement on the Lord's Supper based on traditional theology, and in order to include the humanist leaders from the traditionalist camp, he had long agreed with the Saxon chancellor Brueck to tolerate the Zwinglians and to work toward an "imperial conference on religion" in cooperation with the traditionalists. He must have become uneasy when he saw that this conciliatory position caused the disavowal of the traditionalists who favored compromise and led to the sharpening of the conditions of the diet's decree, but then, after the conclusion of the diet, when he learned of the impending negotiations for an alliance between the evangelical princes and the southern German cities, he really became desperate. The young landgrave from Hesse had already jeopardized the unity of the empire in the "Pack affair," and Melanchthon feared that he, along with his southern German friends, whose revolutionary ideas were known and widely feared in the empire, would precipitate a complete changeover in Christianity and in the empire. Melanchthon saw bloody consequences coming. He laid the responsibility for this upon himself, his yielding and his willingness to compromise. Pricked by his conscience, he turned against the Zwinglian doctrine of the Lord's Supper with a vengeance. With astonishing energy and drive he tried at once to alarm not only Prince John Frederick and his father, Elector John the Steadfast, but also his Nürnberg friends—Joachim Camerarius, Lazarus Spengler, and Hieronymus Baumgartner—against the planned league.

In Saxony, Melanchthon, supported by Chancellor Brueck, soon had his way. By May 19 the elector approved the plan for an imperial conference on religion and had his emissary sound out the Nürnbergers. Luther also joined Melanchthon and on May 22 advised the elector against agreeing to the landgrave's plans for a league, adducing a list of religious and political reasons against it. The two Wittenberg scholars found allies in the free imperial city of Nürnberg and its town clerk, Lazarus Spengler. Although they officially held back in order not to lose contact with Strassburg, the Nürnbergers were

6. Documents in *Deutsche Reichstagsakten,* Jüngere Reihe 7.1, 2 (Stuttgart, 1935; new ed., Göttingen, 1963), appendixes no. 148 (decree of the diet), no. 143 (protest), no. 152 (agreement between evangelical princes and the cities of Strassburg, Nürnberg, and Ulm).

opposed to any exclusively Protestant league and even backed off from the plan for a conference on religion.

According to an agreement made in Speyer, a meeting was planned for Rodach near Coburg on June 6, at which time the league was to be formed. That did not happen. Instead the negotiations broke up over a proposal made by Spengler that the Hessians strongly opposed—particularly on the question of resistance to the emperor. The continuation of the negotiations was first postponed until August 24 in Schwabach but then delayed at the request of Saxony until October 16. It was already clear in Rodach that the landgrave's plans were not going to be carried out quickly. That became even more evident on July 7–8 in Saalfeld, when the diplomats had to leave emptyhanded because the princes did not appear and thus disavowed the negotiations for a league.

In the course of July—secretly and in a way the details of which are no longer known—a decisive process took place; what would later be called the Schwabach Articles came into being. Their purpose was to lay down the theological conditions that the Saxons considered essential for the acceptance of an evangelical league. The Zwinglians were excluded, and the southern German cities were to be forced to an ecclesiastical and theological capitulation. The theological and political foundations for this procedure were certainly laid at the beginning of July in Wittenberg; the elector resided in the city until the eighth of that month. Its theological foundation was formed by the personal confession Luther had attached as the third part of his work *Confession Concerning Christ's Supper* in 1528.[7] Perhaps Melanchthon also made a contribution with his now lost *Enchiridion dogmatum christianorum*. It is not clear whether the articles received their final form at that time or whether the text developed still further. In any case, by the first of August, Luther already considered them normative for Saxon politics dealing with the league. The first decisive step on the road of evangelical confession making had been taken.

At the same time, the conflict over the Lord's Supper once again came into the open. Division among the evangelical estates seemed unavoidable. After the collapse of the Saalfeld negotiations, the imperial cities in southwest Germany, under the leadership of Ulm and Memmingen and through the intervention of Constance, turned to Zurich and Bern for protection; Strassburg stood isolated between the two fronts. Melanchthon announced a polemical work against Oecolampadius and Zwingli in which he would prove by reference to the church fathers that both men had departed from the common Christian tradition.

7. *WA* 26:499–509; *LW* 37:360–72.

The fact that his *Sententiae veterum aliquot scriptorum de coena Domini* came out in February 1530[8] in substantially milder form than could have been expected originally owes to the Marburg Colloquy (October 1–3, 1529). Despite all opposition, the landgrave successfully used diplomatic channels to bring the leading theologians of Protestantism to the negotiating table. Saxon diplomacy pursued a double course: on the one hand, it did not want to force Landgrave Philipp completely into the opposite camp; on the other hand, it did not want to encourage his plans for a league. Once the Schwabach Articles were available, this political position gained a theological basis. After half promising to attend in June, Luther and Melanchthon accepted the invitation to Marburg on July 8. The fact that this date corresponds to the time when the Schwabach Articles were being composed gives a clue to the situation: secure theologically against the entry of the Zwinglians into the defensive league, it was no problem to participate in unity negotiations. The results of the colloquy proved to be greater than the prospect. Of course the question of the Lord's Supper ended in only a half-compromise; the fifteenth of the Marburg Articles brought no agreement on the decisive question of the real bodily presence. But understandings were reached on the remaining fourteen points and many previous suspicions of both sides were thereby firmly laid to rest. Finally, it was agreed that "each side, insofar as each one's conscience will allow, will show Christian love to the other." These agreements became presuppositions that would later prove basic to the work at Augsburg.

Admittedly, the disunity continued a while longer. While the Marburg negotiations were still in progress, Elector John of Saxony and Margrave George of Brandenburg-Ansbach met together at the Conference of Schleiz (October 3–7); the date prevented Landgrave Philipp from taking part. Against the wishes of Hesse and by reference to the Schwabach Articles, the Zwinglians were excluded as "unbelieving and subject to the wrath of God." Those who would not clearly join the other league members in confessing the "principal articles of Christendom" could not be accepted into the league. Similar instructions were given to the princes' emissaries to the coming meeting at Schwabach. The representatives of the cities in southern Germany were to face a solid front on this point; Nürnberg, for tactical reasons only, maintained connections with them.

Thus what was bound to happen at the Schwabach conference (October 16–19) did happen; Strassburg and Ulm rejected the Schwabach Articles and their representatives returned home disappointed. Nürnberg, though in theological conformity with the strict Lutherans, backed off from all alliances, as

8. *CR* 23:727ff.; cp. *CR* 2:18.

Ansbach also finally did. The Schwabach Articles had not achieved their purpose of becoming the foundation for a league; no league was formed. No concerted action against the emperor was possible. He had not given a hearing to the legation appointed to present the appeal in Speyer; in fact, he had arrested some of its members. The purpose of a meeting at Schmalkald (November 28–December 4) was to take a position on this breach of imperial law, but it broke up over the "discord" on the Lord's Supper question; only those who were "of one mind in faith and sacraments" were welcome to attend the negotiations set for Nürnberg on January 6, 1530. Chancellor Brueck was justified in claiming that he had "snuffed out" the landgrave's plans for a league. The question was only whether or not a political alliance was given up for good and whether or not the Schwabach Articles, as they stood, could supply the theological basis for such an alliance. The course of the coming diet at Augsburg answered both questions with a no.

3. PREPARING TO GIVE ACCOUNT
BEFORE THE EMPEROR

Under date of January 21, 1530, Charles V summoned a diet to meet in Augsburg on April 8. At the time, Charles was in Bologna, where he was to receive the imperial crown from Pope Clement VII on February 24. Since the end of 1529 there had been hopes and fears that His Imperial Majesty would step in, suppress the evangelical faith, and abolish the reforms accomplished by the visitations. For Luther and his colleagues, concern for doctrine stood uppermost; they feared for the free preaching of the faith. To the politicians, legal and administrative problems growing out of the reorganization of worship predominated. Despite these differing emphases, questions of doctrine and polity were naturally bound tightly together; it took a considerable time until they could be properly related to one another in the two parts of the Augustana (CA 1–21, 22–28).

The imperial summons designated the chief task of the coming diet to be, in the face of the Turkish threat, "that the holy empire of the German nation might once again be brought into unity." Overcoming the religious division was seen as a means to this end, on the presupposition that a common foundation of faith already existed. Thus the expectation that the emperor proclaimed in his summons seemed justified: "As we all live and battle under one Christ, so all [might] live in one fellowship, church, and unity."

Elector John received the imperial summons on March 11. Preparations for the trip to the diet started immediately. Chancellor Brueck advised that the reform measures previously taken by the government be justified on theological grounds ("methodically brought together in writing with a thorough defense from divine Scripture") and that this document be presented to the emperor for a decision. Accordingly on March 14 the Wittenberg scholars (Luther, Jonas, Bugenhagen, and Melanchthon) got orders from the elector to compose such an opinion and have it ready to present as the basis for discussion at the court at Torgau as soon as March 20. Even though the Wittenbergers had laboriously produced a first draft as early as March 15–16, the discussions at Torgau did not take place before the twenty-seventh. Only Melanchthon represented Wittenberg there. The court left Torgau on April 4, stayed in Weimar from the eighth to the twelfth, and entered Coburg, the southernmost city in Saxony, on April 16, the day before Easter. There was ample opportunity for thorough consultation en route and it continued during the elector's stay in Coburg from April 16 to the morning of the twenty-fourth. They arrived at Augsburg on May 2.

We are not able to establish precisely which opinions and outlines were formulated during this time, principally by Melanchthon. It is still not completely clear which documents belong to the Torgau Articles—a later label—that were supposed to be in the "third red metal-bound chest" in the electoral chancery wagon. It is even more dubious whether there ever was a clearly defined group of documents by a specific time rather than individual opinions differing according to author, place, and purpose, which were presented from time to time. It seems most likely to us that the preliminary material for the "disputed articles," the second part of the CA, was still being put together during the first weeks in Augsburg. At this point we must be content to recount the particular events that occurred in Augsburg from the beginning of May until the presentation of the CA on June 25.[9]

Melanchthon immediately began reworking the materials available to him. Just after his arrival in Augsburg he ran across Eck's challenge to a disputation. The old enemy of the Wittenbergers had gathered long lists of heretical quotations from their works, mixed them with radical expressions from Luther's opponents on the left, and presented the whole collection of 404 articles to the emperor in order to obtain a condemnation of the Lutherans from him. At various points we will identify traces of Melanchthon's coming to grips with these sometimes trivial, but sometimes dangerously distorted, attacks.

Melanchthon hoped to have a first draft ready by May 4 in order to let Luther see it. It took a week longer, and the elector had it sent to Luther on May 11, authorizing him to continue the editing process and to make any additions or deletions. In this form the final document was to be presented to the emperor upon his arrival in Augsburg, which was expected very soon. In

9. For details, see below, pp. 16ff.

his accompanying letter, bearing the same date, Melanchthon conceded the same authority to Luther and explained the motivation of the full draft.[10]

Luther sent the material back to the elector by May 15, saying he had "read over" the "apology." His judgment was both positive and negative: "[It] pleases me very much; I know nothing to improve or change in it, nor would this be appropriate, since I cannot step so softly and quietly." He thus withdrew himself from the task the elector had laid upon him and put the responsibility on Melanchthon, adding the prayerful wish for the "apology," "May Christ our Lord help it to bear much and great fruit, as we hope and pray. Amen."[11]

Both the positive and the negative were meant seriously; this seriousness weighed upon Melanchthon and influenced the confession he authored. Its dependence and distance in relation to Luther must be evaluated with equal seriousness.

These discussions of a newly composed text were interrupted by an episode centering on the Schwabach Articles, which had been written nine months earlier and had been held more or less secret. As a sign of his religious integrity and political loyalty, the elector had sent the text to the emperor at Innsbruck. His courier, the Saxon marshal and councilor Hans von Dolzig, together with two imperial courtiers, Counts Wilhelm of Nassau and Wilhelm of Neuenahr, reached Innsbruck on the elector's special mission on April 30; four days later the emperor arrived. On May 8 they saw to it that the Schwabach Articles came into the emperor's hands, but the Latin translation was poor. At the instigation of the papal legates the emperor answered with an aloofness that amounted to a refusal—a rejection of the elector's mediating efforts that was intensified by communicating through the emissaries that evangelical preaching in Augsburg was forbidden.

The proclamation of this ban on preaching was already known to the elector and Melanchthon when they sent the draft of the Confession to Luther on May 11. Word of the rejection of the Schwabach Articles must have spread through the imperial retinue at Augsburg between May 13 and 15. The effect of both events was shattering. The elector proposed withdrawing to the Coburg in his own territory. His political and theological advisers were certain that the emperor would not handle the religious question as a neutral judge but as a Catholic Christian who was obligated by his high office to defend the Catholic faith. The point of the Schwabach Articles was to testify that the Saxons held to the same faith. The necessity of this testimony, it now seemed, was even more urgent; it could not be met by withdrawing

10. *WBr* 5:nos. 1564, 1565. Melanchthon's letter is in Reu 122*. Hereafter these references to Reu will omit the asterisk.

11. *WBr* 5:no. 1568; *LW* 49:297–98.

those articles—that would be surrender—but could be met only by improving them. Merely giving reasons and defending the measures taken during the visitations would not do in this situation. The development of the Confession up to this point, based on the Torgau Articles, did not probe deeply enough into the theological questions.

Thus an important turning point occurred during mid-May in the work on the Confession in Augsburg. As late as the twenty-second of May, the elector had told Luther that his approval of Melanchthon's draft would permit presenting it to the emperor without further attention. That expectation was illusory. Melanchthon was already expanding and improving the first version of the Confession. He wrote about this to Luther on the same day, May 22, that the elector had written.[12]

Melanchthon began with changes relating to the second half of the articles now before him. He completely rewrote CA 27, less briefly than before. Then he tackled CA 28. In both cases he was uncertain whether Luther would approve the theological bases for his arguments. If only Luther had expressed himself explicitly on these matters in his letter of May 15! The adaptation of these practical articles to the constantly changing situation would have gone easier and faster. Among these changes was the arrival of Landgrave Philipp in Augsburg on May 12, his reconciliation with Saxony, and his anticipated signature of the draft of the Confession. Melanchthon wanted that to happen and hoped that the prince was willing. He did not reckon with a new formulation of the doctrine of the Lord's Supper. A revision of the Schwabach Articles had not yet occurred to him on May 22.

Nevertheless, Melanchthon and his co-workers must have tackled this job with energy during the last third of May. They met daily—according to the report of the Nürnberg delegates on May 28—in order to change and improve "their advice in matters of faith . . . in order to state them in such a way that one could not avoid them but would have to listen."[13] The amendments were also aimed at making the "Catholic" character of the evangelical statements of faith unmistakably clear to adherents of the old religion and to the emperor. The translation of the theological concepts into Latin helped serve this end. It is understandable that the politicians had a voice in these matters, since they had played a decisive role in the composition of the Schwabach Articles and in their use up to this point. On Tuesday, March 31, the work was so far along that the Nürnberg delegates could write out a nearly complete copy of the Latin text. The copy was sent to Nürnberg on the third of June. The next day the text was being reproduced there for the "religious scholars"—with a strong prohibition against its dissemination—

---

12. *WBr* 5:no. 1576. 27ff., 12:no. 4237. 7ff. (*WBr* 5:no. 1576a = *WBr* 12:no. 4237).
13. *CR* 2:71.

and on June 10, Hieronymous Baumgartner, a student and friend of Melanchthon's, was commissioned to put it into "accurately translated German" for the city council. The text of this translation is available to us (Na).[14]

A milestone in the formative history of the CA is the arrival of the emperor on June 15. By his command to take active part in the Corpus Christi procession on the following day, and by the strictly enforced ban on preaching, the ruler forced the evangelical estates into a unified defensive front. The Confession thereby lost its specifically Saxon character; binding on all the Protestants and maintaining the Lutheran doctrine of the Lord's Supper, yet also open to the southern Germans, the Confession now achieved even in phraseology a general evangelical ("catholic") tone.

On June 15, right before the arrival of the emperor that afternoon, the Nürnberg delegates sent a copy of this form of the "Saxon Position in the Matter of Faith" to their town council (Nb). By shedding specifically Saxon terminology they created the hope, even before the threatening events associated with the arrival of the emperor, of a concerted action including at least their city, Saxony, and the margravate, and probably—in their hearts—Hesse as well. The "Position" was immediately translated out of Latin into German, which was the official chancellery language. The text the delegates sent in fact corresponds almost exactly with the wording of the later German version of the CA—at least in the articles that had been completed by that time.[15]

The Protestant unification hoped for by the Nürnbergers on June 15 and forced by the emperor through his hard line on the same day had thus been anticipated and prepared for earlier in the Saxon camp. The landgrave of Hesse had made efforts to take part in work on the Confession as early as May 22, possibly to gain some influence on its formulation. That helps to explain the reserve with which Elector John met the young prince. Even the Nürnbergers, those persistent seekers of an alliance, did not gain a hand in the work until June 18, shortly after the margrave of Anspach. And finally on the evening of June 21, the day that the diet formally opened, the elector invited Ansbach, Hesse, and Lüneburg, together with Nürnberg, to the common consultation in which the theologians and lawyers were to bring the text of the Augustana to completion.

Only three days were dedicated to the task; there was no longer any possibility for basic changes. The Latin text still remained fluid; the textual history of the German version is better documented through the copies prepared for the participating chancelleries: a Saxon copy from before June 15 by Spalatin (Sp.), an Ansbach manuscript before June 16 prepared by its

14. Printed in Kolde; also in Reu, no. 37, 166ff.
15. *CR* 2:105–6; Reu, no. 38, 166ff. For the prehistory and text of Nb, see the index of sources at the front of this volume.

chancellor Georg Vogler (A I), and a Hessian manuscript of about the same
time (H I). Melanchthon himself not only shared in copying out the original
Latin text, he was its chief and most persistent editor.[16]

The solemn presentation of the Confession to the emperor was originally
planned for June 24. At the request of the evangelical estates, however, the
diet convened on the afternoon of June 25 in a special session. The Saxon
chancellor Christian Beyer read the German text. The Latin text, nevertheless, has a value of its own. Both versions are the result of long theological
reflection and numerous preparatory documents. One must begin by considering, analyzing, and evaluating those earlier documents according to their
theological content; only then, against that background, do the official forms
of the final text stand out with their proper and particular value.

4. PRELIMINARY STAGES OF
THE "DISPUTED ARTICLES" (CA 22–28)

The ecclesiastical and legal situation in the empire initially pushed practical questions relating to the reform of worship and church law to the fore
during the composition of the CA. By immense effort and never without the
help of the temporal arm, the Roman church had succeeded in unifying the
worship practices of the Christian West; only reluctantly and briefly during
the Council of Basel did it make concessions to the Hussites in the *Prague
Compactata* (1437). Uniform worship practices together with the religious
and moral principles of education derived from them undergirded the religious and cultural nexus among western nations. In addition, the princely
position of bishops within the empire and their diocesan control—which also
included temporal territories—formed the basis for the structure of the
empire, for the status of the imperial office, and for the balance of political
relationships.

The visitations, carried out most thoroughly in Saxony and Hesse and only
partially in other evangelical territories and cities, had abolished the existing
church structure. The temporal authorities, able to appeal to late medieval
precedents, took over functions that belonged to the bishops' jurisdiction.
The appointment of clergy was shunted away from religious authorities. Even
where traditional patronage rights continued to be exercised, the territorial
powers had the decisive word. They provided for examination and supervision of the pastors and removed the incompetent; the rule of celibacy was
lifted; cloisters and foundations were secularized. In cases where the previous

16. Cp. Heinrich Bornkamm, *Der authentische lateinische Text der Confessio Augustana (1530)*,
Sitzungsberichte der Heidelberger Akademie der Wissenschaften—philosophisch-historische
Klasse 1956/2 (Heidelberg, 1956).

occupants had not already "run off," they were forced to abandon their former common life, given a cash settlement, or if they were too old to find a new occupation, gathered at a central place and provided with care. The cloisters' endowments were applied to local or general religious, social, and cultural functions; in part they were also used for the "common good" of the territory. Generally the Lord's Supper was celebrated in both kinds in the congregations; most of the special votive masses were discontinued, the Sunday mass introduced, and the daily mass replaced by prayer services and religious exercises related to schools. To outsiders it must have seemed that the former church life was completely disrupted. What was new they did not see nor understand nor acknowledge.

The summons issued on January 21, 1530, by Emperor Charles V convoking an imperial diet in Augsburg for April 8 had this whole situation in view, although it did not go into details. It emphasized the Turkish threat and called for unity among the imperial states to avert it. It was clearly stated that religious dissension endangered the empire and that the pope had to cooperate in the "establishment of this unity"; therefore, questions of church law were going to be considered. The use of force was to be avoided, however. Together with the imperial estates, pope and emperor were to do "what was right and honorable"; to that end, "everyone's opinion and viewpoint" were to be "heard and weighed carefully." Thus the emperor implied that, although each side indeed interpreted it differently, the "one Christian truth" would be commonly acknowledged. He urged the estates "as we all live and battle under one Christ, to live therefore in one fellowship, church, and unity."

The base lines of Christian responsibility were thereby laid down for the evangelical estates. They had to account for the newly introduced ordinances and demonstrate their conformity with the common Christian witness. In so doing they had to preserve the unity of Christendom while rejecting uniformity in rites and polity. As a whole, the summons to the diet seemed, especially to the Saxons, to open favorable prospects for future negotiations on religion.

After the imperial summons arrived at the Saxon court in Torgau on March 11, preparations for the journey began at once. The time to April 8 was short, the problems many. Chancellor Brueck did not expect the estates to permit theological debate in their sessions. He therefore advised that a theological brief be prepared. The paper should justify the measures involved "with thorough proof from divine Scripture." On the assumption that the coming diet would be held "instead of a council or national assembly," the elector asked the Wittenberg reformers (Luther, Jonas, Bugenhagen, and Melanchthon) on March 14 to express themselves in the light of the imperial summons "on all the articles concerning which there is declared dissension, both in faith and also in other external church usages and ceremonies."[17]

The consultation among the Wittenbergers took place on March 15–16; its results are available in manuscript E of the so-called Torgau Articles.[18] Here, in the form of an opinion for the elector, are nine points treated in approximately the same order as they would appear in the later "disputed articles": articles 1–3 correspond to CA 22–24; article 4 selects the question of episcopal power of ordination from among the legal issues later assembled in CA 28; articles 6 to 8 are reflected in CA 27 (monastic vows), CA 25 (confession), and CA 26 (the distinction of foods). Article 5 (conditional recognition of the papacy as long as it permits preaching of the gospel) is not covered in the CA, nor is article 9. The latter approves with cutting sharpness the condemnation of the sacramentarians; the elector agreed with a decision of the diet along these lines—in contrast to Speyer in 1529—and remained aloof from any theological and political concessions to them. Thus we see that Saxony maintained the course it had taken since the summer of 1529, and in fact reconfirmed it not only in regard to the empire but also over against Rome. All of this occurred in complete agreement with the Wittenberg theologians without political pressure, in Luther's presence and with his blessing.

On March 21 the elector again summoned his theologians to Torgau to present their draft and to advise him on questions that had arisen in the meantime. Only Melanchthon went, arriving at the court on March 27 or perhaps slightly sooner. There, or more likely during April, after his return or on the trip to Augsburg, he composed a revision of the original opinion (Torg. A). To the degree that it takes the wishes of the politicians into account, it allows us to trace the further course of the official preparations.

At the beginning of A, Melanchthon added a longer introduction, which he intended to expand still further,[19] and in which he emphasized the peaceable and conservative character of the Saxon reformation. As later in the transitional comments between the first and second parts of the CA (see below, p. 45), the orthodoxy of evangelical doctrine is asserted to be indisputable. Equally Christian, therefore, are the innovations in worship growing out of it. They lack only conciliar approval. Is Saxony here picking up again—as later

17. *WBr* 5:no. 1538. The linking of faith and ceremonies here ought not be understood as a division parallel to the CA's two parts. The elector was looking for a theological basis for the innovations that had been carried out in worship and law.

18. The name, already in use by earlier historians, was applied by Karl Eduard Förstemann to six documents he had found and labeled A through F. See Förstemann 1:66ff.; ET: Jacobs 75–98. Reu translates A on pp. 79–91. For the remainder of this section, cp. Gussman 1.1:90ff., esp. 99; and W. Maurer, "Die Entstehung und erste Auswirkung von Artikel 28 der Confessio Augustana," in *Volk Gottes: Festgabe für Josef Höfer* (Freiburg/Basel/Vienna, 1967), 361–94.

19. Cp. his marginal note: "To this effect it is well to begin with a long and rhetorical preface" (Förstemann 1:68; Reu 80).

occurred at the urging of the landgrave—the appeal to a coming council? Or did the elector, who, contrary to Luther, had seen the coming diet as the substitute for a council or national assembly, expect that the diet would approve the Saxon reforms with the authority of a council?

In any case, Melanchthon's draft established unequivocally that the division in the empire that the imperial summons had deplored had been precipitated "principally by certain abuses that were introduced by human doctrines and ordinances." Theological reflection comes more strongly to the fore here than in draft E, which had limited itself more to the enumeration of abuses and their correction. Melanchthon added a completely new formulation of article 1, which dealt with human doctrine and ordinances. By reference to the Saxon visitation he established that the new practices did not conflict with the gospel, that they should be maintained for the sake of peace, and that they were kept with greater devotion and seriousness than the opponents demonstrated. Scripture, tradition, and canon law were then cited to prove that many ecclesiastical usages rooted in the Middle Ages conflicted with the gospel, especially when they involved preaching that one could obtain grace and forgiveness of sins by following them. This article thus lays down the two theological principles that would eventually form the theological basis for the "disputed articles": Church order is obligatory because and insofar as it corresponds to Scripture. Church order never can or should claim to be necessary for salvation. The article on justification through faith alone gives the rationale for all statements about worship and church law.

The subsequent articles of A link up in general with those of draft E. Articles A 2–4 correspond—with slight changes in their order—to E 1–3. In the process, A expands the scriptural evidence and supplements it by including references to the church fathers and canon law. In addition, a detailed theological refutation is directed against the mass as an offering.

Article A 7 corresponds to E 7; the teaching on absolution is expanded in A by a rejection of the enumeration of all sins. Article A 8 continues what E 6 had begun regarding the defense of the elector in the question of monastic life, seeking on the one hand to minimize the "running off" of the monks, and on the other to base monastic reform on theology and canon law. The comments E 4 had made about ordination are now divided into two articles (A 6, 7) by Melanchthon. In addition, A 6 treats the jurisdictional power of diocesan bishops and its relation to the power of the temporal authority; in this discussion, jurisdiction over marriage played a special role. It is conceivable that the court at Torgau showed particular interest in these questions, which had been discussed throughout the Middle Ages and which held the key to the integrity of the nascent territorial states. Ordination, considered in A 7, was also highly explosive politically. In Saxony no one asked the candidate for installation in a parish whether and by whom he was ordained. Marriage of priests was encouraged. Bishops of the old faith had persecuted married priests and employed their power of ordination to suppress evangelical preaching. On this point the gulf between temporal and spiritual princes was the widest. It is here in A 7 that Melanchthon's most intensive efforts at compromise come into play. We will see how they go hand in hand with the composition and application of CA 28.

There were two articles in A that Melanchthon added to his previous document E: A 9 and A 10. The question of invoking saints (A 9) involved worship as well as doctrine; CA 21 places it among the doctrinal articles. Article A 9 also argues on predominantly theological grounds, honoring the saints as examples of faith but rejecting them as intercessors or mediators of grace. Article A 10 defends and extols German hymns.

In A, Melanchthon omitted the article on the papacy (E 5), on fasting and the distinction of foods (E 8), and on the sacramentarians (E 9). Omission of the question of dietary rules can be explained by its minor importance. Inattention to the extremes on both flanks—pope and sacramentarians—corresponds to the middle-of-the-road course of Saxon diplomacy. Many allies in the evangelical camp would have been just as offended by a provisional recognition of the pope as by an uncompromising condemnation of the opponents in the Lord's Supper controversy. Thus, to commit oneself on either flank before the situation demanded it must have seemed to the politicians to be premature and unwise. In both cases Melanchthon complied; still, both papacy and sacraments are questions that constantly dogged the composition of the CA.

Documents E and A are the two preliminary stages of the "disputed articles"; they cover the latter's contents fairly completely. In addition, there are drafts in the Torgau Articles and other places which treat individual questions. We will need to draw upon them in the commentary on specific articles. Moreover, the other traditions, whether dated or undated, whether ascribed to the period before June 25 or to the later settlement negotiations, must be investigated concerning the extent to which their preliminary stages or interpretations contain the "disputed articles." This extensive material makes clear how prominently questions of worship and polity came to the fore at Augsburg and even earlier, and what great pains were taken to solve the theological principles they involved. A historical commentary on the Confession must evaluate this Sitz im Leben properly; in that way the Confession takes on actuality and ceases to be abstractly academic.

At the end of A, Melanchthon had already foreseen the possibility of augmenting the discussion of these practical questions with explicitly doctrinal articles "so that one might see that my most gracious Lord has not permitted any heretical doctrine but has let the holy gospel of our Lord Christ be preached in the purest manner." Was Melanchthon thinking about the Schwabach Articles, which Hans von Dolzig was carrying to the emperor during these days in order to convince him of the harmless nature of evangelical doctrine? This premise is contradicted by Melanchthon's characterization of the content of these supplementary doctrinal articles as "concerning obtaining the forgiveness of sins through faith, as well as how the sacraments are to be used; concerning the difference between temporal authority and the office of bishop, as well as to what degree human church ordinances are to be observed."[20] All of those doctrines—including the forgiveness of sins—emerge more and more clearly in the further development of the "disputed articles" and are therefore not presented in the first part of the CA. We must grant the "disputed articles" a doctrinal character of their own, and we will ask, once we have presented the development in its entirety, why, when, and how the two parts of the CA were put together.

First, we must trace the unique tradition that led from Luther's personal Confession of 1528 through the Schwabach Articles to the doctrinal articles of the CA.

5. PRELIMINARY STAGES OF THE DOCTRINAL ARTICLES (CA 1–21)

In his Confession in 1528, Luther had included the full seriousness of his own faith experience and of his concern for the future of the church. The fact that both of these elements related to the conflict over the Lord's Supper, a conflict that, because of the bitterness with which it was conducted, increasingly called for a settlement, provides the Lutheran confessional development with a special dynamic.

Luther feared that attempts at such a settlement could neglect the concerns of his reformation and could water down his teachings: "Hence lest any persons during my lifetime or after my death appeal to me or misuse my writings to confirm their error as the sacramentarian and Baptist fanatics are already beginning to do, I desire with this treatise to confess my faith before God and all the world, point by point. I am determined to abide by it until my death and (so help me God!) in this faith to depart from this world and to appear before the judgment seat of our Lord Jesus Christ."[21] He therefore had constantly reexamined his confessional utterances in the light of Scripture and was completely convinced of their truth and their agreement with

---

20. Förstemann 1:83–84; Reu 91.
21. *WA* 26:499.16–23; *LW* 37:360. The citations that follow in the text refer to Luther's confession in *WA* 26:499.15–509.28; and *LW* 37:360–72.

the whole church. "This is my faith, for so all true Christians believe and so the Holy Scriptures teach us" (*WA* 509. 19–20; *LW* 372).

It is a Trinitarian confession that Luther sets down, as in the ancient church. The structure of his writing comes from the Apostles' Creed, which he takes as a model. He begins, therefore, with the divine Trinity, the "sublime article of the majesty of God" (*WA* 500.27; *LW* 361) and—to paraphrase the second article—with Jesus Christ, true man and true God (*WA* 500.34; *LW* 361–62). The cross of Christ accomplished deliverance from sin, death, and the eternal wrath of God (*WA* 502.18–21; *LW* 362). His resurrection makes him (according to Phil. 2:9–11) Lord of heaven, earth, and underworld, of life and death, of sin and righteousness (*WA* 502.21–25; *LW* 362). Through the redeeming work of Christ, the Fall, sin, and guilt, which came into the world through Adam, are eliminated; original sin is the negative presupposition for Christ's redeeming act in the cross and resurrection (*WA* 502.25–34; *LW* 362). By these two elements—our bound condition through original sin and Christ's liberating activity—human free will is excluded as a means of achieving righteousness (*WA* 502.35–503.24; *LW* 362–63). The rejection of new and old Pelagians—Erasmus and his followers as well as the scholastics—is the logical conclusion (*WA* 503.25–34; *LW* 363).

It is worth noting that the doctrine of justification is not defined; a special article about it is missing. What is necessary to say on that point is handled within the framework of soteriology and the doctrine of original sin. As in the Apostles' Creed, the bare facts of salvation's history are set down—Adam's fall, Christ's saving act. Out of both of them the consequences for the human need of salvation are drawn. More unusual, however, is the fact that Luther draws out the implications of both of these realities for the social orders in which humanity lives. These structures of society do not pertain only to the original creation (cp. *WA* 500.29; *LW* 361) but are assumed as continuing to exist. Both the Fall and redemption have affected these structures. The "devil's deceptions and errors" (*WA* 503.35–505.28; *LW* 363–65) have perverted them, yet the Christian believer lives in them by God's good pleasure.

The combination of ethics and ecclesiology that Luther works out in the second article of his Confession of 1528 is not unique in the confessional development of Protestantism. In the "table of duties" from the Small Catechism[22] of 1529, Luther concluded his whole catechetical instruction by admonishing "various holy estates and stations" on their office and responsibilities by means of scriptural passages. In the Smalcald Articles[23] he simply

---

22. *BS* 523.30ff.; *BC* 354.1–356.15. In the Large Catechism, Luther discusses the three orders in connection with the Fourth Commandment: *BS* 587.7, 596.17, 598.39, 601.26; *BC* 379.105, 384.141, 385.150, 387.158.

23. *BS* 413.15; *BC* 291.14.

mentions them in passing. On this subject, therefore, Luther's personal confession begins a distinct theological approach.

God has established three holy orders and lawful institutions: the priestly office, the estate of marriage, and civil government (WA 504.30–31; LW 364). They are "according to God's command"—as Luther says of the Sacrament of Baptism in the Small Catechism[24]—and are therefore themselves holy ("pure holiness, . . . a holy work and a holy order," WA 505.2; LW 364); one who serves God in them is a "living saint on earth" (WA 505.4–5; LW 364). And above these three rises the "common order of Christian love," which reaches across all boundaries, serves the needy, and prays for all humankind (WA 505.11–16; LW 365).

These works of love are not prerequisites for redemption; they are its fruits, which we produce through Christ. They do make us holy, but they do not save us: "We are saved through Christ alone" (WA 505.16–23; LW 365). God has set up these orders to show us how we can serve him acceptably in faith, and they are perverted into their exact opposite when we try to save ourselves and escape sin and death by works of our own choosing. Luther vented his fiercest anger against "all monastic orders, rules, cloisters, religious foundations, and all such things devised and instituted by men beyond and apart from Scripture, bound by vows and obligations" (WA 503.35–504.23; LW 363). When monasticism takes this route of self-salvation, it commits a "notorious, abominable blasphemy and denial of the unique aid and grace of our only Savior and mediator, Jesus Christ." The orders established by God belong to the Second Article of the Creed, because through them God has opened to us the way to fulfillment of the loving obedience we, the redeemed, owe him. Orders established by human traditions, however, do away with saving faith.

In his exposition of the Third Article of the Apostles' Creed, Luther related his confession to the external means of grace. The first step is inward: the Holy Spirit witnesses to us in our hearts that, in Christ, God has forgiven our sins and given us everlasting life (WA 505.29–37; LW 366). The Spirit thus brings the work of creation and redemption to completion for our faith and through our faith (WA 505.38–506.9; LW 366). Outwardly this occurs through the preaching of the gospel, baptism, and the Sacrament of the Altar (WA 506.10–29; LW 366–67). All three means of grace are instituted by God, and therefore when they are used in accordance with that institution, they are effective, regardless of the worthiness of those who administer them.

It is in the Christian church on earth that these divine means of grace are actualized (WA 506.30–507.16; LW 367–68). In this context the church is not

24. BS 515.26–27; BC 348.2.

understood as an order instituted by God in which external rites are performed (cp. *WA* 504.31–37; *LW* 364). It is rather the place where the forgiveness of sins occurs, a "kingdom of grace and of true pardon"; outside of it there is no salvation. It is universal in its spread through space and time as the "assembly of all Christians in all the world, the one bride of Christ and his spiritual body." Along with baptism, confession and absolution also belong to this church (*WA* 507.17; *LW* 368); indulgences are a "blasphemous deception" (*WA* 507.28–34; *LW* 369). All false sacraments—sacrificial masses or masses for the dead (*WA* 508.1–12, 30–39; *LW* 369, 371), extreme unction (*WA* 508.17–24; *LW* 370), marriage and ordination (*WA* 508.25–29; *LW* 370), as well as all unnecessary cults and rites (*WA* 509.1–12; *LW* 371), should be eliminated as threats to faith. In harmony with the Apostles' Creed, Luther's personal confession ends with the expectation of Christ's return, the resurrection of the dead, and eternal life.

It is a comprehensive confession, as broad as the Trinitarian confession of the ancient church on which it is based and which it further interprets. At its center, more clearly than in the fathers, stands the saving work of Christ, given to faith and only appropriated through faith. The emphasis on this given and receiving faith constitutes the characteristic Reformation element in this confession. It does not develop a doctrine of faith; it presupposes faith. It describes the means God uses to awaken and sustain it and how God has so ordered human society that this faith proves its worth. These simple statements about God's saving acts and humanity's receptive, thankful faith are the heart of Luther's confession; polemics emerge only on critical points.

Luther's *private* Confession of 1528 was a literary creation; it even appears in a separate printing. The time after the close of the Second Diet of Speyer, however, demanded a *public* confession. We have already (see above, p. 7) noted the presuppositions and concerns that influenced the composition of that document in the summer of 1529, as well as the use to which it was put in the fall of that year at the meetings in Marburg and Schwabach. We now turn to an investigation of the structure and content of the Schwabach Articles as they relate to Luther's personal Confession of 1528.

The seventeen Schwabach Articles[25] depend on Luther's private confession but they are less comprehensive. That stems from the greater restraint they maintain toward both the enthusiasts and the traditionalists. Luther's polemics against indulgences, prayers for the dead, invoking saints, extreme unction, sacramental views of marriage and ordination—even against freedom of the will—are omitted; the antimonastic attack based on the doctrine of the three hierarchies is considerably abbreviated (Schwab. 15); and the

25. They are printed in *WA* 30.3:86ff.; ET: Reu 40–44; also Jacobs 69–74.

hymn of praise for the church becomes briefer and sounds less emotional (Schwab. 12). A pulpit style has replaced theological exuberance in both the positive and negative statements.[26]

In the process, however, significant theological changes take place. Since the moral acts of the Christian, as fruits of redemption, do not occur within the three God-given hierarchies but appear only as fruits of the *Spirit* (Schwab. 6), the ethics of the Schwabach Articles have a somewhat wavering, unspecific, spiritual character; they provide less help in practical matters than Luther offered. Nothing is said concerning the family; they are silent on the structural offices of the church; the office of temporal authority (Schwab. 14) is seen in an eschatological light, which puts more emphasis on its transitory character than on its—expressly stated—origin in the Creator's will.

These differences point to the fact that each of these early Reformation confessions has its own approach. Luther lays a Trinitarian foundation for his Confession of 1528; otherwise his adherence to the form of the Apostles' Creed would have been impossible. The Schwabach Articles, at least up to article 14, are christologically oriented; they deal with the second article of the Creed. Even their Trinitarian starting point (Schwab. 1) climaxes in the divine sonship of Jesus. The strong emphasis on his true humanity (Schwab. 2) is employed to testify to the reality of his atoning suffering and death (Schwab. 3). As in Luther, this work of Christ is confronted with the omnipotence of sin, which holds all of Adam's children in its inescapable grip. They cannot be rescued by any human deed or merit, but only through faith in Christ (Schwab. 4, 5). More clearly than in Luther's work of 1528, Schwab. 5 shows the beginnings of a separate doctrine of justification, though here it is still embedded in soteriology. Nevertheless, the classic references to Romans are cited, and they will later provide the basic concepts for CA 4. In general one perceives a close connection between Luther's exposition of the first two articles of the Creed and the chain of thought in Schwab. 1–5.

It is a different story with Schwab. 6 and 7; despite all dependence in details, the dialectic that emerges here between external Word and internal work of the Spirit, between faith and works, has no parallel in Luther's Confession of 1528. As in ethics, so here in the doctrine of faith itself, Melanchthon's abstract approach comes to expression. We may certainly consider him the chief author of the Schwabach Articles. In Schwab. 6 he teaches us to recognize faith as an inward gift of God given through the Spirit and describes the fruits that this same Spirit of God produces outwardly in

26. Cp. *WA* 26:507.28–509.8, 502.36ff., 503.35ff.; *LW* 37.369–71, 363. It is puzzling that almost all these items reappear in the Torgau Articles and then are transferred to the "disputed articles." The treatment of free will in CA 18 occurs as a supplement to the nucleus of the CA, which is taken over from Schwab. In all these articles the Luther of 1528 once again comes to the fore.

our lives. In addition to this inner action of the Spirit, Schwab. 7 adds the mediating function of the spoken Word through which God bestows both Spirit and faith "as and where he will." In this arrangement of the inner and outer action of God, intensified by counting both sacraments as external signs (Schwab. 8), Melanchthon can appeal to Luther's confession.[27]

And yet the Schwabach Articles pose us some difficult questions in regard to the Holy Spirit. These questions become sharper as the confessional development begun by Melanchthon moves along. For Luther in 1528 the matter is relatively simple: the Holy Spirit is the Third Person of the Trinity, creatively active himself, carrying on and completing the creative and re-demptive work of the Father and the Son. He applies the saving gifts that Christ won for us through his suffering.[28] But in Schwab. 6 and 7 the Spirit does not play an independent role; it appears as a gift given to us by God through Christ. At this point we should not be too hasty in flagging some pneumatological heresy. One can find no fault with the doctrine of the Trinity in Schwab. 1. Rather, we should perceive the difference that arises between a view of salvation that encompasses the Trinity and one that is limited to Christology. Both possibilities for understanding redemption belong to-gether; they condition each other and are not at cross purposes. Thus it remains an open question whether an exclusively christological basis for salvation, following the Schwabach Articles and the Augustana, contains within itself dangerous tendencies that Luther's confession prevents from the outset.

The statements about the church and its sacraments (Schwab. 9–12) belong to pneumatology in Luther's confession. According to him the sacra-ments, alongside and with the Word, are the external means of the Spirit's activity; the church is the place in which this activity occurs.[29] Schwabach articles 9–12 lack a similar unifying focus; their statements float free and are bound together only externally, if at all. In Schwab. 13 the christological framework concludes with the doctrine of Christ's return, although Schwab. 14 squeezes in afterward with its limitation of the restraining power of temporal authority (2 Thess. 2:6) to the time before the return of Christ.

Schwabach articles 15–17 are really supplements that do not fit into the christological framework; their preliminary stages are to be found in the criticism Luther directs against the false sacraments in his Confession of 1528. Luther's temperate judgment on ceremonies is echoed by Schwab. 17. His sharp rejection of masses which are sold or offered appears again in Schwab. 16, although it is divested of Luther's personal recollections and is

27. WA 26:506.7–12; LW 37:366.
28. WA 26:505.38–506.9, 506.12; LW 37:366. Cp. part 2, chap. 1.
29. WA 26:506.10–507.27; LW 37:366–68.

expanded by the demand for both kinds in the Sacrament. In addition, Luther's repeated denunciation of monasticism is picked up in Schwab. 15 and broadened by the demand to abolish the rule of celibacy.[30]

Thus the Schwabach Articles of 1529 are certainly not imitations of Luther's confession from the previous year, although they do carry through its train of thought. They contain nothing that is not already found in the earlier document, nor have they omitted anything essential; they have indeed abandoned the Trinitarian structure without fully working out a christological replacement. The fact that this change sacrificed certain subtle theological bases and connections may have created dangers for the future of Protestant theology; at the time, it was not important. The theological and religiopolitical negotiations of that day needed only a handy enumeration of the points at issue and a usable summary of the Reformation standpoint. The Schwabach Articles provided both and thereby became the basis for the first part of the Augustana.

The adaptability of the content and sequence of the Schwabach Articles to the negotiations is shown by their application to the Marburg Colloquy (October 1–4, 1529).[31] Of the seventeen Schwabach Articles, fourteen were used at Marburg—and in roughly the same order. The difference lies in the article on the Lord's Supper (Marb. 15; cp. Schwab. 10). The Marburg Articles deal twice with works produced by the Spirit and faith (Marb. 6, 10); Marb. 9 on baptism is expanded by Marb. 14, where the legitimacy of infant baptism is confirmed. Lacking are the articles on the church and Christ's return (Schwab. 12, 13). As a substitute for the rejection of monasticism and celibacy in Schwab. 15 and the objection to masses for the dead and the like in Schwab. 16, the Swiss version of the Marburg Articles presents a corresponding addendum (*WA* 30.3:171.10ff).

At individual points, such as in the formulation of the doctrine of the Lord's Supper, a relationship may be demonstrated between the Schwabach Articles and the *Instructions for the Visitors . . . in Saxony*. The latter goes back in the main to Melanchthon, under Luther's constant supervision, and came out in March 1528. It is likely that it was used in connection with the Wittenberg negotiations in July 1529, although its earliest demonstrable use was during the final editorial work at Augsburg in May and June of 1530. When we reconstruct that process we will return to the *Instructions* in dealing

30. Cp. *WA* 26:509.9–12, 508.30–39, 503.35ff., 509.1–8; *LW* 37:363, 370–71.

31. The Marburg Articles are printed in *WA* 30.3:160–71; Reu 44–47; and Jacobs 69–74. In the article in the Elliger Festschrift, mentioned in n. 3 above, we have cited (pp. 145–51) various versions of Schwab. to show how freely the chancellery of Electoral Saxony treated the text; cp. at this point the supplement to *WA* 30.3:13ff. According to this, it is by no means certain whether Melanchthon used one of the editions described in *WA* 30.3:172ff. or some manuscript from the chancellery for the composition of the first part of the CA.

with individual articles. We now turn to the formation of the final version of the Augustana.

6. COMPOSITION OF THE FINAL TEXT

Our attempt to reconstruct the individual phases of the composition of the final text of the CA presupposes the outline of the events in Augsburg that we have sketched for the months of May and June. We now add material from letters of the participants and interested observers, especially the Nürnbergers, as well as sources and preliminary documents that have been handed down to us.

Along that line we first need to consider the further development of the Torgau Articles in the first form in which they are available to us: Torg. A (see above, pp. 17–19). Obviously they were discussed constantly on the trip to the Coburg and during the stay there with Luther. We assume the possibility of changes and expansions in Melanchthon's original wording throughout. It seems likely that in addition to Melanchthon, a lawyer shared in the work on the version we possess. If, as is likely, Justus Jonas had a hand in it, that could only have happened during the journey, because he was still on a tour of visitation at the end of March while Melanchthon was staying in Torgau.

Luther and Melanchthon must have discussed matters and have come to mutual agreements during the days that they both stayed in the Coburg (the sixteenth of April until late evening on the twenty-fourth). That is more than likely when one ascertains the agreement in content between Luther's *Exhortation to All Clergy Assembled at Augsburg,* written at the end of April, and parts of A (concerning relations to the bishops). One would also expect, on the basis of A, that there had been an exchange of opinions over other critical points in the coming negotiations. That brings us, however, into the problem area that will be treated later in the "disputed articles."[32]

Melanchthon continued these endeavors soon after his arrival in Augsburg on May 2. They were set down in a three-part document dating from this time: C.[33] The first part, going far beyond the earlier work of E and A, sets forth the difference between spiritual power (power of the keys) of the bishops (and of the pope) and temporal government. Thus it deals with the question that underlies all of the "disputed articles," a question that found its final answer later in CA 28. Document C also contains two opinions on the ban and marriage questions, clearly recognizable as supplements to A. In the

---

32. See Maurer, "Entstehung" (cited above, n. 18), 370 n. 20. Luther's *Exhortation* is in *WA* 30.2:268–356; and *LW* 34:5–61.
33. Förstemann 1:87ff.; *BS* 120ff.; Jacobs 88–90.

first week of his stay in Augsburg, therefore, Melanchthon had strengthened his text as formulated in A and had further expanded some details.

He must have brought it to a certain point of conclusion by about May 9, because on May 11 the elector sent Luther "articles" that drew upon the preparatory work of the Wittenberg scholars who had put them in a "list." Melanchthon had in the meantime "further revised them and drawn them up in a form." These articles must therefore be derived from the A draft of the Torgau Articles. Melanchthon wrote Luther on the same day, May 11, describing his method of revision: he had made a selection from the material at hand—at least retaining "almost all the articles" of faith—because the emperor did not like verbosity. This selection is defined not only quantitatively but also qualitatively; it is aimed at reconciliation. It is to be "useful and proper" (prodesse vel decere).[34]

Luther sent a brief answer on May 15. It was directed to the elector; the question of the Confession was not raised with Melanchthon. Luther's letter provides no information on the scope or theological content of the material sent him on May 11. Luther touches only on its obliging form, with delicate, but not hostile, irony. Since he was acquainted with its content from the earlier consultations, he did not mention it at all but commented only on the irenic style.[35]

A letter of Luther's from July 21,[36] more than two months later, may provide some information about the material sent on May 11. Luther is strongly critical of Melanchthon, raising again—and in sharper form—the objection of "pussyfooting," and deploring the Augustana's lack of three items he considers essential. The first, on purgatory, is actually not in any stage of the CA;[37] the second, however, on invocation of the saints, is in CA 21 and was already contained in A,[38] although it is missing in Na. The third item, on the pope as antichrist, not only is missing in the Augustana but also does not occur in any of its prehistory.[39] The pope is spoken of as an upholder

34. *WBr* 5:nos. 1564–65; Reu 122. The mention of Eck's 404 Theses is related to these concerns for agreement in Melanchthon. In contrast to the attacks of the old enemy, he wants to apply a *remedium* through a relevant and peaceable presentation. Of course Eck's theses were not restricted simply to doctrinal questions; they referred also to points touched on in the "disputed articles."

35. "I have read through Master Philip's *Apologia*, which pleases me very much; I know nothing to improve or change in it, nor would this be appropriate, since I cannot step so softly and quietly" (*WBr* 5:nos. 1567, 1568.5ff.; *LW* 49:297–98).

36. *WBr* 5:no. 1657.2ff., 8–9 (to Jonas).

37. The *Apology* is the first to mention it: *BS* 255.21, 256.41; *BC* 184.13, 185.26. A hidden polemic might be found in Na 16, but not in CA 17, where the reference to Origen is stricken.

38. Förstemann 1:82–83; Reu 90; Jacobs 85.

39. It first appears in veiled form in Melanchthon's *Apology* (*BS* 300.31–32; *BC* 217.18) and clearly in Jonas's German translation (*BS* 240.8).

of the law, however, in E and C, both times with tacit approval of his temporal power.[40]

From this critical analysis of Luther's correspondence two conclusions follow:

1. Luther is not able to distinguish the completed CA from its earlier stages; in his memory items formulated in previous discussions blended with those included in the final text. Many of his objections about "pussyfooting" concerned sections that he helped to write and that he had earlier approved.

2. In the case of the papacy, however, he could hardly have remembered all the way back to E; that text was completely out of consideration for the last full month of preparatory work, having been replaced by A. This latter transitional text, however, contained nothing on the papacy; Luther had obviously been content with this gap for quite a while. If he then, on July 21, became angry because the CA said nothing about the papacy, he must have remembered that one text had something on the subject. All things considered, that could only have been C. That would mean, however, that in the manuscript sent on May 11, C stood in the place where we now find CA 28. In that manuscript, therefore, was the later "disputed" article; a happy circumstance has preserved the early form from the beginning of May for us.

The chain of reasoning we have forged from sketchy data is admittedly thin, but perhaps it helps us to throw some light on an otherwise completely obscure process. In C, Melanchthon reworked the statements that E had given such a good dogmatic basis; he broadened them and, as Na shows, made them the foundation for the further development of CA 28.

According to his letter of May 22, about this same time Melanchthon also replaced the article on monastic vows (later CA 27) with a new text; the original was too skimpy for him. His reference must be to the formulations of A. The reasons it gives for electoral consent to "running away" from the monasteries[41] are really not adequate to the dimensions of the problem. We can gather from Melanchthon's criticism that this article, in its A form, must have been contained in the draft sent to Luther on May 11. When Melanchthon's letter of May 22 says that he has joined forces with his colleagues to change "much daily" in the articles as they then stood,[42] we must assume that the general revision of the "disputed articles" did not take place until after the middle of May, approximately the same time as the arrival of Luther's letter of May 15. In that case, the draft of May 11, apart from the later article 28

40. Förstemann 1:96 (not in A!), 87ff.; Jacobs 94, 89. The latter version is also in *BS* 120.19ff.; 122.34ff.
41. Förstemann 1:81–82; Jacobs 84.
42. *WBr* 5:no. 1576.27ff.

(= C), would have retained the wording of A by and large. Only after May 15 did Melanchthon and his Augsburg associates undertake the critical reworking, on their own and without Luther's initiative.

The results of these revisions are available to us in Na, the German text of which goes back to the Latin original of May 30. In these four weeks of May—to some degree before May 11, but mostly after—how was the wording of A amended?

Version Na fuses the original ten articles together into seven. The chief omission is the detailed introduction on human doctrines and ordinances.[43] The principal concerns contained in that section, however, appear later in connection with individual questions; the example of dietary laws becomes an independent article in Na.[44] The comments that A makes on episcopal jurisdiction and ordination[45] are smoothly combined in the final article of Na. The articles on invocation of the saints and German hymns[46] are not present in Na and reappear only in the later development.

As far as the *order* of the articles is concerned, Na follows A rather closely, except that the latter framed the whole with two practical demands—the toleration of married clergy, at the beginning, and permission to leave monasteries, at the end. In contrast, Na moves all individual questions to the end under the basic problem of ecclesiastical power, thus showing the beginning of a systematic approach. Document A, of course, had attempted a certain systematization by gathering all the controversial points under the heading "These are the ordinances which cannot be observed without sin."[47]

At this point we cannot carry out an exact comparison of the individual articles from A and Na that agree in content; that will come in due time. We are trying only to mark the total progress made by the end of May.

In that connection it becomes evident that some articles in Na have been more or less broadened in scope, especially the two (on monastic vows and episcopal power; see above p. 18) that were revised after May 15; they have expanded three to four times in size. But even in the articles on marriage of clergy and both kinds in the Sacrament, the biblical citations and testimonies from the church fathers have been materially enriched and theologically honed. The articles on the mass and confession have achieved a theological concentration by the opposite process; the original text has been shortened and tightened.

In summary, one must observe that Na does not leave a single sentence

43. Förstemann 1:69–74; Reu 80–84.
44. Cp. Förstemann 1:72–73 with *BS* 100ff. (Reu 83–84 with *BC* 63–70).
45. Förstemann 1:78–81; Reu 87–89.
46. Förstemann 1:82–84; Reu 90–91. On invocation of the saints, see above, n. 38. German hymns are not mentioned again until Nb (9a.12ff.), dating from mid-June.
47. Förstemann 1:74; Reu 84.

from A unchanged. Of course the previous text still comes through again and again, but in toto it has become something new. This result could only have been achieved through intensive work. That was done in May—how much before the material was sent to Luther on May 11 and how much after, we do not know. It demonstrates a considerable accomplishment, which had drawn heavily on the powers of the participants; it was above all a *theological* accomplishment that corresponded throughout with Melanchthon's plan of May 11: to state "all the articles of faith" in opposition to Eck (see above, p. 28).

That effort alone would make it unlikely that Melanchthon and his colleagues had time to reformulate the doctrinal articles taken over from the Schwabach Articles before May 11. Therefore, it is also unlikely the two-part division of the CA that is first evident in Na existed from the beginning. In addition to these work-related reasons, there is also the fact that no reference to the ongoing work in letters from May can be applied convincingly to the doctrinal articles. The decisive argument, however, is a political one. It is difficult to imagine that the Saxon leaders in Augsburg would have entrusted Melanchthon with a reworking of the articles that, at precisely that time, were being presented to the emperor in Innsbruck by the Saxon councilor Hans von Dolzig as a sign of his ruler's ecclesiastical integrity (see above, p. 12). Would they have wanted to soften their statements on reform at the very moment that they were hoping for imperial approval of the original Schwabach Articles of 1529? That would have been a premature surrender and would have discredited them with the Catholics. On the other hand, a revision sharpening the tone of the original Schwabach Articles would have provoked the emperor at a time when they were looking for accommodation. Both alternatives are out of the question. A refashioning of the articles of faith that were presented to the emperor could not have been considered until after the return of the Saxon emissary from the imperial court. Dolzig arrived in Augsburg from Innsbruck between May 13 and 15. Melanchthon mentions nothing about the project in his letter to Luther on May 22; he could have been working on it secretly, but apparently it was only after this date that he took up the revision of the doctrinal articles.[48] Whether it is conceivable that that was done in the short span of one week—May 23–30—must emerge from a comparison of the Schwabach Articles with the doctrinal articles from Na.

It becomes clear that the basic parts of the seventeen Schwabach Articles are integrated into the eighteen of Na. The last two articles of Na (Na 17, 18) were added during the editing process and supplement Na 2 (on original sin).

48. Cp. W. Maurer, "Studien über Melanchthons Anteil an der Entstehung der CA," *Archiv für Reformationsgeschichte* 51 (1960): 158–207, esp. 161ff.

Melanchthon's respect for his source is so great that he does not dare to work into the wording of Na 2 the compromise he reached with Erasmus in 1527,[49] nor the answer to the questions on the necessity of evil (Eck's 404 Theses, 171–72)[50] and the cause of sin (Eck 86, 331; Reu 101, 115–16) that Eck had raised. Instead, he added new formulations as a sort of appendix. On the other hand, he drops Schwab. 16, because the "abomination" of the mass as sacrifice had already been denounced more urbanely in the "disputed articles." In treating the question of ceremonies, Na 13 combines two closely related articles (Schwab. 15, 17) for basic theological considerations. Furthermore, it uses individual key words from Schwab. 15 as titles for articles that have already been given detailed treatment in the second part of Na.

The regrouping of articles that Na takes over from Schwab. is worth noting. Particularly significant from a theological point of view are these two:

1. The article on original sin, Na 2 (= Schwab. 4), which originally had attached itself to the restatement of the doctrines of the Trinity and Christology in Schwab. 1–3, now divides those articles on traditional dogma into two parts. The christological statements (Schwab. 2, 3 [= Na 3]) are thereby placed in an "order of salvation" sequence. The creative act of God is followed by the fall and restoration of humanity. By contrast with fallen humanity's lost condition in original sin, the soteriological orientation of Christology comes more sharply to the fore. As in Luther's personal Confession of 1528, this contrast ties the doctrines of justification and original sin (as its antitype) most closely with Christology (and that means soteriology). This important change in sequence, which the Augustana maintains right through to its final version, indicates that the ancient church's Christology is not taken over by the Lutheran confessional structure out of mere traditionalism as a relic from the past; it is seen as the indispensable presupposition for the understanding of sin and grace—the central theme of the Confession.

2. Version Na places statements about the Holy Spirit immediately after the christological article and considers them as presuppositions for the bestowal of salvation through Word and Sacrament. In the Schwabach Articles statements about the Holy Spirit do not constitute an independent section; they are spread among the presentations on redemption, salvation, and the appropriation of salvation by faith in the Word (Schwab. 5–7). In this way Na has undoubtedly emphasized pneumatology more strongly and, by its ordering of articles 1–4, has again reached the Trinitarian starting point from which Luther developed his Confession of 1528.

These two last observations lead us to the conclusion that during the

49. Cp. the *Visitation Articles* (*CR* 26:26–28). Cp. also W. Maurer, *Der junge Melanchthon* (Göttingen, 1967–69), 2:481ff.
50. ET: Reu 106.

second half of May in Augsburg, Melanchthon once again took up Luther's personal Confession of 1528 and gave it more weight in his revision of the Schwabach Articles than it had carried at their formulation in July of 1529.

Setting aside subsidiary questions, let us try to summarize the relationship of Na to the Schwabach Articles. The style is notably terser in the articles on the sacraments (Na 8–10). The statements on justification and sanctification (Schwab. 5–7) are also more tightly structured in Na 5 and 6, although the articles on the church and confession (Na 7, 11) are characterized by a certain verbosity in comparison with the Schwabach Articles. The latter have no real counterpart to Na 11. Noteworthy also are the brief comments on Christ's return in Schwab. 13 corresponding to long arguments, later deleted, on the fate of the dead in Na 16. Article Na 15 (on civil life), too, is more comprehensive than Schwab. 14.

All of these observations lead to the conclusion that whenever Na goes beyond its predecessors the formulations are not yet completely polished. The author has clearly concentrated more on the composition as a whole than on individual ideas. The fact that he was still in the midst of his task by the end of May is indicated both by the lack of what would later be articles 20 and 21, although their predecessors were available to him in his material, and by the still preliminary planning for the later article 14 (on church order). In fact Na has provided a number for this article, but no text. The planning was evidently connected with the new arrangement and complete reformulation of Na 4. In contrast to Schwab. 7, Na 4 omits specific reference to the "office of preaching" or the "oral word." It says only "that the Holy Spirit is given through the means of Word and Sacrament"; the institutional reference is lacking. Evidently Melanchthon or one of the lawyers deemed it indispensable, so it was added after May 30.

Therefore, we see that on May 30 the revision of the Schwabach Articles was not yet finished but was continuing. Nevertheless we may be permitted a look back over the work thus far accomplished. The "disputed articles" have been given a provisional form. The opinions and proposals brought along to Augsburg have been critically examined and, to the degree that they were used, have received a new form, except for the two last articles. No further basic changes will be undertaken in the days to come. The reworking of the Schwabach Articles must have occurred in a second round of activity, after the middle of May, because it was not yet finished by May 30. The number of articles that later will constitute the more doctrinal part of the Augustana is still open to additions; most of those already in place still require critical revision, but that will hardly change their theological substance. Above all, the two parts, originally so different in derivation and purpose, have been fitted together into a unity. It is not an organic unity and never will be.

Repetitions and overlappings are not weeded out and will remain. Yet the doctrinal section and the practical section complement each other and have become a unified whole.

Thus, even apart from the accidental documentation, May 30 has a certain importance for the development of the Confession. This date does not mark a watershed in the development of the text, but it is a turning point in the cooperative work between Saxony and the city of Nürnberg. After the first of the new month there was still a great deal to do in regard to the textual formation of the Confession, and there was not much time left before the fifteenth and the twenty-fifth of June. We will attempt to reconstruct the process of development for this time span.

Unquestionably the fifteenth of June forms a real watershed. That is the day on which the emperor entered Augsburg; the battle over the continuation of evangelical preaching in the city and the participation of the protesting princes in the Corpus Christi procession began. On the same day the Nürnberg delegates sent the "German version of the articles" (Nb) of the Augustana back home and clearly differentiated them from the original Latin version they had sent on May 30. In their acccompanying letter they emphasized that the new text had been stripped of its specifically Saxon character and was composed in the name of all Lutherans. They expected that the preface—not yet released—and the conclusions of the Confession would also bear a similarly general stamp.[51]

This second Nürnberg manuscript Nb is by no means an ideal reflection of the state of the text on June 15. One could assume from the intimations of the Nürnberg delegates that the manuscript stemmed from Melanchthon himself, but that is out of the question. The copyist committed grave errors, the worst of which was in Nb 7, where uniformity in rites is indicated as essential for the church.[52] And yet Nb provides the most important stage in the final phase of textual development. It constitutes the end point for the German version of the official text; the remaining textual variations are without material significance.[53] It thus provides the decisive reference point in the textual development, proving that the German version is the original one. The Latin version is subject to two checkpoints. Where it remains at the stage represented by Na, it is obviously earlier than Nb and the present German

51. *CR* 2:105–6.

52. This occurred by the omission of a "not." Nb 2a.17, 1b.3 should have *unzertrennlich* instead of *vunzergentzlich;* 4a.28, *hie* instead of *in;* 9b.17, *fur* instead of *fort;* 9b.18, *nicht* instead of *auch;* 12b.10, *strenge* instead of *sterung;* 14a.2, *wenden* instead of *werden,* 17a.25; *ausgereutet* instead of *ausgebreitet.* Nb 18b.17 lacks *nicht;* 19a.11 should omit *nit.* There are other mistakes. Reu 166–300 prints Nb as no. 38 (the second column of his comparative text of CA) with the errors corrected.

53. For the omission of the anathema in Nb 8, see below, n. 78.

text. Where it differs from Nb, it is later and must have originated after June 15.[54]

Such a comparison also provides insights concerning the relation between the Latin and German texts. The theological language was Latin; the language of diplomacy at the diet was German. The "disputed articles" were, as witnessed by all the preparatory work, conceived from the start in German, since they were intended for the elector and his councilors. The report of the Nürnbergers on May 31 shows that, at that time, work on both a German and a Latin version was underway in the Saxon chancellery. The wording of the report leads to the conclusion that the "disputed articles" were then being sent to Nürnberg in a Latin translation as well, while work on the German text was continuing in Augsburg.[55] In the first half of June, however, reworking must have been undertaken in Latin also, and where Melanchthon edited the various proposals for revision into a comprehensive whole, he made use of the scholarly language. Once the decision for a general Protestant confession had been made and Saxon particularism overcome, which was before June 15, Melanchthon retranslated the now-official text into the German language. Even newly composed articles, such as the forerunners of CA 20, were now also conceived in German. After the completion of the German version, that is, after June 15, experimentation continued on the Latin. To what degree that occurred, and with what success, can only be clarified in the detailed exegesis. The official text is the German one.

Melanchthon must have already begun his comprehensive German editing a few days before June 15 and must have made constant alterations up to the time that the Nürnbergers could make use of the end result. The proof for these assertions comes from two versions of the text that are less complete, and therefore earlier, than Nb but that thus provide us with knowledge of the last phases of its development. There are two copies, one that Spalatin prepared in the Saxon chancellery (Sp.), and one somewhat later, which the Ansbach chancellor Vogler had used in a diplomatic exchange and which must have been composed shortly before that (A I). The two oldest and closest allies, Saxony and the margravate of Brandenburg, attest to the two earliest versions of the general Protestant text.

Document Sp. contains both parts of the Augustana, although neither is complete. Among the doctrinal articles the one on invocation of the saints is still rather undeveloped and was later crossed out by Spalatin himself; the article on faith and good works would be added subsequently and was not yet in its final form. Article Sp. 27 (on monastic vows) breaks off in the middle; Sp. 28 is missing completely. Since the original manuscript of Sp. is complete,

54. In our earlier work on the composition of the CA, we had not yet discovered this.
55. *CR* 2:78.

it must be assumed that Spalatin did not have a full text from which to work. Melanchthon had not released the two final articles because he was still at work on them. The fluidity of the text at that point may also be recognized in Sp. 17 and especially Sp. 23; Nb has numerous stylistic and material amendments, testifying that the original Spalatin copied continued to undergo intensive reworking by Melanchthon. While no further drastic changes were undertaken in the doctrinal articles, Sp. still does not have the "summary of doctrines" which first appears in Nb and which was taken over from there by the German version (*BS* 83c. 7ff.; *BC* 47.1).

The Ansbach manuscript A I stands closer to Nb. Even so, it totally ignores the "disputed articles" and has only the first nineteen doctrinal articles. Those on faith and works and veneration of the saints were not available to the copyist, which means that they were not yet officially adopted. The doctrinal articles that are present in A I, however, later experienced only minor changes in Nb—mostly through the addition of scriptural citations.

We can therefore conclude that Nb reached its final form just shortly before June 15. It is now possible to survey more precisely how Nb differs from Na and thereby discover what had been accomplished in the last two weeks of revision.

For the *doctrinal articles* in general such a survey reveals a stylistic review, a better arrangement of the individual ideas, and an occasional expansion of biblical material or references to the history of doctrine. A noteworthy shift occurs in reference to the relationship between justification, bestowal of the Spirit, and sanctification. This order had finally prevailed after Nb; we will concern ourselves later with the theological considerations that led to it (cp. also above, p. 32). A new addition was the article on "order in the church" (Nb 14 [= CA 14]) already anticipated in Na. Articles Nb 20 and 21 are, as we know, also new to the text.[56]

Beyond those, completely new formulations are rare. The earliest example would be Nb 5, where the wording of Na 4 is replaced by a new and more comprehensive version. Reformulations that go substantially beyond the content of Na are, apart from that of Nb 15, found in Nb 3, 4, and 6 (here, as in Na, the citation from Pseudo-Ambrosius concludes all three articles on justification, Spirit, and sanctification; Sp. and A I had put it at the end of the article on justification).

A striking peculiarity of Nb is its recourse to the Schwabach Articles. In his reworking of Na, Melanchthon apparently paid closer attention to the first stage of the doctrinal articles than in Na and thus brought out more strongly

56. See part 2, chaps. 20–21.

the Lutheran character of the confessional statements. This process is especially evident in the articles on justification (Nb 4–6), but may also be recognized in Nb 15 (on human church ordinances). The question of whether influences from the preparatory work on the "disputed articles" also had an effect on the doctrinal articles need look no further than Nb 20 and 21 for an affirmative answer. Whether and to what degree that influence can be proved elsewhere must be learned from a case-by-case examination later on. The principle of Nb 7, that uniformity of worship neither conditions nor constitutes the unity of the church, is found as early as Melanchthon's formulation of the results of the conference at Torgau (preliminary document A, above pp. 17–18). He adopted it in Na 7, so in principle it accompanied the entire development of the Confession in Augsburg.[57]

Of course, in Nb the "disputed articles" lead a life of their own. In general the procedure is the same as in the first part of the Augustana: individual points are improved in style or changed in content, softened or sharpened, shortened or provided with additions or even transposed. More extensive reworking occurs in the following articles: the article on marriage of priests had already been thoroughly worked over in Sp. 23; in Nb 23, further significant additions are made. In Nb 24—in the main already in Sp. 24—the brief reference to justification by faith, which Na had proclaimed as the formative principle for the mass, offers the opportunity for a sweeping excursus on righteousness by faith and by works, on faith in the reception of the Sacrament, and on the mass as Communion.[58]

Among the later articles, the two last ones are particularly important for us, because the reworking of article 27 was still in full swing when Sp. 27 was being copied, but the work on Nb 28 apparently had not yet begun. Thus the approximately two-fifths of the text of Nb 27 that is covered in Sp. can be viewed as typical of developments that arose in the reformulation process after the beginning of June.

The original framework of Na is better preserved in Sp. 27 than in Nb 27. In its description of conditions in former monasteries and nunneries, Sp. is sharper than Na; the freedom that canon law granted to those living in cloisters is more carefully evaluated than in Na; both the sharpening and the reservation of judgment are continued in Nb. By Sp. the evangelical doctrine of justification is being applied against monastic life, and the doctrine of the estates that Luther in his Confession of 1528 had outlined in regard to the three hierarchies was being developed. The institution of marriage as a part of

57. The principle is not found in Schwab. 12. Cp. Heinrich Bornkamm in *BS* 61.n. 2, 107.22ff., 108.13ff.; Jacobs 76.
58. Cp. Kolde 19, 27–29 (*BS* 97.12–13) with Nb Bl. 9a.29–10a.24 (*BS* 93.5–95.35). The rEspective stages in Reu are (for Na) 224–28 col. 1; and (for Nb) 226–32 col. 2.

creation is given more precise biblical foundations in Nb than in Sp. It is clear right to the end that Melanchthon has looked repeatedly to Luther's pattern from 1528.

This example gives us the picture of a gradual textual revision that constantly applies certain principles to strengthen the argument rather than attempting somewhat radical and sudden improvements. Concerning the practical procedures that led to these results it is difficult to speculate. One cannot state with certainty that committee meetings took place. It is conceivable that individual drafts were circulated and worked on by the circle of theologians and lawyers around Melanchthon and Brueck. This would be the best explanation of how various textual revisions could occur at the same time and then how one or another could be used according to occasion, choice, or coincidence. Melanchthon's governing influence is apparent not only in the continuing application of the same theological principles but also in the unity of style, which is consistent throughout.

It is obvious that Nb 28 received its final form only a short time before June 15. Changes in Nb 28 are not immediately apparent, but they are not unimportant either. Diplomatic modifications and declarations of loyalty alternate with the sharpening of judgments on offensive relationships in political and ecclesiastical life. More important is the restriction of the princely privileges accorded to the bishops and the legal jurisdiction over marriage and tithes that the evangelical rulers were still inclined to concede to them. Even the specifically religious rights of the bishops receive sharper criticism than in Na; lengthy excursuses support this move by adducing arguments from the doctrines of justification and the law.[59]

Thus a serious and profound theological task was carried on up to its temporary conclusion on June 15. In the unsettled days following the arrival of the emperor, during which the evangelical estates were negotiating in preparation for the delivery of the Augustana on June 25, little time remained for further work. At any rate the identifiable corrections in the Latin text do not disclose a unified theological or political tendency. We will therefore have to treat each of the changes occurring during this time span before June 25 at its proper place. As far as the total structure of the text is concerned they carry no more weight than the changes that were made in the Augustana before and during its publication.[60]

7. THE PREFACES

The first opinion (E) that the conference of Wittenberg theologians rendered on March 15–16, 1530, proceeded directly to the questions posed by

59. Cp. Nb Bl. 17a. 26–17b.12 (*BS* 128.20–129.9); 18a.14–18b.14 (*BS* 130.26–131.35). Cp. also below, pp. 62–63.

60. The decisive work is Bornkamm, "Der authentische lateinische Text der CA" (cited above, n. 16).

the emperor in his summons; it had no introductory word. The first one is found in the introduction Melanchthon placed at the beginning of document A, the product of the Torgau negotiations at the end of the month: "Since some accuse my lord, although unjustly, that His Electoral Grace is dispensing with all divine service, and is introducing a heathenish, dissolute mode of life and insubordination, from which the distraction of all Christendom results, it is necessary for my lord . . . to show . . ."[61]

Here Melanchthon speaks personally, directly to the elector. He advises him on how he should defend himself against the objections that have been raised against him. Its view is directed beyond the borders of Saxony to all of Christendom, not so much to the emperor and the coming diet, and only indirectly to a general council; its main audience is public opinion. It is before that jury that the Christian attitude of the elector is to be defended— that he "with the greatest earnestness, desires to introduce and promote true worship which is pleasing to God, and that, to God's praise and glory, he is incurring danger, expense and trouble," and that his whole life has demonstrated him to be a peaceable man.

These presuppositions make one appreciate the fact that the elector has "provided for" the preaching of the gospel and the appropriate administration of public worship in his territory. Melanchthon is not speaking about mere permission; he refers to the measures taken by the ruler as they were being—and had been—carried out through the visitations. Melanchthon defends both the person of the elector and also his developing governance of the church. In matters of doctrine and worship, all has been done in accordance with Christian principles. As far as doctrine is concerned, no special evidence is required. Melanchthon is thinking exclusively about the later "disputed articles." The single point made against them is that they are "innovations" which have been carried out "without consent of the councils"—a lack, one might add, that could and should be remedied at the diet summoned by the emperor. So the conflict—as the Saxons never tired of repeating—lay not in doctrine but only in practical abuses. The following articles were to demonstrate that they had been corrected in a proper way.

With these words, Melanchthon introduces a defense of the Saxon visitations and assembles the relevant arguments. As yet the view is by no means directed to a reformation of all Christendom; rather, toleration is to be given to a territorially limited partial reformation. The great controversy with the papacy which Luther had begun hardly enters the picture at this point; it is of only tangential interest. Despite occasional mention in the intra-Protestant discussion, Luther's concern with the pope ultimately received no attention at all in the final confession. This first preface, written by Melanchthon, is

61. Förstemann 1:68–69; Reu 79 (quoted here).

characterized by a narrow, almost nervous limitation to the specifically Saxon situation.[62]

Melanchthon added this note to the defense of the Christian and political integrity of Elector John: "To this effect it is well to place first a long and rhetorical preface." Although we cannot precisely specify the time when this note was composed—might it have been a suggestion to the politicans?—it must have been before the writing of a second version of the introduction. It leads us to expect a thorough exposition of the Saxon standpoint in the new version.

That resulted in document Ja (*BS* 35–39; Reu 91–95), published in 1912 from the archives in Jena. Chancellor Brueck apparently shared in its composition. The ecclesiastical activity of the elector is not mentioned until its second part (37.5–39.15). The delineation of his character that Melanchthon had attempted in A has been dropped; the Christian motives of his action in the visitations are only indirectly discernible. The presentation is free from effusive apologies and strives for an objective description. One notices the hand of a man like Brueck, experienced in worldly affairs, whose "rhetoric" is not a formal art but practicality.

How has the Saxon elector demonstrated his Christian attitude? He has carried out in his lands the church reforms that the gravamina of the last diet at Worms had demanded (36.30–37.4). The necessity for this course of action became clear to him from the deficiencies of contemporary preaching and from the abuses in worship that were leading the people astray (37.5–23). His purpose in the Saxon visitation is to reform worship and does not, as the opponents allege, indicate the ruin of church life (39.6–15). Evangelical preaching was permitted (37.27–38). It was the defense of the scandalous indulgence traffic that brought confusion into the empire and thus proved the weakness of the previous ecclesiastical system (38.1–17). The prelates looked on without lifting a hand (38.17–24). The called witnesses to Christian truth, however, have freely recognized the truth of the gospel without fear of offense (38.25–39.2). The elector has given them a free hand. He knows, and the emperor should know, "that in matters of faith it is more profitable to allow offenses to arise and increase, than to keep silent or suppress the truth for the sake of avoiding the offense" (39.3–5). A worthy apology for the elector and his territorial reform! It keeps in mind the practical reality as well as the truth of the gospel.

The preface, in addition, opens with a general historical overview (35.3–37.4; Melanchthon's note in A had spoken of "placing first"). Referring

---

62. In our "Studien über Melanchthons Anteil an der Entstehung der Confessio Augustana," *ARG* 51 (1960):158ff., we had not yet given this first preface its due, nor does Bernd Moeller in his noteworthy comments on the composition of the CA and especially its prefaces, in "Augustana-Studien," *ARG* 57 (1966):76ff. Further literature is cited in both articles.

directly to the imperial summons, the preface parallels the planned imperial reform of the church with the measure taken by earlier Christian emperors to further the church and praises them as the fulfillment of biblical instructions (35.3–33). Canon law and the decrees of popes themselves are used to make clear that the new church orders planned by the emperor ought not stem from current church customs (35.34–36.29). The gravamina of Worms in 1521 and Nürnberg in 1522, still unfulfilled, have proved that method to be a dead end. Therefore, the Saxon elector with his visitation program has taken the proper way for reform.

In the foregoing we have understood Ja as a broad exposition and deepening continuation of the suggestions Melanchthon made at the end of March in his introduction to A, which even at that time he indicated was in need of expansion. If this connection is correct, the fragment Wa (*BS* 36.37–39.41; Reu 95–97), from Melanchthon's own hand and described as incomplete, cannot be placed *before* Ja. Then where does it belong? It does not fit into the closed sequence of the introduction to A; we have no reason to assume an unknown preliminary document in addition to A. There is no other choice than to bring it into connection with Ja. Still, there is no gap in Ja where it will fit. It can therefore only have been intended to replace a section of Ja.

Parallels do exist between Wa and the second part of Ja. Fragment Wa also begins with the futile efforts toward reform at Worms and Nürnberg (36.37–37.29); it does not, however, move directly to the Saxon visitations but depicts (37.30–38.37) in the manner of A, and occasionally in the same terms, the previous abuses, especially the indulgence matter.[63] And at the point where Ja speaks about those "to whom God has given grace to understand divine Scripture" (38.25–26), Wa explicitly names Luther, who fought through the indulgence struggle, consoling many consciences with his evangelical preaching and exposing abuses and false doctrine through the emphasis on this chief article of Christian doctrine (38.37–39.41; see also Förstemann 1:80.30ff.).

In contrast to Ja, in Wa every reference to the elector and his work of reform has disappeared and Luther has stepped forward in his place. Which presentation is older? Certainly Ja, if we measure it against A, with its defense of the elector underlined by Melanchthon's marginal note. Fragment Wa is more distant from that document. The reference to Luther, however, fits well with those sections of Ja that go beyond A, primarily the glance backward

63. Moeller's (see n. 62) observation that the section 37.33–40 in Wa has no direct parallel in Ja is correct. The list of abuses in Wa is more comprehensive than the reference in Ja; the contrast is sharper. But that does not lead us to recognize a compelling argument for the priority of Wa. Melanchthon may have taken the reference to Luther in Wa out of A 7 (Förstemann 1:80; Reu 88), where, in regard to division in the church, it is said, "It is to be apprehended that not many Dr. Martins will come after this time, who would control these important matters with such grace, and would avoid false doctrine and war."

from Augsburg, 1530, to Worms, 1521—an account that completed the first part of Ja. That section broke out of the peculiarly Saxon framework of A and grew from an apology for a princeling into an account of ten years of German national history. If the figure of Luther displaces the elector from the second part of Ja, it is because the center of interest has shifted from administrative measure of one terrritory to the religious experience of an entire people, and Luther appears as the author and embodiment of this experience. To the extent that Wa almost completely replaces the end of the first part of Ja and its second part (Wa takes the place of 36.30–39.5),[64] the feeble defense of the elector becomes a fanfare for Luther and his work. In this portion of the draft the vision of a victory of the evangelical confession within all of Christendom occurs for the first time.

When was this preface, in which the first half of Ja is combined with Wa, first gathered into a unified whole? It must have happened before the composition of Na, that is, before the end of May; this becomes clear from the preface to Na, with which we will deal in a moment. But first we must assign Ja and Wa their places in the available span of time. Since A was fully developed during the course of April, Ja also may be dated sometime during the same month. It may have been written down anywhere, either in Torgau or on the journey, but certainly at the latest during the meeting in Coburg (April 15–23). Time enough for the compilation of Ja, which resulted in Wa, is easiest to find in Augsburg; the sending of the first draft on May 11 would then mark the terminus ad quem. In that case the combination of Ja and Wa would have formed the introduction to this draft, and Luther would have been examining this text when he gave his opinion on the entire document on May 15. Perhaps it was precisely the role the preface assigned to his participation in the development of the Reformation that prompted his hesitation.

It may be noted in passing that our suggested preface never goes beyond practical questions of worship; nothing at this point requires us to assume a two-part confession.[65]

Melanchthon's proposal for a conclusion corresponding to the preface builds on the idea that all doctrine is based on justification and forgiveness;

64. In our view, one cannot object to this placement (challenged by Moeller, "Augustana-Studien," 78 n. 9) by saying that the opening sentence of Wa (*BS* 36.36–37) "replaces" the section of Ja on grievances and thus forms a "doublet" to it; it does not replace it but summarizes it in order to provide the stylistic connection to the new formulations. Nor can we accept the "text-critical" objection that compares the corrected phrase 38.36–37 from Wa with 37.27–28 from Ja in order to show the priority of Wa. It is equally possible to imagine that Melanchthon, rather than changing his summary after its conception in order to accommodate it to an apparently discarded bit of Ja, had, without referring back to Ja, corrected 38.36 afterward in order to justify Luther's divine mission—a point that he introduces above and beyond Ja.

65. There is no need to unravel the interweaving of doctrine and church usages (35.8ff.)—of doctrine with preaching, on the one hand, and with ceremonies and administration of the sacraments, on the other (37.8–9), or of reports of church usages and the doctrinal basis for them (39.9ff.).

"Christian and pious" ceremonies should be developed on this basis. Those are the same ideas that Melanchthon used as a rationale for Luther's reforming mission in Wa (38.41ff.). The conclusion, therefore, belongs with the combination of Ja and Wa and came into existence at the same time as Wa or after it. It recalls the imperial summons, from which Ja took its bearings, in its conviction that the emperor's longed-for unity is to be found in the truth of Scripture. It warns of the dangers posed by the radical movements and holds before the ruler the example of Israelite kings who fought against idol worship.[66]

With this appeal to the emperor, the churchwide responsibility that had already found expression in Wa emerges once again. This responsibility is initially laid on the emperor. He must recognize that the issue is not "temporal goods, land, or people, but eternal salvation and loss of souls and consciences," and that God will demand an accounting from him on judgment day.[67] Thus the concluding section offers a suitable supplement to Wa. It belongs to the period of waiting, before the real negotiations got underway. We can well imagine that it occupied an impressive place at the end of the material sent to Luther on May 11.[68]

That framework had hardly any influence on the future development of the preface. Document Na presents an entirely new proposal (BS 39–43, 83df.; Reu 137–43). Its peculiarly Saxon character immediately strikes the eye: the emperor should defend the Saxon elector from charges that have been directed against his church reforms (39.17–40.29). As in Ja (35.11ff., 28ff.), the pious emperor is placed in the line of his great historical prototypes (40.10ff.); his clemency is particularly lauded. Likewise, the "honorable and brave character" of Elector John and his deceased brother Frederick is also emphasized, along with their loyalty to the empire and their love of peace (40.34–50).[69]

This description of the Saxon government's politics forms the background for the justification of its ecclesiastical measures, especially in the case of

66. BS 135–36; Reu 144–45.

67. Melanchthon temporarily took out of Wa the appeal to the emperor, mentioned repeatedly (cp. Moeller, "Augustana-Studien," 79 n. 12) in the omitted part of Ja (BS 36.30ff.), and used it effectively in the conclusion. The final sentence of the omitted section (39.2–5) reechoes in BS 136.6–10; Reu 145.

68. "May God grant Your Imperial Majesty grace and safety for the aforementioned task. Amen" (BS 136.9–10). This prayer expresses both Saxon loyalty to the empire and concern for all of Christendom.

69. The "instructions" for the impending negotiations which were sent with the Saxon emissary Hans von Dolzig on March 16 offer parallels to this self-justification; see Hans von Schubert, Bekenntnisbildung (cited above, n. 5), 244ff. Cp.: ". . . just as our dear brother Duke Frederick, elector of Saxony, of blessed memory and we ourselves have ever and always been most eager (more so, we may say without glorying, than others) and heartily glad to offer His Imperial Majesty our most humble obedience and to assist the house of Austria with friendly and undivided service" (ibid., 250; Reu 77).

visitations (40.30–43.43). We find familiar themes in this major section. The depiction of churchly abuses (41.11–27) stems from Wa (36.38–37.40, 37.40–39.41) as does the view that they were overcome by Luther (41.27–42.15). In the process, however, the positive effects of Luther's appearance are more strongly emphasized than in Wa; these include the concurrence of scholars (41.35ff.), the improvement of church practice even among the opponents of the Reformation (41.46ff.), and the fight against heretics and Anabaptists (41.54ff., 42.2ff.), who in no way owed their start to Luther (42.11ff.).

Thus the defense of the Saxon politics of religion, a premise of A and Ja, is tied to the justification of Luther that we have found in Wa. Both now work together in the description of the Saxon visitations (42.16–43.37) in which we once again find themes from the Torgau Articles, especially version A, tied in with references to the "disputed articles" (Na 22–28)—for instance, the reestablishment of the original mass with examination of communicants, the introduction of German hymns, confession and absolution, and the proper observation of holy days.[70] Especially important, however, is the preview of the regulation of episcopal jurisdiction that will be proposed later in Na 28: bishops are to cooperate with the new church orders (43.10–14); their legal power will not be diminished at all (43.15–21); church property will not be secularized, as in Bohemia, provided the prelates allow free course to evangelical preaching and do not promote ecclesiastical abuses by force (43.22–23).[71] The elector of Saxony is as loyal politically as he is religiously; all civil regulations are maintained as God's ordinance for the sake of peace (43.33–34).

At this point the preface reaches behind the "disputed articles" to the doctrinal articles that have been added in the meantime, picking up the guiding principle of Na 15 (70.21–22) almost verbatim. And right at the end, after recapitulating the most important "disputed articles," the preface leads directly into the "chief article of faith" (43.38–43) which reveals the theological reason for the practical reforms and proves the incontestable Christianity of evangelical preaching. Here, for the first time, the bipolar character of the developing confession is clearly enunciated.

The "summary of the teaching in Electoral Saxony" (83d.26ff.) once again stresses the agreement of evangelical doctrine with Scripture and with tradition properly understood. It blames the conflict solely on the abuses illegally foisted on Christendom. As in the preface and later in Na 28, an appeal is

70. Cp. BS 42.19–22 with 96.33ff., 97.2–3; 42.25–27 with 97.39–41; 42.22–24, 32–35 with A 10 ("On German Hymns," Förstemann 1:83); 42.28–29 with 97.3ff.; and 42.36–38 with 106.32–35 and Kolde 31.3ff.

71. Cp. these proposals with BS 104.30–31; 122.27ff. (also Kolde 28.8ff.); Kolde 29.2ff., 32ff., 31.11ff., 30ff.

made to the bishops: they are not to shatter the unity of the church for the sake of external ceremonies! This same thought is repeated in the transition to the "disputed articles" (84.25ff.) and the Saxon character of the apologetic writing comes once again to the fore.

In the preface to Na the parochial character of the nascent confession had a last moment of glory; it had already been transcended in Wa, and in the final version of the framework (preface and conclusion) its defeat is complete. This version must be dated after the completion of Nb, since neither preface nor conclusion was yet in place when the Nürnberg delegates sent their manuscript home on June 15. The Saxon politicians, more hesitant in this case than Melanchthon in his German version of the twenty-eight articles, had not yet decided whether or not to speak on behalf of all the Lutheran states. One can safely assume from the way in which the Nürnberg representatives comment on this open question that Chancellor Brueck had not yet started on this last version; therefore, it would not have been composed until after June 15. In any case we should recall that the conclusion of Na by no means signified a real turning point in the confessional development. A letter of the Nürnbergers from May 24[72] discloses that Chancellor Brueck was still working on the framework, which would then be sent with Na on May 31. He would have seen no reason to begin immediately on a new concept. That occasion would arise only once the circle of "confessors," including the landgrave of Hesse, had been formed. The general consultation of the evangelical states which finally established the text of the Augustana did not begin until June 21.[73] Brueck would not have begun the final formulation of the framework much earlier. In addition to the official text in German we must also consider the points where the Latin text, just put into final form, differs from it.

Let us begin with the bridge section joining the first and second parts of the Augustana (83c.7–84.24). At this point the Latin version maintains its connection with Na; its first part corresponds almost verbatim with Na's "summary of the teaching." Its second part (83d.6ff.), with its assertion that the old rites have been maintained almost intact, goes back to the preface of Na,[74] and the transition to the "disputed articles" (83d.11ff., 36ff.) even harks back once again to the corresponding sentences of A. The introduction to the "disputed articles" also builds on Na, although it is more explicit in its appeal—even more pressing in the Latin version than in the German—for

72. *CR* 2:62. For the report from June 15, see ibid., 105–6.

73. *CR* 2:124. The diet's proposition of June 20 also influenced the composition; cp. Bernd Moeller, "Augustana-Studien," 81.

74. "For there is no truth to the statement that we dispense with all the old ceremonies and usages; we endeavor to maintain them as much as possible" (*BS* 84.29ff.).

the emperor to understand the cultic and legal changes that have been made.[75]

In its final form, the preface itself represents an entirely new effort. In view of the situation on June 20, Chancellor Brueck had given it a thoroughly political stamp. It clearly falls into two parts. The first (BS 44.2–47.11; BC 24–26.14) sums up events from the issuing of the imperial summons (January 21, 1530) to the presentation of the Confession (planned for June 24 and carried out on June 25). The loyalty and peaceful intentions of the evangelical estates are emphasized by close and repeated connection with the imperial summons; whatever would be specifically Saxon is thus omitted. The entire responsibility for the success of the imperial peace plan is laid upon the estates of the old religion. As the Augustana is now presented, it is up to them to grasp the outstretched hand of peace.

The second part of the preface (BS 47.12–49.14; BC 26.15–27.24) is Brueck's diplomatic masterpiece. In a skillful interpretation of the development of imperial politics from 1526 to 1529 he emphasizes the hope for a general council which had been unanimously and constantly raised by the diets and which the imperial government had repeatedly supported. Thus the emperor becomes the advocate of the conciliar plan; by this means the chancellor intervened in the delicate relationship that existed between pope and emperor despite the friendly negotiations that had just taken place in Bologna. That relationship was constantly endangered by curial reluctance for a council. The appeal for a council by the Protestant estates at Speyer in 1529 had provoked great offense, and now they were creating the impression that a council would fulfill the wishes of the emperor. That was a trump card that had brought Landgrave Philipp of Hesse into the game, and the old statesman from Saxony now laid it on the table; by that move he had hitched the influential and stormy ally on his left to the general Protestant cause. Finally the repetition of the appeal to a council signaled an effective warning to opponents holding to the old religion. If they refused to grasp the hand extended to them, then they were going to be responsible for the domestic political troubles that were bound to follow. And would it really suit them if the emperor, acting over their heads and without regard to the ecclesiastical prerogatives they had acquired since the end of the Middle Ages, made direct contact with the curia and carried out a reform of the church independently of the local rulers?

In his preface, Brueck proved that he had mastered the political art of keeping several balls in the air at the same time. The political side of the confessional structure comes to light here as nowhere else. In fact the Latin

75. The Latin version provides (BS 84.11ff.) in abbreviated form a historical review similar to those in Na (41.11ff., 42.16ff.) and its predecessor Wa.

version strengthens the political elements even more. The German version was intended for the official negotiations of the diet; the Latin version aimed at the imperial chancellery whose non-German officials understood French and possibly Latin. Disregarding textual variants that arise exclusively from linguistic, and usually rhetorical, niceties, some remaining peculiarities deserve notice: In reference to the anticipated mutual negotiations there is a return to the imperial proposal of June 20 (*BS* 46.6–7; *BC* 25.6) and a sidelong allusion to quarreling—among the theologians, of course (46.18). Both references must have found willing ears among the imperial diplomats. Reference to the negotiations at Speyer in 1526 and 1529 emphasized the fact that the emperor had repeatedly ("non una vice, sed saepe"; *BS* 47.14; *BC* 26.15 n. 7) demanded the convoking of a general council; and the flowery language used to refer to King Ferdinand by name ("amicum et dominum clementum nostrum"; cp. 47.27–30) was a well-weighed diplomatic gesture. Also well calculated was the threat to adherents of the old religion of the likelihood of an appeal to a council, in case "the differences between us and the other party should not be amicably settled" (*BS* 48.23–25; *BC* 26.21 n. 1).

The price paid for this new preface's broader view in comparison with its predecessors was that it became completely political. Religious and theological content was concentrated in the bridge section between the two parts of the CA. Do these two dissimilar halves of the framework still fit together at all? To answer this question we draw on a passage from the "summary" which we have skipped up to now (*BS* 83c.8–18; *BC* 47.1 Ger.) contained only in the German version which took it over from the preface to Na (*BS* 41.4ff. [cp. 40.3–4]; Reu 139). There the elector had based the authenticity of his religious commitment to the gospel on the danger to which he was exposing not only his honor and possessions but even his "children and grandchildren." According to the summary, this danger threatened not only the electoral family but also "our own souls and consciences" as well as the consolation of the consciences of believers in general. These statements unify the one-sided political emphasis of the preface with the religious emphasis on responsibility that was present throughout from the beginning. It is on this unity that the agreement between both halves of the framework rests. They are held together by the personal faith stance of the "confessors" of Augsburg. The original particularity of the Saxon elector's defense has been absorbed by this wider solidarity.

This brings us to a decisive question in our preliminary understanding of the Augustana. Who is its logical subject? Whose confession does it represent? This question, however, cannot ignore the fact that the Augustana not only confesses; it also condemns. What do these anathemas imply? Who is confessing?

8. THE ANATHEMAS: WHO CONFESSES AND CONDEMNS?

To confess is also to condemn: so reads an apparently unbreakable law in church history. Reality does not bear this out. The Roman creed, particularly in the form of the Apostles' Creed, has no anathemas, nor does the Nicaeno-Constantinopolitan Creed. Where the Confession is a part of sacramental worship—in Baptism and the Lord's Supper—constantly repeated anathemas would ascribe too much importance to heresies. Even the so-called Athanasian Creed, a doctrinal statement that originated about 500, still did not anathematize by name. That did not appear until later.

As far as its anathemas are concerned, the prehistory of the Augustana is not consistent. Luther pronounced them in his personal Confession of 1528. He used them to testify to the agreement of his Christian faith with that of all Christianity on the following points: in the confession of "the sublime article of the majesty of God" (*WA* 26:500.27, 30; *LW* 361) and the full humanity of Christ (*WA* 501.32; *LW* 362); in the testimony to original sin against new and old Pelagians (*WA* 503.25; *LW* 363); against the Anabaptists (*WA* 506.19–20; *LW* 366) and enemies of the Sacrament (*WA* 506.27; *LW* 367); against the papal antichrist and all heretics, the latter being better than the former (*WA* 507.1ff.; *LW* 367–68); and against the Novatians, who limit the forgiveness of sins to the one-time act of baptism (*WA* 507.15; *LW* 368).

Expansions and abbreviations can be identified when one compares Luther's list with the subsequent development. The rejection of the pope as antichrist is never officially repeated up through the Smalcald Articles. Above all, it is apparent that no negative judgments are expressed by the Schwabach Articles, nor by the Marburg Articles, which depend on them. They hardly appear in the Torgau Articles. Its final version A excludes the possibility of speaking about heretics or schismatics, by its focus on legal or ceremonial ordinances. Of course, in the preliminary form E the elector was advised that at the coming diet, he should "be willing to help, if the sacramentarians be condemned as erroneous heretics."[76] That is obviously Luther's voice. In the second version of E, Melanchthon refers only to the literary battle that was waged from Wittenberg in the Lord's Supper controversy and to the teachings and practice concerning the Lord's Supper which were accepted in the Saxon lands.[77] The preface to Na also boasts of the battle against the "new and un-Christian writings against the Holy Sacraments" waged from Wittenberg and includes both the revolutionary Bohemians and the Anabaptists as disrupters of civil order (*BS* 42.1ff.; 43.22ff.; Reu 141–43).

76. Cp. Förstemann 1:71 with 97; Jacobs 95. Despite Marburg, E continues, "for since they neither will nor can hold our position, they thereby separate themselves from us and it will not do for us to accept their offer as though our teaching were empty or uncertain. Rather we must be certain in such common public articles which must be applied daily."

77. A 4 (Förstemann 1:77; Jacobs 81).

In the process, Na substantially increases the cast of heretics from the ancient church; they are nearly all taken from Luther's Confession of 1528 and indicate its continuing influence. Of the eighteen articles included in the first part of Na, however, ten are without anathemas. None at all occur in the "disputed articles," and with the orientation of Brueck's final preface every attack on left-wing Protestantism also drops out of the introduction to the CA. In addition, Na is the only source that brings up an anathema against representatives of the medieval church. It concerns those who would "require the forgiveness of sins through our satisfaction and not through Christ" (67.32); the final version of CA 12 (sec. 10) maintains the sense of the passage.

The list of heresies received further enrichment in Nb. That did not happen by the addition of condemnations to new points of doctrine which previously had pronounced no verdicts. Rather Nb, like Na before it, generally followed the pattern of Luther from 1528. Where Na had exceeded the standard set there in the doctrine of confession (Na 11), of "civil life" (Na 15), and of the return of Christ (Na 16), Nb followed its example. But, it added still other groups from the heretics of the ancient church, most of them in connection with Trinitarian or christological dogmas (Nb 1); here Melanchthon once again went back to Luther's list from 1528. That is also the case in the article on original sin; Na 2 had passed over the "old and new Pelagians" in silence, but they reappear in Nb 2. Article Nb 5 condemns—without previous example—the Anabaptists because they try to come to faith by the immediate operation of the Spirit without the external Word. In Nb 16 the monks are classed with the Anabaptists (just as in Na 15) because of their perfectionism, and Nb 17 rejects the Jewish eschatological expectation of the conquest of the Holy Land and a thousand-year reign of the holy over the godless.

As the textual rewriting proceeds, a clear sharpening of the tendency toward condemnation becomes evident. The fact that Nb 17, in contrast to Na 16, abandons the express rejection of Origen does not change the picture. The Alexandrian's name does not appear in the final roster of heretics, out of consideration for the Erasmians, for whom he was a saint. But as far as content is concerned, nothing is changed; the Anabaptists who took over that Origenist-humanistic doctrinal heritage still stand under condemnation in Nb 17.[78]

The final text of the CA—in both versions—differs neither in the number of condemnations nor in theological content from Nb. Out of twenty-one

78. The omission of the Donatists in Nb 8—in contrast to Na 7 (BS 62.25) and Luther's prototype of 1528 (WA 26:506.19–20; LW 366)—certainly arises from a scribal error. It reappears in CA 8 (BS 62.13; BC 33.3), which agrees with Nb 8 in all other respects.

doctrinal articles, nine are furnished with anathemas, twelve are not. It is
clear that the false alternatives are emphasized by means of a *damnant* only in
the major issues: the agreement with dogmas of the ancient church; the
doctrines of original sin and of salvation by grace, and of the church and its
sacraments; and in addition, the proper attitude toward the state. These
alternatives also lurk in the background even when they are not especially
singled out by name. For that reason the weight of the condemnations cannot
be judged by the frequency of their appearance. They leave their mark on all
the articles of faith. Therefore it is all the more important to ask how this trait
of the Augustana is to be judged as a whole.[79]

It is immediately apparent that contemporary instances of the condemned
positions are barely described; the opponents are not specifically named.
Zwinglians are the *secus docentes* (those who teach otherwise; CA 10), the
teachers of works-righteousness remain anonymous (CA 12.10), as do the
ethical perfectionists in monasticism (CA 16.4) and elsewhere (CA 12.8).
Obviously the Confession does not intend to brand contemporary false
teachers with a public condemnation. It prefers to choose guarded expressions in referring to them: *reicere*, "reject" (CA 12.10), is the strongest,
and *admonere*, "admonish" (Ger.: "unterrichten . . . lehren," CA 15.2–3), the
weakest. Words like *improbare*, "disapprove" (CA 10.2), or *dem Glauben an
Christus (dem Evangelium) entgegen sein*, "are contrary to the Gospel and . . .
faith in Christ" (CA 15.3), lie more or less in the middle.

Rebuttal in such pastoral terms shows how little the Confession is concerned with heresy hunting. It does not want to condemn but wants to
persuade, and through persuasion to win over. Therefore it neither attacks
nor is defensive—not only regarding political and ecclesiastical measures, as
in the framework, but also in theological doctrines and statements of faith. It
does defend itself against false insinuations (CA 20.1), draws upon testimony
of the church fathers to support its case (CA 18 Ger.; *BS* 73.16ff.) or states
that its own teaching is "not to be accused" (CA 20.35).

Only in opposition to one group does the Lutheran confession make an
exception. The Anabaptists are usually and unrestrainedly condemned as
heretics (CA 5, 9, 12, 16, 17), and even where not mentioned specifically by
name, they are intended. Where they are concerned, there is no question of
consideration or of the understanding born of seeking love. We must admit
this lack openly, and if we explain it by means of the legal situation or
historical circumstances, we still do not excuse it.

The declaration that the Anabaptists are without legal rights goes far back

79. Hans-Werner Gensichen, in *We Condemn: How Luther and Sixteenth-Century Lutheranism
Condemned False Doctrine*, trans. J. A. Bouman (St. Louis: Concordia Pub. House, 1967), 83–
108, treats the condemnations in the text of the CA.

into church history. In this case the reason for punishment was not false teaching but sacrilegious action. Right up to the time of the Reformation the simple act of rebaptizing or the actual refusal of infant baptism remained sufficient evidence for theological and juridical condemnation. Not only the recipient but also the administrator of second baptism was punished; by carrying out the second action the first was declared ineffective and thereby desecrated (Emperors Valentinian I and Valens, 373).[80] Justinian's code regarding heretics confirmed the punitive measures against rebaptizers; as an essential part of Roman law it remained valid as imperial law throughout the Middle Ages. Sharpened by the promulgations against heretics of Emperor Frederick II (1220), the stipulations of Roman law were carried over into canon law. The imperial authorities at Speyer drew on both legal sources on January 4, 1528, when they blamed the Anabaptists for the uprisings and made rebaptizing a capital offense. The Second Diet of Speyer extended this mandate still further. That was the form in which it was entered into the final decree of the diet on April 22, 1529, and recognized by Hesse and Electoral Saxony. It was implemented in the latter territory at least by 1536.[81]

The two Thuringian superintendents, Justus Menius in Eisenach and Friedrich Myconius in Gotha, immediately provided a theological basis for this imperial law on heretics in a work published by Menius and approved in principle by Luther at the end of February 1530. Soon thereafter Luther applied its basic thesis in his exposition of Psalm 82. Even Melanchthon agreed, regretting his earlier mildness toward the Zwickau prophets and hailing the forceful action of the authorities against treason and blasphemy.[82] We must keep this legal situation in mind if we want to evaluate the condemnation of the Anabaptists in the Augustana. It includes not just a dogmatic judgment but also a political one, and for that reason it belongs to the theses on social ethics that are particularly represented in CA 16 (cp. below, pp. 99–101). To that extent the condemnation of the Anabaptists is in a different class from that of heretics in the ancient church.

Certainly the increase in the number of ancient heresies mentioned during the development of the Augustana is connected with the increasing importance of the church fathers in that same development. Especially in Melanchthon's case—and in this regard Luther did not differ from him—our under-

80. Carl Mirbt, *Quellen zur Geschichte des Papsttums*, 5th ed. (Tübingen, 1934), 82.44ff., no. 181 (lacking in the 6th ed.).

81. Gustav Bossert, "Die reichsrechtliche Grundlage zur Bekämpfung der Wiedertäufer" in *Quellen zur Geschichte der Wiedertäufer*, vol. 1, *Herzogtum Württemberg*, Quellen und Forchungen zur Reformationsgeschichte 13 (Leipzig, 1930; reprinted New York and London, 1971), 1*ff.; Horst W. Schraepler, *Die rechtliche Behandlung der Täufer in der Deutschen Schweiz, Süd-westdeutschland und Hessen 1525–1618*, Schriften zur Kirchen- und Rechtsgeschichte 4 (Tübingen, 1957).

82. *WBr* 5:no. 1532; *WA* 31.1:207ff., 210ff.; *LW* 13:61–62, 64–65; *CR* 2:17–18.

standing of the doctrinal condemnations must be derived from his view of patristic doctrinal development. In the process we must avoid assuming the knowledge of the history of doctrine that has been obtained since the Enlightenment. A significant difference exists between that point of view and the perspective of the Reformers. During the Reformation the great teachers of the church, who had confessed the one common truth of Christendom with greater or lesser clarity, were recognized not as individuals but as types; the same thing was true of their heretical opponents. Therefore, the truth the former confessed, as well as the false doctrine the latter perpetrated, remains forever the same. When therefore the old heretical names crop up again in a confessional writing of the sixteenth century, it is not for the purpose of building historical connections between earlier and later doctrinal positions; it is to point out the ever-present danger of false teaching and to urge and proclaim its defeat.

Melanchthon thus starts from a view of history that traces the one unchanging divine truth back through all time.[83] This view also exercised a considerable influence on his understanding of the church and its teaching. Heresy too changes in appearance—that is the sign of its diabolical, lying nature[84]—but it really remains the same. It will never cease in this eon. The legendary Ebion and his supposed contemporary Cerinthus lived on in Paul of Samosata, Arius, Photinius, and Nestorius, and today in the new Samosatenes. They all made Christ into a mere man, denying his divine nature and equating him, as Nestorius did, with the inspired prophets. In this they fell back into Jewish concepts. Cain is their ancestor; Islam has continued their blasphemy against Christ.[85]

Melanchthon can also trace the christological heresy in which the Savior's divine nature is denied back to a dualistic doctrine of two gods in which the eternal and the human Christ are antitheses. In Melanchthon's later writings, Marcion appears as the chief representative of this false doctrine. In this respect Marcion is brought into close connection with the Manicheans.[86] The latter are named in connection with the Valentinians in the confessional writings (as early as Na: *BS* 52.22, 51.3–4). Their abominations (*portenta*)

83. W. Maurer, *Der junge Melanchthon* (cited above, n. 49), 1:102ff. We select the following evidence: "Enarratio Symboli Niceni" (1550), *CR* 23:197ff.; "Refutatio erroris Serveti et Anabaptistarum" (1559), StA 6:365ff.; the later editions of the *Loci*, esp. StA 2.1:164ff.; and particularly vol. 2 of the *Chronicon Carionis* (which is based on lectures from 1559), *CR* 12:901ff.

84. "The devil spreads the same insanity in every age, changing slightly in appearance" (*CR* 12:923). Cp. StA 2.1:211.7ff.

85. The decisive central position that Paul of Samosata—not Arius—occupies in Melanchthon's historical view explains why he added the name in Nb and identified it with his own anti-Trinitarian contemporaries (*BS* 51.6–7; Reu 166). In Islam, which also is added in Nb, Melanchthon sees the completion of this anti-Trinitarianism. He has Servetus studying at an Islamic university (*CR* 12:955). This makes him, in Melanchthon's eyes, a pupil of the Samosatenes (StA 2.1:189.32ff., 194.5ff.).

86. *CR* 12:922, 933, 956; StA 2.1:210.24ff.

consist in having transformed the doctrine of two gods into a gnostic doctrine of many gods.[87] Even in the contempt for authority (cp. CA 16) Melanchthon catches the scent—of course, without naming names—of the barbarism of the Manicheans; later he would try to demonstrate that both rejection of marriage and community of wives occurred not only among the Anabaptists in Münster but even earlier in gnostic-dualistic tendencies at the time of Clement of Alexandria.[88] His relation to Origen was ambiguous while he was editing the Confession[89] and remained so later. He agreed to the condemnation of Origen by the fifth ecumenical council of Constantinople (553), rejecting both the exegetical excesses of his allegorical method and the doctrine of universal redemption, which is dismissed in CA 17.4 without mentioning names. In general, however, the scholar in him carefully reserved judgment on the great Alexandrian. As it was for Origen and his humanistic herald Erasmus, falling back into Jewish legalism and political apocalyptic was an abomination to Melanchthon; the condemnation of Jewish-Anabaptist chiliasm, which finally appears at the end of CA 17.5, reflects his inmost conviction.[90] The damnation of the Novatians had been taken over from Luther's Confession of 1528 as early as the composition of Na.[91] It is a part of the anti-Donatist concern that Melanchthon shared with Luther and Augustine (BS 62.25, 13–14) and that soon found expression in the Loci of 1535 with direct allusions to CA 8.[92] It is clear that the same Augustinian influence was at work in the reinstatement of the condemnation of the Pelagians which had been omitted in Na 2.

What does this historical overview contribute to the interpretation of the specific condemnations in the CA? It may be developed in two directions. First, it proves the thesis that the contemporary opponents to the left of the Wittenberg Reformation are successors of ancient heresies. At the same time, we must observe the limitation of this assertion. Although the difference on the doctrine of the Lord's Supper remained and is clearly expressed in the CA—even if without specifically naming the Zwinglians—those ominous names from antiquity are not applied; the earlier assertion that christological heresies of the ancient church lived on in the "sacramentarians" is not

87. StA 2.1:211.1ff. Later Melanchthon brings the Manicheans together with the *corrupta philosophia* of the Stoics, to whom he ascribes both a cosmic dualism and a corrupt determinism. He does not go into these questions in CA 19, although they are in the back of his mind ("De causa peccati et contingentia," StA 2.1:224; cp. *CR* 12:956). When, on the other hand, in CA 5.4 he attacks other opponents—because of their direct experience of the Spirit—he includes Manicheans, in addition to the Anabaptists, among the enthusiasts who "invented an infused quality without our action" (StA 2.1:245.10ff.).

88. *CR* 12:933–34.

89. Cp. *BS* 72.27. Cp. also above, p. 49.

90. *CR* 12:1052, 939–40, 1015–16, 923. Cp. ibid., 959.

91. *WA* 26:507.15; *LW* 37:368; *BS* 67.9 and n. 3; *BC* 35.9.

92. *CR* 21:508ff.; StA 2.2:487.31ff.

repeated. In contrast, the Anabaptists and the just-emerging anti-Trinitarians are hit hard by the historic parallels. As far as they are concerned, the decision has already been made (see above, p. 50).

But this historicizing of the condemnations also has its good side. The verdict of condemnation that the whole church pronounced from its beginning against every false teaching includes the new heretics. The confessors at Augsburg are not leveling it for the first time; they are really in dialogue with someone else. But they presuppose that previous verdict and make it their own. It is not a tactical move, as some have supposed, but a conviction growing out of history and theology. Whether one can really maintain those condemnations of modern false teachers after the historical basis has been cut away is a theological question still to be answered.

What importance does the enumeration of the old heresies have for the relation with the real dialogue partners at Augsburg—those who held to the old religion? It is not only to defend the evangelical faith and to declare solidarity with all of Christendom through all time. Certainly the condemnations strengthen the assurance given in the "summary" at the end of the first part (*BS* 83d.27–28, 1ff., 83c.9ff.; *BC* 47.1) that the Confession "is grounded clearly on the Holy Scriptures and is not contrary or opposed to that of the universal Christian church, or even of the Roman church (insofar as the latter's teaching is reflected in the writings of the fathers)." But that is still not all. If evangelical doctrine corresponds to the teaching of the ancient church and repeats its condemnations, then the dialogue partners of the old religion are not only obliged to recognize the evangelical truth but must also ask themselves whether they take this truth seriously. Every repetition of ancient anathemas contains within itself a critique of the contemporary Roman church. The church is called to account on whether its original basis has been abandoned and the faith of the fathers damaged by abuses that have crept in over time. The confessors at Augsburg do not use the traditional condemnations with blunt directness as weapons against their counterparts. Rather they inquire to what degree the ancient confessions still maintain real validity in contemporary church affairs, and whether a mutual understanding still might be possible on the basis of patristic faith. This question too has not yet been adequately answered. Nor can it be until we have made a critical evaluation of the special interpretation under which the patristic tradition was picked up in the confession of the Reformation.

Finally, among the preliminary questions we are now considering is that concerning who really is confessing in the Augustana and who is pronouncing the anathemas. The answer is not entirely irrelevant for the interpretation of confessional statements, but it is not entirely clear either.

The reason for this situation is that during the composition and completion of the text, the question of the confessing subject was never clearly answered. It is not possible to repeat the situation in 1528 when one man, Luther, made his confession before God as a testament in the face of death. Who is confessing in our texts? The Schwabach Articles do not say who is speaking through them. They begin with an indefinite "one" and proceed to formulate individual articles in an objective and didactic tone, concluding with another "one" in Schwab. 17. Only the content of this last article, which deals with the abolition or preservation of church ceremonies, gives us a clue that "one" refers to the evangelical authorities who were at that moment carrying out their visitations. Yet, it is not possible to apply that insight automatically to the doctrinal statements themselves.

The situation is somewhat different with the Torgau Articles. Here theological experts are speaking as advisers to their princes: in E it is the Wittenbergers as a whole; in A, Melanchthon as their representative. In the version that was sent on May 11, 1530, to Luther at the Coburg, the prefaces Ja and especially E lead us to assume that Elector John the Steadfast is defending himself personally as a prince of the empire before his imperial lord. In Na as well, the elector is the subject, even if the wording implies that his councilors are stating his case before the emperor. In the doctrinal articles, they report what is being preached in the electorate. In the "disputed articles," they address themselves directly to the emperor, professing their common Christian position and asking his approval for the ecclesiastical changes in Saxony. The subject of this confession is—in what is legally an interesting innovation—the elector together with his councilors, and not his spiritual and temporal estates.

Although Nb (as is the case with Sp. and A I) is written in the passive voice and therefore, as in the Schwabach Articles, originates from an indefinite "one"—the official German text maintains that syntax—the Latin text has a personal subject and repeats it throughout all the doctrinal articles: "Our churches teach with great unanimity, . . . they also teach . . ."[93] Here the Latin text obviously refers to the end of Brueck's preface, which reads, "This is our confession and that of our associates" (*BS* 49.12; *BC* 27.24). The meaning of "our" in this passage becomes clear from the beginning of the preface. The evangelical estates that are to present the Augustana to the emperor are placing in his hands a "confession of our pastors' and preachers' teaching and of our own faith, setting forth how and in what manner, on the basis of the Holy Scriptures, these things are preached, taught, communicated, and embraced in our lands, principalities, dominions, cities, and territories" (*BS* 45.30–46.3; *BC* 25.8). And although the Latin text is abbre-

---

93. Only CA 20, conceived last and originally in German, deviates from the pattern of the Latin version, beginning defensively, "Our teachers are falsely accused . . ."

viated at this point and in the summary, the German summary includes once again the "doctrines that are preached and taught in our churches for proper Christian instruction, the consolation of consciences, and the amendment of believers. Certainly we should not wish to put our own souls and consciences in grave peril before God . . ." (BS 83c.7–15; BC 47.1). Out of all this several perspectives emerge that are relevant to the question about who is doing the confessing.

1. The *bearers of Christian authority* are confessing. In this confession they align themselves both with the pastors and preachers of their realms and with their subjects. Like Luther at Worms, they call upon their conscience, which is bound to Scripture. Because of this captivity to Scripture, they give free rein to the preachers, who are similarly bound, to perform their service. All salvation depends on being so bound. When the imperial estates know that they are responsible for this salvation of the believers in their realms, they do not stand above them, but salvation for the lord is the same as for the subject. All of them together stand under obligation to the same divine truth.

2. It is Chancellor Brueck who formulated those decisive principles of the preface. The summary and the introductory formula for the doctrinal articles, if not stemming directly from him, have been influenced by those same general principles. The *politician* has carefully weighed all that. The duty of the territorial ruler to protect his subjects is an argument in favor of self-determination among the estates, an argument that had already played a role in their achieving and maintaining territorial sovereignty; to apply it in cases regarding imperial law was not without precedent. Consideration for the territorial states is always kept in mind. After all, evangelical preaching occurred in the "principalities, dominions, cities, and territories" under the sole responsibility of the local ruler. Still, each representative of the estates—of the nobles and cities (the prelates who possessed territory are not mentioned before CA 28)—stands in his own place, bound equally in conscience and responsible equally in concern. The territorial rulers' government of the church proves to be wide in jurisdiction but spiritually bound in its actions.

3. Chancellor Brueck is a *lay theologian;* he does not treat these relationships between imperial estates, territorial estates, subjects, and preachers as though he were a theologian but as a diplomat and administrator trained in law. In the preface he presents his simple lay faith. We ought not look for theological mysteries behind his propositions, whether they involve the relation between Christian authorities and their subjects, particularly pastors, or between pastors and congregations, specifically their patrons or rulers. These cases are not thought through in the preface; that will happen either later in

an oblique way in the appropriate article or not at all. One should not apply a theological thumbscrew to the preface.[94]

4. The introductory sentence of the Latin version, "Our churches teach with great unanimity," does not give an adequate grammatical indication of the subject of the Augustana. Rather it abbreviates the more explicit sentences of the preface and the summary; it must therefore be understood in their light and in the light of the following articles. The congregations do not teach; they gather around God's Word (CA 7) and witness to its truth in the power of the Holy Spirit (CA 5) through the believing deed (CA 6). But in this witness they are free—bound to Scripture and conscience precisely like the ruler and pastor. Together with these two other jurisdictions, the congregation takes the Confession upon its conscience. Not in an exclusive sense, but in "great unanimity" with the other two estates of Christendom, the confessing congregation is the subject of the Confession. It confesses and condemns.

94. In the first chapter ("Ecclesiae docentes") of his book *Die Augsburger Konfession und Luthers Katechismen auf theologische Gegenwartswerte* untersucht (Giessen, 1930), Karl Thieme definitely goes too far when he uses this method to validate the right of the evangelical lay congregation.

QUESTIONS RELATING TO
ORDERS

9. DEVELOPMENT OF THE TEXT OF CA 28

The textual history of CA 28 is tightly interwoven with the composition of the Torgau Articles.

The starting point was E (cp. E 4 and 5), which had been composed in March with Luther's help. That document presupposes the continued existence of the medieval hierarchy, but it makes the recognition of that hierarchy dependent on two conditions: bishops must stop requiring vows of celibacy and of the renunciation of evangelical doctrine at ordination; and in the same vein, the pope must give the gospel free course. If these two conditions remain unfulfilled, the supply of clergy will decline; evangelicals will look for other forms of ordination and installation.

Here the problem of ecclesiastical jurisdiction is tackled exclusively from the practical side. Basic considerations of canon law or imperial law play no role. The Saxon territory contents itself with freedom for evangelical doctrine, sets its sights on a reordering of worship—at least as far as installation and ordination are concerned—and settles down to an existence guaranteed by a national church, free of Rome. These were the conclusions drawn from the Saxon visitations.

The challenge to the pope is sweeping; the only thing left for him to do is to accept the measures taken in Saxony.

Legal concerns also seem to be uppermost in an opinion rendered by Melanchthon about March 27 on the occasion of a visit to Torgau.[95]

In this opinion episcopal jurisdiction is approached with the same reticence as in E 4. The topic is no longer ordination but now "spiritual matters" in general. They have slipped out of the bishops' hands; the elector has not taken them away. But he wants to help the bishops—and this is a new note— win that jurisdiction back if the bishops will not use the occasion to burden the poor people's consciences and thereby stir up new unrest and tumult. The

95. *CR* 2:80–81. The basis for the early dating is in W. Maurer, "Die Entstehung" (cited above, n. 18), 365ff.; idem, "Erwägungen und Verhandlungen" (cited above, n. 1), 352–53, 212.

ruler thus wants to work with the proper diocesan bishops in setting up a new ordinance by which evangelical freedom and the evangelical office of the ministry can be guaranteed; that is, he wants to reconcile the bishops to the ecclesiastical situation brought about by the church visitations. He wants to do this for the sake of the responsibility for consciences he holds in common with those bishops.

Melanchthon, certainly in consultation with Luther, developed these principles further.[96] He formulated the position somewhat more sharply: the elector does not desire episcopal jurisdiction, but in the exercise of his duties as patron he wants to protect those of his subjects who are married priests from abuses, and he is not ready to reinstate the previous arrangements. The necessity of sacramental ordination is questioned more explicitly than in E 5. But precisely at this point follows the decisive peace offer that determined the development of CA 28 and the later negotiations at the diet: the elector is willing to yield in all questions of ordination and jurisdiction, wherever he can do so with a good conscience. The reason for this concession is concern for Germany's future. Divisions and turmoil must be put aside. A religious peace will serve that end. The bishops are to accommodate the evangelicals by tolerating the new teachings and not condemning them.

The compromise formulated in A 7 goes beyond the original proposal of E 4 and 5. Melanchthon expanded it further in CA 28 and pursued it to the end of the diet. But first of all he won Luther over to the strategy of unity. Before the end of their ride together to the Coburg and no later than April 23, the two of them must have talked through this strategy one more time. A few days thereafter Luther publicly described it to the German bishops in his *Exhortation to All Clergy Assembled at Augsburg for the Diet of 1530.*[97] In it he not only endorsed Melanchthon's own future attitude but also CA 28 and, along with it, the whole Augustana. In addition he predetermined the course of the negotiations. Of course Luther always emphasized the freedom of the gospel more strongly than the concessions to the bishops. Nevertheless, the compromise he approved sowed the seeds of later dissension that would affect the assessment and exposition of the Augustana.

Probably during the first days in Augsburg—before the first draft of the CA was sent to Luther at the Coburg on May 11—Melanchthon composed a supplement to A 6 and 7 which may have been attached to that draft instead of the later article 28.[98] It deals with legal questions relating to episcopal jurisdiction. Melanchthon approved episcopal excommunication, though

---

96. A 6, 7 (Förstemann 1:78–81; Reu 87–89).

97. *WA* 30.2:335ff., esp. 341.25ff.; *LW* 34:44–52, esp. 50.

98. Designated C hereafter, following Förstemann 1:87ff.; ET: Jacobs 88–90. The first of the three related articles is printed in *BS* 120ff.

only within biblical limits and without extending it to temporal jurisdiction. He thought that pastors ought to be able to call upon episcopal courts to deal with members who despised the Sacrament or who led dissolute lives.[99] Episcopal jurisdiction over marriage should be removed, and canon law on marriage should be replaced by civil law; papal dispensations should disappear.[100]

On these two points, C amplifies suggestions from A 6. In the first section (C 1), "Of the Power of the Keys," the theological problem of the two authorities is tackled for the first time; this theme will form the nucleus of the developing article. The pope is wrong when he uses the power of the keys as a basis for political power over kings. It is rather "only spiritual government, the preaching of the gospel, the reproof and forgiveness of sins, and the administration of the sacraments." This sentence, which is taken over almost verbatim in the final version,[101] is supported by several biblical citations that also reappear in the final edition. These theses were pressed home in reference to the pope; the polemic against him that we traced back to Luther in E 5 is here supported by arguments that had been used by conciliarists in the late Middle Ages.

In accordance with the distinction between the two authorities, no political consequences are drawn from the theological basis. The temporal rights of the pope and bishops remain untouched. But their ecclesiastical right to make laws and grant dispensations is completely denied. In principle the pope (like the bishops) possesses no more ecclesiastical rights than any pastor.

In making that point in C 1, Melanchthon took the decisive step toward the final version of CA 28; it involved the attack on the pope. In the process of developing the article, which had started before May 22, a significant change had occurred. To Luther's dismay, the antipapal polemic was replaced by a discussion of the relationship between temporal rulers and bishops.[102] That move was certainly in line with the proposed compromise. The separation of the two powers determined how far one could go in accommodating the bishops regarding the question of jurisdiction, as well as determining that, in the process, their political position would not be adversely affected. In all the questions of law it discusses, C 1 presupposes the compromise formulated in A 7 and endorsed by Luther's *Exhortation*.

Up to the end of May, Melanchthon moved ahead with his reworking of the

99. C 2 (Förstemann 1:89–90; Reu 125). In his *Exhortation*, Luther also approved such "episcopal power" (*WA* 30.2:342.21–22; *LW* 34:50 and n. 100). The final version (*BS* 120.12–13; *BC* 81.2) speaks of the "violent use of the ban" which "burdened consciences."

100. C 3 (Förstemann 1:90–91; Reu 90).

101. Cp. *BS* 120.27–28 with 121.14ff. (Reu 124 with *BC* 81.5–6).

102. *WBr* 5:no. 1576.27ff. (Melanchthon to Luther, May 22); *WBr* 5:no. 1657.9; *LW* 49:382–90 (Luther to Melanchthon, July 21).

elements available in A and C. What was handed over to the Nürnberg delegates on May 31 in the form of Na 28 was a completely new and more comprehensive text,[103] which contained only traces of A but which was closely tied to C 1. In the distinction between temporal and spiritual government, the agreement extends to word-for-word copying. The justification for temporal rule suffers from an unfortunate comparison between bishops as bearers of temporal authority and the apostles as physicians and craftsmen; it shows that Melanchthon has not yet thought through the problems completely. On the other hand, spiritual power is quite clearly described as the power of the Word. This definition also limits the authority of the bishops as lawmakers for the church.

This point of view also governs the questions of Sunday observance and holy days. Christian liberty is to be protected. Article A 1 had already dealt with such questions more fully—and more polemically. Luther confronted them in the preparation of his *Exhortation*. He sometimes discussed them with sarcasm and sometimes with a certain sympathy for them as instructive "child's play and fool's play" for the young.[104] Throughout that work he deals with practical problems that crop up again in other "disputed articles."

A new element in Na 28 is the concluding warning to the bishops that they ought to exercise great forbearance in all questions related to ordinances. Melanchthon thus recalls the condition he placed on the recognition of episcopal jurisdiction and repeats his willingness to see to it that the spiritual estate does not restore "unity to its own disadvantage."[105] One notices that questions of jurisdiction over marriage which were raised in C 3 are given no attention. Episcopal power of excommunication, treated in C 2, is now extended to cover teaching authority and is closely bound to Scripture (Kolde 29.6ff.). Seen as a whole, Na 28 makes broad concessions to bishops of the old religion. One has the impression that the Saxon court and chancellery were hopeful about the coming negotiations.

In the middle of June, shortly before the arrival of the emperor, the decision was near; the compromise prepared in Na 28 must be put in final form. In the German version which the Nürnberg delegates sent to their town council just before the emperor's entry,[106] it is no longer the elector who speaks, but the whole group of imperial estates who signed the document. The new title, "Of the Power of Bishops," excludes every allusion to the pope.

In general, Nb 28 holds to the pattern of Na. Unclear or misleading

103. In Kolde 26–31; Reu 272–90. Cp. Kolde 63–67.
104. Förstemann 1:69–74, 100–108 (= *WA* 30.2:251–55, 352–53); *LW* 34:59.
105. Kolde 31.16; Reu 288. Cp. Kolde 31.30ff.
106. Citations of Nb will be from the German text in *BS*, which remained almost the same.

passages are expunged,[107] or in some cases, such as in connection with the position of bishops as territorial rulers, they are replaced with more exact formulations. In the process, the theological difference between the two authorities comes more clearly to the fore, and opposition to previous episcopal practice is sharpened to the point of reproaching "doctrines of the devil" according to 1 Tim. 4:1 (*BS* 128.20ff.; *BC* 89.49). The fact that individual bishops have overstepped their authority by issuing regulations about ceremonies is brought up along with proof from canon law that originally there had been greater freedom in the church.

Despite this sharpened tone and content, Melanchthon maintains the original mediating strategy almost intact.[108] He still tenders an official recognition of episcopal jurisdiction. On the other hand, he enumerates the conditions that must be fulfilled if the unity of the church is to be maintained.

Among these conditions are not only, as in Na, the waiving of the requirement of celibacy and the anti-evangelical oath but also the demand for both elements in the Lord's Supper. It occurs here for the first time and is again omitted in the Latin version of the authentic text. A further sharpening consists in the threat of renouncing allegiance to the bishops, following Acts 5:29, if they continue to violate consciences with unevangelical demands.[109]

The changes that the authentic text makes in contrast to Nb and the final German version are insignificant stylistic refinements. The fact that several variations in the Latin text more closely resemble Na may mean that Melanchthon used Na for the final Latin text, which is closer to it than to Nb. In any case, the two texts are not "translations" from one language to the other; each is an independent product.[110]

Once again let us review the textual history of CA 28. A somewhat self-contained development moves from the juridical over into the theological. The key point is the beginning of the development of the doctrine of the two authorities, illustrated essentially by the spiritual. In the final preface, Chancellor Brueck eliminated references to the proposed compromise. Did he consider it politically intolerable, or did he have suspicions about the theological distinction? In any case, the political element needed the theological one, and vice versa. Neither part of the strategy would be realized without the other. Neither was realized.

When we see how all the problems of theology and imperial law that arose from the beginning of the Augustana on are intertwined in CA 28, we can understand the length of time and the care that has been applied to interpret-

107. See my references in "Die Entstehung" (cited above, n. 18), 380ff.
108. Cp. Kolde 31.11ff. (Reu 288) with *BS* 131.36ff. or *BS* 93.69.
109. This too is not yet present in Na. Cp. Kolde 31.30ff.; Reu 288.
110. Details in "Die Entstehung," 383 n. 58. Perhaps this explains why the demand for Communion in both kinds is omitted from the Latin text.

ing the text. Added to that is the fact that CA 28 is related to both parts of the Confession and must be interpreted in the light of both. Communion in both kinds (CA 22), celibacy of priests (CA 23), and the mass as sacrifice (CA 24) were the points at which the conflict with bishops of the old religion broke out first and most vehemently. They were therefore brought up in E and from that time on they always appear in the same sequence. They are among the conditions that characterized the "freedom of the gospel" in the compromise that was proposed to the bishops. All questions of law and worship are connected to that freedom. How, in the process, temporal and spiritual authority are to find the proper relation to each other is determined by the relationship of God's two ways of governing. That relationship was first presented with axiomatic clarity in C 1, the most important predecessor of CA 28. From that source all the articles of the CA, whether dealing with faith or order, receive their characteristic light.

10. GOD'S TWO WAYS OF GOVERNING

At this point we encounter the normative doctrinal issue of the Confession. It lays the foundation for settling the practical questions. Article 28 is not the first place it can be found, but it is clearest there.

Among the Lutheran confessions, CA 28 offers the most fundamental statements about the doctrine of the two ways of governing (two kingdoms). They must be compared with Luther's statements; only in that way can their binding theological force be recognized. In comparing them, however, one must remember that CA 28 is not a doctrinal article; we cannot expect binding dogmatic statements there—in fact less there than elsewhere. Our historical overview has shown us something entirely different: in CA 28 Melanchthon has laid out a well-prepared strategy for negotiation, approved by Luther; it sets the direction for political and theological discussions at the Augsburg diet. The doctrine of the two ways of governing provides the theological basis for this strategy, and we must start out by asking ourselves if this doctrine can be fully dealt with in such a condensed statement written for a specific purpose.

Melanchthon did not wait until the end of CA 28 (*BS* 131.36ff.; *BC* 93.69ff.) to set forth his program for unity. He had made references to it in an anticipatory way throughout the article and thus partially touched upon questions he had already raised in the "disputed articles." Right at the beginning, in the transition from the basic to the practical section (*BS* 123.14ff.; *BC* 83.19), CA 28 protects itself from the revolutionary possibility that the distinction between temporal and spiritual power could somehow lead to withdrawal of the regalia, followed by removal of the bishops (see below). Juridical power, too, including jurisdiction over marriages, is to remain with the bishops (*BS* 125; *BC* 85.29), even though they may have been guilty of much negligence in these matters.[111] In the section on ceremonial questions, which takes up once again almost all the problems of the "disputed articles," the conciliatory attitude of the confessing princes is repeatedly emphasized. They are willing to retain all ordinances that do not contradict the gospel (*BS* 126.3ff.; *BC* 86.34) as long as they are not declared necessary for salvation; for the sake of love and peace the princes will obey the bishops, so that no disorders occur (*BS* 129.27ff.; *BC* 90.55).

In conclusion Melanchthon once again summarizes the compromise proposal (*BS* 131.36ff.; *BC* 93.69): unendurable church ordinances that cannot be observed without sin include Communion in one kind, the law of celibacy, and the oath against evangelical teaching.[112] On these points, without forfeiting their honor and dignity, the bishops could and should give in and abrogate or relax unevangelical regulations. If they do not do that, they continue to force consciences to sin; in that case they cannot be obeyed, and they thus become responsible for the schism and will have to account for that to God. Whoever thinks this language too hard should compare the "summary of the doctrine" which forms the transition from the doctrinal articles to the "disputed articles." Here, especially clearly in the Latin text (*BS* 83c.7ff.; *BC* 47.2), complete toleration of the reorganizations introduced through the visitations is demanded of the bishops, based on the presupposition that the doctrine is the same. This presupposition also underlies the compromise sought in CA 28. Whoever, like Luther, does not share that presupposition, must consider the principles formulated in CA 28 inadequate despite all the desire for unity.

In the preliminary documents, harsher notes were struck; they may still have been echoing in Luther's ears when he received the final text of the Confession during the last days of June. The first Wittenberg opinion (E) had said of the bishops, "However, where they do not relent, they must fall and go to ruin." And when the compromise proposal first surfaced in A, the concern for threatened consciences still was paramount; if he alone were involved, explained the elector, he would "at our own peril, treat the adversaries . . .

111. Na (Kolde 28.5ff.) is much more cautious and indefinite; CA 28 is much more open to compromise. The latter is closer to the starting point of the debate in C (Förstemann 1:89–90; Jacobs 89), which accepts the Donation of Constantine in regard to the pope, and goes on to reject revolt against the bishops and to concede them the power of excommunication. When one remembers the rejection of bishops that dominates E and goes on into A (Förstemann 1:96, 78ff.; Jacobs 94, 82), one detects an increasing accommodation and is helped to understand Luther's growing caution on the question of jurisdiction.

112. It is interesting that the Latin text restricts itself to jurisdiction over clergy and omits the mass; the German at least mentions Communion in both kinds. Congregational worship, which is the focus of CA 22 and 24, does not enter the picture in CA 28. CA 23, at least in the German version, called on the authority of the emperor to oppose forced celibacy; CA 23 Variata vehemently intensified the appeal; CA 28 totally abandoned it.

with still greater rigor."[113] Even in the first version of the preface, which Melanchthon had composed in mid-March while still at the Coburg, the "prelates" appear as blind leaders of the blind who have looked on idly while the people have been led astray. They were counted among the "opponents" who fought the ecclesiastical changes in Saxony without understanding them.[114] It is the preface to Na (*BS* 43.12ff.) that first refers to the planned compromise and asks the bishops to abstain from persecuting married clergy and to recognize the new church orders. In return they are assured recognition of their spiritual power and their temporal possessions.[115] If one reviews this prehistory of CA 28, the inclusion of this compromise with the bishops in its final formulation must seem to be an immense—and unplanned—concession. What is the significance of the doctrine of the two ways of governing for this compromise?

The argument given for it from Luther's doctrine of the two "authorities" appears first in C and is still somewhat inadequate. Melanchthon begins with the pope's claim to be able to appoint and remove kings on the basis of his power of the keys. Melanchthon counters by defining the true *potestas clavium:* "the preaching of the gospel, the reproof and forgiveness of sins, and the administration of the sacraments."[116] These duties, originally laid upon the apostles, constitute the "spiritual authority" that is the "office of bishops *or* priests." Temporal authority is denied them all by the Holy Scriptures. At the same time, however, the divine legitimacy of temporal rule is also recognized; to contest that is to be a rebel. Likewise, the above definition of the power of the keys does not include the creation of new laws and regulations for public worship which are not based on the gospel. If the pope forces them on Christians, the latter must obey God rather than human beings. Especially in the administration of the sacrament of penance the pope has no more power than any pastor.

Melanchthon's starting point in the doctrine of penance and his consequent attention to the power of the keys gives a peculiar stamp to his interpretation of the doctrine of the two ways of governing. On the one hand, it is thereby closely tied to justification. On the other hand, from the very beginning it is grouped with principles of the ecclesiastical office and its ordinances; temporal authority does not contribute anything of its own to this process, but instead it is defined by limiting spiritual authority. Both of these peculiarities become immediately apparent in the way Na 28 presents the material.

Here again penance is the starting point; the distinction of the two au-

113. Förstemann 1:96, 80–81; Jacobs 94, 83.
114. *BS* 38.17ff., 39.6ff.; Reu 94, 95.
115. In Brueck's final preface, the repetition of the Protest of Speyer and the appeal to a future council rule out any compromise with the bishops.
116. Förstemann 1:87ff.; *BS* 120.16ff.; Jacobs 88–89.

thorities serves to console consciences (Kolde 27.3ff.). The functions of the office of the keys are specified exactly as in C (27.6ff.); the office is identical with the office of preaching (27.12ff.). But Na tries harder and more directly to define the limits over against temporal authority. The latter concerns itself only with physical things, but the spiritual power administers spiritual, eternal goods; the Spirit works here through the Word (27.14ff.). The difference between the two authorities thus corresponds to that between body and spirit. That is a typically Melanchthonian contrast, which we do not find in Luther. It allows Melanchthon to come to the remarkable conclusion that the spiritual authority can no more come into conflict with the temporal than singing or arithmetic could (27.20ff.), since they too are "spiritual" activities; the temporal authority, however, protects and punishes only the body (27.24ff.).

Thus the difference between temporal and spiritual authority consists in a division of labor. Each carries out a special mandate. Neither ought to interfere with the other; in particular, the spiritual should not set standards for the temporal or hinder it (27.28ff.). This demand became complicated for the bishops, because they also had temporal power—which no one wanted to take away or could take away (28.5ff.). But this temporal power must be sharply distinguished from their spiritual power; it does not originate in the latter and has nothing to do with the gospel. Thus the distinction between body and spirit helped at this point in the recognition of the princely dimension of the office of bishop within the empire—a prerogative going back to the reforms of Otto I. It was seen from the perspective—whether rightly or wrongly is yet to be determined—that the spiritual could not be affected by the physical. This point of view was applied even to the apostles. They were fishermen, physicians, and weavers, yet they performed the office of preaching. Likewise, the contemporary pastor can live from his benefices and still fulfill the duties of his spiritual office (28.13ff.).

Thus the relation of temporal and spiritual government coincides with that of temporal and spiritual authority (29.2ff) and therefore with the question of the two offices. That is a foreshortening of the Lutheran approach which we must note if we wish to make a theological evaluation of God's two ways of governing. Melanchthon's primary concern in regard to the bishops was that they not confuse their spiritual with their temporal power. Such confusion has led to much war and tumult (26.31ff). Spiritual power consists in preaching and the administration of the sacraments. The sword is denied it; it works "without human power, simply by the Word."[117] Only where it preaches the Word is the Christian obliged to obey it (29.9ff.). These principles are then applied to the validity of church ceremonies and laws (29.12ff.).

117. Cp. Kolde 29.8–9 with *BS* 124.9 (*BC* 84.21 Latin).

At important points Na 28 moves beyond its predecessor C. What the earlier document said about the relationship between pope and emperor is now addressed to the misuse of episcopal power for political ends. The previous improper confusion of temporal and spiritual power is to be resolved by dividing them sharply. No longer is that point supported by a series of proof texts, but it is now rather supported by the incomparable power of the Word of God.[118] On the basis of A, Na (31.11ff.) also develops the plan for unity and appeals to the pastoral gentleness of the bishops.

There are also other places where Na goes beyond C. For Na, abuse of the power of the keys nullifies the gospel and defames the merit of Christ. If the efficacious power of the Word of God constitutes spiritual authority, as the Spirit is bound to the Word, then the false distinction between spirit and flesh is overcome and temporal authority is no longer disqualified as less worthy. On the contrary, Na emphasizes the independence and value of temporal authority, as Luther did.[119] Even the legal rights of the spiritual power were not just delimited but also evaluated positively. They demand obedience. It is owed to them not as institution but on the basis of the Word of God. The power to teach and excommunicate is included (29.6–11). But, if anyone teaches or commands in contradiction to God's Word, he ought not be obeyed (29.11–20).

In this extension of C, Na 28 uses the doctrine of the two authorities to begin to create a basis for the planned settlement. The submission to episcopal power offered in the compromise rests on this duty of the faithful to be obedient. The duty to resist teachings and regulations contrary to the gospel provides grounds for a possible refusal. It thereby limits the legislative and jurisdictional power of the bishops. The individual examples that Na (29.21–31.10) adduces go far beyond what C[120] had mentioned in its brief references to papal dispensations. Those clerical claims are limited not only by the statutory regulations of the Bible but also by the evangelical saving faith itself and by a conscience bound to the Word of God (30.9ff.).

These theological opinions, which go beyond anything in Na's preparatory documents, make its concluding article appear to be a successful attempt by Melanchthon to apply the doctrine of the two authorities to the situation of the Augsburg diet in an effective way. The changes later made in the two final

---

118. *BS* 120.31–37 (Jacobs 89) is replaced by Kolde 27.12–24; only allusions to *BS* 123.27–124.34 (Jacobs, paragraph beginning on bottom of p. 89) remain.

119. Kolde 27.30–28.5. Respect for the temporal possessions of the bishops (ibid., 28.5–6) is related to this view. The somewhat naive reasoning (ibid., 28.13ff.) is still found in the Latin Ansbach and other manuscripts but is discarded by the Saxon chancellery before Nb in mid-June. The manuscripts are to be dated accordingly.

120. *BS* 123.27–124.34; Jacobs 89–90.

versions of CA 28 are only editorial.[121] The more exact references to Gratian's *Decretal* and to Augustine, however, are not without significance. From the passages that are there (II, causa II, q. 7) cited *against* the submission of bishops to lay jurisdiction, Melanchthon picked only those which either treated love and obedience to the bishop by church members (chap. 8) or which left open the possibility of accusation because of deviation from the faith (chap. 13). This is not the first time we have seen the use of canon law as a witness to evangelical truth; in addition to Melanchthon, the Nürnberg town clerk, Lazarus Spengler, was especially fond of this tactic.[122] The fact that CA 28 bases the Christian's duty both to obey and to resist the bishops on the *Decretum* is an especially elegant chess move by Melanchthon, through which he supports his mediating proposal. Obedience results from the irresistible force of God's Word in the spiritual authority. Resistance is necessary, on the other hand, if there is interference with God's Word in the spiritual realm.

After this review of its development, it is possible to list the themes defining the doctrine of the two authorities in CA 28. The starting point is the power of the keys, that is, the spiritual authority which is at work in the liturgical events of confession and absolution. Thus the connection with justification is made from the very start. God effects it through his Word, which is proclaimed with divine authority by his servants. Spiritual authority is therefore concentrated in the liturgical events of an ordered church. It is present in the spiritual activity of the "bishop," which includes administration of the sacraments and discipline over teaching and morals. In the process, a certain narrowing and institutionalizing of the doctrine of authorities is unmistakable. On the other hand, it must be recognized that the narrow focus on the Word preached in accordance with Scripture completely overthrows the traditional hierarchical structure. A bishop possesses spiritual authority only insofar as he preaches. If he is not willing or able to do that, he may indeed hold temporal rule and possessions, but he must permit—in accordance with the presupposition of the plan for unity—free course to evangelical preaching and administration of the sacraments. The evangelical

121. Thus, for example, the high esteem of Na for temporal authority is demonstrated by the fact that the final draft declares both powers, which include the magisterial, as special gifts of the grace of God (*BS* 121.4ff., 8ff.; *BC* 81.4). *BS* 123.12–13 (*BC* 83.19) corresponds to Kolde 28.4, where both powers are commended as praiseworthy gifts of God. Occasionally Melanchthon can play off the physical power of the temporal authority against the spiritual influence of God's Word. *BS* 122.18–20 (*BC* 82.11) is an addition of the Latin version that maintains a dualism expressed in Kolde 27.19ff. and picked up in *BS* 122.13 (*BC* 82.10). The abbreviation of Kolde 28.23–29.5 in the German *BS* 123.22–124.8 (*BC* 84.21–22) is not theologically relevant; it merely adds weight to the assurance of obedience.

122. Cp. W. Maurer, "Reste des Kanonischen Rechts im Frühprotestantismus," *ZSavRG kanonist* 51 (1965): 190–253; and idem, *Die Kirche und ihr Recht* (cited above, n. 1), 145–207.

congregation, however, can—and indeed must—examine everyone who lays claim to the preaching office in their midst. They know the voice of their Good Shepherd; when it is audible in worship they submit themselves to the preaching office with undivided allegiance. When the Word of God is silenced by false teaching and human laws, the believers must obey God rather than human beings. Spiritual authority sets an uncrossable boundary for human-temporal authority.

Temporal authority forms the reverse side of the spiritual. In fact, one can observe that during the course of the editorial work on CA 28, there was an intensification of concern about expressing the divine origin and value of temporal authority. The focus, however, is always limited to institutionalized rule. There is no consideration given to the fact that God's temporal authority ranges far beyond that to include nature and history as well. According to CA 28 it is confined to the body, keeping order in human society through external punishments. Its positive, God-pleasing activity is not mentioned here. There is also no attention given to the fact that there is more to the relation between the two authorities than an unbridgeable difference; there is also a divinely willed connection. To recognize this, however, one must go beyond CA 28 and evaluate the whole tenor of the CA. There the relationship of the two kingdoms forms a basic theme that defines the Confession's total structure. The subject does not arise for the first time in these paragraphs; it is also addressed earlier. Our next job is to compare the doctrinal content of CA 28 with the statements of Luther and Melanchthon on the two authorities.

11. EXPOSITION OF CA 28 IN THE DISCUSSION THAT ACCOMPANIED THE AUGSBURG DIET

Article 28 is not a self-contained dogmatic statement; it represents the result of a lively discussion that began long before 1530, continued between Luther and Melanchthon, and still went on during the negotiations at the diet. Its results are found not only in private letters but also in the journalistic publications by which Luther tried to enter into the process from the Coburg.

In this series, the first place in time and significance goes to Luther's *Exhortation to All Clergy Assembled at Augsburg* (1530).[123] Carefully prepared, this work not only incorporates the proposal for unity that had been agreed upon with Melanchthon and the electoral council (340.20–342.34, 345.20;

123. *WA* 30.2:(237), 268–356; *LW* 34:9–61. Citations in parentheses in the text refer to these editions.

LW 34:49–51, 52)[124] but also offers a whole arsenal of facts and reasons for that proposal. They all are evidence for Luther's evaluation of CA 28.

Almost all the problems Melanchthon discusses in that article and more generally in the "disputed" items of the second part of the CA were already raised by Luther in the *Exhortation*. It demonstrates how heavily Luther had been involved in equipping the Saxons for the diet; E and A were two products of that effort. Together with the *Exhortation*, they provide us with a proper appraisal of Luther's participation in the developing Augustana, especially its second part.[125]

These are, however, reflections after the fact. The top priority for Luther early in 1530[126] was to influence the prelates' section of the diet. He wanted to strengthen the will of the bishops for church reform and to channel that reform in the same direction as the evangelical innovations. He pleaded with them to join the emperor in moving forward with church reform and finally now at Augsburg to take seriously the gravamina as they had been presented at the diet at Worms (268.27ff., 271.24ff., 277.33ff.; *LW* 34:9, 10, 14). He reminds the spiritual lords that in the beginning of his reforming activity he had been an advocate for the bishops in their difficulties with the major orders and the pope (278.27ff.; *LW* 34:14–15).

A pact between Lutheran Reformation and the bishops is still possible, even though their former advocate now steps forward as a preacher of repentance, ruthlessly exposing the chief evils of the church and relentlessly making the bishops responsible for them—celibacy included (336.21ff.; *LW* 34:47). It is a stern love that sketches the portrait of a proper Christian bishop here, not "pussyfooting" like Melanchthon at the end of article 28 out of respect for episcopal dignity, and begging for tolerance. Luther thunders against a clergy that is heading for ruin: "Your blood be upon your own head! We are and want to be innocent of your blood and damnation" (355.29; *LW* 34:60 [cp. 331.25ff.; *LW* 34:44–45]).

Thus, despite all the agreement in specifics between Luther's *Exhortation* and the final article of the Augustana, there is a difference in tone. Does that also imply a material difference in the evaluation of the two authorities? There is nothing to be found on the subject in the *Exhortation*. It does not go into basic theological distinctions, not only because the bishops do not understand them (346.31ff.; *LW* 34:53) but also because the diet should

124. In his *Commentary on the Alleged Imperial Edict*, from April 1531, Luther once again aligned himself with the offer of the previous year (*WA* 30.3:368.18ff.; *LW* 34:92). Franziskus Arnoldi, pastor in Meissen, refers to this passage (*WA* 30.3:432.31ff.).

125. His preparatory materials, discussed and printed in *WA* 30.2:246ff., are also indicative.

126. The *Exhortation* was for sale in Augsburg at the beginning of June; it was written at the start of the Coburg period.

confine itself to simple practical questions "which are comprehensible and certain for all Christians, and which can be fully known by reason" (319.31ff.; *LW* 34:38). A theological difference between CA 28 and Luther cannot, therefore, be inferred from Luther's silence on the doctrine of two authorities in this document. It is rather that Melanchthon was on his own, acting without direct influence from Luther, when he composed C in Augsburg at the beginning of May and then expanded the doctrine further in Na. Previously there had been no theological basis for the compromise Melanchthon was seeking.[127]

Nevertheless, Luther's inner hesitation about the efforts for unity very soon led to a sudden change.[128] It was probably caused by the reports that had been sent to him by his friends at Augsburg immediately before and after the presentation of the Confession.[129] After being partially informed, Luther received additional bad news: despondency from Melanchthon and Brenz, the imperial ban on preaching, the summons to Melanchthon and Jonas from Campeggio, and the limitations that were imposed on the presentation of the Confession on June 25. In this situation, Melanchthon's intention to moderate the basic presuppositions of the planned compromise must have been extremely irritating to Luther, even though his friend reminded him of the agreements made earlier.[130] Luther does not want to bear sole responsibility for it; despite his readiness for compromise he can only concede specifically designated points and even then only to the degree that they are in accord with the gospel.[131]

During these days and in this frame of mind,[132] Luther mounted a new

127. Here also Luther, because of the theological incompetence of the bishops, thinks only of separating their jurisdictional and magisterial functions from the preaching office (*WA* 30.2:240.20ff.).

128. Luther's letter of July 6 to the cardinal archbishop of Mainz (*WA* 30.2:[391], 397–412) shows that by that time he no longer held to the compromise. He considers it no longer possible to produce unity in doctrine, and he asks the cardinal, like Gamaliel, to work toward toleration and peace; at the same time he is quite ready to use Psalm 2 in an attack against princes of the old religion. Luther's other writings from the Coburg—with the exceptions mentioned in the text—belong to this period, when the results of the diet had taught him that the compromise was unworkable. They therefore offer, at best, supplementary commentaries to CA 28.

129. On the twenty-fifth, from Melanchthon, Justus Jonas (twice), and Elector John (*WBr* 5:nos. 1600–1603); and on the twenty-sixth and twenty-seventh, from Melanchthon (*WBr* 5:nos. 1604, 1607).

130. Melanchthon wanted to revise CA 22–24 in order to anticipate the opposition of the other party to the abolition of private masses (*WBr* 5:nos. 1604.16ff., 1607.23ff.).

131. To Melanchthon, June 29 (*WBr* 5:no. 1609.43ff., 84ff.; *LW* 49:326–33). This letter was followed by a broadly worded letter of encouragement on June 30 (*WBr* 5:no. 1611), which did not deal directly with Melanchthon's question.

132. On June 27, "in my raging anger" (*WBr* 5:nos. 1614.47–48, 1654.8). The exposition of Psalm 118, written about June 20 and sent to Wittenberg for printing before the twenty-seventh, does not yet evidence this irritated state, even though it is not without criticism of the spiritual authority similar to that in the *Exhortation* (*WA* 31.1:84.23ff.; *LW* 14:54–55) and also alludes to abuse of the mass and the doctrine of purgatory (*WA* 31.1:131.25ff.; *LW* 14:76). The dedication to Abbot Pistorius in Nürnberg (*WA* 31.1:65–67; *LW* 14:45–46), sent on July 1, sounds a note of peace and joy.

attack on the papists in one of his most vehement polemical writings. It presupposes the Augustana even though it does not refer to it directly. *Disavowal of Purgatory*—the title is meant to be ironic. The Augustana does not mention purgatory. Luther wants to show that this omission does not imply that the earlier polemic against it has been disavowed. This time, however, he does not simply direct his attack against the exegetical and dogmatic arguments, the "lies and abominations," of the sophists. Instead, in countless ways he ridicules the financial practices connected with private masses and masses for the dead. This becomes the characteristic point of the polemic, touching objections that had been raised in the *Exhortation*. This attack strikes the nerve of traditional piety and destroys the cultic and financial basis of the foundations and monasteries.[133] This document makes clear that if church reform is desired, private masses cannot be ignored. It underscores this opposition by the announcement of a new offensive against them. Luther will not abandon the polemic against private masses, nor will he lose sight of this fixed point of reference in planning for unity; he will not make himself a party to such disgraceful abominations.[134]

On July 2, Luther, as he reported to Melanchthon the next day, once again read through the Augustana carefully.[135] The praise he accords it is not materially reduced by his criticism of Melanchthon's expectation of peace. Luther is convinced that their opponents will not satisfy the precondition of the planned compromise, which is freedom for evangelical preaching. On July 5, we find him absorbed in the preparation of the *Sermon on Keeping Children in School*. This work, planned as early as April 1529, and completed in mid-July 1530, avoids all polemics and sounds definitely friendly toward the emperor.[136] But it paints a picture of a future territorial and bureaucratic state in which Rome and the bishops no longer have a role. Theologians and jurists rule, both exercising spiritual and temporal authority. The work is arranged under this double heading; in lively colors it describes the picture of the two authorities that Melanchthon had only sketched in the Augustana. In the process it provides a graphic commentary on CA 28.[137]

In the preliminary notes *regnum spirituale et temporale* is already a strategical

---

133. What is given for the benefit of poor souls serves vile mammon (*WA* 30.2:368.20ff.) Cp. ibid., 375.17ff., 378.29ff., 386.20ff., 387.27ff., 373.5ff.

134. Ibid., 390.16ff., 387.7ff.

135. The first reading assumed here was not of the draft of early May (contrary to Clemen, *WBr* 5:no. 1621 n. 2, but in agreement with *LW* 49:343 n. 6) but of the final edition whose reception Luther had confirmed on June 29 (*WBr* 5:no. 1609.17; *LW* 49:328).

136. Note also the positive assessment of Roman law: *WA* 30.2:557.32ff., 558.17ff.; 26ff., 559.31ff., 561.23ff., 567.27ff., 568.17ff.; *LW* 46:239, 240, 241, 245. It is also intended for the civil legal profession (*WA* 30.2:575.32ff.; *LW* 46:250) and shows a social consciousness: "Children of common people one day must rule the world" (*WA* 30.2:577.24; *LW* 46:251).

137. *WA* 30.2:526.33–34, 554.20–21; *LW* 46:219, 237.

pairing.[138] The connection between the two authorities is more strongly emphasized than their differences, which is in line with the pedagogical purpose of the work. Because it shares the concrete task of CA 28—to set forth the uniqueness of the spiritual office—Luther's approach sees temporal authority as limited to life in time and to ruling with the fist; it is only a "shadow" of the spiritual. That should not be taken as Luther's critique of Melanchthon nor as a fall back into medieval categories; the approach is better interpreted as suited to the traditional understanding of office and to a theologically unsophisticated circle of readers. If this work is to be seen as a response to CA 28, it proves how far Luther had distanced himself from the historic episcopacy and how little he counted on the practical implementation of a compromise.[139]

It was even less possible for Luther to approve this implementation if it were to be bought at the price of further concessions. At the beginning of July, Melanchthon seemed more inclined than ever toward such a move. After negotiations with the papal legate Campeggio ran their course without results, it was feared that the emperor, under pressure from the Catholic princes—especially Duke George of Saxony—would demand retraction of the measures that had been introduced by the visitations. That would mean war. Luther kept a cool head during this dangerous period. He counted much more on a political armistice than on any agreement or toleration in questions of doctrine. But the political and ecclesiastical foundations had been pulled out from under the planned ecclesiastical-political compromise; further accommodations on the questions raised in CA 28 were therefore useless and intolerable.[140]

We can understand why Luther was not exactly enthusiastic about once again becoming embroiled by Melanchthon in a discussion of these questions. The debate that began established the fundamental principles of interpretation for the "disputed articles," and especially for CA 28. Luther had prepared the exposition thematically by means of theses that originally appeared in Latin, because they were intended primarily for the clergy assembled at Augsburg. Here, in contrast to what is found in CA 28, the debate concerns not episcopal authority in particular but ecclesiastical power in general. Luther deals with the church's power to make ordinances, which was the main question at stake in the Augsburg negotiations. He treats it from his

---

138. WA 30.2:509. It is not likely that the draft printed in ibid., 509–10 was written after Luther read the final version of the CA, and so the reference to the doctrine of the two authorities was prompted not by the CA but by Luther's own presuppositions. For an exposition of the draft, cp. ibid., 519.18ff., 554.23ff., 562.27ff.; LW 46:215, 237, 242.

139. Each of the details will be handled at its appropriate place.

140. WBr 5:nos. 1629.8ff., 1630.18ff., 1636.8ff., 1652.2ff., esp. Luther's letter to the elector on July 9 (WBr 5:no. 1633; LW 49:359–65) and its supplements concerning Melanchthon on July 9 and 13 (WBr 5:nos. 1634, 1642).

anti-hierarchical understanding of the church, placing the Word of God above the church and not the church over the Word (theses 1–8, 15). The church, that is, the local congregation rather than the entire church, can make its own liturgical rules as long as they are valid only for itself, do not conflict with the articles of faith, do not harm consciences, do not claim unchangeable validity, and are not impractical (theses 9–13, 18). Celibacy and monastic vows do not qualify; the pastor (prelate) can act only with the approval of his congregation (theses 14, 16, 17). A sharp attack against the heretical papists and an energetic defense against the charge that he himself is a heretic form the conclusion.[141]

To repeat: In this work Luther did not expressly pose the question from CA 28 on episcopal power, but in reality he answered it. Melanchthon raised it again and started out by answering it differently from Luther. His five-point program climaxed in the thesis that the bishops possessed power to rule by human right; on the strength of this authority they could force obedience in questions of order, of public education, and of religious practices.[142] This, therefore, was Melanchthon's understanding of what jurisdictional power CA 28 had conceded to the bishops. And in a supplement he also tossed the matter of votive masses into the debate. If they were to be understood as thank offerings owed to God, then the bishops could require their performance or their maintenance.[143] With that, Melanchthon abandoned the firm basis for the agreed-upon compromise that Luther had just so passionately defended in his work on purgatory.

Luther had to contradict him, and he did. On July 21, he made the counterassertion, "We cannot concede to the bishops, either by ecclesiastical or secular right, the power to determine something for the church, even when it is permissible and good."[144] Luther provides the proof in the form of a scholastic disputation. The thesis is that the primary concern in the making of ecclesiastical rules is not the final cause (*causa finalis*) but the efficient cause (*causa efficiens*); the latter, however, is based on God and his Word (6ff.; *LW* 49:382).

In the process, a distinction must be made between spiritual and temporal authority (10ff.; *LW* 49:383)—taking up the theme that formed the theological basis for the planned ecclesiastical-political compromise in CA 28. Now,

141. *Propositiones adversus totam synagogam Sathanae et universas portas inferorum* (*WA* 30.2:[413], 420–27). It is not possible to prove a direct connection with Melanchthon's inquiry of July 14; in fact the *Propositiones* were available in Augsburg before Luther answered Melanchthon on July 21.

142. See the letter of July 14 (*WBr* 5:no. 1646.31ff.): "I therefore posit that bishops are able to rule by human right" (ibid., 79).

143. *WBr* 5:no. 1655.11ff. (July 20).

144. *WBr* 5:no. 1656.63ff.; *LW* 49:386–87. The following citations in parentheses refer to this letter.

more logically and passionately, every confusion of the two powers is rejected; Christ himself commanded their separation.[145] They must, however, be considered as distinctions between offices, not individuals. Konrad of Thüngen is at the same time Duke of Franconia, therefore a ruler, and Bishop of Würzburg, therefore spiritual leader of a diocese (17ff.; *LW* 49:383–4). He must observe the separation of both functions in principle.[146] Although complete agreement existed between the two correspondents up to this point, the differences began in these propositions with Luther's assertion that no bishop could issue legal regulations without the explicit or tacit approval of his congregation (27ff.; *LW* 49:384–5); if this approval is lacking, the regulations become invalid. The bishops, thinks Luther, would never stand for this limitation of their power; if one were to give in to them here, as Melanchthon had suggested in his proposals on July 14, one would become a participant in all their sins.

But it would be a sacrilege to want to concede spiritual authority over the church to the bishop insofar as he is a *secular ruler*.[147] In this capacity, of course, he can require obedience of his subjects, even in external matters of church discipline like fasting, but the church as church never owes him obedience. If he demands it, even though it be by force and in the emperor's name (65ff., 76ff.; *LW* 49:386–87, 387–88), we must resist to the death. All theologically based attempts at accommodation merely disguise the fact that the bishops want to be temporal rulers and to hold congregations in their power by secular law (111ff.; 389).

Luther's polemic is thus directed not only against Melanchthon's arguments but more broadly against the original plan of compromise for which CA 28 was to form the theological foundation. The article was not invalidated because of Luther's criticism, but it was interpreted more rigorously. The two authorities were maintained, but they were distinguished more sharply than they would have been by Melanchthon. Every appearance of episcopal power to coerce—be it only on the basis of human law—was eliminated. Whatever pedagogical and cultic ordinances in the church were necessary belonged to the realm of temporal power. Melanchthon had declared every sort of disobedience to be sin, explaining that freedom and obedience were irreconcilable.

145. The proof text Luke 22:26 is not cited by CA 28; secs. 5–29 of that article should be consulted in the course of the following discussion.

146. On the difficulties Melanchthon had in presenting this duality and in giving reasons for it, see above, pp. 66–67.

147. "I speak of the church as a church which already has been separated from the political commonwealth," adds Luther (*WBr* 5:no. 1656.42–43; *LW* 49:385); the basic separation of ecclesiastical community and political community, which is therefore the logical consequence of the two authorities for Luther, was not achieved by law in Germany until the nineteenth century.

Luther, on the other hand, found Christian freedom included in obedience to the First Commandment.[148]

The debate dragged on still further, but Luther dropped the matter on August 4. The fact that the *Confutatio* did not pick up on the possibilities for compromise made the discussion superfluous; Luther was tired of hairsplitting.[149] Individual questions also came up. Although they were closely involved with the planned compromise (votive masses, Communion in both kinds), we will not go into their dogmatic content here. In addition, humanistic influences favoring the attempt at unity made themselves felt, both from the camp of Erasmus and Bishop von Stadion of Augsburg and from the court preacher Johannes Henckel and his patroness, Dowager Queen Maria of Hungary.[150] That is an indication of how widespread was the interest, or perhaps "hope" would be more accurate, in the planned attempt at unity. Nevertheless, the matter was already settled, even though the committee appointed by the emperor continued to negotiate about it into September.[151]

The results of this discussion are not insignificant, and they also help in understanding the Augustana. Melanchthon himself stated that he did not want to burden the church with episcopal control again in CA 28 even if he granted them a right by human law *(ius humanum)*; he was concerned not about forms of worship but about bodily exercises with a pedagogical goal. Luther's proof that there were instances in the Old Testament where temporal authority and worshiping congregation had cooperated in cultic reorganization obviously impressed Melanchthon.[152] In the battle over efficient and final causes, Melanchthon's scholarly pride did not want to give up the *causa finalis*. Luther's assertion, substantiated by the authority of the First Commandment, that in the church everything depends on God and his Word, was irrefutable. We must not, however, be misled into thinking that Luther thereby won a debate; he gave a more precise form to the theological basis for the heart of CA 28, the doctrine of the two authorities. The ecclesiastical-political occasion for it became incidental.[153]

148. *WBr* 5:no. 1646.65ff. Melanchthon the pedagogue declares that evangelical freedom is offensive to the common herd: "If obedience is necessary, there is no liberty, because liberty and obedience conflict with each other." According to Luther's interpretation of the First Commandment, "All . . . are ordained into the service of God, so that we all may act, speak, be, and live in the glory and praise of God" (*WBr* 5:no. 1673.24ff.).

149. *WBr* 5:nos. 1674, 1677.16, 1685.17ff., 1671.8.

150. *WBr* 5:nos. 1663.7, 1665.2ff., 1664.11ff., 1665.13ff., 1666.11ff., 1674.appendix 1.

151. See W. Maurer, "Die Entstehung" (cited above, n. 18), 380ff.

152. *WBr* 5:no. 1663.11ff., 19ff. (Melanchthon to Luther, July 27); *WBr* 5:no. 1664.9 (July 28); *WBr* 5:no. 1656.54ff.; *LW* 49:386 (Luther to Melanchthon, July 21).

153. *WBr* 5:no. 1664.4 (Melanchthon to Luther, July 28). See *WBr* 5:no. 1673.12ff. (Luther to Melanchthon, August 3): "For if there is no efficient cause, the final cause is, by necessity, a fiction" (ibid., 20).

On July 20, shortly before Luther prepared himself for his first answer to the question of episcopal power, he began his book *On the Keys*.[154] The inner connection is obvious; it was the office of the keys on which CA 28 had based episcopal power and had thereby developed the doctrine of the two authorities.[155] Luther had already broken with the stiff-necked "grumblers" who would not let themselves be convinced by Scripture. They abuse the power of the keys given to Peter in Matt. 16:19 by using it to rule the church through human law. Luther draws the pope into the polemic, as Melanchthon did in C. He thus corrects the silence of CA 28, which he criticized in a letter to Jonas for excluding the papal question.[156] Opposition to the pope pervades Luther's whole work and is incomparably vehement.[157] The antagonism to CA 28 that breaks out here seems even more unfortunate because there is no difference between Luther and Melanchthon in their understanding of confession; yet how sharply the two associates deviate from each other on the keys, which they deduce from the same theological point of view! For Luther, actual practice is decisive. The bishops do not administer the office of the keys "in faith," but according to "old worldly tradition" the pope wields the "money keys." They know nothing of the fact that the whole church possesses the office of the keys and that it therefore must be conducted according to Matt. 18.[158] Luther is especially sharp and ironic in his attack on the papal power of dispensation. On July 8, in the unity negotiations with Melanchthon, the papal legate Campeggio did not permit the lifting of the requirement for celibacy, but he did state that he was prepared to recommend dispensations for marriage in individual cases; this aroused Luther's bitter scorn.[159]

154. It was certainly finished by the end of August; the manuscript went to Wittenberg for printing at the beginning of September. In the following, we rely mainly on the preliminary manuscript (*WA* 30.2:435–64), never printed, which Luther sent to Veit Dietrich on August 25, and which therefore reflects his attitude at that time. For a comparison of the two versions, see n. 157 below, as well as G. Koffmane et al., eds., *Die handschriftliche Überlieferung von Werken D. M. Luthers* (Liegnitz, 1907), 67ff.

155. The preliminary document C from the beginning of May already bore this title; see above, p. 61.

156. *WBr* 5:no. 1657.9, from July 21, the day he settled things with Melanchthon regarding the power of bishops (see above, p. 75), one day after he had begun *On the Keys*, and shortly after Melanchthon had excluded the question of the divine right of the papacy from the negotiations in Augsburg as a "hateful and unnecessary article" (*CR* 2:183).

157. "Those who do not want to believe in God now pray to the pope" (*WA* 30.2:462.15). Here, near the end of the original document, the polemic intensifies; see ibid., 463.11: "Now where anyone, be he pope, bishop, official, or dean, uses the keys in a way other than that prescribed by Christ, they are not Christ's keys"; the result is "blasphemy." It is quite possible that Luther later dropped the publication of this invective because of the electoral warning on July 21 (*WBr* 5:no. 1658.16ff.).

158. *WA* 30.2:460.32ff., 461.26, 437.21ff., 462.19ff. Matthew 18 is not used in CA 28, where the congregation is given no share in the procedure for confession, except, of course, the right to refuse obedience (*BS* 124.9ff.; *BC* 84.23).

159. Financial abuses and social injustice: *WA* 30.2:440.29ff., 441.19ff. Indulgences: 445.29ff. "Butter letters" and marriage dispensations: 447.9ff. Melanchthon to Veit Dietrich, July 8 (*WBr* 5:447–48; *WA* 30.2:450.27ff.); softened in the later official version (*WA* 30.2:485.23ff.; *LW* 40:350–51).

This example shows how strongly *On the Keys* is oriented toward the negotiations in Augsburg and how carefully Luther watched to see that the planned compromise would not be skewed to the disadvantage of the evangelical party. Basically he did not change the doctrine of the two authorities in CA 28—as long as one does not consider the total rejection of the papacy as a difference of principle. That, of course, continued to be an open question between Luther and Melanchthon. Luther's indifference to the historic office of bishop is revealed at the end of the document by his anticipation that in the future a time would come when the evangelical ban according to Matt. 18 would be reintroduced "and the doctrine of repentance and the keys would again become known."[160]

This discussion has brought us a long way into the later history of CA 28; we now need to investigate, without studying the later works of Melanchthon and Luther in further detail, what they have to contribute to the understanding of CA 28. It is worth noting that the final version of the *Confutatio* does not refer directly to the compromise. The reason is certainly not, as Luther thought, out of fear of answering, nor out of inner uncertainty over against the evangelical confession.[161] Indeed, in their first draft the authors of the *Confutatio* summarily rejected the reordering of church life initiated by the visitations as in conflict with apostolic ordinances, and they held fast to the previous jurisdiction of bishops; the cautious attitude of the emperor moderated their sharpness in the final version, but in essence they yielded nothing. The *Confutatio* played no role in the later negotiations.[162]

In the Committee of Fourteen there was argument over whether the negotiations should begin with CA 28; an agreement on this point would have prejudiced the decisions on the reform measures contained in the other "disputed articles." For this reason the Catholic side rejected that method of procedure and insisted that the agenda begin with the individual questions.[163] The bishops, thought Luther later, understood as little about ecclesiastical power as they did about the theological conditions under which compromise would be possible. One could expect from them no other jurisdiction than that of Master Hans, the hangman.[164] In his printed final report on the Augsburg negotiations, Melanchthon complained about the lack of

160. *WA* 30.2:507.19ff.; *LW* 40:377.

161. *WA* 30.3:285.17ff., 287.18ff.; *LW* 47:22, 24–25. The reformer thought very highly of the Augustana and often made sure that it was not refuted: *De energia Augustanae Confessionis* (*WA* 30.3:389). Also *WA* 30.3:332.24ff., 336.17ff.; *LW* 34:68, 70.

162. Johannes Ficker, *Die Konfutation des Augsburger Bekenntnisses: Ihre erste Gestalt und ihre Geschichte* (Leipzig, 1891), 124ff., esp. 133.19ff.; *CR* 27:177ff.

163. Report of Brueck from August 17 (*CR* 2:285–86). Luther on the committee negotiations, in his *Warning to His Dear German People* (1531; *WA* 30.3:288.16ff.; *LW* 47:26). On the Lutherans' readiness to compromise: *WA* 30.3:278.13ff., 27ff.; *LW* 47:13, 14.

164. *WBr* 5:nos. 1716.31ff., 1707.193ff. Cp. Luther's report to Hausmann on September 23 (*WBr* 5:no. 1723.12ff.; *LW* 49:420–21).

accommodation from the other side, but he stated his continued readiness to
retain episcopal authority, the "polity of the church." In an opinion issued
jointly by Melanchthon and Luther at the end of May 1531, the latter
basically approved of his friend's standpoint. From the perspective of suffering obedience, Luther was willing to accept the jurisdiction of bishops, even
if they "were wolves and our enemies"—"because they still possess the office
and sit in the place of the apostles"—as long as pure doctrine would be
guaranteed.[165]

The theological understanding of CA 28 is not exactly furthered by these
discussions. More clearly than before, Luther, influenced by Augsburg and
post-Augsburg 1530, placed the doctrine of the two authorities in the perspective of suffering obedience. God makes worldly power magnificent
among the godless and through the godless, but he lets his own suffer
distress, misery, and poverty. In the spiritual realm priests and factious spirits
rule the faithful, never ceasing to "cook and brew" the two kingdoms
together.[166]

One of the immediate fruits of these experiences was the realization that
the concept of spiritual jurisdiction applied in CA 28 did not completely cover
the needs and realities of church life. What should be done if the authority of
the bishops completely disappeared? What would then become of excommunication? We noted that Luther said it should be reinstated in an evangelical
form. As late as August 15, 1530, the evangelical princes were still conceding
it to the bishops, but it was only imperfectly exercised in the evangelical
churches. At the same time, the princes were ready to go on recognizing
episcopal jurisdiction in marriage cases; Luther and Melanchthon continued
to make this concession into 1531. The connection between episcopal power
and ordination of pastors was also granted, although from the beginning
there was no unanimity on whether that should include the right of examination and installation. In short, by the end of 1530 it was clear that the scope of
ecclesiastical power was not sharply delimited by CA 28 and that its essence
had not been fully and clearly grasped.[167]

In their attacks against Melanchthon, his critics clearly pointed out these
weaknesses. They feared, as Luther did, that bishops would misuse a power
extending to excommunication, discipline, and ordination as a means to

165. *CR* 2:430ff.; *WBr* 6:no. 1822.appendix 1, 111ff., 124ff. Concerning the renewal of the
Augsburg peace offer in Regensburg (1541; cp. *CR* 6:45–46) and Naumburg (1542), see *WA*
53:129ff. See also Peter Brunner, *Nikolaus von Amsdorf als Bischof von Naumburg*, Schriften des
Vereins für Reformationsgeschichte 179 (Gütersloh, 1961).

166. *Exposition of Psalm 101* (1534; *WA* 51:238.19ff., 239.22ff.; *LW* 13:193, 194).

167. On excommunication, see above, n. 160. See also W. Maurer, *Gemeindezucht, Gemein-
deamt, Konfirmation*, Schriftenreihe des Pfarrervereins Kurhessen-Waldeck 2 (Kassel, 1940), 9ff.;
and Ruth Götze, *Wie Luther Kirchenzucht übte* (Göttingen, 1959), 128ff. On marriage jurisdiction,
see *CR* 2:284; *WBr* 6:no. 1822.appendix 1, 164ff. Cp. *BS* 125.3ff.; *BC* 85.29. On ordination, see
CR 2:313–14.

suppress the gospel.[168] But who should attend to those functions? The legal advisers of the temporal authorities would not bother about these things, prophesied Melanchthon after the conclusion of negotiations with the Committee of Fourteen in August 1530.[169] A unanimous answer to the question of church ordinances was thus not forthcoming. The division of the church would continue to exist and political unity remain in jeopardy. Melanchthon's prophecies were fulfilled in the history of Protestantism. The open questions that were not answered in CA 28 and the compromise negotiations based on it pushed the theological and legal development forward without finding answers that suited everyone.[170] Article 28 thus became the hidden impetus not only for the Augsburg negotiations but also for the history of Protestantism. The official discussion on the doctrine of the two authorities, begun in that article, continues to the present day.

12. LUTHER'S STATEMENTS ON THE TWO AUTHORITIES FROM THE PERIOD BEFORE 1530

Luther had developed the doctrine of the two authorities long before the Diet of Augsburg, not just theoretically, but in thoroughgoing discussion with the powers of his time. In defending anew the position of the conciliarist pioneers of the fifteenth century against papalism, Luther also stripped the episcopal office—as well as the papacy—of its sovereign power. The difference between serving power and sovereign power forms the starting point for Luther's doctrine of the two authorities. It is obtained through a particular understanding of the church and its function; the doctrine develops out of these presuppositions.[171]

The famous distinction between the general priesthood of all believers and the special ecclesiastical office (found in *To the Christian Nobility*) rests on the assumption that in this serving office there can be no hierarchical degrees; where each one serves, no one else can rule the others. There is no special consecration; the only sacramental prerequisite for priestly service is baptism, which consecrates everyone. Episcopal ordination is dropped. Ordination is selection and designation for a specific service; no bishop can carry it out without the cooperation of the congregation. In emergencies the latter can act alone.[172]

168. On these critics, who were also influenced by political considerations under the leadership of Hesse and Nürnberg, see my "Erwägungen" (cited above, n. 1), 386ff., 245ff.

169. To Matthäus Alber in Reutlingen, August 23 (*CR* 2:303).

170. As far as the office of the church is concerned, the development is carried further in Melanchthon's tract *On the Power and Primacy of the Pope* (1537).

171. "The power of the pope is servitude, not dominion" (*WA* 2:676.37). Cp. 677.27ff., 678.6ff., against Emser in 1519.

172. *WA* 6:407.19ff.; *LW* 44:127.

Ordination, therefore, is not a sacrament but a human rite that bishops carry out under papal supervision. For the sake of church unity one can—indeed should—accept it at first, because it really means nothing more than the choice of a preacher. Nonetheless, one must be clear about the abuses that were, and still are, bound up with episcopal power to ordain. Thus from the beginning Luther's reformation takes a critical stance when it makes concessions to episcopal power. The equation "bishops, that is, pastors," *episcopi seu pastores*, by which article 28 relativizes the compromise it offers, is drawn as early as *The Babylonian Captivity of the Church*.[173]

Three years later, in the work *On Temporal Authority*, Luther explains that the church's serving office has nothing in common with temporal ruling power. Here the doctrine of the two kingdoms is explicitly developed for the first time. The relevant section has been the basic nourishment ever since for all those who struggle, then and now, to understand Luther's reformation.[174]

Luther here makes a distinction that encompasses all the children of Adam and that is more profound than the difference between ruling power and serving power, although they are included. Humanity belongs partly to the kingdom of God and partly to the kingdom of the world. Christ is Lord and King in the former realm, and all those who believe in Christ and obey him belong to it. God's Spirit rules their hearts and teaches them directly to suffer injustice and to do the right. They need neither temporal sword nor law. They are few in number.

Most people have little faith, so they try to resist evil. In order to keep "one from gobbling up the other," God has instituted temporal authority in addition to the spiritual. Both authorities are therefore works of God and areas of his activity, related to the two groups of people. By this means the serving and the ruling powers are established anthropologically as well as theologically, and at the same time they are related to the saving act of Christ. Both authorities have their origin in God. He wants to save humanity through Christ, his Word, and his Spirit. He wants to keep the evil of humanity from frustrating this saving purpose of his. Thus the force he exercises through temporal authority serves to further the spiritual authority, which in itself requires no force. The distinction of the two authorities therefore implies that they are always related to each other. One should not assume an absolute antithesis in the doctrine of the two authorities, just as it does not exist between good and evil. It would be a misunderstanding of Luther's teaching on justification to assume that Christians are so removed from the reality of sin that they should not, for love's sake, submit themselves to the restraining power of the sword and, on occasion, wield it themselves.

All of these theological aspects of the doctrine of the two authorities—the

173. *WA* 6:560.20ff., 563.3ff., 564.16–17; *LW* 36:106, 111, 113.
174. Cp. *WA* 11:249.ff.; *LW* 45:88ff.

connection with the saving and disciplining will of God, and with the faith and sin of people destined for salvation—are lacking in article 28 of the Augustana. In that article, Melanchthon gives the teaching in an abbreviated form. That is not to say that those aspects which fade into the background were unknown to him or that he totally rejected them. We ought not forget that he drew upon that doctrine only insofar as it could undergird the planned compromise on the question of episcopal power. He had to clarify, as far as possible, its difference from political power. The problem he was dealing with, it seems, was more one of social ethics than of theology in the strict sense.

The situation also conditioned the statements Luther made on the question of bishops in his work from 1523, *Concerning the Ministry*. Its object is to free the Bohemian Utraquists from the necessity of having their priests ordained illegally by foreign bishops, thus opening a way for them to provide their own church structure. For that reason the polemic against disorder in the church comes to the fore.[175]

The "masks of the bishops" (173.39; *LW* 40:13) incur the wrath of God, because they ordain priests to sacrifice rather than to serve the Word, thus perverting the Sacrament. They use the office of the keys in their self-seeking acquisition and defense of personal power (183ff.; *LW* 40:25ff.). The office of servant, however, tolerates no personal privileges; all church activity, to the degree that it is public, requires the concurrence of the whole church.[176] The right to ordain also belongs to it, especially in cases of emergency when papal bishops refuse to appoint servants of the Word (191.16ff., 194.31–32; *LW* 40:37 and 40).

The emergency situation in Bohemia should not lead one to deduce a general rejection of the historic episcopate. In any case, Luther was not the only one who was under the impression that bishops were not suited to fulfill their spiritual tasks and who was therefore intent on finding a remedy. His opposite number Eck had intervened in Rome on this same mission in February 1523, where he ultimately achieved the transferral of spiritual jurisdiction to the Duke of Bavaria. About the same time, Archduke Ferdinand had pursued similar goals in Austria and finally carried them out for a group of Catholic territories by agreement with the papal legate Campeggio at the Regensburg Assembly in the summer of 1524. At the Nürnberg diet in 1523, the temporal estates took up the gravamina from Worms once again.[177]

175. *WA* 12:(160), 169ff.; *LW* 40:(4), 7–44. Citations that follow in the text refer to these editions.

176. *WA* 12:189.25ff.; *LW* 40:34. On the *ecclesia universalis*, see Johannes Heckel, *Lex Charitatis*, AAM n.f. 36 (Munich, 1953), 170ff.

177. Georg Pfeilschifter, ed., *Acta Reformationis Catholicae*, vol. 1 (Regensburg, 1959), nos. 21ff., pp. 86ff. Luther was still appealing to the Worms gravamina in the summer of 1529 (*WBr* 5:81.93–94). The powerlessness of the spiritual princes, especially in questions of jurisdiction, is reflected in the complaints reproduced in Pfeilschifter, *Acta* 1:no. 164. An unforeseen and un-

After the catastrophe of the Peasants' War it is no wonder that Luther advocated a secularization of the imperial bishoprics in order to seek new officials to discharge episcopal functions.[178]

The tendencies toward secularization were stronger and more effective in the Frankish lands. Nürnberg and the Margravate of Ansbach had already rejected all spiritual claims of the Bishop of Bamberg in their territory before the beginning of the Augsburg diet. The Nürnberg Council constantly fretted that the diet would restore jurisdiction to the bishops, so the Nürnberg delegates offered resistance on this point from the beginning to the end of the negotiations.[179] Margrave Georg, in his first decree concerning the diet on January 29, 1530, had invited the pastors of his realm to bring forward arguments against the spiritual claims of the bishops. The abundant material that he received reveals both the deep antipathy of the lower clergy for their over-shepherds, "true hirelings of the antichrist," and the occasional hope for the restoration of a spiritual episcopacy that would correspond to biblical standards.[180]

Even Luther did not simply condemn the late medieval episcopacy. In the *Instructions for the Visitors* of 1528, the preface of which goes back to Luther, he retraced the visiting function of the archbishop and bishop, rediscovering traces of it in canonical law, and using the later decline to show the necessity for this function. He saw the visitations set up by the elector as the beginning of such a restoration.[181] Nevertheless, in no way did he consider this action, and the ecclesiastical offices it created, a substitute for the historic office of bishop. Of course, if bishops go to war, they disgrace the name of Christ. At home, however, they have a Christian task; they pray, fast, read, preach, and look after the poor, thus fulfilling the commands of Holy Scripture and canon law.[182]

Thus even here, in the treatise *On War Against the Turk*, Luther discovers standards for the proper office of bishop in the distinction between the two

wanted consequence of the Saxon compromise proposal of 1530 was that the decree of the Augsburg diet guaranteed to the bishops their spiritual power of jurisdiction, thus by imperial law putting a stop to the movement for secularization (ibid., no. 161, esp. pp. 493–94).

178. *Thoughts on How Tumult Might Be Stilled at the Present Time* (1526 [1525?]; *WA* 19:446). There are hints of this as early as the end of 1523 in *An Exhortation to the Knights of the Teutonic Order* (*WA* 12:240.10ff., 242.19ff.; *LW* 45:152, 155).

179. Session of May 7, 1530 (Gussmann 1.2:207ff., 1.1:127ff.).

180. *Fränk Bek.*, passim. Positive expressions, which are always based on the equation of bishops with pastors: ibid., 578ff., 600, 615, 624ff.; Gussmann 1.2:45.6ff., 38ff., 46, 46.21ff., 84.36ff., 110.1ff., 114.15ff., 147ff. Such statements are found principally in theologians who were trained in patristics or canon law, such as Johann Rurer (Ansbach), Caspar Löner (Hof), and Johann Beham (Bayreuth).

181. *WA* 26:196–97; *LW* 40:269–73. In the sections on excommunication and superintendents, the bishops are not mentioned. This is all the more surprising because it is to this office of oversight, which also includes the examination of pastors and visitation, that the title of bishop (*episcopos*) originally referred. For christening, cp. *WA* 31.2:510.6ff.

182. *WA* 30.2:111.23ff., 114.4ff.; *LW* 46:165, 167.

powers. This explains how Luther, in his *Exhortation* of 1530, could so harshly attack the clergy assembly in Augsburg and yet at the same time, in his proposal for compromise, directly or indirectly try to make them into servants of the gospel. Article 28 of the Augustana, where that proposal is picked up, is determined by the same intention. In basing the restructuring of the historic episcopate on the doctrine of the two kingdoms, the article follows a development Luther himself had experienced during the previous ten years. It is true that Luther did not limit the doctrine of the two authorities to the distinction between temporal and spiritual offices; it is also true that he started with God's creative and saving will, thereby bringing the different reactions of believing and unbelieving people into the picture. Melanchthon's presentation in CA 28 does not involve these theological dimensions. Although we recognize this lack of depth—also dependent on the situation—we assert at the same time that there is a basic agreement. From May of 1530, Melanchthon built one of the decisive features of Luther's theology into the Confession.[183]

13. LUTHER'S DOCTRINE OF THE THREE HIERARCHIES IN THE AUGUSTANA

Luther's doctrine of the three hierarchies must be taken together with his doctrine of the two authorities. Luther took them together himself in a classic summary of God's four authorities.[184] Of the three traditional hierarchies (estates)—*ecclesia, politia,* and *oeconomia*—rulers and family represent the temporal authority, the church the spiritual. And if we speak of "hierarchies," an expression Luther himself did not use consistently until after 1530, we must go on to say that in the case of the three estates as well as that of the two authorities, we are dealing with spheres of divine rule rather than with this-worldly social domains. Hierarchies and authorities correspond in that God governs the world through them, leading the world toward the goal he has established.

In that context, "hierarchy" refers to the angelic world that, according to the teaching of the Areopagite, also intervened in the terrestrial world and,

183. This is not the place to go into further detail on the almost unmanageable literature on the doctrine of the two kingdoms, so I have limited myself to a brief review of the sources. In the process, I want to emphasize the importance of developing that doctrine from Luther's early writings on, as was done by Johannes Heckel (*Lex Charitatis*, 1953), and not from the textually uncertain series of sermons on the Sermon on the Mount from 1530–32 (as Harald and Hermann Diem did, 1938 and 1947, following Troeltsch and Wünsch). Cp. the collections *Reich Gottes und Welt*, ed. Heinz-Horst Schrey, Wege der Forschung 107 (Darmstadt, 1969), and *Zur Zwei-Reiche-Lehre Luthers*, Theologische Bücherei. System. Theol. 49 (Munich, 1973), and their bibliographies.

184. In the lectures on Zechariah printed at the end of 1527, on Zechariah 1:7 (*WA* 23:511–15, esp. 513.21–22; *LW* 20:168–71, esp. 171). There he says, "The fourth is the temporal authority, which includes governing one's house and the power of parents over their children."

since the High Middle Ages, was thought to determine both religious and sociopolitical existence.[185] Luther was close enough to medieval thinking to maintain the connection between the terrestrial and the heavenly worlds. In the passage from the lectures on Zechariah cited above, spiritual and temporal authority occupy third and fourth place. At the top stands God himself with the authority that he exercises directly within his creation, independently of any creaturely mediation. The authority of the angels—on the second level—consists in the obedient service they render to their creator; they are the external stimulus to human thought and will, and they protect individuals and nations from harm.[186]

God exercises the third and fourth authorities through human beings, although always in cooperation with the angels. He has the gospel proclaimed by apostles and preachers; he creates peace and order through parents and rulers.[187] The *oeconomia*, therefore, as part of the fourth hierarchy, belongs with the *politia* under temporal authority. And if we, as we have done so far in accordance with Luther's customary usage, continue to speak only of temporal and spiritual authority, the *oeconomia* must be classified with the former in order to define the proper relationship between the two authorities. The implications of the commonality of these two estates—the *politia* and the *oeconomia*—for their relationship to each other will be taken up later.[188]

At the time of the Diet of Augsburg, Luther often touched upon the three estates in sermons and academic work.[189] A handy example may illustrate the connection with the developing Augustana.

On April 20, 1530, the Wednesday after Easter, Luther preached at the Coburg, to the elector and his court, on John 21:1ff. Melanchthon heard him. The preacher used the example of the fishing disciples to illustrate "that Christ did not bring in his kingdom in a way that would interfere with other temporal orders"; the preaching of the gospel does not set aside *politia* and *oeconomia*.[190] Suiting his subject to the situation, Luther preaches a sermon on vocation; it addresses the grooms who clean the stable, and the young noblemen of the court who drain their prince's wine cellar and empty his

185. Cp. W. Maurer, *Luthers Lehre von den drei Hierarchien und ihr mittelalterlicher Hintergrund*, SAM, phil.-hist. Klasse 1970/4, 3ff.

186. On the distinction between *opus dei factum* and *actum* in the young Luther, see W. Maurer, *Von der Freiheit eines Christenmenschen* (Göttingen, 1949), 109ff., 130ff.

187. *WA* 23:513.8ff., 21ff.; *LW* 20:171.

188. See below, pp. 163ff.

189. The following discussion gives particular consideration to the conclusion of the lectures on Isaiah that ended on February 22, 1530, and the subsequent lectures on the Song of Solomon, interrupted by Luther's departure for the Coburg, resumed on November 8 after his return and finally ended in mid-1531. The lecture series are in *WA* 31.2; and *LW* 15:189–264 (Song of Solomon); *LW* 16, 17 (Isaiah). The sermons in *WA* 32 comment on the CA from Luther's own point of view.

190. *WA* 32:67.1ff., 69ff.

granary. It also involves the pastors and concludes with the warning that "we should not disturb the social order, but each should tend to his own activities."[191]

In this frame of reference, Peter appears as the model who fulfills a calling in both realms: as apostle he serves Christ with the Word; as parent he cares for his own by manual labor. A full month later in Augsburg, when Melanchthon wanted to make clear in Na 28 that bishops could also wield temporal power, he went back to this example: Peter was a fisherman, Luke a physician, Paul a weaver, and all of them had pursued their trade in addition to their apostolate. Temporal and spiritual calling belong together.[192]

The example shows how the doctrines of the authorities and of the estates have coalesced for Luther and Melanchthon; it also shows how attentively the latter took over these doctrines from his master. The Christian in his or her calling stands under both authorities; if one is not, like the apostle, a preacher, one is nevertheless a hearer of the gospel. The connection between the two authorities thus becomes evident in the three estates. Although *politia* and *oeconomia* properly stand under the temporal authority of God, their bearers belong personally, as Christians, to the *ecclesia*. Likewise the pastor, as a creature of God, has to act and suffer under temporal authority.[193]

Individual statements of Luther that are roughly contemporaneous with the Augustana disclose how the three hierarchies define all of one's existence.[194] The certainty that one is living in a station willed by God comforts the conscience, awakens joy in the adversities of life, and protects one in hours of temptation.[195] God affects each of the three hierarchies through the other two. The Word is at work in the church and teaches one to command and to obey in community and home; in a well-ordered society the fear of God spreads into the homes; God bestows his blessings in all three.[196] On the other hand, Christians in all three estates also experience their share of sin

191. Ibid., 73.6ff., 76.3ff.

192. Kolde 28.5ff. The thought is fundamentally changed in *BS* 123.14ff. (*BC* 83.19).

193. The often-cited distinction between person and office, as Luther articulates it in his preaching on the Sermon on the Mount (*WA* 32:316.15ff.; *LW* 21:23), is thus originally meant simply as an appeal of the preacher for his hearers to prove themselves to be Christians in their own stations in life.

194. Thus Luther—on November 8, after returning from the Coburg—praises the Song of Solomon as a "book for anyone who is tested in his station in life, whether business, politics, or theology, that he may know that his station is a divine creation and institution" (*WA* 31.2:634.29ff.).

195. *WA* 31.2:646.12ff., 733.17ff.; *LW* 15:215, 249; *WA* 32:95.35ff., 96.25ff.

196. *WA* 31.2:698.14ff., 693.23ff., 641.29ff.; *LW* 15:234, 233, 202. It is significant for Luther's relationship to humanism that he considered school to be the wellspring for the three estates (*WA* 31.2:737.3ff., 739.1–2; *LW* 15:249, 250), and in his sermon on April 17, 1530, he recommended pedagogy as the basis for human righteousness (*WA* 32:52.32ff.). Cp. *A Sermon on Keeping Children in School* (*WA* 30.2:508–9; *LW* 46:207–58). Cp., as well, above, p. 73, and W. Maurer, "Über den Zusammenhang zwischen kirchlicher Ordnung und christlicher Erziehung in den Anfängen luth. Reformation," in *Praxis Ecclesiae: Kurt Frör zum 65. Geburtstag* (Munich, 1970), 60–85.

and, as a result, the punishment of God.[197] All three fall prey to specific temptations and afflictions.[198]

If the three hierarchies thus define all of life, and if Melanchthon, as we have seen, took this reality of life into consideration when writing the Augustana, we would have good reason to expect that the doctrine of the three estates also found its way into the Confession. In addition, it formed the basis for Luther's personal Confession of 1528;[199] we will see how Melanchthon constantly referred to it in his formulations at Augsburg. From the beginning his doctrine of the three hierarchies was directed against monasticism, which is most explicit in CA 27 but is at least included in the final editing of CA 28.[200]

That people thought they could earn more merit from God in the monastery than in spiritual and temporal estates (*BS* 112.8ff.; *BC* 72.13) is first inserted in the wording of Na by the revision recorded in Nb, which would put it in the first half of June.[201] Of course, Na had already condemned the monks' idea that their presumed "state of perfection" was preferable to the other estates "which God had instituted." In all the sources the repeated emphasis on God's ordering and command (*ordinatio et mandatum Dei*) is a part of the justification of marriage. It is an especially clear illustration of the divine institution of the three estates, which Luther had cited in his Confession of 1528; conversely, depreciating marriage and despising authority go hand in hand (*BS* 118.8ff., 16ff.; *BC* 79.51, 54).[202]

There are only occasional references to the doctrine of the three estates; in the Augustana the triad is hardly presented in its full form. Article 26, for example, contrasts the meritorious capability of a falsely termed "spiritual" estate with the divinely commanded temporal tasks of parents and rulers (*BS* 102.1ff.; *BC* 65.8–11). The elements of church order contained in CA 14 and 15 are not treated within the framework of the three estates; even CA 20 makes only a vague allusion to them in its list of Christian duties.[203] In its positive section, CA 16 confines its attention to the *politia*, its laws and functions; in its polemic against the enthusiasts, however, it includes the *oeconomia* and, as in Luther's Confession of 1528, places all estates under the

197. Like parents and rulers, Luther the preacher violates God's will: *WA* 31.2:702.26ff.; *LW* 15:236. Cp. *WA* 31.2:728.10ff., 703.7ff.; *LW* 15:246.

198. *WA* 31.2:633.21ff., 636.27ff., 732.22ff.; *LW* 15:211, 247.

199. See above, p. 22; there is an analysis in my *Luthers Lehre* (cited above, n. 185).

200. Here it is only a vague reference to marriage law; cp. above, p. 65. Otherwise *oeconomia* has no place in this essentially diplomatic document.

201. Here Melanchthon is summarizing part of Luther's confession: *WA* 26:504.13ff.; *LW* 37:363–64.

202. CA 23 does base its defense of married clergy on the divine institution of the married state, but the other two estates are not considered.

203. "... diligently engage in callings which are commanded, render obedience ..." (*BS* 81.17–18; *BC* 46.37; not in the Latin text).

claim of Christian love. In this case Melanchthon—more clearly in the final German version than in the Latin—went beyond his source Na 15 in making use of the doctrine of the three estates.

This not very fruitful review of the application of the doctrine of the three hierarchies in both parts of the Augustana confirms two things. First, the doctrine is spliced in fairly late—in most cases after the copying of Na—to individual articles on social ethics on the basis of its practical applicability. Second, these additions echo Luther's Confession of 1528 and show that Melanchthon consulted this earlier document while the text was taking its final form. Nevertheless, two conclusions must be drawn from this evidence: (1) In the doctrine of the two authorities, temporal authority must include parenthood and the ordinance of marriage. (2) That doctrine can be presented in its complete form only when all three estates are developed in succession.

Before that is done, however, we must look at one more factor in the doctrine of the two authorities which we have not previously considered.

14. TWOFOLD RIGHTEOUSNESS

One cannot ignore the fact that in CA 28 there is very little positive comment on temporal authority. The emphasis is unquestionably on the spiritual authority of the bishops or pastors. Temporal power merely provides the contrast. The temporal sword[204] protects body and property; it is concerned not with eternal things but with the things of this world. It executes this function through external force and physical punishment (*BS* 122.1–2, 16ff.; *BC* 82.8, 11). Despite all efforts to honor both authorities as the highest gifts of God (*BS* 123.12–13; *BC* 83.18), there is a certain unmistakable bias against temporal power. This could appear to be inconsistent with the reverence due the twofold activity of God among humankind. That would indeed be the case if it reflected the late medieval subordination of temporal power to spiritual, or if it remained caught in the mystical-ascetic assessment of worldly things that continued to find expression in a Christian humanist like Erasmus. But according to the teaching of the Augustana, God's two ways of governing are to be honored because they both relate to God's action in justifying sinners. This relationship brings a new element into the doctrine of the two kingdoms. Luther and Melanchthon do not work out this relationship in exactly the same way, because it is defined by biblical as well as classical philosophical themes. The Augustana, however, synthesizes these different influences and thereby ties the doctrine of the two authorities to the central concern of the doctrine of justification.

204. *BS* 120.5, 121.6; *BC* 81.1, 4.

We are dealing here with two kinds of righteousness. In a sermon published under this title at the beginning of 1519, Luther distinguished between an alien righteousness, which Christ has obtained for us, and our own righteousness, which grows out of it and makes itself known in self-denial, love, and humble fear of God. The individual Christian's duty of love in no way conflicts with the power to punish and protect wielded by those who occupy public office; in fact even the duties required of authorities in Romans 13 are fulfilled in obedience to God and in love of the neighbor. In this way the righteousness of Christ is more than a private Christian morality; it can be an active public righteousness that punishes and educates the sinner.[205]

Luther also discusses this topic, critically as far as ecclesiastical jurisdiction is concerned, in the preparation of his lecture on Galatians in 1519. He distinguishes two kinds of peace, one granted by the mercy of Christ and the other laboriously and, in the last analysis, fruitlessly sought by human judges. These correspond to the righteousness of the law *(iustitia legalis)* of the Jews and the Christian righteousness before God *(coram Deo)*. There is thus a twofold righteousness: the human and servile kind, taught by Aristotle and commanded by civil and canon law, and the kind that is given by Christ. One is moral and governs civil affairs, but the other is a new kind, a righteousness of faith that Christ bestows on all of his own regardless of their merit, thus fulfilling the Ciceronian ideal in contrast to all human appearances. With these statements, Luther entered the debate on classical ethics. Human righteousness seems to be identical with the classical standards, but in relation to the righteousness of Christ it both loses its value and finds its fulfillment. A key element of the internal struggle between humanism and reformation lies in this tension between human and divine righteousness.[206]

Melanchthon was an active participant in this struggle; as coeditor of the *Brief Commentary on Galatians* he obviously was acquainted from the first with Luther's concept of a twofold righteousness. His own teaching on authority was totally rooted in the tradition of Christian natural law until 1521,[207] although at the beginning of that year, his lecture series on Matthew shows that he had adopted the twofold righteousness view from Luther. He recognizes a righteousness by which one can accomplish good works through one's own efforts but which still does not effect an inner change, and he also acknowledges a righteousness of faith, worked by God, which does convert one inwardly; thus the distinction lies between inner and outer righteousness.[208]

205. *WA* 2:146.29ff., 36ff., 147.7ff., 151.1ff; *LW* 31:299, 300, 304–5.

206. *WA* 2:594.7ff., 488.33ff., 489.21ff., 503.23ff., 504.4; *LW* 27:375, 218, 219, 240, 241.

207. Cp. W. Maurer, *Der junge Melanchthon* (cited above, n. 49), 2:293ff. For the following discussion, cp. ibid., 323ff., 449ff., 457ff.

208. StA 4:170.18ff., 204.19ff.

For Erasmus this gradation of "inner" and "outer" implies a subordination. The inner-spiritual surpasses the outer-material. Even in politics this difference in value surfaces when Erasmus discusses the ideal Christian prince; outward righteousness bears a trace of harshness and therefore of moral inferiority. In his early years Melanchthon was trapped by this Erasmian way of thinking; that is why he was negative toward war and capital punishment. Although he did not reject either one completely, he thought it highly questionable for a Christian to participate in such bloody activities. In a letter written from the Wartburg on July 13, 1521, Luther thoroughly discussed this problem with his young friend, and in the process he supported the doctrine of a twofold righteousness by a comprehensive survey of biblical material. Granted that one cannot deduce the power of the sword from the New Testament, it is, however, presupposed and legitimated there. Granted that the gospel deals with heavenly things, but when Christians use the sword they are carrying out a divinely ordained task. To defend and restore human righteousness is therefore not something inferior; God wills that it be administered along with the divine.[209]

Luther's arguments convinced Melanchthon. Nearly four years later, on April 10, 1525, Melanchthon recounted them almost verbatim to Spalatin.[210] We can note their effects as early as the last parts of the *Loci* of 1521. Melanchthon has adopted Luther's biblical evidence. Offices of authority are necessary; those who occupy them do not sin. In this they are involved with external things that have no more to do with "Christianity" than eating and drinking do. To be sure, this is Melanchthon's old dualism between flesh and spirit lingering on. To the Christian the administration of existing laws is no different from the exercise of other civil callings. Of course, it is in the legal sphere that injustice and power vent their fury, and most people appeal to laws out of pure quarrelsomeness. But that is why spiritual people are needed as judges. Spirit and flesh are at war with each other. Human righteousness is contrasted not with the righteousness of faith but with the righteousness of the Spirit.[211]

Theses on spiritual and corporal government (*regimen spirituale et corporale*) which Melanchthon posed for defense in July of 1522 set righteousness of the spirit (*iustitia spiritus*) over against righteousness of the world (*iustitia mundi*). They are written with an eye to the doctrine of justification. "Spirit" in this instance does not mean human inwardness but rather means the way God acts in exercising his spiritual authority through the Word and office of the gospel.

209. *WBr* 2:no. 418.32–107; *LW* 48:258–62. On that, see Maurer, *Der junge Melanchthon* 2:327–28. A letter to Spalatin on December 21, 1518, shows that Luther himself was still receptive to Erasmian ideals at that time: *WBr* 1:no. 125.

210. *CR* 1:731, and Otto Clemen, ed., *Supplementa Melanchthoniana* 6.1 (Leipzig, 1926), 288, no. 405.

211. StA 2.1:134.37–136.3.

In this sense, Melanchthon has reached the Reformation position. At the same time, the devaluation of worldly righteousness remains. It is a righteousness of the flesh *(iustitia carnis)* limited to external goods and ordinances and enforced by physical means; it is not to be compared with spiritual righteousness. Nevertheless, it is a "good creation of God," as in CA 16; it stands under his protection and can be actively put to use by every Christian. But as a righteousness of the world it concerns only those who lack the spirit of God; it belongs to the realm of sin, death, and punishment. It is clear that Luther's influence has not enabled Melanchthon to overcome his pre-Reformation dualism of flesh and spirit even when he deals with the Reformation doctrine of justification.[212]

Melanchthon also uses the doctrine of justification as the starting point for a compendium he wrote for Landgrave Philipp of Hesse in early September 1524. He calls the young prince's attention to the theological use of the law—through which the activity of the Holy Spirit leads to repentance and the forgiveness of sins—and also to the necessity of human righteousness. The summary sets forth the educational activity of the territorial state *(paedagogia politiae)* which includes not only the younger generation but also civil and religious life together with civil and ecclesiastical officeholders. Of course, a basic distinction is made between this civil righteousness and evangelical righteousness. In practice, however, care must be taken lest false preaching of faith lead people to a false security and, as a result, back into a fleshly righteousness.

Melanchthon thus draws the fine line that the evangelical prince must walk between works righteousness and antinomian libertinism. He urges the prince to use all severity in training people for civil righteousness,[213] which appears here in a new and positive light. Despite all violence and harsh punishment, it is to be preferred to unbridled spiritual excesses. Human righteousness *(humana iustitia)* is an irreplaceable component of evangelical humanism; it is the means by which divine righteousness may achieve its goal in the believer. The more consistently and strictly temporal authorities train people for civil righteousness, the more effectively can the preaching of the gospel produce divine righteousness. When it comes to a choice of means, naturally, there is a qualitative difference between the two kinds of righteousness, but from the point of view of the end God attains, they are of equal

---

212. StA 1:168ff. The problematic appears in pedagogical guise in the fragment "Distinction Between Worldly and Christian Piety" (apparently written by 1521; StA 1:171ff.). Cp. Maurer, *Der junge Melanchthon* 2:448–49, with p. 586 n. 87. Pedagogical applications of internal and external righteousness are also in the letter to Memminger from early July 1524: *Supp. Mel.* (cited in n. 210), 246–49, no. 350.

213. "Epitome renovatae ecclesiasticae doctrinae" (StA 1:179ff.). He uses the proverb (ibid., 183.16–17) "The whip for the horse, the muzzle for the mule, and the rod for the back of the fool" (Prov. 26:3).

value. In this way Melanchthon achieves a synthesis between the Lutheran doctrine of justification and a classical social ethic restructured by Christian humanism.[214]

The two righteousnesses can therefore be evaluated differently, depending on whether they are judged more from the viewpoint of the doctrine of justification or from that of classical ethics, from Reformation theology or from Christian humanism. For Melanchthon, neither of these perspectives is out of the question; even Luther's break with Erasmus did not occur over ethics. Nevertheless, Luther can be very pessimistic about the coercive function of temporal power. It needs to keep "crude people," "the crowd," in prison and chains like wild beasts; they must be made pious by the external means of the sword. In fact, Satan himself is the prince and god of this world, the evil disrupter of all order. From this perspective the sword seems a divine blessing and the peace it defends a heavenly gift. But the qualitative difference between earthly and heavenly righteousness always remains. The latter concerns believers, the former holds the wicked in check so that civil order may be preserved.[215]

Although external righteousness has only a preventive function, restraining the wicked, Luther by no means wishes it to be viewed negatively. Upright civil life, even though it does not suffice in the face of death and God's judgment, can affect human life in society and is therefore valuable and necessary.[216] Human free will is not taken away: it is precisely in *On the Bound Will* that Luther made that point. It is true that the free will cannot act in an upward direction, but certainly it can deal with what is beneath it. It comes into play in the realm of civil righteousness; here people can and should make responsible decisions. The law, even though now obscured by the devil, is written in our hearts. Otherwise, when we hear an admonition, we could not say immediately, "Yes, that's right." Civil laws thus arise out of human wisdom and reason, both of which are God's creations. They are recognized as such in the Scriptures; the theologian can only agree.[217] The two kinds of righteousness belong together from God's perspective as well. The righteousness of faith makes a person devout before God, and the

214. In 1523, when Luther, in warding off Duke George's encroachments, contests the jurisdiction of temporal power over souls and concedes to it only jurisdiction over externals such as body and property, he does not subordinate the physical because it is of less value; he bases his case on the holiness of divine salvation: "Temporal government has laws which extend no further than to life and property and external affairs on earth, for God cannot and will not permit anyone but himself to rule over the soul" (*On Temporal Authority* [WA 11:262.7ff.; LW 45; 105]).

215. WA 18:66.3ff.; LW 40:83; WA 15:228.12, 17.1:467.7ff. (1524–25), 40.1:46.10, 620.30ff.; LW 26:8, 409.

216. WA 29:579.8ff., 32:318.35ff.; LW 21:26.

217. WA 18:638.5ff., 672.8ff., 767.40ff.; LW 33:70, 119, 264; WA 16:447.7ff.; WA 40.3:221.6ff. (sermon of October 1, 1525 [!]). See from 1532, on Ps. 127:1, esp. ibid., 223.1: "Politics and family are seasoned by the law written in human hearts." The theologian was aware, of course, of arrogant opposition to the *iustitia civilis*.

outward righteousness is employed in public office and activities. God maintains them both.[218]

Luther therefore set a high value—all pessimism over sin aside—on both kinds of righteousness. He did not think any less of civil righteousness than the Christian humanists did. And when Melanchthon quoted appropriate statements of Luther, he could be sure that his political ethic agreed with that of the older reformer. As early as December 1529 it was clear to him that the distinction between spiritual and civil righteousness belonged to the category of topics on which the church fathers were not unanimous. He did not seek enlightenment on this distinction from them, nor from Luther. Instead he turned to classical social philosophy, to which he became indebted for a deeper understanding of *iustitia civilis.*[219]

After Melanchthon interrupted his theological lecturing in the early 1520s, classical sources became the focus of his academic instruction. Annotated editions of these texts arose out of this activity as an aid to home study for the students. As early as 1525, Melanchthon published an introduction to Cicero's *De Officiis* which circulated in many editions and became an international success. The same thing happened with the commentary on Aristotle's *Nicomachean Ethics,* which appeared in 1528 covering the first two books and was enlarged in 1532 to include the fifth book. Precisely because these literary aids provide guidelines for political ethics, they permit us to obtain an especially clear picture of Melanchthon's understanding of *iustitia civilis* in its relation to *iustitia spiritualis.*[220]

Melanchthon, then, always measured classical ethics against the standard of Christian faith. His depiction of Aristotle as an interpreter of natural law was important to him as a sign of God's image in humankind, although at the same time he concluded from the imperfections of Aristotelian social ethics that even the noblest human righteousness is imperfect in itself and is intended for completion through Christ.[221] A sharp distinction must be made between *iustitia civilis* and *iustitia fidei:* philosophy per se, with its moral and civil laws, has nothing to do with God and Christ. Its requirements relate only to outward behavior; to the degree that everyone is subject to *iustitia civilis,*

218. *WA* 19:624.30ff.; *LW* 46:95; *WA* 29:598.8–9 (1526–1529).

219. To Theobald Billicanus, December 1, 1529 (*CR* 1:1112).

220. The two prefaces to Ulrich Silling (*CR* 2:452ff., 585ff.) offer interesting details about the lecture process from which these commentaries arose. See Richard Nürnberger, "Kirche und weltliche Obrigkeit bei Melanchthon" (Diss., Freiburg im Breisgau, 1937); Gottfried Weber, *Grundlagen und Normen politischer Ethik bei Melanchthon,* Theologische Existenz heute n.f. 96 (Munich, 1962); and Rolf Bernhard Huschke, *Melanchthons Lehre vom Ordo politicus,* Studien zur Evang. Ethik 4 (Gütersloh, 1968).

221. *CR* 16:277ff. The following comes from the introduction to the commentary on the *Nicomachean Ethics* in the editions of 1530 and later. The introduction is titled "On the Distinction Between Christian Doctrine and Philosophy" and is printed in the notes to *CR* 16:280ff. We can see how this problem was a concern to Melanchthon from the beginning of 1530.

human society depends upon it. Social philosophy, however, knows nothing of the fear and love of God, Melanchthon asserts, as he will repeat shortly in CA 2.[222]

A basic difference between political and evangelical teaching thus emerges in the *Commentary* of 1529. The gospel reveals the eternal righteousness of faith, although it lets us live outwardly according to political laws. Although such laws may vary in details, they should all correspond to reason precisely as all other human ordinances and activities should. Theologians, therefore, need not meddle in the affairs of government; they should restrict themselves to faith. Unbelievers, however, are held in check by political righteousness. The power of the sword and the bishop's power of the Word have nothing to do with each other.[223]

That brings us again to the basic thesis of CA 28. Our review has shown us how it relies on more than the doctrine of the two authorities; it has also disclosed the complex origin of the doctrine of a twofold righteousness as it relates to the function of temporal authority. For Luther, it arises primarily from his doctrine of justification. References to classical ethics, particularly the ethics of Aristotle, play a secondary role. In this world threatened by sin and death, God preserves the remains of a civil righteousness that makes life together possible and that uses force to deter evil people from excesses. From this perspective, *iustitia civilis*, with its protective strength and its educational power, seems to have positive value; in the light of the unrelenting harshness of its means of force and of the evildoers to whom it is applied, it is liable to be judged negatively.

There was no twofold righteousness in Melanchthon's Erasmian origin. The optimism of a *philosophia christiana* permitted everyone to reach, more or less, the goal of a blissfulness based on righteousness. Punishment and the use of force really have no place in this world; a Christian, at any rate, has nothing to do with them. And when Melanchthon encountered pessimism about sin in Luther's and Augustine's doctrines of justification, profligacy seemed as detestable as ever and the concern of temporal authority to keep it within bounds by the use of force seemed unworthy for a Christian. The pure spiritual righteousness of faith was separated from a fleshly one of less value.

---

222. By 1532, in the introduction to book 5 of the *Nicomachean Ethics*, Melanchthon accepts a closer relationship; righteousness is proclaimed not only in Holy Scripture but also in the teaching of philosophers and jurists, "which also is the voice of God" (ibid., 363). The gulf between the two types of righteousness seems to be bridged by a concept taken from Aristotle—*iustitia universalis*, "obedience owed to all laws," which includes obedience to biblical injunctions (ibid., 365).

223. Ibid., 418ff. Melanchthon describes the office of bishop (ibid., 437) in words almost identical with CA 28. Regarding the clergy, Melanchthon speaks as a politician: "We theologians will not eject anyone from the state, but we will remove persons from the government if they propose new laws, and we will ask them to carry out their office and to teach the gospel purely (ibid., 421).

It is Luther who has to teach Melanchthon that God instituted the coercive power of temporal authority in the Old Testament and upheld it in the New. His own pedagogical and political experiences confirm the necessity and the blessing of corrective discipline. In addition, his philosophical teachers from antiquity—Cicero and then particularly Aristotle—help him recognize that *iustitia civilis* is the highest good humanity can attain. His Christian faith values this good as a gift from God the Creator and shows him that the civil righteousness is outwardly identical with that which God demands of everyone; that humankind, under the influence of the Holy Spirit, can recognize its sin by means of this demand; and that *iustitia civilis* thus points beyond itself to the *iustitia fidei*.

In the tension between *iustitia civilis* and *iustitia fidei*, Christian humanism and Reformation theology meet. Luther, approaching the topic from the justification of the sinner, took *iustitia civilis* seriously as a means for educating the people and understood it as a necessary presupposition for the preaching of the gospel. Melanchthon, approaching from a Christianized classicism, learned to appreciate *iustitia civilis*, through Luther's influence, as an indispensable presupposition for *iustitia fidei*. In contrast to the synthetic understanding of the *philosophia christiana*, he recognized the dialectical relationship of antiquity and Christianity, of moral instruction, of law and gospel and humble faith in forgiveness. Thus, from different starting points, Luther and Melanchthon arrive at the same results. And if in the process the understanding of temporal righteousness is in a constant state of flux—to the point of statements on either side seeming to contradict each other in various contexts—it is simply the outcome of that dialectical relationship. The doctrine of a twofold righteousness gives comprehensive expression to the great number of tensions encompassed by that relationship.

Those tensions are the reason that the evaluation of temporal power in CA 28 is not simple. The few passages in the article that deal with it also testify to the various intellectual currents from which they have come—currents we have traced through more than a decade, looking back and forth both at Luther and Melanchthon. The statements of CA 28 regarding temporal authority point beyond themselves to the theses on twofold righteousness contained in CA 18.

Before we deal with temporal government in the next paragraphs, we must sketch out a comparison of the doctrine of twofold righteousness with that of the two authorities (kingdoms).[224]

The two doctrinal complexes are closely related to each other in form and content. In the sources as well as the literature they are hardly to be dis-

---

224. A more precise discussion would once again have to deal with the doctrine of the two authorities in detail; see above, n. 183.

tinguished. Both preserve a dialectical relationship between difference and homogeneity; each part of their dialectical statements appears to correspond to some part in the other complex and, whether viewed from the point of view of God or human beings, to denote the same circumstances.

And yet the two complexes are not perfectly correlated when it comes to origin and content. Luther's doctrine of the two authorities frequently has fragmentary connections with Augustine's *City of God*.[225] As we have seen, he himself developed his doctrine of twofold righteousness out of his doctrine of justification with the inclusion of certain antischolastic traditions. Melanchthon, once he had understood Luther's doctrine of justification, carried the classical tradition further. These different starting points and traditions have given a different stamp, despite all similarities, to the doctrines of the twofold righteousness of human beings and the two authorities of God. It is no small feat that the Augustana was able to hold these two doctrinal complexes together, even if it did not depict their differences more precisely. We will not attempt that either, except by noting the significance of introducing the twofold-righteousness theme into the schema of the two authorities. Perhaps this observation can stimulate further discussion.

It was the connection between the doctrine of justification and the doctrine of the two authorities that anchored the latter in the central teaching of the Reformation. In that way more prominence is given to the soteriological element in God's rule on the left and on the right. The realm of grace is more intimately connected with the saving work of Christ in history; the eschatological orientation is intensified. The relation between the two kingdoms does not arise, as some have argued, from the tension between law and gospel. This tension really underlies the twofold righteousness: *iustitia civilis* is based on the law, and *iustitia fidei* is based on the offer of grace made through the gospel. Only by identifying the doctrine of the two authorities with that of twofold righteousness can the tension between law and gospel be found in the former. And ultimately the introduction of classical ethics in the *iustitia civilis* resulted in a universal broadening of theology, not only in the historical dimension but also in posing new and universal problems for the contemporary proclamation and service of the church.

These connections in retrospect and prospect cannot be drawn directly from the Augustana. They come from the historical and dogmatic presuppositions out of which the Augustana's sections on social ethics arose. We will not pursue them further at this point; we only call attention to them in order to make clear that a commentary that takes seriously the historical situation of the CA can also provide new possibilities for its contemporary interpretation.

225. Cp. Ernst Kinder, "Gottesreich und Weltreich bei Augustin und bei Luther," in *Beiträge zur hist. und system. Theologie: Gedenkschrift für D. Werner Elert* (Berlin, 1955), 24–42.

15. TEXTUAL HISTORY OF CA 16 AND
CA 18, SECS. 1, 2

We are combining the exposition of CA 16 with that of CA 18, sections 1 and 2. These latter paragraphs contain a distinction between *iustitia civilis* and *iustitia spiritualis* which continues the thought of the concluding section of the earlier chapter and which enlarges on the positive side of CA 16. The application of that distinction to temporal authority occurred relatively late (see above, pp. 88ff.); Na still speaks in terms of the individual free will, just as the *Visitation Articles* and the *Instructions for the Visitors* had done when discussing *iustitia civilis*.[226]

We may presume that Melanchthon was prodded to his formulations, perhaps even to the later composition of CA 18,[227] by the objections to Luther's doctrine of the will raised by Eck in his 404 Theses. Eck had not simply gone back to his disputation at Leipzig and the questions about the relation between free will and good works considered there (arts. 31, 36), thereby contesting the *sola fide* of the doctrine of justification (art. 48); nor had he simply derided Luther's *On the Bound Will* (art. 36). He had also accused Luther and Melanchthon of philosophical determinism (arts. 171–72) and ascribed the wretched moral consequences of this doctrine to Satan (art. 331). Eck did not mount an attack against the political integrity of the Lutheran Reformation in this critique of its teaching on the will. But Cochlaeus as early as 1522 had called the theses Melanchthon had proposed on the topic in his *Loci* barbaric and destructive of all order; from then on the old charge of Manichean heresy circulated among the humanists. The question of the will was explosive, both doctrinally and politically.[228]

We therefore need not consider Eck's attack as the decisive impulse for the introduction of *iustitia civilis* and *iustitia spiritualis* into CA 18, which was conceived in the first half of June. Melanchthon had taken note of the attack right after his arrival in Augsburg at the beginning of May, but he had not pursued it. The stimulus arose from Melanchthon himself, out of his continual efforts to come to grips with the objections of his opponents in the old church, with the revolutionary attitude of the Anabaptists, and with the criticism of Erasmus and his humanistic friends. We must search for his personal sources.

In terms of date and content, the composition of the CA stands very close

---

226. *CR* 26:27–28; *WA* 26:226; *LW* 40:301–2. The quotation from Augustine in CA 18.4–6 is limited to civil affairs and private morality. In interpreting *iustitia civilis*, we must keep in mind all that we have heard on the subject from Luther and Melanchthon in statements quoted in previous chapters.

227. See above, pp. 31–32.

228. Cp. W. Maurer, *Der junge Melanchthon* (cited above, n. 49), 2:265–66. Eck's theses are in Gussmann 2 and in Reu 97–121.

to Melanchthon's *Dispositio* on Romans.[229] This short commentary uses the doctrine of twofold righteousness as the key hermeneutical principle for the Bible and interprets Romans from that perspective;[230] human righteousness appears throughout in contrast to the righteousness of faith. Political righteousness, as *iustitia legis,* belongs to the principal office of the law and is constantly allied with its theological use. The relation of theology and philosophy, of revelation and reason, also is governed by twofold righteousness. In brief, all the basic questions that faced Melanchthon in the composition of the Augustana tie in with the relationship of the two righteousnesses. We can understand why he paid attention to this decisive viewpoint in the new version of article 18.

Finally, the distinction between the two kinds of righteousness also underlies the commentary on Aristotle from 1529–30, which ranks just behind the two biblical commentaries in the prehistory of CA 16 and CA 18.1–2. In these three preliminary documents we find archetypes for the formulations in the Augustana. We will have to introduce the appropriate references in the following detailed exegesis.

Statements in the *Instructions for the Visitors* have nothing to do with Luther's Confession of 1528 though written at almost the same time. The latter combines rulers and subjects in a single divine estate of the saved; the *Instructions* focus on the divine authority of the ruling powers and the duty of subjects to obey.[231] The pages of explanation that the *Instructions* devote to this topic are gathered concisely in NA 15 and then expanded somewhat in content at the end of CA 16.[232] In the process, the duty of pastors to admonish temporal authority to act in a Christian way is dropped, as is the duty of the subjects to show honor to their superiors. The influence of the *Instructions* on CA 16 is therefore weaker, both in general and in particular, than the influence of Luther's confession.

The characteristic that distinguishes CA 16 from the *Instructions* and ties

229. The first part appeared during the Diet of Speyer in 1529, and the complete work in 1530 (*CR* 15:443ff.). See below, p. 125, for more on this document, which was drawn upon frequently during the writing of the CA.

230. "It is very helpful in the reading of all Scripture to observe that righteousness is twofold" (*CR* 15:443). At the end (ibid., 487), the relation between *regnum Christi* and *regnum mundi* is called the theme of Romans, and the doctrine of the two authorities is based on it.

231. Cp. *WA* 26:504.30ff., 505.5–7 with ibid., 206–11 (*LW* 37:364–65 with *LW* 40:281–86). The *Visitation Articles* (*CR* 26:12–13), whose much briefer explanations are based on Romans 13 rather than, as in the case of the *Instructions,* on the Fourth Commandment, cannot have anything in common with Luther's confession either. See above, p. 32, on the connection between the treatment of the will in *CR* 26: 26ff. and CA 18. Melanchthon had already established the bond with *iustitia civilis* in the *Articles.*

232. *BS* 70.36–38, 71.20–26; Reu 184; *BC* 38.7; in these cases with the *reservatio* from Acts 5:29, which did not appear in the earlier documents. Compare on that point—in contrast to the spiritual rulers—CA 28.23 and Hermann Dörries, "Gottesgehorsam und Menschengehorsam bei Luther: Ein Beitrag zur Gesch. des Apostelworts Acta 5:29," in *Archiv für Reformationsgeschichte* 39 (1942): 47ff.; reprinted in Dörries, *Wort und Stunde,* vol. 3 (Göttingen, 1970), 109ff.

it to Schwab. 14 is their common dependence on Luther's confession. Schwabach 14 also highlights the sentence from Luther's doctrine of the estates which says that rulers are an "estate ordained by God" and a Christian who is placed in such an estate can "act and serve therein without harm and danger to his faith and salvation."[233] This theme of divine ordinance, weakened a little in the structure of Na 15 but strongly emphasized again in CA 16, remains the formative legacy in the Augustana's doctrine of authority.

As he shortened and expanded his sources, Melanchthon's characteristic handwriting reveals how he reworked Schwab. 14 into Na 15. He reduced the eschatological aspect of ruling power. According to Schwab. 14, it would last only "until the Lord comes in judgment and does away with all power and rule."[234] This end-time view of history, substantiated biblically in 2 Thess. 2:6ff., appears only here in the development of the Lutheran confession and is astonishing in a document that so energetically rejects Anabaptist apocalypticism. The question of whether Luther or Melanchthon would be the more likely source for that view of history is quickly settled in Luther's favor. When and under what circumstances it popped up in the eventful year of 1528 is, of course, no longer possible to ascertain.

Melanchthon, who omitted that eschatological aspect in Na 15, simultaneously expanded the polemic against the Anabaptists. The description of the civil functions that a Christian could undertake[235] also enumerates the objections that the Anabaptists raised against the political order. The listing, in almost all its parts, corresponds to the commands for civil obedience previously stated in the *Instructions*, which had also made occasional references to Anabaptist objections. Naturally, Melanchthon had certain points in mind as a result of his previous literary work. With this enumeration—the individual sections are faithfully reproduced in the final text—and with the condemnations attached to them, Na has already given the final text its characteristic stamp; it seems to be more a rejection of Anabaptism than a disquisition on the essence and task of temporal government. But the appearance is deceptive. The attentive reader must be sure to keep in mind the key concept, which goes back to Luther's confession.

The repeated condemnation in Na (*BS* 70.29ff.; Reu 182–83), where the Anabaptists are specifically named, stems from Melanchthon. First here, and then in the final text (*BS* 71.5ff.; *BC* 37.3ff.), it is combined in a special section with an anathema against the monastic teaching on evangelical perfection; Anabaptism and monasticism appear in the same condemnation. In the process, Na 15 already alludes to the doctrine of twofold righteousness,

233. *BS* 70.29–31; Reu 43.
234. *BS* 70.21–23; Reu 43.
235. *BS* 70.22–28; Reu 182.

which the final text distinguishes as outward and inward righteousness.[236] Precisely this reference links Melanchthon to both Luther's confession and to his own previous work. As Luther, at the end of his discussion of the estates, had tied the three foundations or orders to the "common order of Christian love,"[237] so Melanchthon here bases the external righteousness of temporal government on the "true ordinance of God" by which everyone is to show "Christian love and genuine good works" in his own station in life.[238] Temporal government actualizes the common order of Christian love! Temporal righteousness is enlisted in its service!

Thus the development of the text of CA 16 demonstrates how the stimulus of Luther's Confession of 1528 had an increasingly powerful effect, until it ultimately formed the basis for the article's central point. The additional content—against the Anabaptists and, in the "disputed articles," the fuller polemic against monasticism—is added by Melanchthon in such a way that it obscures but does not eliminate that central point. The teaching on twofold righteousness structures the whole into a systematic unity, and because the beginning of CA 18 ultimately incorporates that teaching too, this unity links the statements on social ethics in CA 16 with the theological anthropology of CA 18.

16. OTHER STATEMENTS ON TEMPORAL AUTHORITY

After our survey of the doctrine of the two authorities in CA 28, we must now consider the article's specific statements on *temporal* authority, giving attention to their growth and content. The relevant passages in CA 28 are those which discuss the relation of the two authorities. Although they invariably make the comparison from the starting point of spiritual authority, they also shed light on temporal authority in the process. A second train of thought makes that clear. We recall how, in the composition of CA 28, the draft of document C (see above, p. 61) drew a sharp distinction between the temporal and spiritual powers of rulers.[239] In that proposal the emphasis lay on the spiritual power, without thereby completely dismissing the temporal. For example, a certain royal luster remains in the evaluation of the imperial system, and some of that luster rubs off on the bishops as well.

Such romantic memories of episcopal rule within the empire make little difference. Melanchthon grants to secular princes the legal jurisdiction that the bishops claimed (sec. 29). The question of jurisdiction over marriage,

236. *BS* 70.33–35; Reu 184; *BC* 38.4.
237. *WA* 26:505.11ff.; *LW* 37:365.
238. *BS* 71.17–19; *BC* 38.5.
239. Secs. 5–19, 29; *BC* 81–83, 85.

brushed aside in Na, is taken up again from C but treated more generally and cautiously than in early May. In areas where episcopal jurisdiction is no longer exercised over matrimonial cases and tithes, the territorial rulers are prepared to step in for the sake of order and the benefit of their subjects (sec. 29). Here temporal authority is shown to be equal to a "spiritual" jurisdiction and in fact really to surpass it.[240] Indeed the final text is much more emphatic than the short note in Na 28 (Kolde 28.3–4; Reu 274) in requiring equal respect from all Christians for both authorities; both are grounded in God's command and are praised as God's highest benefit (sec. 4).

It is striking that, once CA 28 begins to discuss questions of worship and ceremonies (sec. 30ff.), no further mention is made of temporal authority. The separation of the two authorities is carried through so logically that temporal rulers appear to have no role in church reform; even in the other reform articles of the second part they are not mentioned as active participants. One could explain this circumstance by saying that the evangelical estates had no particular need to give reasons to the emperor and the empire about their own participation in the church reforms that had been carried out through the visitations. They adopt the theological rationale provided by the Augustana. That is, they assume political responsibility for everything that had occurred in their territories. They keep quiet, however, about their own active participation and thereby avoid the question of whether or not temporal authority also has the right to cooperate in ecclesiastical reform. In Melanchthon's mind this question would receive an unequivocal yes; he also affirms authority as "good order."

The situation is different in the documents that led up to the Augustana. Both in the earlier versions of the "disputed articles" and in the prefaces, the ecclesiastical activity of temporal authority is clearly given prominence. It is also apparent that originally it was by no means a mere negative counterpart to spiritual authority but that temporal rulers also had positive ecclesiastical tasks to perform beyond the sword and defending the law. Only when these roots are taken into consideration will the full picture of temporal authority presented in the Augustana—as well as Melanchthon's affirmation of "good order"—become fully comprehensible.

We begin with the first opinion issued by the Wittenberg theologians in mid-March 1530 at the behest of the elector, the fragment of the Torgau Articles labeled E.[241] It provides a collection of rules for the elector to follow in his tactics at the coming diet. He can consent to maintaining the connection between absolution and administration of the Sacrament (F. 97.4; J. 95).

---

240. Kolde 65–66 is too one-sided in his application of statements by Melanchthon and Justus Jonas to this addition in sec. 29, and so he overestimates its significance.

241. Citations in the text are according to Förstemann 1:93ff.; and Jacobs 92–95.

He "should be willing to help" (F. 97.16; J. 95) if the diet condemns the sacramentarians as heretics. It would "not be the duty" (F. 96.29; J. 94) of the elector to place monasteries at the disposal of runaway monks who returned. He "neither can nor should consent" to an exclusive position of Communion in one kind or forced celibacy or masses that are private or for sale (F. 93.31, 94.12, 95.13; J. 92, 93). These three points, which form the basis for the later compromise proposal, address the territorial ruler not only as prince of the empire and protector of his subjects but also as a conscientious Christian: he ought not become a party to others' sins (F. 94.34ff.; J. 93). His power extends beyond the rights his medieval predecessors had formerly exercised over a church that was becoming increasingly territorial; he is being confronted by demands of faith that he must fulfill for the gospel's sake by employing the power at his disposal.

This personal evangelical responsibility of temporal authorities becomes much more prominent in A, which of course formed the basis for the later literary development.[242] The speaker—certainly the chancellor when in the singular—who here defends His Electoral Majesty before the emperor and the empire, deals only in passing with the previous situation in church law. The elector has not taken anything away from the bishops but has simply made use of the possibilities that canon law itself provides in the event of its own abuse (F. 78.25ff.; J. 82). He can call upon his right of patronage when he takes capable priests under his wing in opposition to their ecclesiastical superiors (F. 79.17ff.; J. 82). He is within the limits of his temporal powers if he refuses to force his subjects to submit to ecclesiastical tribunals (F. 80.2; J. 83). He gives monks the freedom to leave their monasteries and justifies their motives (F. 81.14ff.; J. 84–85).

With this last example, however, it becomes clear that the prince is consciously overstepping the previous legal limits. He permits existing ecclesiastical abuses to wither away without employing his power to punish (F. 69.14ff.; J. 75–76). He does not force anyone to keep the commandments on foods and·fasting promulgated by the church (F. 73.17ff.; J. 77). He demands proper worship services, pleasing to God, and introduces them; he checks on ecclesiastical ceremonies to see whether they are consonant with the gospel (F. 68.5ff., 15ff.; J. 75). He therefore has set up proper church orders in his territory for the benefit of public worship, particularly the Sunday service, and he is concerned about eucharistic discipline (F. 69.20ff., 76.26ff.; J. 75, 81). For that reason he has recommended to the clergy that they not administer the Sacrament to anyone who has not received absolution (F. 78.2; J. 81). He is watchful over what is taught in his territory so that no

242. Förstemann 1:68–84; Jacobs 75–86.

heretical doctrine will emerge (here referring to the Schwabach Articles, which were in the emperor's hands) and so that the Zwinglians will be opposed in print (F. 74.10–11, 83.23ff., 77.3ff.; J. 78, 86, 81). In all of these functions the Saxon elector knows he is in accord with his colleagues of the spiritual estate. They all seek to provide "true religion and good government" for their subjects, their "most beloved children" (F. 81.3ff.; J. 84). At this point the separation of the two authorities is obviously not observed.[243] It is less than likely, however, after this separation had been made, there would have been even the slightest retreat from any of these princely obligations. After all, an abstract distinction between the two authorities would probably not be enough to dissolve the conscientious obligations of Christian magistracy.

Document A constantly builds on such obligations. The elector appeals to them to justify his participation in ecclesiastical innovations before the emperor and empire. It has all been done in utter seriousness and at personal risk with a desire to serve God (F. 68.5ff., 69.6ff.; J. 75). On account of his conscience he neither would nor could force anyone to fulfill human ordinances that could not be observed without sin. At this point the Protest of Speyer is once again picked up and applied directly (F. 69.28ff.; J. 75). But where the elector is convinced that a true Christian worship service exists under traditional forms, he and his subjects retain it—in contrast to the Zwinglians (F. 77.3ff.; J. 81). Respect for the nation and its people keeps him from making a radical break with the past (F. 80.22ff.; J. 83).

Such claims of conscience must always be acknowledged in the evangelical bearers of temporal authority. They required the princes constantly to intervene in church affairs. The considerations that had to be taken for pastors and members of the congregations in the process are not discussed, but they are nevertheless included in those claims of conscience. All of that must be taken into account when looking at temporal authority as it performs its task among and for evangelical Christians.

In Na there is no further talk of temporal authority's thus sharing responsibility for church reform. In E and A, the elector of Saxony was either advised or defended; in Na, the actual situation is presented objectively and given a theological justification. The teaching and tactics correspond to the style of the later Augustana. All personal allusions are dropped. Only indirectly is it possible to discern that someone ready to take responsibility stands behind the confession. Granted that the hyper-objective attitude underlines the teaching character of the emerging Augustana, but in the case of the article

243. As we know, that difference was not noted before early May; at the conclusion of A (F. 83–84; J. 86), of course, an instructive distinction "between temporal authority and the office of bishop" had already been made.

"On Temporal Authority" there is no doubt that a suspicious shrinkage has taken place. Only what distinguishes temporal from spiritual authority—its external power of coercion and defense—remains discernible; its more positive function, so graphically described in the earlier versions, no longer stands out. In this instance the Augustana does not do justice to the practical realities in the evangelical territories. It was not accurate in 1530 and was even less so later. These areas had developed, along with the distinction between the two authorities, a much more intensive connection and cooperation than was theoretically justified. The gaps in the theological structure, which had existed from the beginning, hampered the full implementation of the doctrine of two authorities.[244]

From this point of view, seen theologically, the preface, transition, and conclusion of the Augustana also play a role. One ought not regard this whole framework merely as a product of Chancellor Brueck's diplomacy; it also introduces a great deal of theological strength. This has already been shown in the history of the development of the prefaces (see above, pp. 38ff.).

As early as Ja, the active participation of the elector in the details of church reform receives less attention than does his responsibility for the whole. According to the pattern of the Old Testament, princes and kings should increase true worship of God and maintain true, pure Christian preaching in the church (BS 35.23ff.; Reu 91–92). Accordingly, the elector has removed abuses in doctrine and ceremonies within his lands, eliminated open blasphemy, and spared simple folk from deception (BS 37.5ff., 23ff.; Reu 93–94). When the preachers and prelates of the old religion failed to act, it was necessary for the prince to give free course to evangelical proclamation (BS 38.1ff., 17ff., 30; Reu 94–95). In so doing, he himself professed the evangelical truth and became its witness.

Here, in the guise of a historical survey of temporal authority, something fundamental is expressed: its bearers are responsible for the spread of the gospel. They must be concerned about proper preaching and worship, as well as protecting the people from being led astray. In Ja, Melanchthon is not developing a theory of ecclesiastical law (ius in sacra). He is really breaking out of all theories on the limits of temporal power through his reference to the obligations of evangelical belief—obligations that even the possessor of temporal power cannot avoid: "No one shall refrain from openly confessing the truth because of the fear of men. For not only is he a false witness who speaks lies in the place of truth, but likewise the one who does not openly confess the truth or does not defend it is a false witness" (BS 38.30ff.; Reu 95).

This confessional courage of the Christian princes lies behind the

244. Cp. above, pp. 64ff., and below, p. 108.

Augsburg Confession; it would not have come into being without it. It remains central, even where it is not emphasized as strongly as in this draft.[245] What the doctrinal statements on temporal authority discuss in detail is already contained in the active confessional stance taken by the evangelical rulers—which exploded all the theoretical considerations. From a legal point of view, this is the legacy of the medieval "defender of the faith." The duty of fighting for the faith—as the emperor expressed it in his summons to the diet—falls both on him and on the Christian estates. Draft Ja of the preface is in harmony with this cluster of ideas, as is Brueck's later and final version (*BS* 44–45; *BC* 24–27). It places Charles V in the line of great emperors of Christian antiquity and the Middle Ages who were protectors of the faith, and it allies with him the princes as "shields" of the pious and God-fearing (*BS* 35.11ff., 25ff.; Reu 91–92).

The draft for the preface to Na, probably composed in the second half of May, heightens the picture of the Saxon elector as a loyal ally of the emperor (see above, p. 43). The temporal authority he exercises resembles that of a medieval ruler. As defender of the faith ("protector of the territory"), he not only defends piety and law but also presents a religious pattern so that "by means of the prince the people will be encouraged in the fear of God" (*BS* 40.18ff.; Reu 138). The Saxon electors—Frederick the Wise is especially prominent—have proved their commitment to the Christian religion by the donation of new church foundations and the support of existing ones. They are as loyal in things churchly as they are in matters political (*BS* 40.36ff.; Reu 139). Although Chancellor Brueck for tactical reasons did not incorporate this "Mirror for Magistrates" in his final preface, it does remain a valid prototype; it supplements the teaching on temporal authority and explains the practice of the evolving confessional state.

The elector of Saxony, though so conservative, is a confessor; he not only exposes the political reputation of his house to grave danger but also risks his "honor, goods, children, and grandchildren." He does so because his conscience forces him to testify to evangelical truth (*BS* 41.4ff.; Reu 139). The details of his activity are only intimated. The example of pious and learned people, and especially Luther's preaching, have set him on the new course (*BS* 41.11–42.15; Reu 139–41). Like its predecessor Wa, Na allows the initiative of the prince himself to fade into the background. The Reformation is no longer seen primarily as a movement of church reform; it is seen as a renewal of biblical truth, the "salutary and comforting doctrine of repentance and righteousness." The elector has, however, supported its spread. He has guarded it against the "seductive and seditious doctrine" of the sacramen-

---

245. It is already fading in the improved draft Wa. Luther rather than the territorial ruler appears as the real confessor. Cp. above, pp. 41–42.

tarians and Anabaptists. He has strengthened its conservative features "whereby authority and civil order are well maintained." He has been attentive to the religious education of the people; "the schools are maintained with great diligence and at great expense to the authorities" (*BS* 43.9; Reu 142). In short, the temporal ruler has become deeply involved in the life of the church. He has not only permitted and approved changes, he has also initiated them. With justifiable pride he can point to the extraordinary achievements that have been made possible through the cooperation of evangelical preaching and magisterial attention (*BS* 42.19ff.; Reu 141–42).

When temporal authority is exercised by an evangelical Christian, it can also be a positive influence on worship and Christian nurture. Therefore, it is by no means limited—as CA 28 makes it seem (that article is not refuted by CA 16)—to the negative functions of punishment and coercion. It is really designed to have a positive religious, spiritual, and cultural effect. If that is no longer discernible at first glance in the final version of the CA's framework, it nevertheless remains a presupposition there as well—although admittedly only by inference.

In the final version it is true that the elector of Saxony is careful not to indicate the details of his personal share in the work of ecclesiastical reform. As far as those details are concerned, he would hardly be in full agreement with all the other signers of the CA. Brueck's preface is so careful to include the evangelical estates within the imperial structure that the confessional conflict becomes almost imperceptible; emperor and empire approach the requested council with the closest possible cooperation. This tactical unity is also intended to further the appeal to the emperor that he not believe the slander of clerical troublemakers but lend an appreciative ear to the initiators of church reform.[246] The fact that the emperor's intervention in the celibacy question, already anticipated in Na, remains a part of at least the German version[247] of CA 28, testifies to the unshaken confidence in him. When he, like a new David, leads his troops into battle against the Turks, he is fulfilling the calling of a Christian prince (CA 21.1).[248]

It is to the same calling that the evangelical princes appeal when they justify their ecclesiastical measures to the emperor and empire. Even though the final version skips the details of reform, the act of confessing at Augsburg makes clear that the princes participate in and take responsibility for the whole. That includes the area of doctrine. They therefore pride themselves on having prevented any "new and godless teaching from creeping into our

---

246. *BS* 84; *BC* 49. Most of this is in only the Latin text.

247. Cp. *BS* 89.11ff. with Kolde 18.22ff. (*BC* 53:14 with Reu 214, 216).

248. The task given to the emperor in the conclusion of Ja, in analogy to the Old Testament monarchy, was much more comprehensive (*BS* 135.41ff.; Reu 145).

churches and gaining the upper hand in them" (*BS* 134.25ff.; *BC* 95.5). Driven by their consciences, they risk their political and religious life for evangelical truth and bind the future of their dynasties to the preservation of right doctrine.[249] The development of patriarchal absolutism into the confessional state is, despite the doctrine of the two authorities, already foreshadowed in the Augustana.

These assertions have been drawn out of the framework of the final version and interpreted against the background of the earlier drafts. In the process we have also recognized the permanent value of expressions that were later dropped, since these omissions can be explained on political grounds. Their point of view, although not expressly spelled out, is nevertheless included in the act of confession at Augsburg and is borne out by it. The reform measures of the temporal authority thus belong to the doctrine on that topic enunciated by the Augustana. Those measures become legitimate in the light of that doctrine at the same time that they illustrate the scope of its application.

Article 16 of the Augustana is to be understood in such a way that these expressions are included, even if the article does not mention any right of the temporal authority to initiate reform. Political reasons in Augsburg prevented it from being made fundamentally applicable, but at the same time political practice was claiming that right. Article 16 remains a monument to this claim, even if it sounds more polemically defensive against the enthusiasts than positively constructive. The description of *iustitia civilis* from CA 18 also must be drawn upon in order to interpret CA 16 and CA 28, and that is also the case in regard to the preface and its preparatory documents. The article is not merely of political importance—even in what it diplomatically does *not* say. It is also theologically significant in its own right.

17. TEMPORAL AUTHORITY AS "GOOD ORDER, CREATED BY GOD"

Article 16 of the CA describes "all government in the world and all established rules and laws" as "good order, created and instituted by God."[250] We have already established that Luther's Confession of 1528 reechoes in these phrases, and that this influence has intensified during the textual development of CA 16 (see above, p. 101). We can also trace back this concept of ordering elsewhere in Luther and Melanchthon, so that we can draw upon

249. They do not want to bequeath to their posterity "any other teaching than that which agrees with the pure Word of God and Christian truth" (*BS* 83c.15–18; *BC* 47.1; only in the German text).

250. *BS* 70.10–13; *BC* 37.1. The preliminary documents and the final Latin version do not speak so sweepingly. Their choice of "good works of God" to designate the ordering, and their use of the plural "orders" give more effective expression to a dynamic and God-centered way of thinking about the topic.

that comprehensive source material in arriving at a well-founded theological judgment.[251]

It is clear that Luther's concept of orders is not determined by medieval traditions, as one could suppose on the basis of its connection with the doctrine of hierarchies. Neither Neoplatonic nor Aristotelian concepts of orders are basic or normative. Rather, everything that is set forth on authority as divine institution is drawn from the Reformation understanding of the Scriptures. We will attempt to lay out the theological motifs and analyze them.

We begin with Luther's Palm Sunday sermon of 1528. Using Philippians 2,[252] he applies the "great work of love" that Christ accomplished for us (91.14) to the ordered life of human society and the three estates (92.17ff.). Christ emptied himself of the form of God and became a servant. Thus God in his power and might condescended to the three estates in order to govern the world thereby (94.5ff.). They are instruments in his hand. They are divine forms, but in their operation they empty themselves. Officials with authority, like the prince himself, become servants (94.21ff.). If they strive for their own honor, they rob and steal the divine honor that has been entrusted to them along with their authority. God wants all offices and estates to take on the form of servanthood.

Here the ideal of the Christian prince, as portrayed in natural law and asceticism, taken over from classical and medieval traditions by Erasmus, and picked up again in the Enlightenment, is conquered by the image of Christian love revealed in Christ. This view excludes the idea that authorities, because of their participation in divine honor, are to be elevated above the mass of humanity—as the system of Dionysius the Areopagite suggests. "The common order of Christian love" in which Luther had included the doctrine of hierarchies in his Confession of 1528[253] also puts its stamp upon temporal authority as a "good order, created by God."

The outworn and discredited concept of orders of creation does not do justice to this nuance. Even the christological reference we detected will not suffice. It could quite possibly mislead us into a blurring of the distinction between the two kingdoms.[254] When Christ told Peter to put up his sword in its sheath, he once again set up that distinction. He did not want the divine order to be destroyed.[255]

251. We will draw principally upon Old Testament commentaries and sermons of the later 1520s and upon works around 1530, but we will not exhaust their resources.

252. WA 27:91ff.

253. WA 26:505.11ff.; LW 37:365.

254. The typological interpretation of the Old Testament increases this danger; see above, p. 105, on the territorial ruler as bishop. In commenting on Isa. 45:1, Luther calls the messianic kingdom of Cyrus, which is a prototype for the kingdom of Christ, a "royal institution" (WA 31.2:356.34).

255. WA 28:250.6.

The divine character of these orders of governance gives expression to God's transcendent might. The royal majesty, whose will is done without opposition, is the created equivalent to the irresistible power of God. God could also govern the world without princes, but he has chosen not to do so. The fact that they bear the mantle of a divinely created office, "sitting in God's place," should only increase their responsibility, not their autocracy. He who created the world governs them as well. Basically, the prince is nothing more than a farmer; he cultivates the land.[256] Or, using another image, God allots princes their power the way a prince allots fiefdoms to his nobles. The great powers too, which Luther rated no higher than Augustine did, were still "God's ordinance and good creation."[257]

Luther's view on good government belongs, dogmatically speaking, to the doctrine of continuing creation (creatio continua). Princes waver in their intentions and actions; God, however, watches unceasingly over human affairs, to the point of frustrating the designs of the powerful. Usually the world is governed by human opinions; God, however, rules through facts.[258] By means of the government, an order he instituted, God carries out everything that happens under the sun. "Under the sun," because there is also a divine activity in heaven, where God acts directly, without human help. In governing the earth, however, he constantly works together with human beings. And this constancy—in contrast to human transience—is the hallmark of divine creativity; everything that God does, including the realm of earthly government, remains forever (in perpetuum).[259] Finally, government as God's good order may be summed up in a syllogism from the Lectures on Galatians of 1531: "God's creations are good; the political order is God's creation."[260]

Over against this steadfastness stands the vanity of human beings and the futility of their political schemes. Where the creator reigns, the creature fades to insignificance. The dissatisfied human spirit flits about in an uncertain future; God stands by his work. The fact that the order is good does not guarantee the goodness of those who occupy it; Luther can speak very critically of the princes, their unjust rule, and the "godless court flunkies."[261]

256. WA 20:152.32ff. (1526); LW 15:136; WA 27:256.23–24 (1528), 28:535.5 (1529), 20:77.2. "[The secular arm] was instituted so that the earth might be cultivated" (WA 20:99.11; LW 15:65).

257. WA 27:205.3 (1528). Cp. WA 31.2:97.1 (1527): "great injustices."

258. WA 20:44.13ff. (1526); LW 15:37. Cp.: "God rules by realities, humans rule by opinions" (WA 20:111.11; LW 15:95).

259. WA 20:182.15ff., 27.14ff., 64.11ff.; LW 15:169, 23 (on the difference between opus factum and actum, see above, n. 186).

260. WA 40.1:395.3.

261. Ibid., 77.2, 64.12, 66.3, 67.3. For his attitude during the Peasants' War, see WA 18:315.20, 399.14, 400.24; LW 46:32, 82, 84. On the court, see WA 19:573.7; LW 14:233. On the "foul" nobility, see WA 19:631.8, 644.15, 654.6; LW 46:101, 117, 128 (more favorably, WA 31.1:223ff.; LW 14:3).

In view of those sins and the consequent judgment, there is significance in the phrase from the *Admonition to Peace* on the Twelve Articles which says that we are to fear God's wrath "if even one leaf rustles."[262]

Luther attributed the scandalous pride of the princes to the fact that they did not acknowledge God as Lord but based their rule on their own power and wisdom. They exploit their divine estate for their own advantage. They consider themselves gods, and they do not hear the voice of their Lord: "Where am I? Where are my commandments . . . ? You have not commanded it, but I, I."[263] In the Old Testament commentaries from the late 1520s, influenced by the Peasants' War, Luther severely chastised this shameless arrogance of his princely contemporaries. Using the example of the Babylonians and their kings, he illustrated the divided nature of the human heart, which wallows in either pride or despair and which, in the "titillation" of victory, is led to the slaughter.[264] God overthrows the "bigwigs" and raises up the destitute; he "laughs and scoffs at them with their clever ideas and exquisite schemes, because he knows that they are futile."[265]

That is not simply a moral condemnation of the political elite with their inordinate pride and lack of consideration; behind it stands a theological judgment. The princes may use their power as their office requires. What God will not and cannot tolerate is that in everything they write their own "I" on their foreheads; for that reason one kingdom tumbles on top of another. It is original sin that turns the princes into despisers of God and humans. In them the Psalm verse (9:2) is fulfilled: the kings of the earth gather together against God. "Everything that is high or authoritative in the world fights against God's Word."[266]

The princes, therefore, possess no superhuman quality just because their office has been created by God. They are his instruments; he works through them and casts them aside if they want to be more than tools in his service.[267] Luther explained this situation as a warning to the German princes in his

262. *WA* 18:297.33; *LW* 46:21. On the judgment of wrath according to Malachi 3, see *WA* 19:410ff.; *LW* 19:212–13.

263. *WA* 31.1:215.4, 216.3ff.; *LW* 13:69, 70 (exposition of Ps. 82:6, from 1530).

264. *WA* 19:372.11ff., 383.9ff.; *LW* 19:173, 185 (lectures on Habakkuk, from 1525). The latter reference paints a frightening picture, arising from the experience of the Peasants' War but directed against the victorious princes: "For the cattle that one fattens one does not raise just for the fun of it or for other purposes but for the kitchen or the slaughterhouse." "God is a great cook and has a large kitchen; therefore he fattens big animals, who are the mighty kings and princes. He fattens them well, so that they—more than anyone else—have an abundance of goods, honor, pleasure, and power. He permits them to be merry and dance. . . ." Cp. also his criticism of the building mania of the new sovereign John: *WA* 19:407.30ff.; *LW* 19:209.

265. *WA* 19:581.30, 588.2; *LW* 19:241, 249.

266. *WA* 40.3:226.8, 227.6, 231.2 (1532), 31.1:27.16ff.

267. This functional character of the organs of government is connected to the distinction between person and office—a distinction incomprehensible outside the context of belief in creation. See *WA* 19:596.20ff., 624.18ff. (1526); *LW* 14:258, 46:94; *WA* 30.2:112.14ff. (1529); *LW* 46:116.

exposition of Psalm 82 during the weeks before the diet at Augsburg.[268] Although they are called gods in that Psalm, it is not just because "all offices of government from the lowest to the highest are God's ordinance" but also because he thereby intends to indicate the difference between his power and theirs: "He wishes to let them be gods over men, but not over God himself." It is always presupposed that God himself sets up all government and maintains it. The rulers as well as the "common people" are subject to him. "He judges the gods, because the government is also his." When rulers and subjects become willful, "they both shall become guilty of death before God and they shall be punished."[269]

On the other hand, the name of the prince is to be spoken with respect and his dignity honored by bending the knee. For where there is no government or where it is not honored, there can be no peace. Every lord and prince is his country's cornerstone, rock, and foundation. Because he exercises the three divine offices of helping, nurturing, and rescuing, he should bear three divine names and be called Savior, Father, and Redeemer. The ruling estate can accomplish innumerable good works, so those who fulfill their office should "share divine majesty and help [God] perform his purely divine, superhuman work."[270] Veneration and condemnation of government—both belong together, and in Christendom they can only exist together; both attitudes are the consequence of government's being both God's institution and his instrument. Obedience too is both required and limited by that double character.

Political obedience is commanded by God. Therefore King Solomon advises that no one should act on his own initiative against the prince. Do what he commands, because he has been appointed by God; the oath of allegiance you have given him has been sworn before God—that is the accepted rule. Obedience to the government is obedience to God. Those who die in obedience—under the emperor in battle with the Turk—die well.[271]

But even if the government can demand obedience in God's name, it does not become deified on that account. It stands in the same obedience to God that it requires of its subjects; before God, rulers and subjects are the same. Because of this common responsibility before God, the rulers cannot demand unlimited obedience.

268. *WA* 31.1:189ff.; *LW* 13:41.

269. *WA* 31.1:191.25ff., 32ff., 192.1, 193.15ff., 21ff.; *LW* 13:44–46. See also *WA* 31.1:215ff.; *LW* 13:69–70. In addition, see the exposition of the Magnificat, which was already completed before the Diet of Worms: *WA* 7:544ff.; *LW* 21:295. On Genesis 21:6, see *WA* 16:533.39ff. (December 1525).

270. *WA* 40.1:100.3–4; *LW* 26:43; *WA* 31.1:192.21, 214.3, 205.17ff., 201.16ff., 23ff.; *LW* 13:44, 68, 58, 54–55. These citations come from the same exposition of Psalm 82 that was so critical of the rulers; see above, n. 268.

271. *WA* 20:152.11ff.; *LW* 15:135; *WA* 18:357.21ff.; *LW* 46:49–50 (decisive for Luther's attitude in the Peasants' War); *WA* 30.2:130.6; *LW* 46:185.

The limits to obedience occur at the point where it demands conflict with God's commandment: "Cursed be all obedience to the abyss of hell if such obedience, whether to government, father and mother, yes, even to the church, is disobedient to God."[272] Because the Sacrament in only one kind is continually required under threat of punishment, administration of the Sacrament in both kinds (see below) not only has become a mark of confessional differences—as in the waning Middle Ages—it is also an occasion to refuse obedience. Government has power only over the body, not over the soul. In matters of conscience, obedience no longer applies. But also where people are too weak to fulfill rigorous demands, one must relax strict obedience and maintain justice. The principle of general equality, of course, which was laid down by the peasants, abolishes that obedience and destroys order. Opposition to that principle does not call into question either natural equality—princes are born and die just like the most humble—or our equality before God.[273]

Obedience to the order set by God removes any possibility of revolution. If one exalts oneself over others and wants to become their judge, the result is nothing but murder and bloodshed. Luther is therefore no hypocrite or lackey of the princes when he does not join Karlstadt's friends in urging the masses to kill princes and rulers. At the same time, Luther also knows that in unsettled times the reproach of revolution can be easily misused; it was even raised unjustly against Christ. There is a limit to the obedient suffering that the pious bear for the sake of their faith; beyond that point, patience would only make the enemy more bloodthirsty.[274]

Thus Luther did not require unlimited obedience; he was aware of the difference between tyranny and government instituted by God. The uncurbed demanding dictator who arbitrarily pursues his own lust for power is outside the purview of the Lutheran Reformation and its confession. It is God who rules the world through his created good orders of temporal authority. They are the instruments he uses to ward off destructive forces and to punish evil. If the governing agencies are foolish or outrageously arrogant, he carries out his ruling will against them. All of this occurs without regard to whether these agencies are Christian or not. The Turks, of course, are enemies and blasphemers of God, so to support them is a denial of Christ. Therefore their

---

272. *WA* 31.1:193.7ff., 28:24.15ff. Cp. *WA* 28:28.35ff. (1528–29).

273. *WA* 30.3:411.20ff., 26:580.9ff., 26ff., 581.19ff., 581.24ff., 20:579.3ff., 143.1ff.; *LW* 15:123; *WA* 25:463.3ff.

274. *WA* 18:73.5ff.; *LW* 40:91; *WA* 18:306.24ff. (1525); *LW* 46:27. Luther condemns the uprising supported by Lübeck (*WA* 19:642.9ff.; *LW* 46:115) and the riots in Goslar in 1529 (*WBr* 5:no. 1432). See also *WA* 28:305.4, 310.4, 30.3:461.18ff., 468.7ff. Hermann Dörries deals with obedience and resistance in two instructive articles: "Gottesgehorsam und Menschengehorsam bei Luther," in *Wort and Stunde*, vol. 3 (Göttingen, 1970), 109ff.; and "Luther und das Widerstandsrecht," in ibid., 195ff.

government is perverted; they lack a "divinely ordained authority . . . to effect peace," even though there is much to be praised in their governing.[275] And there are also unbelieving Christian princes whose rule must be endured and to whom honor and allegiance are due as bearers of the divine office. This situation shows that temporal authority is not a human institution; it is established by God. God works through it. That is worth noting in two respects: first, he uses it to execute justice, and second, he thus binds himself to human reason. In the concept that God, by using human authorities as instruments, enlists human reason in his service, the Reformation doctrine of government approaches the Aristotelian-scholastic doctrine of natural law. We must ask ourselves whether and how they differ.

Human reason was created by God in the beginning at the same time as temporal authority. God does not rule the world from heaven, but through the instrument of reason that he has given to humanity; it is to reason that government is subject.[276] Therefore the best arrangement is when earthly relationships are not regulated by Scripture but when—in contrast to spiritual things—reason decides. Such is the case in marriage law.[277] Legal matters must be freely decided on the basis of equity. The letter of the law should not be rigidly interpreted. Reason must consider the various motives of the people as well as the external circumstances under which the guilty parties acted. "The judge and ruler must be clever and gentle here, measuring equity by reason."[278]

In his *Lectures on Ecclesiastes* in 1526, Luther returns again and again to these decisions of reason. He provides a basic summary and comparison of the idea with the classical doctrine of natural law, in the introduction to his lecture on Psalm 127, begun on July 21, 1532.[279] At first Luther agrees with the old doctrine of natural law from Aristotle, Cicero, and Plato—note the order!—especially in maintaining the principle of causality. But then two essential differences appear. The biblical king pays much greater attention to the experiences he has had of human relationships that are contradictory and that do not neatly fit the rules. Second, he differs from those abstract thinkers

275. *WA* 30.3:123.30ff.; *LW* 38:26.

276. Prior to any specific occupant of these offices of government, it is stated "that God . . . set up secular authority, that he does not rule from heaven but uses for this purpose the reason which he provided" (*WA* 16:356.1ff.). "Worldly rule is subject to human reason" (sermons on Exodus, from August 20 and September 9, 1525; *WA* 16:408.7).

277. *WA* 27:1.19–20 (January 1, 1528), 30:208.20ff., 209.2ff., 244.1 (January 1530). An uprising like the Peasants' War is "against natural law and all fairness" (*WA* 18:304.25–26; *LW* 46:26).

278. *WA* 19:631.12ff., 632.8ff.; *LW* 46:101, 102 (written on behalf of the peasants in 1526 in light of the recent war).

279. Luther attributed Psalm 127 to Solomon: *WA* 40.3:202ff. The following summary is from this source.

in seeing God as the cause of all causes, which exposes the arrogance of human rulers who want to direct political events on their own.

Those who have power on earth do not determine human destiny. That is the foundation of Luther's teaching on government, and that makes it different from all ancient and modern theories of the state. Neither ruling might nor legal skill creates laws. Of course they rest on human wisdom and reason. They do not, however, originate there; they are given. They are God's creation, and they precede all human efforts. Luther's concept of reason is different from that of the classical pagan tradition. Because God has created the human being in his image, he has also implanted there the knowledge of himself. As with all other knowledge, both human social order and law are God's gifts (*ius implantatum et concreatum*). The jurist does not create the law but receives, "finds" it. Human pride dare not turn the God-dependent "receive," *accepi*, into "make," *feci*.

Luther's limitation of natural law is based on his faith in creation; it excludes any self-creating activity of human reason.[280] Thus the lawgiver and judge are not the creator of the law but its receiver and preserver. Conversely, however, it is true on the basis of Holy Scripture that what constitutes temporal authority among various peoples—including the heathen—such as laws, offices, rights, morals, usages, and customs, are sanctioned by God, along with the kings that the peoples have set over themselves.[281] He does not demand that to acknowledge him means abandoning existing law; rather, he lets each nation be governed by its own law. Nor does God conform to the modern practice of applying moralistic standards to existing criminal law, deciding whether it is harsh or lenient; he knows that the temporal sword "out of great mercy must be unmerciful and out of pure goodness must exercise wrath and zeal." One ought not, as reason is inclined to do, mix temporal authority with powerless spiritual authority. What reason can devise

---

280. Ibid., 222.4ff. What was said above (p. 111) about the presumption of rulers is relevant here. Even when they are called masks (*personae et larvae;* WA 16:586.22 [1526], 40.1:174–75 [1531]; LW 26:95), this expression emphasizes God's sovereign rule as creator—and in contrast not only to the princes but also to the peasants. During the Peasants' War, on May 25, 1525 (the day Mühlhausen was captured), Luther described their activity of plowing, harvesting, and sowing as "mere masks," in order to make clear that it was God who laid claim to their service. The use of weapons too (by the peasants or their princely opponents?) is only "shadowboxing" (WA 16:263.1, 6, 11). Regarding the princes, the term "masks" emphasizes both their dignity and their role as instruments. They are creatures of flesh and blood; what distinguishes them is the Word of God that empowers them. To that degree they are "masks of God who are not to be despised, because he works through them." The peasants who took up the sword without a mandate have learned that lesson by their defeat (WA 40.1:548.7ff. [March–April 1526]; LW 26:359). An image of similar import to that of *larvae* or masks (WA 40.1:174.6ff., 175.3ff., 176.13ff.; LW 26:95, 96) is the tournament in which God knocks kings out of the saddle and then lets them remount; both images show how God plays with them (WA 19:360.12ff.; LW 19:162). Cp. WA 15:370.20ff. (1524); LW 45:329.

281. "The Holy Spirit sanctions the temporal rule and authority of all countries and considers them kings" (WA 31.1:234.5; LW 14:14). Cp. WA 31.1:233.22ff., 234.15ff. (1530); LW 14:15.

and set up, there is no need for Christ to do; human law "is your own thing, conceived by your reason and previously created and implanted in you by nature."[282] Thus not only national law like the "Saxon Mirror" holds good, but municipal laws as well.[283] Above them all stands Roman law, the law of the empire. It has replaced the law of Moses, which has become since the time of Christ one national law among all the others, the "Saxon Mirror of the Jews."[284]

Thus the whole realm of justice—in cooperation with human reason—is subject to the divine creative and sustaining will. The specific laws are not divine but human justice. God uses them, however, through the duties of government, to rule the world, and he requires that they be obeyed. The legislators and judges are also responsible to him for the manner in which they apply historically conditioned ordinances in specific cases to suit changing situations. To that end they employ the reason given them by their creator, and they are accountable to him for the way in which that is done. Both judge and accuser stand before God as the accused and become liable to punishment.[285]

Government is an order instituted by God that also subjects the defenders of order to his almighty will. This expresses itself in God's Word; it is the Word that has created the order and also keeps it in existence. Luther's doctrine of orders is scriptural exposition. It does not grow out of anthropological premises, as in the *Politics* of Aristotle, nor out of metaphysical speculations, as in the Areopagite's doctrine of hierarchies. Luther's biblical understanding, however, is not to be traced to a few constantly quoted passages (Rom. 13:1ff.; 1 Pet. 2:13ff.), although they do provide a divine sanction for order and a divine basis for coercive power as well as the duty of obedience, and they set up the divine law to which the peasants erroneously appealed.[286]

It would be a misunderstanding of Luther, however, to interpret his teaching on government in a formal, biblicistic way. The standard for understanding the law is the New Testament's command of love. It is child's play to find

282. *WA* 18:391.30ff., 31.1:241.11ff., 242.12ff.; *LW* 14:22, 23. The limits of this law are drawn in *WA* 31.1:290.1ff.: "The kingdom of Christ is a kingdom of equity and justice. All other kingdoms are unjust, because they are irreligious; God is not feared and honored. The justice of the scribes is very feeble justice." On the kingdom of Christ, see part 2, chap. 5, on CA 3.

283. The exposition of Ps. 82:3–4 (*WA* 31.1:208.30ff.; *LW* 13:62) repeats the well-known admonition from the Small Catechism about the recognition of municipal law (*WA* 30.1:349.17ff.).

284. *WA* 31.1:238.15ff., 241.21ff.; *LW* 14:19, 23; *WA* 18:81.14ff.; *LW* 40:99.

285. In spite of all the stress on strict power to punish, one ought not lose sight of the emphasis on protection and help; government provides protection under the law (*WA* 32:331.12ff.; *LW* 21:40). Note also the etymology of "Ludwig" as meaning "fortification, fortress of the people" (*WA* 31.1:205.30; *LW* 13:59).

286. *WA* 18:303.18ff.; 308.23ff.; *LW* 46:25, 28.

it in the Bible but difficult to fulfill it in suffering obedience. God trains Christians in this obedience so that they accomplish his will by following Christ. Obedience is a function of Christian love. Even the princes, although they occupy a "divine rank," are not certain whether they are doing a divine work until they can relate their action to the command of love. It is not possible, therefore, to appeal automatically to God-given authority and power; one needs to call on reason and conscience in order to fulfill one's task in love. Love grows out of faith. The order of government can be recognized as God's gift only through a faith that clings to God's Word.[287] The enthusiasts reject obedience to the government and consider it (like the Sacrament) an "external thing." But it is "written in God's Word . . . and to be believed that it is God's ordinance." Romans 13 is not a legal statute for those in authority; it is a command to faith. And it is the same way for the people. When they believe the Word of God, they also acknowledge the divine institution of the order of government and are grateful for it. The heathen, "because they know nothing of God, also do not acknowledge that temporal authority is God's ordinance"; they do not render thanks for it and therefore justify the assassination of tyrants.[288] In his next-to-last sermon at the Coburg, on Saint Michael's Day, 1530,[289] Luther has the congregation give thanks "for temporal peace, for a pious prince, and for other similar blessings" at the close of the Augsburg diet.[290] That does not represent an attempt to glorify the office of ruler or its occupant; it is an expression of faith in God's gracious governance of the world.

If we collect these thoughts of Luther, what sort of commentary could we expect from him on the statement of CA 16 that temporal authority is a "good order, created and instituted by God"? Luther's works from around 1530 clearly affirm this thesis; they elucidate it at great length and give it a deep theological foundation. In the process it becomes clear that to understand government as an order of creation one must begin with faith in God the Creator. Government is not an unchangeable structure in which privileged representatives enforce unqualified obedience. Instead, this order, created by God, is subject to his sovereign will. He has not given it over to itself, but he works through it unceasingly toward creating the new. It is he who calls those

287. *WA* 18:309.33ff.; *LW* 46:29; *WA* 27:30.27ff. Cp.: ". . . where there is government, there is a miracle" (*WA* 31.2:590.11–12; *LW* 15:195).

288. *WA* 23:263.17ff.; *LW* 37:137; *WA* 31.2:587.11ff., 590.16ff., 593.23ff.; *LW* 15:192, 194, 195 (abbreviated); *WA* 31.1:79.20ff.; *LW* 14:52; *WA* 19:633.20ff.; *LW* 46:104.

289. *WA* 32:111ff.; here 120.15ff., 117.25ff. In this sermon about angels, Luther puts the princes in their special care (ibid., 115.30ff., 116.6ff.). See also *Luthers Lehre von den drei Hierarchien* (cited above, n. 185), 36ff.

290. The recommended prayer reads, "Dear Lord God, I thank thee that thou hast thus cared for us and protected us by thy dear angels, that thou hast set such princes over us, . . ." (*WA* 32:117.25ff.).

who occupy governmental office into those complex institutions he exposes to continual change; he places rulers and displaces them. They serve him and are responsible to him; he punishes them when they fail in their duty and destroy his order. They serve him by cooperating with him in the maintenance of human order. Because they are responsible to him, they can and must be free to make decisions. That is why their creator also gave them reason. The laws according to which they judge and govern arise out of this reason and must be administered by it.

All people, rulers as well as ruled, are included in this order ruled by God and constituted by authority. They are subject to their creator and Lord. Obedience to him keeps the order secure; all are obligated to such obedience, even those who rule. Of course, they are entitled to special honor, because God acts on his subjects through them. Giving honor to princes and superiors is a part of the subordinates' duty of obedience. All obedience due human beings, however, is limited by obedience to God; where he is respected as creator there can be no unconditional obedience. It cannot be required. A right to resist remains.

Where is the theological foundation for this governmental order created by God? It does not lie in the rationality of the world or of its leading figures and existing laws. The latter are imperfect and sometimes unjust, and those who administer them are occasionally difficult to please or are even tyrants. This order cannot be based on earthly relationships but must be based on God's will as creator. It is given to us because it was given from the beginning by him; just as from the beginning reason was given to us, created in the divine image; just as the laws were given from the beginning, arising from that order and determining its application. This prior gift of government as a divine order of creation cannot be theologically based on an appeal to biblical passages such as Romans 13. Instead it flows out of faith in the Creator God who never ceases to act in nature and history. Even the scriptural passages in which he shows this activity have conclusive force only as supports of this faith in creation.

At this point the contemporary understanding of reality raises questions for this doctrine of government. It also puts the whole Lutheran confession into question. A historical commentary on that confession cannot avoid these questions, but at the same time one must see that they too arise out of a historical context.

Belief in a God-given authority, endowed with divine dignity and requiring obedience in God's name, was smashed, along with feudal culture in general, during the Enlightenment. Efforts to restore monarchy in the nineteenth century failed; the attempts of nihilism to base a new authority on naked power and unscrupulous agitation were exposed. This "de-divinization" was produced by the Enlightenment and the political and spiritual revolutions arising from it. We neither would nor could undo it, but we must discern the causes of the Enlightenment and ask ourselves whether we can conquer them in faith.

The theological Enlightenment of the eighteenth century, which sought to make belief in creation provable, produced intellectual offspring that destroyed that belief in the nineteenth century. The modern world and its theology have destroyed belief in creation, at least in Luther's sense. His doctrine of government, however, rests on that belief and is not conceivable without it.

Without this belief, talk about divine orders of creation makes them appear to be abstract forms, used in reference to an abstract, postulated God from whom no reality and power flow. And the rulers who appeal to him are clever, calculating men, using the religious feelings of their subjects to guarantee their own power by religious claims. They are sovereign, with no authority above them, personifying political rationality. The obedience they demand and get is, to be sure, religiously embroidered by those who still live in pre-Enlightenment traditions; sometimes there are even religious feelings, but they are forced and without religious power. Morality becomes the basis for punishment meted out to the disobedient—as it also justifies moderating the sentence. Those affected, however, reject the punishment covertly—and also overtly when possible—as an unjustified act of force. This sort of state understands itself as the incarnation of a religiously and morally based patriarchalism, but in reality it is an absolute despotism. This was the case with the enlightened state in France which presented itself as a morally absolute divine gift in the ancien régime before 1789 and as absolute democracy after the revolution.

When the Reformation doctrine of government is confronted with this political and social reality, it makes no sense. The remnants of religion and morality that still cling to the state after the Enlightenment appear as hypocrisy. Article 16 of the CA and its foundation in Luther's belief in creation must then be regarded as an obsolete concept. How can present political and civil realities be conceptualized in terms of that belief in creation? What sort of political ethics could that belief develop? Those are unsolved theological problems that cannot be tackled in this context, but the future—and not only that of the Lutheran church—depends on their solution.

Now we need to resume our study by asking whether Melanchthon preserves intact Luther's argument for the central point of CA 16. It is immediately clear that Luther's pupil would have formulated the text of CA 16 differently if he had not been conscious of his agreement with the master. It is easy to demonstrate that he took over the latter's discussion wholesale. Still, that does not let us drop the question of whether his discussion completely corresponds to Luther's in emphasis and purpose. This question, in addition to its biographical and theological importance, has general historical interest as well. For if Melanchthon argues differently from Luther for the statements of CA 16 or occasionally adds other material, one can expect that the pupil and follower would also bring to the explanation of the article themes that were foreign to Luther but that in the course of spiritual, political, and social developments brought about the alterations in the Lutheran doctrine of government which we have just indicated in our preliminary summary of Luther's thought.

We must hasten to add, however, in fairness to Melanchthon, that the works after 1524 in which he developed his doctrine of government were written under the impact of the Peasants' War and were shaped by it. That is true of his work *Against the Articles of the Peasants* from the summer of 1525[291] as well as the section on obedience to the authorities in the *Instructions for the Visitors* of 1528.[292] We will use these writings to propose a contrasting picture—not one that focuses too sharply on details that differ from Luther but one that attempts to reflect the basic color of the total panorama.

Melanchthon, like Luther, has no question about the divine foundation and institution of government (194.32ff.). His first concern, however, is not the origin of this good order in God's creative will. His primary interest is the service this order performs for humanity: that it protects the decent and punishes the offender. In the meantime he does not forget that Christians stand over against this order with inner freedom (195.2ff.) and that they should accept it gratefully as a gift of God's goodness.[293] The emphasis, however, is laid on the fact that government represents God and therefore deserves divine authority and the highest respect. The Christian is to respect the prince's decisions as divine "and what he orders, judges, and sets up is to be considered wisely and lawfully done" (198.28ff.).[294] This respect is also due to tyrants who misuse their power, because government is "a particular order . . . , as the sun is created by God or as God instituted marriage" (231.35ff.).[295]

In order to serve the ends of such good order, the conscience of the bearers of public office must be sure that their work is pleasing to God and that he

291. StA 1:190ff.; "von der Oberkeyt" (ibid., 194–201).

292. Included in an exposition of the Fourth Commandment based on Romans 13 (ibid., 228.30–235.15). The following page numbers in the text refer to StA 1.

293. Ibid., 230.19ff., 26ff., 198.4ff.

294. Also ibid., 230.35–36: "He who therefore wishes to see God in the government will have to love the government from his heart." See also the biblical citations (ibid., 198.34ff.) on princely wisdom and inspiration.

295. Melanchthon does not recognize a right to resist, although he does recognize a right to control the estates of the realm, as in Germany through the electors (ibid., 440).

will uphold them against the malice of the agitators (195.25ff.). On the part of subjects, the divine calling of government should evoke absolute obedience born out of fear of God. This obedience is made specific in the duty to pay financial assessments and other taxes and even to endure injustices (196–97). Melanchthon emphasizes this duty of obedience so strongly—in contrast to Luther—that shirking it falls under God's condemnation (196.25). There is no limit, aside from Acts 5:29 (195.23); instead, "what the rulers order or command is to be upheld as though it were God's order" (234.30ff.). Here obedience to human beings and obedience to God are combined in such a way that the freedom of God's creative will and the resulting value conferred upon the human being are seriously threatened.

When the power of the prince is increased almost to the point of inspiration and his decisions—at least from the point of view of his subjects—are considered infallible, a question arises about the function of reason in governmental activity. Luther would have it regarded as a creative gift of God; he emphasized the responsibility the rulers had toward it. In his popular writings Melanchthon disregards the question of the origin of reason and concentrates on demonstrating that it does not suffice in fulfilling the requirements of political office (198.1ff.). Reason can and must be supplemented. Not infrequently, miraculous interventions of God come to its aid. Above all, reason is instructed to find its guide in the Word of God. The latter not only provides—especially in Romans 13—the basis for the divine origin of government but it also contains a wealth of concrete instructions by which governmental decisions must be guided and from which they derive their justification. The Holy Scriptures in their literal sense, together with the examples they offer, are thus the foundation for Melanchthon's understanding of government. This foundation can shape the exposition of CA 16 just as well as Luther's understanding can.

In the scholia to Colossians, Melanchthon adds an explicit excursus on the doctrine of government.[296] The style is more matter-of-fact, the tone more peaceful, than in the counterrevolutionary works, but the content has hardly changed. As a divine order endowed with divine power, government has the promise of a continuing existence (261.13ff.); subjects acknowledge this divine blessing in intercessory prayer (267.11ff.). Obedience (265.17ff.), punishment (263.29ff., 269.7ff.), and fear (267.28ff., 268.19ff.) characterize the relationship to power; God is the one who as final authority gives government a free hand; aside from obedient suffering there is no possibility for resisting the government (272.8ff.). The interpretation of reason is typical: it does not

---

296. "De magistratibus civilibus et civilibus legibus" (on Col. 2:23; StA 4:260.34–272.12). The scholia appeared in 1527 and were based on a lecture. The following citations refer to that text.

recognize government as a creation of God (262.20ff.); for the people, however, the voice of the law is the voice of God (262.20, 265.29–30). They must obey the government even when they become more sophisticated, "because God has subjected our wisdom to the wisdom of the authorities" (265.34–35).

Melanchthon's *New Scholia on Proverbs* of 1529[297] refers, in accordance with the character of that biblical book, more to individual and pedagogical than to political and social questions; therefore the problem of proper governing receives more attention. Its origin from God serves to underline its duties to him; fear of God and trust in him are the chief virtues of an upright government. Self-reliance and overbearing authority are its special temptations and weaknesses. A godless government destroys all order and discipline.[298]

The princes assume an educational role in relation to their subjects. Their entire domestic policy must therefore be directed toward the furtherance of learning and culture. Punishment is an important means of teaching; those elements of the ancient slavery ethic that entered into Old Testament wisdom literature are quoted with approval: "Fodder and blows and burden for the ass; bread and punishment and work for the slave." Fear, therefore, must rule the subjects: the good prince is like a roaring lion. Fear is awakened and maintained by the certainty that God reveals himself in the punishment imposed by his representatives.[299]

The extrabiblical classical tradition contributed a good deal to this ethic of the state. An ever-changing succession of philosophers, poets, and authors— more from Latin than from Greek literature—with their maxims and examples, alternate with one another in this commentary. The ability of the reason to judge naturally receives high marks. On the basis of the natural laws that God has written in the soul, reason is able to recognize what is right and appropriate and to store it up in a treasury of experiences. It is this treasury—enriched by literary evidence—that is drawn upon when governmental action is necessary.

Of course, reason does not suffice. By itself it cannot recognize God's will any more than it can detect Satan's traps. It does not know how to protect itself from them, and they corrupt it. It is blind, helpless, and disobedient. It therefore needs the supplementary correction of God's Word. Human laws and God's law are designed for each other; human morality must take its bearings from God's Word. What moral reason recognizes on its own becomes a good work only when it is fortified by God's threats and promises. Disciplinary action by a government receives its legitimation only through God's

297. StA 4:305ff.
298. Ibid., 353.30ff., 399.24ff., 423.17ff., 440.12ff., 453.8ff.
299. Ibid., 380.13ff., 431.23ff., 355.4ff., 411.15ff., 22ff., 462.15ff.

Word. Profane authors, it is true, can set up ethical directions, but only the divine will can be effective in real life. Natural law must be supplemented by divine revelation, and only then does it reach fulfillment.

What does this say about the understanding of the order of government? We should get an answer to this question from Melanchthon's commentaries on the social ethics of Aristotle and Cicero, written by 1530. Here again the distinction between *iustitia civilis* and *iustitia spiritualis* is basic; it leads to a significant independence on the part of temporal authority. If the enthusiasts who make the gospel into a political standard are to be rejected, then a clear distinction must be made between political and theological doctrine; the difference is as great as that between medicine and theology. Melanchthon does not hesitate to commend the example of Socrates as worthy of imitation: as the latter wanted to expel poets from the city, so, although we should not chase the theologians out of town, we should exclude them from temporal rule and limit them to the preaching of the gospel.[300]

The independence of reason corresponds to this self-sufficiency of the state. The gospel gives it complete freedom in political affairs. It has free choice among the forms of government; the goal of its activity is the common good *(publica utilitas)*. The church must also recognize natural law as binding, although it refers—especially in the case of punishment—to humanity after the Fall. In its humane tendencies—toward slaves, for example—this natural law, like Roman law, corresponds to biblical demands. The reason for this is its divine origin. Natural law is a ray of truth revealed by God and placed in human hearts. It is clearly distinguished from revelation by the fact that it relates only to outwardly respectable acts.[301]

Melanchthon thus extended the distinction between *iustitia civilis* and *iustitia spiritualis* into the area of knowledge and public order.[302] Rational-moral knowledge restricts itself to this world, theological knowledge to the spiritual and eternal. One is given to humanity through creation, the other rests on the revelation of salvation in Christ. Note that the distinction does not grow out of the doctrine of the two authorities, even though its implications involve that doctrine at many points. The difference and connection between nature and revelation arise out of the collision between classical and

300. *CR* 16:417ff., 421–22. In addition to the example of Karlstadt, who wanted to reinstate the law of Moses, Melanchthon has in mind theologians of the imperial cities—such as Bucer or Osiander—who were active politically (ibid., 447–48). Here he distances himself as a humanist from the theologians; but he himself had certainly been active enough politically. For general background, see also the *Enarrationes aliquot librorum Ethicorum Aristotelis*, which appeared after 1529 along with its introduction (expanded after 1530) *De discrimine Christianae doctrinae et Philosophiae* (*CR* 16:280 n.).

301. Ibid., 420, 435, 437, 279, 443, 451, 536–37, 533–34.

302. As early as his *Epitome* in 1524, Melanchthon extended the *iustitia civilis*, derived from the justification of the individual, to a *iustitia politica*, a governmental program of education (StA 1:184.6ff.).

Christian traditions and the compromise between them. Scholasticism achieved the compromise; Melanchthon took it over. His doctrine of government is also determined by it.

In commenting on the old classical writings about the doctrine of the state, Melanchthon constructed the bond between nature and revelation with the help of the concept of twofold righteousness. It enabled him to take natural morality, on the one hand, and law and gospel, on the other, and interpret each independently, as well as tie them both together. It enabled him to put temporal authority on its own without thereby losing its connection with Christendom or releasing the rulers from Christian responsibility. In this way government is given a peculiar basis that starts out in natural law and ends up as theological. We must now relate it to the doctrinal statements of CA 16.

In good Aristotelian fashion Melanchthon derives government from society and its goals.[303] The beginning of society is found, as in Aristotle, with the marital bond between man and wife. Human beings are destined by nature to the community of the family, but that community presses beyond itself. It binds itself together with other families in a settlement (*colonia*) out of which the city-state (*civitas*) emerges. In the family the relation of superior and inferior is natural; the father rules over wife and children. Some human beings are by nature smarter and stronger, so the duller and weaker ones need their guidance, leadership, and protection. As a result, they crave their company, and in this way the familial group arises, in which the master of the house is at the top and the slaves, along with and under the children of the family, are on the bottom. Thus society structures itself as a fabric of authority; the power to command and the duty to obey arise from purely natural causes. Civil society needs both to exist. It all rests on natural law, although in social ethics as in private morality the principle is the same: natural law *is* the divine law.[304]

The origin of temporal authority is thus traced back to God. After understanding with Aristotle both the development of the family into the state and the principle of hierarchical ordering as immanent occurrences, one then goes on to relate them to God. God has been involved only insofar as he has planted the social drive within humankind. Luther's idea of a spontaneous *creative* will, intervening unexpectedly in the ongoing course of events, is not found in Melanchthon; the foundation for government does not arise from this aspect of God's will. Instead, Melanchthon makes temporal authority depend upon the divine preserving will. To interpret that is no longer the task

303. See *Commentary on Aristotle's Politics* (CR 16:421ff.): ". . . concerning civil society and the offices relating to society." For Melanchthon's views on society, see Werner Elert, *Morphologie des Luthertums* (Munich, 1930, new printing, 1953), 2:28ff.

304. "Civil society cannot be restrained without authority. . . . Meanwhile, the scholastics will remember what I also wrote in the *Ethics*: Natural law is truly divine law" (*CR* 16:424).

of the philosophers but is that of the theologians. They must show how the government's power to punish and educate is necessary for the attainment of *iustitia spiritualis,* and therefore how the gospel requires the data of natural law. They must emphasize to the rulers that their office is answerable to God, and to the subjects that they are to offer obedience for the sake of God's will. The philosophers make clear that the political order was created by God for the preservation of life just as the sun was created to make the earth bear fruit. The maintenance of government, despite Satan's attacks and the wickedness of human beings, is a sign of preservation by God's creative goodness. Thus, as is usual with Melanchthon, civil and spiritual righteousness— nature and revelation—complement each other. The existence of government, if not its origin, is based on God's creative goodness.[305]

Classical and Christian elements shape Melanchthon's understanding of government. That both also underlie his interpretation of CA 16 can be recognized with high probability if one looks into his *Dispositio orationis in Epistolam ad Romanos;* it was published shortly before the diet at Augsburg.[306] Here Lutheran Reformation legacies intermingle with those from the classical-humanistic tradition. As in the commentaries on Aristotle and Cicero, Melanchthon broadens *iustitia civilis* to a *iustitia politica,* making personal morality universal. The political ethic justifies the punitive and educative functions of government; the gospel provides the authorization. When Melanchthon describes these functions in connection with Romans 13, he draws a parallel with the forces of nature: the order of government is created like other natural forces, like the seasons, the times of day, and the course of the stars.[307] It is therefore God's good work of creation; those who hold office can conduct it with a good conscience as pleasing to God. In doing so, however, they are bound to the laws, which, as the comparison with the laws of nature shows, follow their own interior logic. As far as they are concerned, God is the prime mover in an Aristotelian sense rather than the living creator. From that point of view, the Anabaptists and other revolutionaries are not only in conflict with the government but in basic opposition to the whole created order.[308]

Luther and Melanchthon are thus not absolutely identical in the way they

305. See the section "Quod Evangelium approbet politicas ordinationes," in the *Commentary on the Politics (CR* 16:421–22).

306. The first edition (after a part was printed as early as 1529, during the Second Diet of Speyer) appeared in February 1530 and was one of the influences on the formulations of the CA; see W. Maurer, "Studien" (cited above, n. 48), 179 n. 65. The copy in *CR* 15:443ff. contains only a few changes from the original edition.

307. As early as the *Instructions for the Visitors,* Melanchthon compares the creation of government with that of the sun (StA 1:232.1ff.); the image evokes the idea both of life-giving power and of conformity to natural law.

308. *CR* 15:459, 485–86.

argue for temporal authority as "good order," created by God, nor do they contradict each other. In effect, they come out at the same place. All who are called to activity in it are answerable to God—both those who wield governmental authority and those who are trained by it. When this responsibility to a constantly active creator and Lord is taken seriously, it is—on both sides— the expression of a living Christian piety. When it is the expression of an acknowledgment of God-given and unchangeable laws, it leads to an ethical rigor that can easily evoke tyrannical harshness from the rulers and fatalistic passivity or revolutionary resistance from the subjects. The history of the exposition of CA 16 is defined by these tensions; they were present from the beginning.

18. EXERCISE OF GOVERNMENTAL OFFICE

Article 16 of the Augustana contains a list of governmental rights and duties that, as a glance at Schwab. 15 will show, had not been a part of Melanchthon's preliminary documents. He added them to Na 15, which means that he did it during the second half of May. The list is not completely new; it is already laid out in Melanchthon's opinions on the Anabaptists, issued at the beginning of 1528. At their conclusion, he enumerates the characteristic Anabaptist practices.[309] The Anabaptists forbid active participation in the functions of the magisterial office and deny it obedience. They reject its power to judge and to punish. They demand community of goods and prevent the Christian from owning property. They call wealth a sin and reject governmental regulation of trade and contracts pertaining to it, as well as governmental decisions on marriage, family cases, and real estate. In addition, they cultivate a monastic perfectionism.[310]

It is not difficult to find the list from CA 16 in this earlier document. In May 1530, Melanchthon consulted this tract, which had been frequently reprinted. His only addition was the refusal to take oaths. We know, however, that the rejection of the Anabaptists and the warning against them is his particular concern. The positive statements on governmental rights and duties are to be interpreted in the light of their opposites. He also opposes a monastic doctrine of perfection (CA 16.4) that he finds repeated among the Anabaptists.

It is obvious that Melanchthon's rebuff of the Anabaptists did not begin in 1528. On July 25, 1522, right after the first encounter with the Wittenberg iconoclasts, he proposed the thesis that "the administrators of the law enforce

309. StA 1:291.15ff.

310. The list that Melanchthon uses as a basis for his *Verlegung etlicher unchristlicher Artikel* (1536; StA 1:301ff.), is arranged similarly, although theologically it is a step forward.

these [governmental] ordinances without sin."[311] Up to the end of the decade his opposition continued to become sharper. For example, Melanchthon expressed it strongly in the *Instructions for the Visitors*. Faced with the Diet of Augsburg he then summarized the polemic against the Anabaptists in the commentary on Romans 13 in his *Dispositio* on the Epistle to the Romans, thus anticipating the ideas of CA 16. Here again he opposes the "fanatics" who wanted to forbid a Christian to occupy public office, and he encourages rulers to rely on the divine institution of their office. God will protect them against every uprising because he will not permit the distinction between those who give orders and those who obey them to be obliterated.[312]

As in the treatise from 1528 and later in CA 16, Melanchthon's attack is principally directed against the Platonic idea of community of goods and the dream of a new kingdom in which powerlessness and general equality reign. On the other hand, he does not approve of arbitrary government; its law is limited by natural law's demands, which are confirmed in Romans 13. Their stress on fairness (*aequitas*) is also normative for the law of contracts. At this point the jurists and not the theologians must decide.

The theologian Luther, as we have seen, made substantial contributions to the basis of the doctrine of government. He will also have the most important voice on the unfolding of governmental activity. Melanchthon would not argue with either. His statements on good conscience and the loving service of Christian government in CA 16.2 and 16.5 were taken from Luther's world of thought. We do not need to repeat that here.

To put the matter in a proper light, however, we do need to indicate how Luther's polemic against the enthusiastic spirits became sharper as the diet approached. Of course the influence of the Peasants' War had caused him, as he testified in 1525 via-à-vis Erasmus, to intensify his polemic against the spirit-driven "fanatics." In the same period, his sermons rejected the iconoclasts as "apostles of Satan" who replaced Christ with Moses. Satan supports them (Ps. 109:6) and punishes Christendom with their false doctrine.[313] And by January 1528, he could complain in the open letter "On the Rebaptism of Two Pastors," as later in CA 16.4, about the clandestine preachers who drive people from house and home for the sake of rebaptism.[314] Then in 1529, under the threat of Turkish invasion, Luther turned on "mad" people who taught that "it was not proper for a Christian to wield the temporal sword or to govern" and who therefore rejected war against

---

311. StA 1:169.14–15.
312. *CR* 15:485ff.
313. *WA* 18:653.2ff.; *LW* 33:90; *WA* 16:437ff., 19:598–99; *LW* 14:260; *WA* 19:121.16ff., 20:260.13ff.
314. *WA* 26:162.38ff.; *LW* 40:250. Exactly four years later, in January 1532, Luther's work *On the Infiltrating and Clandestine Preachers* appeared (*WA* 30.3:510ff.; *LW* 40:379–94).

the Turks and even went so far as to desire a Turkish government. Unquestionably, a political-revolutionary tendency was emerging among the Anabaptists.[315]

Luther's expressions of displeasure increased before the beginning of the Diet of Augsburg. In his lecture on the Song of Solomon on March 10, 1530, Luther gives a review of his life and work. He enumerates what new and good things the gospel has brought. The result, however, is disappointing: the Word of God has not prevailed. The whole world stands against it; the operation of the spirit is lacking. "I thought that our word would progress in quiet peace and unity. But before we got our bearings one sectarian was here, another there." About the same time, in his exposition of Psalm 82, Luther addressed himself specifically to the Anabaptists, their doctrine, and their legal situation in the evangelical territories. His theological judgment is harsh and decisive; in criminal proceedings, however, he constantly recommends that the government act with a measure of caution.[316]

In April, already on the trip southward, Luther wrote the preface to a work on Anabaptist doctrine by Justus Menius in which he terms the uncalled preachers assassin teachers who, "like the Jews and Turks, concoct a kingdom on earth in which all the godless are to be destroyed, so that they alone shall enjoy good days." Admittedly, he touches only a fringe phenomenon of Anabaptism when he sees in it a fellowship of the sword which—presumably as the instrument of Christ—is to kill the godless by the sword. Even earlier, in his last sermons in Wittenberg, he warned the congregation about the "enthusiasts." They are worse than the papists, ungrateful, fallen away from God's Word, blasphemers given up to their own fancies. Not only is this in the same key as CA 16; the harmony extends even to individual thoughts and sentences.[317]

Therefore, even though Melanchthon is the one who included the catalogue of Anabaptist deficiencies in the preliminary documents for CA 16, not only does the attitude behind it find justification in Luther, but every part of the list of charges—which at the same time sets down the jurisdictions and duties of temporal authority—can be explained on the basis of Luther as well as Melanchthon. In the following we will take up the items of CA 16 in order.

The first and most important item in the catalogue of duties is the administration of justice. It is primarily understood as jurisdiction over punishment; according to Rom. 13:4, the government bears the sword. The Anabaptists rejected this bloody power of punishment. To the degree that they identified

---

315. WA 30.2:107.13–14, 137.21ff., 138.3ff., 139.1ff., 173.10ff.; LW 46:161, 193, 194.
316. WA 31.2:603.20–21 (see also ibid., 601.24ff.; LW 15:198), 31.1:207–13; LW 13:60–67.
317. WA 30.2:213.7ff., 18ff., 23ff., 32:16ff.; here 22.11ff., 24.5ff., 25.2ff. (March 20 and April 3).

themselves with the peaceful tendency to which the future belonged—with the bearers of the staff instead of the sword—they pictured a human society that would be held together without force, simply by common moral persuasion. Luther labeled this rejection of government as plain rebellion and wanted it punished like stealing, murder, and adultery.[318]

Luther had insisted especially emphatically on this strict conception of law since the Peasants' War. Article 16 is the expression of this attitude, because the Anabaptist movement and the peasant rebellion were frequently connected, both inwardly and outwardly. The exposition of this article must keep these ties in mind. At the same time, beyond the historical circumstances, the theological view of law that shaped Luther's thinking must also be evaluated.

There were many complaints about lawlessness, legal confusion, and the breakdown of justice in Germany. Political circumstances were not overlooked as causes for this "lame authority" yet there remained sufficient ground to lash out against despotism and the taking of the law into one's own hands. The admonition to patience in the face of open injustice continued to be necessary; the power of the sword cannot eliminate evil, it can only intimidate and limit it.[319] That was the reason it was necessary that the sword be wielded and terror spread abroad by only one hand. In accordance with the Mosaic and Roman law, Luther also demanded the death penalty for witches because of their demonic magic. In judgment there is no mercy. The judicial office is an office of wrath; the judgment seat is the seat of God, who wills that his laws be upheld. The *lex talionis* is the foundation of justice in the Old Testament, for Moses and the heathen, as well as in nature. The God whose majesty as creator is offended is the author and guarantor of this strict justice.[320]

It is conceivable that well-meaning Christians—not only the Anabaptists— would shrink from the gruesome demands of this God-given office. Not everyone would consider it a comfort to say to oneself, "God acts through the judge and executioner; and 'if the one cuts off your head, it is God who has done it, not the executioner.' " It is hard for us not to dismiss such statements as black humor rather than to take them to heart as testimonies to the frightful wrath of God. We no longer realize that we live so close to the wrathful God; Luther and most of his contemporaries knew it. The Anabaptists are an exception that indicates the trend of the future in Europe and America.[321]

Only against this dark background can we evaluate Luther's positive

318. *WA* 31.1:208.1ff.; *LW* 13:61.
319. *WA* 16:536.35ff., 537.12, 539.27, 549.10, 542.1ff., 20:97.2ff.; *LW* 15:83.
320. *WA* 16:538.8ff., 551.18ff., 552.14ff., 566.15ff., 536.2ff.
321. *WA* 16:549.11ff., 543.1ff.

opinion on the office of judge. He does that soon after his return from the Coburg, in his description of Solomon's royal council as "a fine consistory."[322] Judge and councilors are one. The king has carefully selected them, so that no one would suffer injustice. They are free from all arrogance and greed. There is no corruption among them; eloquence, wisdom, and love hold sway. Love, however, is the greatest of these virtues. Thus peace rules in the land, which echoes with thanks to God for good government. Here Luther has depicted the Christian judge; the picture corresponds to that of the Christian ruler as Luther describes his elector in this lecture. The ideal of the politically active man which Luther presents here was not far from the reality of 1530. It adds some friendly lines to the grim picture of the power of government to coerce and to punish which CA 16 maintains against the Anabaptists.

As we have seen, it is Roman law that Luther uses to illustrate strict justice. Melanchthon speaks of it too, not only with an eye to the emperor and diet but also because he considers it the best form of justice.[323] Luther also prized it and geared his ideas to it. The image of the lictors preceding the Roman consuls fascinated him, because they did not carry books but carried long swords. This terrifying symbol is a sign that the judge dispenses not mercy but fairness (aequitas).[324] Luther demonstrated the strictness of Roman law by Pilate, who had to fear the appeal to Rome. Canon law of the papal church provided him with an illustration of the superiority of the original Roman law, since it formed the basis for canon law.

For Luther, natural, Mosaic, and Roman law form a series. We Christians are not obligated by God to keep the Mosaic law, although it is good and commendable. Luther placed a positive value on many of its precepts. He not only approved of the lex talionis but also wanted to maintain the law of asylum, which of course was not foreign to the Middle Ages.[325] He considered the protection against slander and infamy to be exemplary; the princes of his day should develop family and labor laws for servingmen and maids. He also preferred paying tithes, instead of numerous taxes and fees, to temporal authorities; if he were emperor, thought Luther, he would not consent to the continuation of church tithes but would put them at the disposal of the government.[326]

322. In commenting on the Song of Solomon 3:9ff. (WA 31.2:672–73; LW 15:226). See W. Maurer, "Der kursächsische Salomo," in Antwort aus der Geschichte: W. Dress zum 65. Geburtstag (Berlin, 1969), 99–116.

323. In the final version, keeping in mind the current law of the land; Na 16 does not mention it. See Guido Kisch, Melanchthons Rechts- und Soziallehre (Berlin, 1967), 116ff.

324. "To the extent that you are a proper judge, mercy does not concern you, but when you give attention to fairness, it is an honorable thing" (WA 16:543.1ff., 5ff.).

325. WA 28:331.7ff., 50.27ff., 332.1, 16:572.4ff., 536.3, 19–20, 539–40.

326. WA 16:520.1ff., 522.4–5, 534.24ff., 576.3ff. Most of the citations come from sermons on Exodus preached immediately after the Peasants' War. Their legal content could not be covered completely here, but this does indicate Luther's lively interest in political and social questions.

Luther's treatment of thievery demonstrates that he does not represent a blind retributive punishment. He considered it wrong to hang thieves indiscriminately, as was the custom. The death penalty should be imposed only on kidnappers and extortioners; those who stole objects should be more lightly punished than those who committed crimes against persons.[327] Legal protection of poor people who have no other advocate was a serious concern for Luther; he recalled Jesus, who himself was a nobody (*persona vilis*) as he stood before Pilate. Here and elsewhere Luther lifted out the social elements of the Old Testament law and, where possible, used them to address relationships of his own day. Nature and reason, as well as heathen judges, resist such social considerations.[328]

In addition, Luther cited the heathen Roman law as the basis for declaring the principle of fairness (*aequitas*) to be binding on Christian judges as well. Even the judge who renders strict judgment without respect for persons ought to consider varying circumstances. Luther made a programmatic statement to that effect in 1526, precisely to address judicial bloodletting employed by the princes at the end of the Peasants' War.[329] The letter of the law strictly demands the death penalty for rebellion, which is treason (*crimen laesae maiestatis*). Fairness, however, keeps in mind that although two people commit the same act, their deeds should not always be given the same weight, since motives can vary. The verdict should take such motives into account. This fairness is a "virtue of wisdom" that guides and gauges strict legalism so that each case is judged on its own merits, with the inner attitudes of all parties given consideration. Luther developed this doctrine of fairness on the question of war and rebellion in the light of the rebellious peasants, but he went on from there to apply it also to questions of the legality of resistance to tyrants.

Luther did not base the right of resistance on classical tradition, although he was aware that Greeks and Romans had defended that principle. He preferred to draw on examples and teaching from Scripture. Moreover, the practice of the pre-Christian world contradicted classical theory. "The heathen, because they know nothing of God," have through lack of proper knowledge "rushed in" and let reckless power take the place of law. *Aequitas* can also be injustice. Those who would use it properly must be "clever and pious." They must measure fairness by reason and base reason on love. When fairness masters the law, it does not put it out of business but applies it in such a way that the law of love is fulfilled both for the injured party and for the one who does the injury.

327. Ibid., 537.6ff., 534.11ff. Luther realized the irresistible compulsiveness of many thieves (ibid., 543.33ff.).
328. Ibid., 568.17ff., 573.8ff. (sabbatical year), 569.3ff.
329. *Whether Soldiers, Too, Can Be Saved* (WA 19:631–34; LW 46:101–5).

For Luther, the Roman virtue of *aequitas* is fulfilled in Christian love; only in that way does law reach its goal, and the office of judge its fulfillment. For that reason CA 16 can impose service of the law through government on the Christian. This service and even the use of force that it implies are sanctified through self-sacrificing love.

Thus, as in Melanchthon, a classical-Christian synthesis enters Luther's teaching on government. The reformer, however, handles it differently from the Christian humanist. The latter places classical natural law in a tension-filled relationship with the gospel. For Luther those ethical and legal traditions reach their fulfillment in Christian love. Outwardly the two syntheses are as alike as two peas in a pod. When judged from the inside, from faith in the gospel, the fine distinction becomes apparent. It lies not in theory but in practical action. The judge who is forced to make legal decisions knows that. It is not the same thing to encounter it in the moral responsibility laid upon the judge by the high ethics of classical legal tradition, and to practice it by acting out of the love that recognizes a brother in Christ even in the offender. It is the difference between the law that demands love, and the self-giving love that fulfills the demands of the law—the love that while exercising the office of wrath, nevertheless remains entirely love. This difference also includes a divergent possibility in the interpretation of CA 16. The challenge to place oneself in the service of law and punishment can only be met by the Christian who is conscious of thereby acting in the service of love. The Anabaptists contested such a possibility, because their idea of love was embedded in a legalistic tradition. Melanchthon, the humanists, and others like them saw this tradition fulfilled in Christian natural law. They thus remained within the framework of law and made a fundamental distinction between the service of justice and self-giving love.

19. THE JUST WAR

The Confession adopts the Augustinian doctrine of the just war. To fight a just war (*iure bellare*) is one of the duties of government, and the Christian subject should support it in the exercise of this duty by serving in the army (*BS* 70.14–15, 25–26; *BC* 37.2, 6). In his personal Confession of 1528, Luther did not mention war, nor does Schwab. 14. Article 15 of Na is the first place that Melanchthon discusses the question of war in relation to government, admittedly not yet in relation to the subjects who serve in the army but in regard to the rulers who make war. They are to do it in accordance with their Christian conscience.

The just war is a concept created by centuries of ethical and political thought which our skeptical generation has learned through bitter experience to consider a contradiction in terms. One cannot, at any rate, judge war in the abstract; wars must be considered individually, in the light of their origin, conduct, and effect. The judgment about whether a war is just or whether the participants might at least have the possibility of considering it to be just depends on the presuppositions and circumstances under which it is fought. We will see, however, that, especially for Luther, there were entirely different perspectives for judging a war and that they formed the basis for asking— what was always only a subsidiary question for Luther—about the rightness of a war.

The age of the Reformation was filled with the clamor of war. Even if the military entanglements never reached the magnitude of destruction peculiar to modern mass warfare, life was still dominated by fear of their horrors. Erasmus had repeatedly asserted that war in any case was immoral because it was inhumane; it was widely believed—at least theoretically—that a Christian prince should avoid war under all circumstances. The age was basically not warlike, despite the number and horror of its wars. The Anabaptists to which CA 16 refers were only expressing the tendency of their time when they rejected all war and refused any participation in it. The Augustana, with its talk about just wars, went against this tendency of the time. It obviously thought it possible to evaluate individually the wars that swept through the world in those days.

The Augustana (CA 21) called Emperor Charles an imitator of a true Christian saint (*BS* 83b sec. 1; *BC* 46.1) because he fulfilled his calling by protecting his subjects—a real King David as he set out to make war against the Turks. That war, a particular concern of the Diet of Augsburg, obviously was considered to be a just war. A presentation on the extent and presuppositions of that judgment clearly belongs in a commentary on the Augustana.

Originally, Luther and Melanchthon were not ready to make a positive judgment on the war against the Turks. At that time Melanchthon was totally under the influence of Erasmian pacifism; in his *Rhetoric* of 1519 he roundly rejected the Turkish war. One year later, influenced by Luther's parallel work on Genesis, he conceded that men of God in the Old Testament had the right to wage war in obedience to the First Commandment, so that God's enemies might be eliminated. In the *Loci* of 1521 the right to wage war appears as part of those general human rights based on natural law: it is permissible to take action against those who disrupt the peace, because they inflict harm on the innocent. Thus, at this point a distinction between just and unjust wars is presupposed. Furthermore, shortly before the conclusion of the *Loci*, in February 1521, Melanchthon, using the pseudonym Didimus Faventinus, defended Luther against the charge that he had endangered Christendom by his polemic against the Turks. He argued that Luther had only urged true repentance and opposed papal intervention in political events; they were the reasons for the previous ineffectiveness of wars against the Turks. For three hundred years the Roman antichrist had raged against Christendom with war and murder. Now, to the princes' credit, they had assumed the burden of waging war; they were called upon to employ their power—does that include military means?—against the Roman Babylon.[330]

That was a strange mixture in the young Melanchthon! It included elements of humanism, Luther, and natural law. Subsequently, natural law would become decisive for him. In contrast, Luther's position on the Turkish wars showed more consistency; his original opposition was not so deeply rooted in natural law and was therefore easier to modify later.

In his *Explanations of the Ninety-five Theses* (1518), Luther discusses the necessity of divine punishments, under the fifth thesis. These punishments neither can nor should be removed by indulgences. Among such punishments he includes natural and social disasters in which God can employ Turks, Tatars, and other infidels as his rods of discipline. Those who call for war against the Turks without trying to remove the sinful causes of that punishment wantonly oppose God. It is not the Turkish war as such that is being condemned here but the lack of interest in repentance, which leads to war. The moral judgment is not directed against the justification for war— that is assumed—but against the moral-religious attitude of those who make war. That attitude is the decisive factor in whether or not a war is "just," that is, acceptable to God.[331]

Luther's critique of the curial approach to the Turkish war was condemned by the bull of excommunication. Luther defended himself in the *Assertio*[332] and explained the extent and causes for his shift in attitude on the question of war in his work *On War Against the Turk* (1528–29). His original criticism was directed against papal pretensions in claiming the leading role in that war. Then he recognized the origin and work of temporal government, the doctrine of the two kingdoms was discovered—Luther gave himself credit for that—and afterward princes and lords considered their status an opportunity to serve God. In the meantime, the illogic of the church's previous attitude became clear. On the one hand, people were incited to war; on the other, they heard the commandment from the Sermon on the Mount not to resist evil (Matt. 5:39) praised as an evangelical counsel. There was no way to harmonize the military attitude of the statesman and soldier with the Christian's perspective of peace. That first became possible on the basis of the doctrine of

---

330. See W. Maurer, *Der junge Melanchthon* (cited above, n. 49), 2:149.325–26; *WA* 4:608.1ff. (cp. *WA* 9:353.13ff.); StA 2.1:43.16ff., 1:126.28ff., 130.2ff., 135.34ff.

331. *WA* 1:535.23ff.; *LW* 31:91–92.

332. *WA* 7:140.18ff.; also in *Defense and Explanation* (ibid., 443.4ff.; *LW* 32:89–90).

the two authorities. Luther also believed that the same doctrine governed the Christian's position on war. In those same years after 1518, however, significant changes were occurring in the political and religious situation. At the beginning there had been no external threat; war against the Turks would have involved an attack on them. Now, however, the Islamic enemy had moved much closer; in a few months it would reach Vienna. At the same time, the opposition to the gospel in so-called Christendom had made clear that it did not deserve that name. It did not honor Christ; the enemies of Christ not only were outside, they were in its midst. Pope and bishops conducted a bloody persecution of the gospel. Thus, as Luther stressed repeatedly, they and the Turks were basically alike. If the clerics were going to use the army as a means for their own propaganda, as they had done before, the war was already lost. All of these factors added up to one thing: there was no "Christian" army that could move against the unbelievers. If the imperial forces gathered to face the attacking foe, "hardly five Christians" could be found among them. It was no longer possible to employ the ideology of crusade.[333]

Out of the political changes that occurred after 1518, and out of the ecclesiastical experience he had accumulated in the meantime, Luther drew two basic conclusions on the understanding of the just war. First, a just war is always defensive, never offensive. That is no new discovery; it is a commonplace thesis in ethical thought on war. But given the Reformation concept of government, new conclusions can be drawn. Second, a just war is never a religious war. That is not meant to imply only that a religious reason is insufficient in itself to guarantee the righteousness of a war but is meant to imply also that a war waged in the name of the Christian faith is itself unjust. This assertion not only annuls the medieval idea of a crusade, it also is a condemnation of the religiously tinted ideologies on which the contemporary world has based its wars.

In connection with the first point, Luther wrote, "Whoever starts a war is in the wrong" (*Wer krieg anfehet, der ist unrecht*).[334] This is not a reflection of the *ius talionis* which would label every offensve war a lost war; determinism of that sort, which would ultimately reward the just war, can only grow out of a non-Christian political ethic. The decisive element in the quote from

333. *WA* 30.2:108ff.; *LW* 46:161ff. This is the place to characterize Luther's three major works on this subject. They all forgo a theoretical discussion of the just war in favor of a pastoral, down-to-earth approach. *Whether Soldiers, Too, Can Be Saved* (1526) is, as the title indicates, a pastoral work for professional soldiers. *On War Against the Turk* (1529) offers pastors guidance on preaching about war. The *Army Sermon Against the Turks* (1529) is itself a sermon that interpreted the current situation in an eschatological light, warning and comforting Christians. Behind the different occasions and words of comfort lies the same evaluation of war, and that is what will be elaborated here.

334. *WA* 19:645.9; *LW* 46:118.

Luther is rather its personal focus: the aggressor *is* wrong; he is not merely in the wrong or gone wrong. The bearer of public office is personally involved in the decision between war and peace. What constitutes a just war, appealing to a situation of self-defense, cannot be deduced from universally binding laws; it must be affirmed in personal responsibility. Furthermore, the moment when the situation of self-defense occurs must be awaited in humility; it should not be seized too hastily.[335] It is the personal decision of individual officeholders, not general principles, that determines whether or not a war is just. Respect for this decision is not the result of abstract reflection—for which the average subject is neither equipped nor empowered—but is the result of personal trust.

Making the question of a just war so personal is not attractive to a democratic age; it is offensive. It is in the tradition of patriarchal absolutism of the sixteenth century, a mode of thinking rendered incomprehensible by the presuppositions of Enlightenment absolutism right after the Thirty Years' War. That makes it even more necessary to inquire from a historical point of view about the enduring value of such personal responsibility for the decision on war and peace, even if it is no longer required of autocratic rulers. Only thus can the concept of *bellum iustum*, as presupposed in CA 16, still possess religious significance today.

In the process it becomes evident that the distinction between person and office, which underlies the essay on soldiers, does not inevitably lead to a double standard. That would be a Machiavellian distortion of the distinction. Rather, it intensifies the personal responsibility of the bearer of public office. The officeholder must preserve *iustitia civilis* when opting for war.[336] That can be done only if he also stands up for his people, protecting them and giving them peace. The prince is always a "person for others." He *is* that, not because he personally is a Christian—the opposite might be the case—but because he holds the office. God keeps the "foolish" princes who are always ready to fight in line by giving others fists; one sword keeps the other in the scabbard.[337]

Instruction, therefore, on how one can make war with a good conscience involves more than a doctrine about the just war. The emperor Charles, whom Luther addresses specifically in *On War Against the Turk*, should "simply" defend his subjects because he has been attacked by the Turks. This simplicity is the opposite of political calculation with religious trimmings. God's command for love of the neighbor demands simple obedience from the

---

335. *WA* 19:645.23ff.; *LW* 46:118. In *WA* 19:646.17ff. (*LW* 46:119), Luther uses Frederick the Wise as an example; the waiting game was in fact characteristic of Frederick and his two successors. In this case is Luther the teacher and prototype or the follower?

336. *WA* 19:624–30, esp. 625.1ff.; *LW* 46:93–100, esp. 94.

337. *WA* 19:648.13ff., 21ff., 649.2ff.; *LW* 46:121–22.

emperor. Thus it makes no difference—in terms of political realities—whether or not the emperor is himself a Christian: "The emperor's sword has nothing to do with faith; it is concerned with physical, worldly things."

Luther continues, "Otherwise God will become angry with us. If we pervert his order and throw it into confusion, he too becomes perverse and throws us into confusion and all kinds of misfortune." It is through the office of rulers and not primarily through their personal convictions that they are bound to God's loving will which preserves the life of humanity. Therefore they dare not treat this life carelessly "as though it were up to them whether to rescue and protect their subjects from the power of the Turk or not."[338] A just war is one that satisfies this duty of love, and it is God who demands it. The individual ruler bears personal responsibility before God for war or peace; God's own will has laid this upon him. This responsibility, rather than any ideal concept of the ruler which requires that he enjoy decision making, is the basis for the "personalizing" of the *bellum iustum*. *Iustitia civilis*, which is to be maintained even in war, is not an abstract ideal but the personal loving will of God.

It is at this point that a decisive revolution has taken place between Luther's day and our own. Luther could still reckon with the fact that the princes, even if they were not personally committed to the Christian faith, would recognize God as creator and Lord and would respect his commandment of love. Therefore Luther could remind them of their protective duties and advise the emperor to see his office in the proper perspective: the commandment of God is his battle flag; to fulfill it is to carry on a just war.[339]

The (relative) progress made by humanity in the meantime has led not only to our losing sight of God's command to love, but also to a situation where it is impossible to recognize any element of righteousness in modern mass warfare. For Luther, war was a judgment by which God's righteousness used government to punish evildoers. Just as authorities punished individual offenders, war dealt with "a whole lot . . . at one time."[340] At this point we pass beyond personalism; the "righteousness" of war enters a superpersonal realm. The personal decision of a ruler to fight a defensive war can have unforeseen consequences that extend far beyond the protection of his subjects' lives. God's creative kindness, which desires to preserve individual lives, nevertheless permits collective punishment to be meted out in war. That

338. *WA* 30.2:116–36, with the quotations from 131.8ff., 34ff. (cp. 132.21ff.); *LW* 46:170–92, with the quotations from 186, 187 (cp. 188).

339. *WA* 30.2:134.19ff.; *LW* 46:190. Therefore Luther can even shake off the horror of war. It just appears outwardly to be an "un-Christian work, completely contrary to Christian love"; in reality it is a "very brief lack of peace that prevents an everlasting and immeasurable lack of peace" (*WA* 19:626.6ff.; *LW* 46:96).

340. *WA* 19:628.23ff.; *LW* 46:98–99.

is an act of his punitive wrath which, in war, draws both ruler and ruled into incalculable and unforeseen catastrophes. It is not only the circumstances of modern mass society that undercut the idea of a just war, it is also the terrifying reality of God's wrath, which we are never able to accommodate to our theology or our experience.

Luther's second conclusion—that the just war is not a religious war, and the religious war is not a just war—is one that the war against the Turks prompted him to draw from his teaching on the two kingdoms. The emperor is not to lead a crusade; he is to fulfill his duty as protector. He therefore ought not go to battle with a false self-image or sense of calling. That is the meaning of the warning Luther gives to the emperor: "For the emperor is neither the head of Christendom nor defender of the gospel or of faith."[341] This secularization of the medieval concept of emperor is based on the view that the faith needs no human protection. Those who insist on protecting it overreach themselves. It is humility before God and obedience to his command to love that underlie the correct military attitude and create a good conscience in a just war.[342]

Luther is not the father of the modern ideological war; that is not the intention of CA 16's urging the conduct of just wars. Luther expressed himself on that point with unmistakable clarity at the beginning of the Augsburg diet in his "Schoenen Confitemini."[343] Should the evangelical congregations, pressed on all sides and threatened with a religious war, offer armed resistance? Luther answers in the negative.[344] God rescues his own. He punishes one people through another. He sends "perhaps the Turks or other wrath and plagues of God, bringing death and destruction." Christians therefore have no business defending themselves with force. They kill no one and compel no one. They call on God against their enemies; God works through their prayers.[345]

Luther had advocated this position a year earlier in connection with war against the Turks. He had repeatedly emphasized the inner agreement between the Turks and the pope; they were both smitten by the same blindness. If a defensive war against the Turks was allowed, then should a war against the pope be permissible as well? Luther denied the possibility of a religious war. The pope could be attacked only if he first attacked the emperor; he was

---

341. *WA* 30.2:130.27–28; *LW* 46:185. This is similar to the epilogue to the glosses that Luther later provided to the "two conflicting and offensive imperial commands" in preparation for the imperial diet at Nürnberg in 1524. In it the emperor appears as "this poor mortal bag of worms" who "brazenly" pretends to be the "prime protector of the Christian faith" (*WA* 15:278.2ff.).

342. *WA* 30.2:135.7ff.; *LW* 46:191.

343. On Ps. 118:10ff.; see also *WA* 31.1:14, 73.

344. On Luther and the right to resist, see the remarks above, p. 131.

345. *WA* 31.1:126.22ff., 129.18ff., 127.25ff.; *LW* 14:74, 75.

clearly too weak militarily for that. The Christian ("Christianus") had his own weapons with which to fight the pope.

If there is such a thing as a religious war, then it is neither political nor military but is purely spiritual. This war summons Christianus, not Emperor Charles; its heralds are preachers of the gospel. This is the combat to which Luther encourages Christian prisoners in Turkey. Repentance is the beginning of this spiritual battle, in alliance with prayer—particularly the litany, which is especially recommended to the youth. Indeed, the true spiritual soldiers are always few in number, but they represent Christianity and on them victory depends. They must be urged on by the preachers. To that end—and not to propagandize—Luther depicts the destitution of Christians under Muslim rule, conveys some general knowledge of the Koran, of syncretistic elements in Islam, and of moral and civil conditions, and gives guidance for confessing the faith. This spiritual warfare of Christianus is prerequisite for the victory of Charles.[346]

But does such an attitude not give rise, at least indirectly, to religious wars, by stimulating religious fanaticism of the "God wills it" variety and thus evoking the consciousness of conducting a just war? The question becomes more pointed because Luther increasingly viewed the Turkish war from an eschatological perspective. The theme can be heard as early as the conclusion to the work *On War Against the Turk:* it is an open question whether in an eschatological situation the emperor can count on victory at all or whether Turkish rule signals the prophesied catastrophic transition to the kingdom of God. In any case, the emperor must do what he can and discharge his duty to protect his subjects. In the *Army Sermon* the imminent end is deduced as certain from Dan. 7:3ff. Persecution of the gospel must be recompensed by God's judgment; the Turk is the instrument of this eschatological wrath; in him as the worldly antichrist arise "the last and worst wrath of the devil against Christ."[347]

How is the attitude of Christianus affected by this situation? Awaiting the approaching end may undermine the general's hope of victory, but it makes the battle easier for the simple Christian. According to the testimony of the prophet Daniel, the Muslim empire forms the "little" horn; it has no future. The last legitimate world empire is that of Rome; the Turkish one is only a faint, powerless echo and, in view of the coming kingdom of Christ, only "the last dregs and scuffles." Therefore those who battle the Turks fight against the

346. *WA* 30.2:142.11ff., 143.12ff., 116.33ff., 185.18ff., 120ff., 186ff.; *LW* 46:198, 199, 170, 174ff.

347. *WA* 30.2:143.29ff., 162.20; *LW* 46:198; *WA* 30.2:163ff. (exegesis of Daniel). See also Hans Volz in his introduction to Luther's translation of the prophets in *WDB* 11.2:xxviff., and the literature cited there.

devil's last charge; those who fall in this battle go directly to the kingdom of Christ.[348]

Thus the eschatological situation does not provoke religious wars but rather prepares for a final end to them. What in appearance may goad on the frenzy for war is in reality the expression of a good conscience that ultimate victory is tied not to the imperial banner but to the fulfillment of the history of salvation. It is from this apocalyptic struggle and not from eagerness for war that comes the slogan: "Your fist and spear are God's fist and spear."[349] This must also be the basis for answering other questions posed by similarly sharply turned phrases.

Did Luther not himself dispel misgivings about killing a Turk with the observation that, after all, the battle was "against the enemy of God and the blasphemer of Christ"? Did he not consider that being killed as a Christian, a martyr, and an obedient citizen was an "honorable, holy death"? Luther backs off: he meant all that to be comforting, so that soldiers would not be afraid.[350] But does he not fall back into making devils out of the opponents and producing crusade propaganda that nonetheless turns the war against the Turks into a holy, just war? If Christianus, despite everything, draws his sword in battle for the faith, does not that erase the line between him and Charles? These questions are unanswerable within the framework of a general ideology of war; they lose their sharpness when they are related to the eschatological situation.

Ultimately everything turns on how Luther views the ordinary military service of the individual Christian. Remember that CA 16 lists *militare*, "to fight," in addition to *bellum iustum*. Military service is permitted for the Christian, in fact, under certain circumstances even commanded. We must explain this command in the light of contemporary relationships.

First, to perform military service is a calling, a technical function, and as such does not concern the Christian. Christianus is, in contrast to Charles, a noncombatant. Up to that time only ordained priests held that status; for Luther it is basically true of every Christian. Soldiers form a particular vocational group *(Berufsstand)* and have an ethic peculiar to their calling. That arrangement continued until the French Revolution, when the *levée en masse* called up a national army. Since then universal military service has been the rule, and it has been an open question whether a general civil ethics should supersede a particular military one or vice versa. Right up to the present time it likewise remains unclear whether this open question makes military service harder or easier.

348. *WA* 30.2:171.28, 173–74.
349. Ibid., 174.20.
350. Ibid., 173.4–5, 175.32, 176.22ff.

This question did not exist for Luther and the Augsburg Confession. They confront Christians with the necessity of fulfilling the peculiar demands of military service in their day.[351] They are still in a premodern age; farming and fighting (*agricultura* and *militia*) are still the normal ways of life. The soldier is a vassal and is provided with money and goods as wages for his military service. If someone refused his feudal service on grounds of conscience, he would have to renounce his fealty to his lord. For Luther and the CA, therefore, the duty to perform military service was fulfilled totally within feudal society and its structures. Of course there also was the order of imperial knights. They stood outside society as people "who run around the countryside looking for war," and if they could not find any there was the danger that they would become robbers.[352]

All these people must face the difficult decision of whether or not the war in which they are to serve is a just one. The situation is precarious when one has several feudal lords who, on occasion, could take opposing sides. In such a case, the "hereditary lord and territorial prince" normally takes precedence. Nevertheless, one should always serve him who is in the right.[353]

But can an individual with a limited viewpoint make such a decision properly and—more important—can he carry it out? What becomes of the prosperous peasants who are forcibly drawn in by the insurgents and sent into battle? Must they be treated according to the rule "fought together, caught together, shot together"? In the case of such military service, what is just and what unjust?[354]

The negative side of the case is clear: every uprising is unjust; a right to rebel does not exist. According to "divine eternal ordering of temporal authority," no revolution is legitimate. Even a tyrant cannot be overthrown: "A wicked tyrant is more tolerable than a wicked war."[355] Injustice cannot be punished on one's own authority; it only creates new injustice. That is true for everyone, not just the peasants at the bottom of the social ladder. Revolts of the nobility too are unjust. God has punished the rebellious nobles through the rebellious peasants; he disciplines "one youngster by another." *God* therefore judges injustice, if necessary, by arousing one government against another. He does not need a human uprising. In this case the individual soldier is relieved of the decision between just and unjust.

Then is it also permissible for him to let his conscience speak if his overlord

351. The question in the title itself, *Whether Soldiers, Too, Can Be Saved*, shows that the ethical issue involves a whole class (*Stand*). See above, n. 333.

352. *WA* 19:653, 660.5ff.; *LW* 46:127, 134.

353. *WA* 19:657.11ff.; *LW* 46:134.

354. *WA* 19:630–32; *LW* 46:100–103.

355. *WA* 19:634.1ff., 637.10–11; *LW* 46:104, 109. On parliamentary rights, see *WA* 19:640.20ff.; *LW* 46:113. On the deposing of the king of Denmark, see *WA* 19:641.3ff.; *LW* 46:113.

starts an unjust war? May he then break his oath of allegiance? If the injustice is apparent, he must shun it and take all the consequences. But if the case is not clear, he should "in love" attribute the best to the overlord and fulfill his military duty.[356] His obedience, of course, involves not men but God, who judges the intention of the heart rather than the outward deed. The temporal lord conducts the war; the individual follows him as his subject, which he can do in obedience to God with a good conscience. The reverse is also true: whoever avoids military service—for example, someone in Germany who prefers Turkish rule—does wrong. He breaks his oath of allegiance and becomes a participant in all the atrocities committed by the enemy.[357]

The question about the justness of a war thus concerns a monarch's military subordinates and not just the monarch himself. Each must make his own decision. Here again the judgment on whether a war is just is made personal; there is no blind obedience. But all this presupposes that the individual soldier is set within a previously existing ethic of orders that is by no means exclusively Christian in its expression. It is, however, to be practiced by a Christian when it can be done with a good conscience. Everything done in that way is justified by the divine demand for obedience.

Today one need only speak these sentences to sense how offensive they have become. Is it not necessary to test a given ethic of orders critically on a case-by-case basis? Can a war be just simply on the basis of its cause and without regard to its tactics? And if there was a special social niche for soldiers in 1530 that a Christian might occupy temporarily or all his life, how does a citizen of the twentieth century act when called into military service? On what does one base the decision and its implementation?

Similar critical questions face the whole problem of the just war. The unique context of the final apocalyptic battle immediately preceding the return of Christ no longer concerns our contemporaries. For them it would be out of theological range. The military situation that would face us would be different from that of 1530. Today no Emperor Charles issues to his vassals proclamations directed toward each social order within which each individual must make a decision before God. Today war is an all-out conflict between whole nations from whom mass decisions are wrung by force and propaganda. Certainly it was a historical service of Luther to have introduced the personal dimension into discussion of the just war. But his basing of personalism on God's revealed will of love and relating it directly to that will is a theological move that appears long outdated today. How, in our mass society, can such a personal responsibility before God and man still be maintained by the appropriate elements of a democracy and by individual citizens?

356. *WA* 19:643.13ff., 657.2ff.; *LW* 46:116, 131.
357. *WA* 30.2:173.32ff., 137.21ff.; *LW* 46:193.

It is at this point, in my opinion, that the statements of CA 16 on the just war and on an individual's participation in it require new answers. The concern embodied in the position of the Confession remains, although it can no longer be realized on the basis of the sixteenth century's presuppositions. Christianity must take it up anew within the political and spiritual presuppositions of this century. The solutions that are found must once again pick up the personalism of Luther's concept of man and God. And Christianity must consider how it can see the decision of the individual within the framework of a democracy as a possibility in our day.

20. OATHS

Article 16 of the CA assures the Christian that taking an oath is not in itself a sin, and it requires that he take an oath if the authorities demand it. Not only does that represent a fundamental justification of the oath and a rejection of the Anabaptist exegesis that had deduced a radical refusal of oaths from Matt. 5:33ff. (and Jas. 5:12), it also involves a limitation on the current practice. Only the public oath imposed by the government is permitted; private swearing is branded as a misuse of God's name.

On this point the Confession is not far away from the Anabaptists. As far as respect for God's majesty is concerned, Luther and his allies are not to be outdone by the Anabaptists. God's majesty is not to be dragged into private business and schemes for personal benefit. From this common position both sides level the same criticism at many aspects of public life. The criticism may sound more radical from the Anabaptists, but it corresponds to an old tradition that was also adopted by the Reformers: habitual swearing is a sin; no one should swear to gain a temporal advantage. Melanchthon—citing Augustine—had declared that as early as 1519. One should not require an oath of one's opponent in court. In Christ's eyes simplicity of heart means more than such a forensic act. The testimony of the truth, not a legal oath, is decisive.[358] Luther goes so far as to label the numerous oaths required by the universities as idol-service.[359]

In fact, not only university life but all of political, social, and economic life—to say nothing of the courts—was permeated with requirements for taking oaths. In many places the oath of allegiance was required annually. Social existence in all its aspects rested on people's willingness to take oaths. All feudal relationships were likewise secured by means of oaths; those who broke their vow or fundamentally opposed all vows dissolved the social

358. From the *Annotationes in Evangelium Matthaei* (published in 1523 on the basis of lectures on Matt. 5:33ff. given at the end of 1519; StA 4:157ff.). Prompted by religious concerns, Melanchthon seeks to limit the practice of oaths, if possible, in order to avoid unwitting perjury.

359. *Idolatricum iuramentum* (WA 31.2:652.20).

fabric. Those who took their oath lightly, either out of habit or because the oath was unnecessary, endangered the common life. On the other hand, the abundance of oaths imperiled the holiness of God's majesty.

It is therefore understandable that the pious simplicity of the Anabaptist circles recoiled at these public abuses, rejected all oaths on principle, and contented itself with the plain yes and no required by Jesus. There were, however, factors other than biblicism at work. Manicheism earlier in the Middle Ages had influenced sectarians to refuse oaths on the ground that public authority in Christendom was opposed to God. Anabaptist circles, influenced by apocalyptic, made the same judgment. Whoever agreed with their denial of the divine mandate for government could not allow that government to require an oath. Such a person would have to withdraw from that whole public sphere which was held together by the requirement of oaths, voluntarily assuming the same status of outlawry that a perjurer would incur. The treatment of the question of oaths therefore actually belongs in the article on temporal rule, because government collapses when its divine authority is contested by the denial of oath taking and by equating it—either explicitly or by implication—with powers opposed to God. The conflict over oaths involves the existence of government itself. One need look no further than Luther's doctrine of the two authorities for evidence of that; the connection also became more and more clear to the other Reformers—quite apart from the revolt of Münzer and the peasants.[360]

This political side of the oath issue did not appear at all in early catechization, and even later it was not strong. Luther, beginning with the brief explanation of the Ten Commandments in 1518,[361] was concerned only with warning against perjury and the breaking of vows. This attitude continued through the catechetical sermons and both catechisms of 1529. The warning against perjury and its concomitant misuse of God's name remained in the foreground. The question of whether or not one ought to swear was posed, but not with an eye to the Anabaptists; they were simply dismissed in general as false teachers without any special mention of their rejection of oaths. The question was answered by means of a parallel to supplication: as I can call upon God by prayer in every need, so I can also call on him in the form of an oath if I bring my need or my neighbor's need before him in witnessing to the truth. The Large Catechism enumerates cases where a false oath brought on

360. This is apparent, for example, in Melanchthon's *Verlegung etlicher unchristlicher Artikel, welche die Widerteuffer fürgeben*, published in 1536; here the forbidding of oaths is called "destruction of temporal rule and justice" (StA 1:311.3). In the disputation from December 2, 1536, published by Johannes Haussleiter (*Melanchthon-Kompendium* [Greifswald, 1902], 92ff.), everything points toward the sanctity of oaths.

361. *WA* 1:252.17ff. After 1521, the question of vows was no longer connected to the issue of oaths. The oath of promise is basically set aside; see below, p. 162.

particularly unfortunate results, and it praises a valid oath as a God-ordained means of insuring that justice is done.[362]

Even the sermons on Exodus from 1525–26 treat the command against oaths in the Sermon on the Mount without a polemical glance toward the Anabaptists; the sermons still are aimed at the young and simple folk. The entire emphasis is on God's demanding the oath from us at the instance of government. God is the one who requires it, not our own choice, desire, or mischief. One should not even swear to another's innocence on one's own initiative—out of fear or to gain an advantage. There is a twofold positive justification for taking an oath: either at the command of government in the exercise of its general duty of love and protection, or in behalf of our oppressed neighbor. In either case the oathtaker is fulfilling the commandment to love the neighbor. The motive in doing so is not something specifically Christian but is humane in a general sense; one acts as a member of the kingdom of wrath (regnum irae), not the kingdom of grace (regnum gratiae) of Christ. The commandment against oaths in the Sermon on the Mount relates only to the latter realm. Taking an oath is always an act of faith; the individual testifies that God is trustworthy and that he attends to the sworn testimony.[363]

Luther's first direct confrontation with the Anabaptist exegesis of Matt. 5:33ff. occurs in 1530 in his lectures on the Song of Solomon. The basis for the interpretation has been given: oaths are permitted when required by government or by the commandment to love. Even Christ did not abrogate that position; he only forbade casual swearing. In the process Luther can even—in contrast to the wording of the Sermon of the Mount—approve swearing by the name of an earthly creature; that can occur if God is thereby praised through his creation.[364] That is how far Luther was from limiting in any way the simple call upon the divine majesty in the form of an oath. Gone was the religious starting point he originally had held in common with the Anabaptists.

Even Melanchthon gave up his earlier hesitation; his final standpoint matched Luther's. The divine honor that is to be respected in the taking of oaths is the punitive majesty that confronts the perjurer. To swear an oath is a holy work, because God's honor, the requirements of government, and the well-being of other people all depend on it. The requirement for oathtaking is grounded in the Christian commandment of love, as is the case with the Reformation doctrine of authority in general.[365]

362. WA 30.1:4–5, 30–31, 62–63; LW 51:141–42; BS 572.43ff., 573.22ff., 577.19ff., 576.14ff., 38ff.; BC 371, 372, 373.
363. WA 16:473–76.
364. WA 31.2:651–52; LW 15:217. See also WA 20:152.3ff.; LW 15:135.
365. StA 1:311–12.

21. PROPERTY

Only the Latin version of CA 16 expressly speaks of the Christian's right to own property (*tenere proprium*) and in the same connection requires the recognition of legal guarantees for private ownership (*lege contrahere*). The German version does not go into the doctrine of contracts;[366] it deals only with the simple business activities of buying and selling, which, of course, assume that one has the power to dispose of property. The thesis is directed against Anabaptist efforts to introduce common ownership and against their rejection of the early capitalistic economic system. Thus the Augustana's brief phrases take up concerns that were the objects of lively contemporary debate. The aftereffects of those concerns still govern discussions of social ethics today and raise questions about the current validity of the Lutheran confessions. That makes it all the more necessary to test whether those phrases determine economic and political decisions to such an extent that they still have binding force for our day.

In the process we must keep in mind that communal ideals found hearers in circles other than the Anabaptists and that they were opposed by groups other than the Luthern Reformers. About the time of the diet at Augsburg, Melanchthon republished his commentary on the *Politics* of Aristotle. At the end of the first book he expressly took sides with Aristotle against Socrates and his interpreter, Plato. He argued that Plato's urging of community of wives and goods ran contrary to human nature. Expressing himself positively and in harmony with Aristotle, he claimed that human society is built on property and monogamy; it collapses where they disappear. Melanchthon was amazed that many theologians agreed with Platonic ideas. He did not trace that sympathy back to the Platonic revolution that had influenced European intellectual life for more than a century. Rather he went back to Gratian—certainly correctly as far as practice was concerned—whose decree had related the Christian community of love to the Platonic ideal, thus making clear the affinity between monastic and Platonic forms of community.[367] The communalism of the Anabaptists is certainly no accidental phenomenon that caused the disturbances of the first decades of the Reformation; it reveals traditions that were deeply rooted in the classical-Christian world. Nor did political grounds form the basis for Luther's and Melanchthon's negative response.

The mature Melanchthon of 1530 brings up heavy artillery. The advocates of communalism, he says, start with the condition of humanity before the Fall; we, however, are dealing with fallen humanity. Christian theology inter-

366. Although Na did allude to purchasing and other contracts: *BS* 70.26–27.
367. *Corpus Iuris Canonici* 1, Dist. 8, Gratianus, Pars 1.

prets Aristotle in that way, thus binding humanity to government and its laws protecting private property. Those who would abolish those laws give up the gospel and destroy civil order. Behind these stern judgments looms Melanchthon's constant conviction that natural law is in accord with divine law that is confirmed in the Bible—in this case by the Seventh Commandment, which protects property.[368]

Originally, Melanchthon's rejection of communalism had not been so absolute. His lectures in 1519–20 on Matthew—which depended strongly on Erasmus and his prototype, Origen—called for a communalism of love. This plan, however, respected the variety of talents and avoided a mechanical division of property, while making all spiritual and material goods serve common needs.[369] The communalistic ideal was fulfilled by evangelical poverty, properly understood. In contrast to the monasticism of his day, which Melanchthon rejected as radically as Erasmus had done,[370] a spiritualized image of evangelical poverty was proposed. It did not cast possessions aside but was *in affectu* not dependent on them; the owners should hold property as though they did not have it and should consider themselves the administrators and curators of goods entrusted to them.

The *Loci* of 1521 continues in a purely Platonic way to deduce community of property from natural law. It corresponds to the human society we all hold in common.[371] But it is already apparent that human greed is the enemy of a communalism of love; the latter can only be realized to the extent that the peace and well-being of a community will allow. For that purpose government and the civil laws it enacts are necessary. They see to it that private ownership is for the good of all. Here the Melanchthon of 1521 takes up the doctrine of contracts. They appear to him to be the essence of the Platonic doctrine of the state. In order to further the common good they regulate buying and selling, tenancy and rent, and similar laws of property, thus securing an ordered community life. The spontaneous community of love that Plato wanted has been replaced by the Aristotelian "end" of utility, which is also demanded by most poets and authors. Even slavery is defended on its basis.[372]

Thus Melanchthon has become disenchanted with communalist ideals. Granted, he still maintains the concept of evangelical poverty he developed from Matt. 19:16ff., but it is more firmly tied to property. To be poor means

368. *CR* 16:429–33. A retrospective verdict is once again handed down against Thomas Münzer and Jakob Strauss (ibid., 448). See also W. Maurer, *Der junge Melanchthon* (cited above, n. 49), 2:288ff.

369. StA 4:192–94. In almsgiving, "the context is the community of goods" (ibid., 194.21).

370. "The monks give up their [almsgiving] so that they may accept ours" (ibid., 193.24–25).

371. StA 2.1:42.33–34. See ibid., 43.33–34: "The law concerning community of goods simply arises from the nature of human society." See also Maurer, *Der junge Melanchthon*, 294–95; and Felix Flückiger, *Geschichte des Naturrechtes*, vol. 1 (Zollikon-Zurich, 1954), 151ff.

372. StA 2.1:44.3ff., 14ff., 45.9ff., 29–30.

to administer possessions for others, to hold one's own belongings in common with everyone, to give to the destitute and supply their needs. All of that requires, however, the legal foundations that are recognized and secured through contracts. They provide the means for adjusting the divine and natural laws to changing circumstances. A legal process is followed for which only one principle is laid down in the *Loci: interesse* (the charging of interest) is ruled out.[373]

This introduces the subject that dominated the public discussion in those decades of early capitalism, that also contributed to the social disturbance of the time, and that forms the background for the mention of contracts in CA 16. On what basis might Christians risk their possessions in economic life? The Anabaptists said, On no account, and stuck to the traditional economy of agriculture and exchange. The Wittenberg reformers tried to give both a theological basis and a limit to their yes to modern economic relationships. That did not happen in CA 16. The article therefore derives its chief significance only from the fact that it establishes the participation of the Christian in the accumulation and administration of property. It presupposes economic processes without dealing with them and does not give them any specific ethical basis. Thus the Confession provides no specifics on the matter, although a variety of material is available in writings of Luther and Melanchthon from the same period. By drawing on that material we can gain an insight into the socioeconomic principles followed by both reformers.

Melanchthon is increasingly dominated by his classically oriented view of the state and, in the process, follows a course that leads him steadily closer to his position of 1530. The first step was taken in 1524 when Melanchthon, as he was traveling to his southern German homeland in April, intervened in the quarrels on usury occasioned by the Eisenach preacher Jakob Strauss.[374] Melanchthon brushed aside every theological criticism of usury and tenancy, which were common practices in Thuringia, by pointing to favorable laws that had been sanctioned by the government. Thus the authorities maintain unity and love; there is no question over keeping contracts as long as they are written within the legal limits.

That is a rule a lawyer can advocate, but a theologian cannot advocate it with a good conscience. Melanchthon, however, defended it further with theological arguments. His political passion becomes more apparent after the Peasants' War. To him the demand to hand over all property to communal ownership appears to foment rebellion, both intrinsically and on the basis of

---

373. Ibid., 53.17ff., 22–23, 45.31.

374. See also Hermann Barge, *Jakob Strauss*, Schriften des Vereins für Reformationsgeschichte 162 (Leipzig, 1937), 61ff.; idem, *Luther und der Frühkapitalismus*, Schriften des Vereins für Reformationsgeschichte 168 (Gütersloh, 1951); Clemens Bauer, "Melanchthons Wirtschaftsethik," Archiv für Reformationsgeschichte 49 (1958): 129; and Maurer, *Der junge Melanchthon*, 451–52. See, as well, Melanchthon's report to the government in Weimar (*WBr* 3:276–77).

natural law. The richly developed scriptural warrants for private property serve as the primary divine support for that law, but in the process the central themes of Christian ethics also begin to come to bear.[375] A principal argument is that the duty of love which God requires presupposes one's power to dispose of one's own belongings. Wealth is, therefore, no sin in itself; it is a divinely willed means for benevolence. And because donors can set their own limits, it becomes clear that there can be no forced duty of love within the Christian community; property should always be at one's free disposal. Therefore even the community of goods among the early Christians should not be misinterpreted legalistically. If Christians of that day really felt pressured into giving up their belongings, that force came from persecution and not from the congregation. They knew that if they did not share their wealth with the poor, the government would seize it anyway.

One can ask if Melanchthon is not simply equating the Christian commandment to love with the demands of natural law. If the answer is yes—as it must certainly be—it once more becomes apparent that Melanchthon's concept of property, like his social ethics in general, rests on a synthesis between nature and revelation, classicism and Christianity. One understands, on the one hand, how congenial his economic ethics were to his humanistic contemporaries and with what inevitability they spread. On the other hand, one sees how the confessional statements about property are encumbered for the short- and long-term future when they are interpreted from Melanchthonian presuppositions.

Melanchthon argued from more than the classical-scholastic doctrine of natural law; he was also influenced by the wisdom tradition of the Old Testament. The Song of Solomon was a particularly beloved object of his exegesis. In the *New Scholia* on it that he published in 1529, he treats the problem we are discussing. The fanatics who demand community of goods are presented with the same refutation as before: the disposition of property rests on a divinely willed civil ordinance that is necessary in order that works of love can be performed; it should, however, neither be held sacred nor be despised. It must be administered legally (StA 4:328–29, 351.18ff.). In addition, Melanchthon further elaborated the teaching on contracts from a legal point of view. He did this frequently in the period before and after the Augsburg diet in disputations before the faculty of arts.[376] His suspicion of

---

375. *Adversus Anabaptistas iudicium* presents a detailed justification of private property: StA 1:291–95.

376. Johannes Haussleiter's *Melanchthon-Kompendium* (Greifswald, 1902) lists "De contractibus" (pp. 102–3) and "De contractu redemptionis" (pp. 103–4), both before the end of 1530; "De contractu redemptionis" (pp. 104ff.), from June 1531 (the most detailed); and "De politicis legibus et de vindictis" (pp. 86ff.), from the early 1530s. The ideas and authorities (Baldus, Hostiensis, Panormitanus) cited here reappear later: in connection with the catastrophe at Münster, in the *Verlegung etlicher unchristlicher Artikel* (1536; StA 1:312–13); and in the forties, in the supplement to *Epitome philosophiae moralis* (1546; *CR* 16:128ff.) and in the *Enarratio aliquot librorum Ethicorum Aristotelis* (1545; *CR* 16:495ff.). We do not deal further with these later sources.

economics based on usury is unmistakable. Aristotle had rejected that system, as had older Roman law; the Old Testament permitted it only for non-Jews. The fact that contemporary usage recognizes some broad forms of charging interest ought not be condemned as a sin though. The government has permitted legal and useful contracts involving interest; what it does not allow is forbidden to Christians. Because governmental practices vary it is necessary to reserve judgment. Above all, the clergy dare not presume to have the authority to decide; that lies entirely with the temporal authorities.[377]

We do not do Melanchthon an injustice by tracing a noteworthy secularization in his economic ethics. His call to the Christian for active participation in business and trade, as stated in CA 16, dispenses with all specifically religious motivation. It is oriented completely toward the ordering functions of temporal government—functions that can be traced back to God's will only by following the detour of natural law. This economic ethic dominated Lutheranism through the school of Melanchthon, which spread through all the disciplines and shaped economic life. It then was interpreted into CA 16 without critical examination.

One must ask whether Melanchthon's commentary is really the best description of the Lutheran Reformation's view of property. Luther's statements on the subject start from different presuppositions, treat far different problems, and often come to different conclusions. It is simply that—as in other cases—the "preceptor of Germany" gained a greater influence through his wide circle of students than Luther himself did. The latter's own point of view was hardly known and could have little effect.[378]

In the history of political economy, Luther is a thinker behind his times; he did not advocate the money-economy theories of the day. He stayed with the traditional agrarian economy and used its categories for the theological argumentation of his faith in creation. Those thought forms were insufficient for his contemporaries and even more so for post-Enlightenment thinkers. They offered no stimulation for later theologians.

And yet we dare not forget one thing. When Luther thought about property and its use by Christians, it was from the point of view of a pastor and not a theoretician. He considered property to be a gift of God. It was inconceivable to him that the Anabaptists repudiated private property and trade; he did not spend much energy in contradicting communalism. For him, buying and selling is a "necessary thing," which no one can avoid and which can be done in a Christian manner. Only international trade, which satisfies no necessary needs of life and squanders money outside the country, is on his list of the useless.[379]

377. Haussleiter, *Melanchthon-Kompendium*, 102ff.
378. See also Barge, *Frühkapitalismus* (see n. 374), 40ff.
379. *WA* 15:293.29ff., 294.8ff.; *LW* 45:246.

Pastoral concerns, not economic ones, shape the reformer. He opposes greed and profiteering. He wants to advise merchants whose consciences are bothered by "many a wicked trick and hurtful financial practice."[380] He does not want to propose a national economic program; he is content if a few— those who "would rather be poor with God than rich with the devil"—are "rescued from the jaws of avarice."[381] This reference to the few who are serious about the implications of their Christian faith does not rule out interest in social structures as a whole, but it does rule out the production of detailed proposals for reform. That was a job Luther handed over to the "worldly-wise" as early as 1520 in his programmatic statements directed to the Christian nobility; "as a theologian" he had simply to lay his grievances before them.[382]

The positive proposals that Luther does put forward in his two relevant works must sound wholly utopian to experts. In his "Long Sermon on Usury" of 1520 he recommends three things to believers on the basis of the Sermon on the Mount: (1) Whatever the tax collectors would take from them by force, they should give up voluntarily and, following Christ's example, be ready to suffer even more. (2) If a needy person makes a request of them, they should give as much as is needed, without worrying, trusting that God will not let the giver want for anything. (3) They should lend money to those who ask without requiring interest. If Luther had insisted only on the first of these rules, one could assume that his demand for renunciation on the basis of the Sermon on the Mount (Matt. 5:40) actually put him close to the communalistic utopianism of the Anabaptists or that he was holding to the original ideals of the mendicant orders. The two next points, however, indicate that he affirmed private ownership. Those who give without taking something back and lend without demanding interest must possess property.[383]

The regulation of property does not concern Luther; he is interested in the Word and faith. Christ's Word demands unconditional abandonment of property; Christ's suffering calls his followers to a "peaceful, pure, and heavenly life." This is not a matter of evangelical counsels that we can follow or not; we are bound by a strict divine command that abolishes retribution and forbids the Christian to engage in lawsuits or self-defense. The suffering that God lays upon every Christian is not removed when we become involved in the world's business. But peaceable and loving folk will discover that God will not

380. *WA* 15:293.9ff.; *LW* 45:245. Cp. *WA* 15:294.21–22 (*LW* 45:247), on the purpose of the work *Trade and Usury*; it speaks of the "abuses and sins of trade, insofar as they concern the conscience." As a sermon to a social class, it is related to the *Long Sermon on Usury* (early 1520; *WA* 6:36ff.; *LW* 45:273ff.), which was attached to it in 1524.

381. *WA* 15:293.23ff.; *LW* 45:245. In business (as in the political realm), it is evident "that Christians are few" (*WA* 6:50.31; *LW* 45:294).

382. *WA* 6:466.38; *LW* 44:214.

383. *WA* 6:36.16ff., 41.12ff., 47.4ff.; *LW* 45:273, 280, 289.

let them be totally ruined. Their faith, which gives them patience to endure unjust power, also preserves them despite appearances; it abolishes that principle of natural law which says, "Fight force with force." I act in the faith that God will preserve me even if I spend myself completely for the sake of my neighbor when I support the needy with my property. And the same thing happens when I lend the neighbor money without interest, following a commandment that goes back to the Old Testament (Deut. 15:7–8); it is my duty to do this without any legal assurance, not only in extreme emergencies or just to the rich, but also to the enemy.

Here the relationship to property is developed out of the freedom of faith rather than, as in Aristotle and Melanchthon, out of natural law. The tie to personal property is certainly preserved; on that Luther and Melanchthon agree. But the purpose is not to maintain the divine world order; it is to demonstrate faith in God and love for the neighbor in following Jesus. All the religious and moral themes that Anabaptism took over and developed from the mendicant orders are cleansed and clarified in Luther's teaching on property.

It is not possible to say that it was only the Luther of 1520, not yet experienced much in public life, who thought that way. His *To the Christian Nobility* of the same year demonstrates his knowledge of the world in every sentence. To be sure, Luther's understanding of economic relationships grew through the years. In his sermons on the Decalogue from 1517 he considers interest simply from an ecclesiastical standpoint—as a means for priests and scholarship students to study undisturbed, or to enable the elderly, children, and sick to be cared for by a pension; his principal concern was that pensioners could secure a comfortable income without effort.[384] In the "Long Sermon" of 1520 the criticism goes further and deeper; the earning of interest is not only something new and until recently unknown but is also contrary to natural law and Christian love even when there is no profiteering involved. For in no case will it help the debtor who is in need; it will just make the rich still richer. Everything is oriented toward the advantage of the creditor. He is not taking a risk; it is the already oppressed debtor who must bear that burden. This evaluation of interest presupposes not only a fine ethical sensitivity but also a precise knowledge of economic processes.[385]

In the work from 1524, trade and usury occupy the spotlight, but the panorama also begins to include the interconnections of international trade. The eleven examples from economic life that Luther presents give insight into the manipulations that were common to early capitalism.[386] The experi-

---

384. *Decem praecepta* (printed in 1518; *WA* 1:505.15ff.).
385. *WA* 6:51ff.; *LW* 45:295.
386. *WA* 15:304ff.; *LW* 45:260.

ence Luther cites could not have been gained in little Wittenberg nor from hearsay on visits to, say, Nürnberg or Augsburg. This is an analysis of contemporary economics by a man who, although not possessing the knowledge of a modern historian, yet knows social and ethical life as an educated scholastic theologian. He presents the situation accurately and with a love for the destitute that is matched by critical insight. One can object that such a man has not grasped the deeper threads of economic development; one must admit, however, that he analyzes the circumstances and that he has the pastoral power to evaluate them from the perspective of the highest values of faith and love.

Trade and Usury is a pastoral work. It is not directed to Christians who are suffering from profiteering and are trying to stop it. That had been the case with the sermon four years earlier. This is addressed to the usurers themselves; it describes their practices. It ticks off three rules by which they operate: (1) Without regard for the neighbor, they seek to achieve the highest price possible. (2) They stand surety for one another. (3) They lend at interest. In all of this they seek their own advantage at the expense of the destitute neighbor; they are "cutthroats."[387]

Behind this sharp, radically negative critique of capitalistic developments lies the same understanding of property as in the sermon from 1520: Christian love must shape business and trade; otherwise they become robbery and theft. Economic planning must be determined by trust in God; otherwise the taking of surety, for example, arrogantly replaces divine governance. And lending at interest, entirely apart from the level of the interest rate, is "open and accursed usury." One cannot sidestep God's commandment of love, and private property is subject to it. Granted, only Christians recognize that commandment as obligatory; only they, "the rarest creatures on earth," can keep it.[388]

When Luther says that, he is not being otherworldly. He knows that property can be properly handled only within the Christian community. Only among Christians is credit without interest possible. Only there is one free of those who are so bad or impudent that they want to be fed at the expense of their brother. There also the limits of all charity are recognized, by both sides: primary responsibility extends to wife, children, and servants; only that is available for loan which can then be spared. Although generous love goes beyond reason and fairness, it does not ignore them completely, but in considering them, it observes certain rules that are valid beyond the circle of those who want seriously to be Christians.[389]

387. *WA* 15:294.25, 298.5ff., 301.15ff., 304.19ff., 308.1ff.; *LW* 45:247, 252, 256–57, 261, 265.

388. *WA* 15:294.31ff.; *LW* 45:247; *WA* 6:48–49; *LW* 45:291; *WA* 15:299.1ff.; 301.24, 14; *LW* 45:253, 257, 256.

389. *WA* 15:302.30ff.; *LW* 45:258.

Among them belongs the rule, worthy of consideration by all business people, that says that in buying and selling, all trade should be either for cash or by direct exchange of goods of equal value. Christians should get out of trading companies. If they do lend money at the only possible interest rate—which should not exceed four to six percent—the deal should be tied to a specific object, such as a piece of land. The mortgage should not be a "blind sale" in which the borrower puts up all his possessions as security for the loan. It is always best to link a loan to land and thereby make the yield of a loan dependent on the agricultural economy. Only in that way do debtor and lender bear the same risk. That sort of consideration led Luther to recommend that the Old Testament prototypes of the tithe and the year of jubilee be reintroduced. Unlike Strauss and others, he did not seek to bring a revealed law of God back into force; he saw an analogy between the natural process of harvest and the sharing of risk; the canceling of old debts showed something of the forgiving mercy of God.[390]

In the light of God's mercy, the difference between rich and poor disappears. Granted, a prince must be richer than others;[391] that was why the demand for general equality had a social-revolutionary taint for Luther. But it did not imply that a prince's wealth and power must last forever. Both property relationships and social structures change. What now stands can fall, and the lowly can rise in the service of the church and state. "Then both kinds of government on earth must remain with the poor middle class of common people, and with their children." The children of the poor shall rule the world![392] In the same vein, Luther reacted against restrictions on guild membership. An illegitimate child ought not be barred from joining: "He has been baptized."[393] Servanthood on the model of classical slavery is not part of the view of property held by the Lutheran Reformation. It contradicts natural law, declares Melanchthon; it hinders faith, states Luther.[394] If the sabbatical year mentioned in Exod. 21:2 still existed, Luther would have liked to see such a six-year term of service introduced for menservants and maids; it would provide better obedience instead of the present situation of the servants' lording it over their masters. In any case, the biblical commandment to love has nullified antiquity's slave laws; it would be well if the Old Testament concern for poor fellow countrymen were still practiced. When it

390. *WA* 15:303.19ff., 313.17ff.; *LW* 45:259, 272; *WA* 6:58.6ff., 55.13ff., 56.6–7; *LW* 45:304, 301, 302; *WA* 15:321.14ff., 322.10ff.; *LW* 45:308, 309–10. Luther's principles on the *Zinskauf* first appear in the opinion written to Brueck on October 18, 1523, and in the letter to Strauss of the same date (*WBr* 3:nos. 673–74; *LW* 49:50–55).

391. *WA* 32:307.12ff., 19–20; *LW* 21:12.

392. *Sermon on Keeping Children in School* (1530; *WA* 30.2:577.29ff.; *LW* 46:251).

393. *WA* 15:651.20ff. (sermon of July 10, 1524); see also *WA* 17.2:55.22–23.

394. *StA* 2.1:45.29–30 (*Loci* of 1521); *WA* 16:541.3–4.

is not done, begging takes over. The government should abolish begging for the sake of order.[395]

Begging violates the created order of property, which is maintained and reinforced by *work*. Luther and Melanchthon agree in their high valuation of work. By forbidding stealing, God commands that property be made useful through work. Melanchthon supports this appeal by calling on the Stoic doctrine of duty, which makes each person serve the whole through that person's area of work. Those who prove themselves masters of their property help those who suffer need. A community cannot last if everyone's sustenance is not assured by regular work.[396]

The classical social philosophy on which Melanchthon based this work ethic is supplemented by the Song of Solomon's admonition "Go to the ant, you sluggard." Melanchthon derived the necessity for this reproof out of human fleshly drives. The example of the ant shows that God has implanted the urge to work in his creatures. Human beings defy the divine command. God abhors idleness because of its evil consequences, so he has government force the lazy to work. For us, fear of God and trust in his promise of salvation provide the inner motivation to do what is required.[397]

Luther also appeals to the healthy human urge to work, bolstered by Old Testament proverbs. The world cannot go on if everyone is as poor as a beggar. Heads of households must bestir themselves if they are to support those who depend on them. Of course, "if the Lord build not the house, they labor in vain who build it" (Ps. 127:1); but that only confirms work and in no way invalidates it. Nonetheless, people should not work in vain; that happens when they give themselves over to worry and greed, assuming that everything depends on their own efforts. "Work is your responsibility, but nourishing and managing belong to God alone." A person should work, "but at the same time realize that it is another who nourishes him." "Profit-seeking greed or the lazy old Adam" are therefore enemies of work because they cannot produce that trust.[398]

The same difference between Luther and Melanchthon that we have already discovered in their teaching on property also exists in their understanding of work. Simply put, the humanistic schoolmaster saw work under the power of law; Luther saw it under the attraction of the gospel. For the former, God forced subjects to work by means of government, so that society would

395. *WA* 16:532.16ff., 6:42.1ff.; *LW* 45:281.

396. StA 4:328.15ff.; 355.7ff.

397. On Proverbs 6.6ff.: StA 4:331.30ff., 332.9ff.

398. See *WA* 16:553.28–29: ". . . the meaning of wealth: work faithfully, sell honestly" (sermon from the spring of 1526, on Exod. 22:21). See also *WA* 32:307.1ff.; *LW* 21:12; *WA* 15:366.15ff., 367.2–3, 368.9ff.; *LW* 45:324, 325, 326.

thrive and social and economic relationships would be improved. According to Luther, God preserves the life of his creatures and expects them to respond to this goodness with their trust and their love. A sign of this active relationship to God is their work, whose fruits they share with their fellow human beings, thereby showing them their love.

Because law and justice play a major role in these questions of property and economics, government has a regulatory function. Its office is to hinder robbery, larceny, and indolence. What it can do in the way of positive legislation remains an open question. In no way did either Luther or Melanchthon see government as the source of property laws, nor could a Christian rest easy in settling all questions about property by referring to specific public laws. Luther proceeds very cautiously on this point. The situation varies so much from place to place; no government can operate unto itself; the prince should intervene only in emergencies. In general, one should act in accordance with the customs of the country; local circumstances (market conditions and location) ought to be taken into account. It would be best for the government to authorize experts to supervise and check on things. Moreover, in buying and selling, everyone ought to be able to follow conscience.[399] Obvious abuses should be sternly punished and the evildoers forced to do what is right. Those seeking monopolies should be driven out of the country. If people want the government to keep thieves off the street, they must also grant it authority to protect its subjects from being fleeced by tradesmen. If local authorities do not take care of these cases, then the emperor, kings, and princes should see that the system of capital and interest is reorganized during the imperial diet.[400]

The brief references to property in CA 16 have received different interpretations from Luther and Melanchthon. Luther offers a colorful picture of the social reality of his day; working from Aristotle, Melanchthon brings a stern refutation of communalist ideals. Each uses a different method of argumentation and presentation, but their goal, the rousing of moral responsibility in dealing with private property, is identical. But in harmony with his sharp distinction between *iustitia civilis* and *iustitia divina,* Melanchthon completely omits the faith element in that responsibility and deduces it purely from legal demands; love appears as the fruit produced by this responsibility rather than as the source and power of social transactions. Economic transactions are carried on in strictly standardized forms; one cannot detect a trace of loving spontaneity in them. The relation between creditor and debtor does not contain any personal elements. Melanchthon is

---

399. *WA* 16:554.27–28; *WBr* 3:nos. 673.34ff., 755.33ff.; *LW* 49:54; *WA* 15:295–97; *LW* 45:248–51.

400. *WA* 15:302.14–15, 307.11ff., 311.8ff., 322.19ff.; *LW* 45:258, 264, 269, 310.

completely oblivious to the practical idea of relating borrowed money to agricultural land. He uses canon law to justify the "blind sale" that Luther rejects; he considers reintroduction of the jubilee year to be "revolutionary."[401] Luther's creative imagination, which would see the manifold variety of civil society hidden in new forms, is lacking in the schoolmaster. Of course, Luther's economic ideas are not able to transcend the agrarian concepts handed on to him by the Middle Ages; despite his detailed knowledge of city life, he is never able to enter fully into the thought forms of capitalism. "Increase agriculture and decrease commerce"—this slogan from *To the Christian Nobility*[402] remains determinative for Luther and his followers, and even Melanchthon does not get beyond it.

Yet there are elements in Luther's teaching on property that point toward the future. Although his economic ideas were already out of fashion by the time he developed them, his ethic of love, taken from the Sermon on the Mount, continues to be an effective force in Christian social ethics. Luther did not consider an ethic of love to be a counsel for the elect only, as the Anabaptists and monks did. He discerned in it a binding commandment to which everyone—and not merely that "rare bird on earth," the Christian— was subject. Through the action of government, that commandment was to be enforced among the public at large, even if in weakened form. Here again Luther anticipated the Christianizing of social life, not as Melanchthon did, through the coercive force of legislation based on natural law, but through the gradual radiating power of a giving love that flows from the heart.

Article 16 says that the Christian must possess property. Melanchthon adds an explanatory word: for that purpose, good laws, grounded in God's will and enforced by the government, are needed. Luther, however, comments that God gives us property so that we can serve one another through its proper use.

22. MARRIAGE AND FAMILY

The Texts

The Augustana does not devote an individual article to marriage and family. In CA 16, and as early as Na 15, both institutions were simply enumerated among the civil orders and good works of God in order to condemn Anabaptist practices. In content there is no effort to justify them or to describe how they are manifestations of the creative divine will. In addition, in his *Confession Concerning Christ's Supper* of 1528, Luther had already

401. *CR* 16:134–37.
402. *WA* 6:467.1; *LW* 44:214.

listed marriage, along with the pastoral office and temporal authority, among the holy orders and true religious institutions established by God, thus including it in the refutation of monastic and sacerdotal celibacy. In the process, he expressly identified with the "traditional family"[403] and its large household, including more distant relatives and even boarders, domestics, and the like. According to him, when such a domestic community acts according to God's will, the result is "sheer holiness."[404] At the same time, however, Luther stresses the created, rather than sacramental, character of marriage.[405] Opposition to Rome still outweighs opposition to the Anabaptists.

Articles 14 and 15 of Schwab. say nothing positive about marriage, apart from their polemic against celibacy. The educational aims of the visitation, however, soon forced questions of marriage into the limelight. In the *Instructions for the Visitors*, adultery appears as the chief vice and marital faithfulness as the highest principle of neighborly love; the Fourth Commandment receives detailed attention. Christian government and pastors are being confronted in a new way with legal problems relating to marriage. Caution in these cases is required; pastors are to preach diligently on the divine institution of marriage. Theological grounding, therefore, is not only necessary for polemics; it also forms the basis for instruction in the congregation.[406]

Even so, polemics provide the major impetus to the confessional development. The violation of ecclesiastical laws on celibacy, which was sanctioned in the visitation articles, had to be defended in view of the coming imperial diet. That occurs in E and A of the Torgau Articles through the scriptural proof for the divine institution of marriage. In addition to Genesis 1—3, 1 Cor. 7:28 plays a major role. Those are the same passages that Luther had steadfastly cited in his battle against celibacy. Here too one finds a good deal of caution on legal questions relating to marriage; their answer is left to a compromise between political advisers and canon lawyers.[407]

Document Na and the final versions of both CA 23 and CA 27 continue the

403. Modern sociology distinguishes this from the "great family," in which the married sons and their wives and children live together. That was not what Luther had in mind; see René König, *Materialien zur Soziologie der Familie* (Bern, 1946), 44.70–71.

404. "Again, all fathers and mothers who regulate their household wisely and bring up their children to the service of God are engaged in pure holiness, in a holy work and a holy order. Similarly, when children and servants show obedience to their elders and masters, here too is pure holiness. . ." (*WA* 26:504.35ff.; *LW* 37:364). See *WA* 26:504.30–31, 505.23ff.; *LW* 37:364, 365.

405. "Neither is there any need to make sacraments out of marriage and the office of the priesthood. These orders are sufficiently holy in themselves" (*WA* 26:508.25–26; *LW* 37:370). On marriage as the prototype of the joyous exchange between Christ and the believer, based on Eph. 5:32, see below, n. 440.

406. *WA* 26:203.13, 204.1, 206–211, 225.20ff.; *LW* 40:276, 277, 279–87, 301. See below, chap. 23.

407. Förstemann 1:94–95, 74, 82; Jacobs 93, 79, 84. See also draft C, composed in Augsburg (Förstemann 1:90; Jacobs 90).

scriptural undergirding for marriage with the same biblical arguments. Beginning with Na, Matt. 11:11–12 is added, so that the single life is represented as an inconceivable exception. Nevertheless, the final texts do drop the reference in Na to 1 Tim. 4:1ff., in which forbidding marriage is called a doctrine of the devil.[408] Also, the divine institution of marriage, its mandated character, is emphasized more clearly here than earlier in the Torgau Articles; it is grounded directly in the Creator's will. The final Latin text emphasizes this argument even more strongly than the German version.[409]

Basically there are only a few texts in the confessional writings that refer to marriage and the family; the answers that they give are not well developed systematically. In our commentary we will have to go back to Luther—Melanchthon is not very helpful—in order to grasp the theological background of the confessional statements.

The Theological Basis for Marriage[410]

Luther bases marriage on God's will as creator; it is God's work. These statements are not limited to circumstances before the Fall; they relate to marriage in the here and now. As is the case with the doctrine of the state, the doctrine of the family is tied to *creatio continua*. Although God's creative will had instituted and structured matrimony back in Paradise, he also has maintained and sanctioned it after the Fall. That happens through his Word, not the Bible passages that are cited in theological studies as proof texts for the divine institution of marriage, but a living Word that is active and creative now. Marriage is embedded in this Word as though it were "held in a monstrance," and thus it becomes the vehicle for ever-new creation. Married persons "depend simply on God's Word, and everything that is not God's word strips them naked."[411]

Although Luther can discuss marriage in terms of his doctrine of estates—which seems a form of natural law—this reference to the constantly active creativity of God's Word separates his view completely from classical-scholastic thought structures. Of course, marriage is based on God's command, on his ordering (*ordinatio*); it is a divine "institution." But that is not in the sense of an abstract invariable norm; it is the result of God's living, creative will. In his later years, Luther made the abstract order (*Ordnung*) personal by using "creatures," *creatura*, and thereby included all the persons holding office who

408. Kolde 18.5ff., 19.4ff.; Reu 216.

409. That is a result of the tighter text achieved by the Latin version of CA 23. Cp. CA 23.8, 15, 24, and the added sec. 21 in the Latin of CA 27.

410. Among Luther's writings on marriage these have been especially useful: *Vom ehelichen Leben* (1522; *WA* 10.2:267ff.); *Von Ehesachen* (1530; *WA* 30.3:198ff.); *Auslegung von Ps. 127* (1533); *WA* 40.3:202ff.).

411. *WA* 12:107.23ff.; *LW* 28:19. See *WA* 34.1:53.10, 53.20ff., 55.6ff., 57.26, 59.15–16. Cp. *WA* 17.1:9.12: "God created this estate and added the Word."

carry out God's creative will in the world.[412] His active Word does not set up universally binding laws to which people must blindly conform; it furnishes living human instruments, capable of making decisions, with specific creative tasks and gives those persons the power to fulfill them. His law, therefore, must always be understood concretely. In that respect it differs from abstract natural law. The Sixth Commandment, for example, is a positive demand to be fulfilled from case to case: "Thou shalt be wed, thou shalt have a wife, thou shalt have a husband." It must be understood together with the creative words that institute marriage (Gen. 1:27; 2:24) and which press toward ever-new fulfillment.[413]

It can be shown that the Augustana neglects this dynamic element of the creative divine Word. It gives major emphasis to Melanchthon's interpretation (the unchangeableness of the divine creation, signaled by concepts like *mandatum* and *ordinatio* which Luther, as we have seen, interprets differently):[414] marriage is an inviolate order of creation. As time went on, this reliance on natural law gained ground and pushed aside Luther's belief in Word and creation. That was the result of a biblicistic equating of natural and divine law that Melanchthon maintained from the beginning as his scholastic inheritance.[415] For that reason it is best constantly to compare the social and ethical statements of the Augustana with those of Luther and to interpret them in that light.

According to Luther, the creative Word documents God's will to stoop down to us in love. "Is it not something tremendous that the divine majesty descends to us and creates a child? And he accomplishes his divine work in a masterful manner."[416] He steadily continues what he began in Paradise. He who institutes a marriage today is the same one who ruled creatively in the beginning. This continuation and confirmation of the original state in contemporary marriage does not imply some human integrity that remains untouched by the Fall. It testifies rather to the enduring self-confirmation of the divine Word of creation. Christ has carried it out; his teaching is not meant to break or hinder God's creation and work as it manifests itself in Gen. 1:28. The fact that we are Christians does not eliminate our creatureliness; it holds true "that you are a woman, and I a man." God's spirit

412. *WA* 49:721.29ff. (sermon of April 26, 1545).

413. *WA* 8:573ff.; *LW* 48:331; *WA* 15:667.7, 25:19.7ff.; *LW* 29:20; *WA* 27:25.5, 30.2:61.6ff.

414. See CA 23.8: "For no law of man and no vow can nullify a commandment of God and an institution of God." Cp. the German version (*BS* 87.33ff.; *BC* 52.8); cp. also CA 23.6, 24, CA 27.18b, but also sec. 20. For Luther, see above, pp. 159–60.

415. See also W. Maurer, *Der junge Melanchthon* (cited above, n. 49), 288ff.; and idem, "Göttliches Recht nach den lutherischen Bekenntnisschriften," *Jahrbuch des Martin Luther-Bundes* 18 (1971): 93–104.

416. *WA* 17.1:9.22.

permits "the body its way and its natural work."[417] Luther's belief in creation overcomes the opposition between flesh and spirit from which all asceticism springs.

The Word creates ever anew, and faith, which receives this Word, belongs to it. Reason wrinkles its nose when it hears that the Creator concerns himself with sexual life and the maternity ward; it ridicules the man who looks after a baby.[418] The heathen seek fleshly and worldly lust in marriage, but they do not find it. They praise prostitution in their literature and thereby still lead young students astray.[419] Faith, however, is able to distinguish between marriage and prostitution. It looks to the divine Word and lets itself be guided by it. Only in faith is God's creative will properly fulfilled. Only in that way does marriage move people toward the spirit, and marriage must "be almost purely spirit . . . if it is to go well."[420]

Marriage must be accepted and borne with confidence as God's work on the basis of God's Word; otherwise damage is done and marriage becomes unbearable. Those who cannot interpret their marriage on the basis of God's Word and will should expect little but listlessness and despair. It is also a sign of unbelief—doubt about God's goodness and truth—when the prospect of marriage is thwarted by concern about being able to support a family. Happy and persevering, however, are those who believe from their hearts that God is pleased with the estate of matrimony.[421]

It is amazing how concretely Luther was able to set these theological statements about the purpose of creation, the Word, and faith within the realities of marriage. Certainly, no one before him in Christianity had spoken so realistically of sexual matters. After him, perhaps only the emotional young Zinzendorf was able to conquer narrow pietism in this regard. Luther candidly affirms human sexuality.[422]

Luther thus performs an act of unimaginable importance, both for indi-

417. "That it eats, drinks, digests, eliminates. . . . Thus he does not take from people their male or female form, members, seed, and fruit" (*WA* 12:113.24ff.; *LW* 28:26). See also *WA* 12:113.3ff.; *LW* 28.25.

418. "God, with all his angels and creatures, is smiling—not because that father is washing diapers, but because he is doing so in Christian faith" (*WA* 10.2:296.31–32; *LW* 45:40). See also *WA* 10.2:295.16ff.; *LW* 45:39.

419. *WA* 10.2:297.24ff.; 299.18ff.; *LW* 45:41, 43; *WA* 15:417.26ff. Warning to students: *WA* 10.2:294.8ff.; *LW* 45:37.

420. *WA* 12:107.13ff.; *LW* 28:19. Here nature, spirit, and faith work together in a way "that marriage, by its nature, drives, hounds, and forces people into the most inward and highest spiritual being, that is, into faith" (*WA* 12:107.21ff.; *LW* 28:19). See also *WA* 34.1:53.26ff., 17.1:9.32ff.

421. "There is no greater joy to the heart than to know that God laughs" (*WA* 27:25.15–16). On the joyous estate: ibid., 25.5ff. See also *WA* 10.2:294.25, 298.19ff., 9ff., 302.16ff.; *LW* 45:38, 42, 47. Cp. the warning to Cardinal Albrecht of Mainz, who was to secularize his territory after the Peasants' War: "Fresh and far from the depraved un-Christian estate into the blessed and divine estate of matrimony, there God will show himself to be merciful" (*WA* 18:410.18–19).

422. Among the critics of Luther, such as Denifle and Grisar, these statements were considered particularly offensive; in the popular evangelical image of Luther, they were suppressed.

viduals and for society. It did not achieve its full impact at the time or even afterward, because it was so inextricably bound with the battle against medieval monasticism. It must, however, be seen apart from the latter. The affirmation of sexuality—the confessional writings only make use of it polemically—involves humanity as a creation of God. It should be placed in parallel rather than in conflict with the discovery of humanity which occurred in the Italian Renaissance. We cannot, however, discuss the Renaissance belief in God or creation at this point; we are concerned with Luther's belief in creation, which certainly cannot be brought into total congruity with the Renaissance point of view. We see a new image of humanity emerging from Luther's faith, an image that comes to bear on the understanding of marriage.

Luther wants to encourage W. Reissenbusch, the preceptor of the Antonius house in Lichtenberg, to enter into matrimony with a clear conscience.[423] The vow of chastity is not to be kept; we "all are made for marriage, as the body shows and the Scripture says" (275.17–18). Scripture—that is not the letter of Gen. 2:18 but the "Word of God by whose power seed is brought to fruit in the human body and a man's lusty natural inclination to his wife is created and sustained" (275.25–26). The divine creative Word not only approves the attraction of the sexes to each other, it also awakens it. Those who fight it are opposing God's Word. Luther wants to encourage the monk to entrust himself to that Word. "Your body demands it and needs it" (276.34–35). There is no need to be ashamed of matrimony; to enter it means "to be and to be called human" (277.24).

In marriage, human beings reach their fulfillment as God's creation. That is not only indicated in the divine Word, it is also placed before our eyes in our own body; its members incarnate God's word of creation. He says "your members and vessels are my work." So the monk ought not blame himself if he feels the power of his inner drives. As God's creatures, humans share with all animals the fact that their bodies "must sow and multiply and copulate."[424] In our sexuality we are locked into the laws of everything creaturely, but that does not demean us. Humanity does not consist in overcoming it but in gratefully affirming it as evidence of the divine creative will.

That also implies giving in to the necessity of the sexual drive. It is no more possible to mortify it completely in this eon than it is to live without eating, drinking, or sleeping. When the drive stirs to life, God the Creator is at work and everyone does well to yield. As God's creatures, human beings do not have power over their own lives; man and woman press toward each other and belong together. "Nature wants to go out and reproduce and multiply, and

---

423. For the following, see *WA* 18:275–78.
424. *WA* 15:419.6ff.; 418.5, 12:113.29ff.; *LW* 28:26.

God does not want that outside marriage: therefore, on account of this need, everyone who wants to live in good conscience and walk with God must marry."[425]

To live before God with a good conscience—that is the result of a faith in creation that also includes sexual life as a part of our responsibility toward God. This responsibility lifts sexual love to the pinnacle of mutual consideration between marriage partners. Only in monogamy is this civilized love relationship possible. The strong bond with the partner and the indissolubility of that bond is thus not an outward demand of the law but a necessary result of dependence on the divine creative will; that dependence contains necessary moral bonds within itself. "If you are bound to a wife you are no longer a free lord; God compels and commands you to remain with wife and child, and to nourish and care for them." Responsibility before the Creator rules out an unrestrained sexuality. Sexual intercourse occurs with good conscience "because God has created and prescribed it."[426]

If, however, marriage in the form of monogamy corresponds so completely to the divine creator's will, then celibacy must be contrary to that will. For Luther that is in fact the case. That is why he develops his teaching on marriage almost exclusively in his polemic against celibacy. The celibate state is—as he states in a special section of the *Exhortation to All Clergy Assembled at Augsburg* in 1530—one of the papal innovations "contrary to God's eternal Word and contrary to the ancient blessed custom of Christendom, contrary also to all living creatures and the creation of God himself."[427] Granted, one ought not radically reject celibacy. There are those who by nature cannot marry and those who have been forcibly made unable to procreate. There are also Christians who, by the miracle of divine grace, are able to live in a state of chastity.[428] Still, it is generally true that a man must have a wife; otherwise he remains under God's wrath and disfavor, and the misery of unchastity is then insurmountable. Even pious practices are of no avail. God's creative will (*statutum divinum naturae*) to "increase and multiply" can no more be annulled through prayer than the natural drive can. No one can or should exempt himself from God's mandate.[429]

425. *WA* 12:114.30ff.; *LW* 28:27. See also *WA* 15:418.18–19, 31–32, 559.7ff. Both Testaments of the Bible were the source for Luther's idea that according to God's will, legitimate fulfillment of the sexual drive should occur only in marriage. That corresponds to God's creative purpose, which is intent upon the orderly continuation of the human race. Homosexuality is contrary to God's will; self-pollution was perceived as unclean as early as Old Testament times.

426. *WA* 30.3:243.18ff.; *LW* 46:311; *WA* 34.1:59.24.

427. *WA* 30.2:323.27ff.; *LW* 34:40.

428. Luther always speaks positively about these "spiritually rich and exalted persons, bridled by the grace of God, who are equipped for marriage by nature and physical capacity and nevertheless voluntarily remain celibate." Not one in a thousand, of course, is such a "special miracle of God" (*WA* 10.2:279.15ff.; *LW* 45:21). The division into three categories: *WA* 10.2:277.1ff.; *LW* 45:18; *WA* 15:418.6ff.

429. *WA* 18:410.24ff., 30.2:324.15ff.; *LW* 34:41; *WA* 8:631.4ff.; *LW* 44:338.

In this controversy over celibacy, the evaluation of woman becomes the key point. She is included in the Creator's will as it has just been described. She poses no threat to serving God; rather God has created her and entrusted her to man so that she might help and honor him in conjugal life, just as man honors his wife and not a prostitute. Womanly love is something exalted, willed by God, and not to be despised. By creating woman, God affirms marriage as "divine, noble work"; death in childbirth is a "noble deed obedient to God." Precisely because of his bodily nature, man has no right to exalt himself over woman. He is conceived and grows within her; from her he is born, nursed, and nourished. In short, his "body is for the most part really woman's flesh." Here again, in considering woman we see the biological-anatomical realism that is characteristic of Luther's practical sexual ethics and faith.[430]

In all this, sin is taken seriously. It is not, however, rooted in the nature of woman and actualized in sexual relations. On the contrary, married intimacy is a "medicine" against sexual excess,[431] against the fury of flesh perverted by original sin, and against a man's laying hands on other women. When the papal party denigrated the marriage of priests, Luther could say, on the basis of his understanding of justification, "To the pure, marriage too is pure." He would grant, of course, that sexual intercourse, like any human activity, does not occur without sin; even in marriage one can only speak of a lesser chastity (*inferior castitas*). But the faith that affirms God's creative purpose in marriage perceives not only God's hand of blessing in the fruits of marriage but also knows the power of forgiveness. That faith knows "that intercourse is never without sin; but God excuses it by his grace because the estate of marriage is his work, and he preserves in and through the sin all that good which he has implanted and blessed in marriage."[432]

God's blessing rests upon marriage. He created the two sexes for mutually inseparable union as a means to the multiplication of humankind. Increasing population was still a blessing and not a burden to Luther and his contemporaries. That is the way the Creator shows sexual human beings that he is the benign preserver of human life in general.[433] That occurs not only in begetting and birth but also in care and reciprocal concern. These works of the estate of matrimony seem trivial and mean. "Yet it is from them that we all

---

430. *WA* 30.2:325.15ff.; *LW* 34:41; *WA* 31.1:385, 12:94.17ff.; *LW* 28:6; *WA* 10.2:296.20; *LW* 45:40; *WA* 18:276.4ff.

431. In CA 23.14–15, Melanchthon bases the holy character of marriage and the infirmity of human nature on his philosophy of history: it is because the "world is growing weaker" that marriage is necessary.

432. At the end of *The Estate of Marriage* (1522; *WA* 10.2:304.9ff.; *LW* 45:49). In addition, see *WA* 12:114.12; *LW* 28:26; *WA* 18:410.24ff., 31.1:385, 25:37.4–5, 8:653.25ff.; *LW* 44:375.

433. The divine work of creation is a "nature and disposition just as innate as the organs involved in it" (*WA* 10.2:276.25–26). See also ibid., 276.1ff., 21ff.; *LW* 45:18, 17.

trace our origin; we have all had need of them. Without them no man would exist."[434] To speak of marriage is to talk about humanity and the fulfillment of the creative task, which is a task of love.

The Father of the Household and His Family

There is much talk about "patriarchalism" in Luther and the confessions. What is meant is by no means limited to Luther and Lutheranism but is present in the whole world and the majority of cultures up to the Enlightenment of the eighteenth and nineteenth centuries. It existed in various forms and had a variety of roots. We must consider the theological basis for Luther's "patriarchalism" in order to treat his purpose fairly.

The only part of the confessional writings that deals in detail with the power of the head of the household is in the *Instructions for the Visitors* (see above, p. 158), which goes back in its underlying forms to Melanchthon's *Visitation Articles*. That is the work with the strongest emphasis on popular instruction. The divine institution of marriage is presupposed, though not developed theologically; exposition of the Fourth Commandment, however, occupies a great deal of space. Prominence is given to reverence of children toward their parents and proper discipline of children, in addition to obedience to the authorities. This emphasis is based on the doctrine of law and gospel and is illustrated with a wealth of biblical examples. There is no mention of the role of mothers or housewives; the power of the father of the house is not circumscribed in any way. It sticks to traditional ideas: "The youth were never wilder than they are today," and the rod of discipline cures juvenile folly. The teacher Melanchthon does not get beyond these and similar maxims.[435]

In what way has Luther's doctrine of creation shaped the relation between parents and children? Relying on the biblical creation account, Luther sees woman as a helper to man, but not in the relation of lordship and servanthood. They form a devoted mutual partnership.[436] The Turks with their polygamy have no respect for marriage and they value woman as much as a cow. Among the heathen the wives exalt themselves above their husbands, who consider them necessary evils.[437]

In contrast, Christian faith teaches that "marriage is written in the law of love." From that point of view, even fulfilling the marital duty becomes an act of considerate love, so that "no one is master of his own body, but must serve

---

434. *WA* 10.2:298.27ff.; *LW* 45:42–43.

435. *WA* 26:225.10–11, 206.10–211.36, esp. 207.12ff., 5ff.; *LW* 40:301, 280–287, esp. 281.

436. "For God has created women to be held in honor and as helpers for man, and for this reason he does not wish to have such love forbidden and despised" (*WA* 30.2:325.16–17; *LW* 34:41).

437. *WA* 30.2:126.21ff. (cp. ibid., 190.1ff.); *LW* 46:181; *WA* 10.2:293.10ff.; *LW* 45:36.

the other with it, as is the way of love." Marital fidelity is the basic premise of such love; adultery is the "greatest theft and larceny in the world."[438] Common faith of the marriage partners is therefore desirable but, according to the apostle's teaching, not unconditionally demanded. Marriage is an "outward, physical thing"; it neither furthers faith nor hinders it. Respect for the wife as the weaker partner is a simple human duty; "woman is half child." Compassion for her is really only present where the supporting love that the gospel requires is practiced. Of course woman owes obedience to man, but he must rule "with reason."[439] For Luther, obedience is by no means the main point. The real focus is the necessary compulsion to work. It is something the married couple bear in common. Pain, suffering, and death come from God; marriage is always a heavy burden. But, it is in testing and need that the Creator shares his blessing with the married couple. Children are God's evidence to them of that, and the woman grows into full partnership through this gift. She has the key power at home. She keeps the household running when the husband is absent; she participates in his joys and sorrows. In fact, among believing Christians this partnership deepens into spiritual communion. The joyous exchange between Christ and the believing soul, as Luther's theology worked it out on the basis of Eph. 5:32, is reflected in the peace and joy of wedded fellowship.[440] Christ affirms the divine work of creation and with it marriage as well. Faith grasps this work and is thereby drawn to Christ and strengthened in fellowship with him. The institution from the time of the patriarchs which binds man and woman together is here reestablished by God and the marriage partners. It does not turn out to be a coercive relationship but a bond of common service and mutual love.

There is a corresponding relationship between parents and children. Luther does, however, go more deeply into the tensions that arise with the maturing of the younger generation. In fact he described the tensions with his own father in the introduction to *On Monastic Vows* (1521). In that work, his father, Hans Luther, is the perfect representative of the authority that demands obedience and takes the familiar traditions at face value. The son, who had entered the monastery against his father's will, did not, however, recognize the divine creative Word which was calling him to marriage and thereby to obedience toward the plans his father had made for his future. It took a long time before the monk recognized his self-willed striving as damaging to

438. *WA* 12:101.11 (see ibid., 101.27ff., 102.15ff.); *LW* 28:13–14; *WA* 15:419.10–11, 12:101.22; *LW* 28:13.

439. *WA* 12:120.20ff.; *LW* 28:33; *WA* 15:420.11ff.

440. *WA* 12:120.20ff.; *LW* 28:33; *WA* 15:419.32ff., 12:100.23ff.; *LW* 28:12; *WA* 15:418.6ff.; 419.12ff. (here in reliance on the traditional understanding of the sacrament of marriage: faith, offspring, sacrament [see *WA* 26:522.33: ". . . by its total union it represents Christ and the church"]).

the divine and paternal authority; then, by his free choice, he became fully a son again. Again obedience to parents becomes the highest earthly commandment for him; only his office as preacher and the divine task it entails can limit—or possibly nullify—this human duty.[441]

That is a narrow limitation, and one should not be misled. Obedience to parents was much more strongly endorsed by the Lutheran Reformation than it had been previously. It broke through the monasteries' doors and ultimately tore down their walls. By destroying the idea that the spiritual father stood above the physical one, it annulled a false ecclesiastical authority and opened the way for the claim of the divine creative Word.[442]

God's will as creator, which is realized in children through the service of parents, makes the parents into figures that command respect. There is no greater lordship than theirs, because God shares some of his creative lordship with them. Therefore, it is God that children should see in their parents, and not merely flesh and blood. Father and mother "bear God's Word and will." The duty of obedience and the will to obey are originally implanted in every child's heart by the Creator; that is also true among the Turks. Our hearts remind us that they receive life, sustenance, and knowledge from that obedience.[443]

This domestic obedience—not only from family members but from servants and similar dependents—is more valuable than monastic obedience, because it is not bound to a rule but is fulfilled in a personal readiness to serve. Above all, however, it does not earn merit from God; it does what is actually needed. At the most, monastic obedience can be given a temporary significance; it only makes sense for adolescents. Here we catch a glimpse of the position that is also represented in the Augustana (CA 27.15)—that monasteries were originally schools and that they might fulfill such a role in the future. In that case—and this was the general result among evangelical schools—parental authority was transferred to the teachers.[444]

At any rate, God begins his rule over children at home and commissions the parents to exercise it. Just as he brings children forth from parents, he commands those children to obey them. His creative work continues in their upbringing. And as their creation was a work of his goodness, so is their growth to maturity. Rearing children, therefore, ought to be fundamentally different from the coercion and punishment of the "terrifying" government.

441. *WA* 8:573ff.; *LW* 48:331ff. See esp.: "Continence is not commanded but obedience is . . . (*WA* 8:574.36–37; *LW* 48:333).

442. "After faith in God there is nothing greater than obedience to parents" (*WA* 8:623.5–6; *LW* 44:326).

443. *WA* 16:488.8ff., 491.24, 29:3.1ff., 16:512.3ff.

444. *WA* 8:646.39ff., 628.19ff.; *LW* 44:364, 334. See also W. Maurer, "Über den Zusammenhang zwischen kirchlicher Ordnung und christlicher Erziehung" (cited above, n. 196), 60–85.

Unlike princes and lords, parents are not "our Lord God's jailer, judge, and executioner." They exercise a "loving," a "gentle, noble, merry authority." They take nothing from their children but convey goods and property to them and risk everything, even life and limb, for their welfare. It is not by their power to rule and punish that parents resemble God; it is in their caring and preserving activity. They bring the souls of their children to God; they are "apostles, bishops, and pastors to them in proclaiming the gospel to them."[445]

That is not doctrine divorced from life; the being and doing of the parents belong together. Both are ways of their showing "how God feels about humanity" and that "father and mother are just like God in their office toward children. They are a superb illustration of the divine and fatherly heart's attitude toward us." It is not the wrathful punishing God that children see in their father, but the embodiment of divine love. Their obedience is not forced by fear, it is gratitude for such a self-giving love. In the succession of generations, tensions do not arise; rather love becomes the occasion for sacrificial thanksgiving: our parents brought us into the world; God gives us children for us to rear. If we neglect them, we fail in our creative task from God. If we fulfill it, the result is a "blessed marriage" that mirrors the fatherhood of God.[446]

Because the obedience of children is based on God's Word—always in the double sense of creative, life-giving Word and orally attested word—it has its limits at the point where denial of this Word is required. God and Christ desire to be loved more than father, mother, or children. Luther always basically maintained the limits of parental authority, even after being reconciled with his father. For him there is no unconditional, unlimited obedience.[447]

That is the case not only in basic matters of faith but also when a child approaches marriage. Because of the fact that in adults the drive toward sexual union according to God's creative will is irrepressible, early marriage is necessary. Those who do not marry will commit fornication. Marriage should occur "at least by the time a boy is twenty and a girl fifteen to eighteen; that is when they are still in good health and best suited for marriage. Let God worry about how they and their children are to be fed."[448] Under those

---

445. WA 16:501.3ff., 488.19ff., 25ff., 32:303.30–31; LW 21:8; WA 10.2:301.24–25; LW 45:46. On the office of priest in the home, see Maurer, "Über den Zusammenhang," 75 ff.

446. WA 16:489.17ff., 490.28.33, 501.5ff., 503.4ff.

447. WA 27:201.12ff.

448. WA 10.2:300.23ff., 303.31ff.; LW 45:45, 48. In his lectures, Luther frequently discussed the sexual difficulties that resulted from lengthening the time of academic preparation.

conditions it is necessary that the parents give their consent to the marriage and require obedience to their decision.[449]

Here, however, Luther runs into a problem. Each person must decide personally whether or not God has given him the gift of celibacy. And he must be sure that "God has given me this wife with whom I am to remain."[450] The conflict between caring attachment and vitally needed freedom—both in God's name—is resolved within the family circle. As a pastoral counselor, Luther shared that conflict. His fundamental principle stayed the same: a forced marriage is no marriage in God's eyes, and an engagement made under false pretenses is invalid.[451] That is the point at which the parents' authority ends; they do not have the power to force their children to marry unwillingly, nor ought they use the gospel as an excuse for their abuse of power. Paternal power should not be employed arbitrarily or to the detriment of the children; it should benefit and help them. Children, for their part, should make use of their freedom. There comes a time when they should refuse to be coerced. They should ask for help from good friends, call for the authorities, complain to the pastor, and when all else fails, "cry out publicly." If they fail to defend themselves, then the forced marriage is valid and should stand. Above all, the government has a task to fulfill in this regard. It should take care of a mistreated child the way it protects orphans—acting as a substitute for the physical father—and occasionally dissolving a forced marriage.[452]

God's will as creator, which draws the sexes together, must be acknowledged by authorities at home and in the social order. It grants grown children their freedom.

23. LEGAL QUESTIONS RELATING TO MARRIAGE

This brings us to legal questions relating to marriage and family. Luther was deeply involved with such matters before and during 1530, although he

449. *WA* 15:562.12ff., 17.1:9.40ff. In setting the time of readiness for marriage, Luther follows a tradition that we find particularly in southwestern Germany and Switzerland (W. Köhler, *Zürcher Ehegericht und Genfer Konsistorium*, 2 vols., Quellen und Abhandlungen zur Schweizer Reformationsgeschichte 7.10 [Leipzig, 1932–1942]. In Zurich and Basel the limit for both sexes was 19; in Basel by 1532–33 it was 20 for boys and 18 for girls (in 1529 it was 24 and 20 respectively). In Bern it was possible for children of both sexes who did not have guardians to marry at 16, but that was an exception. In general, however, the tendency was to set later age limits than Luther's. In 1534, Brenz established the age at 25 for both sexes; Strassburg set 24 and 20 in 1531 (25 for both sexes in 1565). The development moved away from Luther as it aimed at a stronger limitation on the freedom of youth. An evaluation of the first volume of Köhler's work, from a legal point of view, is Ulrich Stutz, "Zu den ersten Anfängen des evangelischen Eherechtes," *Zeitschrift der Savigny-Stiftung für Rechtsgeschichte* kanonist 22 (1933): 288–331.

450. *WA* 10.2:302.5ff.; *LW* 45:46; *WA* 34.1:53.34–35.

451. "Because the will is a part of it" (*WA* 25:421.18ff.).

452. *WA* 30.3:236ff., esp. 237.3ff., 238.5ff., 239.5ff.; *LW* 46:304, 305, 307, 308.

did not reach many final answers then or later—and those he did reach were more negative than positive. We must investigate the reasons for this caution more closely.

The Augustana also makes few decisions on such questions. The purpose of the theological discussion on the divine institution of marriage in CA 23 and 27 is the rejection of ecclesiastical laws of celibacy. Section 29 of CA 28 maintains that jurisdiction over marriage, even when exercised by bishops, is a temporal right, and that the temporal authority is to attend to it if the spiritual authority breaks down. The preliminary documents contained in the Torgau Articles had gone beyond that position in many instances. In its article 2, the earlier opinion, E, had opposed making the marriage of priests equal to heresy, and had drawn legal conclusions from this. The later and more detailed proposal, A, took up the defense of clerical marriage and based it—as in CA 23.3ff.—on biblical and historical grounds. Article 6 mounted a pointed attack on episcopal powers of jurisdiction; the failure of these powers precipitated secular intervention. Protection for clerical marriage is a consequence of the territorial lords' rights of patronage. The need occasioned by the spiritual courts' poor practice in handling marriage cases of the laity forced the temporal power to defend public order and private consciences.[453]

As is well known, the seventh article of A contains a compromise offer to recognize episcopal jurisdiction under certain circumstances, but power over marriages is not mentioned. On the other hand, proposal C, which was written in Augsburg at the beginning of May and was later used as a basis for CA 28, contains a section titled "De gradibus consanguinitatis".[454] After excluding any jurisdiction by the curia, it endeavors to delimit the competing privileges of spiritual and temporal lords in regard to marriage cases. That material was not taken over by the Augustana. At the point in CA 28.69–75 where the offer of compromise is picked up again in a weakened form, the celibacy issue is indeed mentioned (CA 28.70), but there is no resolution to the problem of regulating marriage law. The claim of CA 28.29 that such jurisdiction is by human right leaves open the question of who judges in marriage cases. The situation remained up in the air in 1530, as it had been earlier in Luther's treatment of legal questions relating to marriage.

The problem that concerned him most deeply was the question of secret engagements and the marriages they spawned. Spiritual and temporal authorities had long been concerned about the fact that young people, without asking their parents' permission, promised to marry each other with or without witnesses, consummated it, and then brought it to light with all its legal implications. Because of their legal foundations—partly German and partly

453. Förstemann 1:94.25ff., 71.12ff., 74.19ff., 78–80; Jacobs 93, 79, 82ff.
454. Förstemann 1:90–91; Jacobs 90.

Roman law—both jurisdictions were forced to recognize those marriages, even though their legal, social, and educational consequences were obvious. Luther waged a passionate battle against them all his life. In addition to the widely lamented consequences just mentioned,[455] Luther was especially concerned about the crises of conscience that occurred because of ambiguities in the relationship. What happened when one of the two partners—usually the husband—disavowed his never fully public promise of marriage and deserted the other party? What was the legal status of the children in such case? How should some subsequent—and indeed public—marriage be judged by God and man? Was a woman who entered such a second marriage still bound before God to her first husband and therefore somehow an adulteress? These questions of conscience had received different—and in Luther's opinion, false—answers in the previous practice of the church.

Should Luther himself give a binding ecclesiastical-legal answer and then enter church history as the creator of an evangelical marriage code? Zwingli must take this sort of credit, because the Zurich Order of Marriage Courts, of May 10, 1525, which goes back to him, "created new law."[456] That was precisely what Luther did not want to do. He dreaded the "example of the Anabaptists" who "had seized such worldly things for themselves" and had thereby become a "world power . . . above emperor and kings."[457] Nor was he interested in destroying the rule of bishops through the reform of marriage laws.[458] His only binding pronouncements on marriage questions were those made as pastor of his Wittenberg congregation. He harbored the hope that if such experiences and measures from different areas could be brought together, through the help of the territorial rulers a new practice in marriage law might be born.

Luther himself does not want to set up any new law, least of all a spiritual right to coerce. He simply wants to advise a pastor who bears the same responsibility for the care of souls that Luther bears in his own parish. In addition, he intends to give advice to princes who are dependent in marriage cases on the pastoral experience of their clergy and who find existing laws to be inadequate. The laws of both church and state have failed, especially canon law. "The canonists talk a lot about marriage, but nothing worthwhile." They burden consciences and violate reason, fairness, and the law. The decrees indeed contain much that is good, especially from the era of the

455. The authorities vainly tried to prevent the practice by making parents responsible for disinheriting such disobedient children.

456. Walter Köhler, *Zürcher Ehegericht* (cited above, n. 449), 1:26.

457. *WA* 30.3:205.27ff., 206.1ff.; *LW* 46:265–66.

458. ". . . no, I am not destroying it, nor have I ever done so. On the contrary, I am strengthening and confirming it "(*WA* 30.3:210.38–39; *LW* 46:272). This is an anticipation of the unity proposal of April 1530; see *WA* 30.3:211.5ff.; *LW* 46:273.

church fathers. The papal decretals, however, are chaotic and full of contradictions; their interpreters leave much to be desired.[459] The situation is not much better with Roman law. Because it is of this world, it provides the proper basis for a marriage code, for marriage is an "outward, worldly thing" subject to worldly authority. But the Roman law also is interpreted variously; it is precisely in questions relating to marriage that its relation to canon law is most shaky. This uncertainty in the law is what made Luther a counselor on marriage cases. Of course he does not want to be the only one. Life produces legal cases that cannot be settled by the book or written code. Then one or two good pious men are required who give advice knowing that they are in danger of missing the "point of the law" and exposing themselves to criticism. That is also the way that Luther would have others view his own counsel in marriage cases.[460]

Let us return to his battle against secret engagements. The needs of conscience mean more to him at this point than the letter of the law; therefore he also assails canon law in this respect.[461] For Luther the freedom to decide according to conscience is not merely a matter of education but also and especially one of law. He was just as much concerned with comforting the individual conscience as he was with the welfare of the whole congregation. In struggling against secret engagements Luther was fighting for the public nature of marriage. He was also putting into practice one of the strongest tendencies of his time, which was increasingly to make the public church ceremony the basis for a proper marriage. For him public marriage suited the dignity of the creator God: "Marriage is a public estate, ordained by God and not something done in a corner or in the dark."[462] Therefore public witnesses were needed at the institution of the marriage. Having been instituted by God, marriage is divine law that must be publicly recognized "because marriage is a public estate which shall be publicly accepted and acknowledged before the congregation." That is the reason that the public element is constitutive of Christian marriage. Therefore the pastor should not recognize a secret engagement as binding; public tribunals should grant legal validity only to public marriage. The temporal authority should pass appropriate laws, forbid secret engagements, and penalize the man who forces such an engagement by intercourse or who annuls a first engagement by means of a second public one. Thus "through criminal laws and God's Word (which

459. WA 30.3:206.16ff., 27ff.; LW 46:266, 267; WA 15:419.11, 30.3:206.19ff., 208.1ff., 248.1ff.; LW 46:266, 268, 319.

460. WA 30.3:205.12ff., 206.22–23, 222.20ff., 223.20ff.; LW 46:265, 266, 287, 288.

461. A thorough and instructive treatment is in Hermann Dörries, "Das beirrte Gewissen als Grenze des Rechts: Eine Juristenpredigt Luthers," in Wort und Stunde, vol. 3 (Göttingen, 1970), 271–326.

462. A "marriage thief" who marries secretly is not honest and dishonors God and God's Word (WA 30.3:219.21ff.; LW 46:283).

confirms such laws)" order is once again brought to matrimonal relationships.[463]

In this case, order is restored through the temporal sword; Luther's pastoral advice is based exclusively on God's Word; he maintained the distinction of the two authorities with difficulty but with precision.[464] He also observed the limits set by Scripture in relation to divorce. The questions that this area involves agitated Luther very profoundly, especially in the troubled time before the outbreak of the Peasants' War, when the failure of the marriage bond became clearly evident.[465] He was criticized at that time for acting irresponsibly in instances of divorce. He defends himself by confessing that he felt the problems of marriage within his congregation as though they were his own. Although himself unmarried, he was able to place himself in the situation of young couples;[466] he cites the example of Christ, who made our need his own. Papal law does not serve to mitigate this need; Scripture alone can do that. According to Scripture, marriage of a divorced person is adultery; anger and conflict are not grounds for separation, nor are the quarrels that often follow a secret marriage. A marriage can be dissolved only on the grounds of impotence or adultery; death dissolves it in any case. Luther maintains this scriptural position and defends it against papal dispensations as well as against the interpretation of the canonists. At the same time he permits the innocent party in a divorce to remarry. In general a divorce ought not be granted frivolously. Those who wish to divorce should stick it out with each other at least a year. The guilty party should ask forgiveness of his partner, and the pastor should urge the innocent party to grant it.[467]

The case of malicious desertion arose for Luther out of social realities rather than Scripture. Here too he wants to limit the possibilities for divorce; the emphasis is on "malice." The departure of a soldier for war or a businessman for travel is not malice. In these cases the spouse must endure the risk of staying alone; death alone separates. There is also no ground for divorce if a partner must leave the country as a punishment or is convicted of a crime; those married must suffer for and with each other. But if a spouse—usually it would be the husband—actually breaks the marriage and deserts wife and child, then the authorities should declare the forsaken partner divorced after a publicly specified period and make it possible for him or her to remarry. The fugitive scoundrel, however, should be handed over to the

463. *WA* 30.3:207.15ff., 217.18ff., 224.3ff.; *LW* 46:268, 281, 289.
464. *WA* 30.3:206.6ff.; *LW* 46:266.
465. The following is from the afternoon sermon of May 8, 1524 (*WA* 15:558–62).
466. "I do not need a wife, but for the sake of others I am bound to feel as if I were a young boy or girl" (*WA* 15:562.2ff.).
467. *WA* 30.3:216.3ff., 214.25–215.13, 241.2–242.8; *LW* 46:279, 277–78, 310–12.

hangman.[468] In these cases too, Luther's advice, which encourages and defends conjugal love, can include the punitive wrath of government.

24. ECCLESIASTICAL ORDER: TEXTS

Ecclesiastical order is treated specifically in the second half of the Augustana. The basics and many details occur in CA 28 from section 30 on; we will continue here with the analysis begun earlier (see above, chap. 10). Other individual questions are treated elsewhere—fasting in CA 26 ("De discrimine ciborum"); liturgical orders in CA 22, 24, and 25; and questions on the marriage of priests in CA 23 and 27. In the first half of the Confession we find basic considerations on church order, in CA 7 and 15; on special questions of worship, in CA 11 and 12; and on the right to preach, in CA 14. We will begin by examining the relevant articles in relation to their textual histories.

Luther's *Confession Concerning Christ's Supper* from 1528 gives only indirect suggestions in this regard. The basic principle of the Reformation—that in Christianity everything depends on justifying faith—is not consistently applied to questions of worship; it is used only sporadically. Everything related to indulgences is to be abolished, especially masses for the dead. It is worth noting in that connection that Luther proposes a change in extreme unction and develops approaches for an evangelical funeral service. He allows images, bells, mass vestments, church ornamentation, altar candles, and the like; in a postscript he recommends the retention of private confession in order to intensify the comforting power of forgiveness. Among the questions on worship, ordering the priestly office is only mentioned in passing.[469] The sequence constantly makes it clear that for Luther, even questions of order belong to the confession of faith; they are to be addressed from the point of view of justifying faith.

The Schwabach Articles follow Luther's confession almost word for word in relation to private confession (Schwab. 11). While they, like Luther, focus on the comfort of forgiveness, they emphasize more strongly that confession must be free. Consciences should no more be forced in this matter than in the other sacraments or in preaching. In Na 10 and CA 11, this free aspect will no longer be mentioned. But another theme of freedom does emerge that Luther did not address in his Confession of 1528 and that Schwab. 11 mentions only in a concluding sentence: no one ought to be forced to enumerate all his or her individual sins in private confession. The textual development makes it easy to observe how the necessity for spiritual freedom, pastorally established

468. *WA* 30.3:242.9–244.17; *LW* 46:312–15.
469. *WA* 26:507.28ff., 508.1ff., 17ff., 509.9ff., 507.17ff., 504.25, 33ff.; *LW* 37:369, 370, 371, 368, 364.

in Luther's confession from the depths of the experience of salvation, and made valid for all areas of worship life by Schwab. 11, fades away in the later versions of CA 11. Today, anyone reading the article out of its historical context would scarcely imagine the role themes of freedom played in its composition.

In reference to CA 14 it should be noted that this article on order in the church, which includes the activity of the pastoral office, was composed after the completion of Na, placing it in the first days of June. It does not pick up what Luther had written on the office of the Word and its ordering in his Confession of 1528.[470]

Article 15 of the Augustana evolved far beyond its preliminary stage in Schwab. 17. It develops the principle Luther stated many times (although not specifically in his Confession of 1528): that in matters of church order, God's word must be the supreme rule, but that freedom should reign otherwise.[471] It adds the Pauline principle of forbearing the weak, with which Luther had stilled the Wittenberg disturbance of 1522 and on which he based activity within the new evangelical church.

In reformulating Na 13 (Ca 15), Melanchthon abolished the outline provided him by Schwab. 17. He turned the principle of superiority of God's Word in all questions of order into a negative and then made it into a weapon: all human statutes to which the church ascribes merit are un-Christian and injure Christ's honor and merit. Article 13 of Na illustrates the application of this principle to traditional orders. He eliminates the one through whose observance people would justify themselves before God. But the others, which support the peace and unity of Christians—Melanchthon is thinking particularly of church festivals—should be kept in freedom without raising the claim of merit before God.[472]

The final version of CA 15 returns to primary emphasis on the positive significance of church order and goes back to Schwab. 17 and Na 13 in its demand for peace and unity. The principle of freedom of conscience is picked up again from Schwab. 17, adding it to Na 13. In accordance with Na 13, section 3 sets forth clearly the contradiction between a self-seeking striving for merit that tries to make satisfaction on its own through ritual acts and a justifying faith. In this connection it picks up from Na 13 the catalogue of particularly dubious ordinances and acts.

In all of that discussion, CA 15 has already enumerated the grievances that will be treated in the "disputed articles." Section 30 of CA 28 will bring up

470. *WA* 26:504.31–35; *LW* 37:364.

471. On liturgical freedom, see Luther's confession (*WA* 26:509.9–12: *LW* 37:371–72).

472. The distinction between church ordinances that "have been instituted for the sake of good order and harmony" and those that require obedience as a work of satisfaction is taken over by Na 13 from the *Instructions for the Visitors* (*WA* 26:222.19ff., 223.18ff.; *LW* 40:298, 299).

the questions deferred here, one after the other. We will follow this lead and add problems raised in related articles, to the extent that they are mentioned in preliminary stages of the text.

There are only a few traces of the section CA 28.30–68 present before the beginning of the Augsburg diet. The preliminary work for CA 28 in the Torgau Articles (Torg. E and A) says as little about the questions touched upon in the Confession as does the elaborated document C from the beginning of May in Augsburg. In contrast, the first article of A, "On Human Teaching and Human Order,"[473] is a preparatory document for CA 28.30–68. Here the elector of Saxony defends himself against the charge that his territorial church has become schismatic (107.23–108.40), maintaining that the observance of human law could not disrupt the unity of the church.[474]

This document, however, does contrast human ordinance with the divine Word. The doctrine of justification is developed in great detail (108.47–109.19). Measured by that standard, such human efforts are a "public blasphemy and totally opposed to the holy gospel"—criticisms similar to those raised by CA 28.35ff.[475] The alleged divine authority of human statements is combated with the same decisiveness we have found in CA 15 and will discover in CA 28.34ff. and 50ff. Taken together, the commentaries on "human teaching and human order" in this document constitute the source for the article in its final form.

The congruity, however, extends beyond the fundamentals to practical applications. The ordinances by which people erroneously hope to achieve grace and forgiveness are enumerated by Torg. A in almost the same sequence as CA 28.37, 39: "fasting, distinctions in food and clothing, special holidays (feast days), singing, pilgrimages, and the like" (108.44–45). These ordinances are grouped under the rubric "intermediate things," and obtain a positive value as occasions for bodily exercise and for hearing and learning God's Word (109.20–24). These concepts in Torg. A are specifically Melanchthonian in character. The "preceptor of Germany" was always mindful of the necessity for education of the people. We are reminded of the debate he had with Luther over the possibility of obedient submission to episcopal authority (above, pp. 74–75).

In Na 28, Melanchthon uses what his prince brought forward in self-defense and in justification of his visitations, to question episcopal power. He is interested in this basic question: By what right can bishops—they appear here, as in late medieval episcopalism, as the only body with this power—set

473. Förstemann 1:69–74; Jacobs 76–79; reprinted in *BS* 107–9, to which the citations in parentheses in the text refer.
474. Page 37 above shows that this is an anticipation of CA 7, sec. 3.
475. Even stronger in Na (Kolde 29.32–36; Reu 282).

up ecclesiastical ordinances and then legally enforce them?[476] The answer, as in Torg. A, is that such assertions cannot be made in opposition to the gospel (34) because that would not allow those human ecclesiastical measures to be effective (35–36).[477] These are the same programmatic demands that were raised in Na 13 (for CA 15)—agreeing partly even in the way they are formulated. We may assume that the statements in both parts of the growing Augustana had been coordinated in May and that the reworking of Schwab. 17 into Na 13 was therefore going on around this time. The same points are once again present in CA 28.10–52, with section 51 citing the principle of freedom in the gospel according to Gal. 5:1.[478]

The demands raised here are fundamental to all articles of the Augustana that deal with questions of order. They are also of particular relevance in that they provide the theological connection with CA 15, thus bringing congruity to the two parts of the Confession. Article 28 will show their significance for individual problems of order.

In this context, fasting is mentioned particularly often (secs. 37, 39, 41, 44), always, however, in connection with other canonical rules and without specific theological explication. It is treated in a special article ("On the Distinction of Foods," CA 26).

The prehistory of this article goes back to the *Instructions for the Visitors* of 1528. Fasting that lays claim to earning merit must stop—that demand was made as a result of the visitations. One should not, however, consider oneself to be evangelical because one eats meat on Fridays; one is a Christian through fear of God and moral discipline. Furthermore the principle of consideration for the weak also applies: one should not break a fast if that would violate love. Thus there is no absolute prohibition of fasts. On the contrary, the *Instructions* reckons with the possibility that the elector will once again introduce the traditional usage, although only as temporal law, as an "ordinance for peace and love."[479]

The transitional phase of the preceding year had already been worked through by March and April of 1530 as preparations for the diet were being made in the electoral residence at Torgau. First came the bold statement that since the pope and the clergy themselves had not observed fasts, the temporal authorities should leave it alone. Then, however, there was a careful justification for the decline of the old usage: fasts had no meritorious significance; the

476. CA 28.30 (Kolde 29.21ff.; Reu 280). The sections of the article are cited in the following text; Na (according to Kolde) is cited only at points where there are substantial variations from CA.

477. The charge of relapsing into Old Testament legalism was leveled especially in connection with the laws on fasting, and it is in fact more detailed in secs. 39–41 than in Na (Kolde 30.3–5; Reu 284).

478. Na does not have the formulation of justification found in sec. 52.

479. *WA* 26:222.16., 223.20.30ff., 38ff.; *LW* 40:298, 299.

elector had not forced their observance; dropping them is not heresy (canon law itself does not consider it necessary to observe them); in the course of history many rules for fasting had outlived their usefulness.[480]

In contrast to this pragmatic apologetic, CA 26 (as well as its preliminary stage in Na 23)[481] gives more emphasis to principles. It opposes attributing merit to ceremonies—and the consequent obscuring of the doctrine of justification—even more specifically than CA 28 does.[482] The obscuring of justification is mirrored in the obscuring of the divine commandments, which are replaced by human rules, and in the neglect of the divine vocation in family and government. All of that brings with it danger for the Christian conscience and an end to its liberty; Gerson and Augustine, indeed the church fathers as a whole, are summoned as witnesses to that fact. The theological argument is rounded off by a justification for the Protestant polemic and a detailed proof from Scripture. Its basic outline is already formulated in Na 23; CA 26 simply adds exegetical, historical, and rhetorical material.[483]

It is surprising to see how little Melanchthon has taken fasting practices into account in CA 26. At the end of Na, he lists the principles that congregations of Electoral Saxony continued to follow as "serviceable for an orderly life in the church."[484] A supplement in the final version (secs. 30–39), however, once again takes up objections of the opponents, and considerations of a practical and pastoral nature come to the fore: self-chosen mortifications have indeed been rooted out of the congregations, but following the cross of Christ is taught and practiced in its stead (secs. 30–32). Certain ascetic practices have been discontinued; instead the body is to be disciplined through daily work. At the same time, there is still room for such traditional ascetic practice, although it ought not be overvalued (secs. 33–39). Here again we hear Melanchthon the teacher of the masses, who shrinks from every radical break with the past.

Along with fasting, holy days are often mentioned, because they were frequently observed through fasting.[485] It is in connection with the ordinances for holidays that we begin to encounter concrete fasting practices and prescriptions. The first regulation of these practices occurred in the *Instruc-*

480. Torg. E 8 (Förstemann 1:97; Jabobs 95), Torg. A 1 (*BS* 108.44, 109.20ff.; Jacobs 77, 78).

481. Printed in *BS* 100–107 and cited here below.

482. It is more explicit in CA 26.4–7, than in Na (101.30–33). Section 7 deals with the doctrine of repentance from which the understanding of fasting arises. These sections replace the passage in Na (101.32–36) where the opponents are taken to task. That material reappears in secs. 18–21 in another form.

483. Secs. 8–11; Na, 102.33–103.30. Secs. 12–13, 16–17, 42–45; Na, 101.30–102.33, 101.36–37, 106.36–38. Secs. 18–21, 22–29; Na, 104.33–35, 104.35–105.27.

484. Mentioned explicitly are canticles and festivals, and in the final version of sec. 40, the order of lessons; fasting does not appear (secs. 40–41; Na, 106.32–35).

485. When that is the case they have a much more profound influence on daily life and work than when they are marked by special liturgical pageantry.

tions for the Visitors as a part of the visitation process. It made Sunday a legal holiday in Saxony.[486] Manual labor was permitted outside the hours of worship. Because of its teaching value, the sequence of pericopes was to be retained. Un-Christian elements were to be purged from the liturgy. If holidays in addition to Sunday were observed, that was a matter for each congregation to arrange according to its custom. Local pastors should not quarrel over them, nor should they do away with all special services. A table of festivals, which would include some biblical saints as well as days for the apostles and Mary, was recommended, although the details were left open. The dominical festivals—including January 1 and 6 (Circumcision and Epiphany)—were to be retained. In accordance with the apostolic pattern, local customs and complete freedom should reign in all things; the principle of consideration for the weak should also be observed. The only worship services that should cease are those to which some power of satisfaction was being attributed.[487]

The confessional development would come back repeatedly for details from this Saxon holiday ordinance, which also contained the elements of a worship manual. It emphasized the danger that the intensive cultic preoccupation of the late medieval church—especially holidays, singing, pilgrimage, and the like—could lead to human efforts' becoming a means of salvation. In contrast, the intention of evangelical holidays and worship is "for the people to learn and know when they are to gather for worship or perform bodily exercise so that they will thereby become more capable of hearing and learning God's word."[488] It is again from this pedagogical point of view that the introduction of the German chorale is justified; nevertheless, Latin hymns should also be sung as practice for the youth.[489]

Article 28 of CA and the corresponding passages of Na do not simply build on the holiday ordinances introduced in Saxony; instead they look at the whole complex in the light of the question whether the church, through its bishops, has the power to create such ordinances and to make their observance binding for salvation (CA 28.30). To the extent that this question is answered negatively, individual practices are eradicated. The bishops have no right to introduce new ceremonies and ordinances, holidays and fasts.[490] It is wrong to brand physical work on Sundays and holidays or the eating of certain foods as mortal sins (CA 28.41). Such measures introduce servitude into the church, and that contradicts Christian freedom. Clever canonists

---

486. On the Sunday service, see below, pp. 183–84.
487. *WA* 26:222.22ff.; *LW* 40:298.
488. Torg. A 1 (*BS* 108.45, 109.22ff.; Jacobs 77, 78).
489. Torg. A 10 (Förstemann 1:83; Jacobs 85); CA 24, sec. 2. On the Sunday service, see below, pp. 183–84.
490. CA 28.37, 26.2 (Kolde 29.22–23; *BS* 100.23).

have deduced the whole cultic legalism from Old Testament worship in the temple and have constructed a tradition that is supposed to run from the Levitical priesthood through the apostles right down to the bishops (CA 28.39; Kolde 30.4–5). The Augustana makes a radical break with this Judaizing of holidays and worship; it extends the distinction between law and gospel to cultic questions as well.

Therefore it also makes a distinction between Sabbath and Sunday. And the way it draws implications from that for church law is a theological contribution unique to Melanchthon.[491] Canonists had attributed the transition from the Decalogue's Sabbath to Sunday to the authority of the church and had therefore concluded that the bishops and the pope had power over church law. Melanchthon based the introduction of Sunday on the elimination of the Old Testament ceremonial law, including the cultic regulations in the Decalogue.[492] It was the authority not of the church, therefore, but of the word of God that had asserted itself in this change.[493] For that reason, Christian freedom still held true in relation to the hallowing of Sunday.

Melanchthon tied basic considerations on ecclesiastical law to these statements (in reliance on the correspondence with Luther then in progress).[494] There were canonists who did not base the introduction of Sunday strictly on divine law but who permitted relaxations for practical reasons and who mitigated the rigor of the law. Such an application of the Aristotelian doctrine of fairness (*aequitas*) to holiday observances is rejected by CA 28.64: if they are instituted by God, they cannot be changed by human authority; that is no way for a conscience bound to God to find comfort.

At this point, sections 65–68 of the final version add a discussion that involves the whole area of ecclesiastical order. Melanchthon adapted it from Erasmus.[495] The historical survey shows that many once-valid ecclesiastical orders have withered in the course of time and have lost their binding character. For example, no one follows the apostolic council's prohibition against the eating of blood any more; the apostles themselves refused to burden consciences permanently with it. The intent of the gospel to stimulate freedom has constantly demonstrated its power. The New Testament limited not only the validity of church laws in time, but also their strictness. The laws grow old and new customs make them lose their power. They are of human

491. First in Na (Kolde 29.29–32, 31.3–10; Reu 282, 286). And building on that, CA 28.57–64.

492. See also the explanation of the Third Commandment in Luther's Large and Small Catechisms.

493. The precedence of Scripture over church is clearly emphasized in the Latin version of sec. 59.

494. Secs. 64–68; sec. 64 is foreshadowed in Na (Kolde 31.8–10; Reu 286). Sections 65–68 were conceived only during the final editing.

495. W. Maurer, *Der junge Melanchthon* (cited above, n. 49), 2:308ff.

origin and subject to the transitoriness of everything human. That knowledge need not generate a historical relativism, as it did with Erasmus. It can also arise, as it does here in CA 28.65–68, from belief in the eternal validity and the liberating action of the Word of God.

The ordering of worship, naturally, played a role in the discussions of Sunday and festival days, because of the services to be held on them. The same is true of the articles that treat the Lord's Supper and confession (CA 22, 24, 25), so they must be examined for the elements of church order they contain.

Article 25 ("Confession") has the least to be said about it. Among the "disputed articles," this is the one that limits itself most strictly to theological considerations and conforms so closely to CA 11 and 12 that its independent existence can only be explained by the diverse origins of the two sections of the CA. To the extent that it deals at all with practice, CA 25 simply describes how evangelical pastors administer confession and absolution. Such information would be significant for church law only if the legal basis for these procedures was given. That is not the case in the final text, although it is mentioned in the preparatory documents. The elector, according to the first advisory draft, composed while he was still in Wittenberg,[496] declared his consent to having the coming diet—it was considered to be like a national assembly—uphold the obligation of confession and absolution at least before the Easter communion, a requirement in force since 1215. At the same time he argued for dropping the demand that the Fourth Lateran Council had made regarding a complete enumeration of sins. The opinion written fourteen days later in Torgau[497] made the territorial prince the lawgiver for administration of the sacraments, although it traced the declaration of absolution back to Christ's own command.[498] Church order, focused on the inmost area of forgiveness and faith, appears to be an ordinance of territorial government. That is nowhere as clearly evident in the Augustana as it is here.

In CA 22 administration of the Lord's Supper in both kinds, a matter to be regulated by church law, is equally clearly traced back to Christ's command and not to human initiative, whether temporal or spiritual (sec. 1). The situation is the same in the preparatory documents. The elector's role is only protective and permissive. He cannot agree that the approaching diet "should endorse only one kind"; until then he will tolerate distribution of both kinds.[499] This reticence of the territorial prince corresponds to the caution

496. Torg. E 7 (Förstemann 1:97; Jacobs 95).
497. Torg. A 5 (*BS* 97–98; Jacobs 81–82).
498. *BS* 97.39–43. We have just seen that this self-image of the elector as emergency bishop recedes entirely from the final version of CA 25.
499. Torg. E 1 (corresponding to E 3 in relation to private masses). Torg. A 3 abridges but maintains the essence of E 1; on Torg. 4, see below, p. 183.

shown in Saxony regarding the sacramental question since the visitations. In the *Instructions for the Visitors*, not one church ordinance is promulgated, as it might have been in the name of the territorial prince. Rather, the visitors give the ministers pastoral suggestions regarding the knotty issues of administering the sacraments.[500] This method corresponds to Luther's consistent attitude, which took a multitude of individual pastoral decisions and gradually fashioned them into the elements of a church order to which he then ascribed a temporary validity, always open to correction.[501]

In the case of worship services, that means the denial of any generally binding regulation regarding distribution in both kinds. The only binding rule—for the pastor—is that, on the basis of Holy Scripture, both kinds are taught and confessed. There is no compulsion at all, however, for the hearers; that would be "unfriendly, indeed un-Christian." Acceptance of the truth that is proclaimed should be their own free decision. As long as they do not accept it, the pastor may offer them the Sacrament in one kind. It is better to do that than to have these "weak ones" in the faith later confess the reception of both kinds as "sin" or to see them conscience-stricken because they do not dare to receive only one kind. Order, although it can cite the mandate of Christ, bows to conscience, even when conscience is in error. Nor is the pastor bound to this order in his administration of the Sacrament. Although the doctrine is not to be altered, he must adapt his practice to individual consciences. He must treat those who have received the doctrine in faith differently from those weak persons whose consciences still vacillate. The latter are further to be distinguished from stiff-necked people who want nothing at all to do with the Sacrament and who therefore should not have it offered to them. The pastor is free to make his own conscientious decisions in dealing with these three groups. Church order does not relieve him of this task, nor does it merely empower him; it forces him. Order demands that he exercise his spiritual freedom.

This freedom based on the *Instructions* is confirmed in the completed Confession. For that reason the elector hesitates to have the diet force out Communion in one kind.[502] For the same reason, CA 22 is content to develop the mandate of Christ theologically, rejecting any force against those whose consciences are bound by this mandate and who therefore demand that the

---

500. In looking back on their activity, they speak of themselves in the first person: "Accordingly we have instructed pastors and preachers to proclaim this teaching of the gospel concerning both kinds to everyone" (*WA* 26:214.10–11; *LW* 40:289). They repeat these instructions, with the reservation that they "be tried until the Holy Spirit leads us to a better understanding"; thus, they are not ultimately binding ordinances. For the following: *WA* 26:214.28–217.27; *LW* 290–93.

501. See the section on "Christian Freedom" in the *Instructions*, esp. *WA* 26:227.40ff., 228.7ff.; *LW* 40:304.

502. Torg. E 1 (Förstemann 1:93–94; Jacobs 92).

cup be offered to them (sec. 11). The article contains only one legal point; it urges the elimination of processions because the bread and wine belong together (sec. 12). Parading the tabernacle contradicts the intent of Christ's institution.

The ban on private masses—CA 24.13 calls them "bought masses" and "masses in a corner"—was a deeper intervention in the religious life of the waning Middle Ages; the disappearance of mass priests and the redirection of mass endowments precipitated vast changes in social life. The *Instructions* had simply directed, "Memorial masses and other paid masses shall no longer be held," basing the ban on the saving work of Christ and on the intent of his institution.[503] Christian government appealed to Holy Scripture in order to set up binding church orders. It took responsibility for this decision before emperor and empire.

The defense was made by showing the meaning and effect of this renewal on the way the evangelical worship service is performed:[504] Almost all the customary ceremonies are continued. The only difference is the insertion of chorales in German, because all services of worship are to be edifying. Members of the diet who held to the old religion are asked especially to note the reverent attitude with which evangelical congregations approach the mass. That attitude is awakened and strengthened by means of an examination before Communion, "for none are admitted unless they are first heard and examined."[505] In this way a theological bond is forged with CA 25 ("Confession") and the ordering of the preaching mass is traced back to the basic theological theme of the Augustana—God's justifying action through Christ.

The ordering of worship for the preaching mass serves the piety of the congregation, which requires complete freedom. Therefore the Sacrament of the Altar is offered every Sunday, but only to those who sincerely desire to commune.[506] The second draft (A) of the Torgau Articles[507] says that the elector is the one who sees to it that these preaching masses are provided. He does not thereby institute them; Christ himself did that for those who are one in faith and reverence for the sacramental gift of salvation. The intervention of earthly authority in this spiritual event is not, therefore, in order to regiment the spontaneity of faith. It intends only to remove the hindrances that have heretofore stood in the way, thus providing the external prerequisites for fulfilling Christ's command. Church orders, no matter from what

503. *WA* 26:224.3ff.; *LW* 40:299.
504. CA 24.1–9. Na (*BS* 97) only hints (*BS* 97.2–3) thematically at this justification for the action which is so fully presented in the final version.
505. Sec. 6; shorter in the German version.
506. CA 24.34 (*BS* 96.22ff.; *BC* 60).
507. Torg. A 4 (*BS* 96.38ff.; Jacobs 79).

human jurisdiction they arise, are justified only to the extent that they serve the spiritual activity in worship.

The same holds true for the legal regulations regarding the pastoral office which are contested in the "disputed articles." That is less the case in CA 27 ("Monastic Vows") than elsewhere. Here the elector begins by trying to separate himself from any responsibility, treating monasticism as a purely private matter.[508] But it was not possible to maintain this distance in the face of the historical significance of monastic life and the social and ecclesiastical consequences of monks' leaving the monasteries. At the very least the territorial prince had to arm himself against the diet's question of why he had not been concerned about preventing the downfall of a revered institution that had frequently been sanctioned by imperial law. The elector chose to justify his action by means of a full-scale critique of monasticism in general. As in all the articles that treat questions of order, he condemns the meritorious character of monastic asceticism with arguments from CA 23; by opposing the selling of masses in CA 24, he condemns the necessity of monasteries' assuring their economic status through mass stipends.

This polemic against a dying institution provides no bridge to the new church orders required by life in the evangelical territorial churches. Article 27 is important, nevertheless, because here the intrinsic value of these orders is established with respect to temporal and spiritual authority at the same time that their bond with canon law is maintained. Monasticism understood itself, in contrast to temporal authority and parish clergy, as the estate of Christian perfection. This contempt of God-given callings, this flight from the world (CA 27.13, 52–60) has now led to the self-dissolution of monasticism; it indirectly testifies to the necessity of a political[509] and ecclesiastical reordering. The decision of the temporal ruler to take an independent course and his distanced attitude toward monasticism take account of this situation.

The second important reference for the establishment of church order occurs in the way CA 27 uses monasticism to illustrate the proper and original intention of canon law. In the course of history the monks wandered further and further from it, to the consternation of all right-thinking people in Christendom. The vows of novices, especially, were so highly "talked up" that real damage was done to the principle of *aequitas*, a principle characteristic of canon law and endorsed by the popes. The result was that the logic of legal order, which subordinates lower law to higher, was destroyed; human order was preferred to the command of Christ.[510]

508. Torg. E 6 (Förstemann 1:96–97; Jacobs 94); A 8 (*BS* 110.25–28; Jacobs 84–85); Na (Kolde 23.2–6; Reu 250, 252).

509. On CA 27.55 (supplement to the final Latin version), see the discussion on CA 16 above, p. 78ff.

510. CA 27.9 (see Na [Kolde 23.22ff.; Reu 254]), CA 27.25, 31–33, 23.

This positive evaluation of canon law, found more frequently in CA 27 than elsewhere in the Augustana, is at first glance surprising.[511] It is of particular importance for our investigation of church order, not only because it is a means for maintaining a broad continuity of legal tradition but also because it assures the preservation of important legal foundations. Church order cannot establish itself by force; that is demonstrated by the battle against requiring oaths and celibacy. It must maintain the principles of equity and love and then adjust itself to changing historical circumstances. And ultimately it must recognize the divine Word of command as its final authority.

Measured by this standard, the battle against required celibacy in CA 23 ("The Marriage of Priests") also acquires a positive significance. We have already heard the basis for it, drawn out of the nature of marriage. We need to keep in mind that for the medieval church, celibacy had become primarily a disciplinary question, that is, a question of law. Article 23 thus joins previous critics of the church in complaining about the decline of discipline among unmarried clergy.[512] The revolt of priests in 1075 against the Gregorian ban on marriage is cited at every stage of the text's development. That point reveals something of the resentment Germans felt against domination by the Curia and against those who despised the divine mandate sanctioning marriage (secs. 4–9).[513]

The chief offense of the Roman legislation on celibacy is that God's command is annulled by human law. Article 23 prescribes no new discipline for evangelical pastors. Instead, the article uses theological arguments[514] to insure that there will be room for fulfilling the divine command. Within that space everything is based on freedom. No new marriage laws are promulgated. The pastors themselves have taken the initiative. In order to avoid previous offenses they have used preaching to fight for permission to marry (secs. 3, 9). The evangelical princes have granted this permission to pastors and preachers, and they now expect the emperor to confirm it.[515] The ending of celibacy and the freedom of priests to marry are—also because of their consequences for family law—matters for imperial decision. Emperor and princes are defenders of moral law; they must protect public morality against transgressions by the celibate. The emperor is the guardian of the law in Christendom, canon law as well as temporal law. He must restore the original church law that permits the marriage of priests. The bloody persecution of

---

511. There were occurrences elsewhere in the period around 1530, as I have shown in "Reste des Kanonischen Rechts" (cited above, n. 122).

512. Secs. 1–2. See Na (Kolde 17.31ff.; Reu 212).

513. Secs. 12–13; Na (Kolde 18.13–21; Reu 214); Torg. A 1, expanded from Torg. E 2 (Förstemann 1:74, 94; Jacobs 79, 93).

514. From Scripture (secs. 4–9) and tradition (secs. 10–13).

515. Secs. 14–23. The emperor is mentioned explicitly only in the German version of sec. 14—the version read before the diet.

married clergy must cease. Originally church law required only that they be suspended from their ecclesiastical office, but now they are declared heretics, stripped of their rights, and treated accordingly.

Emperor and diet should develop a new set of regulations for pastors, a code that also would apply in all the territories of the empire. It would annul canon law at decisive points. It would assure pastors the right to marry and bind them to the usual civil laws. Thus it would create no new ecclesiastical order. Instead, pastors would be subject to territorial laws that had imperial sanction—a situation that continues through the next centuries. That relationship refers not only to their specifically spiritual tasks and duties but includes their entire life as citizens. Basically their life becomes indistinguishable from that of all other subjects. Thus the elimination of celibacy had legal consequences beyond those of marriage and family. Even though the emperor did not do what CA 23 desired, political and religious armistices and ultimately the Peace of Augsburg in 1555 gave back to the pastors the public and legal standing that at first appeared to be traded away by the elimination of celibacy.

The Augustana gives particular attention to the public and legal standing of pastors in article 14, and to that extent this article belongs with the sections on ecclesiastical order, most of which are located in the "disputed articles." It also brings to focus the problems that arise from the specifically ecclesiastical character of these orders. They are established for the church with its festivals, worship services, and ministers, but at the same time they are legitimated by temporal government through specific legislation or by passive tolerance and recognition. The pastor is both object and executive instrument of these orders. According to CA 14, pastors are rightly called (*rite vocatus*), and within the role of "regular call," they are to "teach publicly." Both the acceptance of this call and exercise of the teaching office presuppose ecclesiastical order. In accepting the call, the pastor is in a passive role, but the teaching function involves a specific way of acting in public. The phraseology of CA 14 does not tell us just how these things happen and what consequences they have for the understanding of church order. This is where commentary is indispensable. We will begin by discussing the composition of CA 14 and its place within the total structure of the Augustana.

This is among the articles that were not written until June. It was not in the Latin text that the Nürnberg delegates received for scrutiny on May 31, 1530, and copied for transmission to their town council on June 3; nor was it available to Jerome Baumgartner for the translation (Na) he worked on between June 10 and 14. He simply left out article 14 in the numbering, as the original had done, and skipped from 13 to 15. That is an indication that article 14 was contemplated by the end of May but was not yet beyond the drafting stage. Its final formulation thus occurs in the first half of June; it is present in Nb.[516]

Its title, picking up the first key words in the text, relates the article to questions of order. "Order in the Church," *Ordo ecclesiasticus*, however, does not refer to the usual ranks of spiritual office that were fixed by canon law, nor does it point to ordination in the sense of an action of installation or consecration. It pays particular attention to the personal dimension of church order—article 15 ("Church Usages") treats questions of practice—but even then it does not present the entire range; it formulates only two basic conditions: that ecclesiastical office is a public office, and that its exercise is tied to a public call.[517]

In Na, the present article 14 was to have been placed between CA 15 and CA 16; the call to an office was thus to have been subsumed under human ordinances in the church. The fact that it was finally placed ahead of those articles does not imply that as a divine call, it is excepted from human ordering (as though divine law were operating here as a factor in human ordering). Instead, it asserts only that human ordinances regarding ceremonies have to serve ordered relationships of a personal nature. False emphases on material or juridical considerations are thus excluded.

As the authors and editors inserted the later CA 14, they certainly had in mind its relationship to CA 5. That article, of course, bears the inclusive title "The Office of the Ministry" and, although it focuses on the spiritual faith-engendering function of that office (see above, p. 36), it also includes the call to it. In CA 14, this preliminary treatment is expanded into a separate article that is placed in the context of orders. Thus a frequently demonstrated basic orientation of the Augustana becomes evident: in the course of salvation, divine events and human concerns for order should certainly meet, just as God and humanity belong together; but they also should be separated from each other like heaven and earth. All the evangelical confessors at Augsburg, including Melanchthon and Brueck, agreed on that basic orientation. The demand for a proper call (*rite vocatus*) arises out of a doctrine of office that is theologically based, and CA 14 must therefore be treated in the context of church order.

516. We can only guess at the reason for this delay. The article was of great juridical importance. It guaranteed to the emperor and the empire that evangelical territorial churches would be well ordered. For that reason it is formulated concisely—and carefully. That would not be accomplished quickly, and it reveals the legal art that we could most readily expect from Chancellor Brueck.

517. It is synonymous here with "church government"—which shares its limitations—and must be strictly distinguished from the "ecclesiastical power" discussed in CA 28.

25. THE CALL TO THE OFFICE OF PREACHING
AND PUBLIC PROCLAMATION

In his enumeration of the "holy orders and true religious institutions established by God,"[518] Luther places the "office of priest" first among the three estates and includes in it "all who are engaged in the clerical office or ministry of the Word . . . , such as those who preach, administer sacraments, supervise the common chest, sextons and messengers or servants who serve such persons." Thus, in contrast to CA 14 and CA 5, here the office is not restricted to proclamation of the Word; it includes services of love and helpfulness. Although this broadening of the preaching office is not particularly emphasized in the Augustana, it is a part of the Confession's basic orientation.

Our task is not, however, to start from the empirical data but to inquire after the basic orientation. Article 5 puts special emphasis on the faith-engendering power and effect of the office. In that respect CA 14 is identical; the two articles ought not to be separated. Rather, everything that pertains to order in CA 14 is deeply rooted in the spiritual. Neither the proper call nor the public proclamation can be correctly understood if they are not derived from the rootstock of all churchly life, where Word, Spirit, and faith play their divine role.

Even before his stay at the Coburg, as Luther busied himself with preparatory work on his *Exhortation to All Clergy Assembled at Augsburg,* he set out an agenda for the church of Christ that began with an "upright office of preaching where God's holy Word is diligently proclaimed and taught according to a pure Christian understanding of it, without additions."[519]

Just as the office depends on the Word, so the church depends on the office. Luther finds the connection between office and Word first in absolution and then in teaching. The consolation of forgiveness comes about through the preaching office; here Word and office become one. The same thing happens, albeit in a process of learning and believing perception, in the application of the "key of teaching." The "general preaching office" serves, in a comprehensive sense, "to proclaim the opening of the gates of heaven to all." The minister of the Word is none other than a voice sounding clearly and consistently from the apostles through their successors to the present day.[520]

Before reflecting on the origin, succession, and activity of the office of the Word, one must be clear about this identification which it has with the effective divine Word of salvation. Everything institutional in worship and

518. Confession of 1528 (*WA* 26:504.30ff.; *LW* 37:364).
519. *WA* 30.2:249.
520. Ibid., 453.20–24, 491.20–22, 492.1–3; *LW* 40:357–58; *WA* 31.2:425.15–20. See Isa. 52:8.

church order that is connected with the pastoral office has its roots in the Word and serves that Word;[521] the remarkable freedom, so offensive to all legalistic Christianity, with which the Lutheran church of the Word treats every question of order and of law finds its basis in the divine depths from which the Word of salvation springs. Even the difference between the institutional office and the general priesthood of all believers is to be measured against that dimension of depth. If the office is identified with God's testimony to himself in his Word, then the voice of the congregation equals the worshipful, responsive reception of that Word.[522]

Luther drew a famous distinction in 1520 between those who come out of baptism and exercise a priestly office to one another, and those who are selected for the estate of priesthood. This distinction is not abrogated by Luther's later understanding of the office nor by CA 14. The congregation does not vitiate the preaching office, nor does the latter vitiate the former.[523] Rather, God's command to spiritual priesthood concerns all Christians; they should fulfill it by praying for the congregation and especially for the pastors.[524]

The gift of baptism does not annul the institution of the office. The Christian should remember with gratitude "that the spiritual estate has been established and instituted by God, not with gold or silver but with the precious blood and bitter death of his only Son, our Lord Jesus Christ." God therefore desires that this estate be highly honored. In it he stoops to serve us, just as he does elsewhere through temporal government. This parallel shows that the institution of the office of preaching is not a special spiritual and sacramental event; it occurs within the three hierarchies through which God rules his creation.[525]

Of course, that does not exclude the special relationship between the office of preaching and Christ's saving work. Preaching does testify to that work and carry it forward. In the process, its connection with Christ's Passion becomes especially evident. We would not have the gospel and preaching if it were not for the "blood and sweat of our Lord." He purchased them by his blood and gave them to us without cost; he paid a price for them, as did the

521. "The episcopal office is established in the Word, and nothing more is needed for this office" (*WA* 27:86.3–4).

522. "And next to the preaching office, prayer is the greatest office in Christendom. In the preaching office, God speaks with us, and in prayer I speak with him" (sermon of May 14, 1531; *WA* 34.1:395.14–19).

523. *WA* 6:408.13ff.; *LW* 44:129. See *WA* 30.2:421.19ff. (summer 1530): "The true church is the number or gathering of the baptized and believers under one shepherd." On general priesthood as brotherhood with Christ: *WA* 15:720.26ff. (sermon on ordination, October 16, 1524). One can preach "in a shepherd's cloak as well as in a chasuble" (*WA* 23:749.32).

524. *WA* 27:129.10–12, 131.3–4. An intercessory prayer of this kind from the first Sunday in Advent 1528, for the absent Bugenhagen, is in *WA* 27:444.28ff.; see also ibid., 512.14–15.

525. *WA* 30.2:527.14–17, 530.20–22, 553.24–25, 564.25–26; *LW* 46:219, 221–22, 236, 243.

apostles through whom the gifts came to us. Christ sealed the covenant between God and humanity; the preacher does the same thing. As Christ's Word is received, a relationship is established between the hearer and Christ. Through his covenant Christ reconciles God and his people. "This office of Christ is transferred to the church; no one should suppose that Christ is dead, but rather that his servants are carrying out his office."[526]

Thoughts of covenant and representation lead to identification. Christ himself is the servant and messenger to whom the office of the Word is entrusted. Where do I find him after his death? "I must look to the office; nothing else will do." Christ is the first in the church to hold this office. Every power connected with it goes back to him, whether baptizing, preaching, or absolution. The preacher is Christ's womb, bearing the believers so that Christ can comfort them and guide them. This communion in Christ fills both preacher and hearer: "When I preach, he preaches in me; when you listen, he listens in you."[527] It continues in the succession of the apostles. Paul, the preacher of forgiveness, starts it off, but the other apostles also were called to the office of forgiveness as early as the Sermon on the Mount. This call is still valid today. Luther recognizes no apostolic succession in the sense of divine right. The preaching office first exercised by Christ and then established for succeeding generations is actually still in force, but that depends upon the content of the call and proclamation rather than the legal form in which they have been transmitted.[528] This content, in turn, is established by Christ's person and work; it is transmitted through the ministry of the preaching office.[529]

This background of the Lutheran understanding of the office must be kept in mind if one wishes to make a proper evaluation of the statements of CA 14 concerning the call to this office. By now it should be clear that for Luther, the legal form in which the call occurs is unimportant; the only necessary thing is that it occurs. The reason, of course, is that one cannot place oneself in the preaching office. It is so tightly bound up with Christ's deed and suffering, with the founding of the church, and with the action of the Spirit in the Word, that no one can assume it independently. The divine call alone, in whatever human form it occurs, is essential for the divine activity to ensue. Because God himself is at work in the ministry of the Word, no one can be

526. *WA* 30.2:583.22ff.; *LW* 46:255; *WA* 31.2:400.28–33.

527. *WA* 15:533.19ff., 29:15.7–8, 305.12–13, 26:6.10–14; *LW* 28:219; *WA* 30.2:112.2; *LW* 46:166; *WA* 20:350.6, 365.1–3.

528. *WA* 29:49.12–13, 32:350.25–30, 37–38; *LW* 21:62; *WA* 29:275.11. See *WA* 29:274.12–14: "To sum up, we will not know Christ or his gifts unless he is preached."

529. "And this suffering and resurrection must be grasped in the preaching office; otherwise no one will learn of it and experience it" (*WA* 29:314.11–12). On the resurrection itself, see *WA* 27:121.3–4.

self-called; only God—even if through human means—can call to this service.

There is documentary evidence that this is an indispensable presupposition for the understanding of CA 14. In the seventh Schwabach article, Saxony identifies the preaching office, that is, the oral Word, with the gospel in the same way that we have found that parallel drawn by Luther, and it also points out the mediating significance of this orally proclaimed Word for the believer. God gives "faith through it as a means by his Holy Spirit, how and where he will."[530] The repudiation of this understanding of Word and office played a special role in the rejection of the Schwabach Articles in December 1529. Martin Bucer, the spokesman for the southern Germans, called the "office and work of teaching" merely the instrument of the Spirit; to restrict God's activity to the administration of such external means seemed to him a denial of divine omnipotence.[531]

These events occurred only a few months before the composition of the Augustana, and they still had a lively immediacy for Melanchthon and Brueck. In CA 5 they reworked Schwab. 7 so that it was limited exclusively to the sphere of salvation without reference to the institutional office, which was along the lines of Bucer's critique. In that way they made room for a new article 14 that seemed to treat the preaching office purely from the perspective of church order. I say "seemed" because CA 5, with its grouping of office, Word, Spirit, and faith, actually forms the background for CA 14. Only in this way can the divine call be made the irrevocable precondition for carrying out the office in a manner pleasing to God; that was Luther's position and the position of subsequent Lutherans whenever they cited CA 14. Luther required this "regular call" (*rite vocatus*) as the consequence of his theologically based doctrine of office. Thus CA 14 forms the bridge from theology to specific matters of church order.

Rite vocatus

The pastoral office—here called the office of comfort—"is weak if it is not authorized and is not pleasing and satisfying to God above all." It is Luther's personal interest in salvation that lies behind his great concern with the saving activity of the office; his insistence on proper calling cannot be based solely on his opposition to the Anabaptists and spiritualists. Clearly, personal possession of the Spirit is not what constitutes a call; the office is not personal but is based on the Spirit and on Christ. The gift of the Spirit belongs to Christendom as a whole, and only through the church's call does the office-

530. *WA* 30.3:88.15ff.
531. See Hans von Schubert, *Bekenntnisbildung* (cited above, n. 5), 122–23, 167ff., 294–95.

bearer share in that common possession. In comforting and teaching, the pastor does not own the Spirit; the pastor is merely a steward. "If that were not so, everything would be up in the air. I would have to be rebaptized tomorrow, because I would not know whether the person who baptized me was trustworthy." One would have to trust the person blindly without asking whether he had the Holy Spirit or not. "But that is what you must know for sure—that he has the authority to baptize, to preach, and to absolve." As soon as he moves from office to person he becomes unreliable. It is the objective givens of the Spirit of Christ that constitute our life and being.[532]

If there is no divine call, preaching is a fiendish temptation for those who preach and for those who hear. Normally the vocation comes through a human intermediary, perhaps by means of a letter of recommendation such as those the apostles drew up for their emissaries. This written procedure can be replaced by an oral one; the preacher is invited by the competent authorities of a town and, on the basis of a sermon and appropriate examination of personal qualifications, can then be called. That sort of right to elect pastors, for example, was probably what Luther had in mind when he initially made that concession to the rebellious peasants. Always included with that, however, was the participation and agreement of the lawful authorities.[533] All of the above presupposes the general priesthood of believers; even the *rite vocatus* is under the Word and not above it,[534] so that every call includes an obligation to which the candidate must submit.[535]

In addition to these calls through human intermediaries, validated by their evoking a God-given inward response, there is also the direct call by God similar to the one Paul received. Luther does not reject such a call out of hand. Nevertheless, one cannot and should not trust it if it is not confirmed by outward miraculous signs; the voice of the Spirit within the heart is not enough. Of course there is an inner and spiritual event connected with external calls as well, even though that event cannot be legally certified. Luther does not consider the external jurisdiction's call to be sufficient either. In such merely human calls he speaks of a call of charity (*vocatio caritatis*).

Alongside the direct spiritual call is the "*vocatio caritatis* . . . that arises out of faith, because you, I, and everyone are in debt to one another."[536] The love

532. *WA* 31.2:702.18–19, 29:305.3–16 (sermon of March 30, 1529), 311.3–4.

533. *WA* 17.1:360.14, 26:21.6–9; *LW* 28:240–41; *WA* 16:34.1ff., 18:298.30–31; *LW* 46:22. On the wishes of the Erfurters for the election of a pastor, see Luther's marginal note, ibid., 534.11–12: "The council, however, has the authority to decide what sort of persons hold office in the city."

534. *WA* 15:720.26ff.

535. Here Luther personally follows the experiences of the early church: "Had my enemies not incited me, I would not have spoken a word, nor would I have been able to convert the whole world" (*WA* 16:35.4–6).

536. *WA* 17.1:362.1. See also *WA* 16:35.1–2, 40.10ff.

of neighbor that grows out of faith is open to being called and pressed into service. The person to whom that happens stands directly under divine orders and need not wait for a miraculous sign. The command to love is God's command; those who follow it are called by God. It is superfluous to stress that this command does not abrogate existing orders but fulfills them. The obedience of love presupposes available structures and creates new ones only in an emergency.

Therefore the legal form of a call makes little difference to Luther; all that is obligatory is that it be issued in conformity with the applicable law—that it be "regular." Later efforts to interpret the "regular" in a ritualistic sense (in contrast, see below, p. 197) were just as wrong as the attempt to read into it a conscious effort to be vague for tactical reasons. It was really not the intention of Melanchthon and Brueck to find a formula that would assure the married evangelical pastor status as a citizen because of possessing a "regular call" under the mantle of canon law. Instead, they adopted Luther's broad view, which, linked with openness to future legal developments, guaranteed a basic legitimacy to the evangelical office of the Word so that it could unfold without restraint.

For that reason, any discussion of patronage or nomination rights to the pastoral office is superfluous. What is valid for one place need not be binding for another. Even application for a pastoral vacancy is possible. Of course pressure is not allowed, but when one hears of a vacancy it is all right to let the authorities know one is interested. If appropriate recommendations are available, a call can be issued. Even Luther himself can extend a call although he has no formal power to do so. There are in fact "brotherly calls through others," which, because they come in the love of Christ, must be accepted in the obedience of love.[537]

Although there is great freedom regarding legal forms, one thing must never be lacking in a call. Those who are to assume a pastorate must "teach the gospel and the faith in complete purity" and are not to besmirch their proclamation with profane or papistic opinions. The certainty of possessing the reliable Word of God supports the pastor and fills his heart with peace and gratitude; it is a gift that can never be used up in teaching and learning. The "purely taught," *pure docere*, of CA 7 forms the indispensable presupposition for the *rite vocatus* of CA 14.[538]

Freedom in regard to legal structure, however, does involve rejection of the traditional form of ordination. In the light of the proposed compromise at Augsburg that would agree to ordination by bishops, Luther's declaration of

---

537. *WA* 26:49.12ff., 51.1ff., 6ff., 5:7–10; *LW* 28:281, 283, 284.
538. *WA* 13:634.13ff., 23ff., 636.1ff.; *LW* 20:103, 105; *WA* 26:19.31ff., 21.1–2, 41.25ff.; *LW* 28:239, 240, 269.

October 16, 1524, takes on special significance. He had said that a new order for ordination must be created[539] because the bishops only ordained mass-priests and in the process demanded renunciation of the gospel; anyone so ordained became a priest of the devil. This sharp language should not in any way lead us to assume that the preaching office was a new office created by the Reformers. It has existed in Christendom since Christ, for teaching, preaching, and admonition have constantly been needed. It cannot be abolished, as the Anabaptists wish it to be, on the grounds that it is a remnant of the papacy. Just as in the case of the Bible, we have the office through the historical medium of the papacy. The pope did not create the preaching office; he found it already in existence. And although the tyrannical enemy now persecutes evangelical preaching, this enemy still cannot hinder God's work, which is allowing the office of preacher to come into its own once again.[540]

Commitment to tradition, however, does not prevent rejection of ordination as a sacrament nor openness to new legal forms for the call and ordering of the office. Luther, as we have already seen in his Confession of 1528 (above p. 188), recognized a threefold preaching office. He did not simply equate the office of bishop with that of pastor; instead, he allowed the higher office of oversight (*antistites*) to continue. Its incumbents are "to oversee all offices, so that the teachers exercise their office and do not neglect it, the deacons distribute goods properly and do not become weary; to punish sinners and invoke the ban promptly so that every office is conducted rightly." In the cities pastors are assisted by preachers. Luther wanted four or five in Wittenberg, related to the quarters of the city; in each case several deacons are also to be assigned.[541]

Luther's renewal of the diaconate is little known and did not last long in Lutheranism. The reason doubtless lies in the fact that CA 14 does not mention this office or a call to it. Now, the induction of a deacon ought not be pictured as institutionalized, as later church orders made it. Here again we have to assume a brotherly call, a *vocatio caritatis*, which would be particularly appropriate to this office of loving service. Luther complained vehemently that it had lost that character and that the pope had made deacons into "epistolers and gospelers." He himself had a clear picture of the ancient church's practice: the deacon is, as servant of the bishop, likewise servant of the congregation. He registers and cares for the poor, visits the sick, and manages church property. Thus the administrative functions receive particu-

539. "Nevertheless in time we will have to ordain preachers" (*WA* 15:720.13–22).
540. *WA* 20:704.13, 26:147.3ff., 13ff., 24ff.; *LW* 40:231, 232; *WA* 27:43.31, 86.34ff. Luther knows of no conveyance of office and Spirit through the laying on of hands during postapostolic times.
541. *WA* 17.2:42.10–14, 335.29–35.

lar emphasis. The fact that deacons were also called upon for preaching, as in the case of Stephen, hastened the demise of poor relief—a gap which was filled by the hospitalers. Deacons need not harbor feelings of inferiority or jealousy; all officeholders stand equal before God.[542]

Occasional statements of Luther,[543] then, indicate that he adopted the traditional threefold division of the pastoral office, but that cannot be considered a contradiction to CA 14 unless one ties the call to the office with the particular legal forms (examination, installation, etc.) that were subsequently introduced in the evangelical territories. If one starts from Luther's view of the *vocatio caritatis*, however, it is possible to assume that a call to the congregational diaconate would come through the congregation. The persons affected by this call usually had been in public service a long time; assuming the diaconate simply broadened their service and gave it a new content flowing from Christian faith and love. Putting it into church law added nothing. It is likely that Luther did not think through this question of order completely, because he did not have people around who could make it work. One thing is clear: these offices derived from the pastoral office—the bishop on a higher level and the preacher on a lower one—serve the truth and the effectiveness of the gospel. That also applies to diaconal service and to the office of schoolmaster, "which, next to the office of preaching, is the most useful, greatest, and best."[544] In its loving service in the world, the office of the Word takes on various forms, depending on practical needs and possibilities. The orders that it sets up do not constitute this office; they just provide its historically conditioned characteristics. That is true not only of the persons who lead worship in the congregation but also of the times and places of worship—"so that it will be preached outwardly and will be visible in time, place, and persons."[545]

If the pastoral office is open only to those who are called, definite assumptions and preparations become necessary for the next generation. Preparatory planning begins as early as Latin school; even when a boy does not continue in school but learns a trade, "he still stands as a ready reserve in case he should be needed as a pastor or in some other service of the Word." For the honor that God confers upon the service of the Word and sacraments applies not only to the pastoral office but to the entire spiritual estate, together with all that pertains to it.[546] And when Luther urges "that children should be

542. *WA* 17.2:335.26ff., 336.12–17, 26:61.9–11, 59.17ff., 24–25, 62.11ff.; *LW* 28:298, 295, 295–96, 300. See W. Maurer, *Gemeindezucht* (cited above, n. 167), 26ff.

543. There is also important material in his lectures on the pastoral epistles. See *WA* 25:1ff.; *LW* 29:1ff. (Titus and Philemon, 1527). Also *WA* 26:1ff.; *LW* 28:215ff. (1 Timothy, 1528).

544. *WA* 30.2:580.19–20; *LW* 46:253.

545. *WA* 34.2:296.7–8.

546. *WA* 30.2:546.24–26; *LW* 46:231. Luther lists "pastors, teachers, preachers, lectors, priests (whom men call chaplains), sacristans, schoolmasters, and whatever other work belongs to these offices and persons" (*WA* 30.2:528.28ff.; *LW* 46:220).

kept in school," he reminds parents of this special value of the spiritual estate, asking them to consider "what good is accomplished by the preaching office and the care of souls"; whoever keeps children from this education destroys "God's foundation and instituted office." In his seminars, which were, of course, not aimed exclusively at future pastors, Luther complains about the lack of suitable candidates. And although he places relatively few demands on them—in addition to the basics, zeal and inner openness suffice—as he looks toward the future of the church he worries about the small number of learned young theologians "who labor in the Word." This lack is a punishment for the ingratitude with which his contemporaries have received the gospel.[547]

The concern for the next generation of pastors, however, reflects more than an educational problem; it reflects primarily an economic one. It is well known that the collapse of the endowment system caused the number of theological students to decline. This was primarily an organizational problem, but Luther saw it as affecting the condition of evangelical congregations and their strength. Where will the regularly called pastors come from if the congregations will not accept them and support them? In 1531, Luther says that in all Christendom there is not a city that supports its pastor. In Nürnberg, for example, citizens do not give their pastors a thing. The incumbents are paid by the council, not out of its own means, to be sure, but out of secularized church property. That is the case everywhere; the pastors never receive their support directly from the citizens or the peasants.[548]

The situation is particularly bad among the peasants and nobles; they try to starve out their pastors. The peasants point their fingers, refuse to greet them and help them, and deny them support. As a result, the pastors' net income has declined; endowments that formerly produced two hundred gulden now hardly bring twenty. It was just as Luther had written in 1526 to the emperor's sister, Queen Maria of Hungary: things had come to the point where "legitimate preachers do not have bread to eat; they all suffer want, trouble, and need. The deceivers, however, have plenty." A pastor had to keep a watchful eye on the yield of the common chest, because that was the source of whatever bread the benevolence of the congregation would provide for him and his family.[549]

Still, this contribution amounted to very little. Neither the pastor nor those studying for that post had anything to live on; the school was unable to continue. Luther complained to his Wittenbergers in a pulpit announcement

547. WA 30.2:532.21ff., 533.28–29; LW 46:223, 224; WA 26:49.20ff., 95.9–10; LW 28:281, 348.

548. WA 34.2:190.8ff. (sermon of September 10, 1531).

549. WA 34.2:157.11–12; LW 51:222; WA 31.2:484.2ff., 26:96.12; LW 28:350; WA 19:613.5; LW 14:274; WA 27:253.5–6.

on November 8, 1528, "You bear no fruit, like a bad tree." If they did not provide anything, he threatened, "I will relinquish the pulpit and teach my students, pauper to paupers, whom you would like to starve to death."[550]

What good is a regular call if you cannot make a living from it? It is certainly necessary because it opens the way to the source of the Word. Those who do not possess it cannot act through the office to save others. It is not bound to specific legal forms; it is immaterial whether the call is issued by the congregation or by some other authority, as long as the right to call is not usurped. In essence it is an act of fraternal love that seeks to bring the gospel to a congregation, and where this love reigns the call has divine approval.

The call is not an act of law but an act of love. It was not turned into a legal process until the 1530s. From the beginning, however, the call involved elements of order. It must be "regular"; that is, it must occur within an ordered framework. Even if the forms could vary in detail, they were still taken over from available traditions. Of course the medieval sacrament of ordination was rejected, but as early as 1524 it was clear that a substitute order was needed. The call presupposes pure doctrine, so it is necessary to establish beforehand that the doctrine has been accepted. Granted that no one can ascertain another's inner state, it is still necessary to demonstrate that a person can read the Bible, understand it, and transmit its content correctly. That is why academic study is necessary. Call to this office presupposes a curriculum and a system of church schools, and that in turn raises pressing questions of church order that had long been the subject of attention by reformers, in collaboration with the Christian humanists. The legal consequences were not drawn, however, until the territories confronted the connection between church order and the calling and installation of pastors. Pastors need helpers for pastoral care in the larger congregations, for education of the youth, and for care of the needy. The office of proclaiming the Word branches out. In addition to *rite vocatus* in its proper sense—pastors and preachers belong together in this category—there are congregational members who combine a civil office with particular ecclesiastical tasks and who are called to that service. Finally, this whole structure of proclamation, education, and social welfare requires a financial base. The general shift in social and economic life made it hard to establish that base, which could only be obtained by mustering congregational self-denial.

All of the above institutional forms demand hard and fast rules. By 1530, the regulations were far from complete, but there was no doubt about their necessity. The existence of an ecclesiastical office based on an orderly call is the presupposition for all church order. That is why CA 14 belongs before CA 15.

550. *WA* 27:409.10ff.

Publice docere

There can be no doubt that the legal nature of the call is connected to the public nature of the proclamation. The claim to teach publicly is legitimated through the call. Without the call, public confusion is bound to result from contradictory teaching. Both Catholic and evangelical territories reacted to such confusion with extraordinary sensitivity, not only to prevent political disorder but also to avoid unsettling consciences. The unity and purity of doctrine is a political and pastoral concern. It can be achieved only under public supervision, and the right of that supervision arises out of the public's authority to call. Public preaching can occur only on the basis of a legitimate call, and those who have been so called take on a public responsibility. Their calling confers a public duty on them within the area of their responsibility, and in carrying out that duty they stand under public protection.

It is obvious that this connection between the legal and the public nature of proclamation is enough to confer a legal character on the preaching office. Even though at first the "regular" may be flexible and undefined—as we saw to be the case—it still contains an element of order. We have already noted the impulses toward church order that grew out of such a call. The public dimension gives rise to still stronger and more numerous impulses. This concept from Roman law was widespread at the time. Every official, even one without special legal training, knew what a public task or a public activity was, and knew too what conditions were connected with each and what obligations and privileges each entailed.

The preacher of the gospel holds a public office. The territorial princes who signed the Augustana granted this office to their preachers and demanded that the empire recognize its public character. The concept of the public official was not yet fully fleshed out in 1530, and the fact that it was developing at about this time out of the structures of the feudal state cannot be explained simply on the basis of the coming of Roman law. A significant contribution also came from the formation of a new class of evangelical pastors with the task and privileges of a public teaching function. The "teach publicly," *publice docere*, of CA 14 plays an important role in the history of jurisprudence.

Yet one should not put a one-sided emphasis on this juridical understanding of *publice docere* in the exegesis of CA 14. No matter how self-evident the Roman law's concept of public office was to people like Melanchthon, it was never dominant in the tradition of the church. There it was remembered that the apostles and teachers of the church entered the public arena only as martyrs, and that service of the gospel took place in the catacombs. The ecclesiastical "public" context was in worship, and *publice docere* meant to preach in conformity with the apostolic tradition and in service of the spiritual unity of Christendom.

Luther derived the public character of his preaching office—except for the special case of his doctorate—from his call, and he considered that public dimension to be a help for his task. But he also knows the legal principle of *notorium facti* (of children talking in the street about their illegitimate origin). That sort of public knowledge also plays a role in the selection of a pastor. One sees a candidate in the pulpit on Sunday or during the weekday services where a chapter of the Bible is studied verse by verse; the whole neighborhood testifies to his blameless life. In such a case the call needs no special legal certification; public opinion is enough.[551] Luther also knows that the effectiveness of a public office depends on the political situation: among the Turks there is no public worship and no one can confess Christ publicly.[552]

In the Old Testament, public proclamation was simply a given. The whole people participated in worship. The prophets confronted them face to face; they did not preach God's judgment and salvation in some corner but at the public gates, corresponding to our city halls and churches. Such open possibilities, however, are limited to certain periods. "In our time," predicts Luther at the end of the 1520s in his lectures on Isaiah, "it will come to pass that that light will be darkened and public preaching will cease; at best it will remain only among private meetings, and in such obscurity Christ will come."[553]

Ultimately the public claim of the gospel is not based on possibilities or circumstances; pastors do not teach publicly because they can but because they must. Christ sent his apostles into all the world to gather congregations of believers everywhere. The salvation that Christ brings with him in his kingdom is for the whole world. He himself preached in the open on the mount. On Pentecost the Holy Spirit acted openly, not in a corner. The servant of the gospel ought to teach publicly too. "The preaching office and God's Word should shine like the sun, not covertly and sneaking in darkness, as one plays blind man's buff, but acting freely in the light of day."[554]

Therefore, to fear no one and to set forth the truth freely and openly is not a test of the pastor's courage; it is a matter of office and command. Those who preach should not wear out and let themselves be chased into a corner, nor should they become impatient and creep away to the wilderness. Public

551. ". . . if we emphasize the matter of the call, we can worry the devil. A parish pastor can claim that he possesses the office of the ministry, baptism, the Sacrament, the care of souls, and is commissioned, publicly and legally. Therefore the people should go to him for these things" (*WA* 30.3:519.29ff.; *LW* 40:385). See also *WA* 30.3:522.2ff.; *LW* 40:387. On the *notorium facti*, see *WA* 26:103.1ff., 7ff.; *LW* 28:359.

552. *WA* 30.2:120.31–32; *LW* 46:175.

553. *WA* 31.2:181.19–20, 425.22ff., 457.30–31.

554. *WA* 13:642.34–35; *LW* 20:113; *WA* 15:533.18ff., 29:308.8, 32:303.17–18; *LW* 21:8.

service demands a person who is willing to risk everything and who is totally committed, who is tough when things are tough, and who will not be frightened or silenced. On the basis of Matt. 5:13, a sermon's permeating effect on the public is compared to the power of salt. It will be rejected by those around it and will bring weariness and pain to those who represent it. But Christ uses this comparison to show that he "does not intend for an office like this to be carried out secretly or in one place, but publicly throughout the whole world." The universality of the church and of the message of salvation entrusted to it become evident in this public claim of the gospel. Public teaching is God's work, which "shines openly in the whole world and lets itself be seen, and for that very reason it is persecuted."[555]

To teach publicly, therefore, is not an offer made to the preacher by a world that is open to the gospel. It is an offer that God makes through his service of the world, and it encounters opposition there. The teaching takes place not in an open public forum but in a world that is hostile and closed. This fact is not at all altered by the legal and public guarantees enjoyed by the ecclesiastical office in the post-Constantinian era and claimed for the renewed evangelical preaching office by the "confessors" at Augsburg in CA 14. Luther appropriates this legally assured public arena, but he bases the task of public teaching on Christ's gospel and the action of the Spirit. Public teaching of the gospel does indeed occur under the protection of the official legal jurisdictions of the world but not under their authority; that authority lies in the gospel itself, and it shows itself in conflict with the world.

Because they hold public office, those who preach face conflict. Luther continually testified to that, and therefore his understanding of public teaching led to the kernel of a pastoral theology that went back to his own experience. Despite all his theological learning, the young Doctor Luther had shied away from preaching, and the longer he lived, the harder it became. All preachers, however, face testing and are the most miserable of all people, on "a road Satan rides." They are like other Christians in military service, although they face particular persecution and danger and are therefore called enemies of the human race.[556] They face a war on two fronts—against the heretics of the traditional faith and against the newly arisen enthusiasts, to whom the office has not been entrusted. The preacher thus lives in constant turmoil, without peace. The public effect of his teaching shows itself in the offense he arouses on every side.[557]

God wills this effect and calls it forth. He does not intend for the bearers of

555. WA 32:320.2ff., 343.24ff., 344.19–20, 351.3ff., 354.10ff.; LW 21:27, 54, 55, 62–63, 66; WA 27:132.27ff.
556. WA 27:286.1ff., 34.2:157.4ff.; LW 51:222; WA 27:251.13–16, 13:625.20ff., 632.12ff.; LW 20:93, 100.
557. WA 32:351.33ff.; LW 21:63; WA 27:77.19ff., 86.15, 2, 17.1:35.14.

this public teaching office to be lazy and to rust. He places them in the arduous battle for the testimony of the gospel and provides his Word and Spirit. It is not just in times of plague that preachers and pastors are "obliged to stay at their posts through death and mortal need."[558] The church that taught publicly in 1530 made its impact through the martyrdom of its preachers. It can have no better defense than their executions. Their blood cries out to God, and for each death he raises up two preachers. Its shepherds serve better after death than in their lifetimes. The disciples of the Shepherd of Bethlehem "believe, preach, are brave, rejoice in the contempt of the world, and praise God." Even when the preachers are weak and the world powerful, God's Word is mightier still and presses on unhindered. Public teaching permeates the world. The "public" of CA 14 points to the world that God has called to salvation. Therefore public preaching knows no boundaries.[559]

On the other hand, every preacher begins by acting within the boundaries of his call; without a legitimate call there is no effective public preaching.[560] The battle against the infiltrating and clandestine preachers forms the negative side of the requirement of public preaching. "God does not violate order"—that is the axiom which argues for a call and which requires a publicly recognized preaching office. Therefore those who deny the public office and fight it are of the devil. "The Holy Spirit did not slither in but flew publicly down from heaven. Serpents slither, but doves fly. Therefore slithering like that is appropriate for the devil, that is for sure," said Luther with his inimitable vividness. The contrast between public teachers and those who slither in is as great as that between heaven and hell; if salvation depends on orderly public preaching, then that makes sense. For that reason the description of uncalled preachers—including even Karlstadt, the doctor of theology and of canon law and the archdeacon of Wittenberg—is unremittingly harsh; further examples would be superfluous.[561]

As we have seen, Christ is the one who institutes the office of preaching and installs in it, so any factious spirit is foreign to Christendom. Regular preach-

558. The quotation (*WA* 23:341.31–342.2; *LW* 43:121), from the work *Whether One May Flee from a Deadly Plague*, refers of course to that situation and applies to all members, not merely the pastor.

559. We here encounter Luther's approach to foreign missions; see W. Maurer, "Reformation und Mission," in *Ihr werdet meine Zeugen sein: Georg F. Vicedom zum 60. Geburtstag*, Lutherisches Missionsjahrbuch, 1963 (Nürnberg, 1963), 20–41, esp. 30–31; reprinted in Wilhelm Maurer, *Kirche und Geschichte* (Göttingen, 1970), 1:159–76, esp. 167–68. On the paragraph, see *WA* 20:371.7ff., 23:749.26–27, 19:246.4–6; *LW* 19:98.

560. On the basis of the Fourth Commandment, preaching in the home continued in use (*WA* 27:48.15ff.). See also part 2, chap. 17.

561. *WA* 20:412.26–27, 30.3:518.21ff.; *LW* 40:384. On Karlstadt: *WA* 18:92.11ff., 97–99; *LW* 40:109, 113–16. In 1530, he said of the Thuringian Anabaptists that "they sneak through the houses and go about the countryside without appearing publicly as the apostles did and as regular preachers do every day" (*WA* 30.2:212.35ff.).

ers rely on their installation and its consequent public responsibility. They battle the clandestine preachers with spiritual means instead of external force. They gather their congregations and seek to instruct them "constantly and conscientiously" not to let an infiltrating preacher come among them. Their chief weapons are preaching and prayer. The means and powers that the preaching office uses to fight are the same as those to which it owes its existence.[562]

The public arena in which teaching takes place is the world where God works through his Spirit. Granted that teaching and hearing of the Word are done by the Spirit in human hearts, he nevertheless accomplishes that from the outside, from the world in which he becomes effective through the Word. For Münzer, the "testimony in my inwardness" is enough; when he latches on to that, he can do without Scripture. For Luther, the preached word is the starting point; that is where the Spirit is. As Moses struck water from a stone, so the preaching office brings the Spirit from the external word "by the word of the mouth."[563]

Thus the preacher is just an instrument like the staff Moses used to strike the rock. The Spirit is also present, of course, but that is not the preacher's personal equipment which can be passed along; it is the gift given to all Christendom, shared through the external word. The preacher is certainly not without the Spirit; the declaration of absolution is a spiritual event. It is not, however, bound to one person but it emanates from Christ, who is at work in the Spirit. To have the Spirit means to teach or to do nothing of oneself without the Spirit. The office remains even when the person misuses the Spirit's gift.[564] Those who receive absolution should not focus on the speaker but rather should keep in mind that "as long as he is dealing with the Word and its ordinances, he is dealing with the Holy Spirit and the forgiveness of sins."[565]

Basically, Luther is skeptical of talk about possessing the Spirit. There is no way to prove that possession. If there were proof—an external fact or an experience that could be confirmed—a person could no longer preach, for he would speak on his own authority and would not need God's Word. It is his calling that reminds him he can indeed be certain of that Word. He has been compelled to preach by other people and continues to preach for their sake. "Therefore I have the proof of the Spirit of love, which does not seek its own but is busy being of service to other people. . . . I am obligated and in duty

562. WA 32:350.28ff.; LW 21:62; WA 29:307.23–24, 30.3:519.8ff.; LW 40:384; WA 17.1:32.16ff.

563. WA 20:780.1–4, 779.14, 26:82.10; LW 28:329; WA 17.2:135.19ff.

564. That is the basic idea of CA 8; see part 2, chap. 23.

565. WA 29:303.22ff., 305.3ff., 19:247.7–8; LW 19:99.

bound to it out of the Spirit of love."[566] It is not spiritual experience that distinguishes the preacher; the *vocatio caritatis* makes clear to him that he is supported by the Spirit-serving love that fills Christendom. It is in this Spirit that public teaching occurs.

The teaching demonstrates its public character as it does battle with the ungodly world. Luther—in contrast to Augustine and the Middle Ages—did not consider the world to be only outside the church, understood in a sacramental sense. The preaching office is to ferret out the world in the midst of the church and to combat it. Thus a good part of the evangelical sermon consists in rebuking evil, that is, preaching the law. In this way the church fulfills its task to teach publicly. The church does not need to generate its public activity artificially; it occurs through preaching the Ten Commandments in their power to reprove sin *(usus politicus)*. To do that is "God's word, office, and command" for the preacher.[567]

In this public office of discipline the preacher is guided by God. He is led to see which people and circumstances require his intervention.[568] God gives him the pastoral love that will accompany the critical word and lead the sinner's heart to repentance. In the process the pastor must adapt himself to people and situations *(esse valde aequus, comodus)* "so that he can help people and improve their habits"; he must keep from becoming a "biter" who overdoes his scolding and misuses his power. It is necessary to differentiate between secret and public sins. To criticize secret ones in public does no good; it just embitters the sinner and makes everyone else proud despisers. But even when it is a matter of public crimes, the preacher ought not name names, because that would evoke division and disorder. In civil matters the public rebuke should be equally severe on town council and on congregation.[569]

Public teaching thus requires humility and self-discipline. A preacher must be a "modest person," not arrogant and overcritical, not vain and ambitious. It is particularly dangerous where there are several preachers at one place. Rhetorical flourishes can do great damage; their jabs and innuendos, their bite and punch can hurt and overwhelm local authorities.[570]

A difficult and dangerous office! Luther advised despairing pastors who could not endure the pressures to throw it all into God's lap and tell him, "If

---

566. *WA* 20:222.34–223.5 (sermon of January 6, 1526).
567. *WA* 27:183.7ff., 184.3ff., 30.2:598.13; *LW* 38:100.
568. *WA* 27:87.28ff. Luther makes this point in the sermon of April 3, 1528, in order that his hearers "might remain steadfast in pure doctrine." On this practical understanding of pure doctrine, see part 2, chap. 23.
569. *WA* 27:88–89, 26:53.1–2, 15.30ff.; *LW* 28:286, 287.
570. *WA* 27:90.7, 257.13ff., 80.23ff., 92.19ff., 26:84.16–17; *LW* 28:332.

you do not preach, I am not able to do a thing." Luther, in his own self-doubt, questioned the effectiveness of his preaching and comforted himself and others with the thought that even Judas the betrayer was one of the apostles. So even if the preacher is no earthly good, the office he has been given is still God's work.[571]

"For I have been ordered and charged as a preacher and doctor to see to it that no one is led astray, and I shall have to give account for that on judgment day." That is the way Luther justified speaking out publicly against the pope in 1530, after the end of the Diet of Augsburg. From the same period comes his warning to all preachers that God has purchased his people through the blood of his Son and "has entrusted them to us and will demand a strict accounting . . . as we well know." Because this highest office with its public claim gives the greatest and requires the greatest, it also imposes the greatest responsibility.[572]

26. ECCLESIASTICAL ORDER AND CHURCH LAW

In the previous section we have considered the office of proclamation of the Word primarily from its institutional side. All salvation depends on the orally proclaimed Word of the gospel, and that is precisely why this proclamation and the sacraments that accompany it must be institutionally assured.[573] The external Word is audible to the ears and issues from the lips of a Christian who proclaims it—not necessarily a winsome person but the one who has been called to tell it to me. The fact that I am addressed or confronted by the saving Word is connected with that call. The institutional assurance depends on the "that" rather than the "how" of such a call. As we saw in the exposition of CA 14, the call is more a "given" than an assurance anchored in specific statutes.

It is a "given" where people who are bound together in the bond of love owe one another the declaration of the gospel. The overall obligation of such a call of love (vocatio caritatis) begins in the family. Father and mother owe it to their children to teach them the Bible; if the parents are silent, they become guilty before God. Beyond this private level lies public teaching. Those who bear public responsibility—as leaders of a political community, as public persons in city and territory, and finally as bearers of a public office—must take care before God and others that the Word is preached among the people

571. *WA* 27:89.3-4, 6-7, 31.2:396.14ff., 28-29, 397.5-6. See *WA* 2:397.2-3: "And I, Martin Luther, if God had not closed my eyes of reason, would have long kept silent in the pulpit and lost all hope."

572. *WA* 32:334.11ff., 30.2:597.29-30; *LW* 38:100. See also *WA* 30.2:111.30-31; *LW* 46:165-66.

573. See W. Maurer, *Pfarrerrecht und Bekenntnis* (Berlin, 1957), 74ff.

for whom they are responsible. This duty is fulfilled when they search for a suitable person to proclaim the gospel and either urge that a call be issued in conformity to the law or extend that call themselves. In this way a *vocatio caritatis* occurs even in the public arena.

As we have seen, the legality of this call is not established through particular ecclesiastical forms and ordinances; it is the result of local circumstances on a case-by-case basis. Because of that, legal provisions that govern public life in other areas also become important for the church. The calling procedure—and the public proclamation resulting from it—thus do not create their own peculiar legal forms but employ those forms that are at hand. The preaching office does not create new laws directly, at least not in relation to the basic structure described in CA 14.

In practice, however, this office is dependent on specific ordinances, some of which are in force and others of which must be created. We have looked at those elements which are mentioned in the Augustana and which are attested in Reformation preaching before 1530. Some of those are traditional elements that are still in effect and claim continuing validity; that claim is examined critically in the Augustana, and in many instances it is rejected. There are, however, other ordinances that are products of the developing Reformation or are instituted independently. And the question arises whether and to what extent such developments are possible at all in the church of the Word. This question about the principle of church orders poses the fundamental problem of evangelical church law. To what degree can it be solved in a commentary on the Augustana?

Ordinances to Be Rejected

In a sermon on the apostolic council (Acts 15:1ff.) preached on June 1, 1524, Luther set forth the principle that all ordinances beyond the Ten Commandments promulgated by the church as binding were "new dreams." He expressly included the mass and vows in that category. To regard the Decalogue as the only source for laws and ordinances—Luther's western European students did that extensively—was a very neat standard for ecclesiastical reform. Was it the only standard Luther applied? At first, only in the negative sense that Moses was superseded; the ceremonial and juridical rules of the Old Covenant, even where they were included in the Ten Commandments, were discarded. The freedom of the gospel invalidated them. That is not to imply that every church ordinance was to be dropped; the relation between freedom and obligation would be grossly oversimplified in that case. Luther looks for a middle way: the Christian conscience can decide freely between "thou shalt" and "thou shalt not." The pope on one side and Karlstadt on the other both impose human ordinances on the Christian conscience as obligations on which salvation depends. "We, however, take the middle course."[574]

For Luther, therefore, there are no Bible verses that immediately justify church ordinances or that invalidate them. There is just one criterion, applicable only by believers, that can be decisive from one case to another. It is the Christian conscience, which is burdened by human requirements and is freed for faith by the gospel. But the conscience is by no means a vacillating and arbitrary tribunal. It does not respond on its own according to its own capabilities; it answers to the address of the gospel that makes salvation independent of all human courts and grants it solely on the basis of God's mercy. This address both frees the conscience and binds it, binds it to the Word of God. The living Word that confronts my conscience liberates me from the claims of human ordinances and binds me to the divine love to which I owe my freedom. Human ordinances within the church are justified only because and insofar as they are expressions of that divine love, that is, to the extent that they serve the proclamation of the Word of salvation.[575]

This view provides a fixed standard—although it must be applied repeatedly, on a case-by-case basis—for deciding which of the existing human ordinances are to be rejected. A couple of examples will illustrate that process.

In the Middle Ages, holy places brought the divine presence especially close to believers. The pilgrimage to Jerusalem was a pious practice up to Luther's time, nurtured by wanderlust and piety. Rome and Trier were pilgrimage goals that lay closer to the Germans. But for Luther there are no longer any fixed cultic centers as in Old Testament times. We can pray anywhere, baptize in the Elbe, and celebrate mass in a field. Christ is our only altar; hearing his Word is the only worship that pleases God. With that, a host of pious usages and holy acts carefully nourished by the church are dropped. The ordinances that have structured popular religious life have lost their binding force.[576] That loss, according to the conclusion of the Augustana (sec. 2), is really a liberation.

574. *WA* 15:588.4ff., 18:76.19–20, 112.20ff., 33; *LW* 40:92–93, 129, 130. The idea of adiaphora that Luther employs here against Karlstadt was also recognized in the *Gutachten* of the Kulmbach pastors (1524) and in the confutation of the papal Ansbach *Ratschlag* (1525): "middle works, that is, those that are neither useful for salvation if done nor harmful to salvation if omitted" (Gussmann 1:1.58; *Fränk. Bek.* 379). Hence it is by no means the expression of an ecclesiastical-political compromise.

575. Instead of a wealth of possible illustrations, just one sentence addressed to Erasmus in *On the Bound Will* (*WA* 18:627.34–37; *LW* 33:54): "Thus the Word of God and the traditions of men are in irreconcilable conflict with each other, just as God himself and Satan oppose each other, each destroying the works and subverting the doctrines of the other like two kings ravaging each other's realms."

576. *WA* 32:38.10ff., 52.12ff., 16:530.26–27, 531.4–5, 16, 576.17ff., 590.29ff. One need only think of the legal questions that had been tied to the multitude of traditionally hallowed places since the second century to recognize the liberating effect of the abolition of such local privileges.

Pilgrimages were a matter of individual preference, but the commandment to fast was a burden that oppressed everyone and strongly influenced public life. Popular customs and church legislation in this area were caught up in a rash of new ordinances (CA 26.2), and the externalizing of spiritual life had led to regrettable results (CA 26.8–9, 12ff.). Criticism of these practices had been raised as early as the New Testament (CA 26.21–29), which made it correspondingly easier for the Reformers.

All the same, they did not want to do away with fasting entirely. Their pedagogical interests dictated the retention of certain bodily disciplines (CA 26.30–39). On this point Luther and Melanchthon were in complete agreement.[577] Both the Old and New Testaments witness to the fact that proper fasting is linked with service to the neighbor, which means it consists of self-giving love and sacrifice.[578] Many contemporary rules for fasting were, however, only superficially based on Scripture. It had already become a premise that fasting rules were not absolutes and that particular human circumstances (sickness, pregnancy, childhood) should be taken into consideration. In a sermon in 1528, Luther went even further: all fasting practices are to be subordinated to the common good. They have no value at all as spiritual rules. Emperor and princes, however, can order fasts if economic conditions demand it; in that case one must obey the command to fast for the temporal good it will do, that is, for the sake of love. If, on the other hand, a spiritual lord tries to force Christians to keep fasting rules by means of hunger or prison, no one should give in to him by word or deed.[579]

The examples cited here do not exhaust the list of church customs and ordinances that were eliminated by Luther's reformation. Something more must be said, however, about changes in those institutions which, in themselves, were continued. Much was in flux. We have discussed the call to the preaching office in connection with CA 14. That concept did more than cause the decline of ordination. Concentration on the sermon, the termination of celibacy, and the "running off" of the monks from the cloister fundamentally altered the public status of the spiritual estate.

Setting up new arrangements for ecclesiastical salaries and the use of endowments became a major task of the visitations. Even though there was concern for preserving the continuity of law, each of the new relationships produced a variety of new regulations. On the whole one must conclude that congregations felt that the offerings required of them for the support of a

577. See also art. 22 of the Ansbach *Ratschlag* (*Fränk. Bek.* 317–18).

578. In his lectures on Zechariah (1527; *WA* 23:292.2ff.), Luther refers with particular emphasis to Isaiah 58, a citation that is not in CA 26.

579. *WA* 23:606.10ff.; *LW* 20:278–79; *WA* 16:560.8–15, 27:364.3ff. On fasts as political measures, see above, p. 177); *WBr* 5:no. 1656.73ff.; *LW* 49:387 (Luther to Melanchthon, July 21, 1530).

pastor's family were more burdensome than before, because much more money was usually needed. Luther's sermons and pulpit announcements reveal some of the consequences of this restructuring of salaries and endowments.

The transformation of the mass had even more dramatic effects on the public. In the distribution in both kinds, every Christian was directly confronted with the fact that the words of institution "Drink of it, all of you" (CA 22.1, 10) had invalidated a host of existing ordinances and usages. The most noticeable was the disappearance of sacramental processions (CA 22.12). The abolition of the sacrifice of the mass by changing the texts of prayers makes practically no impresssion on the public mind. Article 24 does not deal directly with these liturgical changes although it gives the theological basis for them. Instead, the article emphasizes "that almost all the customary ceremonies are retained" and brings up the introduction of German hymns for the congregation as a reasonable and useful innovation (secs. 2–4). Still, if changes even in the public Sunday service were hardly noticeable, the disappearance of votive and private masses did make a deep impression on the congregations. The public ordinances went nearly unscathed. It was more the individual whose personal piety was affected when foundations that had been established for the benefit of a deceased member or for the salvation of one's own soul became worthless overnight, or when fraternal associations that had decisively affected professional and social life suddenly dropped out of sight. The repeal of previous church ordinances became most obvious to the Catholic Christian through the ending of private masses and the disappearance of the mass-priests.

New Ordinances

And yet the beginnings of new ordinances grow out of the decay of the old. Sections 2–4 of CA 24 mention the use of German hymns in the Eucharist. Understanding singing primarily as a means of instructing people in evangelical doctrine rather than as a spontaneous confession of this doctrine— which it also was and is—is especially typical of Melanchthon. For him church order is to introduce doctrine to the untutored and to familiarize them with it.[580] The Ansbach Opinion understood the task more profoundly: hymns and prayers are to stimulate the weak and assist them to love and faith; for the Kulmbach pastors, they are, as are other ceremonies, means to protect worship from disorder. Liturgical order should educate the congregation in a Christian way.[581]

580. As early as Torg. A 10 (Förstemann 1:83; Jacobs 85–86), this educational perspective was transferred from German chorales to other ceremonies and ordinances.

581. Ansbach *Ratschlag*, art. 21 (*Fränk. Bek.* 317; Gussmann 1:1–76). Luther generally envisioned the musical part of the mass in traditional terms, as can be seen from his advice to discontinue the use of the Hallelujah and joyous hymns at the beginning of Lent in 1529 (*WA* 29:37.2ff.).

Access to the mass was the heart of such ordinances. In the Fourth Lateran Council of 1215 the medieval church had made participation in the Easter Communion a duty of every baptized person and had made access to it dependent upon confession and absolution. Luther found this practice of receiving Communion at specified times in Wittenberg, and he could assume it was the same everywhere. He did not abolish it, but he took away its legalistic force. Thus ordered participation in the Sacrament became an established custom in the evangelical churches; there are no statutes to that effect. Of course territorial laws set definite days for the Lord's Supper and impose penalties on notorious despisers of the Sacrament, but they do not require participation. They rely on a tradition carried over from the Middle Ages.

Luther cultivated that tradition in his preaching and instruction. His *Admonition Concerning the Sacrament of the Body and Blood of Our Lord* appeared in the autumn of 1530 while the Augsburg diet was still in session.[582] It is a pastoral work that tries to encourage reception of the Sacrament without forcing it by fixing on specific days. We have an example of the way Luther proceeded from the pre-Easter season of 1529. Christ's words "Do this in remembrance of me" are a command. But the individual Christian is completely free in how to obey it. One is not bound to specific times. The frequency is up to the individual. Luther urges more frequent reception for those not living at home who do not get neighborly reminders, and for "fellow students," teachers, and all adults in general. He also encourages mutual consideration, especially for those who administer the Sacrament. In Wittenberg there are three chaplains and one pastor. They become overwhelmed when too many communicants come at one time. That is particularly true for the eves of festivals when those seeking private confession begin to pile up. Communicants should parcel themselves out before and after Easter; there is still time even at Pentecost.[583]

Here we encounter a classic example of how church order arises in Luther's ministry and how it is handled. Christ's command is not immediately turned into a church law; it is understood as a divine invitation. In its common acceptance of the invitation the congregation creates an ordinance for itself, the details of which are determined by the loving consideration of all for everyone else. External circumstances, therefore, play a decisive role.

Nevertheless, the holiness of the Sacrament itself also makes certain ordinances necessary. "None are admitted unless they are first heard and examined," states CA 24.6; and CA 25.1 equates this examination of faith with the

582. *WA* 30.2:595–626, esp. 598–99; *LW* 38:97–137, esp. 100–101.
583. On this, see Luther's sermons on Judica (March 14) and Maundy Thursday (March 25) of 1529 (*WA* 29:119.5ff., 205.12ff., 219ff.). For the development of ordinances in relation to worship services, see above, p. 181ff.

examination of conscience in confession. The bond between confession and Communion established by Innocent III in 1215 is here affirmed out of a Lutheran understanding of repentance and faith. It proves to be a primary factor in structuring church order, because the examination prior to Communion forms the basis for religious education of adults as well as children and youth. Even family devotions and meditation are oriented toward it.

In his exhortation on the Sacrament from 1529, Luther addresses himself particularly to the young people. They should learn the Ten Commandments, the Creed, and the Lord's Prayer at home, so that they can recite them to the deacons, who will then admit the young people to Communion—one of the roots of confirmation, although the process is clearly understood as being the first of many occasions rather than a once-and-for-all event.[584] Thus through constant use in preparation for Communion, these parts of the catechism will become stamped on individual minds and, more significant, into the daily life of each person. Precisely because the pre-Communion interview is to serve as a confession of sin, the words of law and promise are intended to govern daily behavior by correction and encouragement. Simple Christians are educated in that way; people who are accustomed to living with God's Word, such as "pastors, chaplains, Master Philipp, and similar people who know well what sin is" are exempted from repeated examinations. Those who master the catechism word for word are still a long way from assimilating the content in their hearts, and even when they do, the heart is warm one day and cold the next; Satan constantly tries to snatch the Word away from them. For that reason adults also, especially the parents of catechumens, should attend the regularly scheduled catechetical sermons. Even Luther himself prays the catechism daily. If, however, someone has not learned a thing, then he should be denied the Sacrament on his deathbed—the only use of coercion Luther recognizes as a means of discipline in connection with preparation for Communion.[585]

Luther did not intend to set up a new ordinance by the introduction of a pre-Communion interview. He saw it as an "old, praiseworthy, Christian, and necessary discipline" which was to teach Christians how to live and how to confess Christ. It was the theme of confession that stood out for him in catechetical training. To receive instruction was to confess oneself a Christian; the church that conducted it demonstrated itself to be Christian, as is evident from CA 24.6 and CA 25.1.[586] As children speak the words of the Second

584. *WA* 29:219.10ff.

585. *WA* 30.3:566.31–32, 34.2:195.14ff., 336.22ff., 449.21ff.

586. *WA* 30.3:568.10. The catechism is a "good instructor of the conscience about how to be a Christian and how to recognize Christ" (ibid., 317.32ff.; *LW* 47:52–53). On what follows: *WA* 30.3:367.19–20; *LW* 34:91; *WBr* 5:no. 1572.39ff.; *LW* 49:307 (to the elector, May 20, 1530); *WBr* 5:nos. 1602.49–50, 1590.70ff.

Article, they confess the essence of redemption. The young people of Electoral Saxony, equipped "with the catechism and Scriptures," make the territory a "beautiful paradise" and give the elector in Augsburg the assurance that God is gracious to him. And on June 25, the day on which the Confession was presented, Justus Jonas confessed himself to be Luther's catechetical student by finding his support in the explanation of the First Commandment. "Daily the fruit of the prayers of our Lutheran church and the power and effect of the catechism and children's litanies" show themselves in the fact that the threats of the opponents remain ineffectual.

Thus Luther's admonitions to the youth of Wittenberg fell on fruitful ground. He advises them to attend the quarterly series of sermons on the catechism even during the Advent season, not to desecrate the holy season by degenerate behavior at dances, and not to leave church during the final prayers of the service, especially during the litany. One should never tire of reflecting on the catechism. Luther himself prays it with his children in his daily home devotions—so that no mildew grows on it—and then meditates by himself on a chapter of Scripture or a psalm. And during the loneliness of the Coburg, he once again becomes a student of the Decalogue, learning it word for word like a child, and in the process he discovers that the Decalogue presents the dialectic of the gospel and the gospel uses the rhetoric of the Decalogue.[587]

Catechization and the pre-Communion examination that follows it are therefore not only educational means for the youth and Christian nurture for adults, they also are a way for every Christian to deepen his or her knowledge of Scripture. The public ordinance extends over into private edification and is supported by it. Christians are always students. They are learning from their mothers' laps to eternity; a lifetime is not sufficient to exhaust the resources of the catechism. Luther is a master at this learning process. He meditates on the Bible and catechism daily "as it is taught and made familiar to the children." He daily discovers "that there is always something new to learn from God's Word," and it is from this external Word that all meditation must originate. As a young monk, Luther had adopted the meditation methods of Bernard of Clairvaux, and now they are applied to religious education. Church order as educational order has its roots in the ordering of private devotions.[588] If these roots should be cut off, catechization would become lifeless rote learning, and confession prior to Communion would become an intellectual performance; then church order too would become ecclesiastical

---

587. *WA* 32:65.14ff., 209.13ff., 19ff., 64.24ff., 65.6; *WBr* 5:no. 1610.26ff. (Luther to Jonas, June 26–27, 1530).

588. *WA* 32:136.1ff., 65.15ff., 28:79.6, 31.1:227.13ff., 256.8ff., 29ff.; *LW* 14:8, 38. In the preface to the Large Catechism of 1530 (*BS* 546ff.; *BC* 358ff.), Luther held up his own devotional practice as a pattern for pastors.

discipline. Primarily, however, the imposition and the acceptance of church ordinances is the expression of piety *(pietas)*. Luther put a high value on this deutero-Pauline concept from 1 Tim. 2:2, which also summed up the educational ideals of Christian humanism. *Pietas* is preaching, prayer, and "waiting to see what God would have of us." It is thus not a matter of human virtue, to say nothing of a liturgical attitude; it concerns belief in Jesus Christ and brotherly love. It expresses itself in the mutual affection of parents and children, and even more in reverent worship "in faith and in truth," without externally binding the conscience. The connection between *pietas* and *cultus dei* is preserved, but all legalistic ritualism is sharply rejected. Indeed *pietas* does not involve bodily exercises; it is "for the purpose of meditating diligently. It is labor of the soul."[589]

Opposition to external legalism in worship does not eliminate a pedagogical appreciation for liturgical acts, because they are ordinances that possess educational value. "God intends that, in addition to the gospel, outward acts be instituted";[590] Christ did not reject the various external forms of prayer. When students who act as lectors during worship learn a "good outward prayer that is well constructed," a fine church tradition has been preserved; out of that tradition, church order is born. Of course the danger cannot be ignored: ordinances that are merely adopted in an external manner can be "pure hypocrisy." But when the heart is kindled by human need and God's promise, the gestures become expressions of profound feelings.

Church order necessarily is a part of worship, but worship does not consist in the observance of church order. The value of previously practiced ceremonies is severely questioned because "our religion consists in preaching, praising God, and exalting him, not in ceremonies as the papists teach." God doesn't bother with ceremonies; they are ephemeral, "thread and seam to the outward bag and sack." We human beings put more emphasis on pleasing God by human traditions like fasting and foundations than on obedience to his commandments. True worship consists in heartfelt reverence for God; that is the "royal road." In order to receive the Word of God, people gather for worship: the assembled hearers are the important element. The worshiped God *(deus cultus)* is the God who is revealed in his Word.[591]

589. *WA* 17.1:157.23ff., 25:11.10ff., 26–27; *LW* 29:9, 10.

590. *WA* 16:562.15–16. On what follows, see *WA* 28:74.1ff., 75.5ff., 14, 17.1:429.30ff.

591. *WA* 31.2:318.5ff., 11ff., 562.34ff., 28:672.1ff., 20:95.14ff., 96.1ff., 87.5ff., 31.2:717.5. "If the force [of the text] breaks through, listen and lay aside your wisdom, arguments, and studies, and pay attention" (*WA* 20:88.3–4). Those who would like to trace Luther's battle against externalism in ceremonies back to the "inwardness" of his concept of faith will misunderstand him. He was much more concerned about the hiddenness of God. God cannot be outwardly grasped; he can only be understood in his revealed Word: "God was not willing to become known in his majesty, but through that which he speaks in his Word" (*WA* 31.2:716.17–18). The ordered forms of worship are a part of the Word: "God is worshipped only where his Word, his sacraments, his people and ministers are present in their various orders and activities" (ibid., 717.2–4). On the discussion between Luther and Melanchthon on the idea of *cultus Dei*, see below, p. 225.

Worship has its appointed time on Sundays and festivals. As early as the Old Testament these special days were festooned with laws and ordinances. The replacement of the Sabbath with the Christian Sunday was a decisive factor in early church orders. The meaning of this change is still being discussed in the Augustana (CA 28.33, 57–60, 63) since it involved the hallowed text of the Decalogue itself. Was the replacement of the literal text of Scripture by new regulations really a sign of the spiritual authority of the church? Is that precedent actually a basis for the church's power to create new laws rather than simply to grant dispensations from existing ones? Melanchthon opposed that. Scripture—not the church (sec. 59 Latin)—did away with the Sabbath, since all Mosaic ceremonies lose their force under the gospel. The introduction of Sunday does not create a special spiritual ordinance; it simply specifies one day on which the Christian congregation is to gather for worship (sec. 60). The article views the fact that some other day could have been chosen as a sign of evangelical freedom; the connection of Sunday with the resurrection of Christ is not taken into consideration.

The Sabbath question had already been a subject of controversy between Luther and Karlstadt.[592] On the basis of Col. 2:16–17, Luther had argued for the abolition of Old Testament festival days. Even the Christian Sunday could not be defended by appealing to Moses; it was nature that taught that "one must certainly rest a day now and then so that man and beast might recuperate." Basing a holy day on natural law is compatible with the apocalyptic viewpoint of Isa. 66:23; in the New Covenant a constant Sabbath has dawned.[593] On the other hand, reading natural law in a Christian way also leads one to infer a legal obligation. The Sunday rest should be used for hearing the Word of God; therefore it should not be broken for any reason. Precisely those whose work is the heaviest need to observe the rule. Their spiritual welfare requires that they be united with fellow believers; the same healing aspect applies to family members. Thus Sunday observance is not merely a law enforced by the government; it springs from the Christian congregation's intention and task as a community of love. That is not to exclude the usefulness of Sunday for civil life as well; in fact, such a contribution corresponds to Jesus' precept (Mark 2:27). For that reason,

---

592. In Luther's work *Against the Heavenly Prophets* (1524–25; esp. *WA* 18:77ff.; *LW* 40:93–94). Karlstadt's work *On the Sabbath and Required Festivals* (1524), to which Luther refers, is reprinted in Erich Hertzsch, ed., *Karlstadts Schriften aus den Jahren 1523–25*, Neudr. dt. Literaturwerke d. 16. u. 17. Jahrh. 325 (Halle, 1956), 21–47.

593. CA 28.44, applies Col. 2:16 much more cautiously than *WA* 18:81.26ff.; *LW 40:98; WA* 16:477.6ff. This view gives rise to the mystical interpretation of the Third Commandment which Luther laid out in his *Treatise on Good Works* (*WA* 6:202ff., esp. 243ff.; *LW* 44:21–114, esp. 71ff.) and which Melanchthon adopted in his first *Loci*; see W. Maurer, *Der junge Melanchthon* (cited above, n. 49), 2:298–99. It has a later effect on the Ansbach *Ratschlag* of 1524 (*Fränk. Bek.* 318).

work is prohibited only during the time of worship; at other times people should pursue their occupations.[594]

The church ordinances in use in 1530 and presupposed or described in individual articles of the Augustana are of varied quality and character. Some are taken over from the past or revised; others are newly created. All of them, however, have their common origin in worship, especially in the Reformed Sunday service. In this context old forms are dropped and new ones created. Only a few of them, however, are completely original. The German chorale had medieval prototypes. Catechization of the youth had never been abandoned in the Middle Ages. The educational thrust of Christian humanism revived it; for example, Erasmus urged the linking of admission to the Lord's Supper with the sermons on the catechism that were held during Lent.[595] New, of course, was the extension of this catechetical practice to adult members of the congregation through interviews before Communion and the linking of these conferences with the sacrament of penance. Regardless of the specific objections that might be raised in this regard, it is amazing to see the energy with which evangelical pedagogy permeated religious life, familiarizing young and old with the basic concepts of law and gospel, and enabling them to make a conscious confession of faith. The fact that Luther's two catechisms were written almost on the eve of the diet and served as a direct preparation for it does not diminish the practical value of these edifying works in the slightest; on the contrary, it makes that value clear.

In these efforts evangelical proclamation and Christian pedagogy go hand in hand; out of the indissoluble connection between the two grow ecclesiastical orders. This is the source of their legal character. They are not coercive in the sense of governmental legislation. From their inception they have nothing to do with the police ordinances that the waning Middle Ages had created in the territories. In Christian proclamation and pedagogy it is the spirit of love, given to and transmitted by the congregation, that expresses itself. The Christian ordinances whose origins we have found in Luther and the Augsburg Confession are ordinances of love. The piety behind them is rooted in proclamation and prayer. The constituent elements of church order lie here in public worship; around it crystallizes a structure of ordinances that reaches into the home and into the devotional life of individuals. Nothing is legally prescribed; hardly anything is regulated, and then only in relation to minors and in the power of love. The structure of ordinances as we learn to know it in the Augustana and its predecessors is frail, still in great jeopardy, because it is in the process of growing and developing, but in terms of the

594. *WA* 20:504.7ff., 503.12ff., 27:363.16ff., 364.13ff. On the beginning of a holiday ordinance for Electoral Saxony, see above, pp. 178–78.
595. W. Maurer, *Gemeindezucht* (cited above, n. 167), 43ff.

spiritual norms of life by which it is governed it is clearly discernible. If we may speak of church law in this connection it is only in terms of a law of love. The possibility of such a church law was hotly debated during the composition of the Augustana.

27. THE THEOLOGICAL BASIS FOR
NEW CHURCH ORDERS

It is almost impossible to imagine the difficulty posed by the creation of new church orders for just a few territorial churches in Germany. Official Catholicism simply did not recognize novelty in this field. The legal claim of ordinances was based on their unaltered apostolicity, and Rome felt that local ordinances in the West, with few exceptions, had been amalgamated into its juridical unity. Melanchthon also considered new local ordinances to be unacceptable. He would never have conceded that the Augustana contained any. Therefore he not only asserted the Catholicity of its doctrine, but he also labeled the ordinances that he attacked in the "disputed articles" of the second part as "abuses" that had slipped into practice illegally and that contradicted their original usage. Thus he claimed that the "new" articles were in better agreement with Scripture and ancient tradition and were therefore to be recognized by all Christendom. He felt less certain in these matters of church order than he did on doctrine, however, as he admitted to Luther on July 14, 1530: "In the matter of the mass and the first group of articles of faith, I have been careful enough; on the issue of traditions, I am not yet satisfied with this document."[596]

In fact the committee discussions were centering on the questions of church order, and the evangelical side's compromise proposal—already in trouble—dealt exclusively with those points. We can begin to discover the issues involved by studying the antecedents of the Augustana.

In principle it was clear that, after the Mosaic law had been set aside, no biblical ordinance could be immediately adopted by the contemporary church. New Testament examples, such as the apostolic decree in Acts 15, possessed no legal force; the same was true of the pattern of the apostolic congregations. The only starting point could be the three components by which God himself built the way to salvation: physical baptism, physical Sacrament of the Altar, and oral Word of God.[597] In this respect God himself had established an external ordinance on which the existence of the church depended. If this ordinance was observed, was there any need for human ordinances?

596. *WBr* 5:1646.27–28. The official judgment on the two parts is in *BS* 83c–d; *BC* 47–48.
597. *WA* 18:137.12ff.; *LW* 40:147. The work *Against the Heavenly Prophets* here sets up the counterargument to Karlstadt's motto "Spirit, Spirit, Spirit."

They are indeed needed. Word and Sacrament always involve something physical and concrete, so their spiritual effect is always bound to external conditions. The effect, of course, is the main thing, but the person who longs for salvation must enter into its sphere of influence, and that requires that the external conditions be right. Church ordinances control the entry. In comparison to the external ordinances established by God, they are secondary, changeable, and variable—adapted to human circumstances. Therefore, in contrast to the Roman uniformity of practice, there is no single universal structure of human ordinances that controls that access to the sphere of divine grace with total consistency and immutability. Church ordinances are concrete, changeable, and tied to specific situations; therefore they differ from one another and vary according to time and context. If Christendom is not to set arbitrary limits on the effectiveness of Word and Sacrament, it must constantly seek to update its human ordinances.

There is, however, a unifying theme, an unchanging basic rule on which the success of such ecclesiastical concerns depends; and that is love. "The ceremonial regulations in Scripture are necessary and are to be applied in accordance with faith and love"; the classical example of how that is done is offered by Paul in respect to the circumcision of Titus. Love is the fulfillment of the law. That is what Christ will inquire about on judgment day—not showy church buildings and glittering ceremonies. The latter, however, are not without value, nor does the fulfilling of all love's commandments insure salvation. God himself instituted many ceremonies in the Old Testament. If they are abrogated, God is not displeased, but he is pleased most when the reason for the change is love.[598]

Love, therefore, is what makes human ordinances subject to change. The rules by which love produces those ordinances must always include the reservation that they can be revoked. The classical example quoted frequently by Luther is the apostolic council. It did not, as the scholastics (*iusticiarii*) thought, go beyond the Ten Commandments and invent "new dreams." Rather, it put the Noachic commandments alongside the Decalogue as normative, without intending to burden consciences with them or with circumcision—which was not commanded in the Decalogue. Its stipulations have automatically become obsolete as need for them disappeared. Thus the apostolic fathers were not setting up binding laws but only "customs or usages," without burdening consciences. So in the ancient church, "pure love, service, and support were appropriate, for the good of the neighbor."[599]

598. WA 26:90.13ff.; LW 28:341; WA 27:363.22, 40.2:69.6ff.
599. WA 26:90.16–17; LW 28:341; WA 15:588.4ff., 594.5ff., 26:574.9ff. In the lectures on Titus in 1527, Paul appears as the one who "afterwards, in opposition to the decree of the apostolic council, abrogated" the decisions of that council (WA 25:34.20–21; LW 29:40).

The result of this review is to affirm that the pope has no authority to burden consciences by issuing laws, nor can he set aside existing ordinances. His laws are only to be tolerated if they do not force consciences, because otherwise he "usurps the office of God and sets himself arrogantly in God's place . . . making sins where God does not intend them, thereby slaying souls and binding consciences."[600]

It is simply not important how changes in church ordinances come about, but is important only that they occur. They are effected through the great historical changes that God accomplishes—most notably in the abolition of Old Testament ceremonies in the New Testament. But even the quiet changes brought about by the passage of time remove the old and compel the new. The same is true for the individual. As long as a young monk lives in the monastery without a burdened conscience, monastic orders can be tolerated. The problems begin when the conscience is tested (mit den Anfechtungen). History develops in the same way: circumstances arise that compel a change or at least suggest it. That becomes clear precisely in worship. That we pray is an unalterable commandment. How we pray depends upon the public and private circumstances. They create a host of possibilities that surround prayer as a ring holds a precious stone.[601]

Who in the church has the right to change ordinances? We have just mentioned the possibility that they can become obsolete by their own inner development. Human intervention during that process is not excluded. "The congregation of God [ecclesia dei] has the power to establish ceremonies in connection with festivals, foods, fasts, prayers, vigils, etc., not for others but only for itself; it has never done otherwise and never will."[602] A general principle of legal development is thereby laid down: church ordinances must always correspond to the commonly held faith, yet they cannot claim universal validity. They apply only to the area for which they were instituted. Church ordinances are therefore limited not only in terms of time but also geographically. Who has the right to formulate them? "The pastor or, where appropriate, the congregation," answers Luther in the Large Commentary on Galatians. The congregation decides when worship shall be held. What happens during a service—in addition to administration of the sacraments, hymns, and Scripture reading—is within the jurisdiction of the pastor, who is responsible for the individual actions that are performed during worship or that are connected to it. "Those are our rites, because we perform them according to our own decisions, the stipulation being that love is maintained."

This love is directed particularly toward the young and the weak in the

---

600. WA 18:112.23ff.; LW 40:130. See WA 15:591.7ff., 594.4, 595.2ff.
601. WA 31.2:562.34ff., 15:595.5–6, 30.2:421.30–31, 683.10–11, 13–14, 22–23.
602. WA 30.2:421.1ff. On what follows, see WA 40.1:672.11ff.

congregation. It seeks to rouse them to faith and love through a rich worship experience and through singing and prayer. Love justifies the pedagogical element in church orders; love concerns adults as well as children. Of course it promotes only a "simple and childlike holiness," but if that is understood and is not confused with the true righteousness of faith, it is worth keeping. The simple man is impressed by these childish laws (*pueriles leges*) that seem laughable to the wise; therefore such "magic acts" can influence people just as they do in the temporal realm at coronation festivities. One ought not assume that disdain of the common people lies behind these expressions, as was typical in humanistic circles. In fact God himself is the one who, in the Old Testament, laid down that sort of childish law in order to teach his people. Thus we too should create similar ordinances suitable for educating common people. The only thing to guard against is "taking discipline and morality out of the school and into the church" so that, as happened previously, it finally turns into "pure idolatry." Ceremonies are good for maintaining the difference between what is holy and what is private, but they must not obscure God's Word.[603]

The shaping of church order is rooted in loving concern for the spiritually weak. It is a way of teaching people which takes the reality of existence in the church very seriously. Not all baptized persons live in faith and love. The entire congregation is "still very far" from being Christian, and for that reason there must be external laws such as the one about keeping Sunday holy. True Christians do not need those laws. The whole world, however, is not yet full of Christians, so external ordinances are necessary. Those rules are only a restraint to the uneducated who do not know the gospel "so that they can be kept for the freedom of the gospel which will be bestowed upon them when they believe."[604]

This pedagogical argument was the Achilles' heel of the early Reformation position on church order. It was connected not only to the pedagogical concerns of Christian humanism but also to the moral discipline that the rising patriarchal absolutist state had been developing as early as the end of the Middle Ages. It endangered the distinction between the two kingdoms— as had been the case since the visitations—by blurring the boundary between the coercive power of the Christian state and the loving force of church order. It is true that the pedagogical effect was supposed to be only on those who were unbelievers and not yet Christian, while the true Christians were basically free from all church ordinances and were bound to them only out of love for the weak in faith. But who would want to draw a clear line between no

603. *Fränk. Bek.* 317, 400–401; *WA* 32:52.32ff., 53.7ff., 31ff. (from Luther's Easter sermon at the Coburg, April 17, 1530), 16:561.18–19, 32:54.13ff.
604. *WA* 20:502.8–9, 504.11–12, 16:576.4ff.

faith, weak faith, and real faith? Would it be Christians testing their own faith? If they have grasped the justification of the sinner, they are in no position to make that judgment. A representative of church or civil government? How could that person judge another's faith from the outside? No, precisely because church order, like a tender little plant, grows on the border where faith turns into helping love, it was impossible to bring this love into harmony with the educational practice of the patriarchal state. What we have learned about the beginning of new church orders or the fruitful development of existing ones in the 1520s was not yet completely clear at the time; the relation between law and gospel in this matter required concrete definitions.

The problem was an old one. Melanchthon wrestled with it to little avail as early as 1520–21.[605] It was precisely in relation to church order that Luther gave closer attention to the problem, first against Karlstadt and then in discussion with others. Karlstadt resembled the papists in crushing Christian freedom with his rigid demands, so he too was a "murderer of souls"; Luther confronted him in 1524 with major points of the Christian doctrine, particularly the law for everyman and the freedom of Christian conscience. Next it was the Livonian Christians who had to learn to add love to their freedom in externals and to be ready to give up such freedom for the sake of the common people; their preachers were not to presume upon the freedom of faith but to act out of service to love. Finally Luther had to deal with Erasmus, who scoffed at an easy freedom of confession and penance and who had to be reminded that God's Word brings freedom in the face of all anxiety and human servitude.[606] And to mention another Reformer in this connection, Andreas Osiander in his statement to the Augsburg diet clearly distinguished Christian freedom from all arbitrariness and drew the conclusion that "therefore human order even in the church is not to be rejected as long as it is not set against Christian freedom in the conscience." In his preparation for the diet during March and April of 1530, Luther himself focused on the problem: "ordered, seemly, external ceremonies and worship" belong to the marks of Christ's church, but they must all be tied in with "proper instruction about Christian freedom and about how one may make godly use of external worship."[607]

28. PROBLEMS OF EVANGELICAL CHURCH LAW

The relation between law and gospel, the key question of Reformation theology, is reflected in practical church life by the relation between law and

605. See W. Maurer, *Der junge Melanchthon* (cited above, n. 49), 2:175ff.

606. *WA* 18:112.31–32, 66.3ff.; *LW* 40:130, 83; *WA* 18:419.7ff., 420.1ff.; *LW* 53:47, 48; *WA* 18:627.25ff.; *LW* 33:54.

607. Gussmann 1.1:309.27–29; *WA* 30.2:250.40ff., 251.1–2 (from the preparatory studies for the *Exhortation to All Clergy*).

freedom. For this reason, church practice cannot satisfy rules of casuistry, nor can it content itself with general maxims. Its path must lie between the two extremes. Evangelical church law should point out that path and thus let the tension between law and freedom become vital and fruitful. That is a painful—and not totally achievable—task!

We have seen how this task continually cropped up in the composition and first practical application of the Augustana, especially during the unity nego-tiations with those of the old faith, and how the Reformers constantly discussed it among themselves. It does not directly determine the topics of Luther's writing during his time at the Coburg, but its questions are still evident. Luther's preparatory document, the *Exhortation to All Clergy As-sembled at Augsburg*, and its offer of compromise had to take up a number of legal questions. From the abuse of indulgences to the reestablishment of "schools for poor boys,"[608] it touches on a host of organizational, legal, and financial questions. Its exposition hews to the line of reform proposals that had been made repeatedly since the book *To the German Nobility*. New legal concepts do not appear, nor would they suit a compromise as conservative as the one proposed in the *Exhortation*.[609] Of course, as soon as the impending treaty negotiations went into details, difficult problems would arise.

At the same time we must remember that from the beginning Luther doubted that the compromise would work. As early as the first days of May, in connection with the *Exhortation*, he bitterly noted the slanders with which his opponents persecuted the evangelical teaching, and the proud arrogance and resistance to new ideas on the part of the bishops and princes of the old faith. At first these were confidential expressions spoken in the presence of the trusted Veit Dietrich;[610] but if one also considers the frequent references to the martyr Leonhard Kaiser and others, one understands what Luther feared from his opponents in Augsburg. As early as the middle of June, perhaps influenced by a letter from Jonas, he despaired of a favorable conclusion to the diet.[611] The mischief of the ecclesiastical seducers of the

---

608. *WA* 30.2:281ff., 318.24; *LW* 34:16, 38. The section headings of the *Exhortation* are roughly equivalent to those of the "disputed articles."

609. New legal questions, of course, were in the offing: What should be the relationship between the free proclamation of the gospel and "episcopal jurisdiction" and the installation of pastors, or excommunication and the struggle against heresy (*WA* 30.2:342.21ff.; *LW* 34:50.)?

610. *WA* 31.1:266.23ff., 272.18ff., 296.23ff., 29, 298.6ff. Luther's dictated notes in prepara-tion for the edition of the Psalms that appeared in 1531 are full of references to contemporary events. On the dating, see ibid., 259; the peaceful time before the middle of June was most productive.

611. See ibid., 321.30–31: "Duke John of Saxony has been completely abandoned, and every-one hopes that it will ruin our chances; therefore help us, dear Lord" (on Ps. 17:6). At Psalm 18, Luther interrupted his dictation until June 26 (ibid., 259). The letter from Justus Jonas to Luther on June 12 (*WBr* 5:no. 1587) reported on the tensions in Augsburg on the eve of the emperor's arrival.

people was too great; that is illustrated with apocalyptic imagery in terms of indulgences and purgatory. From the beginning, Luther was fighting mad.[612]

Thus the change that occurred at the end of June and that we discussed above was no sudden event; preparations had been going on for some time. With his *Disavowal of Purgatory*—also conceived much earlier—Luther opened a new offensive. Luther also wants to enumerate in other open letters a list of papal lies and abominations as a warning to posterity. These polemical goals really left no room for the contemplated reconciliation with the bishops; Luther cannot blame a breakdown, as he later often did, entirely on his opponents. Even when he asserts his readiness for peace in a letter to the cardinal archbishop Albrecht of Mainz, on July 6, he is thinking primarily of the political armistice that he energetically pursues in the following months, rather than a compromise over questions of church organization.[613] For him those questions lie behind the reconciliation negotiations only to the extent that he has to reject efforts by the defenders of the old faith to make legal claims that obscure the truth of the gospel. When they demand that the traditional church orders be reinstituted, Luther will not budge an inch, even when they concede two of the former points of compromise—both kinds and the marriage of priests. The problematic of evangelical church law in a positive sense does not even enter the picture.[614]

The same thing is true of the published polemical works. They are, to be sure, supplied with admonitions about church structure, but these exhortations are pastoral rather than programmatic; they are sermons to the various estates, particularly the German psalm expositions. The four sections taken from the brief Psalm 117 are addressed to the nobles and princes; the *Sermon on Keeping Children in School* is intended for citizens and parents; the *Admonition Concerning the Sacrament of the Body and Blood of Our Lord* is directed to the sacramental community, as is the exposition of Psalm 111. Where these works touch on questions of order, they speak to the Christian conscience that is guided by love.

Love does not create Christian ordinances; it recognizes them as givens, works of God. They do not arise out of the creation; they are "all his ordaining and institution which he has set up by his Word and command, so that there are the estates of father and mother, priests, Levites according to

612. *WA* 31.1:294ff. (on Psalm 10, probably dictated at the end of May). The exposition proves that the *Disavowal of Purgatory*, written in July, was not originally conceived after Luther had read the CA and had noted that it omitted the question of purgatory; this is in contrast to O. Clemen (*WA* 30.2:361).

613. Ibid., 397ff.; see also 367.24ff.

614. *WBr* 5:no. 1642.9ff. (Luther to Melanchthon, July 13; quoted in part in Reu 348). On the concession proposed by Duke George and reported through Jonas, see *WBr* 5:nos. 1630.18ff. (and also *WBr* 13:156–57), 1643.13ff.

the law of Moses, manservant and maidservant, marriage, lord and subject, as well as Sabbaths and festivals, worship and church law and the like, all of which are his work or his creation, because he has commanded and instituted them."[615] We again recognize in this list the doctrine of the three hierarchies by which God maintains human life in community. "Church law," therefore, also belongs to the spiritual "orders"; it relates to the New Testament "priests and Levites" and to New Testament holy days and worship. It brings over everything that God "instituted" through those offices and institutions into contemporary church life. Church law is neither human ordinances nor divine cultic law, but God's ordinance, shaped in freedom according to his commandment of love.

Thus, almost in passing, Luther set up a principle for evangelical church law, something he had not done in the more polemic writing of the Coburg period. His work *On the Keys*,[616] which takes up the theme of CA 28, strikes at the heart of papal and episcopal hierarchical claims. Luther repeats the thesis he had proclaimed since 1518: the power of the keys was not given to Peter but to all Christians. It does not form the basis for any human authority to rule over others with laws and dispensations. Laws cover the whole congregation and are simply instructions on what one is to do and to allow. Thus, they apply God's law and in that way form the foundation for the application of penitential discipline, although they are by no means identical with it. Grace and law are two different things as separate from each other as heaven and earth.[617] From this distinction between the two ways of governing, Luther draws conclusions for the understanding of law. Only temporal government has the authority to set up laws. The papal claims are invalid; if they cannot be based on Holy Scripture, the reputation of the "holy spiritual law" amounts to nothing.[618] Any linking of the church of the Word to this law seems excluded.

That is especially the case with Luther's *Warning to His Dear German People*, written in October 1530, and published the following April. The decision of the diet openly proclaims the rejection of the gospel. The offer of peace in Luther's *Exhortation to All Clergy* has been refused. Now one can no longer pray for peace but must brace for revolt and war. Under such circumstances there is nothing left but the refusal of obedience to the militant emperor. The good that the gospel has brought is no longer recognized; evangelical ordinances are reviled. And yet in the midst of all this confusion,

615. *WA* 31.1:399.25ff.; *LW* 13:358 (on Ps. 111:3).
616. 1st version (end of July to early August), *WA* 30.2:435ff.; 2d version (end of August), ibid., 465ff.; *LW* 40:325.
617. *WA* 30.2:443.28ff., 439.2–3, 471.23; *LW* 40:332.
618. *WA* 30.2:472.17ff.; *LW* 40:333. The passage is missing in the first draft—an indication of how Luther's polemic intensified.

"praise God, the form of a Christian church can again be discerned," because the article on the righteousness of faith has remained and will remain. That brings along with it the orderly form of the church which depends on the doctrine of justification. Justification *(Rechtfertigung)* and church law *(Recht der Kirche)* belong together.[619]

Luther's strong emphasis on this connection by the end of the diet is related to an experience that became significant to him only later on. It showed him that it was not enough simply to take the ordinances for church office and worship which were at hand in the *ordo ecclesiasticus* and restore them to their original form, purged of any corruptions that had developed in the meantime. These ordinances also needed a new theological basis that rested on the Pauline doctrine of justification. Luther became aware of this necessity in the middle of July, when Melanchthon, in the light of the impending treaty negotiations, reopened discussion on the compromise that the Electoral Saxons had planned before the diet began and that Luther had made public in May through his *Exhortation.* We have already seen repeatedly that the details of this compromise were by no means entirely clear and that when Melanchthon tried to clarify these questions through an exchange of letters with Luther in July, the understanding of CA 28 seemed in jeopardy.

The only reason for looking at this correspondence again at this point is that it shows how the basic questions of evangelical church law came so clearly into focus for Luther that he never again lost sight of them, as the writings and notes from the Coburg period demonstrate. In fact, they gave him the impetus for one of the most important lines of thought of his later years.

Melanchthon opens the correspondence on July 14 in urgent haste, almost with a certain nervousness.[620] During the painful period of waiting, between the presentation of the Augustana (June 25) and the submission of the *Confutatio* (August 3), the scholars from Electoral Saxony are looking for guidelines to govern the impending theological negotiations. Points for discussion are being raised; Melanchthon struggles with his colleagues for answers. In order to clarify intentions and to build a consensus, he needs Luther's authority.[621] But he is also having his own struggle for clarity. He is satisfied with the doctrinal articles and with the treatment of the mass in the Augustana, but not with the treatment of questions of order; and it is on those points that he anticipates the major controversy with his opponents.[622]

619. *WA* 30.3:276–77, 291.20ff., 317ff., esp. 317.36ff.; *LW* 47:11, 30, 52ff., esp. 52–53.

620. *WBr* 5:no. 1656. Here I insert the following excerpts from letters and cite their number and line in the text: no. 1656 (Luther to Melanchthon, July 21); *LW* 49:378–93; nos. 1663 (Melanchthon to Luther, July 27), 1673 and 1674 (Luther to Melanchthon, August 3 and 4), 1685 (Luther's final word to Melanchthon, August 15).

621. *WBr* 5:no. 1655.13ff., p. 507 (Melanchthon to Veit Dietrich, July 27).

622. Ibid., 1646.16ff., 27ff.

Zwingli's total rejection of liturgical traditions in his *Ratio Fidei* makes the situation even worse (1646.10ff.). Melanchthon cannot shake loose so easily; for him these obligations endure.

Melanchthon lists five sources of ecclesiastical traditions.[623] First, the penitential system with its need for satisfaction, and then those traditions that claim to be eternally valid natural laws. Neither of these first two sources have any binding force, as Paul has shown. That is the basis of Luther's reformation.

Three obligatory kinds of tradition remain: some traditions exist for the sake of church order according to 1 Cor. 14:40; some are for the training of the young; and some are signs of gratitude that arise out of faith. Melanchthon's Aristotelian, goal-oriented thought comes through here, and also his pedagogical streak. These three groups of ordinances are evaluated by the goals they seek: protection of worship from the disorderly and the ignorant, and thankful gestures that testify to faith. These standards reveal the teacher's understanding of worship. Worship is not the exuberant expression of faith but a ritual introduction into the faith.

For that reason worship can also be regulated and required. In these matters of church order Melanchthon is concerned with goal-oriented and goal-setting activities; that means he is concerned with the power to command in the church. Bishops rule in the church by virtue of temporal law (1646.25ff.). That had been recognized by the Saxon compromise proposal and was affirmed in CA 28.19 and 29.[624] How was this recognition to be implemented in the anticipated treaty negotiations? How was it to be supported theologically and limited politically? Here—as Melanchthon rightly sensed—lay the real difficulty. It was natural to expect that the opponents—whether prince-bishops or temporal lords—would make a one-sided appeal to their power (*potestas;* 1646.56ff.). Melanchthon ran into this demand when he tried to base church ordinances exclusively on their pedagogical or edifying objectives. Naturally both sides presupposed that such objectives must be generally in accord with Scripture, although they argued over details. Setting the criteria for these decisions had been the task of the Augustana. Melanchthon should have begun with those criteria when he and his Saxon colleagues in Augsburg prepared themselves for the impending negotiations. The fact that he did not do that made his correspondence with Luther more difficult from the start.

623. The relevant section (no. 1646.31–64) appears not to have been an original part of the letter, because Luther is mentioned in the third person (ibid., 42); it may have been a working paper at Augsburg.

624. In writing to Luther on July 27 (no. 1663.12), Melanchthon appealed to these two paragraphs. Indeed Luther himself had conceded "episcopal jurisdiction" with certain limitations in his *Exhortation to All Clergy* (WA 30.2:342.21ff.; *LW* 34:50).

Melanchthon recognized his difficulties. Deducing the power of bishops from the cultic authority of Jewish and heathen rulers in the Old Testament (1646.58ff.) was an undertaking that offered meager results. Luther interpreted Melanchthon's biblical citations as referring only to temporal political authority and made even that political power dependent on the consent of the people (1656.54ff.; *LW* 49:386). These examples had nothing to offer to the formulation of an evangelical church order; they had more to do with the limitation of princely power by the other estates.

Melanchthon weakened his position even further by the examples he cited out of medieval tradition (1663.15ff.). He himself could not approve unconditionally the self-imposed pious practices that Bernard of Clairvaux had introduced into monastic devotion and that Thomas had tried to justify. Luther, however, rejected them from the start as a transgression of the First Commandment when they posed as divine commands. Luther preferred to discuss them only as private devotion and not as public worship (1674.37ff.). He could not imagine what Melanchthon intended to prove theologically by these examples. In fact they were better proof of dependence on medieval piety and churchliness than on Reformation theology.

We do not intend to elucidate Luther's written replies one by one at this point. We rather wish to show how the arguments they present are also applied in other literary works from this same period and how the total output that is revealed by this comparative method reflects Luther's struggle with the problem of an evangelical church order.

Luther was so greatly aroused by Melanchthon's inquiry of July 14 that, before answering on July 21, he drew up a series of theses that were printed in Nürnberg and reached Augsburg by August 22. They did not refer directly to Melanchthon, but they were intended to provoke the opponents and thus head off the developments expected by the Saxon representatives.[625] With elemental power they attack the question Melanchthon posed about the authority of ecclesiastical acts (theses 1–8): the church may not draw up any articles of faith; it has never done so and never will be able to do so, and the same is true for basic ethical principles (*praeceptum bonorum operum*). In those matters, Holy Scripture is the only source; the church does not make the rules. Instead, it is itself the product of those original doctrinal and moral givens; its goal is set by the divine promises they contain. The divine content of Scripture is the original and decisive authority; the church possesses authority only in a derived form, just as a servant who is authorized to carry the seal of his master.

With piercing clarity Luther here answers the question about church

625. *WA* 30.2:420ff. On their origin and German translation, see O. Clemen, ibid., 413ff.

authority posed by Melanchthon and discussed in the treaty negotiations at Augsburg. It is a theological answer; it deals exclusively with God's will as revealed in law and gospel and manifested in the Creed and the Decalogue. Luther's steadfastness and persuasive power is rooted in the simplicity with which this answer is asserted. It sweeps away the alternatives that Melanchthon raised at the end of his inquiry (1646.80ff.): whether in church order one is to recognize the authority of human powers that have been instituted by God—including bishops who rule by human right (1646.79–80)—or whether consciences are wounded by that authority.

For Luther that question is impossible. In his view both alternatives leave God out of the picture. After all, every human office-bearer derives authority from God, and consciences are bound to him alone. It is no more than collegial politeness when, in his answer of July 21, Luther picks up Melanchthon's use of causal categories and then totally transforms it after brushing aside such scholastic apparatus with supreme irony (1653.5ff.). At the same time, it is a mark of Luther's dialectical superiority that he realizes Melanchthon has not put the question correctly when he asks about the final cause (*causa finalis*) (1656.7ff.; *LW* 49:382); Luther focuses on the efficient cause (*causa efficiens*), because that leads to an inquiry about the person who is authorized to set up the ordinances.

Luther appears, in his letter to Melanchthon—in contrast to his recently written *Propositiones*—to consider the question of ends only in passing (1656.17; *LW* 49:383), but he actually deals with it at a fundamental level. God has appointed two administrations (1656.11; *LW* 49:383) side by side, each with its own authority. He has forbidden them to be mixed. God is therefore the highest efficient cause for everything that happens in the three earthly estates or hierarchies. Therefore the same persons can serve the same divine authority in various capacities, in ways appropriate to each, the Wittenberg "bishop" Bugenhagen also as father, and the celibate Würzberg bishop Conrad von Thüngen also as imperial prince and temporal lord. Luther says he has treated this doctrine of the efficient cause sufficiently in his other writings on God's threefold way of governing (1656.17ff.; *LW* 49:383).

These distinctions have three implications for the Augsburg negotiations:

1. A bishop cannot impose an ordinance on his congregations by virtue of his own authority without their explicit or implicit consent. As bishop he has no ruling power over his congregations. They are free lords and, with their bishop, are bound only to God's law. Church law consists in the bishop and congregation's applying God's law together, adjusting it cooperatively according to circumstances (1656.27ff.; *LW* 49:384).

2. As temporal lord—Conrad von Thüngen as Duke of Franconia—the

bishop does not have the coercive jurisdiction over his church, as church, that he has over the civil community. That limitation is required by the difference between temporal and spiritual power—a difference that must be preserved at the risk of one's life (1656.38ff.; *LW* 49:385).

3. As prince, the bishop may exercise the same power of command over his subjects that other princes exercise. Here, as elsewhere, force is part of the realm of temporal authority or of paternal power. Under no circumstances, however, should this force be transferred from the temporal to the ecclesiastical community (1656.44ff.; *LW* 49:385).

We find the clearest and most basic expression of Luther's doctrine of the two kingdoms in this letter of July 21, written at the moment when everything at Augsburg hung in the balance. The conservative attitude on the existing orders of the empire is unmistakable. And yet what revolutionary effects must be generated by this doctrine of the two kingdoms and of God as the ultimate cause of all ecclesiastical and political events. Some unresolved questions arise. The centuries-long unity which existed between the princely and episcopal offices would dissolve if a bishop were to conduct his office in an evangelical manner. It was clear that in Germany, in contrast to England and Scandinavia, the existing episcopal office could not be transplanted into the new relationships. Questions also are raised about the governance of the church by territorial princes, as that practice had developed since the Saxon visitations and had been given its religious blessing—in Luther's eyes too— by the confessional act at Augsburg; whether its subsequent development corresponded to Luther's idea must, according to Holl, be investigated afresh. Above all, the basic demarcation between civil and ecclesiastical communities had implications far beyond the sixteenth century and into the nineteenth. Luther certainly realized that such a demarcation would give an independent status to the sphere of church law. Even though his distinction between church law and secular law (1656.63; *LW* 49:386) echoes terminology of the past, his exclusion of all external force from the sphere of church law laid the foundation for an evangelical church order.

Luther went far beyond Melanchthon on this point when he—if only for the sake of argument—conceded to the bishops the power to rule by human right (*iure humano*) and seriously considered that Duke George in Dresden could secularize the bishoprics in Ducal Saxony and Bohemia as a Counter-Reformation measure (1646.79, 1656.104ff.; *LW* 49:389). Luther further widened this distance from Melanchthon in the *Propositiones* when he applied the principle of God's sole authority in matters of church order to concrete cases.[626]

626. *WA* 30.2:421 (theses 9–18).

He drew fairly narrow boundaries. Ceremonies could not and should not contradict the God-given Creed and commandments. They should not extend beyond the circle of the congregation itself; they are valid only there and are not immutable. They ought neither bind nor confuse consciences. They are also limited by their workability; in addition to being grounded in the Word of God they have to be based on practical reason shaped by love. Celibacy and monastic vows violate these principles; therefore no congregation can permit these medieval vestiges to remain in its midst.

Even before the letter of July 21, but in conformity with it, Luther had defined the relationship between congregation and bishop (proposition 16 speaks of "pastor or prelate"). Congregational orders can only be established by the agreement of both parties. The pastor has the right and duty to propose new ordinances and to recommend the amendment or abolition of surviving ones—all of this, however, only with the concurrence of the congregation. The scope of this relationship remains undefined. It is assumed that all the baptized who believe belong to the congregation. The jurisdiction of the pastor can just as well encompass a province as a city, or even the whole world; there is room for division into bishoprics, and even for a reformed papacy.

In a brilliant, almost lightninglike flash of insight—certainly there were only a few hours available for the composition of the *Propositiones*—Luther sketched the outlines of an ordered church reform that would span all of Christendom. The proposal was certainly not intended to be a document for the negotiators in Augsburg, but it does indicate the goal Luther would have liked to see realized. The correspondence between Luther and Melanchthon is governed by scholastic terminology, which does not permit such clear statements as those revealed in the preceding *Propositiones*. Instead, Luther presses for the sole significance of the efficient cause in contrast to Melanchthon's one-sided preference for the final cause. If God as the efficient cause is not the starting point, then everything else is pure fancy or even idol worship (1673.20). Stated without the stilted Aristotelian terminology: it denies the First Commandment. There, in God's insistent word of command, the effective cause for every legitimate occurrence in the church can be found. Apart from it neither princes nor bishops have any power to set up binding ordinances in the church. There is no ecclesiastical authority without reference to God's Word (1674.7ff., 53ff.).

Certain basic themes of the perspective that was first suggested in the *Propositiones* and then further developed in the letters to Melanchthon also occur in other drafts from Luther's stay in the Coburg, especially in the poorly titled fragments "On the Power to Make Laws in the Church" (*De potestate leges ferendi in ecclesia*).[627] As in the letters—although not yet in the

627. *WA* 30.2:681ff. On these notes collected and transmitted to posterity by Veit Dietrich, see below, n. 638.

Propositiones—even the most pious among the bishops is denied the power of command in the church. As proof, passages of the New Testament are cited which speak of the serving role of the disciples.[628] The *Propositiones* had spoken less of the personal ruling power of the prelates than of the power of approval that belongs to the church in general; this power had played a role in anti-Reformation polemics.[629] Here Luther understands it to be judicial authority and contests the church's right to it as early as the *Propositiones*, in the August 15 letter to Melanchthon, and also in the "De potestate." In other words the church possesses no decision-making authority (*autoritas iudicalis*) over the direct divine testimonies. Only one judge can approve; that means God instead of the church, not the church instead of God.[630] Luther likes to illustrate the difference between God's power to establish law and the church's power to exercise jurisdiction by the analogy of the master who signs and seals his decisions and the servant who checks the authenticity of a seal, recognizes it, and then does what his office requires.[631]

Thus, the church cannot establish its own jurisdiction but can only acknowledge the jurisdiction given it by God. This limitation also involves the doctrine of the two kingdoms. What is legitimate for temporal authority in its own realm, namely, the enforcement of law by coercive power, is denied to ecclesiastical authority. Luther speaks of that only in passing in the *Propositiones:* by treating ceremonial questions with the same dignity as doctrinal ones the papacy is mixing what God wants to have rigidly separated. It is in the letters to Melanchthon that the distinction of the two kingdoms in relation to the jurisdictional claims of the bishops is stated in classical fashion. The bishop cannot make anything obligatory; he can only confirm what has been established by God and accepted by the congregation. This is the sphere of spiritual freedom, not of human lordship; the congregation dies for its freedom. The negotiators in Augsburg should never tolerate the tyranny of the bishops.[632]

In the *Propositiones*,[633] Luther had called this overstepping of boundaries by the spiritual authorities heresy, and in the process, through a more detailed analysis of the concept of heresy, had condemned the opponents'

628. Ibid., 681.3ff. The use of *causa efficiens* indicates that this fragment is later than the correspondence (ibid., 681.14).

629. Ibid., 420.18, 23, 25; 686.31ff., 687.3ff. The notes refer to the connections that exist between the *Propositiones* and the fragment *"De potestate."*

630. Ibid., 420.19, 23, 687.3, 10ff.; *WBr* 5:no. 1685.18ff. The fragment is probably later than the letter. Notable is the logical pattern of major and minor customs, which can be seen as a unifying element of style.

631. *WA* 30.2:420.26, 687.14ff.

632. Ibid., 422.6ff.; *WBr* 5:no. 1656.27ff., 81ff.; *LW* 49:384, 388.

633. *WA* 30.2:422-23. One can imagine that Luther already had the carefully constructed set of theses 20-39 on hand when he had to answer Melanchthon's question on the ruling power of bishops by return mail. The theses would then have been an offensive arsenal already in reserve. The *Exhortation* had already denounced the proceedings against married priests (see above, p. 71), as had the *Sermon on Keeping Children in School* (ibid., 585.25ff.; *LW* 46:256).

practice of convicting married priests of heresy and handing them over to the Inquisition. In his letter to Melanchthon of July 21,[634] Luther does not go into the individual sins of the bishops but places them broadly under the ban according to Matthew 18 because of their open tyranny; only public repentance can free them. In "De potestate," Luther uses laws regarding heresy as the basis for this break.[635] The bishops want to rule, and they have destroyed the church. Their misuse of Scripture and their contempt for their office show that they are enemies of God.

Later notes show that Luther continued to wage the battle against the heretical papal church from the Coburg. The opponents appeal to their possession of the gospel and the sacraments, as well as to their preservation of the apostolic succession. Historical examples, however, show that such possessions do not eliminate heresy. Only when the papists are ready to confess the misuse of their Lord's gifts can they again be recognized as true servants of God.[636]

This discussion of the true and false church is connected to the question about the efficient cause of church order, because it arises out of the relation between church and Word of God. Only when the church accepts the Word of God—as the faithful servant accepts the master's seal—do its ordinances have validity and obligatory force. God is the creator of the church; it is his creation. He speaks his authoritative word of command, and the church follows it. The church is under God's Word. It testifies to the gospel, and without it no one would know what the gospel is. To be sure, the gospel can exist without the church, but not the church without the gospel.[637] That, however, is the situation in the papal church; spiritual laws have abolished God's Word.[638] Christ and his apostles did not found the Word on the church but founded the church upon the Word. God's Word assures us where the church is, and not the other way around. The canonicity of the four Gospels does not rest on the approval of the church; the approval itself presupposes recognition of the gospel within the church. Augustine's frequently quoted saying about the connection between gospel and church is wrongly interpreted if one concludes from it that faith depends upon the church rather than the gospel.[639]

634. *WBr* 5:no. 1656.82ff.; *LW* 49:388.

635. *WA* 30.2:681.15ff. This is another summons to repentance.

636. Ibid., 684.20ff. The attack against the heretic Roman church is carried on under the slogan *mendacia*, "lies," in ibid., 685.8ff., 686.18ff.

637. Ibid., 681.33ff., 682.4ff.

638. Ibid., 473.15ff.; *LW* 40:334. This harsh judgment makes its appearance in the second version of the work *On the Keys*, which means at the end of August 1530; the intensification of the first version occurred after the end of July. The fragments we have discussed should probably also be placed within this same month-long period.

639. *WA* 30.2:686.31ff., 687.8ff., 35ff., 688–690. One could entitle the whole section from 681.1 to 690.12 "The Church Is Not Mistress Over God's Word." The present title which we have used in referring to the work seizes on just one key word from the first line of text. Augustine's famous phrase about gospel and church (*Contra epistolam Manichaei* 5.6, *MSL* 42, 176) may be found as early as 1520, in the *Babylonian Captivity* (*WA* 6:561.3ff.; *LW* 36:107).

Thus, in the summer of 1530, Luther was prompted once again to lay a theological foundation for church order. He began from the well-known doctrine of God's two—or three—ways of ruling. That doctrine makes it impossible to transfer worldly coercive power to the church. Behind this distinction, however, lies the question of spiritual authority, and this is where reflection on the efficient cause plays a decisive role. God alone possesses the authority to order and to make laws. The church acts legitimately only when it follows his Word in obedience. Thus reflection on the efficient cause defines the relationship between church and divine word of command. Only when the church acts in accordance with that Word does it act legitimately; then it is an ordering power according to God's will. God's Word prevents the church from acting independently in matters of law.

Luther's concern about a theological foundation for church order thus involves central issues of Reformation theology. To what extent is it linked to the doctrine of justification? This final question forms the bridge between the first and second parts of this work.

29. CHURCH ORDER AND THE DOCTRINE
OF JUSTIFICATION

In his letter of July 14, by which he opened the debate, Melanchthon wants this question to receive as little attention as possible. When Luther deals with episcopal power, he is not to bring in the freedom of the believer that grows out of justification. The Pauline dialectic between freedom and obedience is not suitable for the simple Christian, because Paul's subjecting himself, on occasion, to the Jewish law makes it hard for his followers to grasp it.[640] At the beginning of his response, Luther does not discuss this criticism of Paul by Melanchthon. Only after the collapse of the first phase of the committee negotiations at Augsburg on August 15 does he protest that Paul is the only authority who has made apostolic—and that means legitimate—decisions about questions of church order. No law applies here; here reason loses its power. Here only the Holy Spirit can be fully and completely judge. Melanchthon's rational structure of the four causes for church order is rendered totally useless by this inconceivable reality. Law belongs to no one within the church; no one may consider himself a *causa efficiens*. Nor is there a final cause in the church, because everything necessary is already there. Furthermore, these are all spiritual and eternal matters that, like faith and love, human beings do not define; they are laid down in God's Word. This Word, communicated by God and believed to eternal life in the power of the Spirit, makes all ecclesiastical laws superfluous.[641]

640. *WBr* 5:no. 1646.65ff.
641. Ibid., no. 1685.17ff. The item printed as Beilage II to no. 1674 (pp. 529ff.) is closest to no. 1685 in content and may, as the conclusion of the debate, also belong to the same time period.

Church orders, therefore, cannot be enacted by human beings in connection with human laws or in analogy to them; for that reason, nicely balanced committees such as the Committees of Fourteen or Six formed in Augsburg are in no way competent to make binding decisions in church law. From the perspective of the apostle Paul, people who believed as Luther did should not let themselves become involved in such efforts. But would that not open the door to an ecclesiastical chaos that would do more damage than any lack of uniformity in ordinances and usages, a chaos that would feed unbelief and harm souls? The articles on order in the Augustana have shown, and the accompanying commentary has confirmed, how seriously Luther and Melanchthon tried to face these dangers. Luther continued these efforts during the treaty negotiations without support from Melanchthon.

In that regard, and in the light of his concluding statements in the letter of August 15, major attention must be given to Luther's interest in Paul. By August 24, when he announced the never-completed work "On the Article of Justification" *(De iustificationis loco)*, he was nearing the end of his Pauline studies, in which he reexamined, and then adopted, the doctrine of justification in the Augustana.[642] Luther's fragmentary notes for the work, which we owe to Veit Dietrich's diligence in collecting such materials, as well as the marginal comments in the 1530 edition of the New Testament, indicate the state of Luther's doctrine of justification at that time; they also illustrate his understanding of the church. The exposition of the first twenty-five Psalms must also be taken into account.[643] This material was dictated by Luther to his amanuensis Dietrich off and on during almost the entire time in the Coburg. And finally, the falsely titled "On the Power to Make Laws in the Church," written during the same period, stands in close connection with the discussion between Luther and Melanchthon on traditions.[644]

Among the exegetical-devotional works, Luther's exposition of Psalm 117, completed at the beginning of August, reveals his struggle with questions of order; the sections "On Revelation" and "On Admonition" are especially illuminating.[645] By applying the implications of his understanding of Paul's soteriology to ecclesiology, Luther pronounces historical-theological judgments that demonstrate the new Reformation breakthrough more clearly than in almost any other writings. These judgments put the question of church law on an entirely different basis, so that they excuse Melanchthon's vacillating

642. *WBr* 5:no. 1693.11.

643. *WA* 31.1:263ff. On dating the individual copies, see ibid., 259.

644. *WA* 30.2:(677), 681ff. The title is taken from the introductory sentence: "I do not find the power of proposing laws in the church to be approved, but to be condemned." If one wishes to consider the collected fragments as a unity, they ought to be titled "The Church Is Not Mistress Over God's Word."

645. *WA* 31.1:233ff., 251ff.; *LW* 14:14, 32.

attitude in the treaty negotiations and even make his counterparts seem to be truly committed to tradition. In Psalm 117, Luther finds an "extremely remarkable secret which was barely known even in the days of the apostles and now, under the papacy, has completely faded away." It is not that church order goes back to some ancient Christian legislative right that was discarded under the papacy and now has once again been discovered by the Reformation. Rather, from the fact that Paul proclaims the abrogation of the Jewish law it is concluded that the kingdom of Christ "is not a temporal, passing, and earthly kingdom, to be ruled by laws and judgments; it is a spiritual, heavenly, and eternal kingdom that must be ruled apart from and superior to all laws, judgments, and external means."[646]

This relativizing of human laws in the light of the boundless gifts of Christ's kingdom could be understood in the sense of Luther's two-kingdom doctrine and as therefore implying that spiritual law was superior to earthly law. Luther, however, sees it differently. He recognizes that political societies "must have their laws, customs, and ways so that they can judge, punish, protect, and keep the peace," and that occasionally they will alter them. God lets both government and household authority have their own integrity. But according to the First Commandment, he demands that he alone be recognized as God, that human worship not exalt human holiness, and that human pride not disgrace God's honor.[647]

That approach does away not only with liturgical ceremonies but with every ecclesiastically sanctioned rule of conduct that claims an intrinsic religious value. God himself demonstrated that by his destruction of the temple in Jerusalem, and the "finest government and law on earth which has set itself up" independently of God is not exempt from his judgment. The dissolution of monasteries and foundations during the Reformation signifies the same thing. God testifies that a "Christian is something higher and very different from all worldly and spiritual rights, laws, external holiness, government, and anything else you can name."[648]

Placing the kingdom of Christ and the Christian over all church law does not, however, imply doing away with it completely; it means the annulment of all its salvatory functions. The Christian stands *above* church order; measured against that standard, "worldly and spiritual" laws occupy the same level.[649] The separation between worldly and spiritual rule ought not be

---

646. *WA* 31.1:233.17ff.; *LW* 14:14. Paul requires something higher "than outward, temporal justice, laws, or ceremonies" (*WA* 31.1:233.28; *LW* 14:14).

647. *WA* 31.1:233.32ff., 235–238; *LW* 14:14, 15–20.

648. *WA* 31.1:239.6ff., 17ff., 241.12ff.; *LW* 14:20, 22.

649. Here Luther means the same thing as in his Confession of 1528 (*WA* 26:505.11ff.; *LW* 37:365), where he places the "common order of Christian love" above the three orders or institutions established by God.

equated with the difference between the kingdom of Christ and earthly social institutions together with the various principles of order essential to their existence. The "pure holy works" that belong to the pastoral office or the service of the Word and that constitute spiritual rule[650] presuppose church orders differing from canon law in character and in worth. During his last months at the Coburg, Luther studied the theological and legal peculiarities of these orders thoroughly, although he did not emphasize them.

What he does emphasize is the Pauline approach and, based on that perspective, the rejection of the legal structure of the Western church. The point remains that the church, in the sense of the Apostles' Creed and CA 7, is holy and is able to incorporate only what is divine and holy in its statutes. Therefore it cannot legislate anything that conflicts with what God has declared in law and gospel, anything that would force the conscience committed to God to depend on human statutes, or anything that would break the bond with the *sola fide* and the grace that alone can justify.[651] The doctrine of justification, with its message about the forgiveness of sins and the freedom of the Christian, emphasizes the spiritual character of the church so strongly that no ecclesiastical law could possibly be derived directly from it. This doctrine really forms only a negative criterion against which all ordinances of the church are to be judged. In this way the principle that governs all the articles on church order in the Augustana is confirmed from Paul: every church order that claims to be necessary for salvation and binds consciences is opposed to God and must be abolished. Every institution that claims to be a means of salvation is a sign of Satan's church.[652]

Now, that does not mean that the church should not and cannot enact binding statutes. The opposite is true. But these ordinances are limited to the open space where the Spirit acts through Word and faith. That means that they are external (*foris*); they regulate the relation of persons to one another in the light of the Decalogue. They are therefore under the divine command of love which defines all other interpersonal relationships in government and family. The "ordered" church thus forms one of the three hierarchies by which the common life of humanity is maintained and peace and concord promoted.[653]

The church thus exercises an ordering power within the area delimited by

650. *WA* 26:504.31ff.; *LW* 37:364.

651. "The church set up nothing that binds or justifies the conscience before God, but it has left conscience free, to be justified in grace alone, and to be preserved by faith alone" (*WA* 30.2:684.13ff.). See also the continuation of the quotation in n. 653.

652. Ibid., 685–86.

653. "In outward matters, however, [the church] legislates for peace and concord among human beings, as is the case with other civil and domestic laws. Such laws are to be held in great honor because they do not harm faith and are conducive to peace. Yet even in these matters the church is not to act contrary to the commandments of God" (ibid., 684.15ff.).

law and gospel. In its divine origin and in its goal oriented toward the realization of love, that ordering power corresponds to the powers exercised, each in its own sphere and in its own way, by government and family. Thus our question about the Lutheran understanding of church order leads us back to the doctrine of the three hierarchies or ways of governing. We must discover what answer it yields in this context.

Government and the preaching office, as well as the physical and spiritual goods produced as the fruits of their activity, are to be gratefully accepted as signs of the sustaining goodness of God.[654] "All his ordinances and institutions"—thus not only the political and domestic estates but also the "priestly estate" and liturgical rules ("Sabbaths and festivals, worship and church law [!] and the like")—are "his work or his creation, because he has commanded and instituted" them. God, therefore, does not make statutory ordinances; he sets up individuals who rule the community according to his Word and who make rules—but not unchangeable ones that are independent of its consent—for the community's Christian life together. "One should laugh in one's heart for joy upon finding for oneself a status that God has instituted or ordained."[655]

In describing these orders Luther gives prominence to the civil element. Here God's righteousness clothes itself in "natural" and "imperial" law; it is the realm of the jurists. But the church also, to the extent that it lives under ordinances, is tied into this legal structure. Its unique status arises not from its special ordinances but from the specific character of the preaching office. Whether in the temporal or spiritual realm, God intends "to create right and righteousness and thereby to maintain peace." So in Christendom, as in the government of the children of Israel, "temporal authority and external priesthood" stand in a complementary relationship to each other. Precisely because Christ does not give his people a new law, the congregation can and should transfer ordinances from the realm of politics and domestic life to the area of life where God's Word is operative. Seen in that way, the church as social structure does not possess a unique "form." Its form is recognized where young and old know the catechism, that is, where evangelical preaching is accepted and "pulpit, altar, and baptismal font" have been restored to their rightful place. The decisive thing is what happens spiritually, not the ordering of how it happens.[656]

In his private pondering on these principles, Luther tried to formulate the issues of church order by means of the scholastic tension between substance

654. WA 31.1:367.17ff. (on Ps. 23:1).
655. Ibid., 399.26ff., 34ff., 408.35ff.; LW 13:358, 368.
656. WA 31.1:409.34ff., 410.10ff., 25ff., 411.3ff.; LW 13:369, 370; WA 30.3:317.32ff.; LW 47:52–53.

and accidents.[657] In his Word, God has established everything that is essential to the ceremonies; beyond that nothing is necessary. Thus God's Word presents the substance; the accidents are time, place, forms, and related circumstances, that is to say, everything that human ordinances can determine. Those things are optional, but everything that pertains to the Word-substance element is essential.

In his subsequent reflection on this theme, Luther came to the deeper insight that God and the Word of faith transcend the difference between substance and accident.[658] God's work is the substance; variable church ceremonies are accidents that may or may not be present. On that basis, church actions commanded in God's Word are legitimate; ceremonial embellishments are accidental additions, like a golden ring that surrounds a valuable gem. Luther enumerates the divine commandments and shows how they are translated into action. Taking prayer as an example, he lists all the modifications by which it can be enriched. In so doing, he gives an interesting overview of the liturgical possibilities available for public and private worship. None of them is universally binding, although, of course, some may be prescribed locally and amended at any time. Thus they do not abolish God's ordinance, although they are to be carried out in the spirit of love.[659]

657. At first, in the concluding letter to Melanchthon on August 4 (*WBr* 5:no. 1674.17ff.); then more fully, but right afterward, in *WA* 30.2:683.6–684.6. The subject was explored as early as the *Propositiones* (between July 16 and 19); the relationship between articles of faith and ceremonies, treated in theses 18ff. (*WA* 30.2:421–22), is just touched on in connection with the question of Scripture (ibid., 686.31–688.6). One becomes aware of the comprehensiveness and variety of the lines of thought.

658. *WA* 30.2:683.7ff.

659. Luther ends by pointing to the opposite image, to the "false stone" in the golden ring, the self-selected works by which one hopes for self-redemption (ibid., 684.2).

PART TWO

THEOLOGICAL PROBLEMS

CLASSICAL CHURCH DOGMA

1. TEXTS

The Augustana does not simply take the texts in which Christianity had stated its faith officially since the Council of Constantinople in 381 and repeat them word for word. It interprets and modifies them. This fact soon makes clear that we are dealing not with a formal repristination but with a theological renewal arising from an inclusive understanding of Reformation theology and, in turn, affecting that theology. The return to the confession of the ancient church did not occur under dogmatic pressure or because of state-church legal requirements. Further support for these observations comes from the fact that although CA 1 and CA 3 follow the text of the Nicene Creed, Luther's interpretive exposition, on which our commentary is based, prefers to work from the Apostles' Creed, which Luther explained in a popular and pastoral manner in his two catechisms of 1529.

In order to understand the developments that took place, we will refer to the texts of the individual articles and explain them by using the theological statements of the Reformers, especially Luther. In his "testament" of 1528, which was issued as an appendix to his last great work on the Sacrament of the Altar, *Confession Concerning Christ's Supper*, Luther made his own contribution to the ongoing confessional development of the church. He assures us that he has "by the grace of God . . . most diligently traced all these articles through the Scriptures, [has] examined them again and again in the light thereof, and [has] wanted to defend all of them as certainly as [he has] now defended the Sacrament of the Altar."[1] He begins with the sublime "article of the majesty of God, that the Father, Son, and Holy Spirit, three distinct persons, are by nature one true and genuine God, the maker of heaven and earth." Luther further confesses "that the Second Person in the godhead, viz., the Son, alone became a true man." And "third, I believe in the Holy Spirit, who with the Father and the Son is one true God and proceeds

---

1. *WA* 26:499.26ff. (= *BoA* 3:508.1ff.); *LW* 37:360. (I provide references to the Bonn edition where possible.)

eternally from the Father and the Son, yet is a distinct person in the one divine essence and nature."[2]

The important thing in these texts is not that minor variations here and there in the traditional wording suggest the possibility of small interpretive shifts; the scholastic art of formulation had done plenty of that before Luther got involved. More significant is that the Nicene Creed—its use in the mass gave it priority over the baptismal creed—is a stylistic masterpiece that incorporates all the central confessional statements. Luther's Trinitarian confession is the basis for his theology, including its reforming elements. The Trinitarian character of his theology in no way eliminated or set aside its reforming character. The confession of the triune God and the incarnation of the Son presupposes all Reformation principles, including the justification of the sinner. Those who assume the opposite turn the whole thing upside down and allow it to collapse, since one cannot think coherently while standing on one's head. The foundation and cornerstone of Reformation theology is that every internal and external action of the Trinity is directed toward the salvation of the world: "These are the three persons and one God, who has given himself to us all wholly and completely, with all that he is and has. The Father gives himself to us, with heaven and earth and all the creatures, in order that they may serve us and benefit us. But this gift has become obscured and useless through Adam's fall. Therefore the Son himself subsequently gave himself and bestowed all his works, sufferings, wisdom, and righteousness, and reconciled us to the Father, in order that restored to life and righteousness, we might also know and have the Father and his gifts. But because this grace would benefit no one if it remained so profoundly hidden and could not come to us, the Holy Spirit comes and gives himself to us also, wholly and completely. He teaches us to understand this deed of Christ which has been manifested to us, helps us receive and preserve it, use it to our advantage and impart it to others, increase and extend it. He does this both inwardly and outwardly—inwardly by means of faith and other spiritual gifts."[3]

Luther's Trinitarian confession is also the foundation for all that follows, to the degree that every Lutheran confession is built upon it. In 1528, the visitations began on a wider scale. They were Luther's brainchild, and although he was not the original author of the *Visitation Articles*, he did do the decisive editing. The *Instructions for the Visitors* of 1528 presupposes Luther's great *Confession Concerning Christ's Supper*. Naturally the sublime mysteries of the divine majesty are not discussed in this practical work designed to educate

2. *WA* 26:500.27–29, 33ff., 505.29–31 (= *BoA* 3:508.11–14, 18–20, 511.12–14); *LW* 37:361, 365.

3. *WA* 26:505.38–506.9(= *BoA* 3:511.21–34); *LW* 37:366.

the people; it is content with the acknowledgment that "God is the one who threatens, commands and alarms." Above all, he is God as lawgiver and punisher who is impressed on the minds of children through their memorization of the Creed on Sundays.[4] That was the laborious way in which the learning of the Christian faith began to take place, and that was the artless reduction to legalism that first brought the faith to simple folk. The confession starts out as nothing more than a defensive reaction against unbelief and heresy; it is in this primitive form that the deep meaning of Trinitarian faith begins to work itself out.

We do Melanchthon an injustice when we link him with this mnemonic reduction of Luther's Trinitarian theology, even if this reduction determined Protestant classroom teaching for centuries. The poor quality of this teaching method, exhibited here at the beginning of the evangelical confessional process in the *Instruction for the Visitors*, shows us how laboriously and imperfectly Luther's original intentions struggled for expression in the subsequent confessional development. His Trinitarian statements are not blithely accepted as traditional teaching; they are inserted in the thought process that was beginning to work through the principles of the theology of justification. That was Melanchthon's real concern. The confessional development up to the completion of the Augustana presents a reformulation of the Trinitarian statements and of the christological statements associated with them. This reformulation did not result in an alteration but resulted in an enrichment. The important part of the process was that the doctrinal content of Luther's Trinitarian theology was taken beyond the first communities of citizens and peasants which simply reproduced its content in a primitive way, and was made available to the preaching clergy (the first phase: the Schwabach Articles). But then these pastors who had embraced evangelical doctrine had to be directed toward a Reformation theology that was unified within the empire and that incorporated earlier confessional approaches in its general outline (the second phase: the final version of the CA).

The road from the visitations to the Schwabach Articles has more than a diplomatic, confessional-political course. It also has a theological-spiritual character, which we now consider in light of the Trinitarian doctrine. In Schwab. 1, 2, and 3, that doctrine is presented in a publicly binding form for the first time. Of course this maintains its adherence to the official, imperially sanctioned doctrine, which had been in effect since 381; but more important is its connection with the salvation event. This is not the place for a theological analysis of the three articles; we will just compare their wording with that of Luther's personal Confession of 1528. It is striking how strongly all three

4. *WA* 26:202.36,230.37; *LW* 40:275,308.

articles rely on Scripture, not only in the strictly Trinitarian statements of
Schwab. 1[5] but also in the more christological ones.[6] Exegesis is always in the
foreground. Article 1 of Schwab. deals with the divine unity of the Son with
the Father; Schwab. 2 emphasizes the true humanity of the Son; Schwab. 3
stresses the indivisible unity of the humanity and the divinity. These systematic concerns are less apparent in Luther in 1528. The heretics he rejects in
every article were figures from the christological tradition of the ancient
church.

The Schwabach Articles do not lack such historical references, but it is a
theme from salvation history that predominates: unity between the Father
and the Son endures forever (Schwab. 1), the Son alone received body and
soul from the virgin Mary in the incarnation (Schwab. 2) and as God and man
walked the road through crucifixion to resurrection (Schwab. 3). To summarize: the Schwabach Articles see the Trinity as a historical event; the unity
between the divine Trinity and the human nature aims at the salvation of
humanity.[7] Such an approach can be seen as a reflection of the Apostles'
Creed, or as an echo of the *propter nos* of the Nicene Creed and the *pro salute
nostra* in the so-called Athanasian Creed (there is quite a lot in common
between Luther's exposition and this late Western confession). The fact
remains that a christological-soteriological creed reaching far back to the
beginnings of Western confession making comes to light again in Luther's
Trinitarian confession and finds extension in his theology. Closely tied to that
is the fact that Schwab. 1–3 provides a biblical basis for its christological
declarations by a well-thought-out chain of scriptural statements.

Thus there were theological differences between Luther's personal Confession of 1528 and the Schwabach Articles that were the result of deliberations
of a commission during the early summer of 1529. Melanchthon was a party
to those discussions. We shall weigh the differences later, but now we shall
pursue the further development of the Trinitarian doctrine.[8]

5. *WA* 30.3:86.10–15.

6. Ibid., 87.7–10, 20–23.

7. " . . . for us men suffered, crucified, dead, buried . . . " (*WA* 30.3:87.13–14).

8. I have argued that this development followed an uncertain course during the year, in the
article "Zur Entstehung und Textgeschichte der Schwabacher Artikel," *Theologie in Geschichte
und Kunst: W. Elliger zum 65. Geburtstag* (Witten, 1968), 134–51. No substantive changes were
made. In article 1, the Marburg Articles make a point of the agreement between the Wittenbergers and the Swiss (and the southern Germans) on the Trinitarian faith, and they also add
historical data: the Nicene Creed was adopted by a council in 381 and since that time has been
"sung and read . . . by the entire Christian Church in the world." Article 2 emphasizes the
antithesis between the incarnation of the Son from the Father and the birth by "the pure virgin
Mary." Out of Schwab. 2's refutation of ancient christological heresies, Marburg takes just the
incarnation of the Son through the cooperation of the Father and the Spirit. Article 2 of Schwab.
relates the unity of body and soul to the God-man; Marb. 2 to one born of the pure virgin Mary
(the human side is more strongly emphasized). In article 3, Marb. omits discussion of the participation of God and man in the suffering of Christ; the unity of the two natures gets more
emphasis. The breadth of Luther's Trinitarian and christological thought and his efforts to be
conciliatory to the Zwinglians are both obvious.

In that connection we must not forget that these principles were given an independent development in the catechisms through the visitation program in the territorial churches. Closest to the emerging Augustana in content—although quite different in wording—is Luther's Large Catechism, which appeared in its first edition during the winter of 1528–9 and in its final edition the following spring. While Luther's "testament" of 1528 reveals the deep sources—to the extent that they can be plumbed—of his Trinitarian faith in God, the catechetical efforts of that same year relate to congregational preaching and catechesis. The students—always seen as beginners—and pastors are to learn how to preach on the three articles of the Creed in such a way that faith is given the strength to fulfill the Decalogue and that no one, therefore, gains and sustains his life from himself. A practical approach of that sort describes creation, redemption, and salvation in the simplest terms. In this respect it is much better than the petrified exposition in the *Instructions for the Visitors,* but it does not match the profundity of the tradition that Luther revitalized. If we now wish to portray the textual formation of CA 1 and 3, however, we cannot start from the graphic and visual terminology of the catechism.

We must begin with Schwab. 1–3. Its structure is modeled after Luther's personal confession. The "sublime article of the majesty of God"[9] leads to the emergence of the second article, on the "Second Person in the godhead,"[10] and then, far removed from statements about salvation or the mediation of salvation and its socioethical consequences,[11] to the "Holy Spirit." To be sure, there are some problems; the articles almost completely ignore pneumatological concerns, and the Christology in articles 2 and 3 differs between incarnation (in art. 2) and saving act (in art. 3).

In Schwab. 1, Saxony—in harmony with the Schwabach negotiations, which later collapsed—professes the decrees of Nicaea (325) and begins with a pointed statement about the unity of the divine essence, without at first being able to do justice to the problem of the three persons. Their unity seems, in fact, to be seen more clearly in the creative activity of the triune God than in the general activity of the three persons. Although Luther's faith in the Trinity finds expression in his personal confession and in its powerful concluding summary,[12] Schwab. and the entire subsequent Lutheran confessional development limit themselves to the relation between the Father and the Son, thus laying the foundation for a "binitarian" confession of faith. At least the procession of the Son and the Spirit from the Father is retained in

9. *WA* 26:500.27ff. (= *BoA* 3:508.11ff.); *LW* 37:361.
10. *WA* 26:500.33ff. (= *BoA* 3:508.18ff.); *LW* 37:361.
11. *WA* 26:505.29ff. (= *BoA* 3:511.12ff.); *LW* 37:365.
12. See above, pp. 239–40.

Schwab. 1, thus taking the Western *filioque* into account. Luther's list of heresies has been dropped, and in its place Schwab. 1 presents detailed proofs from Scripture.

From its roots in Luther's personal Confession of 1528[13] through Schwab. 2 and 3 to the final version of the CA, Christology appears as a particular way of confessing the Trinity. The incarnation of the Son is always seen as a manifestation of the triune God. The Son, born of the Father in eternity, remains eternally "true God by nature." In 1528, Luther called him the "middle person in God"; in him God bonds himself to humanity. The statements about his true humanity and about Mary agree with classical Christology, and they emphasize the true humanity of the Redeemer. It is noteworthy that, in order to strengthen this element, the indivisibility of the body and soul of the human Jesus is emphasized. Such formulations, and their support from the historic struggle against heresies, disclose the concerns Lutherans had during the Lord's Supper controversy about maintaining the unity of divine and human natures in the reception of the Sacrament—a good example, by the way, of a concrete application of classical church dogma. The list of heretics that Luther compiled and Schwab. included relates to this concern. Characteristic again are the scriptural proofs, which Schwab. develops beyond Luther's beginnings.

By the end of May 1530, Melanchthon had expanded these first efforts into the version called Na.[14] He gave Schwab. 1 a new introduction, geared toward Saxony and based on Nicaea, but in the final version this addition lost its special character through the elimination of exclusively Saxon elements. In the doctrine of the Trinity, Melanchthon added a series of divine attributes that described the Trinitarian unity more exactly, in accordance with the learned tradition. He outlined in more detail the basic concepts of being and person, thus preparing for the philosophical character of the final version.

Article 3 of Na combined the christological articles Schwab. 2 and 3 into one. Melanchthon's knowledge of the history of doctrine shows itself when he terms the incarnation the assuming of human nature by the Son of God, thereby basing both the personal unity of the two natures and their indivisible cooperation on the saving activity of Christ. To tie together all these themes, which he gathered out of the tradition stemming from Luther, and then to bring them to bear on the disputed unity of the two natures in Christ's saving work, is a theological tour de force by Preceptor Philipp, although it is barely recognizable in his later version of CA 3. (On the other hand, new themes come to expression, such as looking back to the doctrine of original sin which Melanchthon had inserted in the meantime in CA 2, and looking forward to

13. *WA* 26:500.33–505.28 (= *BoA* 3:508.18–511.11); *LW* 37:361–65.
14. The page and line numbers for its text are according to Kolde.

Christ's ascension.) Both of these themes occur again in later revisions of the Augustana.[15]

Compared to the lapidary brevity of Na 3, Christ's redeeming work outside the realm of history finds a new form of expression in Nb 3. In both versions Christ's suffering and death are called a sacrifice that was accomplished "not only for original sin but also for the actual sin of all mankind"; Nb speaks of the sacrifice effective "for all other sins" which "propitiates God's wrath."

The additional reference to Christ's propitiation occurring in Nb shows that Na has given a new twist to the understanding of the christological article. We saw that in Luther, it arose out of the doctrine of the Trinity; under Melanchthon's further theological revisions in Augsburg, it has crept over into soteriology and thereby into the doctrine of justification.

Let us now observe how this development shows up in the final version of the Augustana. The decisive push comes from the insertion of the doctrine of original sin (Na 2) into the Trinitarian-christological articles. It happened before the composition of Nb and after the Schwabach Articles had been sent to the emperor, which would put it sometime during late April 1530. The process shows with what concentrated energy Melanchthon addressed the central theological questions once the "disputed articles" had been more or less completed. Among the most important of those questions was the doctrine of original sin. In his first years at Wittenberg, Melanchthon had defended this doctrine against Eck and the scholastics. It appeared again in the struggle with Erasmus, challenging Melanchthon to new answers. And finally Eck's 404 Articles summoned him to these problems in Augsburg as well. He posed them in CA 2,[16] but he also treated them within the framework of a total theological perspective.

He placed CA 2 between CA 1 and CA 3, between the Trinitarian doctrine of God and Christology, certainly not just because he wanted to handle the former abstractly and the latter in a soteriologically concrete way. There are other theological motives at work. As Melanchthon jotted down a few familiar phrases on the theme in Na 2, he had greater things in mind. He wanted to clarify the concept of rebirth by showing that Christ's saving act restored the state of humanity before the Fall. In that way Christology was given a soteriological slant, and the doctrine of the Trinity, despite any conceptual abstractions, was also aimed in the same direction. Thus the sequence of the first articles gains new significance: after humanity lost access to the triune God through its sin, Christ opened a new way by his sacrifice.

The concern of the doctrine of justification is thereby integrated into

15. Na 16 and CA 17 link the ascension with the last judgment; the conclusion of Na 3 establishes the lordship of the One who ascended into heaven.

16. See below, p. 271.

Christology. Before we demonstrate this in detail, we need to establish the theological connection that carries it throughout the Augustana.

God (CA 1) sends to fallen humanity (CA 2) Christ the Redeemer (CA 3). This deliverance and renewal is accomplished in the justification of the sinner (CA 4); through the beneficial influence of office, Word and Sacrament (CA 5), new spiritual powers and forgiveness are given to humanity (CA 6). These powers carry out their historical work within the one, holy, Christian church (CA 7), and although that work is continually threatened by hypocrites (CA 8), it continues to exist. That work occurs in the sacraments (CA 9 to 13); its existence is humanly guaranteed through the activity of the spiritual office and by church orders (CA 14, 15), for which civil order provides the presuppositions (CA 16).

A few articles sprinkled in subsequently give support to what has gone before (CA 18 and 19 to CA 2; CA 20 to CA 4 and 5; CA 21 to CA 4). Articles 22–28 deal with current questions on order that are based on the theological foundation of the first part.

The influence of soteriological thought on traditional Christology can be followed in the transition from Nb 3, which also involves a changeover from German to Latin wording in CA 3. Tiny textual changes mark the shift: Christian redemption is expressed in CA 3.3 by the phrase "that he might reconcile the Father to us," *ut reconciliaret nobis patrem,* thus replacing the reference to propitiating God's wrath in Nb 3; at the same time, the process is further clarified by the distinction between original guilt and actual sin, in continuation of CA 2. In Christology proper, the phrase "took on human nature" is reintroduced from NA 3, the Son of God is called Word, in accordance with the most ancient tradition, and in section 5—as in Na 3— the ruling power of Christ's kingdom is particularly emphasized. In this developed form, CA 3 is the standard for the understanding of Christology.

2. TRINITARIAN AND CHRISTOLOGICAL CONFESSIONS IN LUTHER'S SERMONS AND LECTURES

Werner Elert[17] and Erich Seeberg[18] have accustomed us to seeing articles 1 and 3 as derived from the imperial laws of Theodosius; it has therefore become widely popular in evangelical theology to trace the Trinitarian and christological articles back to late antiquity and to see in them a legalistic and rather rigid element of that tradition. These observations are not completely wrong, but the fact that they do not fully describe CA 1 and 3 may be seen by

17. Werner Elert, *The Structure of Lutheranism,* trans. Walter A. Hansen (St. Louis: Concordia Pub. House, 1962), 1:200–201.

18. Erich Seeberg, *Luthers Theologie,* vol. 2, *Christus, Wirklichkeit und Urbild* (Stuttgart, 1937), 380–81.

a glance at Luther's writings, where these central questions of the Christian faith are treated with great seriousness and never as edifying platitudes.

These are basic questions for Luther; he is therefore untiring in holding them up to congregations and new preachers. Opportunities were always there in preaching, especially at Christmas, and in exegesis, whenever the texts lent themselves to that topic. In every case it is obvious that for Luther the speculative and dogmatic interests were not central. He was always concerned about the supreme article, the essence of the Christian faith. If it is maintained, all of Christian truth remains secure. In this "compendium of salvation," the church triumphs over the world.[19] "I believe in Jesus Christ"—a Christian should so fix this article in mind that there is no room for lies or error; without that, everything is lost.[20] "Our cause is based on that, so that we may not be worried by those who persecute us. And our chief article is Jesus Christ." Where that article is not accepted, the mystery of lawlessness will be revealed, according to 2 Thess. 2:8ff.[21]

Thus knowledge of the articles of faith does not involve abstract, nonbinding truths but the very foundations of faith. Luther defends them, knowing well that they will be subverted by the enthusiasts after his death. That is not yet completely clear, "but if it goes that far, instead of the gospel we now have, terrible deception will reign." Where people hold to faith in God the Father, Son, and Holy Spirit, they will also believe in the divinity of the man Jesus; where that is not the case, the Sacrament is trampled underfoot, because to deny that Christ suffered according to his divinity is to deny the Sacrament. Such principles of faith contained in the Creed also provide the criterion against which the truth of faith statements is to be measured.[22]

In opposition to the increasing adulteration of the creedal text by the enthusiasts, who deny any physical concreteness (Jesus being creator of heaven and earth, Mary being a virgin, Pontius Pilate a heathen governor), Luther sets forth his unshakable faith in the Scripture, which testifies to tangible revelations: by their witness heaven and earth strengthen belief in God.[23] The heart of all Christian proclamation is that Christ has come in the flesh; enthusiasts and scholastics contest that.[24] Thus the doctrine of the Trinity does not lay out an abstract doctrine; it describes the course of

19. *WA* 20:800.22ff., 31ff.

20. *WA* 29:126.2ff. Cp. *WA* 127.5–6: "For if the second article of the Creed lies, then there is nothing left but the devil."

21. *WA* 29:131.11ff.

22. *WA* 20:581.9ff., 432.14ff., 603.13, 725.8ff.

23. "Heaven and earth confirm my faith, my belief in God" (*WA* 27:57.23ff.).

24. Luther cites his Wittenberg teacher Mellrichstadt by name (*WA* 20:730.13ff.). The plan of salvation is summarized in the incarnation: " 'Jesus Christ, the Son of God, comes into this world and comes in the flesh.' The Holy Spirit proclaims this Jesus. If something agrees with this doctrine, accept it; if not, reject it" (ibid., 725.8ff.).

revelatory events that runs from Christ to us and then forward to Christ again.

A special way of knowing is necessary in order to understand the divine threefoldness. In a Passion sermon of 1529, Luther makes a distinction in Scripture between naming and knowing.[25] We name things that are and remain outside us; naming involves an objectivizing of externals. Knowing is a mutual participation about which the learned know nothing. Spiritual insight is knowing: "What we know does not consist in our doing, wisdom, righteousness, or glory. For he who declares himself righteous boasts, he does not change God." Knowledge of the triune God, therefore, is the insight of faith, upon which justification is based. It is free from any elements of classical metaphysics, even though the ancient Creed is locked into them.

Luther wants to bring about such knowledge of the triune God through the practice of the articles of faith. They are all "very difficult and sublime, which no one can grasp without the grace and gift of the Holy Spirit. I speak and testify to that as one who has more than a little experience. . . . Select an article out of the faith, whichever one you will, whether the incarnation of Christ, the resurrection, or anything else, and you will have nothing left if you grasp it with your reason." He makes that most clear in his Christmas sermon: "true God from true God, true man from true man, and what he was before the world"—that is its theme. It does not deal with ancient events but deals with the present gift of eternal life.[26] Practiced that way, faith in the Trinity conflicts with faith in reason. Trinity and incarnation have nothing to do with speculation. Luther cannot answer the sharp questions posed by the scholastics and contentious spirits. What is necessary is knowledge of one's sins, and that is not found just anywhere; it lies nearer to us than our own body and soul. Human metaphysics separates God and humanity from each other; it also tries to bring humanity close to God apart from Christ. Christians, however, are to keep their reason in check; otherwise they will not hold to a single article of faith.[27] Mary is a model of this simple openness; questions about divinity and humanity do not exist for her; there exist only questions concerning her maidenliness and modesty. It seems suspicious to the rational enthusiasts that God would busy himself with creation or other physical things that are connected with the incarnation. They would rather see fire consume heaven and earth, because they are not spiritual. Faith, however, is strengthened by having Christ, who was born of Mary and crucified under Pilate.[28]

25. See WA 29:124ff. (sermon of March 14, 1529).
26. WA 32:57.16ff., 27:529.1–2. The "compendium of salvation" reads, "Man and true God, and in this God and man we all have eternal life" (WA 20:800.31ff.; LW 30:327).
27. WA 32:131.1ff., 29:361.1ff., 166.1–2.
28. WA 27:74.34, 57.23ff.

Everything depends on the immediate historical concreteness: "He who was God's Son came to us, in order to show himself to us in the flesh"; God's Son was sent into the world so that we might live through him. It is in Jesus' being God's Son that we discover that God loves us.[29] The incarnation of God is the sign of his love toward us. That puts the judging ability of our reason to shame; from the beginning, God dealt with us in a way that allowed unbelievable things to happen to us. All the statements that address the incarnation of Christ are in themselves inconceivable; only those who accept the witness of Scripture in faith grasp the meaning of the biblical accounts that constitute the confession. Creedal faith, therefore, includes statements that can be understood only from Holy Scripture.[30]

It would appear natural to subsume Luther's creedal faith under late medieval skepticism, which also understood creedal declarations as biblically based statements about otherwise incomprehensible events. Luther's confession, however, is not a submission to the irrevocable truth and logical power of certain biblical statements but rather a belief that their truth is firm and unchangeable because it is grounded in God's love and faithfulness.

3. UNITY OF THE DIVINE BEING IN THREE PERSONS AND THE INCARNATION OF GOD

Article 1 of the CA testifies to "one divine essence" (*unitatem essentiae divinae*). The terms used here are not word for word the same as those used in the official confession of the ancient church. They avoid abstractions and prefer, as did Luther's personal Confession of 1528, expressions about concrete divine activity. Luther also took this approach in his sermons and addresses of the late 1520s. In the process, the biblical background causes a recasting of the vocabulary, so that a shift occurs within the Trinitarian statements. In the prologue to John, for example, Luther finds the relation between God and the Word formulated not in terms of unity but in terms of their connection with each other and the world. Luther then, however, quite incidentally introduces the notion of "natures" and ties the one divine nature to the three persons.[31] We find no critical reflection about the divine nature, and no hint of the dangerous consequences that might arise from the application of that concept. Luther is a biblical theologian who accepts the dogmatic tradition at those points where he can interpret it biblically. His Trinitarian and christological statements are to be explained on the basis of the concept of eternal life.

29. *WA* 20:729.4, 741.2–3, 755.2
30. *WA* 27:2.11ff., 43.10, 14.3ff., 26ff.
31. "One God by nature, and this God is three" (*WA* 15:801.9ff.; on John 1:1).

This procedure is applied more effectively and fruitfully in the exposition of Phil. 2:5ff. It involves the *morphe theou*, which Luther translates as "appearance," thus finding a counterterm to "being," *essentia*. God has his being in himself; he is concealed and unfathomable. If God hides himself and does not disclose himself, obviously nothing can be said about him. He is silent, and we have nothing to say; he is, and all we can do is recognize his presence. Here the divine majesty encounters us in its nakedness, the sun without concealing or protecting shade. Luther often warns his students that when they come across testimony to the fearful majesty and its terrible works, they not seek to explore everything or presume to speak about God: he does not want us to name him in that way. "You cannot get together naked to naked."[32] It is in his "form," his "shape," that God makes his appearance; no longer can he be spoken of as incomprehensible, because he shows himself, according to his divine essence, by visibly bestowing himself in teachings, miracles, and other works.[33] According to his nature, therefore, God does not simply rest in himself; he breaks out of himself and deals with the world. He *was* in the form of God, but he *shows* himself as having been that. "The being is hidden, but the showing occurs openly; the being *is* something, but the appearance *does* something or is itself a deed."[34]

Luther cannot understand the first article, *de unitate essentiae divinae*, in the sense of a substance at rest; coming out of biblical terminology and its visual language, he thinks of being as something real and effective. Speech about God always describes his actions. That is demonstrated in witness to God the Father, to the king and his kingdom, to his works, and to his gifts. It is impossible for this image-filled language about God's actions to pile up proof texts. But we must understand how God's action in the various sets of images derives from his single purpose. That purpose includes humanity in our creaturely state: "God not only loves me but also comes to me to be human with me; he becomes what I am."[35] Here the relationship and the activity that were just illustrated in the distinction between "being" and "self-disclosure" are completely reversed. Humanity is and remains; it is God who ceases to be what he is and was. Luther bases this radical change in God's being on his love. That is the heart of his life and actions. That is what gives the being of God a new face.

Corresponding to God's being are his attributes. They are listed for the divine essence, in CA 1.2, and for the three persons, in CA 1.3. One looks in vain for a similar sequence of terms in Luther—although the Athanasian

32. "Non potes nudus cum nudo congredi" (*WA* 31.2:38.24). See also *WA* 31.2:38.19ff., 16:85.3, 17.2:238.28ff., 239.5ff., 240.8ff.
33. *WA* 27:93.18, 29ff., 29:269.3ff.
34. *WA* 17.2:239.17f.
35. *WA* 29:643.9ff.

Creed has something similar. There are, however, specific parallels in form as well as content. Yet a detailed examination will show that not all the parallel terms are congruent with Luther's list. There are more agreements with the medieval exegetes who speak of God's attributes in terms of the *via negationis* or the *via eminentiae*. But on closer examination it is exactly this Neoplatonic style of expression that has few parallels in Luther. In listing the divine attributes, Luther stands independent of the tradition as formulated by CA 1. God lives in an eternal spiritual realm; mercy, truth, and love constitute his essence. He is governed by righteousness, peace, and bliss; comfort, goodness, and fullness of life emanate from him. Those are the marks of the divine essence. The goods and gifts of his kingdom are not physical but spiritual and eternal.[36]

God's essence is *eternal*. That is central to Luther's idea of God. The eternity of God is the mark of God's unique nature and also of the relationship between the persons. To be eternal is to have no beginning and no end; it is to be outside time. There is not, as the "Arians" wished, a middle ground between temporal and eternal. The "quality" of the eternal is not accessible to reason but can only be grasped by faith.[37] Luther's view of the God of the first article is defined by the Johannine concept of *eternal life*, which in turn cannot be separated from the life and nature of Christ. The divinity of God as seen in the first article cannot be treated independently of the kingdom of the Son, which is filled with life, comfort, and bliss. The kingdom of Christ is inseparably bound to the nature and essence of God. Thus a proper understanding of the doctrine of God leads us to the mystery of God's incarnation.

The essence of God manifests itself in the fact that Christ "alone has the power to confer eternal life, which can only be received by his decision." Thus the essence of God does not rest within itself but communicates itself in the eternal life that is incarnate in Christ and, through him, given to his own. And so Luther sees the quintessence of this theology to be "The man [Jesus] is true God, and in this God and man we all have eternal life."[38] All speculation about the true nature of the divine majesty is thus swept away. God is only to be grasped in Christ and in the spiritual experience of our believing heart. "Father and Son have eternal life, eternal righteousness, truth, and all things in themselves." In us, the opposite of all that is found—sin, death, and despair—so we turn to the One; Father and Son unite themselves with us. Christ, who is eternal life, devours death and turns it into God's righteousness.[39] Luther's only way of speaking about the essence of God is to identify it

36. *WA* 13:320.42–43; *LW* 18:241.
37. *WA* 15:801.9ff.
38. *WA* 28:111.18, 20:800.33; *LW* 30:327.
39. *WA* 20:611.9ff.

with eternal life and equate it with the saving work that Christ accomplishes in the sinner. Time and again Luther directs his congregation away from the naked God of metaphysical speculation and toward the God who is attested in his Word. Luther warns, "If you want to be secure against death, sins, and the like, don't let yourself be told that there is a God other than the one who has been sent. Begin your wisdom and knowledge with Christ and say, 'I know no other God than in that man, and if another is pointed out to me, I close my eyes.' "[40]

The divine majesty cannot be grasped in itself but can only be grasped in the self-revelation of its love. The abstract terms that disguise this fact in the list of divine attributes in CA 1.2 are replaced in Luther's own writings by descriptions of the attributes that express the loving activity of God. This description occurs precisely where the threefoldness is developed out of the unity, that is, in CA 1.3. The three persons are "of the same essence and power, who are also coeternal" (*eiusdem essentiae et potentiae et coaeternae*). Essence and power indicate God's divinity itself; Luther understands eternity as God's supertemporal saving will. The "coeternity" of the three persons is a way of saying that the three persons do not form an abstract unity but that they are carried along by the same saving will.

To believe in life eternal (*credere vitam aeternam*)—that is the article that ties together the Apostles' and Nicene Creeds. Luther made this observation and then put it to use theologically. The last article is also the greatest because it summarizes the spiritual gifts that came into the world through Christ's mission. This mission disclosed the depths of God. The heart of God let the Son be born, die, and rise again; those who believe will be saved.[41] One does not understand the doctrine of the Trinity as soon as one knows that God is the Father and has a Son; one needs to discover the intention of his will and the craving of his heart. Then it is not that the way to heaven opens but that one sees God pointing into the depths. The simplest understanding of God is belief that Christ has come from the Father and that he has returned to him again.[42]

The self-giving of eternal life to the world implies the sending of the Son. Christ comes to us on earth in order that we might live in him. It is again through the Son that we know God loves us; his boundless saving work assures us that he is not angry with us. In that way the mission of the Son discloses itself to us: he comes not to judge and to slay but so that we might have life in him.[43] Eternal life—that is the one essence that binds the three

40. *WA* 28:101.4.
41. *WA* 28:43.8ff.; see *WA* 31.2:72.2ff.
42. *WA* 28:65.25ff.
43. *WA* 20:741.2ff.

divine persons together. It is an essence that does not rest in itself but imparts itself.

It discloses itself to us mortals in the Son and imparts itself to us. The Son is one with the Father and the Holy Spirit through the power of the Spirit, and that is true of the Son made flesh and not just of him who sits on his heavenly throne in eternal majesty and harmony. Thus Luther understands and proclaims Augustine's doctrine of the Trinity in a new way. It is the "common article of faith, that Christ's flesh is full of divinity, full of eternal good, life, and salvation."[44] Luther hardly ever spoke about the eternal procession of the Son from the Father, because a God of self-communicating everlasting love poses no problems on that point. This eternal power of love was present before the creation of the world; it is precisely as the bearer of eternal love that the Son participates in the creation and the preservation of the world. For Luther the divinity of the Son is a necessary consequence of the faith experience of receiving eternal life.[45] One need only stick to this experience; nothing can be known of God *before* the sending of the Son. There is no need for a semidivine intermediate being between the creation of the world and the incarnation.

The *birth of Christ* as a human being from the womb of Mary is an event of an entirely new creation. Those who worry about the preexistent Christ lose themselves in visions and in the stupid disputations of contemporary heretics.[46] But we do need to look at what God has done ex nihilo. That includes the communication of eternal life through Christ; God gives his eternal life to Christ, and Christ gives it to us. Christ's incarnation and our fellowship with him are two sides of the same coin.[47]

The creation account declares that according to his deity, all things are in Christ (*secundum deitatem omnia sint in Christo*). That does not only mean that the incarnation provides the key to the created world; it also ties that world to the creator God through Christ. As a result of the incarnation of God in Christ, the whole creation is manifest in him. To talk about the two natures of Christ does not mean that the divine and human natures are baked together like two kinds of dough in one cookie, but means that they are inseparably

44. WA 23:251.20ff.; LW 37:129. Luther appeals to Hilary's *On the Trinity* in 1527 against Zwingli (WA 23:251.20ff.; LW 37:120).

45. ". . . that Christ must be true God because he alone has power to bestow everlasting life which can be received only through acknowledging him" (WA 28:111.18). On what follows, see ibid., 96.18, 110.15.

46. WA 20:602.1ff. See also ibid., 19ff.: "Our heretics have begun to discuss how the humanity can be separated from the divinity: the divinity cannot be heard, but the humanity can."

47. Thus we can say to Christ, "Dear Lord, you have taken my sin upon you and have become Martin, Peter, and Paul; you have therefore destroyed my sin and swallowed it" (WA 32:47.18ff.). The ascension provides the opposite pole: "We are ascended with Christ, because his resurrection includes us, so that it is our true resurrection" (WA 34.1:471.12ff.). On *creatio ex nihilo*, see WA 20:486.33.

joined together in personal unity. When Luther speaks of Christ, the concept of person predominates; he declares the unity of the Son with the Father: the Son is true God and man. Christ the man is creator of heaven and earth because of the divinity that is within him. The glory of the human race lies in the fact that we are related to one who shares our nature and yet possesses a glory that surpasses all other natures. Furthermore, God does not remain within himself, disengaged, but is active in humanity. By coming to us, God does not remain in his divinity but "lowers himself into flesh."[48]

This union of divine and human natures occurred in the womb of the virgin Mary. Christ was born not of a nun, but of a virgin. Mary's virginity was hidden; outwardly she lived as a married woman and her divine Son was a "legitimate child." Incarnation is the taking on of the human nature created in the womb of Mary; any other conjecture would be nothing but storytelling. Christ is a human being like you and me; everyone can say of him, "He is my God, and he has taken on my nature, flesh, and blood." If it were otherwise, Mary would be a "ghost" and Christ would not be a true, whole human being in body and soul. But in fact he is, and at the same time the Father's "natural and born Son"; Luther expressly rejects an adoptionist Christology.[49]

Evidence for these same disputes with contemporaries can be found in the other Reformers, and the issues play a role in the preliminary stages of CA 1 and 3. The indivisible unity of the divine and human natures is emphasized in CA 3.2. The true humanity of Christ in body and soul,[50] as well as the participation of the human nature in Christ's suffering and glory, is asserted in Schwab. 2 and 3, and it is also maintained in Na 3—more strongly than in CA 3. There are plentiful examples for every one of these statements in Luther's writings from the 1520s. They show how powerfully the problems of the Trinity and Christology had gripped minds of that period; it was by no means a matter of dragging out defunct traditions.

There is not much material on this theme to quote from Luther's wide-ranging discussions with Zwingli, the Swiss, and the southern Germans. None of those theologians had any problem with the inner bond between the divine and human nature in the man Christ, but they found it impossible in God. The discussions on that point, especially during the Marburg Colloquy, probe deep into evangelical hermeneutics and into the formation of the evangelical confession. A sentence like Luther's "Divine majesty gives itself

48. "What, therefore is Christ? A person who is Lord and man" (*WA* 20:520.1ff.). See also *WA* 20:559.2, 27:128.8, 73.7–8, 126.18–19, 127.9ffg

49. *WA* 32:295.12ff., 296.3ff., 88.21ff., 34.2:492.11ff., 27:485.4ff.

50. The references to the Christology of the ancient church are given in *BS* 54 n. 2, 55 nn. 1–2.

in the flesh"[51] touches most sensitive points about the Trinity, Christology, and the understanding of the historical revelation of Christ. Although we cannot go into details at this point, we must keep in mind the background of these great debates on the Trinity and Christology—debates with which Protestantism is still not finished.

The doctrine of the incarnation also involves *pneumatology*. He who was born of woman through the incarnation and became "our fabric" (*unsers Tuchs*) is nevertheless not born "of and through the flesh." "For the Holy Spirit came that the Maid might become pregnant in the flesh, but not of the flesh." The begetting Spirit was a "new power, not rooted in the flesh," who "in a sublime and marvelous way" accomplished his work in the body of Mary without the cooperation of any human activity.[52] The phrase "conceived by the Holy Spirit" assures the full humanity of Christ in body and soul, but at the same time it assures the entire sinlessness of the Redeemer; both assertions were contested by the enthusiasts of Luther's day. In addition to bringing knowledge of the essence of God the Father, the incarnation brings knowledge of the power of the Holy Spirit to create anew. In a catechetical response from June 1, 1528, Luther said, "You know who the Son is: he is true God with the Father and the Holy Spirit, creator of heaven and earth, born of the Virgin."[53]

It is proper to summarize the doctrines of the Trinity and the incarnation in the same paragraph, because that makes clear how the triune God does not rest in himself but overflows with creative love. The entry of the Son into the world of death and his return to the glory of eternal life is the foundation of the Christian faith and of all Christian wisdom and knowledge. "It is an unspeakable grace," declared Luther on the Annunciation (March 25) in 1528, "that on this day the Lord himself clothed himself in our flesh and blood."[54]

The Trinitarian event of eternal love, which reached its climax in Christ's humanity, was planned from the beginning of creation. This is the way Luther explained the connection between the doctrines to his students as an introduction to his lectures on 1 John (begun on August 19, 1527).[55] Christ is true, eternal God, the image of the Father from the beginning of the world, and also true man, temporally limited, the human mediator of a God we can neither see nor hear. As such, he is not a phantom but really human, a

51. *WA* 17.1:152.3–4.
52. *WA* 20:407.18ff., 35ff.
53. *WA* 27:171.8; see also ibid., 485.4ff.
54. *WA* 28:64.5–8, 27:48.4ff., 73.3ff.
55. *WA* 20:602ff.

person, familiar to us. One ought not speculate how this human person can be separated from the divine; after all, only the human, that is Christ's Word, can be heard.

This person of the human Jesus is one, consisting of two natures inextricably bound together. Anything said of one nature concerns the other as well; rational objections ought not be raised at this point.[56] One ought not deny that Christ, even in his divine nature, can suffer; in that way, one denies his divinity. The two natures form one person. Also, whatever is said of one person of the Trinity includes the others. Luther justifies this inclusion of the incarnation of the Second Person in the doctrine of the Trinity. "I know no God except in such humanity"[57]—that is the climax of Luther's Trinitarian teaching.

In his sermons, as well as in doctrinal works, Luther explained this connection by analogies. The simplest image is that of the human body, whose members taken together constitute the whole person.[58] The interrelationship of cross and resurrection provides both an illustration and a basis for the close connection between the two natures. Both natures participate in the birth, the cross, and the suffering. Humanity sees only the human, but faith says, "That is God"—"and yet God is not seen" (et tamen Deus non videtur).[59] The connection between human and divine natures is not only explained by faith through individual examples, but the faith process itself is an example of such a supernatural union. Luther compares it to the two natures in Christ: the righteousness of faith corresponds to the divine, and the works of faith to the human. Faith and works belong as inextricably together as the two natures in Christ; one person results in both cases.[60] In view of the negotiations at the end of the Augsburg diet, Luther formulated the matter more precisely in his manuscript copy of the New Testament.[61] He began with justification. Faith and works are inseparable in it; once again, faith corresponds to the divine, and works to the human nature. Both belong to justification, for there is only *one* righteousness. Likewise, in Christ, God and man form one person, and body and soul, one man. When the unity is dissolved, the components also disintegrate. That means, although Luther did not draw this conclusion, that when the bond between God and man is

56. In these lectures, Luther drew the christological consequences of his battle against Zwingli. We will not consider the question of the *communicatio idiomatum* which was a part of that controversy, nor will we discuss the related doctrine of ubiquity. Cp. *WA* 23:141.11ff.; *LW* 37:62.

57. *WA* 20:605.9. Once again confirming that the bond between Trinity and incarnation is not a metaphysical entity but the creative power of the Spirit: "Father and Son have eternal life, righteousness, everlasting truth, and all things in themselves. . . . We unite in one, the Father and Son sharing with us" (ibid., 611.9ff.).

58. *WA* 20:603.22, 27:127.1ff.

59. *WA* 27:127.9ff.

60. Ibid., 127.1ff.

61. *WDB* 4:448.11ff.

broken, the Godforsaken man falls prey to death; then eternal love would—
unthinkably—form a closed circle.

4. EFFECTS OF THE UNITY OF THE
DIVINE AND HUMAN NATURES

In Christ the divine and human natures are inextricably connected in the
unity of his person. Article 1 of the CA infers this theme from the doctrine of
the Trinity. Article 3 elaborates it: "one Christ, true God and true man." This
theme has further consequences for our participation in eternal life. The
consequences are drawn by CA 3 in relation to the historical events of Christ's
life. Here it once more becomes clear that the self-revelation of the triune God
has effects within history and that all metaphysical speculation about it lacks
substance.

"God's Son took on human nature." Two natures, divine and human,
thereby are inseparably bound together in the unity of his person. A twofold
"truly" confirms this union: "truly God and truly man" assures the integrity
of both natures; "truly suffered, was crucified, . . . " assures the com-
pleteness of the human nature. Birth and death are designated as the two
pillars of Jesus' mission—reconciliation with God and atoning sacrifice for
humanity. The simple wording of the Apostles' Creed, which the article uses
as a basis and then carries further, is here interpreted with a "for us" in the
sense of the "for us" in the Nicene Creed. Then, following the resurrection
and exaltation of Christ, the article ends with a perspective on the finite
course of saving history (sec. 5). We here skip over what we have already
explicated on the incarnation and concentrate on the parts taken from the
Apostles' Creed.

1. The *assuming of human nature* by the Second Person of the godhead is,
of course, not a theme of the Apostles' Creed. The idea is not in Schwab.; it is
first adopted in Na, deleted in Nb, and retained only in the Latin version of
the official text. The formulation underscores the principal concern of the
article, which is the original independence of the human nature. For Luther
this concept of "assumption" is completely foreign. For him the important
thing was not the assumption of Mary's specific corporeality but the endowment of the whole human race with the divine nature. This glory transcends
all natures. In general, Luther thinks of Mary's conceiving by the Holy Spirit
as the starting point of the incarnation,[62] although he gives little theological
attention to the gestation process as such. Those who believe in Jesus'

62. *WA* 16:228.9, 34.2:492.11, 27:73.7ff., 20:327.3f., 407.18ff. provide examples for the *as-
sumptio carnis.*

miraculous birth are really only those who know who this child is and why he came into the world. Faith clings to the "for you."[63]

2. The *unity of the two natures* can be understood both from the side of the reconciling will of the Father—of the incarnation of God—and from the historical event that occurs through the man Jesus, who obediently assented to that will and fulfilled it. The birth of the Son takes place because the newborn accepts it and the suffering it brings, all the way to the cross and resurrection. The depths of God's saving purpose are thus matched by the power of faith among those destined for salvation.[64] Our faith is not simply directed to the divine nature insofar as it is distinct from the human; it embraces the *whole* Christ: "If I believe in the human Christ, I believe in the whole person."[65] Luther considers it dangerous to speak broadly about a "humanity" of Christ. That was not what was crucified; it was the human being Jesus who was given up to death as man for mankind and who yet was the only-begotten Son of God. Granted, all these statements of faith contradict human reason, but if we drop one article, we lose them all.[66] "Historical" reason does indeed contest the unity between the man Jesus and the triune God, but this unity conforms to the believing testimony of Scripture and to humanity's faith in salvation.

3. In all this, an emphasis remains on the "true man" in addition to the "true God." Luther recognized the difficulty that late medieval piety had in acknowledging the full humanity of the God-man. It was quite common to preach a Christ who, as man, appeared separated from God. Luther himself recalled in 1527 that for twelve years he had to study the phrase "believe in God the Son" and that he had not yet stopped learning from it.[67] He who was conceived of the Holy Spirit by the virgin Mary is a "complete man in both body and soul," including his sinlessness. All pious activities (*tota nostra exercitacio*) are directed toward this man; no one can hold to a God without Christ. One cannot speak "metaphysically" of either of the two natures. The Old Testament speaks allegorically of this man with the name Israel—a man who, through God's grace, becomes master of God, so that God does what the man wills.[68]

63. *WA* 32:262.7ff., 263.9; *LW* 51:212, 213; *WA* 34.2:496, 11ff.

64. "The Christian sees the profundity of God through the gospel" (*WA* 28:43.12ff.). "It is not something invented by human beings; it is because the Father loves us" (ibid., 64.19–20).

65. *WA* 20:604.12–13; see also ibid., 604.4ff.

66. *WA* 20:603.14ff., 32:59.16ff., 62.12ff.

67. "I always say, and you remember at my death, that all the devilish teachers begin by preaching a God separated from Christ, as we formerly heard in the schools" (*WA* 28:101.1ff.). "Because I believe that Christ on the cross has real flesh and blood and is also God, and that this person who is God risked his flesh and blood for me" (*WA* 16:228.7ff.).

68. *WA* 27:485.7ff., 31.2:516.28ff., 15ff., 29:361.1ff. Israel is "a man made by God and empowered by God . . . , who is a lord in God, with God, and through God, able to do all things" (*WA* 7:597.17–18; *LW* 21:351).

4. The real human birth of the God-man is addressed by all of these statements; the Christmas story is fully echoed in theological reflection as well as in popular piety. This leads to further steps: that this man "suffered, was crucified, dead and buried" is self-evident to popular belief, although it has not been completely understood theologically. Christ, as a man, can certainly suffer and die as we do, but how is that possible if he is inseparably bound to the divine nature? It is well known that in his controversy with Erasmus, Luther went back to the "theopaschite" formula of the Alexandrians and maintained that God participated in the experience of pain, death, and hell; he based this view on God's all-pervading nature, his ubiquity. It is ultimately a consequence of God's having lowered himself into human flesh; nothing that happens there occurs without God's participation. The godhead is not idle; God is active among the human race. He is active, but he is not recognizable by reason. On this point faith must hold to God's Word. Faith in Christ grasps him in his earthly appearance; in justification, faith is always bound to the man Jesus and ascends from him to the godhead.[69]

5. Through his suffering and death, Christ *reconciled* the Father to us and became a *sacrifice* for all our sins. There is no mention of *reconciliation* in the German version of the final text (nor in Nb), and the same is true of Na and Schwab. In the final editing of CA 3, Melanchthon reached all the way back to Luther's original Confession of 1528.[70] There the concept of reconciliation is rendered as "payment," *Bezahlung,* which clarifies the logical subject of reconciliation as it was retained by CA 3.3: God is reconciled to us and not we to God. The reconciling sacrifice is not an act of atonement that Christ might have brought to God as our representative; it is a direct gift of ours that influences God. This train of thought clashes with the reference in Luther's confession to the "innocent lamb" who bore our sins. Therefore, the line of thought based on representation remains brief in *BoA* 3:509.10ff. (*LW* 37:362); in CA 3.3 a shift has occurred through the reference to God's active assumption of guilt—a shift that is eliminated by the abbreviation of the German text.[71]

Regardless of the details, atoning power is attributed to Christ's sacrificial

69. *WA* 18:623.14ff.; *LW* 33:47; *WA* 27:126.18ff., 127.9ff., 23ff. CA 1 avoids the depths of the problem. See also *WA* 31.2:432.20ff., where at the end of the lectures on Isaiah (1527–30), Luther rejects the necessity of Christ's suffering punishment in the world; from an external point of view, Christ's suffering was deserved. Thus CA moves within Luther's sphere of thought when it avoids references to the conflict with Erasmus.

70. *WA* 26:502.30ff. (= *BoA* 3:509.10ff.); *LW* 37:362.

71. We note here that revisions of the text have created certain ambiguities in their wake. One thing is sure: during the final editing, Melanchthon worked with Luther's original text, but in the ultimate editing of the Latin text he introduced confusion by overinterpretation. It seems likely that these revisions are connected with the introduction of the doctrine of original sin into CA 2.

death. These statements are most closely related to the explanation of the
Second Article in the Small Catechism. There too the innocent suffering and
death of Christ are seen to have a redeeming and atoning effect; 1 Pet. 1:18–
19, with its Old and New Testament parallels, provides a biblical pattern.
During the period of composition of the catechisms, Luther made use of
these texts, especially in his lectures on Deutero-Isaiah, thus providing the
basis for the expansion in the CA text. We are not able to go into the
differences here.[72] One should not overestimate the influence of these and
similar passages on Luther's understanding of salvation. He also used other
christological statements as a basis. Of course, he does reject the "Pelagians"
who deny a representative suffering of Christ for our sins. He can also employ
the parallels between God's incarnation and the divinizing of the human
nature it effects, or the traditional *exitus-reditus* schema, in order to explain
liberation from sin; naturally, justifying faith in Christ always remains the
presupposition for the forgiving grace. The most picturesque analogy is that
of the worm and the fishhook, used frequently elsewhere, but throughout the
typical Easter sermon at the Coburg (April 17, 1530) and in preparation for
the Augsburg diet. The worm the fish seizes represents Christ's human
nature and the sharp hook the ultimately victorious divine nature. The
triumphant deliverance is the product of cooperation between the two.
Luther has many ways of explaining the act of salvation.[73] His palette is
colorful and his ways of expression various as he clarifies the central
christological statements of the Second Article in the Apostles' Creed.

6. The *descent into hell and the resurrection* form the counterpart to the
section on suffering. The first appearance of references to the *descensus ad
inferos* is in both final versions of the text of CA 3, so it must have been added
during the first half of June. At that time the difficulties of the phrase, which
would soon agitate the theologians, were as yet unknown. Granted that
Luther had provocatively explained during the conflict with Erasmus that
God could be in death, hell, and even more abominable places,[74] his followers
under Melanchthon's guidance had not recognized the meaning of the
provocation. They did not take seriously the implications of Luther's doctrine
of ubiquity and so they missed the point at which the old doctrine of God in
the early confessions was decisively breached.

Even the corresponding recognition of the continuation of sin in the
justified person, who is constantly aware of inner sinfulness yet remains
within the scope of forgiving grace, is a break with tradition. The other

72. *WA* 31.2:226.16ff. See also the joyous exchange in *WA* 31.2:282.6ff., 20:611.14ff.
73. *WA* 28:6.9ff., 27:126.28ff., 20:403.6ff., 28:64.5ff., 32:40ff.
74. The pious do not shrink from saying, "God is in death as well as in hell, and in things
more horrible and filthy than them, such as the privy and the sewer; indeed, as Scripture testifies, God is everywhere and fills all things" (*WA* 18:623.14ff. [= *BoA* 3:114.8ff.]; *LW* 33:47).

extreme is that the doctrine of the two natures is transferred to justification, a move so bold that it can only be understood in the light of Christ: he is in his human nature so closely united with the divine that he was actively involved even in the creation of heaven and earth. That corresponds to what happens in justification, where the righteousness of faith is connected to divinity, and the good works to the human nature.[75] Justification is a mirror image of the doctrine of the two natures.

Thus the descent into hell opens up theological topics on which Luther had already achieved new insights during the years before 1530, and for which the way had been paved by the understanding of Easter even earlier than that. Easter too is a battle between God, or more particularly Christ, and death and the devil. Confessing the resurrection includes the acknowledgment of the facts that come with it. Christ dies as a sinless man, so he does not fall under the power of death; the person of the God-man remains alive in the midst of death. That God, however, who raises the dead to life gives humanity, as opposed to other creatures, power over sin and also power over death. Luther's vividness in portraying God and humanity becomes clear in this earth-shaking struggle in which the *efficacitas* of the triune God unites itself with the power of the New Creation over humankind. It demonstrates that Luther's teaching on the Trinity and the incarnation is shaped by a dynamic view of salvation that was indeed hinted at in the original confession (1528) but that first comes to full expression in Luther's theological statements.

Luther's original thoughts on these matters, like the lapidary phrases of CA 3.2ff., seem to lack the richness of the traditional variations on this theme and even to fail to match his own overflowing wealth of thought on salvation. The extent of the gap can be shown by the distinction between original sin and actual sin that was drawn in Schwab. 4 and Na 3, as well as afterward. It does not fit into the connection between Trinitarian and christological statements in the original confession, nor is it yet present in Schwab. 2 and 3; it first appears in Schwab. 4, which runs parallel to the development of the doctrine of original sin. Only after this doctine split the original connection of the Trinitarian and christological statements was it possible to establish the distinction between original and actual sin. Its content has hardly anything to do, however, with those sublime articles on God and Christ; instead it forms a later rhetorical bridge from CA 1 to CA 3, composed between Schwab. 1–3 and Na 3, which would put it in the second half of April.

75. "Because here [in the creation] one thing depends on the other, two things are spoken of as though they were one. Thus the righteousness of faith is divinity, which accepts the works as though they were humanity, the two making one person, just as divinity and humanity are in Christ" (*WA* 27:127.16–18). On the doctrine of the two natures and justification, see above, p. 256. On the section as a whole, see also *WA* 17.1:298.6ff.

5. THE KINGDOM OF CHRIST

The sequence of the earthly works of the *vere deus–vere homo* is brought to an end by the reference to the ascension, although that does not bring the earthly work itself to an end. Christ carries out his work from this time on as the one who "ascended into heaven, and sits at the right hand of God." From now on and from that position, he will "eternally rule and have dominion over all creatures." Thus section 4a still belongs within the sphere of Christ's earthly activity; his heavenly rule begins in 4b. Of course, since it is from God's right hand, the rule includes all earthly creatures, both the pious and the impious. It fights the battle of Christ and his faithful against the demonic powers, and finally Christ, as judge of the living and the dead, gains the ultimate victory.

What a story, filled with tension and pressing onward to the end of all things! The beginning of world history leads to the end. The salvation-history aspect of the Confession, which became apparent in details such as the insertion of CA 2 between CA 1 and CA 3, now appears in its entirety; tied to this aspect is the general eschatological tone. The decisive thing, however, is that the course of salvation history and its eschatological end in grace and judgment are seen in terms of the kingdom. The controlling images are *regnum* and *dominatio Christi*. The heavenly lord, sitting at the right hand of the Father, rules his kingdom. That kingdom includes all creatures and thus relates to universal history. It sanctifies the believers and thereby brings the saving work of Christ to general fulfillment; and since the final judgment is carried out within its framework, saving history also includes satanic destructive history. In both heavenly curse and heavenly blessing, however, world history and saving history, creation and chaos, are bound to the perfecting of the world.

That is a view of God's kingdom without precedent in the Apostles', Nicene, or Athanasian Creed. We can still follow the development of this grand structure through the composition of the final text. There are not yet any traces in Schwab., but the eschatological viewpoint is picked up in Luther's revision of Marb. 3, which concludes with reference to the last judgment. Article 3 of Na goes back beyond this ancient baptismal statement and further elaborates the end of the article. From the Second Article of the Apostles' Creed come the phrases "ascended into heaven" ("afterward ascended into heaven") and "is seated at the right hand of God the Father Almighty" ("that he sits at the right hand of the Father"). The concluding phrase of that article in the Apostles' Creed follows with scarcely any alteration.

Article 3 of Na adds the following phrases after the reference to Christ's sitting at the right hand of the Father: "and eternally rule, make just, holy, and alive, and protect everyone who believes on him through the sending of the Holy Spirit into their hearts." The concept of the *regnum Christi* is not yet there, but ideas like the eternal reign to the end of time, sending the Holy Spirit into hearts and thereby justifying, making holy, giving life, and protecting believers provide the individual elements of a theology of the kingdom of God. They permit us to observe the pneumatic side of the Trinitarian event in the power of the Spirit over humanity. In the German text of CA 3, two things are combined in one: Christ rules over all *through* the Holy Spirit. The Latin text, however, makes a sharper distinction. Christ rules over all creatures directly. The spiritual, inner event in the hearts of believers, however, is caused indirectly by Christ's sending the Spirit. Conceptually, this approach merely reflects Luther's distinction between *regnum externum* and *regnum internum* without emphasizing it. But we can still see how, right up to the final days of completing the text, people in Augsburg were struggling with formulations that would be faithful to Luther.

There was already mention of the sending of the Holy Spirit into hearts by the end of Na, and in his Confession of 1528, Luther had praised the Holy Spirit "as a living, eternal, divine gift and endowment," although he concentrated basically on the forgiveness of sin.[76] In the confessional development proper—apart from Luther's personal writings—we find no trace of such thoughts, except that famous parallel enumeration of terms in the Small Catechism where the work of the Spirit is directed toward faith and salvation. Here in CA 3 the Trinitarian statement is completed and rounded off, bringing world events and salvation events (for the individual as well as for all of Christendom) to one divine conclusion. In the kingdom of Christ— understood as *regnum internum* as well as *externum*—the creation and preservation of the world, together with the salvation of the world and the individual, come to fulfillment.

Seated at the right hand of God, the risen Lord rules his kingdom. Article 3 of the CA reaches its climax by describing this kingdom in key words. The kingdom is stamped by the unique character of its king. Luther spent twelve years meditating on the fact that this king was God's Son. The Son dwells, like God himself and his kingdom, in hiddenness. He cannot be known frontally, by his face, but only when he is turned away. His reign is marvelous and unusual, mysteriously contrary to all our reason, nature, and wisdom. He governs us in the same way that he is governed by the Father.[77] His realm is a kingdom of grace, of help, and of comfort for all poor sinners. The nature of his kingdom is understood only when one pays attention to the office,

76. *WA* 26:505.32 (= *BoA* 3:511.15); *LW* 37:366.
77. *WA* 25:447.15ff., 19:152.2, 153.27.

rather than the names, of those who exercise authority there. Royal and priestly functions are united; the royal authority protects, and the priestly reconciles.[78] It is an eternal kingdom. It begins with Christ's baptism and remains to the end. Its stages are unknown, even though a series of pious leaders can be recognized. Beyond that, all that is known is that it will last until the final return of Christ. All who allow themselves to be governed by God's mercy and truth may live in this kingdom. Christ reckons among that number all who do battle in his kingdom against evil desires.[79]

Yet he is not only a king who demands but is one who gives. As king of mercy he wants us to trust his mercy. According to Philippians 2, the royal Lord became a slave and does a servant's work; he is in the service of love. As in CA 3.4 his external kingly reign corresponds to his inner power over hearts. As head of those who belong to him, he is united in love with his body and thereby reflects his own Trinitarian unity with the Father. It is only out of this spiritual bond that a kingdom can come into being in the first place. As king, Christ reigns over a people; the faithful cling to him and he to them. As God, he rules over all creatures. As a human being, he is just like me.[80] Divine and human natures rule all creatures and direct human beings from within through the Holy Spirit. Seen as a whole, the realm of this king of grace is a strange kingdom; its king is filled with might and with utmost weakness, seated at the right hand of God and hidden in the world.[81]

The personality of the ruler defines the character of his realm: he rules a kingdom of grace. Within it, powers of grace flow abundantly to the faithful; the sick and the infirm are gathered there. In peace and gratitude they rejoice in reconciliation with God. From his throne the heavenly king gives life to souls through his Word and grants them forgiveness. He has the message of salvation proclaimed to all people. He lifts the condemnation of sinners. All are called to this kingdom of mercy. He pours out the comfort of the forgiveness of sins upon everyone.[82]

The law does not count in the kingdom of Christ. The kingdom is like a hospital in which Christ is the director. Along with forgiveness goes cleansing, the "sweeping out" of sin. In the kingdom of Christ, the Christian is both "sinner and not sinner" (*peccator et non*), ever remaining dependent upon the activity of the Holy Spirit, just as Christ remains the king of righteousness (*rex iustitiae*).[83]

78. *WA* 19:156.20ff., 13:609.5ff.; *LW* 20:71.
79. *WA* 15:421.30ff., 515.4, 429.9–10, 432.6.
80. *WA* 20:295.9, 308.2, 375.7ff., 376.21ff., 520.1ff., 573.7ff., 546.9ff.
81. *WA* 34.2:57.8ff., 59.6ff. See also ibid., 75.5ff. (sermon of August 4, 1531).
82. *WA* 13:477.31ff., 464.16ff., 15:480.10ff., 13:243.10–11, 38ff.; *LW* 19:5–6; *WA* 13:505.38ff., 506.8ff.; *LW* 18:358–59; *WA* 15:698.1–2.
83. *WA* 15:725.7ff., 728.18ff., 729.2ff., 731.5ff.

Thus the sermon on Christ and his kingdom which we have here compiled from fragments of Luther's sermons and expositions turns into a sermon on the kingdom of God under the sign of the returning Christ. Christ's kingdom rules human history, which in turn is defined by the history of Christ. Strictly speaking, the latter is not history, since the Son is coeternal with the Father. But even though he participated in the creation of the world, he entered into solidarity with the human race through his incarnation in Mary's womb. To that degree even the kingdom of Christ became a part of human history.

All the Old Testament prophets were oriented toward the coming Christ and his future kingdom, so that certain events in the Old Testament foreshadow that kingdom; the unity of the biblical proclamation in the Old and New Testaments is related to the unity of the kingdom. It becomes apparent beforehand in the incarnation of Christ, as well as in the universal significance of Jerusalem, prefigured in the temple and fulfilled in the work of Christ. At the end of time, Abraham's blessing for the nations, the universal kingdom of David, will come to pass. Old and New Testament histories of the kingdom overlap one another.[84]

In the New Testament the message of the angels on Christmas Eve already announces the breadth and majesty of Christ's kingdom. It begins concretely in the baptism and death of Christ, who is also a sign of the duration of the kingdom to the time when all his enemies will lie at his feet. In the meantime there is the period of the peaceable kingdom, when Christ provides believers with all the gifts and goods he obtained after his ascension to the right hand of the Father, and when God's love, begun in the sending of the Son into the world, is fulfilled in the blessed in heaven.[85]

This kingdom of love is also the place where the gospel is proclaimed in the world. As in the Synoptic parables, Christ is the heavenly householder and his disciples are the messengers of the gospel. "Because Christ sits in his kingdom and rules the world through the Holy Spirit, the gospel begins."[86] New members are continually brought to the kingdom by constant preaching. Through the gospel, the king also rules the proud and rebellious, subduing them outwardly to the power of the kingdom; he thus has both political and spiritual power at his disposal and is both king and priest forever.

Thus Luther's doctrine of the two kingdoms belongs intrinsically to this eschatological view of the dominion of the ascended Lord who rules his kingdom from the right hand of God, as it is described in the Third Article of

84. *WA* 13:88.1–2; *LW* 18:79; *WA* 13:243.10–11; *LW* 19:5; *WA* 13:660.12ff.; *LW* 20:140; *WA* 15:480.10ff., 505.16ff., 764.21ff., 23:526.27ff., 553.25ff.; *LW* 20:186, 217; *WA* 31.2:63.23ff.

85. *WA* 15:478.16–17, 479.14ff., 32:165.21, 15:542.18ff., 564.17ff., 637.9–10, 679.27ff.

86. *WA* 20:285.11–12; see also ibid., 235.9–10. On the following, see *WA* 20:497.17, 31.2:28.5ff.

the Apostles' Creed. As long as his lordship is not yet complete, that is, until his coming again, the kingdom of Christ and the kingdom of the world must appear to be separate from each other. At the same time, both pious Christians and the godless multitude live under his dominion. The two kingdoms can be differentiated as a kingdom of mercy over against a kingdom of mercilessness, wrath, and disfavor. Believers are also subject to the devil's jurisdiction, but the more they are beaten down, the more they can glory in mercy.[87]

Under the heavenly reign of Christ, and in expectation of his final judgment, it is important to come to terms with the existence of the two kingdoms. It is a "great and difficult office for a man to rule in that second [kingdom?], whether it be spiritual or corporal rule, by the prince's office or by mine," declared Luther on February 28, 1529.[88] At this point we cannot explicate his doctrine of the two kingdoms in relation to the Third Article (see above, p. 263); we can only use examples to show that it finds its place in such a context. Its statements about the spiritual kingdom are drawn from the evidence that salvation history presents about the kingdom of Christ as a kingdom of mercy (see above, p. 264). The difference between the two kings results from the gap that exists between their realms; the crucified king rules in heavenly majesty, the earthly king in human sovereignty.[89] The difference between the two kingdoms is primarily one not of power but of quality. The spiritual kingdom is not equipped with weapons but has only the office of preaching as its instrument; by this means the preachers attract the masses and gather new people. Through this Word the laws of earthly power are invalidated; for example, freedom replaces the command about the Sabbath. The two laws run parallel to each other; one is not to make the spiritual law into an earthly one. Christ's kingdom is spiritual and is indeed here on earth, yet it is not earthly. Christ's kingdom existed alongside David's kingdom in one nation, Israel, although the former existed invisibly in Word and faith.[90]

Christ's spiritual kingdom is defined through the power of the Word, which is mightier than all created things. It enters into the heart and devours everything that opposes Christ's lordship. Through it the one person of

87. "Here therefore the kingdom of Christ prides itself in being a kingdom of mercy. . . . In this kingdom there is pure mercy, even when he punishes us the most. There is another kingdom of mercilessness, wrath, and disfavor" (WA 17.1:326.10ff.). "If this doctrine were accepted, the kingdom of the world would be in ashes. The kingdom of Christ and of the world must be separated. This speaks of the kingdom of Christ, which is of no concern to the masses. All of us, Christians and unbelievers, are subject to God" (ibid., 333.15ff.).

88. WA 28:524.9ff. On the following, see WA 27:259.10., 407.9ff., 409.1ff.

89. "Thus the mode of ruling is different in the kingdoms of the world and of Christ. In the kingdom of the world, the prince or king alone is free; all others are servants. But in the kingdom of Christ, Christ alone is the servant, and we are free" (WA 31.2:70.32ff.).

90. WA 13:326.25ff.; LW 18:250; WA 13:475.17ff., 608.25ff.; LW 20:70; WA 15:690.2, 691.12ff., 693.13ff., 695.15–16, 17.1:193.22ff., 20:558.6ff., 31.2:72.1ff.

Christ, divinity and humanity united, comes to expression. Christ gives himself to us through the Spirit as a gift in our hearts. Only faith, not works, forces its way into the heart. The kingdom thus founded is not perceptible to the senses; it thwarts all sensory expectations and has a spiritual and eternal character. The earthly sense of the person of the world aims at making a physical kingdom out of it. In the distinction between the two kingdoms we once again encounter the difference between faith and works.[91] It is certainly not adequate to separate the two kingdoms by the categories of visible and invisible. When the kingdom of Christ is described as within us, the intention is to express its ubiquity as well. Like its Lord, the kingdom of Christ is nowhere and everywhere, in order to fill all things.[92] The two kingdoms correspond to the two natures of Christ. We recall (see above, part 2, chap. 4) that faith corresponds to the omnipresent divinity of Christ and visible works to his humanity. The exalted humanity struggles for the kingdom, but it attains victory because of the hidden divinity. The invisibility of the kingdom corresponds to faith hidden in God; its visibility, to work which pushes for deeds and action[93]—or to illustrate it by the crucified king himself, "In that kingdom is supreme power and profoundest weakness."[94]

6. THE RETURN OF CHRIST

The resurrected Christ, exalted to the right hand of God, rules his kingdom spiritually, that is, through the Holy Spirit, to the end of the world. The confessions of the ancient church have much less to say on the work of Christ and the condition of his kingdom during this intermediate state than we have just finished elaborating out of CA 3 and its parallels. Before Luther there was no total concept of a theology of the kingdom of God in the sense that it can be found in his writings—the two-kingdom doctrine is merely a modest abridgment of the whole—however much individual elements of his thinking were present among spiritualists and apocalypticists. Among the ancient confessions, the Apostles' Creed gives a twofold reference: at the end of the Second Article, it points to Christ's return and judgment, and at the end of the Third Article, to the final resurrection and eternal life. The Nicene Creed speaks in somewhat greater detail of the kingdom of eternal glory after the ascension of the Son to the right hand of the Father and then, in the appendix to the Third Article, of the general and final resurrection of the dead and of the life of the world to come. Although packed with content, the creeds never

91. *WA* 19:500.25ff., 25:51.19ff., *LW* 29:64; *WA* 27:800.2ff.
92. *WA* 17.1:211.12ff.
93. *WA* 40.1:417.8ff.
94. *WA* 34.2:59.6–60.1.

speak of that intermediate state between the resurrection and the return of Christ which the third article of the Augustana describes. We have seen how, as the text was reworked, it was elaborated along lines that we could trace back to Luther. We can follow a similar process in relation to the return of Christ.

We find a first step in that direction in Schwab. 13, which paraphrases the final sentence of the Apostles' Creed. The judgment of the living and dead is depicted in images that Luther also uses: deliverance of the believers from all evil, and punishment of unbelievers and the godless with the devil in hell. Luther had already included all of these elements in his personal Confession of 1528,[95] so to that extent Schwab. 13 depends on him, even to details including the rejection of a doctrine of final restoration. We find echoes of Schwab. 13 in Na 16, which in turn forms the basis for CA 17. Article 16 of Na goes beyond its original in Schwab. 13 by identifying the dead with those who are bodily resurrected and by stressing that the condemnation of the damned and the devil to the pains of hell is eternal. A rebirth of all things will not take place, contrary to the position of Origen and the Anabaptists—nor will there be a physical restoration of Jerusalem and the promised land, nor a final battle in which the pious annihilate the godless and bring in a millennial kingdom. It is a total rejection of contemporary apocalyptic.

The end of CA 3 mentions the return of Christ quite simply by referring to the Apostles' Creed. All fanciful, unbiblical embellishments are dropped. Just as the beginning of the Trinitarian self-unfolding is hidden in the darkness of divine mystery, so speculation about the end of all things must be pushed aside.

In Luther's writings it is never easy to draw the line between the session at the right hand of God and the return of Christ. Basically that is because the intermediate state has fluid borders, and in any event, eschatological events cannot be set into a chronological system: that was even true in the Bible! As kingdom of mercy the reality of the resurrection extends far into the last days; it works secretly in the world through Word and faith.[96] A forgiving rather than a condemning righteousness reigns; the faithful are justified, made whole, and freed from sin and death. In the world, tensions remain. The Lord who lives among us as hidden and weak continues to be a stumbling block to the human race, even though in the end he will sit in judgment over his despisers.[97]

In no way is this intermediate state to be equated with hell. Prior to the day

95. *WA* 26:509.13ff. (= *BoA* 3:514.38ff.); *LW* 37:372.

96. "Christ prepares, strengthens, and establishes this kingdom in the world through the word and faith, although in a hidden way" (*WA* 31.2:72.3–4).

97. "A delightful kingdom in which mercy flourishes" (ibid., 5ff.). See also ibid., 72.8, 79.8ff.

of judgment there is no separate place for condemned souls. According to the biblical witness, the devil does not sit in hell but sits in an intermediate region from which he rules the world. If sheol is a particular location, then it is the place of the final fear of death, where God's wrath works itself out at the last day.[98]

For most people the intermediate state is the sleep of death. The dead feel nothing, unconscious of time over a period of days and years. There are those whose bodies rest in marked graves. Some, however, have been completely removed from the earthly realm. Only their souls sleep outside the physical world in a hidden place, unknown to us, which as an "underworld" is distinguished from our spatial existence. Luther is quite cautious in describing these intermediate states; much remains mysteriously hidden.[99]

The world does not know these secrets of the soul's life. If, as occurred in the Averroist controversy,[100] the immortality of the soul is contested, human beings are looked upon as animals. Still, one should avoid disputes about these questions. There is no need to rack one's brains; Plato and Aristotle do not have the last word either. "Enjoy what is at hand and do not pry into what is not yet known"—that is Luther's motto.[101]

Thus the intermediate state introduced by Christ's resurrection is not free from temptations. Those are conquered, however, through faith in Christ's uninterrupted reign. People who are tempted consider themselves to be captive to demonic powers, but in faith they know that they are in the realm of the powerful Word that promises them healing forgiveness. This promise is like a point. Temptation is removed in the "now." It ought not be considered eternal; it is only an appearance that will be gone momentarily. Luther can testify to that out of experience. The mathematical point (*punctum mathematicum*) is in reality an eternal point (*punctum eternum*).[102]

Thus the experience of faith from the grace-filled kingdom of the Resurrected One already extends into the ultimate state of fulfillment after the second coming. Luther, however, is cautious and restrained about describing these things. Instead, he urgently warns of the signs indicating the end of the world; like Elijah, the first doomsday witness, he preaches vigilance. The same task was assigned to the prophetic witnesses to the destruction of Jerusalem; they were to warn of the end of the world. The present bloody

98. *WA* 17.1:255.12ff.

99. *WA* 20:168.29ff.; *LW* 15:157. The *mortui extra locum* are the true saints who, after the resurrection, will exist free of time and space (*WA* 20:163.1–3; *LW* 15:150).

100. See Carl Stange, *Die Unsterblichkeit der Seele* (Gütersloh, 1925), 81ff.

101. *WA* 20:70.4ff., 72.9ff.

102. *WA* 31.2:446.5–6. "The best remedy is to turn your gaze away from the visible to what is invisible" (ibid., 6–7); the believing conscience reaches, from afar, the state of being under the lordship of the Resurrected One as though it were immediately present. The believer discovers "all our trials to be momentary and that disdain to last a very short while" (ibid., 445.23–24).

persecution of evangelical Christians by tyrannical rulers and seditious spirits is one of the apocalyptic signs, as are astrological changes in the atmosphere and the stars. In 1524, the year of the threatened end of the world, Luther carefully observed the cosmic movements, and his early hope that their frequency would decrease was disappointed. The world continued to get older, and the proverb held true: "The older, the sparser; the longer, the worse."[103]

One can see that Luther shared in the general expectation of the approaching end of the world and that he paid attention—although with some aloofness—to the signs of the times. Nevertheless, certain criteria can be deduced from an analysis of his understanding of the intermediate state between the ascension and the second coming. The idea of judgment fades; the gruesome late medieval pictures of punishment have disappeared. The righteousness that forgives has supplanted the righteousness that condemns. When the places of sacrifice and judgment disappeared, the *punctum mathematicum* went with them; the new heaven and new earth, created by God, will last forever. There Christ and all his faithful will act as priests eternally. What Christ began in his resurrection is now transformed into inexpressible eternal life. It is not possible to state what eternity is; only faith can grasp it.[104]

Thus the circle is completed. That which occurred before the beginning of the world—the communication of eternal life from the Father to the Son and from the Son to believers through the mediation of the Holy Spirit—is now completed in eternity. Eternal love encompasses itself.

---

103. *WA* 20:590.3ff., 29:611.14ff., 618.5, 16ff., 619.2ff., 622.5ff.

104. "I, Martin Luther, do not possess the perfect, but I learn and am occupied with it. Therefore I say constantly, 'This is but a moment, it will not endure' " (*WA* 31.2:446.15ff.). See also ibid., 584.30ff., 437.11ff.

SIN AND FREE WILL

7. TEXTUAL HISTORY OF CA 2, 18, AND 19

The statements of the articles on original sin, free will, and the cause of sin (CA 2, 18, 19) not only are connected thematically but also have common roots in the tradition. Without going into the individual relationships, we will limit ourselves to the interconnectedness of the themes that are found in Luther's *On the Bound Will* and in his Confession of 1528.

At the end of *On the Bound Will,* Luther himself identified this coherence. He derived the rejection of free will from God's foreknowledge and predestination; it applies to all creation. Behind it is the enmity of Satan toward Christ and his kingdom. This merciless captivity to the power of evil can only be lifted by Christ's redemption.

Out of this series of negative statements comes the positive confession that Luther compiles at the end of his book: (1) All salvation depends on God's unerring knowledge and will.[105] (2) Therefore human free will is excluded.[106] (3) Satan's destructive power is broken.[107] These three conclusions flow out of the redeeming power of Christ. The concluding thesis of *On the Bound Will*[108] brings these three principles together. The abolition of human free will and the bondage of humanity through original sin—a bondage that only Christ can remove—constitute the theme of Luther's book. The structural connection of the three theses determines its literary form. Although we cannot trace that structure here—that would take a commentary on *On the Bound Will*— we can pick up the three confessional statements that are finally laid down in CA 2, 18, and 19.

Luther's preliminary formulation against human good will—that it is not good in itself, and that the attempt to realize it does not come from us— corresponds in every way to the assertion of the Confession of 1528 that

---

105. *BoA* 3:291.23–25.
106. Ibid., 25–28.
107. Ibid., 28–36.
108. "Si credimus . . ." (ibid., 291.41–294.4).

praising free will only nullifies the help and grace of Jesus Christ.[109] One must bear in mind, however, the two qualifications Luther mentioned in 1525 but did not repeat explicitly in 1528. The first rejects Augustine's contention that the free will can do nothing but sin. The second opposes a thesis of Wyclif that occasionally appeared in Luther's polemics as well—that one may not speak of a free will at all.[110] By thus explicitly distancing himself in 1525 from the original and the late medieval radical Augustinianism, Luther takes the same position on the question of the free will that would influence the Lutheran confession from 1528 on.

Likewise, the later development of the doctrine of original sin is already sketched in *On the Bound Will*. Because the free will is unable to do the good, the result is an unbreakable bondage to sin and guilt; only Jesus Christ, through his sacrifice, can abolish it. No one but God himself can extricate us from our entanglement in the power of evil. In his Confession of 1528 Luther draws all of these conclusions: free will is not able to do anything, so Christ is our only helper and source of grace; outside of his lordship, sin, death, and the devil ply their trade. Original sin is therefore not a weakness or a defect; it means abandonment to eternal death. All that Luther confessed in 1528 had been clearly evident in 1525. To deny Luther's confession is to abolish all the articles of faith. He states as much in *On the Bound Will* where he cites Paul's observation that the revelation of God and Christ is no more than foolishness and scandal in the eyes of the heathen. Erasmus is on the same level with them because he defends free will. And in a positive vein, "to believe in the One who is both God and man, who for the sins of humanity both died and rose again and is seated at the right hand of the Father"—this confession of Christ, summarized in the Nicene Creed, is the starting point and heart of Luther's confession in 1525 as well as in 1528.[111]

Thus the connection of the three articles, 2, 18, and 19, is discernible even before the Confession of 1528; it goes back to the roots of the confessional development in the ancient church. We now will trace the development in detail up to June 1530.

In its original form of 1528 the article on original sin (later CA 2) echoes the dispute with Erasmus; those who see original sin merely as a "weakness or a defect" are certainly to be found among Erasmus's followers in German-speaking areas to the southwest. They are the "new Pelagians." Their identification with real Pelagians refers broadly to the Pelagian controversies at the time of Augustine. Characterizing original sin as a "very great sin" comes from quotations out of Paul and the Psalms.

109. Cp. ibid., 160.6–8, with ibid., 509.15–17.
110. Ibid., 160.6–23.
111. Ibid., 258.27–29.

The text of Schwab. 4 smooths out the wording of 1528. The character of original sin is more profoundly and precisely described. It "condemns and eternally separates from God all men who come from Adam." After the Fall a total and general captivity to sin occurred. Only Christ's work on our behalf frees us from that captivity. By his suffering he has done enough to cover all sins, both original sin and its consequences, and has completely done away with them.

The tightly packed biblical and Pauline statements of Schwab. 4 were essentially weakened under Melanchthon's influence and with Luther's consent. There is no talk of original sin; interest in popular education may have motivated Melanchthon's reticence on this point. He paints the profound moral corruption of the general masses in vivid colors, adding the terrible wrath of God and the punishment he inflicts upon sin. But Melanchthon does not move on to the threat of eternal judgment; he demands that sinners repent and make satisfaction for fear of God's judgment, assuring them of forgiveness that will be given in response to their earnest prayer, as God has promised.[112]

Those are different tones from the one we pick up from Luther's *On the Bound Will* or his Confession of 1528; the prophetic witness to God's judgment and salvation has become a vice squad's warning with threats and prodding. It is precisely in those confessional articles whose origins are tied to Luther's *On the Bound Will* that this difference comes into play, as will become clear in the further development of the Confession.

It was Melanchthon who took the decisive steps toward the final formulation of CA 2. The text he presents in Na 2 presupposes Schwab. 4 and shows only minor deviations from it. Article 2 of Na repeats the statement of Schwab. 4 that through Adam's fall all humanity is born in sin. Gone is the comment on the Pelagian idea that original sin may also be termed a "weakness or defect." Instead, Melanchthon accepts a formula that has become classic because of him: original sin describes a condition in which human beings are "without fear and trust toward God, full of concupiscence, . . ." He is speaking about an "inborn sickness" that condemns us and delivers us over to eternal death if we have not been reborn by baptism. We observe two things in this formulation by Melanchthon: the psychological basis and the connection with baptismal grace. These two additions of his require further discussion (see below, p. 276).

In the middle of June, Nb 2 shows minor changes from Na 2 which are passed on almost word for word into the final German version of CA 2. It is doubtless more pointed to say that since the Fall all persons ("from their

112. *WA* 26:205.17ff., 3ff.; *LW* 40:278.

mothers' wombs") are involved in the covetousness of original sin. That must go back to the exegetically based assertion in Luther's Confession of 1528 that "in my mother's womb I have grown from sinful seed"[113]—another indication that the final editing of the German text was carried out in the light of Luther's confession. A second observation points in the opposite direction. In the final German version, original sin is identified with an "inborn sickness," which is a return to the original interpretation of the sin as a "fault."

From Nb 2 on—in contrast to Schwab. 4 and Na 2—CA 2 contains a rejection of the Pelagians, who oppose original sin. Article 2 of Nb sees them as glorifying our natural powers and correspondingly downgrading the suffering and merit of Christ. The Latin text strengthens the christological concern by another addition. In a phrase reminiscent of CA 4, it castigates the efforts of human reason to deny original sin and thus to achieve righteousness before God by its own powers.

This defense of the justification of the sinner over against an assumed free will represents a certain connection between CA 18 and CA 4; it strengthens the hypothesis that CA 18 may have been on hand during the final editing. We have already treated (pp. 89–97) the difference between civil and spiritual righteousness, which also directs us back beyond its location in CA 16 to the problem of justification. Our earlier suggestions about the original links connecting hereditary sin and the doctrine of the will (see above, p. 272) make such relationships appear more plausible.

Luther's Confession of 1528 begins with free will and then moves on to the doctrine of original sin. As in all of Luther's literary work, the emphasis is on the problem of the will; for him everything else is derivative. Article 2 of CA places the doctrine of original sin between the two creedal statements, which follows the example of Schwab. and does it more logically. The result, however, is that all connection with the doctrine of free will is lost. For Luther, on the other hand, it is typical that in 1528 the condemnation of the free will led to the polemic against the Pelagians. The christological interest is again in the foreground; the free will acts "diametrically contrary to the help and grace of our Savior Jesus Christ." Outside of Christ "death and sin are our masters." Therefore any praise of free will is "sheer error."[114]

The development of the article on the will is not shaped as much by Luther's thought of 1528 as by the conclusions Melanchthon drew from the conflict with Erasmus. From the beginning it was known that the Wittenberg humanist did not share Luther's views wholeheartedly and that he had misgivings about their pedagogical application. These misgivings became especially acute during the visitations. By agreement with Luther they were

113. WA 26:503.33–34 (= BoA 3:509.33–34); LW 37:363.
114. WA 26:502.35ff. (= BoA 3:509.15ff.); LW 37:362.

cautiously expressed in the *Instructions for the Visitors*[115] and thus were in a position to influence statements in the Confession.

In the face of revolutionary attitudes, Melanchthon speaks "modestly" about the possibility of freedom of the will. On no account may it be asserted in opposition to governmental authority. Christian freedom consists primarily in the forgiveness of sins and the readiness to love and to serve which that forgiveness conveys. The power it possesses is therefore chiefly a protective and comforting power engendered by the Holy Spirit; it has no creative potential. This embedding of the justified Christian within the civil order is far removed from the Lutheran "freedom of the Christian" with its spontaneous exuberance. Luther is better at maintaining the total lack of freedom of the sinner who opposes God side by side with the freedom of the believer.

Even Melanchthon, however, is not completely satisfied with his preliminary solution in the *Instructions*. As the Thuringian visitations were getting under way, he was in Jena because of the plague, and there he lectured on Colossians,[116] explaining the relationship between philosophy and theology by reference to the problem of free will. Thus before Luther clarified these questions in his Confession of 1528 from the standpoint of his theology of the will, Melanchthon had already dealt with them on his own philosophical premises. The final formulation of CA 18 and—as we shall see—of CA 19 is to be understood in this light.

Melanchthon's starting point is the rejection of a deterministic misunderstanding of predestination. The power to act has its origin, wisdom, and strength from God. That implies, however, that we cannot freely command these goods; we must accept them gratefully from his hand. But above all we cannot please God by these natural powers; we cannot by ourselves "produce true fear of God and true confidence in God nor the other spiritual emotions and dispositions [*motus*]." By this formula, later picked up in CA 18, Melanchthon intends to establish the difference between natural and spiritual powers of the will, or between a natural and a Christian spiritual attitude. By reaching back to the distinction between *iustitia spiritualis* and *iustitia naturalis*, which were the product of other theological concerns, Melanchthon gave new currency to the scholastic distinction between nature and grace; natural ethics, fed by ancient springs, is raised to a higher level by the gracious activity of the Spirit.

In the process, the free will is robbed of its power. It relates to eating and drinking, seeing and hearing, and reproduction—in short, everything that humanity can produce by itself. In the spiritual relation to God, the free will cannot do a thing; this realm of the spiritual life is completely closed to

115. *WA* 26:226ff.; *LW* 40:301–2.
116. Printed in August 1527 with an excursus on free will (StA 4:221ff.).

unbelievers, who often lack even the *iustitia civilis* that is possible on this level. God thus punishes them for their sinful nature. The nature of *iustitia civilis* reveals itself in the active and passive elements of the punishment, just as salvation reveals itself in the *iustitia spiritualis*.

In the preliminary statement on free will in Na 17, Melanchthon relies in general terms on Augustine for his presentation of the difference between external and internal-spiritual righteousness. In June of 1530 he went back to earlier literary formulas, so from Nb 2 on he applies the classic formula for original sin: human beings without God are from their mothers' wombs "full of evil lust and inclinations," without "true fear of God" and without "true faith in God" (cum peccato, hoc est, sine metu Dei, sine fiducia erga Deum et cum concupiscentia).[117] This Melanchthonian formula for original sin avoids all substance-language and is tied, as Luther intended, to the doctrine of the will.

Opposition to free will and assertion of original sin had a longstanding connection with the question of the cause of sin. Luther pursued this question in his Confession of 1528. In his condemnation of free will there, he attributed all help and grace to Christ, saw death and sin as masters of the sinner, and called the devil "our God and prince" who holds us in his captivity and service.[118] In that way the question about the cause of evil was taken out of metaphysical categories and placed in the realm of sin and grace.

For Melanchthon too the emphasis was on themes of practical piety. He explains in the *Instructions for the Visitors*[119] that people tested by tribulation should keep their vulnerability to temptation in mind and consider "how the devil always knows in what way he can entice us into evil, bringing temporal and eternal shame and misery on us." The devil is the enemy of free will. God, however, protects us so that our freedom is not lost in affliction and we do not fall victim to temptation. We should each keep our weakness in mind and consider that we cannot keep our heart pure by ourselves and that we are threatened by God's anger. Those who believe and pray will be protected from the devil by the Holy Spirit.

Those are the powerful tones of a simple lay piety which can also be found in Luther; there is no confessional ring to them. At Augsburg, Melanchthon tried to translate them into theology. In Na 18, he tackles the question of the cause of sin by using the concept of nature. God created human nature, but

---

117. Almost word for word in the preface to *Dispositio orationis in Epistola ad Romanos* (1529; *CR* 15:443): "[Human reason] is without fear of God, without trust in God, and has concupiscence and all sorts of evil feelings." With minor variations also in ibid., 448 (top) and 450 (middle). The dialectic between *iustitia civilis (politica)* and *iustitia fidei* is in fact a recurring theme in the *Dispositio*.

118. *WA* 26:503.20ff. (= *BoA* 3:509.17ff.); *LW* 37:363.

119. *WA* 26:212.10ff.; *LW* 40:287. Cp. *WA* 26:226.19ff., 227.22ff.; *LW* 40:302, 303.

that does not imply sin. Sin came from the will of Satan, and the godless support him in it. How the devil and his followers get to that point is not explained. The fact remains that those who turn away from God fall prey to demonic corruption. The corruption comes from the devil; help is from God.[120]

It is obvious that this justification of the God-given nature in Na 18 is connected to the assertion of the natural free will in Na 17 (CA 18). *Iustitia civilis* is based on God's creative will, which is not set aside by original sin or abolished by human wickedness; they only confirm it. In Melanchthon's mind the three articles (CA 2, 18, 19) form a unity that upholds God's glory as creator alongside humanity's fall into evil. The inner connection of the three articles, already established in the conclusion of *On the Bound Will* (see above, p. 271), has remained intact throughout the development of the text.

Excursus: Melanchthon and Luther on Original Sin and Free Will

After the conflict over the doctrine of the will became generally known through Luther's answer in *De servo arbitrio*, the public discussion of the questions raised remained remarkably cautious. In occasional utterances Luther did indeed give some sharp answers, but he never offered another exposition of the unsettled issues. It was not until his Confession of 1528 that he repeated his theses in brief and precise form (see above, p. 271). Neither his contemporaries nor those who came after him recognized that those theses represented his theological legacy—just as the whole conflict over the will received less attention than it deserved, even in the church that bore Luther's name. The underground rumblings among the evangelical parties may be regarded as talking around the question rather than setting great store by it.

Of course Melanchthon is not to be held completely responsible for the further development of the doctrines of the will and of original sin. He did, however, set the tone for the way things went, and to the extent that the process began before 1530 it belongs to the prehistory of the Augustana. His *Scholia on the Epistle of Paul to the Colossians* of 1529 is determinative.[121] Right at the beginning he defends the new theology against the vulgar charge that Luther is the originator of sin, but he moves God's actions so close to natural phenomena that the activity of the devil and the ungodly are explainable by philosophy.[122] God wants to act through freedom in all that he has created, but the devil and evil humanity misuse that freedom and do evil. This freedom involves all natural human characteristics and activities. In it we can do everything within our natural powers and abilities. But reason is one of these natural gifts; it forbids us to do evil. Through it God's Spirit works in the heart; by it God sets the limits for freedom. The Spirit punishes the sinful nature. In the conflict between

120. Na 17 reappears in the final versions with very few changes.

121. The *Nova Scholia in Proverbia Salomonis ad iusti paene commentarii modum conscripta* (1529; StA 4:305–464) has a basic pedagogical attitude very close to that of Proverbs, but it avoids dealing with concrete issues.

122. Melanchthon's concept of nature stems from the classical rather than the biblical belief about creation: "I will make God not the author of sin but rather the preserver of nature, giving both life and activity—which the devil and unbelievers do not use in the right way" (StA 4:222.16ff.).

the divinely created nature and the Spirit, sin becomes apparent; punishment puts an
end to the conflict. Theoretically it is impossible to resolve the antithesis between
human freedom and sin. God confirms it and annuls it through the punishment we
humbly accept, thereby coming to faith by means of sorrow and repentance.[123] The
puzzling relationship between original sin and freedom is solved through the fallen
sinner's being brought by punishment to freedom. For Luther, God's punitive righteousness leads us ever deeper into the abyss of his judgment; in Melanchthon, the
guilty person's culpability leads through judgment and forgiveness to salvation.

In the process the tension between *iustitia civilis* and *iustitia spiritualis* is lifted.
According to civil righteousness one acts in accordance with the prescriptions of
natural conscience; that is what public law demands and that is what the government
enforces by means of rewards and punishments. In this area the natural powers come
into play. Nothing that occurs in this way affects the God-relationship; it remains in
the realm of our natural endowments. Of course there are situations where the
demands of the natural law prove to be more than we can fulfill. Then, however, God's
Spirit grants new powers. They exceed the natural means of the *iustitia civilis*. They
are new creations and confer unknown possibilities for renewal and life. Adam's fall
has been overcome; the Spirit bestows new power.[124]

Thus Melanchthon repeatedly arrives at the formula that describes natural freedom
and that CA 2 turns into a negative to define the essence of original sin: the person
filled with the Spirit can "fear God, believe in God, and love the cross."[125]

If reason alone cannot fulfill the righteousness demanded of it, then God must be
implored to "guide every part of our life and all our actions, watch over us, and show
us the way, so that we see our weakness with spiritual eyes and attain knowledge, so
that we are cleansed and led by his Spirit."[126] The Spirit thus supplements what we
cannot carry out with our own natural reason. In order to fulfill the divine purpose of
salvation, we are to recognize our need and pray with contrition and faith. This
synergism is a carbon copy of that of Erasmus, and it is the direct opposite of the
unfree will.

In this way, Melanchthon affirms the necessity of philosophy; it too supplements
the activity of the Spirit. Human beings by nature possess access to truth and
morality. They recognize not only moral demands but even their nature, measure, and
number; they can build houses and heal diseases. According to Ovid, ethics, natural
philosophy, mathematics, and medicine[127] are holy seeds of the understanding. Of
course, that philosophical knowledge is often deficient and erroneous, lacking true
reason. Even eloquence, the queen of sciences, often makes mistakes in its arguments.
By God's will there is a gulf between the gospel, as the doctrine of spiritual life and
righteousness before God, and philosophy, as the knowledge of bodily things; reason
cannot bridge that gulf. "Scripture, not reason, is to be consulted concerning the
articles of faith."[128]

123. Ibid., 223–24.

124. Ibid., 223.10ff.

125. Ibid., 222.31. "Love of the cross" here indicates a link with medieval cross mysticism,
just as elsewhere we can see a connection with the doctrine of "affects": ". . . human nature
according to the natural man cannot produce true fear of God, true faith in God, and the other
feelings [*affectus*] and spirtual impulses" (ibid., 223.1ff.). Reason cannot summon these powers
without the help of the Spirit (ibid., 223.23ff.).

126. Ibid., 225.26ff.

127. Ibid., 230–32.

128. Ibid., 241.10–11; cp. ibid., 225.14ff.

Reason and revelation are mutually in need of supplementation—that is the view of the scholastics and Erasmus, and of Melanchthon as well. This is the point where Melanchthon did not appropriate the Lutheran doctrine of the will and grace.

In his Confession of 1528, Luther bases the rejection of the free will on the argument that Christ alone is our help and comfort and that all other power comes from the devil.[129] The exposition of CA 19 will cover what it is necessary to say about the devil in this connection.[130] Here we must note that the reference to the devil is not Luther's only explanation. He has many reasons for the rejection of free will. The most profound is certainly a statement in a sermon from 1525 which may have stimulated Melanchthon's unknown formulations from 1527 to 1530; it corresponds to Luther's basic thesis that the sin of the unbeliever is that "in temptation it is not possible for the flesh to believe in God, to trust God, to know what is true and what is promised to his servants."[131] Those who are in danger do not talk about free will; they cling to God's Word. The blind do not rely on their free will; they get up and seek help. The thesis that we are to do what is in us and then God will give us his grace contradicts the realities of life; when someone smart like Erasmus speaks in that way, he contradicts himself. The battle that must be waged against free will is at the same time directed against worldly wisdom in general. But even monastic asceticism based on reason and free will becomes a disgrace.[132]

Out of these negative statements comes an understanding of nature antithetical to that of Erasmus and the classical world. For Luther, human nature is basically corrupted (*pestilens*), because it flees from God. Its inborn powers count for nothing, and preachers who praise its perfection contradict reality. In their blindness, the children of Adam, possessed through their flesh by the devil, do not know God. God's dealings with sinners seem incomprehensible to them. They do not understand the distinction he makes among them. He hates only those who do not want to see themselves as sinners; to those, however, who recognize themselves as such he is gracious. This reversal of human judgment also changes the evaluation of all human relationships. God is the enemy of all who do not want to be sinners.[133]

Where human beings, on the basis of a confused mixture of free will and divine grace, join together for common action, they lose their clear judgment. This is the point of departure for Luther's rejection of Erasmian synergism. That is why he so passionately and persistently attacked human free will.[134] But the Holy Spirit is no skeptic; he demands clear confessional decisions and abhors wishy-washy reflections. He does not imprint dubious opinions on our hearts; he gives unwavering certainty. He creates new human beings with clear judgment who know how to avoid evil and do good, and who thus become free from sin and death. They judge everything and are judged by no one.[135]

129. *WA* 26:502.35ff. (= *BoA* 3:509.15ff.); *LW* 37:362. Cp. above, pp. 271–72.

130. See below, p. 281ff.

131. *WA* 13:431.19–20; *LW* 19:119 (on Habakkuk 2). The same idea is at the end of the *On the Bound Will* (*WA* 18: 786.17ff. [= *BoA* 3:291.41ff.]; *LW* 33:293).

132. *WA* 17.1:58.1ff., 59.12ff., 62.13–14, 244.10–11, 441.24ff., 18:667.21ff.(= *BoA* 3, 157.19ff.); *LW* 33:112. Luther's sermons from 1525–26 provide a still-unexhausted source for statements on the dispute about the will.

133. *WA* 16:297.8ff., 17.1:59.12, 17.2:219.24ff., 31.1:377.23ff.

134. "perpetuo asserui" (*WA* 18:756.6ff. [= *BoA* 3:255.28ff.]; *LW* 33:246).

135. *WA* 18:605.30ff., 630.1ff., 653.13ff. (= *BoA* 3:100.29ff.), 120.32ff., 141.32ff.; *LW* 33:24, 58, 90; *WA* 17.1:59.10–11.

That is connected to the fact that the Spirit gives a twofold judgment. There is an external one that is heard publicly, and an internal one that makes itself known in silence. The external judgment, on the basis of Scripture, recognizes no free will; the inner one convicts itself inwardly from the words of Scripture just as God judges us. The defenders of free will know nothing of this discriminating power of the Spirit, because its decisions occur in the hidden depths of the conscience. This is very close to the Melanchthonian distinction between outward and inward righteousness. But that which is expressed in Melanchthon as a tension, based on God's creative will, between reason and Spirit, is stretched in Luther to an unbridgeable opposition in fallen humanity which can only be overcome through the new creativity of God's gracious will. What for Erasmus and, following him, Melanchthon runs along an indefinable border between the moral will of human beings and the saving will of God stands for Luther as irrevocable grace over against the uncertain human will. The "dogma" of free will, dark and dubious in itself, has nothing to offer Christians; they should consider it a fairy tale. The Christian articles of faith, however, are not only completely certain for Christians but are also confirmed to other people through clear and plain statements of Scripture. Melanchthon's statements in CA 18 do not measure up to these requirements; they do not attain the heights of Luther's teaching on the will and grace.[136]

Luther wastes no time on speculations about the possibilities and limits of free will. He demands complete agreement with his rejection: "I advise everyone to show respect," he warns his readers.[137] If anyone tries to avoid a decision by appealing to the ambiguity of Scripture, Luther lets that person know that Scripture is unequivocal and clear and that it rejects free will. Much, however, is hidden in God, including the boundary between his will and ours. We ought not rack our brains over it—as Melanchthon does in CA 18—but ought to hold to God's clear Word, which establishes his sovereign freedom to decide without consulting our wills. The inquirer will not find an answer in the natural freedom of our political and ethical decisions, as CA 18 does. The answer is given once and for all in God's self-revelation that took place in Christ and is confessed by the church.[138] Although Melanchthon's reference to the human freedom which is guaranteed by natural law may thus assert a relative claim, it has no relevance to the fundamental problem. The truth of Scripture is authenticated to us not by natural revelation but by the revelation that occurred in Christ.

Thus for Luther the sovereign freedom of divine grace and the nonfreedom of the human will are indissolubly bound to the Trinitarian self-revelation of God in Christ's saving work. In a deeper sense than Melanchthon intended, CA 2 stands between CA 1 and CA 3: original sin is not only a connecting link within saving history between God's creation of the world and its redemption through Christ; the conquest of original sin by means of true fear of God and true faith, which means the conquest of evil lust and inclinations, occurs as God's free act in Christ—as an inner necessity of the self-unfolding of divine love. And the freedom of the human will in ethical political decisions is only an apparent freedom in the light of this self-unfolding of divine love. In a strictly theological sense, CA 18 does not belong together with CA 2.

136. *WA* 18:656.21ff. (= *BoA* 3:145.20ff.); *LW* 33:95.

137. *WA* 18:787.13 (= *BoA* 3:293.6–7); *LW* 33:295.

138. "The supreme mystery has been revealed—that Christ, the Son of God, has been made man, that God is three and one, that Christ has died for us and will reign eternally. Are these things not known and sung even in the byways? If you take Christ out of the Scriptures, what will you find left in them?"(*WA* 18:606.26ff. [= *BoA* 3:101.25ff.]; *LW* 33:26).

8. THE CAUSE OF SIN (CA 19)

In his Confession of 1528, Luther spoke of the cause of sin only in a side remark and without ever using that precise expression.[139] In rejecting human free will, he relies upon the work of Christ, against which sin, death, and the devil have no power. Without Christ, humanity is captive to the devil and is the property of sin. These evil powers make the intrinsic freedom of the will impossible. The question of the origin and limits of natural freedom thus includes within itself the question about the cause of sin.

Of course Luther never posed that question. For him it is clearly unnecessary; it is the power of sin that concerns him. As early as Na 18, Melanchthon, however, feels himself compelled to justify the majesty of God the Creator over against demonic power—a speculative question that had been answered in the same sense as Melanchthon's Na 18/CA 19 by the decree of Innocent III in 1215 against the dualism of the Cathari. Thus his answer lies on a different plane from the other articles in the Confession. Nevertheless, it would be well for us to ask what Luther would say about the "will of the devil and of all the ungodly which, as soon as God removes his hand, turns away from God to evil" (CA 19).

For Melanchthon, therefore, the devil is only the indirect cause of sin. It occurs when the perverted human will despises God, and he therefore withdraws his hand. The devil, therefore, is not an active cause; he stands between God and humanity so that when we flee from God we fall prey to the devil. It is a subtle dialectical game that preserves human freedom over against God and the devil just as the latter then acts in freedom over against God and the people who fall away from God and into the devil's hands. We wonder to what extent Luther too took up this dialectic and affirmed these complicated relationships between freedom and necessity.

Luther and Melanchthon share at least one thing in their understanding of CA 19: they both begin from the situation of the tempted person. That is a considerable step, because it takes the wind out of all those speculative tendencies we have encountered in Melanchthon from time to time. The sin in which the freedom of the will is lost arises out of that freedom, and God does not break or bind the free person who willingly falls into his hands and accepts what God has given as his own.

The tempted person falls prey to Satan and loses his freedom! Theologically that can be understood in different ways. There are one-time, final temptations, such as those of the martyrs whom Satan seized through the hands of tyrants and executed. In those instances the fatal temptation meant the entrance into life; Satan lost the game. But there are also extended

139. See above, p. 271.

temptations in which the tempted, as described in CA 2, no longer have any fear of God or any confidence of faith. Such persons think Satan is master of the world, against whom Christ and his kingdom are impotent; they consider themselves to be perpetual prisoners, incapable of anything but evil. Luther uses the biblical example of someone possessed to describe the fate of one who is held captive by the devil in original sin and who therefore loses all the gifts that had been received from God—especially the knowledge of God.[140]

In Luther's more popular expressions of his views on temptation,[141] the fundamental direction of temptation theology (Anfechtungstheologie) is not abandoned. The devil is always near; one ought not think he is far away. He attacks not only the soul but the body as well. It is his natural role to corrupt everything. He has a kingdom; he is the ruler of this age (deus seculi). He thus fights against Christ and his kingdom. God battles him with his Word. The devil places this Word in doubt and thus gives people an uncertain conscience; that is what happened in Augsburg among the bishops and princes of the old faith.[142]

All of these descriptions of the devil and his goals and activities can be found in Melanchthon as well as in the edifying literature of the time.[143] Everywhere the theology of temptation (Anfechtung) accompanies belief in the devil. The unique thing about Luther, however, is that for him the work of the devil leads to the conquest of temptation. The tempted believe themselves to be thrown in prison among hostile demons. But faith crowds what is visible out of sight, and the believers hold on to nothing but the Word. They say, "I am not in prison, but in tranquillity." They repeat the same word of promise over and over and in that way steady their conscience. The angry punishment of the disturbed conscience seems to last forever, but in God's presence it is a momentary act. Luther recalls personal experiences where such an indignatio punctualis disappeared in the twinkling of an eye.[144] His theology of temptation aims at such a victory.

From that point of view the statements of CA 19 take on new meaning. They are not primarily descriptions of how the corrupted will falls prey to the devil; they quietly presuppose that God does not withdraw his hand forever from fallen humanity but always holds open the possibility that they will turn back to him and thereby be rescued from temptation. Understood in this way, CA 19 forms the background for satanic temptation—a background that may

140. WA 29:618.18ff., 15:431.18–19, 18:786.7ff. (= BoA 3:291.28ff); LW 33:293.; WA 17.2:219.24ff.

141. The fine dissertation by Hans Martin Barth, "Der Teufel und Jesus Christus in der Theologie Martin Luthers" (Göttingen, 1967), is basically correct in not delving very far into Luther's more popular descriptions.

142. WA 32:112.19ff., 113.5ff., 114.29, 119.6ff., 172.11ff., 125.14, 119.16ff.

143. Barth provides evidence in abundance elsewhere.

144. WA 31.2:445.28ff., 446.9ff.

be obscure but that is also illuminated by God's gracious will. It is no longer merely a matter of maintaining that temptation and sin have nothing to do with the Creator's intention: that would be simply an apologetic attitude. It is also a matter of maintaining that faith is always there to overcome the onslaughts of Satan.

We can best recognize the progress made in this matter when we draw a comparison with the statements on the devil in the decree of Innocent III from 1215.[145] There too God the Creator is exonerated from responsibility for the existence of the devil by placing the latter originally among the good angels and blaming the ancient fall on him. Humanity then becomes guilty by allowing itself to be drawn into Satan's snares. This position preserves divine freedom in relation to sin. The whole cause, however, is then laid at the door of the devil; humanity remains stuck in sin. Article 19 of the CA, on the other hand, describes sin as letting oneself fall into Satan's power, and thus ascribes a passive cooperation to humanity. The freedom of all parties is preserved to some extent, and the dualistic impulses of the confession of 1215 are overcome. One thing, however, is not clear, and that is the most important point about the Fall for Luther: faith breaks Satan's chains and brings fallen humanity back into the divine fellowship of grace.

145. "For the devil and other demons are indeed by nature created good by God, but what they do by themselves is evil. In fact man sinned at the prompting of the devil" (*Lib. Decretal* 1.1).

FAITH AND GOOD WORKS

9. TEXTS

Luther's great personal Confession of 1528 does not contain a formula for the doctrine of justification; the later article 4 of the Augustana did not grow out of his wording. Luther never developed this doctrine systematically but always developed it exegetically. Even his attempt to provide a summary in 1530 at the Coburg, his "De loco iustificationis"[146] remained a torso. It does show his powers of formulation, but he was not equally enthusiastic about making balanced formulas binding on his church.

Thus even Luther's statements on the justification of the sinner are really nothing else than exegetical paraphrases of the Apostles' Creed.[147] The focus is on Christ and his work. He is "my Lord and everyone's Lord." He "has suffered, been crucified, died, and was buried for us poor sinners; thereby he has redeemed us by his innocent blood from sin, death, and the eternal wrath of God." Echoes of the Catechism, which was just being written, are obvious. All salvation depends on the death and resurrection of Christ. No one can become blessed "except through the one righteousness which our Savior Jesus Christ *is* and *has given* us, who has been placed for us before God as our only mercy seat (Rom. 3:25)." The nature of Christ's righteousness becomes clear. A commentary on CA 4 will have to be especially attentive to these points.

These points are no longer so easy to recognize in the development that took place over the summer of 1529, leading from Luther's confession to the Schwabach Articles. In between lies the *Instructions for the Visitors*, which, although it was completed in the spring of 1528—approximately the same time as Luther's confession—represents a completely different stage of theological development. Before the visitations were over, Melanchthon and Agricola had engaged in the first antinomian controversy. With Luther's

146. *WA* 30.2:657ff.
147. On the following, see *WA* 26:501.34, 502.19ff., 25, 504.17ff., 505.16 (= *BoA* 3:508.35ff.), 509.4–5, 510.4ff., 39–40; *LW* 37:362, 364, 365. See, in addition, the explanations of the second article of the Creed in the Large and Small Catechisms.

support, Melanchthon had carried the decisive points; Luther's final editing of the *Instructions* shows how far his influence reached.

That can also be seen in the *Instructions'* explication of the doctrine of justification. By requiring that one should "preach the whole gospel," it puts the call to repentance before justification: "Without confession there is no forgiveness of sins." As faith in Christ, justifying faith includes repentance.[148] That then raises the question of how the law that leads to repentance relates to faith in forgiveness, and how works that are good and pleasing to God come out of the cooperation between divine demand and the faith that God works in human beings. These are questions with which the doctrine of justification, particularly in the form Melanchthon gave it, had continually to deal. They require a constant distinction in justification between human faith and action. The doctrine has to take a process of the inner soul that has its cause in the saving action of Christ, but describe it in terms of internal and external reactions—not in the interest of somehow constructing a psychology but for educational reasons. When preaching justification, one is confident of arousing in the hearers those dispositions of emotion and will to which God predisposed them by the proclamation of law and gospel. That is a different doctrinal starting point from the one given in Luther's explanation of the Second Article of the Creed. There the description is not of present processes that God is carrying out in human beings, but of God's action in the suffering of Christ who has been exalted to be our Lord. The difference of approach certainly ought not be magnified into an antithesis. But it is clear that the doctrine of justification develops differently as an explication of Christology, or more precisely soteriology, from the course it takes as a description of an event between God and humanity, with particular attention being given to human experience.

The approach of Luther and Melanchthon is first made confessionally binding in the fifth of the Schwabach Articles.[149] Luther's confession is the basis of the text, with the references to Christ's suffering and redeeming sacrifice further strengthened, partly through repeated borrowings from Luther's Catechism. And yet certain differences can be detected. Material in Luther's confession that paraphrased the Apostles' Creed now becomes the component of a systematic theology in this document meant for Schwab. The doctrine of justification is tied not to the Christ-event but to original sin (Schwab. 4). It is impossible to free oneself from that sin through good works; justification can happen only "if without all merits or works, we

---

148. *WA* 26:202.8ff., 16ff.; *LW* 40:274, 275. Luther worked out an agreement between Agricola and Melanchthon (*WA* 26:202.32ff.; *LW* 40:275, 275 n. 10). For the teaching on repentance in the *Instructions*, see below, pp. 409–10.

149. *WA* 30.3:87.32ff.

believe in the Son of God, who suffered for us. . . . This faith is our righteousness; for God reckons and regards as righteous, godly, and holy, and presents with the forgiveness of sin and life everlasting, all those who have this faith in his Son: that, for his Son's sake, they are received into grace, and are his children in his kingdom. . . . "

Expressions that will later occur in CA 4 are already being shaped in this document, and in the process, the sorting out of the idioms taken from Luther's confession continues. Without pursuing its theological significance at this point—the shift in emphasis from Christ to our faith comes immediately to mind—we note that in Luther the "one righteousness" is that "which our Savior Jesus Christ is and has bestowed upon us, and has offered to God for us as our one mercy seat." Article 5 of Schwab., however, equates faith with righteousness: "This faith is our righteousness; for God reckons and regards as righteous, godly, and holy . . ." In other respects the article still has not attained the clarity of sentence structure and conceptuality that we will admire in the final version of CA 4. But it does surpass the *Instructions* both in linguistic expression and in richness of thought.

Thus, even though the deviation from Luther is not great, it will make the issue of faith and good works increasingly important in the further development of the article on justification. That issue will determine the systematic context of the article.

The doctrine of original sin in Schwab. 4 forms the negative presupposition for Schwab. 5. The doctrine of justification in Schwab. 5, in turn, results in the articles on the good fruits of faith worked by the Spirit (Schwab. 6) and the work of the Spirit through the spoken Word (Schwab. 7). Thus the statements on justification ought not be interpreted in isolation. They belong to a context that is deeply interwoven with the structure of the doctrinal articles and that gives them their theological unity. The art of systematics is truly at work here, and I do not hesitate to give Melanchthon the credit. Just as he brought the tensions between sin, law, and grace to bear in his *Loci* of 1521,[150] he places the nascent Lutheran confession within the polarity of sin and grace, developing the doctrine of justification out of his pedagogically based pessimism about sin. That involves a different systematic from Luther's christological line of argument. Even though Luther's use of the sequence of the Apostles' Creed may still have some influence on the external structure of the Schwabach Articles (see above, pp. 241ff.), the internal structure of this first general Lutheran confession is fundamentally different from that of Luther's private confession. He did not relate the doctrine of original sin to justification. He did indeed reject the advocates of free will, the

150. See W. Maurer, *Der junge Melanchthon* (Göttingen, 1967–69), 2:264ff.

new and old Pelagians, but primarily because they disregarded Christ's redeeming sacrifice. Without Christ, however, "there is no power or ability, no cleverness or reason, with which we can prepare ourselves for righteousness and life or seek after it."[151] Thus Luther does not bring original sin and justification into a logical relationship with each other; each is independently tied to Christ and his work. It is from that perspective that they gain their light and their brilliance in Luther's personal confession.

By comparison with Luther's confession, we have established that Schwab. 5 does not identify justification with Christ but with faith. In so doing we have hit the nerve that connects Schwab. 5, 6, and 7: the faith in the Son of God of which the cited Scripture passages speak (Rom. 4:22, 10:10; John 3:16) is God's work and a gift of the Holy Spirit, and because it is "an efficacious, new, and living thing," it "produces much fruit" (Schwab. 6). It is effected, however, through the Spirit-laden oral Word (Schwab. 7). Thus, according to the Schwabach Articles, faith and Spirit constitute justification; it is effected by both, and both operate through good God-pleasing works. This spiritual event, however, is only outwardly connected with Christ's saving work; at this point the article on justification still lacks depth.

Melanchthon worked on that problem when the failure of the Dolzig negotiations in Innsbruck (see above, p. 31) made it necessary to incorporate the Schwabach Articles in the growing Augustana. We note the following effects of that process:

1. The connection between the doctrines of justification and original sin is formally detached and, in terms of content, made less tight. That occurs through the fact that original sin is discussed earlier—in Na 2 after the doctrine of the Trinity and before Christology—so that the articles dealing with justification and faith (Na 4–6) are directly connected to Christ's person and work, although it is true that the soteriological theme is not worked out as carefully here as in Schwab. 5–7. Article 5 of Na has dropped the negative statements about human bondage to sin, death, and the devil because of original sin, so that—going further than Schwab. 5—the inability to perform works of satisfaction is discussed entirely in the light of forgiveness and justification before God. There is no longer much evidence of Melanchthon's pessimism about sin.

2. The regrouping of the Schwabach Articles affects not only the placement of the doctrine of original sin but also the arrangement of the statements on justification (Na 4–6). The faith-producing activity of the Holy Spirit by means of the Word is placed first in Na 4. That anticipates Schwab. 8, where, of course, the offer and the gift of the Holy Spirit are considered together and

151. *WA* 26:502.35ff. (= *BoA* 3:509.15ff.); *LW* 37:362.

are made dependent on both sacraments as well as on the Word. At the same time, however, the content of Schwab. 6 is also included. The connection between Word and Spirit, emphasized in both Schwab. 6 and 7, is now made only once, in Na 4.

3. The placement of Na 4 before Na 5 subordinates justification to the activity of the Spirit—a true expression of the young Melanchthon's spiritual theology. It is not so glaring in Na 5, because there God's forgiving and justifying action, the freedom of his grace and Christ's saving work—in harmony with Schwab. 5—are central to the content; it maintains the connection with Luther's approach. Echoes of it are still to be found in the completely new formulations constituting the second half of Na 5.[152] They pick up the closing scriptural quote from Schwab. 5 (John 3:16) but tie this key soteriological passage with Gal. 3:14, in a theological link to the gift of the Spirit promised to Abraham. Thus the article on justification (Na 5) is put in the framework of Melanchthonian pneumatology; this emphasis on the Spirit forms a new and independent element in Lutheran confessional development.[153]

Article 6 of Na speaks of the active power of faith. The fact that, according to Schwab. 6, the good works of faith are necessarily performed by the Holy Spirit is explained in Na 6 by the phrase "God has willed it"; only in that way are they pleasing to God. Thus Na 6 does not put the primary emphasis on good works but puts it on the central core of justification, the free gift of grace. One can see that Na 6 is not yet fully developed; it is more like a duplicate of Na 5 and Schwab. 5. The common bond of Na 4–6—faith produced by the Spirit—is more prominent than the individual differences. By this time, the basis for justification which Luther's confession provided is barely detectable.

That is why the theological foundation of Melanchthon's doctrine of justification in Na 4–6 is still unclear and tentative. In Na 4, faith appears as a fruit of the Spirit acting through the oral Word. According to Na 5, the gift of the Spirit and the forgiveness of sins and the justification it brings are mediated through the forgiving power of Christ.

In Na 6, the major theme is our acceptance (*acceptatio*) by God's gracious will, a theme mentioned previously in Na 5. This bundle of themes common to the three articles is neither tied together nor differentiated. The editorial work did indeed bring a tighter style than that of Schwab. 5–7 but no greater clarity of thought. The continuing uncertainty is also illustrated by the shifting sequence of the three articles.

152. Kolde 12.26–30; Reu 172.
153. In this context we should point out the quotation from Ambrosiaster that will be evaluated below (pp. 350ff.), as an element of patristic tradition added to Na 6.

Clarity is not achieved until the final version. It sets up the final, logically cogent sequence of the three articles. After presenting the process of justification in CA 4, it gives its basis in God's present action through Word and Spirit (CA 5) and its divinely acceptable effect in our good works (CA 6). Although justification forms the thematic core for these three interrelated articles, it is basically part of one event for which God repeatedly creates a new beginning by his spiritual rule in Word and Sacrament, and which continues in the good works of the faithful. In this spiritual continuum the individual phases are cleanly separated from one another and yet interrelated. The final text is therefore tighter and clearer than its predecessors; repetitions are eliminated. Article 8 of Schwab., the article that listed Word and sacraments, is dropped, and Na 4, which came out of it, is absorbed by CA 5.

In this arrangement, CA 4 is the "chief article," the article upon which the church stands or falls (*articulus stantis et cadentis ecclesiae*). In it one can see what progress Melanchthon made in describing the doctrine of justification during June 1530, up to the date of presenting the CA. The beginning of the article (sec. 1) is repeated almost verbatim from Na—more closely in the German version than in the more polished Latin. The christological-soteriological reference (sec. 2) is expanded in CA 4. In the German version, Christ's vicarious suffering and its consequent gift of forgiveness, righteousness, and eternal life are cited as the basis for justification; the Latin picks up the *acceptatio* theme from Na 5 and connects Christ's sacrificial death with the concept of *satisfactio*, thus taking over more of the traditional conceptual language than the German version does.[154] That includes the concept of the imputation (*imputatio*) of faith which is common to both versions. The entire newly formulated text is oriented toward the Epistle to the Romans; previous New Testament citations are replaced by a general reference to Romans 3 and 4.[155]

Article 5 of CA, like CA 4, represents a decided improvement and clarification of the preparatory documents. In light of the weak and unsatisfactory formulations of Na 4, a stronger reliance on Schwab. 7 is understandable. The latter provides[156] the equation of the "preaching office or the oral Word" which will have such important consequences later (see below, pp. 348–49); by clearly placing Word and Sacrament together as "means of the Holy Spirit," CA 5 goes beyond both of its predecessors. The famous formula in

154. For its derivation, see below, pp. 316–17.
155. Allusions to Schwab. 5 that are not covered in Na 5: the impossibility that a man can "by his powers or through his good works" (*non. . . proprius viribus, meritis aut operibus*) deliver himself from original sin (*WA* 30.3:87.35); the vicarious suffering of Christ (ibid., 88.5); and above all, the reference to the imputation of our faith (ibid., 88.6–7). Melanchthon therefore had Schwab. 5 in mind or in hand during the final editing of CA 4.
156. Perhaps Na intended to use it in the still-missing article 14.

CA 5 on the Spirit who awakens faith "where and when it pleases God" (ubi et quando visum est Deo) is taken over from Schwab. 7.[157] The rejection of the Anabaptists, barely mentioned at the end of Schwab. 7 and openly expressed in Na 4, becomes an official condemnation in CA 5. When one reviews the article as a whole it becomes clear that it has taken over the classifying function that was originally unique to Schwab. 8; it prepares for the arrangement of the following group of articles.

In comparison with the two preceding articles, CA 6 seems more like a postscript, although, as we have seen, the question of good works had been a central concern since the visitations. While Schwab. 6 had said that living faith brings forth good works in the power of the Spirit, the emphasis in CA 6, as in Na 6, lies much more on the divine requirement. At the same time, however, the works produced in this way are kept separate from all meritorious acts, as was the case in CA 4. Finally, the rejection of meritorious works is based on the tradition of the ancient church. The only time that the articles on justification mention the *sola fide* is in a citation from Ambrosiaster attributed to Ambrose, and not in the words of the author himself. In this traditionalism, as well as in the stress on the divine will, we see Melanchthon at work. The biblical image of good fruit never gets fully used; the gushing fullness and freshness that poured out in Schwab. 6 have dried up in CA 6.

The transition of the three articles from Na to the final text did not occur as directly as we have described it. There is the manuscript Nb, which the Nürnberg delegates sent home on June 15, and we can look at it in relation to the copies by Spalatin (Sp.) and Vogler (A I). There is hardly any difference between Nb and the final German version. Spalatin, however, has obviously used a version of the text that was different, and therefore earlier, than Nb; apparently he translated that earlier text freely. Although we may charge the paralleling of related concepts that arises from that process to Spalatin's account, the fact that the citation from Ambrosiaster (*BS* 60.12ff.; *BC* 32) that now stands at the end of CA 6 is found at the conclusion of the fourth article in Spalatin's copy[158] and that the citation of Luke 17:10 is still missing indicates that Sp. relies on a version of the text available previous to Nb. The same is true of Vogler's translation. It is very free in some places and smooths out the original; here too Ambrosiaster is cited at the end of article 4 and the quotation from Luke is dropped from the very independently treated conclusion of article 6. We thus see that the work of revision was still going on around June 15—admittedly without changing essentials—and that the text was not at all sacrosanct.

157. God "through the same [oral Word], as a means, bestows faith by his Holy Spirit, as and where he will" (*WA* 30.3:88.27–28; Jacobs 71–72).

158. The later shift shows, moreover, that the final editing considered CA 4 and CA 6 as a unity.

Seen as a whole, the three articles on justification in their final shape had gained much in form and content during the course of their development. But if we trace the result back to the beginning we will have to recognize that there are discrepancies. The doctrine of justification in the Augustana is not monolithic: it shows cracks and flaws. In the course of its development the christological-soteriological approach of Luther recedes into the background; correspondingly, the role of Christ in justification becomes more and more difficult to understand theologically. When the emphasis is on describing what occurs to faith, it is hardly possible to keep one's eye on God's activity in justification; technical terms like *satisfactio, acceptatio,* and *imputatio,* which are emphasized in the final Latin version, are heavy with tradition, it is true, but they are not thereby any more graphic. And it is precisely the last version of CA 6 that assumes—rather than explains—the central problem of the Reformation's doctrine of justification, the connection between faith and good works. By moving the focal point from Christology to anthropology, Melanchthon created the problems that would henceforth determine the doctrine of justification for Protestantism.

In the Augustana the doctrine of justification also developed an offshoot that has no direct connection with the section CA 4–6. It is CA 20 ("Faith and Good Works"). It is one of the appendixes to the first part and was not added to the whole until late, say, the beginning of June.[159] Its original form (B) may go back as far as the prehistory of the diet; the original tenor of the text and the fact that it was transmitted with the Torgau Articles argue for that dating.[160] Like them, it purports to be a report of electoral consultations about the coming diet; it counters the objection of the old faith that evangelical preaching of justification forbids good works. The topic is handled as an open discussion: thus far the opponents have had nothing solid to say on the subject; they have only taught foolish and harmful things about good works, nothing appropriate. In defense, the "report" describes the content and effect of preaching faith; the connection with good works is assumed rather than explained theologically.[161] A glance at possible preliminary forms of Nb—in addition to the early text from the Torgau Articles—may also

159. It first appears in Nb, and in that form it is taken over almost without change into the final version. The German version is the shorter one and probably also the earlier. It remains an open question whether the article in the final version was conceived at the time of its inclusion in the ultimate text or whether it was already at hand. The similarity with B could argue for the latter conclusion.

160. Förstemann designates it B in vol. 1 of his sourcebook (pp. 84ff.; Jacobs 86ff.); we use that designation.

161. It employs a style, linking historical narrative and polemical reasoning, that is related to the drafts for the preface, and it was probably written at about the same time. See *BS* 39.9, on how good works are not forbidden; see *BS* 37.32ff., 38.12ff., on abuses. It is remarkable that the final version (CA 20.3) increases the list of abuses and names things that Luther had enumerated in his preparation for the diet (*WA* 30.2:252ff.). I therefore conclude that Melanchthon edited at least the introduction to CA 20 at an early date; see above, n. 159.

afford an insight into the composition of the article. Vogler did not copy it in A I; Spalatin probably did not find it in his original source but copied it down afterward out of an independently circulating source, making some stylistic changes in the process.[162] In spite of that, linguistic defects of the original remain; fortunately Nb eliminated them. A corrupt spot in the text is refashioned better by Spalatin than by the final version.[163] From there on, he goes his own way; Spalatin replaces the reference to Hebrews 11 that *BS* 80.2ff. takes over from Nb with a reference to Ephesians 1. These examples too show us the detailed effort that was still being given to shaping the text in the middle of June.

Although the final version of CA 20 has not completely abandoned the narrative style, it does achieve a greater dogmatic precision. *Sola fide,* already applied as a formula in the preliminary document B, now actually becomes the organizing principle.[164] Proof texts from the Scriptures and the church fathers are expanded—an indication that Melanchthon's editing of the text was not completed all at once. That and the inclusion of CA 20 in the final text makes clear that the relation of faith and works posed an unsolved problem to the author; he had to tackle it again and again from various angles. This shows that the Augustana's doctrine of justification is not a doctrinal edifice filled with compelling conclusions; it is the expression of a theological struggle to find the proper fit between divine and human activity.

From this point of view, one may also ask whether CA 21 ("The Cult of Saints") belongs more among the doctrinal articles than in the "disputed articles" on worship and church order. For Luther, who took a position on the issue in his great Confession of 1528, it is clearly a matter of doctrine—even where he is rejecting ecclesiastical abuses. He always sees Christianity as the "kingdom of grace" in which the article on forgiveness of sins is put into practice—even at those points where, in connection with indulgences and purgatory, he deals with invocation of the saints.[165] His central concern in this case is that "Christ alone should be invoked as our mediator." There is nothing in the Bible about the invocation of saints; therefore faith has nothing to do with it. In general, Luther declares himself to be in agreement with those before him—like the Wycliffites—who opposed the veneration of saints; thus this is not a special point of attack for him.

It did, naturally, become a focus of Reformation preaching through the attack on late medieval liturgical abuses; in the *Instructions for the Visitors,* it is clearly inserted in the section on human church order, especially the orders

---

162. On the relation with the article on the cult of saints, see below, n. 170.
163. Cp. Nb 5a, 6 with *BS* 79.16 and Förstemann 1:325, last paragraph and nn. 5, 6.
164. *BS* 76.36ff., 26ff.
165. *WA* 26:508.15ff (cp. ibid., 507.7ff. [= *BoA* 3:513.35ff.]), 512.32ff.; *LW* 37:370, 368.

for holy days.[166] Luther's concern, however, forms the core: "For Christ Jesus alone is our mediator who represents us." That is also the one point on which questions of worship are related to the doctrine of justification. The *Instructions for the Visitors* takes a positive approach to the lack of biblical evidence and sets up principles for the proper and scriptural veneration of saints. The biblical characters are held up to us "as a mirror of the grace and mercy of God"; they show how we become blessed "by the grace of God through faith." Thus they are examples to comfort us and to stimulate faith and good works so that we practice them and grow in them.[167] These points of view have decisively influenced the Lutheran confessional development, have eliminated the threat of iconoclasm, and have maintained the continuity with tradition—especially in the arts.

The statements of the Torgau Articles of April 1530[168] may be seen as a summary of what is contained in the *Instructions*. The focus is on Christ's unique status as mediator, as was the case in Luther. A scriptural proof for the proper veneration of saints is added; the veneration is based on their exemplary faith and life. Invoking them, however, or even counting on their merits, is rejected because it would diminish the honor of God and Christ.

In his *Exhortation to All Clergy*, Luther sharply attacks the veneration of saints without direct reference to the Torgau Articles. The bishops are made responsible for the abuses. They have added the merits of the saints to the treasury of good works that the church claimed to administer in its indulgence practice, and they have thereby corrupted faith in Christ's atoning work. In particular, they have replaced Christ with the virgin Mary, "that holy noble person," as a mediator for poor sinners.[169] Here Luther maintained the soteriological attitude that characterized the nascent Lutheran confession without directly quoting the wording of his private Confession of 1528.

It is not surprising that he deals primarily with intra-Protestant problems in the Schwabach Articles, and even more in the Marburg Articles. In both cases, veneration of the saints is not considered. Nor does it occur in the revision of these articles; at the end of May, in Na there is still no trace of the later article 21. It is no longer possible to discover what considerations led to the move back to Torg. A 9 in the first half of June. The discussion of veneration of the saints before the diet would certainly escalate the conflict

166. *WA* 26:222ff., esp. 224.26ff.; *LW* 40:297, esp. 300.
167. *WA* 26:224.32ff.; *LW* 40:300.
168. Torg. A 9 (Förstemann 1:82–83; Jacobs 85). Taken from Förstemann: *BS* 83b.
169. *WA* 30.2:283.30ff., 299.19–20, 295.27ff.; *LW* 34:17, 26, 24. The last citation shows Luther excoriating the innovations of the late medieval cult of saints, particularly as it developed in popular piety regarding the Fourteen Helpers in Need (see *LW* 34:24 n. 32, 42:119, 119 n. 2).

with popular piety and thereby exacerbate the situation of the Protestant "confessors."

In any case the new title in Nb, "On the Deceased Saints," already makes a polemical point; the final German version goes back to Torg. A 9: *De invocatione Sanctorum*. In other respects, Nb is absorbed into the final text with very few changes (reference to Rom. 8:24).

That transition did not occur without consideration being given to editorial changes, which can be seen by a comparison between Nb and Spalatin's version. In contrast to what becomes the official text, Sp. shows a certain floweriness of language; we do not know whether to attribute it to the author or to his source, but in the latter event the source must have been very closely related to Nb. At crucial points, however, Spalatin is briefer than Nb. He connects the examples of faith and good works provided by the saints in a unified and terse way, whereas the final text differentiates more minutely. Even the theological basis for Christ's saving mediation provided in Nb is abbreviated by Spalatin; Nb's concluding reference to 1 John 2:1 is missing entirely.

Thus Spalatin's text proves to be preliminary or subsidiary to Nb. The uncertainty of the author is demonstrated clearly by the fact that he subsequently crossed out the whole article in his manuscript and replaced it with "On Faith and Good Works."[170] The process shows that the group of coworkers vacillated on whether the article on veneration of the saints should be taken over from the Torgau Articles and included in the doctrinal section. It was finally done, not because of a desire to protest against abuses and to sharpen the polemic but because of the intention to emphasize more strongly—along Luther's lines—the christological-soteriological concern.

That is the principal difference between the final version of CA 21 and its original predecessor in Torg. A 9. The soteriological side of the matter now becomes even more central: "Christ is the *one* mediator" (1 Tim. 2:5). Around this scriptural passage the authors of the article (i.e., of Nb)—even more than Spalatin[171]—have built a whole defensive wall of biblical and theological statements, all of which emphasize the unique significance of Jesus Christ as the mediator of salvation. Because of these statements, CA 21 must be classified with the articles on justification.

The prehistory of CA 21 leads to the conclusion that it is not feasible to draw a sharp distinction between questions of theology and those of worship

170. Its numbering is altered accordingly; cp. Förstemann 1:322 n. *. Vogler's copy A I lacks both articles.

171. The parallel between Emperor Charles and King David, and the reference to war against the Turks—which the emperor mentioned during the opening of the imperial diet on June 20— suggest that Chancellor Brueck had a decisive part in the consultations on the text (Förstemann 1:297ff.). Brueck himself referred to the Turkish War in his preface (*BS* 44.9; *BC* 24). The preface to Na presents Theodosius, Charlemagne, and Henry II as prototypes of the emperor.

and administration. That is true, however, of the entire CA. The division into two parts cannot be carried out precisely; even the "disputed articles" of the second part contain doctrinal statements about justification.[172] We cannot expect them to be as detailed as the articles of the first part. But, for example, a sentence like "The Scriptures teach that we are justified before God by faith in Christ"[173] is certainly a terse summary of the basis on which sacrificial and silent masses are rejected. Article 26 also repudiates meritorious ascetic works by citing the righteousness of faith, defends itself against the charge that it wants to forbid good works, and praises those good works that occur in the fulfillment of one's calling.[174] Finally, even the polemic against monasticism must be placed in this context. The monk wants to obtain forgiveness of sins through acts of satisfaction and in so doing he obscures God's Word, particularly in reference to the righteousness of faith.[175] The doctrine of justification thus permeates the entire Augustana and thereby proves itself to be the "article on which the church stands or falls."

10. IUSTIFICARI CORAM DEO (CA 4, SECS. 1, 3)

The phrase used in this title is emphasized only in the Latin version of CA 4; in the German text it is replaced by a reference to receiving the forgiveness of sins. In the confessional tradition stemming from Luther it does not appear until after the Schwabach Articles. Although, as we shall see, its use is not limited to Melanchthon, he does prefer it. The *Visitation Articles,* where it is first used publicly, show (*BS* 57.4) that it comes originally from Ps. 143:2 Vulg.: "None living is righteous before Thee"; the terminology is finally taken up by Na 5. In his translation, Spalatin prefers talking about the righteousness that counts before God (Rom. 1:17). To understand what the phrase means, we must begin with Melanchthon's works.

In relation to CA 4 and the following articles, we are in the fortunate position of having almost contemporary material from Melanchthon's hand. In May 1528 he lectured on Romans; Luther, who told of this, expected a published version. In actuality a dedication by Melanchthon to his *Dispositio orationis in Epistola ad Romanos* appeared during the Second Diet of Speyer, a portion of the book was published in 1529, and a complete and revised text in

172. Even though the sources make a distinction between doctrine and order, one ought not question the fact that originally only the articles on order were envisioned; the references to doctrinal positions did not presuppose from the beginning that Schwab. would be used in the composition process.

173. CA 24.23. Similar as far back as Torg. A 4 (*BS* 96.13ff.; Jacobs 80). In Na (*BS* 97.12; Reu 226).

174. CA 26.4, 10, 20, 30. Torg. A 1 (*BS* 108.47ff.; Jacobs 77–78).

175. CA 27.44, 48ff.; Torg. A 8 (*BS* 111.27ff.; Jacobs 84). To be included in the same connection is the disavowal, already suggested in Na 15, of the ascetic ideal of perfection in CA 16.4.

February 1530. The work does not provide a commentary on Romans but analyzes the rhetorical conventions determining its structure.[176] This procedure required the capturing of fundamental Pauline ideas in the formulations of the epistle's text, or at least the extracting of such formulas from it. In the case of the Augustana's articles on justification, it gives us the inestimable advantage of being able to trace their thought content back to its earliest context and to evaluate it in its original sense. That is especially true of formulations which, like the title of this chapter, were adopted in the last—the Augsburg—stage of the text's development.

At first glance it is not possible to establish the meaning of the words *coram Deo* that are appended to the justification formulas in the *Dispositio*. Even if they were missing, no essential feature would be lost.[177] In most cases the concept emphasizes the immediacy of the faith relationship that constitutes justification "before God." It can also be used to express that immediacy from God's side, as when he teaches us righteousness through the gospel or promises us forgiveness without our aid. In this respect, the *coram Deo* and the imputation of righteousness are closely related.[178] This connection has no deep theological foundation; it cannot be identified earlier than 1527, that is, before the citation from Ps. 143:2.

Behind it, naturally, is Luther's influence. The *coram Deo* is quite familiar to him from the psalms and the prophets; he frequently used the expression at crucial points. He does not understand it as a theological formula but understands it as a central biblical statement. In the Magnificat (Luke 1:48), Mary rejoices that God has *looked upon* her low estate. When God turns his face toward someone—as Luther establishes throughout the whole Old Testament—he grants that person the essence of grace and blessedness. A proper respect for Mary will see her placed thus before God. But Luther reaches even deeper into the scriptural context, back to the idea of the "passive righteousness of God" (*iustitia Dei passiva*) which was so significant in his early years. In Hebrew the righteousness of God meant that which we have from God and before God (*quae ex Deo et coram Deo habetur*). And from Paul

176. In my "Studien über Melanchthons Anteil an der Entstehung der CA," *Archiv für Reformationsgeschichte* 51 (1960):179 n. 65, I have dated the first, incomplete form of the *Dispositio* to March 1529. Luther's statement to Spalatin (*WBr* 5:no. 1426.9ff.) appears to press for a later dating. The text in *CR* 15:443ff. is from the edition of 1539, but it hardly differs from the original.

177. E.g., in the description of our status according to Rom. 3:21 (*CR* 15:41); likewise in the *Commentary* (1532; StA 5:32.21ff.).

178. ". . . righteousness before God is to believe that our sins are forgiven for Christ's sake" (*CR* 15:443). Likewise: "Righteousness before God is to believe" (ibid., 451); "Whoever believes in Christ is righteous before God" (ibid., 452). The reference to Christ is not dropped: "The righteousness by which we are justified before God, indeed, is to believe in Christ" (ibid., 477). This makes the difference over against a philosophical understanding of righteousness (ibid., 483). Cp.: "The righteousness of God, by which we are righteous before God, that is, by which God reckons us righteous . . ." (ibid., 451–52); ". . . that before God those who believe are held to be righteous . . ." (ibid., 446).

himself comes language about righteousness that counts before God (2 Cor. 5:21), "that makes a person pious for God."[179]

What counts before God is the opposite of what humans think. What happens *coram Deo* evokes the opposite: *coram Deo* versus *coram mundo* or *coram hominibus*. Granted it is not an absolute antithesis; what happens before God removes the contradiction. "A gracious God and a real sinner must meet"—that is the meaning of the contradictory event. Before the world, we appeal to our own accomplishments; before God, we must each give account and receive according to how we have lived. Before the world, Abraham is a child of Adam; before God, he is the father of the faithful.[180]

Before God, therefore, everything is reversed in comparison to the world. In the world, civil righteousness that we all perform out of our own capacity is important; we do it for the sake of human recognition. God, however, searches the heart; where he does so, it becomes pure. Before him human beings are sinful and dead; at the same time they live in the Spirit because God looks upon them as righteous. Before God, we are all sinners, man and woman; at the same time we are before him in grace. Before him the most zealous follower of the law can least fulfill that law. Before God, our works of the law are simply condemned as lawlessness;[181] all our fame is vanity before him.

Thus to stand before God means to stand under judgment. We are before him like the possessed mute in Luke 11:14ff. Before God's judgment seat all nations, heathen and Jewish, are judged. That which is without faith lacks righteousness and is therefore sin, because before him there is no middle ground between righteousness and sin. Moses is right in warning us to fear him. No one can offer an excuse to him; each must openly confess. For where God is to forgive sins, they must be true sins.[182] Those who understand this abandon every boast before God and even every act of their own that claims value before God.[183]

The concept *coram Deo* thus belongs together with the rejection of "our own merits, works, or satisfactions" in CA 4; it testifies to complete subjection to the judging and pardoning will of God.[184] But that is not all. Those who thus place themselves before God unconditionally will also experience

179. *WA* 7:567.24ff., 568.34; *LW* 21:321, 322; *WA* 18:769.1f. (= *BoA* 3:270.34–35); *LW* 33:265; *WA* 19:624.30ff.; *LW* 46:95.

180. *WA* 30.2:657.18–19, 40.1:379.9–10; *LW* 26:240; *WA* 15:675.17.

181. *WA* 19:624.30ff.; *LW* 46:95; *WA* 30.2:661.19ff., 25ff., 18:765.15ff., 769.10–11 (= *BoA* 3:266.12ff., 271.2–3); *LW* 33:259, 265.

182. *WA* 17.1:134.31ff., 18:761.18, 763.40, 768.15–16 (= *BoA* 3:261.26–27, 264.26–27, 270.2–3); *LW* 33:253, 257, 264; *WA* 28:688.3–4, 15:674.21ff.

183. *WA* 29:585.34ff., 17.1:191.9–10.

184. Human attainment "is nothing; that is, it counts for nothing before God other than to be reckoned as sin" (*WA* 18:752.12ff. [= *BoA* 3:251.13ff.]; *LW* 33:240).

divine forgiveness. The space they enter "before God" is also the field of activity of divine grace. Luther here draws on spatial concepts for clarification: those in the political sphere cannot distinguish righteousness; that only happens "in the theological and spiritual sphere before God" (in loco theologico et spirituali coram Deo).[185] *Coram Deo*—that is the renewing and creating reality in which God does his hidden work of salvation. Those who wish to participate in it must stand before God and be born from God. They are not moral examples as Erasmus taught in reference to the centurion Cornelius (Acts 10:2); they know nothing of their own righteousness. But they are pure before God, acceptable to him. They need no works to achieve that, other than the knowledge of Christ ("that I know what he has done for me").[186]

In this reality defined by God and Christ, exposed to the will of judgment and grace, human beings "stand" before God. The dialectical tension to which they are exposed must not mislead us into reducing the event of justification, where God and humanity simultaneously act in opposite ways, to a mathematical point. The "standing before God" is not, of course, a permanent situation, but a state of life *(Lebensstand)* which determines one's whole existence. The righteous person *lives* before God, not on the basis of demonstrable personal achievements but because "he has the testimony to Christ that the Spirit gives."[187] That is a life without law, but not without love and not without the neighbor.[188] The rhetorical contrast "before God–before the neighbor" is not a material one; both sides are designed to be mutually complementary. "Before God" means pure grace, no merit; we are responsible, however, for our neighbor's being served. That is the basic thesis of Luther's essay on freedom: in God's freedom, a lord; in relation to the neighbor, a servant. And as in 1520, so now in the sermons of 1529, this thesis leads back to Christ; Christ stands before Pilate as the guilty one, not for himself but for me. Before God too he is guilty, not for himself but for me. For me who cannot fulfill the law, he has fulfilled it. "No one is righteous before God except through the blood of Jesus Christ."[189] The sacrificial love of Christ unites God's judgment and grace; it also causes the one who stands before God to stand at the service of the neighbor as well.

To summarize: Although for Melanchthon *coram Deo* was a phrase whose

185. *WA* 40.1:92.8–9. In the conflict over grace with Erasmus, the issue was not "what we are on earth but what we are in heaven before God" (*WA* 18:781.6ff. [= *BoA* 3:285.25ff.]; *LW* 33:384–85).

186. *WA* 17.1:121.5–6, 276.5–6, 18:739.9ff., 769.7–8 (= *BoA* 3:236.19–20, 270.42–43); *LW* 33:220, 265.

187. *WA* 17.1:261.23ff. See also the sermon "The Christian Life: How It Is to Be Lived for God" (ibid.).

188. *WA* 40.1:270.1ff., 306.1, 18:752.4 (?) (= *BoA* 3:251.2–3); *LW* 33:240; *WA* 29:114.11.

189. *WA* 28:354.8ff., 20:622.5–6.

meaning unfolded only imperfectly and with difficulty, at most indicating the incalculable nature of justification, in Luther the doctrine of justification comes to its fullest and broadest expression in the image of standing before God. In the process the concept is modified in many respects by the total biblical revelation and is illustrated by the image of Christ. The tension in which humanity stands over against God thus becomes apparent: in us nothing, in God everything; in us total sin, in God totally pardoned. This tension is set up by God and thus is bearable; God places the sinner in judgment and at the same time surrounds the sinner with the gaze of his grace. The space where the soul stands before God is not only the place before the steps of his judgment seat but is at the same time the sphere of a spiritual event that purifies, changes, and renews. Of course that does not happen instantly and once and for all; it is rather a steadily motivating process of the Christian life which is sustained by the Spirit of Christ's love. With him, the Crucified, we stand before God as those who for his sake receive grace in judgment and pass on the love of Christ to the neighbor. In "standing before God," forgiveness of guilt and new life in the Spirit are imparted for Christ's sake. Thus the opening phrase of CA 4, *coram Deo*, includes all the main themes that are contained in CA 4–6.

11. IUSTIFICARI GRATIS PER GRATIAM DEI (CA 4, SECS. 1, 2)

Article 4 of the Augustana speaks (in reference to Rom. 3:24) about the connection between justification and the favor of God in two different ways. At first the article deals in sharp antitheses; we become righteous freely *(gratis)*, not "by our own strength, merits, or works" (sec. 1). Then it lets the believers be "received into favor" (sec. 2), as if healing divine existence were a room into which faith would grant admittance. It is immediately clear that no actual contradictions lie hidden behind these different modes of expression. As Melanchthon says in his commentary on Romans from 1532,[190] the *gratis* serves as a *particula exclusiva* to limit the misunderstanding of justification, and it represents an element of style that is particularly prominent in CA 4. The *in gratiam recipi*, "received into favor," represents the result of justification in a metaphorical way. The combination of both ways of speaking, the thesis and the antithesis, characterize the doctrine of grace in the Augustana.

They are previewed in the writings of Melanchthon, especially in the stiffly formal phraseology of the *Dispositio* of 1530. Here the formula *in gratiam*

190. StA 5:108.16. Neither *gratis*, "freely," nor *in gratiam recipi*, "received into favor," can be traced back before Na despite the quotation from Rom. 3:24 containing both these phrases which we have used as the title for this chapter.

recipi is particularly frequent; it stands for the heart of the Christian understanding of faith. We see from that, that Melanchthon understood it quite
abstractly; its cognitive value is not transposed into figurative terms.[191] This
abstract formality is somewhat softened by the frequent reference to Christ:
the Father receives us into favor for the sake of the Son.[192] The exclusive
gratis is occasionally added to this formula quite nonchalantly; that is how far
Melanchthon is from playing off the thetic and the antithetic concepts of
grace against each other.[193]

That also becomes clear when we look at the word *gratis*, which is not used
so frequently, but which is always given special emphasis. In the standard
formulation in the *Dispositio*,[194] the antithetic expression *gratis* complements
the thetic one *in gratiam recipi:* whoever believes himself received into favor
for Christ's sake also knows that he cannot point to anything he has earned
through the law; to that extent the *gratis* is interpreted as *sine lege*, "apart
from law" (Rom. 3:21). Only in that way does the necessity of Christ's
incarnation become comprehensible.

In the *Dispositio*, Melanchthon emphasizes strongly that he sees the understanding of the doctrine of justification as totally dependent on the *particula
exclusiva, gratis*, "freely." He takes the theme of Romans from Rom. 1:17 and
then draws the negative corollary: we cannot be justified by our works.[195]
This, however, is an irrationalism of a different sort from Luther's. Melanchthon sees the illogic in the doctrine of justification precisely at the point of the
gratis, that is, in the contradiction of human rational expectations. For
Luther, however, grace becomes the evidence of God's hidden wisdom, which
no human being can discover. That wisdom can only be grasped under its
opposite, that is, under the cross; and only there can it be maintained.
Behind it stands the "secret anger that God threatens through his Word." We

191. "This faith always comprehends the knowledge of Christ, by which the Father receives
us into favor" (*CR* 15:454). Reason knows nothing of this reception (ibid., 483).

192. Ibid., 443, 454. Cp. ibid., 445: "The righteousness of God is to believe that because of
Christ we are received into the Father's favor without our merits. . . ." This is Melanchthon's
definition of human standing before God in Romans.

193. It is worth noting that the phrase "received into favor" fades into the background in the
Commentary on Romans of 1532 and finally disappears. Is that connected to the equating of *iustus*
and *acceptus*? In any case Franciscan theology from Bonaventura on broadened the doctrine of
the *acceptatio*. The comfort of grace does not violate God's absolute freedom because it is based
on the divine *acceptatio* rather than on the meritorious powers of humankind. So too Luther in
his *Lectures on Romans* (*WA* 56:41.2; *LW* 25:35; gloss on Rom. 4:4); see Ficker's *Kommentar*.
Friedrich Loofs, *Leitfaden zum Studium der Dogmengeschichte*, 4th ed. (Halle: M. Niemeyer,
1906), 823ff., traces the adoption of the acceptatio doctrine by the *Apology*. At about the same
time, Luther uses the concept in the *Large Commentary on Galatians* (*WA* 40.1:233.7). See below,
n. 350.

194. *CR* 15:451 (cp. ibid., 482); StA 5:31.36.

195. "Humanity is not righteous by nature, nor can it be justified by its works" (*CR* 15:447).
As in all Reformation writing, the polemic against works righteousness is so frequent in the
Dispositio that we will only give a few prominent references: ibid., 451 (restatement of the *Propo-
sitio*); 452 (*iustitia civilis* included in the antitheses to the *gratis*); 473 (election traced back to
God's free grace). On the two last points, see below, pp. 341–42.

feel this anger together with the hatred and disdain of the world; these are the husks in which grace is concealed from us.[196] The law and its works are public, accessible to human reason. *Gratis,* the *particula exclusiva,* can only testify that grace is grace, but it cannot make its nature comprehensible.

Melanchthon stresses a series of consequences from his antithesis. The most important: from the fact that the law does not work faith comes the freedom of the believer from the law. In the course of its conceptual definitions, the *Dispositio* broadens the opposition to works righteousness in various ways. The gift of righteousness, of course, does not do away with *iustitia civilis.* Those, however, who rely on the powers activated by that grace and on the works of God it effects and who do not accept the divine gift really blaspheme God and profane his grace. The righteousness that is understood in faith as the gift of God goes far beyond the civil righteousness that is required in the second table of the law. Christ is not a lawgiver; he is the Redeemer. The natural law that Paul recognizes in Rom. 2:14ff. and that makes possible moral decisions between good and evil is limited and made worthless by the renunciation of human powers. That also leads to a limitation of philosophy. The moral directions that Paul gives in the final chapter of the Letter to the Romans are also accessible to human reason; to that extent heathen philosophy and Christian faith agree. But the reason has no inkling that "we are freely made righteous before Christ [!] when we believe that we are received into favor by the Father for Christ's sake."[197]

The "freely" thus gives particular emphasis to the paradoxical character of the divine act of grace, but it makes no direct statement about the content of this act. When Melanchthon distinguishes between grace as free divine kindness and as gift of the Holy Spirit, he falls back into his old ideas of spiritual grace that is poured into the heart and then enlivens, renews, and leads the believer.[198] We must ask whether Melanchthon has here fallen back into the infused grace of the Middle Ages, and whether, under the distinction between thetic and antithetic concepts of grace, there is not a hidden conflict that also has repercussions for the understanding of CA 4.

This question brings us to Luther. How did he combine these two aspects of the idea of grace? In the section of *On the Bound Will* where he quotes the passage from Romans mentioned in the title of this chapter (Rom. 3:24), he understands the two sides as a unity.[199] The graciously given righteousness is

196. "Outwardly grace seems to be pure wrath, so deeply it lies hidden under the cover of two thick hides or skins" (*WA* 31.1:249.16ff.; *LW* 14:31). Cp. *WA* 31.1:248.29ff.; *LW* 14:30. See also *WA* 26:16.11; *LW* 28:234.

197. *CR* 15:452, 450, 448, 483.

198. The *donum gratiae* (gift of grace) is identical with the Holy Ghost, "who is poured into the hearts of those whose sins are forgiven, who sanctifies and gives life and brings forth a new creature" (ibid., 458). Cp. ibid., 446ff.: *de vi gratiae.*

199. *WA* 18:769.25ff. (= *BoA* 3:27.20ff.); *LW* 33:266.

free; the gift of grace is separated from all meritorious efforts by the *particula exclusiva*. In contrast to Erasmus, Luther opposes the scholastic doctrine of *meritum de condigno*. It does not, as the humanists thought, make possible a minimum activity of the free will; instead it takes away the gracious character of justification. The mystery of the gracious choice that justifies a person without merit while rejecting one who apparently has plenty is neither explained nor transcended by the doctrine of merit that Erasmus shared with the Thomistic understanding of grace.

In his *Disputatio* of 1530 Melanchthon too affirmed the irrational character of the Reformation doctrine of justification, and with that he joined Luther's antischolastic and anti-Erasmian polemics.

In his *On the Bound Will,* Luther carried on this battle on a wider front and in the most pointed fashion. He sounds almost like Marcion when he declares that grace is received "so very freely" that one can neither have an idea it exists nor precede it with efforts and exertions. If one posits the sole activity of God, then the thesis follows that we cannot ascribe merit and reward to ourselves but that God's Spirit works both in us. That also corresponds to God's majesty as creator. Everything that we have and are comes from him. We cannot prepare anything that he has not already made. Even the kingdom of heaven is prepared for the children of God from the foundation of the world (Matt. 25:34); the kingdom creates them for itself, they do not earn the kingdom. If we reverse this relationship, we sin against God. Apart from *iustitia civilis*, the free will is "guilty of unbelief" (*crimen incredulitatis*); all of our own powers, exertions, and efforts come under this verdict.[200] And the point of this judgment is directed not only against scholars like Erasmus; in August 1530—at the time of the greatest tension in the unity negotiations at Augsburg—it was aimed at the great and the humble in the world at large. No one can earn God's inexhaustible gifts; we all, however, have earned only unending wrath, death, and hell by our idolatry, ingratitude, scorn, and every sort of sin.[201]

That is a direct proof ad hominem; Luther addressed it to Christians in his sermons and elsewhere. Without our merit, solely through God's grace—that is the "chief part of our Christian faith, to be sought and acted upon everywhere in the Scriptures." Luther can also argue from the common understanding of benefice (*beneficium*); it is given to one who has not earned it, without being requested. He can also appeal to common experience: that which we have and do on our own is not Christian. That opens the way to

---

200. Free will is "constantly guilty of the sin of unbelief, with all its powers, efforts, and enterprises" (*WA* 18:769; *LW* 33:266). On the whole section, see *WA* 18:775.23–24, 696.7ff., 694.22–23, 26–27, 769.17ff.; *LW* 33:276, 155, 153, 266.

201. *WA* 31.1:243.20ff.; *LW* 14:25 (exposition of Psalm 117).

such subtle concepts as the passive righteousness of God (*iustitia Dei passiva*) that human beings receive without their help; that explains the "received into favor," *in gratiam recipi*, precisely. And even the general formula *ex opere operato*, which every prospective priest learned about the sacraments before his ordination, was drawn into the argument over grace. Those who want to obtain grace simply through works, without faith, destroy themselves.[202] Or in plain language, those who want to make a show of their works before God turn him into a junk dealer from whom they can buy grace. "These good works and everything else are lost when they come before God."[203]

Thus in Luther's sense the *gratis* in CA 4 denotes the worthlessness and transitory nature of human capabilities and merits, while the *in gratiam recipi* indicates the value and lasting nature of the divine act of favor. It is therefore dealing with two sides of the same thing. Being accepted into favor denotes a new status in which we are placed by God. The manifold spiritual gifts we thereby receive (1 Cor. 12:4ff.) result from the unity and the continued functioning of this divine act. It is God's "grace or favor when he turns away his wrath and looks upon us graciously through his Word, forgiving all our sins and therefore making our hearts confident and joyous toward him."[204] This is Luther's way of describing the effect of the divine blessing that is understood as a continual promise of grace. When God gives his Word, he causes his face to appear bright and happy "like the dear sun when it rises and spreads its rich splendor and warm light throughout the world."[205] Justification by grace is more than a doctrine one can absorb by hearing. It is a new birth; born of God, the evil person becomes good and does good to the neighbor.[206]

To be received into favor, therefore, means to enter into a new realm of life. Luther did not hesitate to use images from nature for that event of justification any more than the New Testament did. Certainly the most frequent and most vivid is the image of the heaven of grace into which the believer is received—not, of course, by being lifted up into a reality above the earth. Heaven arches *over* the earth, and the believer remains *on* the earth.[207] The believer cannot sin or be in sin, because overhead arches the heaven of grace, infinite and eternal. And if one does sin or fall, one still does not fall from

202. One ought not overestimate Luther's polemic against scholasticism and make it the characteristic theme of the Augustana. Even in the *Large Commentary on Galatians*, of 1531, where he speaks most polemically, he just touches on scholastic concepts like *actus eliciti* without getting into an intensive debate with them. Cp. *WA* 40.1:226.7, 230.3ff.

203. *WA* 31.1:254.28ff.; *LW* 14:36; *WA* 17.1:419.11ff., 40.1:41.1ff., 217.5ff., 32:107.11ff.

204. *WA* 30.3:578.19ff.

205. *WA* 30.3:576.32ff.

206. "To be born of God is to acquire the nature of God" (*WA* 20:692.4–5). Cp. ibid., 1ff.

207. On the following: *WA* 31.1:245.22ff., 246.26ff.; *LW* 14:27, 28 (exposition of Psalm 117, August 1530).

under that sky—unless one wants to go with the devil to hell. For God rules over sin, death, and the devil. And God sees to it that these powers look like nothing more than dark clouds that we see with our physical eyes against a visible heaven. They cannot rule over the heaven of grace; they must remain under it and let this heaven rule them until they finally vanish. Believers see it stretched out above them without any help on their part; they look at it when they sin or feel sin, and comfort themselves with the sight, apart from any merit or work of their own.

Less graphically but always clearly and concretely, Luther equates the heaven of grace with the heavenly compassion that governs us and is greater than every sin that occurs on earth. Luther can also identify the kingdom of grace with baptism. I can fall out of baptism, the ship of grace, but the ship does not sink because of my falling and wavering; I can once again reach the rescuing hands. Sin has lost its power over those who stand under grace, unless they freely give themselves over to its jurisdiction.[208] To be received into favor is valid once and for all. The reliability of this event is based not on our efforts but upon the faithfulness of God. He gives us his Word, and then we are blessed by the light of his face.[209]

Luther also refers to this state of grace with the word "peace," *pax*. The word of grace and the peace of God are not separable. And that brings us to the real meaning of justification, the forgiveness of sins: "Grace forgives sins; peace quiets the conscience."[210] Those who are received into favor are at peace in their consciences. Indeed, CA 4 puts "received into favor" and "sins forgiven" side by side, although it does not expressly mention a conscience at peace. That does occur, however, in a relatively detailed manner in CA 20.15–22; in reference to Rom. 5:1, Melanchthon emphasizes the comfort that the doctrine of justification brings to weak and terrified consciences. In so doing he goes back to a central theme in Luther's theology of testing *(Anfechtung)*. It is a theme that breaks through even in the year of the Augustana,[211] despite the clouds obscuring the heaven of grace. This experience of comforting consciences stands as the principal achievement of Luther's Reformation in opposition to the works righteousness of the medieval church (Ca 20.19ff.)

In Luther's view the worst consequence of works righteousness is the bad conscience that can never rest. Those who are held by God's mercy have a quieted conscience. "Faith is nothing else than a good conscience." The heart defiled by sin remains troubled; it becomes pure through faith in God's mercy, and a pure heart produces a good conscience.[212] Through the influ-

208. *WA* 29:573.1ff., 31.1:250.19ff.; *LW* 14:32; *WA* 27:125.6ff.
209. See above, n. 204.
210. *WA* 40.1:73.1–2.
211. See above, n. 205.
212. "It is first necessary for the heart to be pure; then a good conscience follows" (*WA* 26:11.5; *LW* 28: 226). Cp. *WA* 26:11.2ff. On the same point, see *WA* 29:27.12ff., 20:718.19–20, 26:25.18ff.; *LW* 28:246.

ence of grace, faith and love in close cooperation create the new human being.

To summarize a few findings of this chapter: We cannot understand the doctrine of justification in CA 4 simply from the antithetic sense of *gratis*, that is, simply as a contrast to works righteousness. It has a positive sense that spans the whole realm of reality. Those who are made righteous are received into God's favor. They live here on earth under a new heaven. Sin still continues to assault them, but it cannot remove the heaven of grace from above them. The tension between testing and grace cannot be rationally understood, much less resolved. Thus the doctrine of justification is subject to a mystery that the unbeliever cannot understand and that the believer must humbly accept. Scholastic efforts to formulate the doctrine fail to do it justice; it is not theology's task to get to the bottom of it. The Augustana did not intend a purely forensic doctrine of justification; even more sharply than scholasticism, forensic logic is in conflict with the images Luther uses to illustrate the reception into favor. He and Melanchthon use similar terms to describe the help that grace brings to troubled consciences. This suggests that the thetic side of justification, as we have indicated, has not yet been adequately presented. Its content, that is, the forgiveness of sins, needs further elucidation.

12. REMISSIO PECCATORUM (CA 4, SEC. 2)

Article 4 of the Augustana teaches that those who believe in the forgiveness of sins effected through Christ will be justified; the German version adds the further benefits of "righteousness and eternal life." Document Na had put "forgiveness of sins" and "righteousness before God" as synonyms prominently at the beginning of the article; Nb and the final German version followed its example. The fifth Schwabach article had presented the antithetic side of justification in all its breadth and had preceded the final version and even Nb in tying together the forgiveness of sins and eternal life. Article 20 of the CA again goes its own way on this point. As early as its preliminary form in the Torgau Articles, the forgiveness of sins and the mediation of grace were tightly bound together.[213] The final German version picks this up in relation to the forgiveness of sins, but the Latin version, in heavy reliance on the Latin of CA 4, inserts "received into favor" and gives it an even stronger christological underpinning than CA 4.[214] We can see that the equation of justification and the forgiveness of sins goes far back in the development of

213. Cp. *BS* 79.28ff.; Jacobs 87.

214. *BS* 77.1ff., 34–35, 37; *BC* 42.9. The remarkable relationship between the Latin texts of CA 20 and CA 4 at this point makes the hypothesis of a late editing of these texts—after June 15—likely. At these points, Spalatin still agrees generally with the German text of CA 20.

the Augustana and that it is only relatively late that it diminishes somewhat in favor of other themes.

In his *Dispositio* of 1530, Melanchthon presented the connection between justification and forgiveness of sins in detail—considering the brevity of the presentation. To be righteous before God means "to believe that our sins are forgiven for Christ's sake."[215] Because he understands justification as the gracious fruit of Christ's suffering (see below, pp. 310–11), he formulates the thesis that "justification is the remission of sins."[216] This equation of justification and forgiveness arises from the terrified conscience produced by the law; the old triad of sin, law, and grace, which formed the basis for the early stages of the *Loci* of 1521, asserts itself again in the *Dispositio*.[217] But the forgiveness of sins—and this was not yet so clear to Melanchthon in 1521—also includes the comfort of consciences and the gift of the Holy Spirit. Now, grace comprises two parts; in addition to the forgiveness of sins, there is the gift of the Spirit.[218] The terrifying and the comforting of consciences stand in correlation with each other; statements of CA 20 on that topic[219] are closer to the *Dispositio* than to the completed article on justification in the Augustana.

For Luther too the decisive Word of God is not the terrifying word of the law but that of saving grace.[220] Forgiveness of sins—that is the "major high article" of the Apostles' Creed, "which, where it is rightly understood, makes a real Christian and gives eternal life."[221] The meaning of the forgiveness of sins is contrasted with civil righteousness that is ultimately dependent on coercion and punishment. Here Luther is concerned with righteousness before God, which is heavenly and which leads to eternal life.[222] The article on forgiveness of sins involves the teaching that "makes us and names us Christians and that distinguishes and separates us from all other saints on earth": those who live by forgiveness have dismissed all righteousness of their

215. *CR* 15:443–44. The continuation of the passage equates forgiveness with reception into favor: ". . . or that for Christ's sake we are received into the Father's favor." Cp. ibid., 451, the last six lines.

216. Ibid., 454, last third. Cp. a few lines farther: "justification is nothing else than that sins are not imputed."

217. Ibid., 457–58.

218. Ibid., 458–59, 466 bottom.

219. Secs. 15–22; see above, p. 305.

220. ". . . in which is offered the forgiveness of sins, proclaiming, 'Believe in me and you shall be saved' " (*WA* 29:117.2ff.).

221. Ibid., 564.15ff. Here we are analyzing Luther's sermon on Matt. 9:1ff. preached in Marburg on October 5, 1529, at the conclusion of the Marburg Colloquy. We use the Wittenberg printing of 1530, which was probably produced with an eye to the diet at Augsburg.

222. Ibid., 569.25ff. Cp. *WA* 15:531.35ff.: "When God begins to forgive, it is forever." It therefore is valid throughout one's whole life: "This forgiveness endures as long as you live, as you hear in the First Gospel." Forgiveness is not a one-time thing; it is an "enduring quality which hovers over us always" (*WA* 34.1:469.8–9).

own.[223] That is difficult: it is hard to distinguish between righteousness before God and outward righteousness. This is the reason that the preaching of the apostles was scorned. The evangelical preaching today, says Luther, is likewise taken so lightly that anyone who hears it once wants to be a master and doctor immediately. Luther himself, after more than fifteen years as a preacher, still cannot boast of his mastery; he can only warn his colleagues in the pulpit about self-satisfaction.[224] Its cause is the overvaluation of reason. It can indeed understand proper civil behavior, but not the righteousness of faith; therefore it is defenseless against temptation. "In short, according to this article, it is completely beyond human sense and reason, art and ability, for us to rise above or go beyond earthly righteousness."[225] Human beings are split; good works count only for this outward life, and those who deal with God on the basis of works learn that before God neither our own sins nor our good works count. All that matters is Christ and his forgiveness.[226] Sin, of course, can still be detected daily; my conscience condemns me and holds God's anger before me. But precisely for that reason divine forgiveness is decisively important; the power of sin makes clear that forgiveness "is not a joke but absolutely serious." "Forgiveness cancels all sin and wrath, so that sin cannot push you into hell nor your piety lift you into heaven."[227]

Because of forgiveness, the Christian is lord over sins, death, and the devil; one can and should hold this principle above everything in heaven and earth. At the same time, however, one should regard one's own sinful state and recognize how little one has formerly understood the word of forgiveness and put it into "practice and existence." It is impossible to exhaust the meaning of this word; all the more reason for a Christian to deal with it constantly and intensively.[228]

223. *WA* 29:570.15ff., 22ff. Cp. *WA* 32:166.4–5: "If it is forgiveness, it is not deserved."

224. *WA* 29:570.28–571.24. Cp. *WA* 32:164.4: "The rude masses do not know what the forgiveness of sins is." One person does not inquire at all about sin; others do not take it seriously because they are not humble enough (ibid., 165.4). We will not entrust ourselves to God's grace and therefore will not tolerate even the most necessary article (*WA* 28:567.3). We do not want to feel that it concerns us, "but the forgiveness of sins affects and concerns you and me" (ibid., 272.1–2).

225. *WA* 29:571.25–572.18. Being a Christian is "amazing, which cannot be understood by anyone rationally, but only be believed by faith, because reason cannot grasp that the same person is saint and sinner."

226. *WA* 29:572.26–33. In 572.34–573.24, Luther anticipates the image of the heaven of grace that, almost a year later, he will again set forth in his exposition of Psalm 117. Cp. above, pp. 304–5.

227. *WA* 29:573.25–38. The difference between my sinfulness and God's forgiveness is discussed in ibid., 574.18–39. This homiletical use of the *simul iustus et peccator* shows that Luther sees it as a key part of the doctrine of justification but also of practical piety. Friedrich Loofs, *Leitfaden zum Studium der Dogmengeschichte* (cited above, n. 193), 713–14, was generally correct on this point. Luther describes the conflict of the Christian in his exposition of 1 John in 1531 (*WA* 20:630.8ff.): "The Christian is divided: he is a righteous man, pious and holy, that is, a blessed spirit, a son of God. But in the flesh he still has sin, does sin, and daily is indebted to God. But because the spirit rules and is superior to sin, his sin is not imputed to him."

228. *WA* 29:575.14–36. On the two last sections of the Marburg sermon, which deal with the christological basis for the forgiveness of sin and its dispensation in the church (ibid., 575–82), cp. below, pp. 311–12.

The article on forgiveness of sins does not treat a "doctrine" but treats an incomprehensible reality of God that is nonetheless experienced through faith. In his Marburg sermon of October 1529, Luther expressed this experience in a way that can claim to be binding; we therefore have a right to use it as a standard of interpretation for the official confession. To be sure, it does not answer all the questions about the forgiveness of sins that Luther posed for himself at the end of the 1520s, nor even those that could be answered strictly within the confines of a congregational sermon. Among those are particularly the relationship that exists in God between grace and forgiveness of sins. The two are inseparable. Grace is favor *(Gunst)* and is thus a word, a promise of forgiveness. It is God turning to us and proclaiming his will. It occurs "when he averts his wrath and regards us graciously through his Word, forgiving us all sins and thus making our hearts confident and joyful toward him."[229] In this word it is the gospel, in contrast to the law, that speaks.

What is the believer's position regarding the law? It accuses us as children of Adam, rules over us, and makes us sinners according to earthly righteousness; seen from Christ's perspective, however, we are free from the law. This dialectic between law and gospel is no more prominent in the Augustana than in Luther's Marburg sermon; the Confession agrees with the simple proclamation in that it does not speak dialectically.

To be forgiven from sins also means that I am totally freed from them. They may still be there, but they are covered, buried, interred. They no longer rule over me; I no longer ask about them; I have my constant refuge in the article on forgiveness. To the extent that I believe in Christ, I no longer have sins; to the extent that I live in the flesh without faith, they remain.[230] It is not the task of the preacher to develop the tension that exists in an individual within the *simul iustus et peccator,* nor does it belong among the statements of the Confession.

13. PROPTER CHRISTUM (CA 4, SEC. 2)

Justification occurs freely *for Christ's sake;* for his sake we are received into favor, our sins are forgiven (CA 4 Latin), and we are given righteousness and eternal life (CA 4 German). One cannot stop, therefore, with the idea that justification occurs "freely"; reception into favor and forgiveness of sins should not be separated from the saving work of Christ "who by his death made satisfaction for our sins" (CA 4.2 Latin). In the Lutheran confession,

229. *WA* 30.2:578.19ff.; *LW* 46:251. Cp. *WA* 29:117.1ff.
230. *WA* 40.1:233.8ff., 367.5ff., 445.9ff. It is no accident that these passages come from the *Large Commentary on Galatians.*

justification and Christology are inseparable; therefore we must always consult CA 3 for an understanding of CA 4 (see above, pp. 259–60).

All the developing stages of CA 4 maintain this connection between Christ's work and justification. We have already seen how Luther's personal Confession of 1528 is structured entirely within a paraphrase of the Second Article of the Apostles' Creed: Christ redeemed "us from sin, death, and the eternal wrath of God by his innocent blood." He has "taken upon himself this guilt and sin [of Adam] as an innocent lamb, paid for us by his sufferings, and . . . still intercede[s] and plead[s] for us as a faithful, merciful Mediator, Savior, and the only Priest and Bishop of our souls." To wish to be saved by one's own power is a "notorious, abominable blasphemy and denial of the unique aid and grace of our only Savior and mediator, Jesus Christ."[231] Justification of the sinner occurs only through Christ.

Melanchthon's *Visitation Articles* stated independently from Luther's personal Confession of 1528 that it is not because of our merit but because of Christ *(non propter nostra merita, sed propter Christum)* that our sins are forgiven; here the "freely," *gratis,* in its exclusive sense is given christological content. The reception into favor and the concomitant gift of the Holy Spirit occurs "for Christ's sake."[232] The *Instructions for the Visitors* is dominated by the same alternatives: sins are forgiven "not because of our merits but for Christ's sake."[233] In the same vein, Schwab. 5, and Marb. 7, which relies on it, teach that believers, for the sake of God's Son, "are received into grace, and are his children in his kingdom." Surprisingly, Na 5 replaced the phrase "because of Christ," *propter Christum,* with "through Christ," *per Christum.*[234] In addition to Nb, manuscripts of Spalatin and Vogler also correspond to the final German text.

The *propter Christum* also played an increasing role in the textual history of CA 20. It occurs only once in the preliminary document B of the Torgau Articles, where it is used in an exclusive sense to rule out human participation in the forgiveness of sins.[235] It is also noteworthy that the final version of CA 20 interprets *propter Christum* by the concept of a "mediator" who recon-

---

231. *WA* 26:502.20–21, 31–34, 504.16–17 (= *BoA* 3:508.39–40, 509.11ff., 510.2ff.); *LW* 37:362, 364.

232. *BS* 57.1ff., 7–8.

233. *WA* 26:203.23, 25; *LW* 40:276.

234. ". . . that our sins are forgiven through Christ and that we are received into favor" (*BS* 57.15).

235. *BS* 77.37; Jacobs 86. Otherwise B uses the less exclusive "through Christ" (*BS* 78.37, 79.28, 80.32; Jacobs 87–88), which is preserved at the corresponding points in the final version (*BS* 79.13, 16; *BC* 44.23, 24 Latin). The significance of Christ's merits—as opposed to human merit—becomes stronger in the course of the textual development. For the same reason, the idea of redemption is inserted by the quotation from Pseudo-Ambrose that is contained only in the Latin version (*BS* 77.25; *BC* 43.14).

ciles the Father to us.[236] In any event, it is clear that CA 20 is affirmative toward the *propter Christum,* even if it interprets it in its own way.

At the beginning of his *Dispositio,* where he defined the status—that is, the scope—of the Letter to the Romans, Melanchthon proposed the phraseology that is faithfully interpreted by the statements of the Augustana's articles on justification. He understands Christian righteousness to be the "faith that we are received into the Father's favor for Christ's sake," that therefore Christ is called mediator and propitiation, and that we are "justified for his sake freely, without our merits."[237] And as early as the first version of CA 20, justification and the forgiveness of sins are found to be identical.[238] We recognized the reception into God's favor as an essential part of justification in which the exclusive ("freely") and the positive ("received into favor") concepts of grace partly overlap. In the *Dispositio,* as in CA 4.2, both sides of grace are frequently bound together by the *propter Christum.*[239] The whole saving work of Christ is aimed toward justification.[240]

In the *Dispositio,* Melanchthon posits this connection chiefly by means of formal theses.[241] Luther explained it theologically by means of an example in his Marburg sermon of October 5, 1529.[242] The whole work of Christ, from his incarnation to his death on the cross, is the treasure for which the forgiveness of sins is given to us. It took the application of such a gift, such an "expenditure," to extinguish God's wrath and reconcile the Father, making us his friends.[243] Hence Christ's vicarious atonement is the basis for our justifi-

236. *BS* 77.3; *BC* 42.9. The Latin text also adds "propitiation" from Rom. 3:25; cp. below. Spalatin shows no changes in the text, and the article is missing in A I. Biblical concepts that interpret the *propter Christum,* "through Christ," are present as early as A 9 of the Torgau Articles (*BS* 83b.22ff.; Jacobs 85). Cp. CA 21.2: Scripture sets Christ before us as the "only mediator, propitiation, high priest, and intercessor." See also the Scripture passage in sec. 4.

237. *CR* 15:451 top. The first clause, "because we are received into the Father's favor for Christ's sake," is repeated almost word for word in the beginning of CA 4, sec. 2; the third clause, "because for Christ's sake we are freely justified without our merits if we believe," is found at the end of CA 4, sec. 1. The *propter Christum* is introduced in the exclusive and positive sense of the doctrine of justification.

238. Cp. *BS* 77.37; Jacobs 86 (". . . when he believes that, for Christ's sake, his sins are forgiven, and grace is granted him") with *CR* 15:443–44 (". . . to believe that our sins are forgiven for Christ's sake, or that we are received into the Father's favor for Christ's sake").

239. "We are received into the Father's favor for Christ's sake" (*CR* 15:444, last third). ". . . that we are received into the Father's favor for Christ's sake, without our merits" (ibid., 445 last third). "We believe that we are freely received by the Father into favor for Christ's sake" (ibid., 445 top). ". . . that for Christ's sake we are received into the Father's favor, that because of Christ there is righteousness and life, because of Christ we are truly the objects of God's attention, that we are defended by God and preserved" (ibid., 477 middle; content of the apostolic preaching).

240. "Why will Christ come? He does not come so that the law may be carried out . . . but so that he may freely give righteousness and the Holy Spirit to believers" (ibid., 482 middle).

241. The key formulation occurs as early as the scholia on Colossians (1527; StA 4:239.24–25), in the famous excursus on Col. 2:8; it serves to point out the uniqueness of the gospel in comparison with philosophy: ". . . that for Christ's sake God forgives our sins and receives us into favor."

242. Cp. above, p. 309. Cp. also *WA* 29:575.37ff., where in the second part of his sermon Luther describes how Christ earned our salvation.

243. *WA* 29:575.39ff., 576.21ff.

cation; it makes all our meritorious works worthless. That treasure is made available to the individual through the spoken Word and the public preaching office and not through some special secret revelation within the heart.[244] The justification won by Christ is mediated only in that way and in no other; with that reproving glance at the enthusiasts, Luther's Marburg sermon comes to an end.

It lays open the key themes by which Luther describes the connection between justification and Christology: the infinite guilt of humankind, God's unappeasable wrath, and Christ's infinite love. These are themes that were given a special character by Anselm in the medieval tradition but that are as old as Paul. The question whether CA 4 is inextricably bound to the Anselmian doctrine of redemption or whether the understanding of the *propter Christum* flows directly from Scripture can be decided only from the statements of Luther the exegete and preacher.

Luther took the dry formulas of Melanchthon's doctrine of justification, as they appeared in the *Dispositio* before the Augustana, and clothed them with the living flesh and blood of his biblical exposition. Although that did not make the Reformation doctrine of justification more logical, it did make it more understandable for believers. Let us first look at those statements of his which speak directly about the *propter Christum*. We will surely be surprised at how little explanation there is of these statements; they simply repeat broadly traditional religious attitudes. God grants all salvation for Christ's sake.

Thus the beleaguered heart prays, "Father, for Christ's sake have mercy on me." The faith of the Second Article of the Creed "which children pray" expresses itself in, "No one but Jesus Christ, God's Son, alone died for our sins"; our works are thereby excluded. The forgiveness of sins through Christ is the cornerstone on which our faith is built. We are justified through Christ, not through the law. The Christian religion is thus defined as "trust in the mercy of God for Christ's sake."[245]

But what is the basis for such trust? A change occurs in God's attitude. "The most holy Christ turned the judge into the Father and gave you all that he had—righteousness." This transformation of God occurs in heaven. There Christ presents his righteousness before the face of God and represents us. God, in turn, requires that we look to the Christ who justifies us; then, for Christ's sake, God forgives our sins. By believing that Christ has done everything for me, I come to God.[246] Accordingly, what happens for Christ's

244. Ibid., 579.23, 28.
245. *WA* 40.1:428.4–5, 30.3:367.19ff.; *LW* 34:91; *WA* 20:283.4ff., 26:15.14ff.; *LW* 28:232; *WA* 31.2:54.30.
246. *WA* 20:391.20ff., 574.3ff., 16:532.13, 17.1:375.3.

sake is a complex event in, by, and through Christ; between Christ and God, and thus in God himself; and between the believer and Christ (or God).

Let us first consider the Christ-event itself. At its center stands Christ's cross and death; what happened for Christ's sake is concentrated there. Around 1530 we find Luther speaking about that event more in traditionally defined images from the late medieval piety of the cross than in clear theological arguments. During the year of his stay at the Coburg, Luther received from Electoral Prince John Fredrick the gift of the "Luther rose" carved in stone for him as a seal. Luther accepted the gift as a symbol of his theology: it is defined by the cross "to remind myself that faith in the Crucified saves us."[247] And back in the midst of the tumult of the Peasants' War, he had proclaimed the password "Christ dead and resurrected for us," *Christus pro nobis mortuus et resurrexit*, rather than an attack on images, to be the essence of righteousness. He gave his lectures on 1 John in 1527 under the motto "No one is righteous before God except through the blood of Jesus Christ." Although he remains bound to the religious tradition, he knows that many of his contemporaries—the followers of Erasmus are especially mentioned—considered it to be ridiculous foolishness; how can the God-become-man die? The answer is not new; Peter Lombard shaped it out of the piety of his day and impressed it upon learned and simple souls: "Those alone are Christians who believe that Christ suffered for us and died as the Lamb of God for our sins." This sacrifice of Christ is the foundation and cornerstone for our salvation through Christ's work and not our own. He completes this work by drawing us into his death and resurrection through the gospel.[248]

The Luther of 1530 also has the guides for meditation provided him by medieval monastic practice. Those who wish to understand Christ's struggle on the cross and its meaning are to compare their own sins with the burden that Christ bore for them. Then they realize that they are enemies of God, so much so that the sun will not shine on them nor the earth bear their weight. When they thus apply Christ's suffering to themselves, they also come under the curse that Christ took upon himself. Hence believers must always look away from themselves toward Christ. They should not ask, "What sinful thing have I done or what merit have I earned?" Rather, they should ask, "What has Christ done for me?" Conversely, God places his suffering Son before him, sees the believer bound to Christ and for Christ's sake overlooks the sin still clinging to us. Between the sinner and God stands Christ's merit. The sinner's crime brings about Christ's suffering; he takes God's wrath upon himself and bears our sin.[249]

247. *WBr* 5:no. 1628 (= *BoA* 6:316.2ff.), *LW* 49:356–59.
248. *WA* 17.1:191.9–10, 20:622.5, 40.1:361.6, 30.2:433.20–21, 20:778.7, 17.2:374.8ff., 25:411.22–23.
249. *WA* 17.1:70.11ff., 27:104.15, 40.1:164.5ff., 366.10ff., 27:105.12, 6.

For Christ's sake we are justified in the face of God's wrath. That seems, in fact, to be Luther's solution for the connection between Christology and justification. It suggests the Anselmian interpretation of the Christ-event. This idea, however, which actually determined the post-Melanchthonian doctrine of justification, does not do justice to the diversity of Luther's christological statements. It was not just Christ's death to which he connected justification; he interpreted it from the entire saving work of Christ.

God set the incarnation of the Son as a sign of salvation for us sinners.[250] The power and truth of Christ's resurrection, comprehended in faith, show the way to salvation and freedom from works. The divine and human natures interact in the resurrection; the same occurs in justification. Faith corresponds to the divine nature, works to the human. Justification is not only represented by the person of the Resurrected One, it depends on him. Christ's transition from earthly to eternal life *is* our righteousness. Christ effects salvation when he binds sin, death, and the devil and puts them under his feet as his prisoners. Although our bodily resurrection has not yet occurred visibly, eternal life for the justified, though still invisible, has already begun. Christ's resurrection and ascension, as well as his place at the right hand of the Father, are mine; I sit in the Father's lap. It is in the Resurrected One that my faith recognizes its righteousness.[251] For my sake, Christ not only died but also is resurrected. I am righteous not only because of his death but also because of his life.

The life of Christ is a unity, bringing together his incarnation, suffering, and heavenly reign. Therefore our justification, which occurs for his sake, is not limited to the single event of his crucifixion; it takes in his entire life. At the cross, I hear only the accusation; my hopeful faith, however, holds to the heavenly Christ, who intervenes before God in my behalf, and whose death guarantees life for me. He is the same Christ yesterday, today, and forever. The gospel that testifies to him is valid for the beginning, middle, and end of the world and always says the same thing. If, for Christ's sake, we receive righteousness from it, that does not happen only with respect to his atoning sacrifice on the cross. Abraham was justified through faith in the coming Christ. In this faith the fathers of the past are one with their future sons; they are all directed toward the whole Christ. It would be wrong merely to wait for the coming Christ; that would be a denial of God's deed in the One who came.[252] Granted that this saving act of God is central, it nevertheless has a "before" and an "after." It is only in this total context that the sacrifice on the

250. *WA* 26:26.15–16; *LW* 28:247.
251. *WA* 27:124.3, 125.19ff., 127.15ff., 28:47.9–10, 21ff., 32:42.30ff., 34.1:409.14ff., 472.4ff.
252. *WA* 25:12.7ff.; *LW* 29:11; *WA* 19:395.5ff.; *LW* 19:197; *WA* 40.1:377.7ff., 378.1ff., 390.1ff.

cross holds meaning for us. Luther thinks in terms of salvation history; Anselm, of logical structures. Therefore Luther's *propter Christum* cannot be interpreted by means of Anselm.

The articles on justification in the Augustana present us with a series of christological titles taken from the New Testament which can clarify the content of the *propter Christum:* redeemer, mediator, propitiation, intercessor—almost all from the textual history of CA 20—and, from Luther's writing of about the same time, satisfaction and savior *(salvator, servator).*

Among these titles, mediator is the most frequent, the broadest, and the best known. Luther indeed uses it in connection with Romans 8:34 in the sense of entreater or intercessor, but he puts the emphasis on the element of helpful exchange.[253] Later statements by Luther deduce Christ's function as mediator of salvation out of his God-manhood. Jews and Turks appear before God without a mediator. And those who regard Christ only as judge also lose sight of his intercession. But Christ mediates eternal salvation; the title of mediator appears in close connection with that of savior and deliverer *(salvator, servator);* anxious souls sigh for the mediator. It is he who brings about our righteousness.[254] To become righteous for Christ's sake, therefore, means—entirely apart from any particular theories of atonement—that Christ makes righteousness available to us by bridging the gap between humanity and God. The christological presuppositions for this thesis are only implied here, but they will be discussed later (see below, p. 326).

We also just mention in passing the noun form *propitiator* of the concept that comes from Rom. 3:25. It presents the counterimage to Christ the universal judge; it is the epitome of mercy and forgiveness, without even taking the ritual dimension of atonement into account. Thus the fact that we become righteous for Christ's sake is demonstrated by an actual image of faith rather than being developed out of some theological doctrine.[255]

From the realm of images we move to the realm of law when we speak of Christ's work as a redemption, on the basis of Rom. 3:24. It is possible to recognize that Christ has thus made us righteous, and any further drawing on Anselmian theories of satisfaction is unnecessary. Christ's blood buys our freedom from sin and death; the fact that God sent his Son into the world in order to bring this valuable gift shows how precious sinners are to him. Luther picks up this redemption theory from Paul, and unwittingly he turns it into the idea of the exchange: Christ sold his scalp for our life. In doing so he differs from Abraham, the bearer of the promise. Abraham believes;

---

253. "If he is our mediator, then he takes what is ours upon himself and in return we take what is his as if it were ours" (*Advent Postil* [1521], *WA* 10.1:2, 31, 13–14).

254. *WA* 29:577.20, 30.2:658.15ff., 26:37.10ff.; *LW* 28:263; *WA* 40.1:232.1, 25:37.11ff.; *LW* 29:44.

255. *WA* 30.2:671.3–4, 34.1:471.7ff.

Christ, however, acts, saves, and justifies. This distribution of grace continues in the sermon, where it becomes the treasure of salvation and spreads its benefits further.[256]

Luther's exposition of redemption and its application in the sermon is extremely clear in illustrating that righteousness is possible for us because of Christ. Nevertheless, it only hints at what actually goes on between God and the believer in the process of justification. One thing is clear: the action is God's alone. "I am inwardly redeemed by God"; alien works, not my own, make me free. The event itself remains obscure; the only certain thing is that Christ's blood has something to do with it. Blood and death effect redemption; without both there is no deliverance. Here all human power and reason amount to nothing. Redemption from death makes life possible. But many people despise both, just as sick persons will sneer at the doctor. Christians will recognize their sins, but they also know that Christ has borne them and that we are free of them.[257]

Luther repeatedly said that these were homiletic statements that tried to communicate direct impressions; they were not theories: "I say to Christians, 'You have the redeemer Christ. He died for you and redeemed you from death. If you find someone else who has not died for you, do not believe in him.' "[258] What God did in redeeming us through Christ is so provocative and susceptible of misunderstanding because God's Word is not unambiguous. Luther preaches seriously about the forgiveness of sins through Christ, but at times he speaks as though he was not taking it seriously. One must hold to the serious Word, at the same time taking one's baptism seriously and, like the Canaanite woman, "casting God's Word aside for the sake of God's Word."[259]

It is hard to believe that we are made righteous for Christ's sake, not because of the difficulties that accompany the doctrine of vicarious satisfaction—we saw that Luther stays within the limits laid down by Paul on that point without drawing on the authority of Anselm—but because of the difficulties in speaking about God and his justifying activity. It is only when we overcome those difficulties here that we will be able to explain the *propter Christum* in Luther's sense. That, however, also requires us to draw upon his understanding of the concept of *satisfactio*.

Here we leave the biblical vocabulary; the Vulgate speaks of God in terms of *sufficentia*, the compensation for deficiencies, but not of *satisfactio*, or obligatory compensation. Luther had a feel for the secular use of the word:

256. *WA* 26:25.31ff., 26.15–16, 37.24ff.; *LW* 28:247, 264; *WA* 40.1:390.1ff., 20:780.16ff., 757.2ff., 16:607.2ff., 17.1:290.1ff.

257. *WA* 17.1:374.6ff., 15:675.14, 27:81.20ff., 82.4, 20ff., 83.23–24, 125.8ff., 167.4ff., 31.2:433.20ff., 434.13ff.

258. *WA* 28:599.6ff. (sermon of August 15, 1529). A constant element in sermons on redemption is the reminder "I cannot praise redemption if I do not mention Satan and its other enemies" (ibid., 607.2–3).

259. *WA* 20:283.4ff.; cp. below, pp. 328–31, on faith and temptation (*Anfechtung*).

satisfaction is given when business people reach an agreement or when an evildoer is executed. But when it comes to God the problem is one of being acquitted at his bar of justice; human beings can contribute nothing to their own defense.[260] In matters of conscience we bring no capacity for satisfaction. At this point, Christ steps in as our representative. We sin; he makes satisfaction. He deserves impunity; we actually possess it. He who should have peace receives punishment *(disciplina)*; conversely, those who merit discipline have peace. "It is difficult to recognize who Christ is."[261]

In an image drawn from Isaiah 53, Luther calls this relationship with Christ an "amazing exchange" *(mirabilis mutuacio)*. He thus sees it in terms of love rather than as a legal transaction. Christ bears our sins; by him we are redeemed. In Luther's view, our justification for Christ's sake is not a matter of recompense, with guilt, wrath, and punishment being weighed against one another; it is an incredible game of love that can be described more precisely by the image of the joyous exchange.

We must begin by emphasizing the incomprehensible nature of this event. It really does not explain anything; mystery upon mystery remains because we are dealing with God's own being. In the justification that occurs for Christ's sake, God's wrath is bought off. That is inconceivable, because God is here acting in contradiction to himself by annulling his threatened punishment by a demonstration of love. For our sake Christ has taken God's wrath upon himself; the Father sent him for that purpose, and we should thank him for it. Christ's role as mediator does not rest simply on his nature as God and man. He also takes an active part in placating the wrath that God directs against humanity because of its transgressions, and that human beings in turn direct against him because of his words and deeds. Through his self-giving he has satisfied the divine wrath and righteousness for us. Here Luther rejects two misunderstandings and quietly corrects ideas from his own past. The suffering Christ ought not be taken simply as a type of the suffering Christian; he is rather the true purchase price for the forgiveness of sins. And that brings the second idea to light: God's wrath is not a false hypothesis but sober truth. If it were otherwise, his mercy would also be a fiction and our faith would be futile.[262]

260. *WA* 30.2:657.6ff., 18–19.
261. *WA* 31.2:435.9ff.; cp. ibid., 434.13ff.
262. *WA* 27:105.6ff., 167.4ff. Christ "has become the price by which satisfaction is made for divine justice and wrath on our behalf. Some people think that Christ's death has been set as an example, a type, an ideal of Christians. This is preaching scarcely half of Christ. He truly is the price of redemption, which God elsewhere calls the forgiveness of sins. The wrath of God is real, not imaginary. It is no joke. Were it false, mercy would be false. You see, as wrath is, so is the mercy that forgives. May God avert that joke from us. When genuine wrath is at its highest, so is genuine mercy. Thus most truly has Christ taken the wrath of God upon himself and has carried it on our behalf. He takes this upon himself not only as an example, but he is the very true price that is paid for us. If he has placed himself in his own person to turn away wrath from us, he has established himself as the price for us. If he is the price, he has given not gold or silver but himself" (ibid., 26:37.26ff.; *LW* 28:264). This statement from the spring of 1528 (*Lectures on 1 Timothy*) anticipates the explanation of the second article in the Small Catechism.

One has to respect the energy with which Luther rejects an abstract interpretation that would argue away Christ's role in justification. Otherwise our righteousness would be imagined, our faith weak, and the seriousness of the encounter with God a fantasy. It is precisely this lack of abstract thought which underlies the difference between Luther and Anselm. Anselm tries to use a process of logical deduction to base the God-humanity of the Savior on the total original fall of humanity and the infinite sublimity of God. For Luther, the personal unity of the two natures and God's holy wrath form the presuppositions for the justification of the sinner. He sees the crucial element as being the unification of the believer's life with Christ, in which the loving wills of Father and Son meet. Justification of the sinner occurs in such a manner that sinners no longer make satisfaction on their own; instead they let reconciliation with God happen to them through the Lamb who bears all sins. The seriousness of the divine punitive wrath lingers on in the fear with which sinners cast aside their own works in order to entrust themselves completely to God. And furthermore, from the human side, the seriousness with which believers live out their righteousness testifies to the new reality that has come to them in justification.[263]

The uniting of the believer with Christ clarifies the mystery of justification for Christ's sake. In Anselm it is metaphysical principles—the holy righteousness of the Father and the divinity of the Son—that form the basis for justification. For Luther that basis lies in the believing union with Christ in the "joyous exchange" by which the believer receives righteousness and Christ takes the burden and punishment of sin upon himself. In his sermons of 1519 and 1520, Luther developed this image of the joyous exchange in a graphic and edifying way. The basic outlines had been sketched out in mysticism and theology since Bernard of Clairvaux. Luther brought it up as early as his lectures on Romans.[264]

The idea of our being granted Christ's innocence in exchange for our sins was an element in the Passion meditations of that time. Isaiah 53 gives shape and color to that image of grace which we are to make our own. The conquest of sin, hell, and death is made visible by Jesus' suffering on the cross. Its "token" is the Sacrament of the Altar, which assures us that we participate in what we see. In baptism, God binds himself to us with the promise that he will not "reckon" our remaining sins to our charge.[265]

263. WA 29:578.9, 16ff., 31.2:85.32ff.

264. Walter Allgaier, "Der 'fröhliche Wechsel' bei Martin Luther" (Th. diss., Erlangen, 1966; pub. 1973), 66ff. Relying on this basic work, I restrict myself to developing the theological themes. For its connection with the Christology of the early church, see my study Von der Freiheit eines Christenmenschen (Göttingen, 1949), 36ff.

265. On imputation, cp. below, pp. 331ff. Here we need only note that the idea belongs entirely within the context of the sacramental realism under discussion here. Cp. Meditation on Christ's Passion (1519; WA 2:137.14ff. [= BoA 1:156.10ff.]; LW 42:8); Sermon on Preparing to

In the context of our commentary it is important to show that Luther's statements about the joyous exchange are not limited to the early years of the Reformation. They can be traced through the 1520s and they reach a climax during the period of the diet at Augsburg. Nonetheless, in the process certain shifts in accent may be observed. The one-sided connection with Passion meditations fades, and Easter begins to play a larger role.[266] The exchange no longer covers only human sins and Christ's death. Christ takes my sin upon himself and also my death; he dies for my sin, and I will not die. Thus something more than an exchange is involved; it becomes an identification. "He has crept into me so fully that he has all of me." "Christ becomes me and I Christ." Any actual identity of being, however, encounters a twofold obstacle at this point. One element is the battle against guilt, and the other is in the divine-human character of the person of the Savior. The enemies of Christ revile him as a sinner, but his innocence is "too strong, gobbling up sin and death." The mystery of Christ's commitment to sinners permits no false confidence. And the incomprehensible love of God in allowing the God-man to die for us remains a deep secret until God lets it be known through the preaching of the gospel. Our identity with Christ stems from the Word that testifies to his works. In this Word, by which he informs us of his presence, we also hear the distance that still exists between us and the Son of God.

Thus, for Christ's sake, the Christian becomes righteous, a child of God; born of God, he obtains God's nature.[267] Those are strong words with which to describe the connection between human beings and Christ and on which to base Christ's justifying activity. Nevertheless, they do not portray justification as a transformation of "substance" comparable to the scholastic doctrine of the infusion of grace. On the contrary, this Christ-piety is based on a faith relationship with Christ. The qualitative difference between Christ and the believer continues to exist: "The Christian is a son of God by faith, corresponding to what Christ is by nature." Only on the basis of this qualitative distinction can the similarities between Christ and the believer be properly appreciated: according to his human nature, Christ saw nothing of his divine

---

Die (1519; *WA* 2:689.30ff., 697.17ff. [= *BoA* 1:166.4ff., 173.20ff.]; *LW* 42:105, 114); *Sermon on the . . . Sacrament of the Holy and True Body of Christ . . .* (*WA* 2:748ff. [= *BoA* 1:202ff.]; *LW* 35:45ff.). See esp. *WA* 2:748.17f. ([= *BoA* 1, 202.31–32]; *LW* 35:58): ". . . through the interchange of his blessings and our misfortunes, we become one loaf, one bread, one body, one drink, and have all things in common." In baptism, "he pledges himself not to impute to you the sins that remain in your nature after baptism, neither to take them into account nor to condemn you because of them" (*Sermon on the . . . Sacrament of Baptism* [1519], *WA* 2:731.4–6 [= *BoA* 1:189.10–12] *LW* 35:34). The classic reference to the joyous exchange in the treatise on Christian liberty: *WA* 7:25.26ff. (= *BoA* 2:15.28ff.); Bertram Lee Woolf, *Reformation Writings of Martin Luther* (London: Lutterworth Press, 1952), 1:363.

266. On the following, cp. the Easter sermon of April 16, 1525, *WA* 17.1:187ff.

267. "To be born of God is to acquire the nature of God" (*WA* 20:692.5). In that way the moral character of the righteousness mediated through Christ is fully preserved: "Therefore he who is truly born of God acts justly and takes care of the neighbor."

nature during his suffering on the cross. The same is true of human beings according to their outward existence; they do not detect the faith that makes them children of God. It is sin, not faith, that can be verified outwardly.[268]

The Christ who has suffered for our sake and has thereby given us righteousness is also one with us in temptation (*Anfechtung*). Only where the idea of satisfaction deals with this identity[269] does it have anything to do with justification. Luther had reached clarity on this exposition of the joyous exchange as early as the mid-twenties. Then in his statements during the Augsburg diet and immediately thereafter he completed this line of thought[270] and strengthened his understanding of the *propter Christum*.

In that light our justification rests on our relationship with Christ, "which gives and assigns to us everything that Christ is and has"; it consists in gift-giving love, not in works and achievements.[271] Their worthlessness is demonstrated and righteousness is given by the fact that Christ takes our sins upon himself and thereby destroys them.[272] He personifies all criminals; he has committed all our sins—not on his own but as the representative of all Christendom (*in suum corpus*).[273] He is the Lamb of God, given for us; all of Scripture and the Nicene Creed testify to that. As far back as Isaiah 53 the suffering servant illustrates the theme of redemption. One ought not press legal language for such a concept, nor should one take literally the picturesque expressions describing the community of faith.[274] Scholasticism of the Middle Ages or after Luther may have been more rigorous in conceptualization, but Luther did not use that approach in his doctrine of justification.

14. PER FIDEM: THE FAITH THAT JUSTIFIES (CA 4, SEC. 2)

The idea of faith links together the individual statements of the article on justification. Although "by faith" seems to be just one expression among

268. *WA* 17.1:72.11ff. (sermon of March 6, 1525). Here the tension of the *simul iustus et peccator* (cp. above, pp. 308–9) is based in Christology and frustrates all human desires for deification.

269. The congruence is far from complete, particularly because the approaches are so different.

270. Some sermons from 1530 and 1531 (*WA* 32, 34.1) are important here, but especially passages from the *Large Commentary on Galatians*, *WA* 40.1, 2. It is remarkable how, in Luther's fragmentary *De iustificatione* (*WA* 30.2:657–76), composed in midsummer of 1530, the christological statements fade into the background. It may have something to do with the polemical nature of the situation.

271. *WA* 32:84.20ff. In this early sermon at the Coburg (April 21, 1530), Luther has the Christian say, "I will not share my good works with you, and do not share yours with me; rather hang them on the public gallows between the stinking thieves."

272. "My sin is in Christ; the sin that damns . . . and the justifying righteousness is grace in Christ" (*WA* 40.1:276.2ff.).

273. This representative role is a result of his birth from the virgin Mary: "Christ is not born from the Virgin in divinity but as a sinner who does and commits all our sins, not committing them of himself but bearing them in his body" (ibid., 433.8ff).

274. Ibid., 437.1ff. All salvation is granted through Christ "by the cementing, the gluing of faith, by which we are made to resemble one body in the Spirit" (ibid., 284.6–7).

others in the series of adverbial qualifiers that are part of the statements on justification, it is actually the one that gives each of the others its specific character. To endure judgment "before God" is possible for the justified only by holding to faith. To be justified "freely" means that "our own merits, works, and satisfactions" are replaced by the faith that is none of these three but is solely a gift of grace. A grasp of the promise of righteousness "for Christ's sake" can only occur, as we have seen, in faith; that is what creates the bond with Christ through the joyous exchange and thereby reconciles the believer with God. The doctrine of justification is the doctrine of faith. Faith and righteousness are not two related complexes of ideas; they are two sides of the same coin.

In the same vein, CA 4 (secs. 2, 3) adds clauses that once again emphasize this foundational connection. To be justified by faith means that we "are received into favor and that sins are forgiven on account of Christ, who by his death made satisfaction for our sins." The German version of CA 4 formulates the content of faith somewhat differently: it puts stronger emphasis on Christ's role in justification—the forgiveness of sins is a result of his enduring suffering for our sake—and it adds that eternal life is given along with righteousness. In either case, justifying faith is inseparably linked to Christ and his saving work. As a human attitude effected by God, faith is defined primarily by its relation to Christ, rather than by how we see ourselves.

What now appears in both final versions as added material in a twofold form was originally a single statement in Na (*BS* 57.14–16)—the statement that faith brings the forgiveness of sins and reception into favor. From this point of view, the final Latin version—except for one minor transposition—is closer to Na than the German version is. The latter—as is the case with Nb (therefore in mid-June, 1530)—has a greater wealth of expressions for the same content. In any case, the final German text for this section is later than the Latin.

Both final versions, however, drop the scriptural evidence (John 3:16; Gal. 3:14) that Na uses as a christological basis for justification. Nonetheless, it continues to have theological relevance as a witness to the fact that the Reformation doctrine of justification is to be traced back directly to Holy Scripture rather than to medieval constructs. Additional proof of this fact comes from Schwab. 5, which also provides scriptural evidence in abundance and hands it on to Na. Although as early as Nb the *per fidem* becomes the conclusion of the definition of justification proper, relegating the original statements about faith to a supplementary clause, one is still aware—particularly in the German version—that the connection between Christ and faith remains immutable. Modern exposition of this article cannot overemphasize this close connection between the *per fidem* and the *propter Christum*.

Just how close the connection is may be seen from our frequently demon-

strated observation that Luther's Confession of 1528 does not set up a formal
doctrine of justification but presents it in a paraphrase of the three articles of
the Apostles' Creed instead. In that way the christological approach is
grounded in the Trinity. When Luther repeatedly asserts that he believes in
these articles "from the heart," he is repeating faith statements from Scripture that are binding on all Christians.[275] But in Luther's personal confession,
faith signifies more than agreement with traditional facts and truths; it is a
conscious yes to accepting what God has given us for our salvation, just as a
no is its rejection. That gift consists primarily in the fulfillment of those
things God has assigned to each estate in the three hierarchies.[276] In 1528,
Luther built the christological reference of faith snugly into our creaturely
relationship. Christ's work for us corresponds to what the Father and Creator
does for us; it is imparted to us through the gifts given us by the Holy
Spirit.[277]

What Christ does for us is closely tied to the works of God the Creator and
the Holy Spirit; faith opens itself to these works and then acknowledges them
by praising and honoring God. Thus confession is not merely the recounting
of biblical truths and events; faith is itself a divine gift, by which the believers
are "adorned, raised from the dead, freed from sin, and made joyful and
confident, free and secure in their conscience."[278] That Trinitarian approach
makes it possible for Luther to join the objective side of salvation history with
the personal experience of salvation. For the reformer, subjective and objective elements in the process of belief that have steadily lost contact with one
another since Pietism and the Enlightenment maintain an inner connection
with one another through the Trinitarian connection of faith.

The *Instructions for the Visitors* doubtless took over this Trinitarian reference
from Luther's confession, which had been composed shortly before in the
same year, 1528. Preaching on the faith encompasses creation, redemption,
and sanctification.[279] This preaching, however, is primarily instruction, advice, and exhortation for the plain folk of the congregation; the "articles of

275. "This is my faith, for so all true Christians believe and so the Holy Scriptures teach us"
(*WA* 26:509.19–20 [= *BoA* 3: 515.5–6; *LW* 37:372).

276. "For God wishes us to perform such works to his praise and glory. And all who are saved
in the faith of Christ surely do these works and maintain these orders" (*WA* 26:505.21ff. [= *BoA*
3:511.4ff.]; *LW* 37:365). See below, p. 347.

277. "The Father gives himself to us, with heaven and earth and all the creatures, in order that
they may serve us and benefit us" (*WA* 26:505.39ff. [= *BoA* 3:511.22ff.]; *LW* 37:366). After
Adam's fall, "the Son himself subsequently gave himself and bestowed all his works, sufferings,
wisdom, and righteousness, and reconciled us to the Father, in order that restored to life and
righteousness, we might also know and have the Father and his gifts." On the distribution of
these gifts, "the Holy Spirit comes and gives himself to us also, wholly and completely. He
teaches us to understand this deed of Christ which has been manifested to us, helps us receive
and preserve it, use it to our advantage and impart it to others, increase and extend it."

278. *WA* 26:505.31ff. (= *BoA* 3:511.15ff.); *LW* 37:366.

279. Cp. *WA* 26:231.1–14; *LW* 40:308.

faith" are conveyed to them as information. In this vein there is no more discussion of the self-surrender of the triune God and of the thankful reception of this Spirit-wrought gift than there is of the central significance of Christ's sacrifice. At the same time the edifying relation between the *propter Christum* and the *per fidem* is maintained throughout: God forgives us without our merits for Christ's sake. "That is satisfaction. For by faith we attain to the forgiveness of sins if we believe that Christ has made satisfaction for us."[280]

But for Melanchthon, who was the principal author of the *Instructions,* the emphasis lies not on the christological reference of faith in forgiveness but on the fact that true faith is not possible without contrition. The suffering Christ is the pattern for the contrite sinner.[281] Contrition and faith are inseparably connected; that is Melanchthon's chief concern. It even defines the christological reference of faith. A false faith is one that accepts in carnal security the forgiveness of sins as a result of Christ's suffering, without at the same time feeling any contrition or grief for sin.[282]

Thus for Melanchthon the function of faith in relation to Christ is defined somewhat differently than in Luther's Trinitarian way of thinking. Therefore in studying the development and interpretation of CA 4, it is necessary to ask what image of Christ is being linked with faith in each particular instance.

In this connection, the Schwabach Articles occupy a special place, both in terms of content and in terms of time, midway between the early confessional texts of 1528–29 and the final versions. Although nothing remains of the Trinitarian reference, Luther's christological concept still exerts a powerful influence. "But the only way to righteousness and deliverance from sin and death is, without any merits or works, to believe in the Son of God, who suffered for us, . . . " This key passage in Schwab. 5 influenced the German version of CA 4 down to minor details. If Melanchthon's finely chiseled phrases are apparent in the smooth formulations of the Latin text of CA 4, Luther's Christ-piety speaks through the German version.

The relation between faith and good works, which was a matter of urgency as early as the preliminary Torgau work and was confirmed anew at the end of the editorial process on CA 20 at Augsburg (see above, p. 292), did not exactly encourage a close bond between faith and Christology. Nonetheless, the preliminary draft of CA 20 does see good works growing out of faith in Christ.[283] Its final version (sec. 9) gives greater emphasis to the personal side

280. *WA* 26:222.3–4; *LW* 40:298.

281. "If Christ has had to suffer so much on account of our sins, how much shall we have to suffer if we will have no part of contrition, but rather despise God?" (*WA* 26:221.4ff., 12ff.; *LW* 40:297).

282. *WA* 26:217.34ff.; *LW* 40:293. Luther expressly confirmed this thesis of Melanchthon against Agricola in the introduction to the *Instructions for the Visitors* (*WA* 26:202–3; *LW* 40:274).

283. ". . . when he believes that, for Christ's sake, his sins are forgiven, and grace is granted him. Only this faith makes one just and righteous in God's sight . . ." (*BS* 77.35ff.; Jacobs 86).

of faith in Christ. He "alone is the mediator who reconciles the Father;" the self-righteous despise Christ. In CA 20, Melanchthon laid particular stress on the element of personal decision that typifies faith's connection with Christ.

Thus, in summary, we may conclude that in every stage and expression of the doctrine of justification, the Augsburg Confession relates faith closely to Christ, although that may take various forms. Given this, how does the *per fidem* in CA 4 make its contribution?

Christ is the Lamb of God who died for us. That is the content of the Bible; it is also the content of all Christian confession since the Apostles' Creed. That is the way one recognizes Christians; they believe that Christ suffered and died for us. They differ from other people in their dependence on Christ in faith and in their confession that he is the one who bought them with his blood and made them members of his body.[284] Thus, justifying faith does not consist in imitating Christ but consists in being focused on him; we are justified not through the faith with which Christ believed but through the faith with which we human beings believe in Christ.[285]

Such faith makes us righteous. "Christian righteousness before God is to believe in the Son." It is the "trust of the heart in God through Christ." "For Christ's sake this faith is reckoned as righteousness."[286] "Our faith depends only on Christ, who alone is righteous . . . because his righteousness stands before God's judgment against God's wrath and for me."[287] This relationship with Christ and our exchange with him occur in the objective context of salvation history. We are dead through Adam's alien sin; we are to live through Christ's alien righteousness. This righteousness, however, belongs to faith. "Because you believe in me and do not doubt Christ, you shall be righteous," says God's judgment.[288] And this righteousness is eternal in value and duration, because it is the eternal righteousness of the Risen One.[289]

Thus from the viewpoint of faith, righteousness comes to be understood as a result of communion with Christ. "Faith grasps Christ, the Son of God, who was given for us. By grasping him in faith we possess righteousness." The trust of the heart grasps an invisible reality and in so doing has Christ himself present. Only by such faith are we Christians, "one cake with Christ"; through faith "I put on Christ and, conversely, he me"; I lay "all my misery on him, and in return he lays all good things on me." The interchange

284. *WA* 40.1:437.1ff.; 20:381.15ff.; 31.2:433.20–21.
285. *WA* 31.2:120.33–34.
286. *WA* 40.1:366.6ff.
287. *WA* 25:35.1–2, 37.12; *LW* 29:41, 44.
288. *WA* 40.1:233.6–7. See *WA* 31.2:85.34–35: The merits of the monks and their righteousness are masks, but justification is reality. "It is no mask or appearance that we die because of someone else's sin; it is fitting that we live by another's righteousness."
289. *WA* 32:41.32ff., 42.30ff., 43.13–14.

is effected in a joyous exchange through faith; the one occurs because of the other.[290]

Luther's graphic language ought not lure us into oversimplifying faith's unity with Christ. Christ is enthroned behind dark clouds; faith recognizes him by reaching into the darkness. Faith looks to the coming Christ, just as Abraham was justified by his confidence in the Christ to come. Fathers and sons live in the same faith. But to wait for Christ today the way Abraham did is to imply that God has done nothing in the meantime. Abraham believed in the promise; we believe in the fulfillment that Christ brought through his redemption, although as yet it is complete only to believing anticipation.[291]

To believe in the invisible Christ means to leave behind everything that is ours and "to leap into Christ." "It is impossible to believe"; we are too lazy to do it. Mere empty thoughts and intentions do not do any good. The important thing is to lay hold of Christ in faith ("but who believes in him, in him?"). Taken as an emotion, faith is just "a little tiny box," but it contains a costly gem, more valuable than heaven and earth.[292]

Faith's unity with Christ differs from mere mystical inwardness in that it is completely directed toward the life of Christ. It is the entire Christ through every step of his saving work who is grasped by faith and who justifies. Basic to it all is the incarnation; on that depends the truth of the Word on which faith is grounded. Even though Scripture occasionally speaks about faith in an absolute or abstract sense, justification requires a concrete faith that does not simply regard the man Jesus according to his human nature but sees him as the Son of God. Only on that basis does his claim to proclaim the Word of God become credible.[293] "Thus one goes to heaven if one believes in the only-begotten Son who was born and suffered."[294]

Christ's incarnation is mirrored in his birth and crucifixion. The "for me" of justification to which faith clings has its true ground in the crucifixion. My heart remains fixed on Christ, who was crucified and condemned for my sake and not his own. Faith holds Christ before its eyes. It asks not, "What have I done or failed to do?" but, "What has Christ done and accomplished?"[295] Thus death and resurrection are seen as one. It is in connection with the resurrection that faith demonstrates its victorious power—that it is not a mere opinion but a "brave hero who is to cling courageously to the words 'I

290. *WA* 40.1:297.5ff., 229.4ff., 20:677.2ff.
291. *WA* 40.1:288.15–16, 377.7ff., 390.1ff.
292. *WA* 27:122.27ff., 173.9ff. Cp. ibid., 172.6ff.
293. "If we believe in the Son of God, we have proof" (*WA* 20:784.8ff.). On the difference between *fides abstracta* and *fides concreta* (*incarnata*): *WA* 40.1:414.8ff. Cp. ibid., 415.10ff.
294. *WA* 29:387.22ff.
295. *WA* 40.1:459.2, 164.5ff.

believe in the resurrection.' "[296] The message of Easter proclaims victory over the devil and the world. It is vital to us, mired in sin as we are. In it "he extends himself as wide as the world is," having his victory over sin and death proclaimed for our benefit. Only faith is able to receive this effect of the resurrection.[297]

This is how faith achieves union with the Risen One: if I believe in Christ who was raised from the dead, I am where he is. The testimony of the Risen One is the only way to heaven. There is nothing else that justifies before God. "To be with Christ means to believe in him, so that we enter into the being he has."[298] This faith in Christ justifies before God. Luther has God summarize it by saying, "If you want to reconcile me, believe my Son, who was born and suffered; if you believe that, you will be righteous." Faith creates reconciliation with Christ, with God, and with our neighbors. Conversely, one can also say that Christ our mediator reconciles us with one another and enables us to trust in God.[299] Faith and Christ perform the same function in establishing a community of love; unity with Christ through faith is the presupposition of community between God and humankind.

Through this faith, human beings are justified.[300] The "righteousness of faith" deals with the specific concern of CA 4. "Christian righteousness before God is to believe in the Son." "To believe in Christ and justification by faith is the chief article of the gospel." "He who believes has righteousness." "Their [the disciples'] righteousness was faith in Christ."[301] It would be easy to add to this series of quotations from the time around 1530. That is because of the various relationships in which we have found faith to be involved. They presuppose the essential difference between the righteousness of faith and the righteousness of the flesh: they count only "spiritually before God." The righteousness of faith is not a formal quality that can be acquired through training or habit, nor is it a product of reason as cultivated by the followers of Erasmus and the monks.[302] If justification is the same as belief in Christ, the Son of God, then it is evidence of the hidden divine wisdom, and human reason can neither discover it nor comprehend it. Righteousness can come only from faith; therefore the justified person is free from everything that can be measured by human standards. "Through faith alone will you become a son of God." As such, we participate in Christ's righteousness and purity.

296. *WA* 29:333.14–15. Even the first disciples considered faith in the resurrection to be acceptance of a myth (ibid., 292.11); it is still viewed that way today, especially in Italy (ibid., 335.3).

297. *WA* 27:118.30ff. Cp. ibid., 124.3: "The resurrection cannot be grasped except by faith."

298. *WA* 20:318.20–21, 615.24ff., 29:82.1ff.

299. *WA* 40.1:365.12–13, 27:303.6ff., 167.4ff.

300. "It is through faith we have righteousness" (*WA* 40.1:297.7).

301. *WA* 40.1:366.6, 26:67.14; *LW* 28:308; *WA* 25:43.15; *LW* 29:53; *WA* 27:249.9.

302. *WA* 40.1:392.8–9, 225.10, 226.7, 363.8.

Faith is the shrine that bears the costly treasure of this righteousness. "If you believe, you have him; if you do not believe, you do not have him."[303]

Christ's righteousness is the righteousness of God, and the justified person shares it. "I am built upon God's righteousness, which is God himself; he cannot reject it because he would be rejecting himself." It is eternal as he is. Eternal too is the forgiveness of sins that we receive through it; therefore our faith can depend on it absolutely. In his debate with Erasmus, as in his early theological work, Luther places this understanding of the righteousness "which God has," an understanding gained from Hebrew linguistic usage, in parallel with *gloria dei*, which is peculiar to God and which is acknowledged in praise and thanksgiving. "You have Christ if you believe in him; give glory to God the wise, the powerful; you thereby give him righteousness, praise him, and give him divinity."[304]

Faith affirms God by acknowledging that he is righteous; that is the most profound basis for the connection between faith and righteousness. "Faith justifies because it gives God the recognition due him; whoever does that is righteous."[305] This recognition of God is possible only through Christ—in two senses. Christ makes a Father out of the judge; he also represents God's eternal righteousness. "If I bore the sins of the entire world, I would believe in the eternal righteousness that sins cannot annul; then all sins are obliterated because this righteousness is mine." In God there is nothing but righteousness; therefore Christians should know that they are free from all sins.[306]

Corresponding to this incomprehensibility of divine righteousness is the antirational character of human faith. Believers possess an unspeakable treasure that cannot be expressed by tongue or pen. Faith trusts in the midst of darkness; in adversities and troubles it finds its only support in the naked Word. The victories it wins are not obvious. The acts of God on which it relies appear to reason as ridiculous, silly, and unnatural; that is particularly true of the incarnation and the crucifixion. Carnal reason cannot fathom this faith whose mysteries are not worth a penny. Human reason wants to specify time, place, and means to God before it will believe; therefore God's deeply hidden wisdom goes far beyond all reason and experience of the human mind.[307]

303. *WA* 26:16.9ff.; *LW* 28:235; *WA* 18:784.10ff.; *LW* 33:290; *WA* 27:127.19ff., 172.6ff.
304. *WA* 17.2:450.29ff., 29:569.19ff., 570.1ff., 18:769.1ff.; *LW* 33:265; *WA* 40.1:369.2ff.; *LW* 26:233. In his dispute over justification, Osiander thought he could appeal to such passages in Luther's works; see Martin Stupperich, *Osiander in Preussen 1549–1552* (New York and Berlin: Walter de Gruyter, 1973), 130ff. and elsewhere.
305. *WA* 40.1:360.10ff.
306. *WA* 20:403.32ff., 692.1ff.
307. *WA* 40.1:361.6ff., 29:387.24–25, 20:526.26ff., 19:381.20ff., 387.3ff., 394.15ff.; *LW* 19:183, 190, 197.

The nature of faith can also cause difficulties. The enthusiasts take it lightly, thinking that one can grab hold of it all at once and conquer the nasty world completely. Again, a proper understanding of the forgiveness of sins does not relate it to persons other than ourselves—then it obviously has nothing to do with us—but rather relates it to our own situation. Then it hits us; it concerns each of us personally, but no one wants to believe that. Therefore even the message of grace appears intolerable. And finally, it is impossible to tell outwardly whether someone is righteous through faith; for that reason believers are still to this day condemned. In short, faith is a mystery, a holy secret (Eph. 5:32), not only because it lies hidden in the heart but also because it deals with the invisible as though it were right at hand.[308]

All of that is to say that faith is constantly exposed to testing *(Anfechtungen)*. In August 1530, as the treaty negotiations approached their climax, Luther spoke of the necessity of testing, by means of the image of the sky of grace.[309] Temptations are like clouds that crowd the horizon and that we cannot disperse by our own powers. But the sky is above them and will cause them to disappear, and then faith once again, without having done a thing, can exist in pure peace and joy.

Testing, however, is not just an outward threat; it is a part of the condition of faith. In the sermon, faith hears of something hidden that exists contrary to all appearances; faith remains forever dependent on that hearing, because what it sees are only masks. Faith is always struggling; God conceals himself from it, and the more deeply God hides himself, the more faith is challenged to cling to God's Word. Sin snaps at us; faith holds to God's mercy all the more. Although Christians try to avoid sin and strive for the good, we never remain free from sin. But we do not give up our hold on God, nor do we despair in our sins. Thus, justified faith is always tested faith.[310]

That is tied to the fact that faith still remains under sin despite its bond with God and Christ. The tension between sin and grace, the paradoxical situation of the believer—righteous and sinner at the same time—is not discussed in CA 4 or in its immediate predecessors, even though it provides the indispensable foundation for the Reformation doctrine of justification. It was not only in the major lecture series on Galatians (1531) that Luther mentioned this paradox; the series was the continuation of efforts, begun the previous year at the Coburg, to present the doctrine of justification in a systematic way. Further evidence from this period, cited in the following discussion, can be found in the more homiletic lectures on 1 Timothy (1528;

308. *WA* 40.1:509.1ff.; *LW* 26:329; *WA* 28:271.5ff., 567.3–4; 27:249.9ff., 26:60.11ff.; *LW* 28:297.

309. *WA* 31.1:245.34ff.; *LW* 14:27. Cp. above, pp. 304–5.

310. *WA* 31.2:85.32–33, 57.31ff., 27:333.18, 335.5ff., 26:11.2; *LW* 28:226; *WA* 31.2:10.8.

WA 26), the sermons of 1528 (*WA* 27) and the lectures on Isaiah, which lasted into 1530 (*WA* 31.2). It is clear that Luther did not hesitate to introduce students and congregations to the more complex problems of the doctrine of justification.[311]

Luther began quite early to deal with the fact that "remnants of sin" remained even in the justified;[312] he solved the apparent contradiction that arises from that fact by recourse to his understanding of faith. "Where Christ is believed, sin no longer exists; it is in fact dead, buried, destroyed. But it remains in the flesh, where there is no faith; but because one believes, the sin is not imputed."[313] In faith, therefore, the sin that is still attached to the flesh is canceled. But because of that remnant of sin, the righteousness of faith is in itself not complete; it is just a formal righteousness (*iustitia formalis*). Faith is never more than the beginning of righteousness, but for its sake the sin that is still present is overlooked. There are circumstances in which faith and sin can exist together. Only one thing is impossible: that faith could tolerate the presence of a mortal sin. Then faith would indeed be a useless quality (*otiosa qualitas*), as Thomas called it in regard to infused grace, and as the enthusiasts speak about it without keeping Christ in mind.[314]

But the only way to solve the riddle of how faith and sin can exist side by side is to begin with Christ. To the degree that we are in Christ, no sin will be found in us; it has no right to us. We stand entirely under grace and are free from death and the law. Because faith clings to Christ, is glued together with him, and becomes one person with him, a man becomes Christ, who says of himself and that person, "I am that sinner because he clings to me and vice versa." And he who has become free by faith in Christ says, "My sin is in Christ," and so he can condemn the sin. This sin, eliminated by Christ, swallows up the sin I condemn; "justifying righteousness is the grace of Christ."[315]

In Christ and in his sin-concealing grace, the tension between sin and righteousness is eliminated. And in that way faith that makes Christ and his grace its own constantly overcomes this tension. Faith overcomes it if and insofar as it is in Christ. But that means that it is always in motion, always a

---

311. Cp. also: "The Christian is at the same time sinner and saint, enemy and son of God" (*WA* 40.1:368.9). "The Christian is a sinner yet righteous. That is a rare person. If he is not a sinner, he does not obtain the forgiveness of sins" (*WA* 29:576.14ff.; see also ibid., 577.1ff.). "The Lord gives his Spirit that we may believe; the actuality and the truth are there, the weak faith in us" (the lecture on the "state of Christianity," September 3, 1527, *WA* 20:637.13–14). On the Christian: "Because of this faith he is righteous, although in himself a sinner" (*WA* 34.1:471.9).

312. E.g., in the work against Latomus (*WA* 8:57.3ff.; *LW* 32:157). Cp. W. Maurer, *Der junge Melanchthon* (cited above, n. 150), 2:276ff. See also below, p. 334.

313. *WA* 40.1:431.7, 445.9ff.

314. *WA* 40.1:363.8, 366.10ff., 367.6ff., 228.12ff., 545.6ff., 27:173.8ff.

315. *WA* 26:15.11ff.; *LW* 28:232; *WA* 40.1:284.5ff., 285.5ff., 276.2ff.

living power, and never a useless quality of the soul. The result of this tension-filled activity of faith is that it never stays at the same level. It certainly knows about levels but they do not lead upward in a planned sequence. It recognizes growth too, although the growth does not happen through organic development. The life of faith is lived in stages of greater or lesser perfection, of feast and famine, of climbing upward and falling back.

Faith that is always beginning is imperfect faith. "As long as I am in the flesh, sin clings to me, but because of faith it becomes invisible when I cling to Christ." The forgiveness of sin gets us started; we no longer think about sin. Nevertheless, its reign in us again becomes apparent no matter how much we wish to separate ourselves from it. The new being comes into existence only when faith and love join. Faith becomes more effective the more love in Christ becomes effective. Sanctifying love keeps on working in the believer, even though some defects still remain. As justified persons, we may seem to live for the first time without guilt, but in fact that is not the case, because we cannot always love. Although after we come to faith, the grosser carnal sins fall away, there is no Christian on earth who can say, "I am without sin." But even in the midst of temptations by which sin threatens us, we can testify that the sin has been forgiven.[316]

This peculiar floating situation of faith corresponds to the situation of this time in the world, between the ascension of Christ and his return. In faith, my heart has withdrawn from everything earthly and is with Christ. I participate in his victory; no one can condemn me. But believers still live among the temptations of this world. In this eon the law under which the creation began is still in force. God creates out of nothing; the visible comes forth from the invisible. The power of the Risen One acts visibly in the believer.[317]

That effect is always incomplete. And as long as the process does not go far enough, there will always be strong and weak believers. "Faith brings with it a measure or a distinction of gifts." According to Rom. 1:17, we are to grow "from faith to faith." Therefore we must constantly learn in faith that we conform ourselves to Christ's death. The "milk faith" or "young faith" is still faith, even when it quite naively clings to Jesus' Word and calls on him for help. But such faith must not stay drowsy and lazy, content with its own imperfection. There is an increasing faith, and compared to that the imperfect faith is nothing. The joy of a beginning faith is only partial; it becomes complete when it grows through writing and meditation.[318]

The Bible too speaks of the first fruits of the spirit (Rom. 8:23), for whose

316. WA 40.1:366.10ff., 26:25.13ff.; LW 28:246; WA 20:295.17ff., 309.12ff.
317. WA 20:318.20ff., 27:399.5ff.
318. WA 26:75.36; LW 28:320; WA 20:267.17ff., 527.24ff., 528.3ff., 612.1ff.

preliminary and various expressions the Christian must be grateful; they assure us that our prayers are heard. Prayer compensates for any lack of the Spirit by overcoming the remaining effects of sin. Thus the Christian life never stands still. Faith presses on (Phil. 3:12) toward perfection. Initial faith must become stronger and better. It is not perfect all at once, although there are moments of perfect faith, as in the case of the Canaanite woman (Matt. 15:22). That shows that faith is not something temporary, like foam on water, but that it takes possession of one's whole heart. Above all, the forgiveness of sins is an offer that remains throughout our life; faith, even though it may fall a hundred times, gets to its feet again and again.[319]

Thus even the weak stand in faith. God holds them fast, even when they do not hold themselves completely to his Word but treasure other things more highly. But God does not want them to remain stuck in the first stages of faith. He sends them temptations to urge them to grow. Moderate faith, miserable faith (*modica fides, misera fides*)! But faith is a very delicate structure that must be tended carefully. Luther himself, who teaches it daily, is never beyond the danger of losing his trust in God. We are saints and yet are not. Our holiness consists not in what we have already achieved but in the forgiveness of sins. It is assuredly there, but we have still not grasped it completely—just as the resurrection of the flesh is certain although we do not yet see it. In the same way, eternal life has begun for the justified; it is there— and so sins, unholiness, and death have disappeared—even though it cannot be felt and empirical people cannot recognize it. We can no more see our holiness than we can see Christ.[320]

15. IMPUTED FAITH (CA 4, SEC. 3)

Thus faith both leads us into a tension between sin and righteousness and leads us out again. Out of this tension arises the form of the doctrine of justification that we customarily call imputative in contrast to effective. According to CA 4.3, "God will regard and reckon this faith as righteousness" (*Hanc fidem imputat Deus pro iustitia coram ipso*).

This statement on imputed righteousness, drawn from Rom. 4:3, appears late in the history of the text of the Augustana. Melanchthon had passed over it at the end of May in his editing of Na and did not add it to the wording of the official German text until the beginning of June (Nb). Nevertheless, closely related statements can be found in Schwab. 5 and Marb. 7.[321] Thus

319. *WA* 20:791.6ff., 793.9, 630.8ff., 15:717.3ff., 17.1:81.4, 15:531.35ff.
320. *WA* 27:397.2ff., 28:66.1, 3, 31.2:426.19ff., 34.1:469.10ff., 470.2ff.

321. It is not faith, according to the literal meaning of Schwab. 5, but the person (because of that person's faith) that God "reckons and regards as righteous, godly, and holy" (*BS* 57.26; Jacobs 71). According to Marb. 7, it is on account of faith that "God reckons and regards us righteous, godly, and holy" (*BS* 57.37; Jacobs 71). Thus the imputation originally referred to a person rather than an attitude. CA 20 and its draft do not mention imputation.

the idea of imputation had been part of the background of the doctrine of justification for a long time. It did not just emerge out of difficulties in interpretation, possibly as an independent development by Melanchthon. We have already established (see above, p. 297) that Melanchthon had made explicit statements about the imputation of faith in justification as early as 1527 and that he had investigated the problem further just before Augsburg. Even prior to that, several profound statements of Luther were available. One ought not dismiss imputation as un-Lutheran nor attribute statements of the reformer that were made after 1530 to influence from Melanchthon. Luther took over the doctrine from the tradition familiar to him, but he developed it independently on the basis of his unique combination of Christology and faith (see above, pp. 223–24, and below, p. 340). The idea of imputation in post-Luther theology, therefore, does not represent the growing influence of Melanchthon. Before one makes an assertion like that, one ought also to inquire about Luther's influence in each individual case.

The locus classicus for "reckoning," *imputare*, is found in Romans 4 in connection with God's estimation of Abraham;[322] God reckoned his faith to him as righteousness. Thus in adopting the idea of imputation, Luther was primarily taking over a biblical way of thinking rather than a scholastic doctrine. In his discussion with Erasmus, Luther explicated this text in greater detail:[323] in grace, God imputes righteousness without regard to merit; righteousness given graciously is imputed righteousness. Imputation is thus understood as more than a particular aspect of justification; as in Paul, it is seen as the entire event of grace. The righteousness of faith is based not on some work of ours but on the "God who is benevolent and who imputes out of grace."[324]

If in this discussion with Erasmus, Luther adopts terminology that is also found in scholasticism, it is more unconscious than intentional. He only wants to bring out the meaning of the doctrine of justification in the words of the apostle. That occurred both in 1525 and later. In a sermon from 1526,[325] Luther describes how sin remains even in believers but how God "for the sake

322. WA 18:772.18 ([= BoA 3:274.35]; LW 33:271) points out that the idea appears there ten times; *reputare* and *imputare* are equated. In this, Luther adopted a correction of the Vulgate made by the humanists. They replaced *reputare* by *imputare*. Erasmus, above all, suggested not only *imputare*—as Valla and Faber did—but also *accepto ferre;* Reuchlin even proposed *computare*. Cp. Ficker in WA 56:277.8ff.; and LW 25:264. Cp. also Rolf Schäfer in StA 5:126 n. 6.

323. WA 18:771.34ff. (= BoA 3:274.5ff.); LW 33:270. Also by appeal to Psalm 32: "Blessed is the man to whom the Lord imputes no sin." Cp. the earlier WA 18:769.24ff. (= BoA 3:271.20); LW 33:266. See also above, p. 303.

324. WA 18:772.12 (= BoA 3:274.27); LW 33:271. On the closeness of this concept to acceptation, I point particularly to WA 18:769.8–9. ([= BoA 3:271.1]; LW 33:265): "This pleases God, God approves of this, this he considers worthy and accepts." See also below, pp. 335ff.

325. WA 20:309.12ff.

of faith" forgives these remnants of sin, that is, does not impute them:[326] a forgiven sin is simply no sin at all. In answer to the question of how such a nonimputation of sin can occur, Luther points to the superiority of Spirit to flesh.[327] By possessing the Spirit, a Christian is righteous and blessed, thus overcoming the remaining sin through the fact that it will not be imputed.

During the Augsburg diet, Luther fought his traditionalist opponents with the help of the doctrine of imputation. They asserted that almsgiving made the heart pure and pleased God. Luther countered that faith is what does those things and thereby creates righteousness before God who sees the heart. That implies, however, that although humanity in its physical nature remains captive to sin, "God reckons us righteous because of the belief of our hearts" and lets our flesh and sin have their own way until the day of judgment. Every "holy sinner" commits sin in each good work.[328]

Luther's teaching on imputation, therefore, presupposes the equation "righteous and sinner at the same time." It solves the inherent contradiction by pointing to the immeasurable mercy with which God rewards faith. Thus it forms a contrast to the calculating into which the later doctrine of imputation degenerated. Luther developed the imputation model fully in his major commentary on Galatians in 1531.

Here too the basic assumption is the fact that within the justified there remains a sinful remnant that cannot be conquered in this world. Luther describes the nonimputation of this remaining sin by showing how the believer can constantly flee to the word of forgiveness and, through that forgiveness, have the sin "covered" (Rom. 4:7) so that it is no longer seen by God.[329] The continuing activity of that sin results in a loss of faith. God, however, "reckons this imperfect faith as perfect righteousness."[330] Thus imputation deals with the weakness and deficiency that sin causes in faith. In the process it becomes clear that the relationship to God and Christ created by faith is fundamental to justification. Faith is "trust of the heart through Christ toward God." This faith is "imputed" to the sinner "as righteousness for Christ's sake."[331]

It is God who imputes faith to the believer for Christ's sake and who does

---

326. "As long as one holds fast to faith, although one has sin, God does not impute it" (ibid., 309.15).

327. In the exposition of 1 John (1527; ibid., 630.8ff.).

328. *WA* 30.2:661.10–30, esp. 26ff.

329. *WA* 40.1:233.8ff.

330. Ibid., 366.9–10, 367.6ff.

331. Ibid., 366.7ff. One can just as well say, "The imputation occurs for the sake of faith or of Christ." Two things belong together: "(1) Faith which holds Christ and has him present the way a ring holds a jewel. (2) He who is found to grasp Christ with such faith will be reckoned as just by God" (ibid., 233.2ff.).

not impute the sin that still remains. But as with justification in general—in which God acknowledges us as righteous and we God—so it is with imputation. It is reciprocal. Human faith attributes to God wisdom, goodness, omnipotence, and everything divine; to that degree, Luther can say, "Faith is the creator of divinity." Likewise God, despite the sin that still clings to us, imputes everything good to us for the sake of this faith.[332]

For Christ's sake the sin that still clings is not imputed to the believer. "Where one believes in Christ, there is no longer any sin; it is dead, buried, destroyed. It remains in the flesh, however, to the degree that one does not believe; but because one believes, it is not imputed." Luther has God say to the justified sinner, "Because you believe, I will not count, punish, or condemn these sins, but I will have them forgiven and covered, not for your sake or because of your works and worthiness but for the sake of Christ in whom you believe; because you believe in him, your faith does everything. Thus the sinner is at the same time sinner and saint, enemy and son of God."[333]

From all this we can conclude that for the Luther of the *Large Commentary on Galatians*, justification and being declared just are one and the same. As he did in 1521,[334] Luther can here speak of a twofold justification corresponding to the twofold gift that God thereby distributes. For both aspects of justification, the forgiveness of sins is fundamental. For initial faith (see above, pp. 329–30) it effects only a preliminary righteousness (*iustitia formalis*); with regard to the still remaining remnants of sin, it is righteousness by imputation.[335] Both aspects, however, belong together according to Rom. 4:3. Because the *iustitia formalis* permits the continued existence of sin in the justified, there is need for the imputation that alone can annul the sin before God.[336]

Thus the doctrine of imputation is not a single aspect of the doctrine of justification, nor is it the perfected version of that doctrine. It completes the doctrine of justification by providing its necessary supplement. What human faith has achieved by the reception of the forgiveness of sins and by spiritual communion with God in Christ is confirmed and completed by God, despite all remaining sinfulness, through the promise of total righteousness before him. In this way everything that was effected through Christ and that

332. Ibid., 360.3ff.

333. Ibid., 445.9ff., 368.5ff. Here Luther continues, "The sophists do not understand that; they urge us to live such holy lives that there will be no sin in us."

334. In *Against Latomus* (WA 8:105.36ff.; LW 32:226).

335. "I am righteous through the remission of sins (1) through the gift of initial faith a *formalis iustitia* . . . , (2) through imputation" (WA 40.1:408.6ff.; LW 26:260).

336. On Rom. 4:3: "'It was reckoned to him as righteousness.' Why does Paul make this addition? Faith is a formal righteousness, but it does not suffice, because there are still remnants of sin in the flesh" (WA 40.1:363.8–9).

happened in reciprocal exchange with him is presupposed and perfected. The concluding statement in CA 4.3, "This faith God imputes for righteousness in his sight," thus summarizes the entire content of the article. The doctrine of imputation must therefore be understood—even in Luther's perspective— as the essence of the doctrine of justification.

Excursus: Imputatio and Acceptatio

As we have seen, the doctrine of justification is firmly embedded in the thought world of the Bible, especially that of the apostle Paul. That does not mean, however, that it has lost its relationship to scholastic terminology. At the same time, it maintains its connection with Holy Scripture. The Reformation doctrine of justification rests on a new exposition of a biblical concept that had already been adopted by scholasticism.

We have already[337] pointed out that Luther developed the biblical understanding of justification according to Romans 4 during his controversy with Erasmus in 1525. In that process he supplemented the biblical concept of imputation *(imputatio)* with that of acceptance *(acceptatio)*. The association of these two concepts was familiar to scholasticism since Duns Scotus. In addition, the collection of terms *acceptare*, *acceptus*, and *acceptatio* was traditional in the LXX and the Vulgate.[338] Of course, the medieval teachers did not give specific attention to these biblical associations. Their interest was directed toward the philosophical concepts that would help to describe the relationship of humanity to God and especially to the granting of salvation.

In that effort, the major concern of the late Middle Ages was to maintain, in addition to the freedom of human action pleasing to God, the sovereignty of the divine saving will. The apparent contradiction that this creates is solved by means of the concept of *acceptatio*. "Acceptance" denotes that ordering of God's will which sets a human good—whether a natural gift or a later attainment—on the road to blessedness. Thus human merit is presupposed; the accepted person *(homo acceptus)* is at the same time *meritorius*.[339] Corresponding to the free act of human love in which the natural will takes precedence over love given by God, there is a freely granted acceptance on the part of God *(voluntas divina acceptans)*. Such was God's decree for every act of forgiveness according to his ordered power *(potentia ordinata)*. When it happens according to his absolute power *(potentia absoluta)*, it becomes a matter of predestination, and eternal salvation is the result.

We can see how closely this theory of acceptance is connected to the Reformation doctrine of justification. It is true that the influence of divine grace on the attaining of human merit is diminished; the individual's moral will becomes predominant. But the individual steps before God in a direct encounter, leaving behind the supernatural

---

337. See nn. 322–24.
338. References in Werner Dettloff, *Die Lehre von der Acceptatio divina bei Joh. Duns Scotus mit bes. Berücksichtigung der Rechtfertigungslehre*, Franziskan. Forschungen 10 (Werl, 1954), 3–4 (hereafter cited as Dettloff 1). Also in Werner Dettloff, *Die Entwicklung der Akzeptations- und Verdienstlehre von Duns Scotus bei Luther*, Beitr. z. Gesch. d. Philos. und Theol. d. MA 40 (Münster, 1963), 2 (hereafter cited as Dettloff 2). Supplementary observations in Carl Feckes, *Die Rechtfertigungslehre bei Gabriel Biel und ihre Stellung innerhalb der nominalistischen Schule*, Münsterische Beiträge 7 (Münster, 1925); Johann Auer, *Die Entwicklung der Gnadenlehre in der Hochscholastik*, vols. 1 and 2 (Freiburg, 1942–51); and Erwin Iserloh, *Gnade und Eucharistie in der philos. Theologie des Wilhelm von Ockham*, Veröffentlichungen des Instituts für Europäische Geschichte 8 (Mainz, 1956).
339. Dettloff 1:53–54.

nexus of salvation in which the world redeemed by Christ is led toward salvation.[340] The ethical-religious decision of the individual is the human basis of justification.

This approach to the Reformation, however, is blocked by a great chasm. Although late scholasticism varied in its assessment of the role God's grace played in transactions involving merit, all of its branches held human merit to be the indispensable presupposition for divine acceptance; it seemed indispensable because that was the only way to preserve human freedom. Anything else would make the favored human being into a block or a stone.[341] To love is to be free. God has ordered things so that a deed of love meets with divine approval (*acceptatio*); our merit is rewarded *ex gratuita acceptatione divina*. It therefore remains an open question whether, as Thomas taught, the habit of grace which God created brings about the acceptance or whether, following Scotus, its objective basis is laid in the divine ordinance (*potentia ordinata*). Human merit and divine approval work together to the extent that God's will arranges it so. He offers a reward for an act foreseen from eternity which God himself caused.

Luther's doctrine of justification protests against this attribution of merits. When it speaks of imputation, Luther's teaching means something completely different from the attribution that is spoken of in connection with *acceptatio*. The two concepts are intrinsically very similar.[342] Scotus rightly terms as *actus imputabilis* the recognition of human merits that follows acceptance.[343] Attribution of merits and bestowal of divine approval form a single indivisible event. It thus becomes evident that acceptance does not involve a change in the divine will. It is human beings who change by accumulating merits or by working off debts. Thus the forgiveness of sins is not a divine act of grace; it is the recognition, pleasing to God, of a change that human beings undergo intentionally. Ockham was stronger than Scotus in his emphasis on God's making up his own mind on the basis of his *potentia absoluta*. For Ockham, imputation implied liberation from incurring punishment rather than actual remission of sins.[344]

We would go far beyond the bounds of this presentation if we were to follow all the ramifications of the doctrine of imputation and acceptance after Scotus.[345] But it is obvious that Luther—and Melanchthon too, as we shall see—developed their own understanding of justification by coming to grips with that doctrine. To that degree this struggle belongs in a commentary on CA 4.

Luther's first lectures (the earliest lectures on the Psalms and the lectures on Romans) make clear how intensely this discussion with the past stirred him.[346] They show us how early and how consistently Luther pondered over the late medieval tradition.

340. Auer, *Entwicklung* 2:254, shows that in Scotus the structure of the supernatural is shattered and that he "replaces the capacity for grace with the final effect of grace, the divine effect of acceptance." "The analogy of being is broken; faith and knowing are split."

341. As is well known, this analogy used by Scotus (Dettloff 1:67 n. 204) played a significant role in the Flacian controversies.

342. That is the case as early as Rom. 4:5–6 Vulg., where the gracious reckoning of righteousness is rendered as *accepto ferre*.

343. Dettloff 1:120. Cp. Dettloff 2:223, 233, 235, for the references to John of Ripa (ca. 1350); and cp. Dettloff 2:315 for the references to Gregory of Rimini. Dettloff also points out (2:289) later alterations that are sometimes perversions of the Scotist doctrine of acceptance.

344. "Non imputati ad poenam" (Iserloh, *Gnade*, 98). Cp. ibid., 89ff. Then the imputation because of Christ's work follows (ibid., 99). For Biel, see Feckes, *Rechtfertigungslehre*, 94.

345. The treatment of this theme remains an unfulfilled fundamental requirement for the understanding of the Reformation doctrine of justification.

346. Here again we cannot go into all the ramifications; we restrict ourselves to the two concepts in the title of this excursus.

The first statements demonstrate how hackneyed the concepts of the acceptance doctrine had become and how only the minimum content of that doctrine had been maintained. From God's point of view, *acceptare* means that he is pleased to accept the spiritual goods he has given humanity, such as purity of heart, and conscience, and the day of salvation (*tempus acceptum*) he has determined.[347] From the human point of view, *acceptare* denotes the acceptance of the Word of God—the reception of the Spirit as the seal of faith or the reception of absolution (in which the limits of papal power of the keys remain questionable)[348]—and also the acceptance of the external privileges that pagans see as proofs of divine grace, and the acknowledgment of God's law. This application of the cluster of concepts associated with *acceptare* had not become evident in the classical representatives of the theory. These examples demonstrate how vague the outlines of the acceptance doctrine became after Scotus. Luther, however, was acquainted with the whole complex and came to grips with its core despite all the deficiencies of its details. In the process, he rejected Ockham's thesis that acceptance was a pure act of will by means of the *potentia absoluta* without any personal bestowing of justifying grace.[349]

In the background stands Luther's rejection of an abstract, "idle" grace that nullifies the lively, active effectiveness of God's Spirit in the here and now. The struggle against the traditional acceptance theory is thus fueled by specifically religious impulses. The Leipzig disputation resulted in the attack on the "subtlety of Scotus" (*subtilitas Scotica*) that calculates the divine act of acceptance by hairsplitting and makes it depend on human merit; the decisive element is, after all, divine forgiveness.[350] As early as the Heidelberg disputation in 1518, Luther viewed divine forgiveness as the action on which the acceptance or nonacceptance of the sinner depended. God's mercy saves real sinners, not apparent ones. The decisive thing is not the measure of human merit but a declaration of acquittal that rests on Christ's righteousness.[351] Where Luther saw himself differing from the acceptance theory of the late medieval authorities was in his conviction that God forgives sinners out of a free and gracious attitude. Only when *acceptatio* is understood in its biblical context can the concept be used as an expression of the doctrine of justification. Of course it

347. *WA* 3:116.18., 307.34–35. The rich collection of material on this topic at the Institute for the Late Middle Ages and Reformation, at Tübingen, was made available to me by Dr. Oberman, to whom my sincere thanks.

348. *WA* 3:189.22., 336.31, 1:66.1–2, 56:177.31–32, 197.27, 198.3; *LW* 25:158, 180, 181; *WA* 1:585.23ff.; *LW* 31:176. Passages on the *acceptio personarum apud Deum* according to Rom. 2:11 and pars. are out of our purview. See, e.g., *WA* 4:128.35–36, 108.6, 56:21.17, 22.9ff.; *LW* 25:18; *WA* 5:430.15.

349. "God cannot accept man without his justifying grace" (*Disputation Against Scholastic Theology* [1517], thesis 56, *WA* 1:227.4–5). See also *WA* 1:227.1ff.; *LW* 31:13.

350. *WA* 2:420.10ff., 17ff. As late as 1531, in the *Large Commentary on Galatians* (*WA* 40.1:230.14ff.), Luther interpreted the acceptance doctrine accurately, but he rejected its implications for the *merita de condigno* and contrasted it with the teaching of faith.

351. "Therefore, it is the sweetest righteousness of God the Father that he does not save imaginary but saves, rather, real sinners, sustaining us in spite of our sins and accepting our works and our lives, which are all deserving of rejection. . . . I therefore say that every good deed is both accepted and not unaccepted, and on the other hand, that it is not accepted but unaccepted, for he forgives through mercy that which is less worthy of being accepted. This, however, is unaccepted, that is, sin, insofar as it is an action of the malice of the flesh . . . but he pardons and deals sparingly with all our actions. Those opponents of ours, however, imagine that there might be someone whom he would accept without pardon, which is false. When therefore he pardons, he neither accepts nor does not accept, but he pardons" (*WA* 1:370.9ff.; *LW* 31:63–64). Similarly, *WA* 2:420.11ff.

then is also appropriate for the explication of the acceptance doctrine—provided Luther's terms are met and acceptance is understood as God's purely gracious act.

This understanding of imputation can be found as early as 1516 in the exposition of Rom. 4:4. Luther calls the imputation of the righteousness of faith to Abraham an "entirely gracious acceptance on the part of God,"[352] completely disregarding any merit because of works. If the scholastic acceptance doctrine went back to the word *imputare* precisely to denote the imputation of human merits, Luther took the opposite course. God's gracious forgiveness consists in not reckoning sins; we become righteous through the imputation of faith.[353] The contrast to the scholastics is that they make grace into a duty. God's acceptance, however, does not rest on external fulfillment of the law.[354] Here in the lectures on Romans we can already see the way being paved for the explanation of the doctrine of imputation that we heard in Luther's sermons around 1530: sins that still cling to us after we believe in forgiveness are covered by Christ's righteousness and are not charged against those who believe in him.[355]

Thus Luther's adoption and reinterpretation of the acceptance doctrine stays the same from his first lectures to his commentary on Galatians. That is an indication of how deeply he is imbued with the doctrine of imputation.

Before we close this circle from 1516 to 1531, let us make a few spot checks on the course of development taken by the two terms in this excursus during the period of time under study.[356] In the *Works on the Psalms*,[357] we recognize how markedly the derivatives of *acceptare*[358] give way to the simple *accipere*, thus emphasizing pure receptivity toward God.[359] The believer receives spiritual benefits that go beyond those directed toward salvation, as in traditional teaching, and that reach into life itself: the grace we receive works, keeping us in communion with God. God himself becomes our inheritance. Humble faith receives the Holy Spirit who produces new powers that in turn evoke the grateful proclamation of grace and make people gentle and meek.[360]

"God, who tests and searches hearts, accepts."[361] This "acceptance" is more definitely a juridical act than it is in Scotus. God not only establishes a person's "status" but also draws consequences for acceptance or rejection. Grace and judgment intertwine, but in such a way that forgiving mercy has the lead. *Acceptatio* sets up a living relationship between God and humanity, with God providing the mediation

352. ". . . acceptance solely through the graciousness of God" (*WA* 56:41.22; *LW* 25:36).

353. *WA* 56:271.20–21.; *LW* 25:259.

354. "Nor does he want to accept the law as being fulfilled according to the substance of the act" (*WA* 56:279.5–6.; *LW* 25:266).

355. *WA* 56:347.9ff.; *LW* 25:336. See also (continuing the quotation in n. 351) *WA* 1:370.27–28 (*LW* 31:64): "And thus he accepts his own mercy in our works, that is, the countenance of Job, namely, the righteousness of Christ for us [Job 42:8]. For this is the propitiation of God who forgives and makes pardonable our actions. . . ."

356. Because we discussed *imputatio* in detail earlier (above, p. 332), we concentrate here on *acceptatio*.

357. 1519–21.

358. *Acceptatio* occurs only once, and then in an allegorical interpretation of Ps. 3:4 (*WA* 5:84.6ff.); it is never used in a scholastic sense.

359. "We are his vessels and instruments; we neither receive nor give any power unless he himself gives it or receives" (ibid., 258.40–41).

360. Ibid., 522.30, 454.38, 559.12ff., 663.30, 553.38, 128.21.

361. Ibid., 237.14.

through Christ and his Word. Christ's words must be taken as simply as possible; unbelievers hear them but do not accept them.[362] In the *acceptatio* human beings are accepted by God, and themselves receive divine grace. Thus there is no earning of merit or divine recognition of merit, as in scholasticism; there is an exchange in which God acts graciously and human beings accept this divine act in faith. Tied in with this transformation of the original doctrine is the reduction of the artificially construed *acceptatio* into a simple *accipere* (*recipere*). The "received into favor" of CA 4 is an expression of this simplification. The question of the apostle Paul "What have you that you have not received?"[363] is in fact the simplest guide to the core of justification.

As is well known, Luther illustrated the gift character of the Sacrament by interpreting the words of institution as a testamentary promise, particularly in *The Babylonian Captivity*. Here *acceptare* refers unequivocally to the person who is given a gift despite any unworthiness. The promise "believe and receive" is an indivisible unit.[364] It seems as though Luther, here at the climax of his Reformation battle, completely forgets the acceptance doctrine that was transmitted to him during his student years.

That was not the case, however, as demonstrated by the controversy with Jacob Latomus that Luther carried on during his stay in the Wartburg in 1521. In contrast to his Louvain opponent, Luther did not hesitate to take up the old weapons, partly to reforge them but also to wield them against the received theology. For him, as for Scotus much earlier, Christ is the prototype of humanity accepted by God; as the source of grace, he is "alone pleasing and acceptable among mankind."[365] Likewise, the accepted person is received in grace and stands fully in God's favor. As early as 1516 and 1518, Luther's polemical writings[366] asserted that in God there is no longer any vacillation between acceptance and rejection. The person as a whole is pardoned; there is no longer any possible reason for God's wrath. "The total person is totally accepted and sanctified." Sin still remaining in the justified is "sin without wrath."[367] In this context, justification seems to be a process that begins in communion with Christ and is completed in him, but that could never be content with a one-time acceptance.[368]

The samplings we have taken from Luther's writing before 1521 show that the reformer never adopted the acceptance doctrine uncritically, but that even when he used the customary terminology he reinterpreted it in the sense of his own doctrines of justification and grace. *Acceptatio* is reception into the state of salvation; the meaning of this doctrine is that the Christian has only what has been received. For years Luther used *acceptare* only in this sense. In the process the meaning has shifted completely. It is not God who accepts humanity; this sense is retained only in the formal parallelism

362. Ibid., 439.15, 138.32.

363. 1 Cor. 4:7; *WA* 5:169.23ff. Cp. ibid., 258.40–41.

364. *WA* 6:517.38ff., 519.34ff., 520.27ff. (= *BoA* 1:449.23ff., 451.34ff., 452.31ff.); *LW* 36:43, 46, 47.

365. Dettloff 1:184ff.; *WA* 8:106.25ff.; *LW* 32:228.

366. See above, p. 337.

367. *WA* 8:107.1ff.; *LW* 32:228.

368. "Not to stop with what has been received" (*WA* 8:111.34; *LW* 32:235). Cp. *WA* 8:31ff. That the *acceptatio*—in contrast to a self-willed vow—is an intentional and continuing process is described by Luther, in *On Monastic Vows* (1521), with reference to the sacraments (*WA* 8:661.36–37. [= *BoA* 2:291.29–30]; *LW* 44:389): "We are always quite sure what to receive or suffer, and that is things from God." See also the catechetical sermon of May 28, 1528 (*WA* 30.1:22.20): "Baptism, that is, receiving, lasts continually through all of life."

of *iustus* and *acceptus*. It is rather human beings, justified by God, who accept the gifts of grace to which God has given them access.

Of course, when Luther defends his doctrine of justification, he deals with the scholastic theory of acceptance, and in a polemic way. The controversy with Latomus in 1521 represents only one episode. The conventional scholastic wisdom on this subject did not catch Luther's attention again until the negotiations at the Augsburg diet, when the debate over fundamental principles flared up and Luther took the first steps toward joining it by planning a work on justification. He immediately picked up the controversy again with his second *Commentary on Galatians* in 1531.

Luther's battle, as always, was against the doctrine of merit. Neither those merits that are based on our natural abilities prior to the reception of grace (*merita de congruo*) nor those that come later through the cooperation of grace (*merita de condigno*)—in short, no good works—are accepted by God; nor do they open the way to an inflowing of justifying grace. Justification, therefore, is not an inherent quality of the heart; such a quality could not be called righteousness in any formal sense. That would contradict the teaching of the apostle Paul. It is a monstrosity of the sophists. Luther's students are to understand those doctrines—not, of course, to approve them—but to be able to carry on the battle against their milder forms as presented in Scotus and Ockham.[369]

This polemic against the scholastic acceptance doctrine also included a critique of its understanding of imputation. Both ideas are contrary to Scripture because they refer to meritorious works. These works result in the *acceptatio;* and the imputation takes them into account without considering that the heart is corrupted by sin even when no major vices are apparent. This view sees imputation and acceptance as inseparable; the first is the presupposition for the second. Luther, however, takes the opposite view in both cases. He is not concerned with an acceptance of works (*acceptatio operis*). For him *acceptatio* refers only to Christ, for whose sake God accepts the sinner.[370] Imputation does not mean taking moral achievement into account but rather means the regular overlooking of our defects and crediting of our faith in Christ. Our righteousness is God's fusing together of the faith of our hearts and his own imputation. "Christian righteousness before God is to believe in the Son."[371]

Thus the connection between imputation and acceptance for Luther is completely different from that of scholasticism, because he excludes the idea of merit. *Acceptatio* and *reputatio, fides* and *Christus*, belong together. Faith clings to Christ, and because of this faith the believer is recognized as righteous. "Therefore God accepts, that is reckons, you as righteous solely because of Christ in whom you believe."[372] To this positive imputation of Christ, Luther connects the nonimputation of sins; this too he can call *acceptatio*.[373] Sin still clings to believers; in this life believers are never pure in

---

369. *WA* 40.1:225.15ff., 226.20; *LW* 26:127, 128 (cited from the printed edition of 1535, which modifies Rörer's manuscript in some details). In similar statements (*WA* 40.1:230.3ff., 17ff.; *LW* 26:130), Luther seems to approve the content of *acceptatio* (*WA* 40.1:231.14–15; *LW* 26:131), but he calls its connection to a system of infused grace and works a "dream." Cp. Luther's positive verdict on *acceptatio* further on (*WA* 40.1:233.7; *LW* 26:132).

370. God says, "If you wish to placate me, believe in my Son who was born, suffered . . ." (*WA* 40.1:365.12; *LW* 26:231). *Deum placere*, therefore, means to make oneself pleasing to God, so that he accepts you.

371. "Therefore faith begins righteousness, and imputation perfects it until that day. Therefore righteousness is divinely united out of faith from the heart and imputation from God" (*WA* 40.1:364.8ff.). For the paragraph, cp. ibid., 364.2–366.10.

372. *WA* 40.1:233.23–24; *LW* 26:132. On the whole subject, see *WA* 40.1:233.2–234.5; *LW* 26:132–33.

373. *WA* 40.1:233.25ff.; *LW* 26:132.

themselves; God must continually see to their purification. We always have recourse to Christ as the guarantor of our forgiveness. A Christian, therefore, is not someone who has no sin or who does not even feel it, but someone to whom it is not imputed. Weak faith cannot exist without such nonimputation; it cannot come to fulfillment.[374] If we inquire about the basis for such a transformation of the scholastic acceptance doctrine, Luther himself gives us the answer. All distortions of the doctrine of grace, works, and merits are like heads of the same serpent. This evil creature is called reason.[375] The rational thought of theologians trained in classical philosophy collides with Luther's biblically nourished concreteness. Luther's theology attributes everything to inconceivable grace and unprovable faith. It sees acceptance as an inducement to faith, by which in turn God makes everything acceptable and pleasing to himself.[376] It sets up an image of the way of salvation, beginning with initial grace (*prima gratis*) that makes the individual pleasing to God and that proves itself in grateful love toward God and the neighbor.[377] Pleasing and acceptable—that describes both the Christian who lives in faith and the martyr who dies in faith.[378]

This excursus was necessary for a proper understanding of Melanchthon's doctrine of imputation in relation to Luther's. We have already said a little about its beginnings. It is evident that it presupposes the late scholastic acceptance doctrine, either in its original form or in the recast form we have met in Luther's work. The question is whether Melanchthon developed the doctrine further or whether he simply passed on the tradition. It would be a mistake at this point to say that Melanchthon had a special doctrine of justification in contrast to Luther's, as has been the custom since Holl; one must always keep in mind that both Wittenbergers were dependent upon the scholastic doctrines of imputation and acceptance.

One can begin with the *Dispositio* of 1529–30—that is, before the composition of the CA, where this dependence is already apparent. The Pauline statements in Romans 4 provide the starting point.[379] According to them, *imputatio* refers initially to the person who is to be justified; it signifies the gracious nonimputation of that person's sins. Only in this way does it become sufficiently clear that law and good works contribute nothing to justification.[380] This is the sign of the divine intention to justify—not by compensating for human sins and thus providing a reason for their nonimputation—that exists only in the divine will to forgive. The divine will foresees that sin will always cling to human fleshly existence, but it also sees that it will

---

374. "Faith begins righteousness and imputation perfects it until the day of Christ" (*WA* 40.1:364.27–28; *LW* 26:230). For that reason, Luther speaks of a "free imputation" (*WA* 40.1:43.24; *LW* 26:6). There is just no element of calculating credit in Luther's theological thought.

375. ". . . which is the fountainhead of all evils" (*WA* 40.1:365.18; *LW* 26:230).

376. ". . . the excellence of faith, which makes everyone pleasing and acceptable to God" (*WA* 43:328.32; *LW* 4:269).

377. *WA* 43:606.37ff., 614.19–20; *LW* 5:258, 269.

378. *WA* 43:607.25, 625.23, 646.8; *LW* 5:259, 285, 315.

379. *CR* 15:453ff.

380. Ibid., 451–52.

nevertheless reach the goal of the law, which is blessedness, just as it is still able to fulfill the Ten Commandments in the power of the Spirit.[381]

For Luther the cause of the imputation was the righteousness of the believer, even though it was only a start and needed to be completed. What still remained was not imputed; the process of justification seemed to be an unending one that, because of our faith, God considers already completed.[382] Melanchthon interprets the whole process from the point of view of fulfilling the law. Even where empirical persons in an attitude of faith have not completely fulfilled the law, that perfection is granted. God sees the law as a whole in circumstances where a person has fulfilled only part of it. In that case God contents himself with recognizing the new spiritual stirrings that faith has aroused, just as the faithful believer recognizes the whole will of God, despite individual mistakes he has made.

In this event of justification—encompassing human faith and the nonimputation of remaining sin—Melanchthon finds the Pauline answer to the Anselmian question, Why did Christ come?[383] Through his death, the Son offered satisfaction for sins and thereby assured that the law could be fulfilled before God and for humankind.[384] That is the objective background on which that fulfilling of the law rests.

It is questionable whether a doctrine of imputation rooted in this understanding of the law can be related to acceptance. That would be possible only if one could render reception into divine favor by means of the biblical concept of atonement. Melanchthon says of the faith that lets itself be accepted in grace, "This faith appeases God's wrath."[385] "Received into favor," *in gratiam recipi*, is a formula for justification in CA 4.2 which we have already noted as appearing in the *Dispositio* (see above, pp. 300–301). If it is also identical with "appease God," then Melanchthon has tied imputation to the Anselmian doctrine of atonement as well as to the late medieval doctrine of acceptance, admittedly in such a way that it is not identical with the motifs of either. Instead, in this early phase of his development he interprets it out of his understanding of the law and thus takes over the concepts of the medieval tradition while completely reinterpreting their content.

In the *Apology*, from the winter of 1530–31, three new points of departure may be observed:

381. "But whoever believes in Christ is already righteous before God, so you have the end of the law even though sin still clings to your flesh" (ibid., 452).

382. As Holl rightly stated, although he overlooked the importance of the idea of imputation.

383. *CR* 15:444–45. Paul wrote to the Romans, "that he might teach the chief article of Christian doctrine not only to the Romans but to the whole church. For if one is not acquainted with this article it is impossible to understand why Christ came" (ibid., 445).

384. Ibid., 467, 482.

385. Ibid., 444. Cp. the bottom of ibid., 453 on the faith of the pre-Christian Abraham— "faith which believes God to be satisfied, propitiated, which trusts in the help of God." This faith includes (ibid., 454) "that the Father receives us into favor."

1. Here the concept of imputation is explained in a way that leads to a juridical connection with the law. Imputation becomes a "forensic" act; God as judge acquits the sinner and declares the sinner righteous.[386]

2. In this act the "alien righteousness" of Christ is communicated to the sinner through faith.[387] Although in the *Dispositio* (1529–30) imputation was, as formerly in Luther, the nonimputation of sin still clinging to the believer, now just one year later Melanchthon sees it as an imputation of a righteousness not originally belonging to the believer but won by Christ. There is still no talk of the merit of Christ, but there is talk of his obedience—typically, indeed, obedience "to the gospel"; in that way, faith took on Christ's saving deed.[388] Just as in Luther's picture of the joyous exchange, here in Melanchthon an exchange takes place between Christ, the rich bridegroom, and the believing soul, the poor little whore, who receives spiritual goods from him. The exchange, however, is not made at a joyful wedding; it is a legal transaction in which God rewards faith by imputing to it what still remains to fulfill the law—whereby God himself makes full satisfaction to the law.

3. The imputation of Christ's alien righteousness thus makes no essential change in the believer and therefore it does not initiate an effective renewal. What does occur is described in the *Apology*[389] by means of acceptance language. Imputed righteousness signifies "that we are made acceptable to God".[390] The phraseology that Melanchthon uses here sounds Scotist. But the meaning he attaches to it points to God's ordinance of grace, as in Luther, although it is true that Melanchthon sees that idea of ordinance as primarily directed toward the law—as was the case with Scotus.

That becomes apparent, as we have seen,[391] through the fact that righteousness is brought into connection with obedience to the gospel. Indeed obedience to the law and the righteousness of the law that grows out of it are imperfect and are unacceptable to God; they do not reconcile us with him, nor do they make us acceptable to him. The reconciled person is thus the accepted person; *acceptatio* equals *reconciliatio*.[392] For the Melanchthon of 1531, therefore, the acceptance doctrine flows into the doctrine of reconciliation, but both are directed toward total fulfillment of the law. Faith that receives the forgiveness of sins constitutes this reconciliation and effects this fulfillment; all three elements make us acceptable to God.[393]

386. See Apology IV, sec. 305 (BC 154), on Rom. 5:1: "In this passage, 'justify' is used in a judicial way to mean 'to absolve a guilty man and pronounce him righteous.' "

387. The "for Christ's sake" of CA 4 becomes in Apology IV, sec. 305 (*BC* 154) "on account of someone else's righteousness, namely, Christ's, which is communicated to us by faith."

388. Apology IV, secs. 306, 308 (*BC* 154, 155).

389. Ibid., sec. 307 (*BC* 154).

390. ". . . by it we are made acceptable to God because of God's imputation and ordinances" (ibid.).

391. See above, #2.

392. Apology IV, secs. 181–82 (*BS* 196.14ff.; *BC* 132).

393. *Acceptos Deo*, in Apology IV, secs. 112–16 (*BC* 123). Cp. sec. 86 (*BC* 119).

Thus, in the *Apology*, Melanchthon continued the course Luther had begun, linking the doctrine of reconciliation to imputation and building it fully into the acceptance doctrine. In the process he completely transformed the latter, but he did follow Duns Scotus in directing it totally toward the fulfillment of the law. Then in his commentary on Romans of 1532, one year after the publication of the *Apology*, Melanchthon further shaped the doctrine of imputation in the light of his earlier synthesis.

In the *argumentum* that Melanchthon puts at the beginning of his exposition of Romans, he brings all three elements together in the definition of his doctrine of justification. Righteousness means "that man is reconciled to God and reckoned as just, that is, acceptable to God and a son of God because of Christ through mercy and that this mercy is certain, and that it must be established by faith that we have certainly been accepted because of Christ."[394] Here *reconciliatio, imputatio,* and *acceptatio* are inseparably united in a way that gives them fresh nuances of meaning.

1. We encounter the equation "reconciliation, that is, acceptance." Human beings become acceptable to God and received into communion with him not through an inconceivable and unprovable act of will but through the mercy of God, to which he himself testifies in his Word, grounded in biblical history and still active in the history of the contemporary community.[395] To be received into this historical connection is the fulfillment of acceptance in its simplest and unscholastic form, as we found it presented in the "received into favor" of CA 4,[396] and as it repeatedly comes up in the formal equation of *iusti* with *accepti*.

By being embedded in the reconciliation through Christ, the late medieval *acceptatio* is brought into relationship with God's loving will instead of merely with his historical activity. Scotus's God of philosophy becomes again the zealous God of the Old Testament, who not only punishes sin but also lets himself be reconciled for Christ's sake, and who makes peace.[397] By receiving a person into communion with himself, God brings peace and creates a good conscience. Originally so abstract, in its reinterpreted Reformation form the acceptance doctrine moves closer to life and to reality.

2. Then there is the equation of reconciliation with imputation. Both concepts refer to the forgiveness of sin that is granted the sinner on the basis of the promise of faith and the mercy of God demonstrated in Christ. For Melanchthon this cluster of terms expresses the proper meaning of the

394. StA 5:32.21ff.

395. " . . . wherefore the gospel proclaims another sort of righteousness, which is reconciliation or acceptance through mercy" (ibid., 124.18ff.).

396. Cp. StA 5:135.18.

397. Ibid., 66.13ff. Cp. ibid., 136.12ff.: in the controversy over good works, the issue is "how God's wrath is to be satisfied."

righteousness of faith.[398] In this way he keeps the tightest possible hold on the forensic meaning of imputation precisely because of its polemical value against the medieval doctrine of infusion. Faith is not a new quality to be assessed, given on the basis of achievements or merits.[399] Rather imputation itself is an expression of divine mercy; to trust in that mercy means to be reconciled and to be made pleasing to God (*reconciliari et acceptari*).[400]

For Melanchthon, as for Luther, *imputatio* in the sense of the nonimputation of sin is associated with the ongoing impurity of the believer. But in contrast to Luther, Melanchthon sees the imputation as filling up what is lacking, so that perfection before God might be restored. Nevertheless, we still await complete renewal. We are righteous only in faith and hope. Justification is an eschatological event. Before it occurs, sin and faith work themselves out side by side. The more faith grows, the more sin is repressed; this happens through God's wrath and punishment.[401] The dialectical tension of the "sinner and saint at the same time" is not maintained by the simultaneity of God's judging and gracious will, as is the case in Luther. Instead it is dissolved through a process in which successive purifications correspond to the gradual growth of faith. Melanchthon was certainly sensitive to the fact that this could lead his doctrine of justification back into scholastic tracks. He avoids this danger by drawing, of all things, on the late scholastic concept of *acceptatio* in Luther's modified sense. Although sin continues to reign, we trust "that we are righteous, that is, accepted, not because of our renewal but for Christ's sake."[402]

In that way the paradoxical tension of the Lutheran doctrine of justification is basically broken. Our still-sinful natures really have no further role to play after God has acquitted us. The law thus attains its ultimate recognition, not by us—because of our continuing sinfulness—but in God's steadfast will to accept. That same will also forms the basis for the constant divine forgiveness by which God's justifying verdict removes our ever-present weakness; his mercy makes us acceptable to him despite our persistent unworthiness and impurity. Forgiveness of sin and acceptance are likewise enduring and constant.[403]

3. Thus in 1532, *reconciliatio*, *acceptatio*, and *imputatio*—three entirely biblical terms—become a tightly braided wreath in Melanchthon's doctrine

398. Ibid., 159.17, 141.24.

399. Ibid., 106.20ff. Ibid., 107.1ff., shows that Melanchthon drew the "forensic" idea out of the tradition.

400. Ibid., 101.1ff. On the threefold meaning of *reputatio* which also manifests its giftedness, see ibid., 101.26ff.

401. Ibid., 159.34ff.

402. ". . . righteous, that is, accepted, not because of our new nature but because of Christ" (ibid., 160.18–19).

403. Ibid., 134.6ff.

of justification. The latter two terms obtained their specific nuances in the late scholastic period; the idea of reconciliation was decisively shaped during high scholasticism by Anselm and Peter Lombard. Luther decidedly recast all three on the basis of his scriptural understanding, and Melanchthon built on those presuppositions. Basically, therefore, he did not differ from the reformer.

The doctrines of acceptance and imputation in particular were not just developed after the Augsburg diet in contrast to Luther. Both doctrines were already in evidence before Augsburg and were more fully defined in agreement with Luther. That is particularly true of imputation as presented in the *Apology*. Both of these originally late scholastic concepts were employed in the controversy with Counter-Reformation theology. The battle began right after the end of the negotiations in Augsburg and was fought principally over the doctrine of justification. In the years that followed, the doctrine itself remained in the form it had received in the Augsburg Confession, but it was developed further for polemical purposes. For that reason it was right and necessary that a historical commentary on the Confession should describe the first steps in that direction.

Luther and Melanchthon took these steps together, but the major burden of the technical discussion fell on Melanchthon. We must credit him with conducting it in his own way, both in form and in content. Thereby certain nuancing took place. In our exegesis of his writings between 1529–30 and 1531–32 we have just shown how this nuancing affected the three concepts we have been discussing. The results may be summarized in thesis form:

1. In the doctrine of reconciliation, Melanchthon relied more heavily on Anselm, although he did not adopt the basic thesis of *Cur Deus homo*. Instead, he basically remained attached to Luther's concept of the joyous exchange, even though he rationalized it and eliminated the imagery.

2. In the doctrine of imputation, Melanchthon brings out the forensic side of justification more clearly after 1532—although not yet in the *Apology*. Probably because of the immutable validity of the law, however, he makes no attempt to base the necessity for this doctrine on the continuing presence of sin in the believer. It is employed instead simply as a protection against misunderstanding grace and faith as substances. There is a connection in method between this abstract interpretation of imputation and its original understanding in scholasticism.

3. In contrast to this conception, and in heavy reliance on Luther, Melanchthon understood the doctrine of acceptance as purely a doctrine of grace. Acceptance by God is, although not initially and not exclusively, an expression of justification.

4. Melanchthon did what Luther consciously did not do: he maneuvered

these three traditional doctrinal complexes so close to one another that they largely overlapped. In that process the most strongly biblical idea, *reconciliatio*, showed the greatest power of assimilation. That means that *acceptatio* lost its abstract character and took on elements of biblical saving history; the same may be said for *imputatio*.

16. FAITH AND WORKS (CA 5, 6)

Article 5 of the Augustana ("On the Preaching Office," *De ministerio ecclesiastico*) and article 6 ("On the New Obedience," *De nova oboedientia*) further develop the thought of CA 4. The two articles are to be read in the light of the statements in CA 4.2 and 3, on the nature and effect of faith. They continue the train of thought by answering the questions, How do we obtain such faith? (CA 5) and, What are its fruits? (CA 6).

When Luther was formulating his concluding confession in the conflict over the Lord's Supper early in 1528, the present structure of thought in CA 4–6 had not been developed. Of course the question about the cause of faith had already been raised: the creator of faith and of all the spiritual gifts connected with it is the Holy Spirit. Luther did not consider any institutional intermediary. He says, "For this is our assurance if we feel this witness of the Spirit in our hearts, that God wishes to be our Father, forgive our sin, and bestow everlasting life on us."[404] Thus the inner effect of the Spirit by means of faith remains in the foreground, and the external mediation through the spoken Word and the physical sacraments is traced back to the Spirit.[405]

In his confession, Luther speaks of the "ministry of the Word" (*Pfarramt* or *Dienst des Worts*) in connection with the three hierarchies that God has established as "holy orders and true institutions" (cp. above, p. 22, and below, p. 383). Here the office of preaching, together with marriage and temporal authority, is subordinated to the "common order of Christian love."[406] The idea that a way to salvation would be opened thereby is expressly excluded; that happens only through faith in Jesus Christ. Even the godless can dabble in the "holy things" connected with the preaching office. The bishops or pastors are not "heads or lords or bridegrooms" of the church but "servants, friends, and—as the word 'bishop' implies—superintendents, guardians, or stewards."[407]

404. *WA* 26:505.29ff. (= *BoA* 3:511.12ff.); *LW* 37:365.

405. *WA* 26:506.10–29 (= *BoA* 3:511.35–512.13); *LW* 37:366–67. The anti-Donatist orientation is indeed applied to the preaching of the gospel, but still Spirit and faith are only loosely connected with that preaching; at any rate, they are not made an indispensable condition for its reception. See below, pp. 360ff.

406. About the same time, Luther used this subordination as the basis for the visitations (*WA* 26:197.20; *LW* 40:271).

407. *WA* 26:504.31ff., 505.11ff., 506.33ff. (= *BoA* 3:510.18ff., 512.17ff.); *LW* 37:364, 365, 367. On the doctrine of the hierarchies, see below, n. 471.

We must admit that in his Confession of 1528, Luther did differentiate between the preaching office as an office of temporal order and as an institution mediating spirit and faith, but he did not explain the connection between them. Even the Augustana did not achieve complete clarity on this point. Melanchthon made his own task easier during editorial work at Augsburg by inserting a new article, CA 14, which forms a transition to the questions of order in CA 15 (cp. above, p. 187).

In the *Instructions for the Visitors* of 1528, a literal interpretation can pose an obstacle to understanding the genesis of justifying faith. The visitation was seen primarily as a project for educating the people. The poor condition of public life in general was attributed to previous degeneration of this function. Preaching was expected to improve the situation—hence Melanchthon's controversial, but ultimately successful, demand that the preaching of the gospel be tied to preaching of the law and penitence. The children must be taught to make confession. Urging good works was to take precedence over preaching the gospel and forgiveness. The effect of this preaching is more to awaken "serious and genuine repentance and fear of God" than to bring "peace, comfort, and joy."[408]

The development of the later so-called Schwabach Articles during the summer of 1529, which was nearly at the climax of the conflict with the enthusiasts, explains the passion and detail with which Schwab. 6 and 7 treat the effect and cause (the sequence is reversed from that of CA 5 and 6) of justifying faith. But the fight against works righteousness is also emphasized strongly. That occurs at the beginning of Schwab. 6: no human effort can produce faith in us. It is God's work and a gift of the Holy Spirit, who is given through Christ.[409] Thus the pneumatological themes that Luther had put forward in his confession of the previous year are picked up again. They are also continued in Schwab. 6 in relation to the fruits that the Spirit produces through faith: praise and thanks for God, love and service for the neighbor.

Thus Schwab. 6 prefigures the structure of cause and effect that later will shape CA 5 and 6. In this connection Schwab. 7 is almost superfluous. It would be no more than that if it were not considered in relation to Schwab. 8 and 11. Then the emphasis in Schwab. 7 falls on the institution of the "preaching office, or the oral Word"; the connection with obtaining justifying faith is only a rhetorical link. Gospel and sacraments in Schwab. 7–11 are defined in the sense of Luther's Confession of 1528 as means of salvation.[410] In this context the allusion to obtaining justifying faith is appropriate.

In the final version of CA 5, as indicated by its title, "On the Preaching

---

408. *WA* 26:195–96, 202, 219.9, 227.6, 203.21ff.; *LW* 40:269, 274, 295, 303, 276.
409. Cp. the beginning of Schwab. 5.
410. *WA* 26:506.10ff. (= *BoA* 3:511.35ff.); *LW* 37:366.

Office," this allusion from Schwab. 7 gets far too much emphasis. Basically Schwab. 7, like Luther's confession and Schwab. 6, points to the Spirit-engendered Word as the source of faith and its fruits.

The redundancies and obscurities of Schwab. 6 and 7 make it clear why Melanchthon undertook major abridgments and revisions on both articles during the first weeks in Augsburg. Thus in Na 4 the connection with justifying faith is loosened in style and content; there is a one-sided emphasis on opposition to the spiritualism of the Anabaptists. The article continues the practice of Luther's confession in referring to Word and Sacrament. Reordering puts Na 4 ahead of Na 5, which is on justification. More closely than in Schwab. 7, Word and Sacrament are set forth as the sole means of grace.

Article 6 of Na posits the connection between justifying faith and good works without giving a theological explanation for it. As in Schwab. 5, the meritorious character of works is vigorously denied, although no direct borrowings from Schwab. 5 can be detected.

The manuscript Nb—drafted in the middle of June and taken over in the German version of CA 5 and 6 almost without change—shows crucial alterations. It is significant that Nb establishes the present sequence of the two articles; it makes a clear distinction between the cause (Nb 5) and the fruit (Nb 6) of faith. In addition we can see a stronger reliance on Schwab. 6 and 7 for individual formulations, although there is an unmistakable tightening in style.

Article 5 of Nb (equivalent to CA 5 German) adopts the beginning of Schwab. 7 by equating the preaching office and the "oral word" (that is, the gospel) and adding the sacraments. In Schwab. 7 (cp. Nb 6), the description of the gospel still referred to the effects of faith, but Nb 5 limits itself to the origin of faith out of Word and Spirit, rejecting other means more specifically than Schwab. 7 did. It is in this connection that the Augustana first talks about the merits of Christ, which are contrasted with human merit. That is a noteworthy extension of the basic thought of CA 4. The Latin version of CA 5 somewhat obscures this extension by simply repeating formulations from the Latin version of CA 4.2. The added condemnation of the Anabaptists in Nb 5 was foreshadowed, in content at least, by the conclusion of Schwab. 7.

Compared with Na 4, article 5 of Nb represents an obvious move back toward Schwab. 7; at the same time it sounds very like what became the definitive version in CA 4; in fact it partially surpasses CA 4. Article 4 of Na remains one-sided in its concentration on Word and Sacrament as the means of grace that awakens faith, thus staying completely in line with Luther's Confession of 1528. In its repudiation of the Anabaptists, Na remains in the tradition stemming from Luther; the content of the rejection reminds one of the end of Schwab. 7.

Thus the editing we see in Nb 5 has brought something decidedly new out of the article; it is tightly written and packed with several theological topics. Article 6 of Nb makes a weaker impression. It depends directly on Na 6; there are few borrowings from Schwab. 6. The rejection of faith as a human work, which stands at the beginning of Nb 6, forms its real subject and takes up a lot of space. In the process the description of justification gets a new expression. Further, the rejection of human merit is underlined in the final version of the article by the citation from Luke 17:10. Preparatory work for Nb 6 limited itself to one quotation from Ambrosiaster's commentary on 1 Corinthians. It was used later and came to be seen as a patristic summary of the doctrine of justification. This is notable also because it is only here in connection with this doctrine that we find a specific reference to "faith alone." From this we may assume that by the end of May, Melanchthon had come to see the present articles CA 4, 5, and 6 as a unit.[411]

The concluding editorial work on the Latin version of CA 5 and 6 is principally stylistic in character. The cumbersome sentence structure in the major part of CA 5 (= Nb 5) is simplified. Turning the first clause (sec. 1) into an independent sentence creates an important statement about the ministry of the church, but the relation of that ministry to justifying faith is presented in a fairly complicated way (sec. 2; cp. above, p. 349). Although the institution of the office seems basic to obtaining the Spirit (according to sec. 1), it is (according to sec. 2) Word and sacraments as instruments of the Spirit that produce faith through the hearing of the gospel. In that sequence the institution of the office starts the chain, but it does not initiate anything, particularly when everything depends on the sovereign and unfathomable will of God, which lets the Spirit work "where and when it pleases God." Thus God cannot be institutionalized in this chain that leads to faith. Instead it points to the next links after the office, to Word and Sacrament; they are instruments not of what is human but of the Holy Spirit. He is the decisive member; faith is worked through him. How the Spirit uses the Word as his instrument remains an open question; the one thing established is that it is a matter of the "physical," externally audible Word. The clarification brought by stylistic improvements in the Latin version does not eliminate the unanswered questions.

Article 6 of Na presupposed "good works" as the result of justifying faith, and required them. Since Luther's sermon of the same name in 1520, the good works commanded in the Decalogue were put in an indissoluble connection with faith. Article 6 of Nb added to them the "fruits" of faith that had already been mentioned in Schwab. 6 and 7. This parallelism of "good fruits"

411. For CA 20, see below, p. 351.

and "good works" was established as a divine postulate in Nb 6. Only during the final editing of the Latin version did the editor have to become aware of the difference between fruit and work. He speaks—without any analogy in the German text—about "bringing forth fruits," thus letting the "fruits" arise out of the creative power of the Spirit. On the other hand, he traces "works" back to the divine command one must fulfill for God's sake. This legalistic side of the matter occurs only in Na and Nb. If Melanchthon—who is certainly the final editor—supplements that side by reference to the productive power of the Spirit, he is touching on a problem of his theology of the Spirit that has concerned him from the beginning:[412] that of how the working of the Spirit and obedience to the law fit together. In CA 6, he only indicates this problem; he does not solve it. It reaches deep into his understanding of justification.[413]

We have already dealt with the development of CA 20 insofar as it discusses the major themes of the doctrine of justification (above, pp. 305–7). According to its own title, however, the article deals with the relation between "faith and good works." To what degree does the history of the text also consider this relationship?

Neither in the available preparatory work for the Torgau Articles nor in CA 20 itself do we find any systematic development of the relationship. In fact, at first both documents seem to present a work ethic based solely on law—one that is not directly connected to justifying faith. They also emphasize heavily that it is inadequate for attaining salvation. To some degree the line of thought is related to that of Na 6, both in the legalistic basis for good works and in the rejection of works righteousness. The final version of CA 20 differs from its predecessors—although it is, at the latest, contemporaneous with Na—only in its fuller presentation of the doctrine of justification (secs. 9, 10) and in the citations from tradition, where the final Latin version supplements Pseudo-Ambrose with Pseudo-Augustine (secs. 12–14).

Despite this somewhat wooden and mechanical stringing together of elements we have seen elsewhere, the final version does try to derive good works from faith and prides itself on being able to show "how good works may be done" (sec. 35). It does that by referring to the Holy Spirit, who is received by faith, renews hearts, and awakens new stirrings in them, so that good works are brought forth.[414] Following Pseudo-Ambrose, faith is called the "mother of the good will and the right deed" (sec. 30), a reference to the patristic sources of the Melanchthonian doctrine of the Spirit. The conclu-

412. Cp. W. Maurer, *Der junge Melanchthon* (cited above, n. 150), 2:385ff.

413. The changes in the Latin text cited here are to be dated relatively late. They are not in Sp. and A I, but of course those documents also lack the quotation from Ambrosiaster that was already available in May, so they are certainly not complete.

414. Sec. 29: "to bring forth good works." This is similar to the Latin text of CA 6.

sion of the first draft (*BS* 81.26ff.) already used the Pauline doctrine of the Spirit in a sense that depicts the Holy Spirit more as a protective force than a productive one. The sequence transmitted by Wackernagel shows the same interpretation. How good works come forth from the Spirit is not really made clear in the article.

It is questionable whether and to what extent CA 21 ("The Cult of Saints") is connected to justification. For example, if one looks at Luther's Confession of 1528 on veneration of the saints,[415] it is clear that issues of church order are central. The rejection of indulgences leads to hesitation on intercession for the dead, and this abstinence in turn forbids invocation of the saints (cp. above, pp. 293–94). Luther, however, reserves his own judgment and cites with approval the criticism by unnamed predecessors: one thinks immediately of Wycliffites, Hussites, and perhaps even of Münzer's rejection of the veneration of saints. But in this connection we need to remember the riots over images in order to understand that these liturgical questions could lead to dangerous controversies. For that reason, Luther finally shoves them aside and cites two dogmatic axioms that are both closely connected with justification: (1) Christ alone is to be invoked as mediator. (2) There is nothing in Scripture about the invocation of saints, and therefore one ought not hope to obtain a hearing through them.

It is obvious that for the *Instructions for the Visitors*, the veneration of the saints posed primarily a liturgical problem; in the section "The Human Order of the Church" it is treated in connection with Sunday observance, that is, in connection with the hearing of God's Word.[416] Here invocation of the saints and their intercession for us have no place; as in Luther's confession, the motto is "Christ Jesus alone is our mediator who represents us."[417] Beyond that, however, there is a personal connection to faith and justification. The saints are "held up before us as a mirror of the grace and mercy of God." Like Peter and Paul, all the other saints were made blessed by the grace of God through faith. They are given to us as "examples" in our weakness so that we will be stimulated and exercised in faith and good works.

The saints are examples, models of justifying faith! The article is thereby removed from liturgical orders and shifted to the practice of faith. As far as the doctrine of justification is concerned, CA 21 has the indispensable task of translating it into practical life, not only in personal contemplation but also in common worship. Evangelical Christendom shows proper honor to the saints by competing with them in faith and good works. In them the evangelical

415. *WA* 26:507–8 (= *BoA* 3:513); *LW* 37:367.

416. *WA* 26:222ff.; *LW* 40:297.

417. The quotations from 1 John 2:1 and Rom. 8:34 are basic to the further development of the text; see above, p. 295.

sermon finds its practical and historical references, its examples. In this respect the sermon is also a biblical testimony; the biblical witnesses are the true saints who are attested in Scripture and retained in the calendar.

At the points where the Schwabach Articles make Christ the "only way to righteousness" (Schwab. 5) and use that as a basis for freedom regarding ceremonies (Schwab. 17), they do not go into the veneration of saints. The second, larger draft of the Torgau Articles,[418] however, adopts the positive theological perspective on saints taken by the visitation instructions, although its primary interest is in undergirding the new practices in worship.

The Torgau draft gives its major attention to the significance of saints as examples for the strengthening of faith. They are thereby rejected as intercessors; it is not their merits that bestow grace upon us, Christ is the only mediator. He wants to be claimed himself as helper, just as a prince wants to exercise his right to pardon without the intercession of members of his court. Furthermore, in addition to the ideas on justification that we can trace back to Luther's confession, a new element appears in this article: the reference to vocations. One follows the saint's example of faith according to one's vocation. The biblical models are individualized and thus made productive for Christian life in the world of work. The fruits of faith show themselves according to each person's personal, social, and historical relationships.[419]

Nevertheless, there was no immediate pursuit of this fruitful stimulus from the Torgau Articles. Up to manuscript Na, that is, to the end of May 1530, Melanchthon and his friends did not devote their editorial work at Augsburg to the veneration of saints. It was not until Nb 21—in the middle of June— that the problem was again taken in hand, this time with vigor; that almost completed the final German version of CA 21, except for minor modifications.[420] Liturgical practice is completely dropped. The theological basis is essentially that of Torgau; no new theological elements appear, except that the strengthening of faith and the experience of grace (*BS* 83b.4–5; *BC* 46.1) are more strongly emphasized than in Torgau. The exemplary role of the saints for fulfilling one's vocation in the evangelical sense is fondly depicted (*BS* 83b.7–13; *BC* 46.1). The expansion of scriptural citations is especially noteworthy in this late version of the article. As in Luther's Confession of 1528, the biblical basis for the cult of the saints is removed (*BS* 83b.14–15; *BC* 47.2). Instead, the justification theme is supported biblically by a series of Scripture passages[421] showing that Christ is the sole mediator. That gives

418. A 9 (Förstemann 1:82–83; Jacobs 85).

419. In the earlier articles on justification, this side of the doctrine is not considered (not even in CA 6). But see CA 21, sec. 1, on King David as a prototype for Emperor Charles in the war against the Turks.

420. Note the polemic title of Nb 21, "On the Saints Who Have Died," which was not picked up later.

421. This process combined the examples from the *Instructions for the Visitors* (*WA* 26:224.29–30; *LW* 40:300) with those from the Torgau Articles (*BS* 83b.24–25; Jacobs 85).

the final stamp to the character of CA 21.

Spalatin's copy of the article shows that there were hesitations about the final version.[422] Note even its position. Originally it bore the number 20 and preceded the article on faith and works that was later so numbered. Later, however, it was stricken completely, so that once again there was no mention of the veneration of saints. Spalatin's original wording varies from Nb 21 at many points; one might almost take it for an earlier form. The scriptural evidence for Christ's sole mediatorship is still incomplete, and the reflection of Luther's explanation of the Second Commandment in his Small Catechism that appears at the end of the last sentence has no parallel in the tradition of this article.

In contrast to the German version of CA 21, which goes back to Nb 21, the final Latin editing shows some characteristic changes. That remembering the saints consists in "imitating" their faith and their good works can no more be derived from the previous history of the text than it can be supported by the evangelical doctrine of vocation (sec. 1). Christians do not fulfill their callings by imitating exceptional people but they fulfill them by obeying God's commandment in whatever responsibilities they have. This context of faithfulness in one's calling, however, takes some of the force out of the marked emphasis on the sole mediatorship of Christ (secs. 2–3); instead of pointing to his significance as Savior, it could also signify the exemplary nature of Christ's representative obedience in suffering. This danger is not entirely removed, either, by the use of a single biblical text, 1 John 2:1, which—echoing the Second Commandment as Spalatin did—is understood as a proof text for the kind of worship most acceptable to God. There is an unmistakable weakening in the concern for justification in this final editing of CA 21. The interest in the divinely approved ordering of worship that accompanied the development of this article from the beginning asserts itself in the concluding version of the Invariata; it will emerge completely in the Variata editions.

A host of theological motifs are at work in the Augustana's basic and subsidiary articles on the doctrine of justification. We must attempt to bring better order to this variety than we have done, both from Luther's perspective and in dialogue with Melanchthon.

17. PREACHING OFFICE AND GOSPEL (CA 5)

The preaching office is instituted by God so that we may obtain justifying faith. Article 5 of the CA (and parallels) does not discuss the nature of this institution nor does it disclose its legal implications. That is not picked up

422. Förstemann 1:322.

until CA 14,[423] although fixed ideas about it exist from the beginning. The emphasis in CA 5 falls entirely on the effect of preaching in creating faith;[424] there is no immediate basis for thinking about constitution and order here, although, naturally, indirect connections are present.

If we want to understand the meaning of the term "ministry of the Word," *ministerium verbi*, we must, like Luther, inquire what "to minister" means in biblical usage. The equation of "servant" and "apostle of God" in Titus 1:1 provides the chief evidence for designating every servant of the Gospel as God's means of proclaiming the Word of God.[425] The servant is thus given a divine commission so that he must declare, "Thus says the Lord." He is relieved of all human service; he is neither a court attendant nor a hired hand but the attendant and servant of God. Therefore he ought not be a "dumb dog" (Isa. 56:10) that leaves the flock of Christ defenseless. Even if he should be executed for his preaching, dead preachers have a greater effect than live ones.[426]

Luther puts the earthly servant of Christ in the closest possible relationship to his heavenly Lord. As Christ forms the link between God and humanity, his servant is meant to bring God and the nation into relationship.[427] The office of the Word is one of the visible signs under which God's Spirit performs his work, the sign of the effective power of the New Testament. This mediating function consists of intercession. God has made his servants kings and priests to exercise the same mediating office that Christ had. How miserable the paid intercession of the papal minions looks by contrast! Christian service consists of mutual intercession. Those who do not practice that will eventually lose their faith. Next to preaching, prayer is the greatest office in Christendom. Every Christian embraces everyone else through such prayer; it encompasses all humanity, even enemies, blasphemers, and Turks.[428]

The preaching office does not exclude the general priesthood. Article 5 does not intend to establish the institutional means by which one comes to faith; that is based on the individual responsibility of every Christian. Even the emergency baptism administered by women provides the preaching

423. Cp. pp. 186–87.

424. Cp. Schwab. 7: the "office of preaching or oral word."

425. "Every minister ought to glory in this, that he is an instrument of God through which God teaches, and he ought not doubt that he is teaching the Word of God" (*WA* 25:7.4ff., 15ff.; *LW* 29:4).

426. *WA* 31.1:198.12ff.; *LW* 13:51; *WA* 31.2:466.5ff., 20:371.1ff.

427. "For as Christ is the bond between God and humankind, so any minister is an appointed bond for you, so that you are strengthened in your ability to believe. . . . Thus a minister of the Word is a bond in whom God and people are brought together" (*WA* 31.2:400.28ff.).

428. *WA* 31.2:119.1ff., 499.1, 503.30ff., 15:432.26ff., 34.1:218.11ff., 395.13ff., 27:131.3ff., 251.18, 440.28ff.

authority for every Christian—man, woman, and child—who has the opportunity. As bearers of the Holy Spirit, they are judges over all creatures in
heaven and earth. The sermon of the Magi (Matt. 2:7) before Herod is a
model for the priestly activity of all Christians. Everyone is an evangelist, but
order must be maintained so that doctrinal confusion does not arise. Basically, Christ is the real preacher; all must conform to him. When it is a
question of true doctrine, all Christians are to be counted as priests and are to
exercise the correct office. As early as his stay at the Coburg, Luther spoke
about mutual conversation (*mutuum colloquium*) in this connection.[429]

It is apparent that preaching office and general priesthood, church order
and individual spirituality, make demands on each other and are not mutually
exclusive. That can only be the case because the Augustana does not tie the
idea of an official institution to the term "preaching office" but thinks rather
of a spiritual occurrence that encompasses all Christendom, even though it is
concentrated in individual persons who are at times designated for that
function. The reality of this occurrence has its basis in God and Christ. Every
person, whether pastor or other member of the congregation, is bound in a
special way to that basis, when it comes to spiritual activity. The servant form
of the preaching office directs them to Christ, who was a servant according to
Philippians 2. Like him, all preachers but also all other office-bearers of
Christendom, are divine figures.[430] Ministers are messengers, angels. Their
honor, however, lies in their lowliness.[431] In that respect they are like Christ;
their symbol of office is the slain Paschal Lamb. Their spiritual warfare
against opponents and their personal self-sacrifice through the purging of
their passions—these are the only sacrifices that matter in the New Testament. Thus they glorify Christ alone and do not seek their own fame or
profit. All ecclesiastical dissension arises from the vanity of office-bearers.
Only where that vanity is overcome can their representing the suffering and
risen Christ and their preaching of judgment and repentance become
believable.[432]

The responsibility assigned to the preaching office results from this spiritual quality rather than from its hierarchical position. It corresponds to the
divine character of the office. Sermons preached in this office reach their
hearers, including the pastor himself. He must "tweak his own nose" when

429. WA 25:16.17; LW 29:16; WA 15:433.2ff., 684.7ff., 27:512.14 (a similar example involves
the shepherds of Bethlehem who preached in their herders' cloaks and not in surplices, WA
23:749.25ff.), 31.2:270.9ff., 14:533.18ff., 31.2:692.14ff.

430. "Through our tongues we are instruments through which God preaches. Thus all offices
in the world are divine in form. We are not God or Christ, but in this one particular we take on a
divine form" (WA 27:94.15ff.).

431. For this reason, Luther ridicules the Areopagite's doctrine of hierarchies: WA 13:604.2,
40; LW 20:63–64; WA 13:538.12ff.; LW 18:377.

432. WA 16:226.15–16, 31.2:503.30ff., 13:634.23ff.; LW 20:103; WA 27:80.23ff., 101.15ff.,
121.4ff., 10–11, 20:779.4ff., 784.1.

he preaches to others. He is, according to the biblical title of bishop, an overseer, "afflicter," and pastor of souls who not only exercises discipline concerning the Lord's Supper but who also decides, in the case of an individual's spiritual gifts, what is lacking in that person's soul or faith. In that respect the preacher is like Saint Christopher. Indeed, his office is the same one that Christ took upon himself in the church; like Paul, he distributes the treasure of redemption. On the day of judgment he must give an accounting for his hearers' reception of the divine gift; that lays an unbearable burden upon him.[433]

Luther himself tried to avoid that burden. His attempts in this direction, as is often the case with events in his life, should not be traced back to a particular conflict. They are rather a product of his special concept of the seriousness of the preaching office. He shaped it on the pattern of the Old Testament prophets who "wanted to ward off punishment and make the people pious." Like them, the preacher has to carry out the office of punishment; he ought not relinquish it to the crowd. But the preacher is not only wearied by public resistance in the congregation, he has the added sense of his own inadequacy. His overestimation of himself bothers him just as much as his personal lack of spiritual knowledge. When Luther recognizes this attitude, especially in talented preachers, he advises them to "throw the keys at God's feet" so that God would preach or administer the sacrament of confession without human mediation. The best preacher becomes increasingly aware of his ignorance. Thus Luther, after originally considering himself thoroughly suited to the pulpit, later mounted it only with hesitation—and then chiefly out of dutiful love for the congregation. Negative self-criticism, too, kept him from preaching for extended periods.[434] The idea that preachers suffer under their own imperfection corresponds to Luther's personal experience.[435]

He is supported both in his inadequacy and in his gifts by the example of the great teachers of the past: Augustine, Jerome, and Cyprian. The series of witnesses of the gospel extends back to the apostles; the true apostolic tradition relies on the living influence of the divine Word, just as the irreconcilable opposition between that Word and human traditions enslaves consciences. The decisive element is always the continuity of correct teaching rather than the succession of people and institutions.[436]

433. WA 27:85.23ff., 307.12ff., 385.9–10, 26:6.10, 41.25–26; LW 28:219, 270; WA 32:319.3ff., 324.11ff., 343.29–30; LW 21:26, 32, 44.

434. An interesting admission in WA 31.2:397.2–3: "And I, Martin Luther, if God had not shut my eyes of reason, would not long ago have ceased preaching and lost all hope."

435. WA 19:357.2ff., 389.9ff.; LW 19:159, 192; WA 20:184.2, 27:80.23ff., 89.6ff., 286.1ff., 20:222.32ff., 31.2:602.10.

436. WA 31.2:505.33ff., 425.16ff., 18:655.11ff., 741.29ff., 751.29ff., 627.34; LW 33:93, 224, 239, 54; WA 32:345.15ff.; LW 21:56. On the connection with the Old Testament patriarchs: WA

Therefore, that part of the *ministerium verbi* which is tied to legal forms is of no value in itself; it forms just the exterior shell for the spiritual relationships and effects. Naturally a congregation must maintain its pastor financially; if it refuses to do so, it denies itself the truth of the gospel.[437] In the calling of a pastor, in itself an external and legal matter, the spiritual relationship becomes especially evident. It is connected to the divine worth of the preaching office. The young Luther had not recognized that, nor had he even let Paul be his teacher in that respect. Later he knew that because God's Spirit participates in the call, he bestows a passive holiness similar to that which is conferred through preaching, baptism, and the Lord's Supper. And the effective authority of the preaching office depends upon the call: "No one can hold an office without and apart from a mandate or a call." Only those who are called to preach have the dauntless security to testify to God's Word; they alone conquer the fundamental temptation of the preacher, spiritual pride. Their hearers are convinced that "now God himself is preaching to our hearts." This is why the apostle Paul boasted of his call, and Luther himself would not have dared to preach in a church of the pope if he had not been called to do so. The necessary presupposition for the call is not the inner whispering of the Spirit—Luther reports Thomas Münzer's confession "The testimony in my inwardness is enough"—but is the outward attestation through fellow citizens and spiritual or temporal superiors, which may possibly be preceded by a personal declaration of readiness. Exceptional learning, particularly when it is combined with vanity, does more harm than good; an ignoramus (*idiota*) who conducts his office by the book, on the other hand, may not accomplish much, but he doesn't hurt much either.[438] In summary, a call is necessary for the preacher in order to tie him totally to his divine commission and to free him from his own vanity. It is also indispensable for the congregation, so that it knows that God's Word is active in its midst, giving it a bond with all of Christendom. The public character of the preaching office, which has been impressed upon the preacher ever since Christ and the apostles,[439] demands a public authorization; that authorization is expressed by means of the call.

Ordination belongs in the same context. Luther considered its reintroduction for evangelical clergy, in contrast to previous practice, as early as October

16:414.5ff. The fruit of the evangelical preaching office in the rising generation of theological students corresponds to the example of the schools of the prophets in the Old Testament: *WA* 31.2:65.23–24, 513.36ff.

437. *WA* 16:576.34–35, 27:253.5–6, 411.3ff., 26:95.31ff. (in contrast to the Waldensian preachers), 101.7; *LW* 28:349, 356.

438. *WA* 40.1:62.11–12, 63.6ff., 70.1ff., 30.3:521.9–10; *LW* 40:386; *WA* 16:587.27, 594.14, 26:41.9ff.; *LW* 28:269; *WA* 34.1:422.12–13, 26:82.15, 61.6–7, 51.1ff., 55.4ff.; *LW* 28:329, 298, 283, 289.

439. Christ intends that this office "be conducted publicly through the whole world and not secretly or in one place" (*WA* 32:351.3ff.; *LW* 21:62).

1524. That became a reality with the ordination of Georg Rörer on May 14, 1525; in addition to Luther and Bugenhagen, Melanchthon, the mayor, and a judge also participated in the laying on of hands. But the liturgical action of ordination is not the only expression of the public character of the preaching office. The general priesthood—perhaps in a prayer service at home—makes everyone who loves the divine Word into an ordained priest (sacerdos ordinatus) who intercedes for all people.[440]

The universal nature of the preaching office, which not only addresses all people but also is laid upon all groups and ranks of the congregation by virtue of the general priesthood, is based on the all-encompassing claim of God's Word. The preaching of the gospel gathers all peoples, calls them to judgment, and shows them salvation in Christ. Christ is the central point from which all rays illumine the world. He is the real preacher, whose comforting office gives life to all the world. These first fundamental statements by Luther make clear from the beginning that he does not consider the evangelical preaching office to be identical with the service of a city pastor in Wittenberg or of a village pastor in the neighborhood.

Salvation is dependent not on the institution of preaching but on the universal nature of the Word. Luther can say that if Christ (Mark 16:15) had not sent the disciples to all creatures, "I would neither let myself be baptized nor accept the faith." Because the divine promise includes all humanity, therefore even me, "[I] bet one hundred thousand hells on that word." And because that Word accuses all humanity, even the most pious, before the tribunal of God, the whole world falls under judgment. Thus the people of God cannot be recognized by any personal characteristics, but "where the Word is, there is the people of Christ." For the preaching office this means that pastoral care has no other task than to testify to the naked Word; blessedness does not come through the suitability of the preacher but through the power of the divine Word. "If the preacher is certain to have God's Word and to preach nothing else, and if it is rightly received, then the name of God is rightly honored and he can be rightly invoked." And thus it cannot be the preacher's task to arouse piety or to communicate it. The hearers are only instructed to accept the Word or reject it. The preacher is saved if he manages to do that. For him it suffices to know, "Thus saith the Lord." A good preacher will therefore avoid moral sermons and will flatter neither the common folk nor those in power.[441]

---

440. *WA* 15:720.20ff., 16:226.12 n., 27:130.14–15, 129.10. The only exclusion from the *publicum ministerium*—in the light of the biblical examples of religious functions by women—are women who are married (*WA* 26:46.9ff.; *LW* 28:276).

441. *WA* 13:115.33, 635.9ff.; *LW* 18:114, 20:104; *WA* 15:533.18ff., 16:386.6ff., 17.1:244.11ff., 16:312.3ff., 472.3ff., 116.11ff., 25:7.4ff., 15ff., 24.25ff., 29.1ff.; *LW* 29:4, 27, 33. On the "tongue that has been taught" (Isa. 50:4), see *WA* 31.2:412.15, 601.10ff.

The authority of the office of the Word rests neither on the legal and social position nor on the educational level of those who bear it, but upon the power of the Word of God. The statement of the apostle Paul that the gospel is the power of God is the basis for the doctrine of office in CA 5. Only on that ground can one dare to make the bold statement "The teaching Christian [thus not only the ordained minister but also father and mother] is the true God on earth."[442] It would be terrible arrogance if that Christian made up his teaching out of his personal experience of the heart; the teaching Christian would be replacing God's will with personal ideas. This is the key point on which Luther bases his resistance to the enthusiasts. Their inner word, which they say is the voice of God, is a human word, and is vulnerable to the objection that it is human opinion. God always speaks through the external Word and always acts in the sacraments through external events. One cannot and should not put the sound of the Word and the external elements in opposition to the real spiritual event. "If the external word is a human one, then I am lost, and later I will think that what my heart says is from the Holy Spirit."[443]

In order for the preaching office to communicate the Holy Spirit, as stated in CA 5, one must presuppose that it does not identify its activity with the Spirit but identifies it with the visible Word and sacraments. The outward signs are nothing in themselves. God, however, can make something out of them. He does not act without results; "God does not speak in vain." Therefore one cannot separate God's activity (ordinatio) from the Word. The preacher does not create the divine Word but accepts it in faith and in the process saves himself and others. So, like Christ, he becomes a connecting link "in whom God and people are reconciled."[444]

18. GOSPEL, SACRAMENTS, AND THE SPIRIT (CA 5)

Gospel and sacraments are the means (instrumenta) through which God gives the Holy Spirit (CA 5.2). This does not imply a particular difference between gospel and the sacramental means of grace, because God's Spirit works through visible means without differentiation. God instituted both Word and sacraments and, through them, gives the Spirit free rein. Bishops and pope do not possess it by virtue of their office, through special consecration. The preacher communicates it just as much as the midwife who baptizes a baby. There is no distinction in rank between preaching and administering the sacraments; the authority involved is one and the same. Luther rejects

442. WA 20:683.11.
443. WA 27:77.5ff. Cp. ibid., 76.5ff., 21ff., 231.1ff.
444. WA 27:231.6ff., 136.4–5, 31.2:400.28ff.

Zwingli's demand that the preaching office be placed over the baptismal function. Of course Christ's words of institution determine sacramental action, and to that extent the Word is superior. But what Christ did not expressly forbid may happen spontaneously. It is impossible to separate the external oral Word and the physical signs, on the one hand, from the internal process of Spirit and faith, on the other.[445] But we ought not reverse God's order: first the Word is heard, and then the Spirit comes giving faith "where and in whatever way he wills."[446]

The Word brings the Spirit. "Where the Word is, there is the Holy Spirit." Even the voice that was revealed to Paul from heaven could not have been perceived inwardly if it had not been heard outwardly. The external Word is decisive. Therefore the Spirit ought to be tied not to a "spiritually motivated" person but always to the office. It is Christ who bestows the Spirit rather than the baptizer, preacher, or confessor. The Spirit is the comforter because he repeats the Word of Jesus; he does not speak to us directly but speaks in such a way that he places Jesus' Word in our hearts.[447] And those who hold an office cannot, and should not, rely on personal spiritual experiences but should rely rather on the commandment of love that impels them to service of the neighbor—against their own feelings and wills.

The certainty of justification rests on these objective givens; they remain bound to the sway of the Spirit in the preached Word. But it is just as urgent that the Word not be separated from the Spirit; the Word of Christ is spiritual. That Christ is our food can only be understood and effected through the Spirit-filled preaching of Christ. Nor can a dead preoccupation with words exclude the fact that something spiritual happens: "The Holy Spirit sinks into your heart and kindles it, so that you truly know and love Christ." It is of nothing less than the coming of Christ that the Spirit speaks; he effects that coming. The Holy Spirit is not idle but is always actively at work.[448] This activity is not limited by time or space. The Holy Spirit preaches openly (*manifeste*), not in a corner. That is a consequence of Christ's resurrection. The preaching office was instituted at Easter, as was the gift of the Spirit. The resurrection testifies to Christ's victory over his enemies. What his suffering had accomplished was made known to all the world by the resurrection and proclaimed through the office of preaching. The Christ of Easter is the real preacher; it is him we hear when we hear the gospel. God's Word is his own voice. Those who do not hear it in the Scriptures know

445. *WA* 32:137.10, 249.1ff., 30.3:111.8, 128.2; *LW* 38:15, 28; *WA* 17.2:114.25ff., 115.28ff., 18:136.9ff., 139.2ff., 20ff.; *LW* 40:146, 150.

446. See below, pp. 363ff.

447. *WA* 31.2:19.16, 40.1:142.3ff., 29:304.10, 305.3ff., 20:396.33ff., 222.33ff.

448. *WA* 31.2:268.21–22, 15:433.7, 468.21ff., 566.5ff., 551.33–34, 685.32ff., 20:504.34, 704.3–4.

nothing about it. Even the heathen are called to the gospel and to faith by the preaching of the Spirit. Faith therefore is imparted through the gift of the Spirit and not through human efforts.[449]

Ever since the first Easter, the preaching of the Spirit has followed a pattern among humankind. Centurion Cornelius was the first in whom this development took place. By the standards of the Old Testament, he was righteous and holy; therefore he could accept the witness of the Spirit concerning the coming Christ. The Word received by the heart "meets" the Spirit, and the Spirit causes faith to grow. Thus Spirit and Word are continually changing places with Christ. The external Word remains unintelligible when the Comforter, the Spirit, does not teach it, that is, when he does not repeat what the apostles once heard from Christ. When that teaching does occur, it begins a process in which the hearer of the Word is struck to the heart by the fiery tongues of the Spirit. Christ speaks in his Word; the Spirit teaches by giving life to what Christ has said. The sermon in itself is just the first stage. Faith climbs higher by being taught by the Spirit and ultimately receiving the Spirit into its heart. Basically, Word and Spirit are on a par; the same divine power is at work in both. Where the Spirit is, there is the Word; and where the Word is, faith is also present, producing its fruits. They, in turn, cause persecution, and that leads to deliverance.

Thus an individual development takes place in the believing soul. There are parallels in the church. There too Spirit and Word are simultaneously present. First for the teacher, where Spirit leads to Word. Then for the hearer, who first hears the sound of the Word and then perceives the Spirit. In both cases, whether individual or for the whole, development means more than a temporal movement in one direction; it implies a lively movement back and forth that produces steady spiritual growth. Luther explains it by the wording of the Third Article of the Creed: where the Spirit and the Word are, faith follows and with it the forgiveness of sins, all of which together form the basis for the church.[450] The Spirit-filled Word spoken of in CA 5 is never associated with the law but is always associated with the gospel. Wherever the Holy Spirit is, one finds the gospel and with it the forgiveness of sins; the Holy Spirit does not wield the sword any more than Christ does. His gospel is the Word of righteousness and grace; the law is the office of death. The task of preaching consists entirely of bringing Christ near to us. Initially that is an external service that conveys the external clarity of Scripture. But the decisive step is when preaching leads to the appropriation of Scripture's inner clarity.

449. WA 30.1:308–9, 20:350.5ff., 365.1ff., 390.3ff., 27:14.1–2, 121.4, 40.1:151.7ff., 330.12ff., 36.3–4.
450. WA 40.1:330.12ff., 338.10, 27:396.33ff., 424.10ff., 15:686.30ff., 31.2:499.16ff., 24ff., 32–33.

That can only happen through the testimony of the Holy Spirit who ignites the words by means of true faith. And those who thus attain their own understanding of Christ lead others to him.

Making God's Word our own through the Spirit is therefore not an external process of learning; it is an inner event, which Luther expressed in the language of late medieval mysticism, anticipating the terminology of later evangelical mysticism. It is these terms, rather than the forms of Aristotelian dialectic cultivated and passed on by Melanchthon, that CA 4 and 5 use to convey the doctrine of justification. Therefore the statements concerning the connection between Word, Spirit, and faith in CA 5 belong to the heart of the evangelical doctrine of justification.

At the same time, these statements extend into the evangelical understanding of the church. The church does not achieve perfection through the law. Instead it follows the Christian commandment of love, which bids us support the weaker members. Up to that time church practice had been precisely the opposite. It set up ideal requirements in the name of God and condemned those members who did not fulfill them. Where the gospel reigns, however, the church is like a hospital where weak and strong live together; each is dependent upon the other and bears the other's burden. The Christian life is a mixture of power and powerlessness. Imperfection remains, but the Spirit works on. He makes it possible for the proclamation of the gospel to awaken faith and sustain it; he explains the gospel and makes it understandable.[451]

19. THE POWER OF THE SPIRIT TO CREATE ANEW (CA 5, SEC. 2)

In CA 5.2, the Holy Spirit, communicated through Word and Sacrament, is recognized as having the power to produce faith "when and where he pleases." This thesis forms the capstone for the CA's doctrine of justification. Here the creative power of the Spirit is presented as the presupposition for the ability of Word and Sacrament to produce faith. As the essence of justification, God's grace and the merits of Christ are anchored in pneumatology. Only then is the doctrine of justification complete; without acknowledgment of the Spirit, it remains incomprehensible.

It has been popular to see that phrase "when and where it pleases God" as a predestinarian touch and to trace it back to the influence of Erasmus and the southern Germans. Melanchthon is made responsible for the phrase. That is obviously wrong, as has been clear for a long time from Heinrich

451. *WA* 17.1:43.19ff., 244.5–6, 31.1:58.12–13, 20:784.1, 18:609.4ff., 653.22–23 (the difference between *claritas externa* and *claritas interna* is discussed in Friedrich Beisser, *Claritas scripturae bei Martin Luther*, FKDG 18 [Göttingen, 1966], 82ff.); *LW* 33:28, 90; *WA* 27:142.2ff., 31.2:312.10ff.

Bornkamm's note on the text. Bornkamm refers to Luther's polemic against Karlstadt (*Against the Heavenly Prophets*), where the sentence in question appears almost word for word.[452] Neither Luther nor Karlstadt, however, is dealing with predestination. Indeed, Karlstadt's spirituality completely eliminates the external mediation of Word and Sacrament in the achieving of justifying faith; it derives such faith exclusively from the free activity of the Spirit, whose unimaginable gift it is to justify a person through faith alone.

In the work against the "heavenly prophets," Luther's opposition to Karlstadt took a realistic line. The Spirit who acts freely in the Word punishes the world because of sin, so it is never simply a promise of grace. It is rather an impenetrable mystery of God whether the Spirit acting through the Word is received as judgment or as God's gift of salvation. If one wants to use the idea of predestination in this connection (one could also speak of *acceptatio*), one must keep in mind that there is no talk of selecting certain people from among the hearers. The point really is that God has not so bound the achievement of faith to office, word, and faith that the freedom of his will is lost. Only with this observation is the Reformation doctrine of justification complete; it could not be left out of CA 5. Melanchthon took it over from Luther.

At the same time the passage from the work against the "heavenly prophets" does not provide the first and only reference that Melanchthon had to consider. Luther described the incomprehensible nature of God's activity through the Spirit in many very diverse ways. At first he seems to echo the statements of the spiritualists literally, as when he uses the language of mysticism about the experience of the virgin Mary in his exposition of the Magnificat: ". . . thus she is illuminated and taught by the Holy Spirit. For no one is able rightly to understand God or God's Word; it comes without means through the Holy Spirit."[453] Granted that as early as this, the end of 1520, Luther already sees this experience as inseparably linked to the testimony of Scripture, without which there would be no spiritual experience. That God acts "without means" certainly does not exclude God's activity in his Word; it expressly includes it. But the emphasis is always on the Spirit. And the crucial point is that the Spirit "does not operate in comprehensible ways";[454] he maintains his unpredictable mystery. In his debate with spiritualism, Luther clearly recognized, even in his occasional concessions to mystical language, that the duality between the fleshly and the spiritual brought with it a rationalism that did not correspond to the divine activity of grace.

452. *WA* 18:139.2ff., 20ff.; *LW* 40:148–49.
453. *WA* 7:546.24–25 (= *BoA* 2:135.34ff.); *LW* 21:299.
454. *WA* 7:551.31 (= *BoA* 2:140.30); *LW* 21:304. Cp. *WA* 7:556.12–13 (= *BoA* 2:144.26–27); *LW* 21:309): The Spirit is that which "makes incomprehensible things possible through faith."

This insight of Luther's, sharpened during the debate with the "heavenly prophets," remained the touchstone for differentiating him from Erasmus. I have shown in another work[455] that the antithetical title of his book *On the Bound Will* does not indicate the real issue: the subject is not primarily the question of the will. Rather Luther stresses the assertive character of Reformation theology in contrast to Erasmus's skeptically tinged relativism. The doctrine of justification rests on the fact that the promise God gives in his Word is unshakably and inalterably clear. The Spirit of God who is active in it carries out his work in an unpredictable way; what he does must be accepted without question. This God is free and blows "not where we will, but where he himself wills." The salvation of God is not distributed to us according to our powers or calculations; it depends solely on God's action. Without that action all our deeds are evil. Where the Spirit of God is not at work, human action in relation to God is—"by immutable necessity, not by coercion"— culpable, even though reluctantly so.[456] Thus the Spirit encounters human beings in opposite ways; some in mercy, some in condemnation. And one cannot oneself determine in advance which of these ways it will be.

So the question is not the predestination of humankind but the freedom of God's Spirit. When the Spirit enters our heart by means of the Word, he creates something new that is pleasing to God. Of course the heart can draw back from the divine touch. But there is never any middle ground between the yes and the no; the Spirit presses for a decision from those who are called to faith. "The Holy Spirit is no skeptic; he does not write dubious things or mere opinions in our hearts. He writes firm assertions that are more sure and lasting than all experience and life itself."[457] Justification rests on this security, brought about by Spirit-induced faith in the Word. If faith were in predestination, that security would be destroyed. In contrast, when the Spirit works through faith in the Word, the faith already includes that sovereign power of God to act which human beings cannot predict.

Melanchthon brought this central element of Luther's theology of the Spirit into the Augustana. We cannot tell exactly whether he made use of Luther's heritage of late medieval mysticism as it was found, for example, in the exposition of the Magnificat or whether he picked up statements from the struggle with the spiritualists or even from the battle against Erasmus over the will. In any case he granted the phrase about the free action of God's Spirit a key place in CA 5. Furthermore, that did not happen right at the end of the editing process; it was prepared well beforehand. Article 7 of the later

455. See my article "Offenbarung und Skepsis," in Maurer, *Kirche und Geschichte* (Göttingen, 1970), 2:366–402, esp. 368–69, 377ff.

456. *WA* 18:602.14–15, 634.15ff. (= *BoA* 3:96.29–30, 125.15ff.); *LW* 33:18.

457. *WA* 18:605.32ff. (= *BoA* 3:100.31ff.); *LW* 33:24.

Schwabach Articles already traced the power and fruit of faith back to God, who caused it to happen "how and where he will." Therefore the phrase had already been adopted in midsummer 1529 by the commission of Wittenberg theologians that, under Luther's authority and with Melanchthon's active participation, produced those articles that began the development of the evangelical confession. The later history of the phrase[458] shows that CA 5 in its present version grew out of the discussion with spiritualism in the widest sense (including Erasmus). It intends not only to trace justification of the sinner back to the external means of Word and Sacrament but also, as Luther made clear especially in *On the Bound Will*, to ground the creative power of those means in the free and sovereign authority of God's Spirit.

The final version of CA 5 is another demonstration that Luther and Melanchthon worked together and that Luther had the decisive role. A key element of Lutheran theology of the Spirit was built into the article of justification in Schwab. 7 as early as the summer of 1529; Melanchthon made room for it in the final version of the Confession beginning in June 1530. The basis for the connection between Word, Spirit, and faith was thus finally laid.

In the final version of CA 5, especially in section 3, Melanchthon repeated the classic formulations of the doctrine of justification from CA 4—in this case, particularly section 2. That was not accidental. Article 4 gives a somewhat abstract presentation of justification; CA 5 makes it concrete. It introduces theses from Luther's teaching on the Spirit that illustrate the "before God" *(coram Deo)* of CA 4. The gift of forgiveness of sin is not just traced back to the external Word and Sacraments. Behind that giving lies the constantly repeated creative spiritual event. Nothing in this event is predetermined, nothing can be "mechanically" calculated in advance. In this instance, God acts to save or not according to his sovereign will of grace. And so the Reformation doctrine of justification here reaches the limits of what can be taught. Only if these limits were exceeded—which is not the case with Melanchthon—would the doctrine of justification lose its power for faith.

20. FRUITS OF FAITH (CA 6)

The connection CA 6 makes between Spirit, faith, and work was recognized and expressed by Luther long before the CA, probably most clearly in his "Sermon on Good Works" of 1520. In that sermon, good works are characterized as being effected by the Spirit in faith. The Spirit challenges faith, and faith does the good work. Only what comes from faith is a good

458. The *ubi et quando visum est Deo* is indeed still found in Schwab. 7 but is gone by Na 4; perhaps it is omitted in order to avoid drawing too sharp a line over against Erasmus and the southern Germans. "Where he will" and "where and in whatever way he will" are used of the Spirit in the parallel statements from Marb. 6 and 8.

work; no other kind can exist before God. The reason is that only the former is without sin; a work is good when it is done under the forgiving mercy of God rather than out of our own powers. In that way, Spirit, faith, and work are all anchored in the gospel of Christ; he is the source from whom faith flows.[459]

Becoming one with Christ is not only the presupposition for justifying faith[460] but also the basis for the love that "bears all things." Here faith and love are not separated. Together they constitute the Christian life. The dialectic at work here covers not only our thoughts but the whole reality of our life. The tension between faith and love corresponds to that between grace and law. Through faith, Christians are free from law; in love and obedience, they are subject to it. Both together constitute the new—and that means the active—person. The peculiar dialectic of the treatise on *The Freedom of the Christian* defines the doctrine of justification and also the doctrine of good works. The exuberant fullness of the Spirit flows over faith and works; the wealth of spiritual experience calls forth an abundance of fruits in which the exuberance of the Spirit (*spiritualis affectus*) makes itself known.

We cannot here follow in detail the connection between these themes in Luther through the 1520s. Certain especially emphasized landmarks of the development are unmistakable. The beginning of church organization and educational work was a watershed. About 1524—before the outbreak of the Peasants' War—the decisive perspectives were clearly established. The tension set up in the "Sermon on Good Works" and the treatise on Christian freedom is maintained in all the written and oral sermons. An exposition of the prophet Micah from 1524 speaks of the "fixed order" that ties faith and works together.[461] It reveals an unmistakable liturgical approach to the event of faith: justification forms the highest step, which is followed by the praise of God in thanksgiving, and finally by good deeds done to the neighbor.

This approach directs attention to the direct relationship between one person and another. The Christian life is based entirely on fear of God. This legal element is characteristic for both rulers and ruled. We should serve our neighbor through bodily discipline; faith does good works through obedience.[462] This tendency toward legal narrowness which appears here so early (and in Luther himself, not only in Melanchthon, although in both cases in the classroom context) constantly endangers the relation between faith and good works. Indeed, in his lectures on Habakkuk from the same period,

459. *WA* 6:204–16 (= *BoA* 1:229–41); *LW* 44:23–39.
460. See above, p. 318.
461. *WA* 13:291.24.
462. "The fear of God is faith; it is always present" (*WA* 13:471.4ff.). Summarized in ibid., 471.7: "This is the sum of the preaching of all the prophets."

Luther himself sees this relationship destroyed by more than pedagogical considerations; the difficulty lies deeper—in the common people who do not want to accept justifying faith and in the preachers who do not insist strongly enough on works.[463] The sermon of 1520 had a simple and solidly based solution to the relationship, but it was not able to prevail. In his interpretation of the basic message of the Reformation in Hab. 2:4, seen in the light of Rom. 3:28, Luther complains about the stubbornness and lack of faith among his followers.[464]

We have previously heard similar complaints given as a reason for his weariness of preaching;[465] he overcame that weariness through the inseparable connection between the preaching of the gospel and the spiritual fruits flowing from it, fruits that assure we can never lose the promise of the forgiveness of sins. After the revolution of the enthusiasts and the peasants, that is, after 1525, Luther grouped Word, Spirit, and faith more firmly together than ever before; in so doing he took the most important step, in terms of consequences, for preparing the way to CA 6. In October 1525, after the end of the Peasants' War and just before the Marburg Colloquy, he proclaimed the certainty that "where God's *Word* is preached, there also its fruits must follow and be. Because we now have God's Word, God's *Spirit* must also be with us; and where the Spirit is, there must faith also be. It is there no matter how weak it may be, whether one sees it or not."[466] We are dealing here with a postulate of faith that rests on an empirically unprovable postulate of history. Article 6 of the CA is based on the same postulates; it arises from the bitter experiences of the years 1522–29. The statement that good works proceed from Word and Spirit is a principle of experience in only a very limited way; it rests essentially on the power of the Spirit, who, contrary to appearances, performs good works when and where he will.

Article 6 is not a general principle of doctrine; it is a statement of faith that applies in specific instances. For its hearers, every sermon brings curse or blessing. The effect of faith does not depend on the person of the preacher, whether pastor, father, mother, or neighbor. It is the mystery of divine creative growth that determines where fruits will spring forth. It is not the fruit that makes the tree, but the tree the fruit. God rules the world in a wonderful way; he never gives the fruit everywhere and to everyone but always contrary to blind reason.[467]

463. "Faith is not preached to believers; love is what the faithful should hear. . . . One cannot preach faith enough to the hardhearted, because they do not understand faith and the gospel. We who have the Word and faith in God through Christ do not understand love and service. The former do not want to stop talking about works; we do not want to start. They want works without faith; we want faith without works" (*WA* 15:435.1ff.).

464. *WA* 13:434.5ff.; *LW* 19:123. Cp. *WA* 15:435.1ff. (see n. 463).

465. See above, p. 357, and on this passage, *WA* 19:138.8ff.

466. *WA* 17.1:434.11ff.

467. *WA* 25:285.1–2, 27:232.25ff., 17.2:34.31–32, 15:660.16ff.

After the experiences of 1525, the wonders of the effects of Word and Spirit became greater and greater for Luther.[468] The sorely tested evangelical preacher sees Word and work coincide; their fruits spring forth without human aid. The Christ who testifies to himself in his Word is the sole model for the preacher; his public witness cannot remain hidden, Luther assures his hearers on May 28, 1525, in the bloody days after the end of the Peasants' War. At a time when the bloody justice of the princes reigned so terribly, Luther proclaimed the external righteousness of love, a sign to everyone that there were still Christians who gave a good account of themselves before their neighbors. He applies the old familiar distinction between entering (*ingressus*) and exiting (*egressus*)[469] to good works. Faith is turned inward, dealing with the self; love is directed outward toward works. The Holy Spirit must "pour in love together with faith." "Where the Holy Spirit is, there must love and everything be." Infused faith and infused love flow together.

Faith and love belong together by nature, like the divine and human natures in Christ. But faith is the schoolmaster of love; love is subordinate to faith. According to God's will, faith engulfs all cares, so God has forbidden the preacher to worry about anything except passing on to others that which has been received from God. Faith receives the spiritual gifts inwardly; love shows outwardly what it has received. Thus faith is the stronger part. Because it is "one being" with love, "one work or deed" arises from it. Knowledge is not enough; when faith increases, it becomes "strong and mighty," love becomes "warm and fervent." In fact in this context Luther can even speak of deification. Faith intends to work so completely and powerfully in us "that we are entirely turned into gods." This goal of the life of faith also includes the good works proceeding from faith.[470]

It is striking that this talk of the union between the Spirit, faith, and its fruits uses imagery that reminds us of the language of mysticism. Indeed the images are found in Luther's writing before 1520, but not in the works for instructional purposes from the twenties, although they appear again at the end of the decade. There is no trace of them in CA 6; the organic image of the tree and its fruits is pushed aside completely. For example, where Luther uses the image of the three familial estates[471] that originated with Jerome, the biological references are ignored entirely; it is a matter of *creationes* over which no human being can exercise control. To the degree that the Reforma-

468. *WA* 17.1:261.25ff., 376.9ff., 17.2:97.7ff., 164.15ff.

469. "It enters through faith in God; it goes out through love to the neighbor" (*WA* 17.2:277.24, on John 10:9, from June 6, 1525).

470. *WA* 17.1:451.3–4, 242.6; *LW* 12:194; *WA* 17.1:417.15ff., 23ff., 428.34ff., 429.1ff., 438.11ff.

471. See also W. Maurer, *Luthers Lehre von den drei Hierarchien und ihr mittelalterlicher Hintergrund*, SAM, phil.-hist. Klasse 1970, 4:passim. Cp. *WA* 20:263.5ff., 13.

tion doctrine of justification has a practical effect on Luther's preaching, it differentiates between external works and those that come from the heart, between human and Christian love.[472]

This distinction, of course, relates to the origin of love and good works, not to their quality. In that respect, Luther says, "Love toward God is the same as that toward the neighbor." Its special hallmark and divine requirement is that it does not seek its own.[473] To the world it is unknown. The world does not know the truth of the Christian faith, and therefore it does not know brotherly love; it consists of hypocrites and idlers. Outward righteousness is only an illusion; that which stems from faith is inward and hidden from human eyes.[474]

The good works of that inward righteousness consist of pure preaching of God's Word to serve the neighbor. They climax in the sacrificial offering of one's life. Not only do they follow Christ's example, but they also make believers children of God and sisters and brothers of Christ. Exemplary fulfillment of Christ's deeds in works of mercy and love is the true fruit of the Spirit. Thus the unity between the hidden promptings of the Spirit and the outwardly visible works of the Spirit lies in Christ, that is, purely in the spiritual realm.[475]

It must be noted how greatly the pedagogical and ethical impulses in Luther's preaching on good works diminished in the course of the 1520s; indeed, apart from the sermons on the catechism they disappeared altogether. There is much less talk about good works than about the fruits of faith. They are not brought forth by our own initiative; the tree on which they grow stems from God, and therefore the fruits do too. The ground they are rooted in, faith, is hidden in God. The fruits that appear make a righteous person known, but only to other persons, not before God; before him only faith justifies. Thus the fruits are to be judged differently before God (*coram Deo*) and before men (*coram hominibus*). They constitute human righteousness only, not the hidden divine kind. Therefore human beings also have "two natures" or two kinds of righteousness, one before God and one before other human beings.[476]

This passage, from a sermon of July 1526,[477] has a different ring from other contemporary expositions of Matt. 7:16. Luther completely omits the

472. "Christian love is different from human love. . . . Worldly love considers where it can obtain something" (*WA* 20:480.20ff.). Cp. ibid., 475.4ff.
473. *WA* 20:514.2, 516.1–2, 701.4ff. See also the exposition of 1 John 3:2 (1527; ibid., 697.9): "It is necessary to love one another, to gain a most kind heart, a flowing brook to the neighbor."
474. *WA* 20:74.19ff.; *LW* 15:62; *WA* 20:467.2ff., 475.4ff., 714.19ff.
475. *WA* 20:693.9ff., 697.12, 701.4ff., 17.1:37.8–9.
476. *WA* 20:467.8ff.
477. *WA* 20:467.2ff.

imperative of the law on which CA 6 bases the insistence on good works "as God has commanded." There is no statement that the "good works commanded by God" must happen "because it is God's will." We have ascertained that this legal tendency dwindled for Luther during the course of the 1520s. An increasing amount of space is given to themes of spiritual communion and exchange with Christ, and to dialectical tension between hiddenness and being revealed, or between inner and outer. And to the same extent the bond between faith and its fruits is drawn ever tighter. For Luther the ethics of love grow directly out of the doctrine of justification; for his contemporaries, even the evangelicals, the two are stuck together from the outside. That is also the case in CA 6, where guiding principles and concepts from past definitions are tacked onto the body of the article and brought to a conclusion with a quotation from Ambrosiaster that simply strings together the basic statements of CA 4–6, on belief in Christ, salvation apart from works, faith alone, and receiving forgiveness of sins by grace.

21. THE CULT OF SAINTS (CA 21)

In the discussion of the textual development of CA 21, it was made clear that only a part of the article was related to the doctrine of justification. It is to that section only that these additional paragraphs will be addressed.[478]

It is predominantly negative toward veneration of the saints. Luther exposes the danger of the cult of saints by numerous examples, both anecdotal and theological. He knew from his own experience and that of others that Christ was represented as a judge and that mediation of salvation was attributed to the saints. Nonetheless, the Holy Spirit is really Christ's instrument and no help from the saints is needed.[479] At one time breaking away from them was difficult for Luther. But to the degree that he was able to do so, his doctrine of justification disclosed the damage done by veneration of the saints.

At the same time, the images of the saints were inseparably tied to church tradition. One cannot lose sight of the fact that Luther always understood as saints the more prominent biblical figures, the lawgivers, prophets, and kings of the Old Testament—even those the biblical tradition rejects—and the apostles and other figures of the New Testament. His rejection of the cult of the saints did not shake his understanding of the Bible but instead reinforced and reestablished it. Despite the false impression spread abroad by the naming of saints by medieval church councils, only the towering figure of Augustine deserved a place alongside the evangelists, John the Baptist, and

478. On the question of order and law, see above, pp. 232–36.
479. *WA* 20:390.2ff., 30.2:644.10–11; *LW* 35:199.

the apostle who was second only to Christ as a preacher—Paul. And in these matters even Augustine did not give proper consideration to the biblical witness in addition to church tradition.

In the course of time, Luther also passed increasingly sharp judgment on the cult of Mary. By the mid-1520s the debate over the Mother of God was decided. On the basis of her biblical role, Mary has a special status. She who must have feared that she would lose her son is our pattern in times of temptation; her faith that she would bear a child although a virgin makes her a witness of faith to the whole world. As the one who suffered at the cross, she is the greatest of all martyrs; her cloak offers a shield and protection in danger. But we will not and should not make her into a goddess, placing her at Jesus' side. We praise her because the Divine Majesty chose her as the mother of his Son.[480]

In addition to the biblical saints, and perhaps Augustine as well, there are the saints of the church, like Jerome and Gregory, Agnes the singer of praise, and Bernard, equipped with the gifts of order and rule. As teachers of righteousness, however, their luster fades in comparison with the apostolic preaching of grace. Huss too, and his co-workers before and after him, along with many others of the baptized, were given great and holy gifts by God. Of course, where God is praised, Satan also celebrates his triumphs. That was Luther's testimony when, on June 16, 1524, the bones of Saint Benno were displayed for veneration in the cathedral at Meissen.[481]

Undoubtedly Luther, as a child of his time, regarded the medieval veneration of saints with a good bit of skepticism. But when he expressed that skepticism, it arose out of the Reformation gospel and not simply from medieval thinking. It is initially peasant realism that makes him want to regard the saints as really dead. "The bodies of all the saints lie in the ground and are sinful and have died in sin."[482] He thereby denies that the departed saints intercede for us; to expect that of them would be to make them into "gods" and patrons. We know nothing about the state of the departed saints; at least they do not invoke one another.[483] This common-sense approach to weighing matters beyond our grasp is Luther's necessary counterpart to justifying faith, where God declares himself directly through his saving Word.[484]

Luther's criticism of the saints is bound to the Word. Their example is not

---

480. *WA* 15:642.37ff., 643.5ff., 27:22.33, 23.9ff., 74.1ff.
481. *WA* 15:636.22ff. Cp. ibid., 416.21ff.: "examples of the saints which fool us completely." On Huss, see *WA* 26:168.12ff.; *LW* 40:256.
482. *WA* 30.2:369.39–40.
483. Ibid., 694.1ff.
484. These discussions are connected with Luther's supplement to the CA, *De loco iustificationis* (ibid., 674ff.).

sufficient if the Word does not supplement it. On the other hand, the true saints are those who undergird the Word of preaching with the sacrifice of their lives. Therefore, in Luther's lifetime there were "saints" in the church; they were the evangelical martyrs who had sealed their preaching with their blood. The evangelical saints speak not through the relics they leave behind but through the Word that is still received from them, confessed and believed after their death. In a sermon (April 8, 1526) during the days before the First Diet of Speyer, when there were threats of an intensified enforcement of the Edict of Worms, Luther made the conquering power of the evangelical martyr-sermon into a new type of "saint" that had forerunners and successors in Christian missionary preaching beyond the limits of confession or time.[485] This marks a new understanding of the martyr saint. The understanding itself becomes the preacher, and when it is proclaimed, Christ himself is present in its words.[486]

Christ preaches in every true sermon. Through the Word the congregation—and Christ himself—find their saints. Christ is the "saint of saints" (sanctorum sanctus). All others preach like him according to the measure that God has allotted them. In this light, how many great saints there are! Christ is the head of all saints; he has spirit, power, and authority within himself; he is the source of all preaching. "From him flows all holiness." There is therefore a total difference between Christ and other saints. Every saint is, in his own right, no better than any other in respect of holiness; Luther himself is a "wretched sinner" (miser peccator).[487]

Therefore no one should martyr himself or let himself be martyred by the preachers of holiness, nor should one make meticulous comparisons with others to see who is the holiest. We all have only the one Christian faith, and not a Marian or Petrine one. Holiness is concerned only with what is Christian; the Holy Spirit effects that throughout Scripture. All holiness depends on the person of Christ. His word, preached and believed, creates holiness through the Holy Spirit. It is not to be grasped by reason. Holiness is a heavenly gift of the Spirit which operates in earthly humanity. "We have a heart that rejoices in Christ and finds peace in him."[488]

As is the case with Luther's doctrine of justification, community with Christ constitutes the core of his teaching on the saints. The saints represent the existence of the state of righteousness made possible through Christ. In

485. "For he who is a Christian and preaches him [i.e., Christ], does not act of himself; it is Christ. When we hear the gospel, we hear Christ himself, and it is his own voice and his Word that is spoken" (WA 20:365.1ff.).

486. Similarly from the Easter Tuesday sermon of April 3, 1526 (WA 20:350.7): "When I preach, he preaches in me; when you hear, he hears in you."

487. WA 20:390.6ff., 444.1–2. Cp. ibid., 539.21ff.

488. Ibid., 390.19–20, 479.32–33, 611.4, 390.2ff., 425.13, 750.12ff.

this state, holiness is yoked with sinfulness: *simul iustus et peccator.* It all depends on Christ; all the merits of the saints disappear in his presence. No matter how highly Mary is honored, she did not die for us as Christ did. He alone is the Lamb of God. Everything else that Scripture may say about human holiness has its reference point in him. Any polemic against the saints is in fact preaching Christ. "We have not preached vehemently against the saints but have primarily dealt with Christ," said Luther in defending the discontinuation of festivals of the saints in the summer of 1529. Collecting indulgence benefits that are based on the merits of the saints devalues the suffering of Christ and corrupts faith in it.[489]

The veneration of saints is made so human that the saints become visible objects of God's forgiveness. The greatest saints are sinners; their deaths at the stake—even when it comes to biblical witnesses and prophets and present-day martyrs—testify to their sinfulness. As the reliquaries of the saints were once adorned with gold and silver, now their true holiness is honored by obeying one's parents; the bones of our parents are the true reliquaries of the saints. The battle against the saints is not a matter of unmasking holy pharisaism or of exposing apparent saints to all the world through the judgment of God; the true saints, condemned utterly by the world, are the more holy the further down God presses them.[490] The saints present the pattern of what it means to be justified; the more the world despises them, the closer they are to God.

And as saints, the justified realize the true Christian community of love. Through the Word they live, as we saw, in Christ, and Christ lives in them. In that state one cannot live for oneself alone. Those who rightly preach the Word cannot help serving their neighbors; they share the riches of the divine Word with them. Sharing in the Word is the sharing of the saints in Christ; by all becoming Christlike, each saint becomes a saint to the neighbor. The early church's understanding of *communio* is preserved into later times by Luther's understanding of *communio sanctorum.*[491]

Thus the communion of saints arises out of the unity of faith in Christ that occurs through the Word. Luther worked on this reinterpretation during the 1520s, and it became the position of CA 21. He ties the article on saints to preaching and hearing within contemporary Christendom. Under Christ as its head, its members are bound by Word and Spirit to Christ and to one another. The listening church is also the loving, mutually giving church. Thus Luther's early exposition of article 21 combines the key themes of his doctrine of justification—the themes concerned with the exchange between

489. *WA* 29:413.7ff., 243.8ff., 30.2:283.30–31.
490. *WA* 16:249.3–4, 491.4, 493.5ff., 17.1:331.26–27, 244.32, 4.2.
491. *WA* 20:703.1–9; cp. ibid., 683.10ff., 693.8ff. (fall 1527; on 1 John 2, 3).

Christ and the sinner through faith, as well as those which describe the mutual love of the faithful in terms of sacrifice and prayer. Hence, CA 21 has a strong internal bond with the group of articles on justification (CA 4–6, 20).

It is an open question whether those themes are also directly reflected in the text of CA 21. A look at the content of CA 21 can provide a quick affirmative answer. The negative paragraphs (2–4) refute the abuses of the medieval cult of the saints with arguments that can be amply supported from Luther. Paragraph 1 traces the true meaning of venerating the saints back to the faith relationship to Christ and the love relationship to the neighbor. That double reference goes back as early as the Torgau Articles (A 9), but it is barely visible, and that only now and then, in Luther's semi-official preparations for the Confession.

It is more important to ask whether and to what extent Luther's interpretation of the christological connection between Christ and justifying faith—or generous love—played a role in the final explanation of CA 21. To say that remembrance of the saints should lead to imitating their faith certainly does not plumb the depths of Luther's doctrine of justification, and since imitation is not community of faith, it is no different from the vague exhortation for one to practice the good works of the saints in one's own calling. Although the war against the Turks has a prominent role in this passage, it by no means exhausts the Lutheran view of vocation, nor does it involve the militant spirit of Lutheranism beyond the fact that Melanchthon, acting here as a political orator, is trying to stir up the enthusiasm of the princes of the empire for war.

The theological significance of the article lies in its rejection of the common abuses on which the cult of the saints depended heavily. In this rejection, it adds to the titles that CA 3[492] had given Christ (sec. 2) and it emphasizes the intercessory power of Christ (sec. 3).[493] Intercession is not, however, justification. One can find nothing in these Melanchthonian additions to compare in content or depth with the corresponding statements of Luther. Those statements obviously exercised no direct influence over the final version of the article.

492. See also above, n. 236, on CA 3.
493. In the German version of CA 3 (*BS* 54.20; *BC* 30).

THE CHURCH AND ITS SACRAMENTS

22. THE CHURCH (CA 7, 8): TEXTS

The most important definitions of the church occur in Luther's fundamental Confession of 1528 rather than in the Augustana. The latter sometimes curtails and sometimes elaborates his basic points. Luther describes the church as the essence and source of all spiritual gifts that God has given the world through Christ. The church and its servants are distinguished from all earthly powers and institutions. It is Christendom, a universal entity spread throughout the whole world among all peoples. It is a spiritual entity, spiritually gathered "in one gospel and faith." It is subject to one spiritual head, Christ, and is his spiritual body and bride. It is opposed by the papacy, which is the "true realm of antichrist, the real anti-Christian tyrant, who sits in the temple of God and rules with human commandments."

In the church, "wherever it exists, is to be found the forgiveness of sins," so that it is "a kingdom of grace." In it are found the "gospel, baptism, and the Sacrament of the Altar, in which the forgiveness of sins is offered," and there they are "obtained and received." That does not happen at one time only, in baptism, but whenever one needs absolution up to the time of death. "Outside this Christian church there is no salvation or forgiveness of sins, but everlasting death and damnation," despite the appearance of many good works.[494]

An exact analysis of these statements, which often border on being hymns, is no more possible here than it would be to show the sources for each of the references. That can happen only to the extent that we compare Luther's confession with other statements of his about the church. The later formulations from the confessional development that climaxes in CA 7 and 8 often seem like an abstract from the Confession of 1528. They reveal what Melanchthon and the "confessors" at Augsburg considered to be the significant

---

494. This text, somewhat smoothed out here, is a core element of evangelical confession and should precede all statements on ecclesiology. It is found in *WA* 26:506.30–507.16 (= *BoA* 3:512.14–41); *LW* 37:367–68. It is abstracted in *BS* 61 n. 1.

elements in the Reformation understanding of the church. It is for that purpose that we will now analyze the development of the text up to the final versions of CA 7 and 8.

A literary comparison of Schwab. 12 shows it to be an abstract of the Confession of 1528.[495] Three theses reappear: (1) There is a "holy Christian church" on earth. (2) It is nothing else than "believers in Christ." (3) It is where "the gospel is preached and the sacraments used rightly." These three basic principles again form the foundation of the evangelical concept of the church: universality, essential connection with Christ, and dependence on Word and sacraments.

The principles are varied slightly in Schwab. 12. The nature of the church includes its remaining "until the end of the world," according to Matt. 28:20. If this statement in Schwab. 12 is taken to refer to time as well as space, then it is an abbreviation for the more detailed geographical and eschatological descriptions in Luther's confession and a support for his apocalyptic statements against the papacy. The bond between the church and Word and sacraments is found in Schwab. 12.3. The whole article is undergirded by a christological foundation.

Article 12 of Schwab. also has additions to the earlier confession. There are three in particular:

1. The continuing existence of the church to the end of the world provides a certain substitute for the colorful eschatology of Confession 28. The substitution of Matt. 28:20 for the apocalyptic biblical quotations is in the same vein.

2. The faith in Christ which constitutes the church is connected to the "above-mentioned articles and parts"; it is therefore confessional faith.

3. Believers are identified as those who "for this suffer persecution and martyrdom," which signals the substitution of martyrdom for the earlier eschatological accent.[496]

Comparison from every angle shows what a strong foundation links Luther's confession to Schwab. 12. The freely formed content of Luther's confession is recast and poured into the text of the treaty for the future defensive alliance. The form becomes tighter, but the content remains unabridged. Its universal breadth transforms it into a new ecumenical understanding of the church.

In its first half, Na 7 picks up the three basic principles that Schwab. 12 had taken over from Luther's confession. They are formulated more concisely than in Schwab. 12; the additions and clarifications we had noted are dropped. Melanchthon limited his editorial work on the first half of Na 7 to

495. Henceforth abbreviated Conf. 28.
496. Items 2 and 3 point to the confessional conflict.

this tightening and concentrating of the text. One can see how consistently Melanchthon maintained the connection with Luther's original confession.

The second half of Na 7 (and the corresponding part of CA 7) is a different matter. The break in the text comes somewhat earlier than the point where CA 7 and CA 8 will later be divided. It begins where the criteria for church unity are set down in positive and negative terms (CA 7.2 and pars.). This unity is not a matter of urgency in Luther's confession; it is presupposed but not defined. That occurs in another source which lies behind the second half of Na 7 and CA 7–8; we now turn to that source.

To the first part of the most developed and most complete draft of the Torgau Articles, which we call A, Melanchthon and his co-workers at Torgau gave the title "On the Doctrines and Ordinances of Men," which Luther subsequently accepted.[497] The section begins with a justification of the visitations on the part of the elector. The opponents have wanted such changes to take place only with papal approval; otherwise they raise the objection of schism. In defense, the electoral government appeals to the obedience we owe to God alone (Acts 5:29) and bases the unity of Christendom on the unity of doctrine and sacraments:

> On that account, the unity of the Christian church consists not in external human ordinances; and therefore we are not members cut off from the church if we observe dissimilar ordinances from one another; and for this reason, the holy sacraments among us are not invalid.
>
> For dissimilarity in external human ordinances is not contrary to the unity of the Christian church, as is clearly proved by *the article that we confess in the Creed: "I believe in the holy catholic church." For since we are here commanded to believe that there is a catholic church, that is, the church in the entire world* and not bound to one place, but that wherever God's Word and ordinances are, there is a church, and yet the external human ordinances are not alike, it follows that this dissimilarity is not contrary to the unity of the church.

The italicized material is taken almost word for word from Luther's confession. There are also additional concepts that can be found more or less strongly emphasized in Luther, such as the rejection of unified hierarchical structures and of geographical limits on unity, and the appeal to God's Word as the basis for unity. The Torgau Articles also contain canonistic proof texts that were later used in CA 26.

CA 7–8 follow Na 7, although independently, in relying on the Torgau formulations; thus they once again give account of their connection with Luther's confession. In the process they emphasize Word and sacraments as the positive elements of unity.[498]

Nevertheless, Na 7 (and consequently CA 8) has taken the approach of

497. Förstemann 1:69ff.; Jacobs 76ff.; here quoted according to *BS* 107.22ff.
498. The new formulations of CA are considered below, pp. 388–89.

Luther's confession and developed it independently, so that the ecclesiological confession of the Augustana has its own unique character. Article Na 7 bases the relativizing of outward church ordinances on Luke 17:20, a biblical passage that spiritualizes true church unity more than presenting it in a positive light. Article 7 of the CA therefore replaces it with Eph. 4:5-6. Article Na 7 makes a really new contribution through the contrast between "true believers" and the "many hypocrites and evildoers," that is, between the "proper" church and the "wicked" priests who might still administer the sacraments within it. This anti-Donatist touch grew out of the objection that Lutherans were schismatic, which had been faced in the Torgau Articles; it is strengthened by the anathema at the end of CA 8. These inclusions form a good counterweight to the spiritualizing sound of the "Christian church, properly speaking," and they allow Melanchthon, as author, a chance to use his Augustinian tradition. The Donatists are substituted in CA for the Novatians, who were singled out in Luther's confession. There is no counterpart in that earlier document for the balancing of spiritualism against Donatism in the CA. The citation of Matt. 28:20 recalls the antipapal polemic of Luther's confession, although it certainly does not match the urgency of his apocalyptic mood.

The literary composition of the Augustana is particularly easy to trace by means of CA 7 and 8. The foundation and starting point for CA 7 is Luther's Confession of 1528 as it was shortened and concentrated along the lines of Schwab. 12. Article 8 of the CA goes back to the key phrases of Torg. A 1, where the electoral council defends the integrity of its visitation project— again with ties to Luther's confession—by asserting that many ceremonies are superfluous and that its own reform of worship is within the law. The spiritualizing of the concept of the church, on the one hand, and the reference to Augustinian ideas of sacrament and office (anti-Donatist principles), on the other, shaped a concept of the church that was essentially foreign to Luther but that achieved fundamental significance for the future theology of his students. It does give us some technical information about the editorial process. The first sentence of the third part of the Apostles' Creed forms the foundation and starting point for all the participants—for Luther himself, for the electoral advisers in Torgau, and for Melanchthon as their representative in Augsburg. The electoral advisers had obtained the foundation for their church visitations from that understanding of the church. It gave them (a) the justification for a break from Rome in matters of worship, in order to carry out their own reform based on evangelical preaching and administration of the sacraments; (b) the excuse for the fact that the reform remained incomplete in the congregations because of the "admixture of hypocrites and evil persons" (adherents of the old faith and ministers who made only outward accommodation to the reforms); and (c) a new understanding of the mixed nature of the newly organized congregations, in which the objective basis of Word and sacraments produced a whole spectrum of "Christians, properly speaking." Indeed it took a great deal of independent reflection upon the heritage of thought from the ancient church as well as that stemming from Luther before this classic document of Lutheran ecclesiology could come into being.

23. THE THREE CONSTITUTIVE ELEMENTS OF THE CHURCH

From Luther's personal confession through Schwab. and Na we found three constitutive elements of the church: (a) its universality as assembly of the saints (congregatio sanctorum); (b) its bond with Christ; and (c) its bond with Word and sacraments. These three basic ideas are deeply rooted in Luther's oral and written statements from the years prior to 1530.

"One holy Christian church" will exist forever. This assertion reaffirms the early church's confession "I believe in one holy church" (Credo in unam sanctam ecclesiam). Luther was not mechanically parroting a rigid tradition; to him the Nicene Creed, especially by its use in worship, is a continuing testimony of the Holy Spirit that confers authority on the preacher.[499] It testifies to the truth of the Christian faith in all the world as well as to the continuing existence of Christianity from the beginning of its history.[500]

At the same time, it testifies to God as the creator and Lord of the church. He rules it "from the beginning and authoritatively through his Word"; the church handles the Word only "passively and supportively; it is God's creation." Every teacher of the church must know that and act accordingly.[501] The church makes known God's claim to lordship through its preaching, and the fruits of this Word become evident through the church's obedience to that claim.[502] The church is God's maid and servant; it hears and does nothing beyond that which it knows from his Word.[503] "Because the church is born from God's Word, we should not accommodate the Word to the church but rather the church to God's Word," state the Nürnberg Articles of Inquiry of 1528.[504]

Thus the church is obedient to the Word of God and does not change it; rather it lets itself be changed and mastered by the Word. If it does not do

499. WA 34.1:463.3ff. The choirboys sing it "happily and boldly."
500. WA 27:52.19ff., 26:168.27ff.; LW 40:256.
501. WA 30.2:681.34–35, 682.1–2, 685.1.
502. WA 29:481.4ff., 483.10–11.
503. WA 28:25.19ff.
504. Fränk. Bek. 469; cp. the opinion of Johann Beham-Bayreuth from 1530 (ibid., 566).

that, it is the church of the devil, who from the beginning wanted to set himself above God. It is the gospel that created the church, and not the other way around; the church received the gospel and believed it.[505] That is how the bond with Christ is expressed. The church is built on him; that is, it believes that Christ is our righteousness. To deny faith means to take Christ away from the church.[506] It is upon this preaching of Christ that the church has lived from the first. The church is the bride of Christ, he is its bridegroom—that is how the imagery of the Song of Solomon describes their mutual relationship. It has the same spirit he has, indeed it lives in the same spirit as Christ does in the same divine life. God and Christ have passed the same judgment on it: its portion is the same righteousness that Christ possesses. Bride and bridegroom have everything in common.[507]

This unity of the church was also described by the term *congregatio*, which was used by Luther in his Old Testament exegesis long before the composition of the Augustana. It clearly preserves the image of the one flock: "There is one flock, one church, *congregatio*, of one doctrine."[508] It is not formed, as "crazy clever reason" and the world imagine, by chance and "blindly" through mere coincidence,[509] but in the way that a nation is gathered and dwells together. According to Genesis 1, a "congregation" is founded and created and then "confirmed and established by a special word of God."[510]

Therefore, that which holds the *congregatio* together is God's will to create and, let us add, God's will to save. Thus unity is the essential element of the congregation; unity of doctrine is included. Therefore the teacher of the flock must be someone who continues in right doctrine rather than some vagabond.[511] An "orderly assembly" belongs to God; he tends it as his own work. The Holy Spirit is his creative instrument; it gathers the congregation and preserves it in faith in Jesus Christ. It creates a life in it that is pleasing to God and humanity.[512] In the church people are brought together (*congregati*) in such a way that those who have fallen prey to sin are set right again. The church is armed with Word and deed through the power of the Spirit.[513]

Thus, for Luther the word *congregatio* is tied to inherently biblical concepts. By playing on the Greek word *koinonia*, "fellowship," as it appears in

505. *WA* 26:568.23ff., 29:17.1.
506. *WA* 16:331.1ff., 40.1:575.3.
507. *WA* 17.1:439–43.
508. *WA* 31.2:677.14.
509. The origin of the Reformation vocabulary is to be found in the language of the Old Testament and not in the late medieval vocabulary influenced by ideas of natural law.
510. *WA* 31.1:193–95; *LW* 13:45–48.
511. "A teacher of the people is to maintain purity of doctrine and not wander around" (*WA* 31.2:676.9).
512. *WA* 29:374.19ff., 82.6–7, 605.9.
513. *WA* 20:796.17, 721.15.

the account of the decision of the apostolic council in Gal. 2:9, he can say of the church that we have *communio* in doctrine, everyone has the same gift, we preach the same. In short, he makes statements similar to those he usually makes about *congregatio*, even though he is not fond of the term *communio* otherwise. And he takes the "that all may be one" in the high-priestly prayer in the sense of an identity that excludes all symbolism. We are one body with God and Christ—"a holy *communio*, not a likeness [*similitudo*]." He who attacks a Christian attacks the entire body.[514] *Congregatio* is a unity that does not arise from human will and ability. It comes into being by God's hand and is preserved through the activity of the Holy Spirit. Even when the dead are gathered for the universal judgment in the valley of Jehoshaphat (Joel 3), Luther says that "they are gathered [*congregantur*] under the Word of God."

The congregation of the saints (*congregatio sanctorum*) does not form an assembly totally composed of holy people; it is a mixture with the ungodly. In using the term, Luther anticipated Melanchthon's problems in CA 8. When the congregation gathers around the office of elder, ambition creeps in.[515] Luther first applies the phrase about sinners in the congregation of the righteous from Psalm 1:5 to his students: "They are neither teachers nor learners; they remain themselves because of their frivolity and willfulness." And he anticipates what Christ will say at the judgment: "I have a Christendom which of course should and will become one, but that has not happened yet because many in it are still weak. The single essence is there, but it depends on faith alone; to the extent that it is present, so is unity."[516]

Thus the congregation is split into more and less believing people; even obvious unbelievers belong. Thoughts of the gathering of those who "seriously want to be Christians" are heard throughout the 1520s although they tend to be directed more toward social ethics.[517] As in his Confession of 1528, Luther begins from the three groups (hierarchies): spiritual rule or the preaching office, temporal rule, and domestic rule. They are all three included in the "just group" (*rechten Haufen*) of the chosen children of God and of all saints on earth, "who are the true Christians." Abuses in the three estates are painted in lurid colors: "There is neither respect for God nor timidity before men," but the faithful little group testifies to fear of God and remains pious. It is hidden in the three groups, although few in number, and is gathered out of them by God. For its sake, God preserves the three groups

514. *WA* 40.1:189.4ff., 28:147.27ff., 149.7–9, 156.8.

515. "It is a natural sin that, where there is a congregation, where there is a church, one is prone to attach oneself to anything lofty" (*WA* 26:96.27–28; *LW* 28:350).

516. *WA* 31.1:265.24–25, 28:189.31ff.

517. Cp. the *Exposition of Psalm 118* (1529–30; *WA* 31.1:87ff.; *LW* 14:56 [Ps. 118:4]). The theme also appears in a sermon from September 12, 1528 (*WA* 28:132.23ff.). On the doctrine of the three estates, cp. above, pp. 85–89.

and, in the process, the whole world; without the pious it would disappear like Sodom and Gomorrah. On the other hand, the good group is persecuted by the other three. In anguish and need, it experiences the "beginning of eternal life" with comfort and help of which the world may not share the slightest drop.

The contrast between pious and worldly[518] thus runs right through the congregation; as the congregation of saints it is in no way a self-contained sociological structure. It is like an army ravaged by civil war; in the eyes of the world, it is a horrible thing; it is of no reputation before the world, but only in the eyes of God. Indeed, the church is holy despite the many evil persons within it. From the beginning of the world there have been much better people in it than in the church. "God preserve me from that Christian church in which there are only holy people. I would rather be in one with the weak and persecuted."[519]

Thus, the contrast that defines life in the congregation leads us to the tension between holy and unholy in the church; in contrast to his preface to the *German Mass* of 1526, Luther now does not make the tension visible by a legal and liturgical structure. He maintains the tension, beginning with himself: "When I look at my person, it is never holy, but if I look at Christ, it is holy, for the sins of the whole world are not there when we look at Christ." Theologically considered, sin is no longer in the world; looked at rationally (*secundum rationem*), however, the world is full of sinners. That has its consequences for the *congregatio sanctorum*. Its sanctity is only beginning. It should say of itself, "I am in sin, a sinner and nevertheless holy, for I believe that the body and blood of Christ are given for me and that this forgiveness of sins endures forever because sin certainly continues to exist." "There is no sinner as great as the Christian church."[520] It is holy, as Luther put it in opposition to Erasmus, "by the rule of love, not by the rule of faith." In its holiness it is hidden from the eyes of the world; its hiddenness indicates its holiness before God.[521] Thus I can confess in the Apostles' Creed, "I believe . . . one holy Christian church."[522]

In this church, the gospel is "preached in its purity"[523] and the holy

---

518. The former have the Word of God and the latter suppress it (*WA* 28:132.23ff.).

519. *WA* 31.2:723.6, 749.22ff., 750.2–3, 727.6ff., 15ff., 18:651.7–8; *LW* 33:87; *WA* 27:538.3ff.

520. *WA* 40.1:445.2ff., 34.1:208.11ff., 276.7. We state in advance that these two statements from 1531 are subsequent to the change that accompanied the spread of the doctrine of justification.

521. "The church is hidden, the saints unknown" (*WA* 18:652.23–24 [= *BoA* 3:141.1–2]; *LW* 33:89). Cp. *WA* 18:651.24ff. (= *BoA* 3:139.39ff.); *LW* 33:88.

522. "Where that Christian church is, all sins are forgiven, for such a Christian assembly is the kingdom of Christ which he boasted of before Pilate" (opinion of Johann Beham-Bayreuth [1530], *Fränk. Bek.* 571). Cp. ibid., 566–67.

523. It is here assumed once and for all that for Luther *docere* = "preach."

sacraments administered "according to the divine Word" (recte). The holy Christian church bases itself on Word and Sacrament.

We have already spoken of the Word of God as the sign of divine lordship over the church. Now it must be developed in its universal significance. The church is obedient to Christ under God's Word.[524] It extends into the world. Using the example of the kingdom of Solomon, Luther shows how the gospel spreads across all provinces, everywhere awakening a few out of the masses to faith and gathering them into a congregation. Christ himself did not do mission work, but his apostles did after Pentecost; in tongues of fire the gospel changed human hearts, conquering national boundaries. Luther himself remembered his Italian trip, where he was able to make even the Italians understand his preaching.[525]

In CA 7 as well as in Luther's preaching, however, the main emphasis lies on the pure proclamation of the gospel, that is, on preaching against heretics. Pure docere (to preach purely) does not aim primarily at preaching correct doctrine but aims mainly at the inner communication of the truth of the gospel by the power of the spirit. It is the spirit's work "to build up the Christian church, to grant forgiveness of sins, to raise the flesh from the dead and to give eternal life." "Our salvation is in the fact that we hear the Word of Christ; then the communion of saints (communio Sancta) occurs."[526] The church, however, is primarily the subject, not the object, of pure doctrine. It is the congregatio that "believes purely" that which it teaches, and "when you have learned that, you can defend yourself" against the false prophets. The church preaches the gospel and confesses Christ; then the fruits of love follow.[527]

The spirit follows the Word of Christ; where the spirit goes, the fruits spring forth. Doctrine testifies to the truth (vera doctrina), and the Spirit effects its recognition; its strength operates powerfully even among those who resist. The heart of this doctrine does not refer to Christ's rules about what we should do and permit; it refers to the gospel with its promise of grace. Luther summarizes that for himself: "I let myself be comforted, help my neighbor, suffer . . . , wait for eternal life; that is the teaching of Christianity."[528] The firmness of the struggle against heresy does not exclude ardent love for the

524. It grows under this Word: "The church is greater after Christ than before" (WA 31.2:681.1).

525. WA 31.2:737.15ff., 20:285.17ff., 395.24ff.

526. WA 29:363.14ff., 365.2, 366.12. Cp. ibid., 374.19ff.: "The Holy Spirit, by its work and the teaching of the apostles, gathers the church, builds it up in unity, and keeps it in the faith of Jesus Christ."

527. WA 29:481.18ff., 483.10ff.

528. Ibid., 365.11–12, 425.14–15, 559.3–4, 487.18. On October 5, 1529, after the end of the Marburg Colloquy, Luther preached on the forgiveness of sins, "that you may see the agreement of our teaching with the teaching of your preachers" (ibid., 564.10–11). In this article, therefore, he was seeking pura doctrina.

irresolute and weak. True doctrine is the teaching of Christ, not preaching the law. The struggle involves the whole congregation and not just individuals; it is in the congregation that the doctrine must endure and the sun of righteousness shine. The stubbornness of evil preachers who corrupt the purity of Christian teaching must be opposed just as consistently.[529] In the process one must wait with patience to see what will come of suspicious teaching. In the end the sects turn out to be in the lap of pure doctrine. No arrogance! Let every Christian, whether teacher or learner, act with humility toward others and let the grace of the Holy Spirit rule; passion is excluded.

These personal statements produce a different picture of Luther from the usual image of someone who was quick to judge heresy. Of course, one must insist on the fundamentals of the original doctrine; otherwise one loses certainty and steadfastness.[530] The original doctrine of the church reaches back to the origin of the creation. In the beginning God sent his son. From the beginning this God is the true one; a new God, who required human efforts rather than Christ, would be a fictitious God. A doctrine that preached such a God would not be true. A new doctrine would require a new form of worship. What confusion would then arise in Germany! Reason and the impending council would combine to form a new church out of the numerous sects. So many new teachers have already appeared that we have all we can do to preserve "the dogma." In the history of the church the number of pure teachers has always been small; only Scripture is pure. "Beware of those who teach something different from what the apostles taught."[531]

One theme runs through all these statements: the pure doctrine is the old; every new one is heretical. The psychology of heresy handed down from Christian antiquity is therefore normative for Luther, although he measures heresy against Scripture rather than against traditional dogma. The old doctrine that counts against the newly devised one is that of the apostles Peter and Paul. "Beware of new doctrine and preserve the old!" The gospel remains ever new, but the old man does not understand it. Preachers should beware of formulating new articles; where those do show up, preachers should be as careful as they would be of the devil. False doctrine flourishes; the more impure it is, the more adherents it finds.[532]

The new false doctrine is from the devil, the antichrist! He wants to stamp out all of Christ's teachings in the name of the Christian church. In his desire to persuade humanity by force to accept false doctrine, he transforms himself into the shape of God and perverts consciences in doctrine and life. The

529. WA 20:601.6–7, 617.4ff., 647.3ff., 667.10.
530. WA 20:668.15, 675.13, 685.16–17, 24ff. Thus the concept is not foreign to Luther: "Our foundation is first 'Jesus the Son of God died' [Rom. 4:25]."
531. WA 20:655.13ff., 673.6ff., 674.4–5, 744.2–3, 748.1–2.
532. WA 29:429.5–6, 20:647.20ff., 23:413.36–37, 419.6–7; LW 43:152, 158.

vagabond preachers are his instruments; they do not let pure doctrine be heard.[533]

In addition to the pure Word, to "administer the holy sacraments in accordance with the gospel" is a constitutive sign of the one holy church. In this case, therefore, it is a matter not of a formulation of doctrine but of a proper administration of baptism and the Lord's Supper as they were instituted. This already sets up the theological and practical problems that will be treated in CA 22 and 24.

Let us turn our attention particularly to baptism. As early as the Wittenberg disturbances, with the Anabaptist polemic against infant baptism, Luther cited the undisputed usage of the church as a principal argument. The church had always baptized children and had never turned against that custom. If infant baptism were wrong, then the church had always confessed a false faith. The opposite is true; it always confessed what it believed.[534] Infant baptism is therefore an inseparable part of the early church's confession.

Luther also held this conviction at the end of the 1520s, when the battle against the Anabaptists reached its climax. Even his opposition to the papacy took second place to this issue. There is no denying that in the old church much of value, "indeed everything that is Christian and good," is to be found. Under the papacy, "there is true Christianity, even the right kind of Christianity and many great and devoted saints." Therefore, "if they would permit baptism and the Sacrament of the Altar to stand as they are, Christians under the pope might yet escape . . . and be saved."[535] Luther's opposition is directed primarily against alleged Lutherans who claim that the "baptism is not valid because the priest or the one who baptized did not believe." But God allows the papal baptism to stand and considers the evangelical Christian properly baptized. If it were otherwise, there would have been no baptism and no Christianity for the last thousand years. Then the Apostles' Creed would have been wrong. Christianity is the bride of Christ and has "his Spirit, his Word, his baptism, his Sacrament, and all that Christ has." Although, according to 2 Thess. 2:4, the devil may sit in God's temple, the church is nevertheless "not a haunt of heretics but true Christendom, which must truly have a proper baptism."[536]

The objection that an unworthy, unbelieving priest could not administer an effective sacrament is not convincing; the power of the sacraments is based on

533. *WA* 29:108.1ff., 306.10ff., 20:672.15ff.
534. *WA* 2:424ff. (= *BoA* 6:91.13ff.); *LW* 48:365ff. (Luther to Melanchthon, January 13, 1522).
535. *WA* 26:147.16ff., 149.1–2; *LW* 40:231, 233.
536. *WA* 26:163.11ff., 168.27ff., 169.5ff.; *LW* 40:250, 256, 257; *WA* 18:649.26ff. (= *BoA* 3:137.36ff.); *LW* 33:85.

the words of institution rather than on human sanctity. Holiness thus derived applies even to the enthusiast preachers except, of course, those who basically deny the reality of the sacrament altogether. Once again the universality of the church is involved; it is spread around the world wherever there is baptism. Cyprian's rejection of heretical baptism was therefore misguided; even the papists carry out a valid ministry. That they misuse the name of the true God in the process is a quite different matter.[537] From the perspective of this understanding of the sacraments, there cannot be different confessions. Or is it possible that the contrast between the true and false church preserves church unity? Are there indeed two churches reviling and excommunicating each other? No, Luther leaves the use of the name Christian church to the judgment of God. God decides who has lost that name and who keeps it. But no one can dispute the claim of a church to possess that name when the church has preserved the gospel and the preaching office, and has maintained baptism and the Lord's Supper according to Christ's institution. The fact that Roman priests revile and slander that which the evangelical church does in the name of Jesus reflects on themselves. The unity of the body of Christ rests on the faith of those who accept the gospel and the sacraments; this bond of faith cannot be broken. A similar point of view enables Luther even to justify the existence of Christian sects. His proposal sounds almost as ingenious as the Hegelian concept of the idea: the true foundation of Scripture would not have been found without the attacks of heretics; Christians become stronger through the onslaughts of the devil. "Christian life is military service [*militia*], and God is the Lord of hosts" who leads his own onto the field of battle.[538]

24. UNITY AND MULTIPLICITY OF THE CHURCH (CA 7, SECS. 2ff., AND CA 8)

The multiplicity of the evangelical church is thus already implicit in the expressions Luther uses to illustrate the central elements of the true unity of the church. We have seen that Melanchthon took over the relevant sentences from the Schwabach Articles and that they in turn went back to Luther's Confession of 1528—sometimes word for word.[539] Thus the theological statements do not go much beyond what we have already investigated.

The second half of CA 7 is an inversion of what section 1 had established with the help of familiar sources: the true unity of the church rests on Word and Sacrament. The devaluation of ceremonies is a theme running all through

537. *WA* 29:173.1ff., 40.1:71.6ff., 34.2:433.1ff., 12ff., 27:52.19ff., 42.10–11.
538. *WA* 34.1:432.9–10, 433.1ff., 16ff., 437.7ff., 17.1:140.11ff.
539. See above, pp. 377–78. See also *BS* 108–9; Jacobs 76.

the "disputed articles." The reference to Ephesians 4 nicely summarizes the biblical passages mentioned in Torg. A 9.

Article 8 of the CA once again explains what the *congregatio sanctorum* is, by means of words and ideas we have amply investigated in connection with CA 7. The anti-Donatist principle is vigorously underlined in the condemnation (sec. 3), more explicitly in the Latin version than in the German.[540] Thus there is no part of CA 8 that shows any advance in Luther's doctrine of the church. It holds fast to those points which A 9 established in order to justify the Saxon visitations.

25. THE SACRAMENTS (CA 9–13): TEXTS

The articles on sacraments in the Augustana have a twofold root, and that is clearer in their case than with most of the other articles. One element remains embedded in Luther's Confession of 1528, as was the case with previous articles; the other is found in the official explanations that led to the production of the Augustana. Private documents of both reformers from the preceding years must also be considered where necessary.

In the Confession of 1528, which began the development of the Augustana, Luther gave a general definition of the sacraments. He ties the three sacraments to the activity of the Holy Spirit, which communicates the Word and conveys salvation; by this means Christ's beneficent gift of salvation is imparted, received, and preserved. Inward and outward gifts are not pitted against each other in terms of value; they are bound together by Spirit and faith.[541]

The Spirit thus rules in a threefold way: through the Word of forgiveness, through baptism, and through the Sacrament of the Altar. This compartmentalization lingers on in the Augustana, which, although it does not name three sacraments, does tie confession and absolution together and make them part of the use of the sacraments (*usus sacramentorum*). Luther relates all the sacraments to their saving use more than the Augustana does; educational and psychological definitions fade into the background. According to Luther, the activity of the Spirit "inculcates the suffering of Christ in us and brings salvation for our benefit."[542]

Luther's understanding of baptism is similar. Just as there is only one gospel for the forgiveness of sins, so there is only one baptism. The same divine ordering is at work in both areas; neither is nullified by wrong use.

---

540. Numbers 13 and 28 of the *Concord of the Churches of the Reformation in Europe* (the Leuenberg Concord) barely touch the problem of CA 7, 8.

541. *WA* 26:506.3ff. (= *BoA* 3:511.28ff.); *LW* 37:366.

542. *WA* 26:506.12 (= *BoA* 3:511.32); *LW* 37:366. The difference becomes most apparent when one compares the simple sentence with the rhetorical structure of CA 13.

The crucial point is not the legal status or the belief of the one who administers the sacrament but the fulfillment of the command to baptize. Anabaptists and Donatists have thereby excluded themselves from the Sacrament of Baptism. With a light touch, Luther omitted all dogmatic argumentation in these remarks and related the use of the sacraments exclusively to the fulfillment of their divine institution.

The same concern governs his discussion of the Sacrament of the Altar, which was practiced and interpreted in so many different ways.[543] These many differences in theological meaning required, however, a statement of faith. Luther's confession says that "in the Sacrament of the Altar the true body and blood of Christ are orally eaten and drunk in the bread and wine. . . . " To this first formulation of the doctrine of the Lord's Supper, which we can trace right through to the completion of the Augustana, is added an anti-Donatist reservation, as was the case with baptism: " . . . even if the priests who distribute them or those who receive them do not believe or otherwise misuse the Sacrament." Here, in lapidary simplicity, the Sacrament is grounded in God's Word and ordinance, rather than in human belief or unbelief. Those who change any of this, as the enemies of the Sacrament did in Luther's day, pervert God's Word and ordinance and therefore have no Sacrament but "only bread and wine."

Luther, however, did not limit the threefold sacrament to the two external functions of Baptism and the Sacrament of the Altar; they include the functions of forgiveness contained in confession and absolution.[544] Forgiveness is not only received in the one-time act of baptism; through the gospel it is continually offered, obtained, and received. The church is a "kingdom of grace and of true pardon"; therefore, outside its territory "there is no salvation or forgiveness of sins."

This view provides the occasion for Luther's anger against the indulgence system to break out again. As at the start of the Reformation, the polemic is ignited by the misuse of the sacrament of penance. If one follows Luther in including penance and private confession among the sacraments—they were added to the second printing of the Confession of 1528[545]—it is clear why Luther's reformation was more than a mere elimination of the sacramental church of the Middle Ages; he was concerned about renewing it in the center of its sacramental life, in the practice of penance. Thus the sacraments are tied to the ethical demands of his Confession of 1528, particularly the renewal of the three estates or orders under the "common order of Christian love."[546]

543. *WA* 26:506.21ff. (= *BoA* 3:512.4ff.); *LW* 37:367.
544. *WA* 26:507.7ff. (= *BoA* 3:512.32ff.); *LW* 37:368.
545. *WA* 26:507.17ff. (= *BoA* 3:513.1ff.); *LW* 37:368.
546. *WA* 26:504.30ff. (= *BoA* 3:510.17ff.); *LW* 37:364.

In that way the reform of evangelical worship leads to the renewal of social life. It also explains why evangelical confessional development centers on the conflict over sacraments, which is summarized here in articles 9–13.

The trail that leads from Luther's Confession of 1528 to the Schwabach Articles of 1529 is no longer apparent in all its details. The research of Hans von Schubert tells us that an early draft by Luther of that later alliance's confession was taken as the basis for the Marburg Articles. A closer examination of reports of the Marburg Colloquy, however, makes clear that, at the beginning of the negotiations, Luther provided the landgrave with seven theses directed against the Swiss and the southern Germans.[547] From July 1529 on through the days of Schleiz and Schwabach, the general Protestant confession grows within a Lutheran framework. The original version of the Schwabach Articles follows Luther's earlier work almost literally,[548] but it lacks the general definition with which he tied his teaching on the sacraments in 1528 to the imparting of salvation in the church. Baptism and Eucharist as "external signs" (Schwab. 8) are added to the sole means of grace in the oral word. The article on baptism (Schwab. 9), relying on Luther's Small Catechism, makes a distinction between the simple water and the creative Word of God. The doctrine of baptism is developed in the dialectic between visible element and Spirit-filled Word, between external and internal event. While this approach follows Augustine, it also depends on the catechetical tradition represented through Luther. It supplants the Confession of 1528. For example, the latter's reference to the biblical emphasis on *one* baptism (Eph. 4:5) is missing, as are Luther's central themes of divine ordinance and right use of the sacraments, as well as mention of the anti-Donatist principle. In general, the understanding of baptism in 1528 far exceeds that of 1529; there is no dependency in thought or style between the two texts.

Article 10 of Schwab. follows the same pattern of external-internal and material-spiritual that Schwab. 9 used; this polar tension gives rise to the nature of the Sacrament of the Altar. This tension had to be made plausible in the contemporary debate: "According to the Word of Christ," the body and blood of Christ are truly present in bread and wine. As with Baptism, the creative Word makes the Lord's Supper a sacrament. We quote once again from Luther's eucharistic formula of 1528: "The true body and blood of Christ are orally eaten and drunk in the bread and wine." There is a clear difference, though not a contradiction, between the lively description of a

---

547. The "anonymous" version of the Marburg Protocol—in contrast to Hedio's version—mentions only the Strassburg theologians. Therefore Jacob Sturm felt that it was his Strassburgers who were primarily under attack; cp. *WA* 30.3:111.11ff., 149–50. The sequence of Luther's first polemical statements is related to that of the Schwabach Articles. The Marburg Articles show even more parallels in thought to the Schwabach Articles.

548. On the text of Schwab., see W. Maurer, "Entstehung" (cited above, n. 8).

visible process in 1528 and the schematic presentation of a parallel between internal and external content in 1529. Despite the polemic against the "opposing party," there is no condemnation of Donatism, which would have highlighted the peculiarity of a real presence known only to faith. Thus in the 1528 version it is only a logical paradox, not a reality of faith. The addition to Schwab. 10 attempts to remedy this situation by making both sacraments dependent on the gift of faith. In the Torgau Articles the elector's advisers presented a description of what happens in the Sacrament that offers nothing new in terms of content, but it does overcome the stiff abstraction of Schwab. 10 by more vivid language. "And the people are diligently instructed that in the Lord's Supper the body and blood of Christ are present and that they are given, for thereby one strengthens faith that consolation is received, that Christ wishes to be ours and to help."[549] Although it is not possible to establish any further influence of this unique sentence upon the eucharistic tradition, it gives the simplest description of the role that faith plays in the Sacrament of the Altar.[550]

For Luther in 1528, confession was only an addendum; in Schwab. 11, it precedes penance. In both documents the basis is the same: negatively, there should be no legal coercion to enumerate sins; positively, the comfort of forgiveness is beneficial. Luther speaks of this comfort and, as a result, of penance much more fully than Schwab. does. He also makes the connection with baptism that is missing in Schwab. 11. What happens once and for all in baptism is constantly offered anew in absolution.

It is apparent that, in contrast to earlier parts of the articles on the sacraments, here the connection with Luther's Confession of 1528 is much looser. Evidently Luther's direct influence had diminished considerably by the time of the formulation of the Schwabach Articles. Their revision during the months in Augsburg shows, in individual cases, that the process was reversed; Luther's thought occasionally breaks through again. We will now trace the articles on the sacraments—with the exception of the article on the Lord's Supper, which requires special treatment—through Na and its reworking to the final version.

In Na 8, baptism is oriented exclusively toward infant baptism and the rejection of the Anabaptists. Echoes of Luther's Small Catechism are gone, as are reminders of his Confession of 1528. All that remains is that children are accepted into grace by God.

Private confession gets strong emphasis (Na 10), although the full enumer-

549. A 4 (Förstemann 1:77; Jacobs 81).

550. Melanchthon had already provided a similar instruction on the Lord's Supper to pastors in his *Instructions for the Visitors*. He recommends study of the church fathers and gave directions about what should be done with those congregational members who held to the traditional mass.

ation of sins is rejected. These latter two articles show particularly clearly that there has been no attempt at theological reflection.

Article Na 11 gives a much more detailed treatment to Melanchthon's central theme of penitence. The understanding of penitence as a constantly repeated baptism is taken up from the Confession of 1528.[551] The idea that adult baptism is a sort of general absolution, which was common among some Anabaptists, is rejected. It asserts the obligation of the church to absolve repentant sinners, thus opposing the pressures of ecclesiastical politics that dominated the practice of penance in the medieval church. The description of penance around the two poles of contrition and hope remind us of the *Instructions for the Visitors,* with its twofold demand for recognizing one's sin with a contrite and fearful conscience and for receiving absolution through faith in the gospel.[552] These thoughts, reinforced by mention of satisfaction through Christ alone, move us into the theological circle that Melanchthon occupied all his life. It is in Na 11 that that position first becomes evident in the general confessional development. In this article the church reached a breakthrough from which it never retreated.

In Na 12 we have, for the first time since 1528, a general statement on the sacraments, although it no longer has anything in common with Luther's general definition of them.[553] Melanchthon and his Augsburg co-workers reached back to the distinction between external sign and creative Word, which we already noted in connection with the two principal sacraments—especially with Baptism, following Luther's Small Catechism.[554] The sacrament is not only a badge of identification among humankind, but it is first and foremost a testimony of God's saving will for the strengthening of our faith; the sacrament gives faith assurance of the divine promises. The sacraments thus promote our understanding—which marks a fundamental difference from Luther—but to that extent they do not incorporate us in spiritual communion with God and Christ.

In the three solid weeks between Na and the textual revision of Nb we find characteristic changes in the wording of the other articles on the sacraments (again skipping the article "De coena domini").

Sharper formulations are inserted in the article on baptism (Na 8; now Nb 9). Baptism not only includes a demand on Christians (that "children should be baptized"), but also an inner spiritual necessity ("that it is necessary and that grace is offered through it"). The article speaks only of the offer of grace and not of the reception of grace—a weakening also present in the

---

551. *WA* 26:507.14ff. (= *BoA* 3:512.39ff.); *LW* 37:368.

552. *WA* 26:202.26ff.; *LW* 40:275. This passage harks back to the traditional trio of sorrow, confession, and satisfaction, which also is recalled in Na 11.

553. See above, p. 389.

554. See above, p. 391.

final text. On the other hand, Nb 9 is stronger in no longer saying that children are "brought before God"—which could imply merely the liturgical act—but in saying rather that they are "committed to God and become acceptable to him."

As far as private confession is concerned (Na 10; Nb 11), the existence of this institution is permanently guaranteed ("not allowed to fall into disuse"), and Ps. 19:13 is used to support the impossibility of complete enumeration of individual sins.

The long section of new material on repentance in Na 11 is tightened up stylistically in Nb 12, and its main point supported by Matt. 3:8. The most important change is that the mechanical parallelism between contrition and faith is refashioned into what became a classic paradox: "to have contrition and sorrow, or terror, over sin, and yet at the same time to believe the gospel and absolution." Article Nb 13 makes a typical change in the definition of a sacrament in Na 12, by insisting on the claim, as well as the gift, of faith ("to awaken and confirm faith").[555]

The focus of interest at Augsburg was on the question of the Lord's Supper. Upon its answer depended both the legal status of the evangelical princes within the empire and their relation to the Swiss and southern Germans. The article on the Lord's Supper thus had to maintain the substance of the faith that the medieval church had preserved. It is therefore understandable that there is less emphasis on the specifically evangelical statements with their ties to the doctrine of justification, and that, on the other hand, the core of the Reformation did not get so much attention that it would seem to counteract the more rational elements of Zwinglian teachings on the Sacrament. In the heat of the conflict, this complicated set of relationships was not very noticeable. It became critical when the inflexibility of the emperor seemed to make a move toward the southern Germans necessary. The two elements—preservation of content from the early and medieval church and openness to radical innovations—that had struggled with each other since before 1530 had to work toward a certain synthesis once the emperor's obstinacy became evident.

The critical observer will detect the juxtaposition of those two elements in both the Latin and German final versions of CA 10. At the same time, one is able to recognize the intrinsic problem by looking at the development of the two formulas through the successive documents:

1. "[I] confess that in the Sacrament of the Altar the true body and blood of Christ are orally eaten and drunk in the bread and wine" (Luther's Confession of 1528).[556]

---

555. It should be pointed out once again that the official German text is unchanged from Nb.
556. *WA* 26:506.21ff. (= *BoA* 3:512.5–6); *LW* 37:367.

2. "They are to believe that the true body of Christ is in the bread and the true blood of Christ is in the wine" *(Instructions for the Visitors)*.[557]

3. ". . . that there is truly present in the bread and wine the true body and blood of Christ according to the word of Christ" (Schwab. 10).

4. ". . . that the Sacrament of the Altar is a sacrament of the true body and blood of Jesus Christ . . . although at this time we have not reached an agreement as to whether the true body and blood of Jesus Christ are bodily present in the bread and wine . . ." (Marb. 15).

5. ". . . that in the Supper the body and blood of Christ are present . . ." (Torg. A 4).[558]

6. ". . . that the body and blood of Christ are truly in the Lord's Supper and are distributed, and those who teach otherwise are rejected . . ." (Na 9).

7. "The true body and blood of Christ are really present in the Supper of our Lord under the form of bread and wine and are there distributed and received. The contrary is therefore rejected" (Nb 10).

We will not go into the individual exegesis of these formulas from the time prior to the summer of 1530, but a quick survey shows that in Luther's statement from the Confession of 1528 (first in the list), everything is oriented toward the oral consumption of the body and blood in the bread and wine, and that the full burden of this statement is not expressed again until Nb 10 (seventh in the list). The second through sixth formulas in the list are definitions of essence; they disregard the process of sacramental eating. The sixth at least allows for the distribution, although not for the acceptance and reception, of the food. In other words, these formulas seek to approach Luther's point of departure in varying degrees, but only the last one reaches it—whether completely or not remains to be seen.

There is a series of quotations from Melanchthon that shows us the origin of those statements about essence. The formulas may all be traced back to the sentence "Christ's body and blood are present in bread and wine."[559] It is never stated that baldly, but it is elaborated in various ways. That Christ is *truly* present is mentioned in the third, sixth, and seventh formulas, in addition to the first. The adverb is lacking entirely in the fifth; in the second, third, and fourth, it becomes an adjective: the "true" body, the "true" blood. The expression is ambiguous, because a spirit (not a spiritual) body can be set in opposition to the real historical body of the Resurrected One.[560] The subtle

557. *WA* 26:213.21.; *LW* 40:289.

558. Förstemann 1:77; Jacobs 81.

559. We provide the literary evidence for this key statement of the Melanchthonian doctrine of the Lord's Supper, which also forms the central declaration of CA 10 in the Latin version.

560. In no. 7, the adjective and adverb are found in the same sentence. On the issue, see *BS* 64 n. 1. It shows that even contemporaries did not understand the real Lutheran meaning of "truly."

differences in terminology show that philosophically trained dialecticians had a hard time understanding Luther's description of a spiritual event. His description of a process turned into an analysis of a condition.

Our next task, however, is to follow the further development of the wording. The seventh formula (which is Nb 10 and therefore the German version of CA 10) shows only the final form of the German text. It goes beyond Na 9 in saying not only that the body and blood of Christ are present and distributed in the form of bread and wine but also that they are actually received. The text presses beyond all abstraction to the concrete process of the sacramental meal. But when we compare it with the final Latin text of CA 10, we find the opposite. Its backbone is formed by Melanchthon's core sentence, "The body and blood of Christ are truly present and are distributed to those who eat in the Supper of the Lord." Luther's codicil is not forgotten, however; the "truly" links the statement with the "true" of his 1528 confession. The reference to "those who eat" picks up the actual consumption mentioned in the German version. It does not, however, adopt the German text's phrase "under the form of bread and wine." That phrase goes back to the early scholastic sacramental doctrine that was struck down by the decree of Innocent III in 1215. Thus, both the Reformation presuppositions of the phrase and their Melanchthonian stamp are sacrificed in the interest of continuity with the Middle Ages. One must acknowledge the wisdom of the final editors who weeded out that overstatement of the doctrine of the Sacrament from the Latin text. Finally, it is noteworthy that the official rejection of opponents, which was not directly stated in Schwab. 10, appears in Na 9 and in both versions of CA 10, albeit in milder form and without naming names.[561] Of all the articles of the Augustana, CA 10 exhibits the most complicated process in the total development of its text, and that has made a variety of interpretations possible.

26. BAPTISM (CA 9)

There are many discussions of the Augustana's doctrine of the sacraments, and even more on its relation to Luther and—to a lesser degree—to Melanchthon. But we do not intend to make use of them here, nor will we evaluate the Reformers' doctrine of the sacraments by that of the Augustana in order to obtain some critical standards. Our task is much simpler. It is to reveal the background against which the five articles on sacraments (CA 9–13) are placed. We must consider more than just doctrinal statements that influenced

561. See Heinz-Werner Gensichen, *We Condemn: How Luther and Sixteenth-Century Lutheranism Condemned False Doctrine*, trans. Herbert J. A. Bouman (St. Louis: Concordia Pub. House, 1967), 89ff.

the formation of confessional language. Sermon statements, particularly those of Luther, that allow us to recognize the themes of pastoral care in the Confession are also important. Precisely because subtle theological questions lie behind the various confessional statements, it is important not to overestimate those subtleties but to appreciate the pastoral themes that are the primary interest of the scriptural expositor and preacher. Furthermore, because these themes still have some importance today, a historical commentary on the articles dealing with sacraments is relevant to the present situation in theology and church life.

In the second half of the 1520s, it is not only Luther's literary work that reaches a marked richness of content; the exegetical legacy of the Wittenberg professor also demonstrates particular power—as does the increased preaching activity occasioned by Bugenhagen's frequent absences. The testimonies that we derive from these sources will not only confirm Luther's doctrine of the sacraments but will particularly emphasize those of its elements that become barely visible or disappear altogether in Melanchthon's smooth formulations. Only against such a background can the confessional statements on the sacraments achieve their real power.

The article on baptism immediately confirms these observations. In general, all that CA 9 says about baptism is that grace is offered in it and especially that children should be baptized so that by this grace they may be brought to God and become acceptable to him. All the emphasis is obviously on the defense of infant baptism. Luther's Small Catechism had already gone far beyond these ideas, and there are plenty of other statements that give a more comprehensive picture.

Baptism is an actual offer of grace. If this is disputed, then baptism is impoverished and remains nothing more than the sign of individual righteousness of those who are baptized later in life. In the case of a child it simply expresses the hope that the child will someday become righteous. A baptism of that sort thus has nothing directly to do with grace and the forgiveness of sins; it is no more than a sign of membership in the Christian community. Luther correctly understood this evisceration of the Sacrament of Baptism as the expression of an ethical optimism that basically denied the sacrament.[562] From a rational point of view, baptism would be a work one performed or had done to oneself. But the promise of baptism is not bound to human deeds, not even to the presence of faith. In baptism someone other than I is acting: I am baptized; that is, I receive and undergo an act from without. Baptism is a divine work. And therein lies its sacramental character. Although Luther is conservative in his position on baptism, and although he respectfully main-

562. *WA* 28:574.1ff., 30.3:111.16, 27:134.13ff.

tains the traditional images describing the baptismal event—washing, bath, submersion, drowning—he nevertheless emphatically distances himself from all the symbolic ritual acts that were in use from the old church. As a sacrament, Baptism is God's effective deed; it rests solely on the effective word of his institution. But it is thereby also God's compelling command, which no Christian can evade. God, the true God who created heaven and earth, has instituted baptism. It does not go back to a human deed or to an earthly historical development; it has come from heaven. "No one should create worship for God."[563]

The Augustana is never as strong as Luther's doctrine of the sacraments in affirming that God acts with sovereign power in the sacrament and that his will and command are decisive here. That means, however, that the word of institution is the only fundamental factor in baptism: "For our baptism is not valid without the Word of God." "Just as the sign is of no avail without Scripture, so it is with baptism without the Word." That is why baptism occurs in the name of the triune God. God, not the priest, is the baptizer. Christ is the baptizer; we are baptized on his cross, and the fruit of his redemption is applied to us.[564] If we add that the communication of baptismal grace from beginning to end is evidence of the work of the Holy Spirit, then we will understand that for Luther, baptism in the name of the triune God is not a matter of form; the sacrament is embedded in the saving activity of God. Because of that, none of it is from our side, not through the liturgical action and even less through the person who receives baptism. Baptism is exclusively God's work through God's Word.

With that, something decisive is said that Luther never tired of affirming: in baptism human faith is not active, it merely receives. This principle prevents confusing faith with a general spiritual aptitude. Luther thus considered baseless the objection of opponents that infants possessed neither speech nor reason. No one knows what happens to them in baptism. But he nevertheless had every reason to be thankful to God for the blessing of baptism. "Whether I have believed or not, I have followed the command of God and been baptized and my baptism was correct and certain. God grant that whether my faith today be certain or uncertain . . . nothing is lacking in baptism. Always something is lacking in faith."[565]

The counterthesis of the Anabaptists states, "I was baptized as a child; I did not believe. Therefore I must be rebaptized; my baptism was not proper." In reply, Luther cites the basis of baptism: "Baptism remains, even when it is

---

563. "Nemo soll dei cultum facere" (*WA* 16:178.8ff., 179.8ff.).
564. *WA* 16:275.5–6, 17.1:98.9–10, 27:33.7, 136.19–20, 134.7ff., 36.3, 26:40.23–24; *LW* 28:268.
565. *WA* 26:157.8ff., 165.34ff.; *LW* 40:243, 253.

misused by those who administer it or by those who receive it." "Therefore baptism is to be considered a blessed, holy, divine work whether the one who baptizes be good or bad."[566]

One sees that Luther did not misinterpret the anti-Donatist principle in a traditionalist way; he filled it with new content from his newly won understanding of the sacrament. When the sacrament receives its meaning and power from God's word of institution, it does not depend on the piety of those who participate.

That may be true for the one who administers baptism, but does it also apply to the one baptized? Luther argues from the revelation of salvation as a whole. "If baptism were improper, God would not have bestowed the Holy Spirit and his gifts." Thus the certainty of my baptism is a result of the Trinitarian self-revelation of God. Luther appeals to the external verbal promise, and it is precisely its externality that the enthusiasts contest. But if that is abrogated, then grace is eliminated as well.[567] It is the fact that the Holy Ghost is constantly at work with his grace that accounts for the constant effectiveness of the existing practice of infant baptism.

If it were not proper, God would not have preserved it for so long. But it has existed since the days of the apostles. "There has not been improper baptism through 1528 years." "What God ordained is proper." Therefore the church has not made a mistake in practicing infant baptism. Through the uninterrupted flow of church history, baptism has been available to each generation. Where it has been administered as it was instituted, it has remained valid even though one or another of those who received it may have misused it. "Baptism . . . in itself is proper and ordained of God." It is therefore precisely God's command that is violated when this chain of succession is broken. In reality a rebaptism is simply not possible. God's activity, which extends over the whole world, cannot be disputed and brought to nothing. Baptism is valid whether one believes or not.[568] If the Anabaptists base the invalidity of infant baptism on the existence of the God-defying papacy, Luther appeals to the intact institution: even under the papacy the command to baptize is valid, as is the Trinitarian formula and the use of water.[569]

In the light of this unchangeable tradition, subjective faith does not mean a thing. No one can appeal to it. Ask those who have received rebaptism whether they now believe; they cannot give you a certain answer. It is just as impossible to prove in any given case that a child is without faith. The

566. WA 27:38.14–15, 18–19, 42.10.
567. "His ablatis ablata dei gratia (WA 27:20.28–29). "Faith should be based on God's Word instead of the Word of God on faith" (ibid., 44.8–9). Cp. ibid., 52.28.
568. Ibid., 36.3ff., 27ff.
569. Ibid., 42.23–24.

command to baptize is so sure that even Anabaptist leaders, if they follow that command properly, can awaken faith by their words. On the other hand, if a considerable number of parents were to refuse infant baptism there would soon be a decline of Christianity, so that no more than a tenth of the population would be baptized and the majority would become nothing more than Turks and heathen. Those who still went to church would follow the well-known example of early Christianity and not let themselves be baptized until their deathbed.[570]

A certain concern for the continuation of church life is thus part of the picture when Luther argues so vehemently for infant baptism and is so proud that there are no Anabaptists in Electoral Saxony. It is regrettable that up to the Revolution of 1848 the state required baptism and, although it rejected the necessity of confession, did not make infant baptism voluntary. The theological motives behind this practice are obviously secondary; they may be traced back to the understanding that God's grace in baptism addresses the entire world, and that those who despise it commit sin. After the collapse of the state church this requirement of baptism which is presupposed—although not directly expressed—in CA 9 was no longer binding.

Luther's traditionalism, which in this case worked itself out in both positive and negative ways, finds its counterbalance in the relation of infant baptism to circumcision. The Reformers who came out of biblical humanism, Melanchthon included,[571] assumed a connection between the two. Luther asserted the opposite. He recognized the typological function of circumcision as practiced by Abraham, the father of faith, but "that does not concern us heathen." It is only as an example of Abraham's tested faith that it still has any relevance to us; in itself it is nothing. Circumcision "was"; baptism "is." It is a sign of the grace in Christ that God now does without the power of the external sign. In itself that offensive rite was a symbol of God's "foolish dealing" with his people. In that respect—and only in that—Christian baptism corresponds to circumcision; it is indeed a foolish thing that a person would submit to baptism. Otherwise, circumcision is at an end now that Christ has come.[572]

These are merely marginal notes we have added to the discussion of CA 9 on the basis of roughly contemporaneous citations from Luther in order to illustrate his theological views. They show that the Confession reveals only a small segment of the Lutheran doctrine of baptism. That doctrine rejects any typological interpretation; baptism is understood entirely in relation to Christ and relies on him for its saving effect. This position overcomes any spir-

570. *WA* 26:154.1ff., 164–65; *LW* 40:239, 251; *WA* 30.2:595.4ff.; *LW* 38:97.
571. Cp. W. Maurer, *Der junge Melanchthon* (cited above, n. 150), 2:406.
572. *WA* 16:50.4, 429.3ff., 27:2.32–33, 17.1:1.6ff., 22.

itualistic weakening of baptism more clearly than CA 9 does. Baptism does not merely require Christian behavior, and in that respect it is not just an external sign of joining the church. It bestows the forgiveness of sins along with all spiritual gifts. The Holy Spirit is the mediator of these gifts; the person who receives them is inwardly changed.

It is God's creative Word that produces this renewal through baptism. Baptism is not just instituted by God. The words of institution are not only words of command that carry out an ordinance of God; they are creative words of grace. That is expressed in the Trinitarian baptismal formula, which brings the event of baptism within the Trinitarian process of salvation, tying it to the Confession's central statements on salvation. Faith makes that creative event its own. The act of confession is receptive rather than typically "active." The person *is* baptized; it does not matter who does it or under what authority it is done. This is the point on which the contrast between the Anabaptists and the basic Reformation position becomes most sharply evident. The evangelical understanding of the sacraments becomes clear: the action of the sacrament rests on the power of the words of institution; hence the passive attitude of the person baptized. These presuppositions form the basis for the anti-Donatist principle that Luther adopted out of the tradition of Cyprian and Augustine, a principle that is not expressly stated in the Confession.

Thus baptism as infant baptism lies within a broad theological and ecclesiastical framework that cannot be detected in the simple words of CA 9, and therefore one must consult Luther's statements from the same years.

27. THE LORD'S SUPPER (CA 10)

The last remarks on baptism are even more relevant to the article on the Lord's Supper. The key sentence of CA 10 is lapidary in its brevity, which conceals the important statements more than it explains them. Even if one adds the details, it scarcely goes further than merely asserting the real presence. The German version, with its inclusion of language from the decree of Innocent III in 1215, still is more allusive than definitive. If we want to obtain a clear picture, we have to put CA 10 alongside statements of Luther from roughly the same period. Only then is it possible to derive a Lutheran doctrine of the Lord's Supper from the article. Such a method will protect that lapidary core of which we spoke from inappropriate abridgment of content, as well as from unwarranted conclusions.

When we look at the final text, we must once again remind ourselves of the variety of interpretations that exist between the German and Latin versions of CA 10. Some expressions may be rhetorically redundant without any significance for the content, as in the "true" and "really" of the German version. Other expressions might support a spiritualizing understanding of the Latin text. The German text says that bread and wine are "distributed and received"; the Latin says "distributed to those who eat in the Supper of the Lord." In the German version the real presence in distribution and reception can be divided into two concrete acts; in the Latin text, distribution and reception form a self-contained process and the presence of Christ fills the entire course of the meal. One ought not infer a basic difference from this. The German version of CA 10 need not lead one to assume that the real presence is reduced to the moment of reception.

It is a different matter with the added phrase "under the form [*sub specie*] of bread and wine" in the German version. Scholasticism spoke of the two "forms" of which the laity could receive only the substance of the bread. One could infer a polemic against the denial of the cup in CA 10, as it had been expressed in the Torgau Articles[573] and would later be presented explicitly in CA 22. But it is more likely to be an effort at underlining conformity with the tradition of the real presence. One could interpret the text in a way that would assume a change of the bread into the body (so that only the empty form remained), but that is rendered superfluous by limiting the real presence to distribution and reception.

The reference to the decree of Innocent in the German version of CA 10 is a unique occurrence in the development of the article; it has no forerunners in the prehistory of the article and no consequences in its later history. Nevertheless, the core idea that "the body and blood . . . are really present in the Supper of our Lord" must be understood in the light of the whole tradition. Our task here is to explain the development of the article, showing what personal concerns of Luther played a part in supplementing or refining it. One ought not expect a full presentation of Luther's doctrine of the Lord's Supper.

We ought not underestimate Luther's personal experience with the Sacrament of the Altar; it made it impossible for him to deny the real presence, as many of his humanistic contemporaries tended to do. The real presence had never aroused doubt in him, but he had felt tempted to give it up. He reported in a letter to the Christians in Strassburg at the end of 1524 that five years earlier he would have been glad to leave traditional realism behind, because "I realized that at this point I could best resist the papacy. . . . But I am a captive and cannot free myself. The text is too powerfully present, and will not allow itself to be torn from its meaning by mere verbiage."[574] He must follow the words rather than follow reason, which is based on the

573. Torg. A 3 (Förstemann 1:74–75; Jacobs 79–80; BS 85.26ff.).
574. WA 15:394.12ff., 19–20; LW 40:68.

appearance of the bread on the altar. The word to which he knows he is bound is not a legalistic interpretation of the words of institution, but the saving Word of salvation which holds within itself the treasure of redemption. Misuse cannot keep it from being God's ordinance *(ordinatio)*. It is not an allegorical sign that requires further interpretation. It is rather the mark that is put upon a Christian the way an owner's sign is branded on a sheep at shearing time.[575] The Word binds faith to the Sacrament, because it is the essence of God's saving will. "The gospel is purely the offer of grace; therefore the Sacrament is not poison but a remedy of grace: it provides deliverance from a bad conscience."[576] Christ is to be taken as the content of all the words of Scripture, even those, like John 6:51, which force us toward a spiritualistic interpretation. By the same token, any sacramental materialism is also excluded. For to eat Christ's body means to believe in him, and that occurs through preaching rather than through physical acts. Just as the body takes in food and the two become one, so there is a spiritual eating that creates union with Christ. The spiritual process is not merely a reflection of the physical one; the two processes are inseparable. The spiritual act of faith assumes that Christ's flesh and blood are given for us, and this acceptance in faith is not possible without the physical action.[577]

In his sermons, Luther clarified the transition from spiritual to physical and back by means of words from the Gospel of John. The bridge between the two spheres is not built by us; it is presented to our view when we look at the cross. God offers up body and blood for us in death; we accept the saving fruit of this death for us and in faith eat and drink what he has done. Faith is the decisive element in this process of mediation. It "ascertains that the body and blood of Christ are communicated *substantialiter* in bread and wine to those who truly receive."[578]

In order to illustrate sacramental Communion to a village congregation, Luther explained the mystery of the joyous exchange, the same exchange he used to clarify the justification of sinners.[579] Christ takes my sins upon himself; I assume his grace. Thus for Luther the doctrines of justification and

---

575. *WA* 26:41.27; *LW* 28:269; *WA* 27:15.37ff., 36.19–20, 56.4ff.

576. *WA* 17.1:172.24ff.

577. *WA* 15:465.12ff., 16:225.8, 229.6–7, 305.1.

578. Our unity in faith with the crucified One corresponds to the unity of Christ's flesh and blood with the bread and wine in the Sacrament. In the introduction to a Maundy Thursday sermon, on April 13, 1525, in a village church near Wittenberg, Luther defined it in this way (the preacher demanded this Latin formula of his simple hearers): "It is to be firmly believed by all the godly that in the Supper of the Lord, the body and blood of Christ are truly present and given to those who receive" (*WA* 17.1:174.1–2). Similarly: "True faith, however, believes for certain that the body and blood of Christ are given substantially and truly in the bread and wine to those who receive" (ibid., 174.14–16). I have not been able to ascertain the pre-Reformation source for such a formula which could be assumed to be familiar to a rural congregation.

579. See above, pp. 318ff.

real presence belong firmly together; that is why he felt the dispute over the Lord's Supper touched the nerve of faith. After Communion, Christ says to the believing soul, "Now you have my righteousness, life, and blessedness, so that neither death, hell, nor any misfortune will overwhelm you. As long as I live and am righteous, you too will remain pious and alive."[580]

Christ gives me his body and blood, so that I possess both for eternity. "But if that is true," then it is also true "that Christ's righteousness and all that is his is mine as well." "Christ and I are blended together, so that my sin and death become his and his righteousness and life become my own. In short, a joyous exchange takes place. The Father lays all of my sin on him [Christ]. . . . In this faith I approach the Sacrament: that the body has been given for me, the blood poured out for the forgiveness of sins, and that faith does not believe this because of something tangible [ex sensu aliquo] but because of God's Word."[581]

To believe means to eat. That is figurative language which is not easy for everybody. It is the expression of a spiritual eating. God speaks with human-kind through the word of promise; we receive the Word in a spiritual eating (manducatio spiritualis) that presupposes receptive faith. If the bodily eating occurs in faith, it becomes spiritual; the earthly food becomes spiritual.[582] The equating of earthly and spiritual food, of eating and believing, can only be grasped and duplicated when one accepts a Christology in which God takes on human flesh and the human nature is made divine in faith. And because, in that process, faith has no power to produce but merely receives, the critical factor in the sacramental event is the objective course of the Word rather than subjective belief. "Whoever eats the Sacrament has the true Sacrament, whether that person is a believer or not."[583] Thus, in the course of the dispute over the Sacrament, what seemed a casual comment in Luther's discussion of baptism becomes the momentous watchword concerning oral reception by unbelievers.

Sacramental eating is an objective action. But subjective belief in receiving the Sacrament is not excluded. Those who go to the Lord's Supper should examine themselves beforehand as to whether they desire it with a believing heart; if they are without faith, then they would despise it. Only those impelled by heartfelt pangs of conscience ought to go to the altar.[584] On the other hand, a false objectivity is also wrong. Our altar is the place of preaching, not a sacramentally hallowed place. Our altar is where Christ is,

---

580. WA 15:498.21–24.

581. WA 17.1:175.2–5, 8–15.

582. WA 30.3:119.5, 133.21–24; LW 38:21.

583. WA 27:36.19.

584. Admonition Concerning the Sacrament of the Body and Blood of Our Lord (WA 30.2:601.7ff.; LW 38:104). See also WA 16:232.7.

above the heavens, and therefore not bound to any fixed spot. It is where God is, therefore everywhere, right or left, in death as in life, in a sacred space or robe or not. He who sits at the right hand of God shares in God's ubiquity.[585]

The doctrine of ubiquity is a key principle in the dispute over the Lord's Supper. For Luther the preacher, it is the simple expression of the intimate communion between the believing communicant and the body and blood of the heavenly Lord. By speaking the words of institution, the Lord binds himself to the believing soul, wherever that soul may be. This word of grace is unlimited in its effectiveness; wherever it is, spiritual eating takes place. To eat is to believe; those who experience that are together with their heavenly Lord wherever he is.[586]

This line of thinking has led to talk of a new metaphysics in Luther, because the barriers of space and time are conquered in the intensity of experiencing God. Luther does indeed describe experiences that go back to sacramental mysticism from the Middle Ages. But they are not significant as pious experiences of the believer who, in a joyous exchange, transcends the limits of space and time. It is not a matter of incomprehensible ecstatic experiences, as claimed by many medieval mystics and still given to Spanish mystics during the decades of the Reformation. For Luther, it is the simple folk in town and country in and around Wittenberg who let him teach them how to make the body and blood of their heavenly Lord their own through spiritual eating so that they become physically and spiritually one with him in faith. The religious immediacy in which that occurs shatters all limits of scholastic and metaphysical descriptions of the world.

The communication of attributes (*communicatio idiomatum*) is a pillar of Luther's doctrine of the Lord's Supper. Although he did not use it in teaching the congregation, it was of service in academic instruction. Here again Luther starts from existing relationships. The students will one day become preachers. Their sermons will have the same content as the proffered Sacrament: Christ. "In Communion the body crucified for us is given." "I preach this Word in which the treasure of redemption is wrapped."[587] In both cases the whole Christ, God and man, is communicated. Redemption is "God in substance and true nature." The God-man of the Redeemer cannot be separated into two persons, divinity and humanity. The entire Christ is active in Word and Sacrament. Those who pray to him address both his divinity and his humanity.[588]

The communication of attributes is a christological statement about the

585. *WA* 16:450.22, 26ff.

586. "Where the Word of God is, there is spiritual eating. Whenever God speaks to us, faith is required, and such faith means 'eating' " (*WA* 30.3:119.5; *LW* 38:21).

587. *WA* 26:40.29–31, 41.26–27; *LW* 28:268, 269 (lecture of February 5, 1528).

588. *WA* 26:92.18ff.; *LW* 28:344.

inseparable unity of the divine and human natures. It is the presupposition
for preaching Christ as well as for the real presence of the body and blood of
Christ in the Supper. The Christ to whom the sermon testifies, testifies to
himself in the Sacrament. In both cases, Christ offers himself in bread and
wine; Word-event and sacramental event are one, and faith grasps both in that
unity. Thus it becomes apparent that faith lays hold of the true and total
Christ in the words of institution and becomes one with him. To believe is to
eat. That is true because Christ is present for the believer as God and man and
is accepted as the pledge of redemption.

The divine and human natures in Christ are one and interchangeable! On
that fact rests the unity of bread and wine with Christ's flesh and blood; we
are dealing with the flesh and blood of him who ascended and is exalted, who
represents in his person the unity of divine and human nature. And to these
two circles, representing the unity of God and man, of exalted flesh and
earthly matter, is added a third circle unifying the believing Christian with
the person of the God-man and his earthly incarnation in the Sacrament of
the Altar. One must first comprehend how these three circles intermesh if one
hopes to understand the connection that exists between Christology and
Sacrament, on the one hand, and reception in faith, on the other. And then
one will appreciate Luther's concern about the future of Christianity when he
heard Averroes, the new convert to "heathenism," joke about Christians as
the worst people on earth, who "devour their own God," and when he hears
how his own followers are insulted as "cannibals" during the conflict over the
Lord's Supper. He calls it a "scandal of reason" that despises God's marvelous
acts.[589]

When one can appreciate the connection between faith in Christ and faith
in the Sacrament the way Luther does, then the "doctrine" of the Lord's
Supper becomes more than a conceptual abstraction; it is faith in a miracle.
The Lord's Supper is primarily a miracle to be adored. "If I eat Christ bodily
in the bread," explained Luther at Marburg on October 2, 1529, "that ought
not be understood as ordinary eating [humilis intellectus]. It is a good gift of
the Holy Spirit; therefore it is not ordinary and common but a sublime eating
[sublimis manducatio], because we can believe those words that the body of
Christ is here."[590]

As Luther wrestled at Marburg with the understanding of the Lord's
Supper, he saw the unity between faith in the Sacrament and in Christ as
something wonderful and sublime. The mind of faith encompasses the unity
of God and man in Christ and of bread and body in the Sacrament. The
parties that argued about these realities in scholastic and philosophical

589. WA 19:484.9, 499.13–14; LW 36:336, 346; WA 27:2.1–2.
590. WA 30.3:114.11ff.; LW 38:18.

terms—and Luther held his own in those battles—really missed the best part.

For the marvelous and the sublime is a category that has had its place in the worship of God from time immemorial. Luther prayed and explained the psalms from the beginning of his life as a monk, practicing the daily sacrifice of praise. And he also knows the lament of the prophets concerning the vain babbling of lips and a sacrifice rejected by God. He combines this knowledge with the experience of the justification of the sinner who offers his sacrifice of praise to God out of the depths of guilt, and he includes the encounter with Christ, "our altar," who sits at the right hand of God, everywhere present and near when we pray.[591]

Toward the end of the imperial diet, Luther, influenced by the impending termination of the unity negotiations in Augsburg, revived youthful memories about the mass as a sacrifice of praise. His object was to extract an evangelical meaning out of the sacrifice of the mass, in order to conquer both the Roman concept of sacrifice and the impoverishment of the Sacrament by the rationalism of the Swiss and southern Germans. Luther urges his followers to participate in the Sacrament "out of love and thanks to my Lord and Savior who has instituted it in honor of his suffering in order that I might use it and give thanks for it." This fulfills Christ's instruction "Do this in remembrance of me." It includes the memory of his suffering as well as the thank offering which that suffering now prompts us to bring.[592]

Luther knows that these ideas bring him into dangerous territory. The papists could accuse him of falling back into traditional "sacrificial" theology and then just renew the usual sacrifice of the mass. Luther, however, sees the difference clearly. It is not a matter of the mass as a work or a memorial whereby one increases the treasury of one's good works or meditates on Christ's suffering; it should be a thanksgiving to God for the abundant blessings he has made available to me through Christ's sufferings: "As a sign and confession of such thanks and praise, receive the Sacrament with joy."[593] Nor should the distinction between priest and laity be drawn anew, so that the priest might apply the fruit of such thanksgiving to other believers; all communicants receive the same gift and show the same gratitude.[594] Luther's theory of thank offering maintains all the achievements of the Reformation; it preserves the omnipresence of the body and blood as well as the unity of the

591. *WA* 16:605.8ff., 530.22ff., 531.16ff.

592. *WA* 30.2:609.15ff.; *LW* 38:115.

593. *WA* 30.2:610.6ff., 10ff.; *LW* 38:116, 117.

594. *WA* 30.2:612.6ff., 613.12ff.; *LW* 38:119, 121. The "restitution" of church goods demanded by the party of the old faith at Augsburg becomes groundless if those goods were the expression of a sacrifice of thanksgiving (*WA* 30.2:613.19ff.; *LW* 38:121).

divine and human natures. These gifts are the occasion for praise and thanks from those who have been filled with salvation.

One can understand why Luther's teaching on the sacrifice of praise is the least known and least durable part of his sacramental theology. The polemic against the standard theory of the sacrifice of the mass was incomprehensible and annoying to traditional believers. To the new believers in Zurich, Basel, and Strassburg, the connections in terminology and content with medieval ways of worship must have seemed offensive. It could only remain an episode in the history of the Wittenberg theology; the era of the treaty negotiations at Augsburg was too short for it to have any effect. The circle of Luther's students was too small; otherwise, during the time of Luther's isolation in the Coburg, they would have been able to think beyond the limits drawn by Melanchthon.

When one compares CA 10 with the ideas on the Sacrament that Luther developed in the years leading up to 1530, one notes with sorrow what little place those ideas found in the Melanchthonian development of the doctrine. We have been able to find the fundamental core statement that establishes the real presence relatively early in Luther; Melanchthon picks it up, but it remains undeveloped. His statements on the Lord's Supper thus become somewhat wooden. They are either formulated to communicate so carefully that an intentional ambiguity cannot be avoided, or they are abrupt condemnations that are consciously vague in naming persons, as in the Latin version of CA 10, or that can be exceedingly harsh, as are those against the Anabaptists.

Luther usually describes his doctrine of the Lord's Supper without fireworks or cutting irony, although these are not entirely absent. For the most part, however, he uses sermons addressed either to a congregation[595] or to students preparing to be pastors.[596] One is amazed at what Luther expected of his hearers and what he burdened them with on such occasions: difficult doctrinal complexes like *communicatio idiomatum* and the doctrine of ubiquity. How did the reformer arrive at such expectations? The answer is obvious, but it is difficult for today's reader. The doctrinal points in question are of a christological sort. And when it came to understanding the doctrine of the two natures, Christian congregations of the early sixteenth century were still at home. And even though the simple audience did not take in all the subtle niceties and sometimes followed the learned discussions with more stubborn tenacity than profound understanding of the issues, it was in agreement on questions of Christology, and it was certainly able to gauge the theological consequences of such questions. That is why the controversies over the

595. I refer to the Wittenberg village congregation; see above, p. 404.
596. See above, p. 405.

Lord's Supper penetrated so deeply into the spiritual life and the theological conscience of simple Christians, sometimes involving polemical consequences—even though not always clear to the nth degree.

Melanchthon, however, sought to avoid those consequences. The "pussy-footer" tried to soft-pedal the polemic element in his formulations. He put the key statement—concerning the real presence of the body and blood—in as elementary a way as possible, rejecting speculative conclusions; theological profundity could be annoying to him. This is not the place to trace lines back from Melanchthon to scholasticism or forward to Erasmus. He was aware of these connections and defended or contested them in his writings. But in formulating the Confession, he speaks so simply that deeper lines of theological thought are not unearthed. That is the weakness of his neat statements, his simple diction, and his resilient polemics. The consequence of that for the doctrine of the Lord's Supper, which concerns us here, is that the connection between Christology and Sacrament remains largely in the dark; Luther's deepest thoughts do not come to bear on the point. Statements that undergird the real presence, as ubiquity and *communicatio idiomatum* do, and doctrinal items like Communion as a sacrifice of praise, can simply disappear and then be taken up again in later discussion, albeit with a good chance of being misinterpreted and polemically twisted.

Luther's thoughts are often deeper and clearer than those of the official confession. They must be drawn upon if one is to hear what this confession really has to say.

28. CONFESSION AND REPENTANCE (CA 11, 12)

We have already become acquainted with the early stages of the articles on confession and repentance in the confessional writings, in connection with our study of the texts for baptism and the Lord's Supper.[597] In the course of the independent development of both articles, which really belong to the sphere of private pastoral care, questions of a more practical nature predominate.

In the *Instructions for the Visitors*, and even more in the Torgau Articles of the following year, the early concern is that the medieval institution of confession not fall into disuse but that it be maintained in its true biblical meaning.[598] In order for that to occur "with utmost seriousness," the *Instructions* and the electoral government rely on the hearing of confession that, after absolution, admits one to Communion. This maintains the connection be-

597. See above, pp. 389ff.
598. *WA* 26:202, 217–18, 220ff.; *LW* 40:274, 293–94, 296–97; Förstemann 1:77–78; Jacobs 81–82.

tween the Sacrament of the Altar and the practice of confession that was introduced in 1215. In contrast to the Roman usage, however, the obligation to confess and the requirement for complete enumeration of sins were discontinued. Remorse in confession and pain in repentance are to remain direct effects of the Spirit and faith. Those are the basic requirements for confession, and they are maintained right through to the wording of the Augustana.

The institutional aspects of confession and repentance thus move further into the background; in the *Instructions*, that occurs under the direct influence of Luther, who finally sided with Melanchthon in the latter's conflict with Agricola over the necessity of repentance and its relation to faith. Entirely apart from the question of how extensively Luther himself participated in the editing of the *Instructions*, the demand for "contrition and sorrow over one's sins and sincere fear of the wrath and judgment of God" goes right to the heart of the Lutheran doctrine of justification and is identical with Melanchthon's teaching on repentance. The pastoral principle of arousing people to fear and faith is central to Luther's explanation of the Ten Commandments. Thus one cannot consider Melanchthon's demand for repentance a regression, as Agricola did, but rather must see it as a deepening of his teaching on that point which occurred under Luther's influence; from the *Instructions* on, it defined the development of the Lutheran confessions.

At first, of course, institutional themes like freedom of practice and the justification of private absolution predominate in Schwab. 11 and Na 10. Article Na 11 adds a special section that picks up the basic outline of absolution almost word for word from the *Instructions* of 1528. It is followed by rejections of the Novatians—taken from the Confession of 1528[599]—the Roman doctrine of satisfaction, and the Anabaptist doctrine of perfection.

Article Nb 12, and consequently CA 12 in its German version, bring scarcely any changes in the text. They do, however, put stronger emphasis on the polarity—picked up from Luther and Melanchthon—between contrition and sorrow over sin, on the one hand, and "yet at the same time," the centrality of the assurance of the gospel, on the other. In this respect, CA 12 provides an important supplement to the teaching on justification. The doctrine of the fruits of repentance, hinted at in Na 11 and picked up again in the same brief form by the Latin version of CA 12, reaches its fullest biblically based expression in Nb 12, which is also CA 12 in the German.

The foregoing provides the key to everything that CA 12 says about true repentance. It gives expression to Luther's earliest and deepest experiences. Those who do not feel their sin and the curse that comes with it do not repent and do not become righteous. Conversely, those who feel themselves con-

599. *WA* 26:507.14ff. (= *BoA* 3:512.39ff.); *LW* 37:368.

demned do penance. Contrition's grief over sin covers all of life and includes its renewal. We are never able to put ourselves into that state of grief and thereby begin the renewal by ourselves. It depends upon God's Word, that flitting bird, truly reaching the heart. In a sermon, Luther recounted a personal experience from the same day. He had come from confession dissatisfied, and the devil questioned whether his contrition had been sincere. Then he took heart by deciding to base the forgiveness of sin not on his own contrition and sorrow but on the divine word of forgiveness that had been addressed to him.[600]

The result of all this was that confession no longer held the highest rank in the administration of the sacrament of penance, as formerly; the consolation of absolution became the principal thing. Of course, those who neglect confession or speak disparagingly of it also despise the word of forgiveness and therefore God's Word in general. But the important thing is not the total examination of conscience and the complete enumeration of sins. Luther provides his hearers with a model confession that they are to use: "Sir, many sins burden my conscience, because through them I have offended God. Among them, however, is a particular one; I ask that you lift me up with God's Word and comfort me with the forgiveness of all my sins." In contrast to previous practice, everything in this confession depends on personal humiliation before God; shameful sins are only to be mentioned and confessed when it is absolutely necessary.[601]

"Absolution is the principal part of confession, on which to rely the most." In it one grasps that on which all else depends: the forgiveness of sins. Replacing this word with human prescriptions or indulgences is like "mixing the dregs and the clear broth together."[602] In contrast, the decisive element in the Lord's Supper is the promise of the forgiveness of sins; it consists of an absolution. The close and, in terms of content, necessary connection between sacrament and absolution rests on this equation rather than on ecclesiastical law.[603] It is in the light of this event in which Lord's Supper and absolution are bound together that confession, too, attains its real depth. If it were not for the word of absolution, confession would abandon us to the wrath of God. The soul trembles, quakes, and despairs when it discovers its sin. Only when

---

600. "Those who do not feel sin and all their accursedness do not do penance, but neither are they saved. And the rest who feel themselves condemned are the ones who do penance" (WA 15:629.22ff.). "To do penance is when our former life grieves us and we condemn the way we lived and begin a new life" (ibid., 629.34f.). "Penitance is perpetual and lasts as long as a person lives (ibid., 629.37). Forgiveness of my sins does not consist in confessing them but consists in the word spoken by the priest, 'I absolve you' " (WA 27:45.5ff.). Cp. ibid., 44.35ff.

601. WA 17.1:177.3ff., 12ff. The simple formula of absolution is "I give to you the remission of sins" (ibid., 171.15–16).

602. WA 17.1:177.3–4, 30.2:288.22. Cp. WA 30.2:288–92.

603. WA 17.1:171.16ff.; cp. ibid., 172.25–26.

we accept the promise of freely given grace dare we grant that the sin we feel in our heart is not sin before God. Like Jonah, who is thrown into the sea, penitents must leap from the safe shore of this life into the abyss where there is neither feeling nor seeing, no longer any support or footing, and commit themselves "freely to God's supply and deliverance."[604]

Seen in this way, confession and absolution are complementary and reflect the same theological aspects. The description of confession in CA 11 does not plumb the depths of the troubled conscience that Luther reported from his own anxiety over confession—that feeling "that every misfortune overtaking us is God's wrath, and all creatures think it is a real God or God's wrath when it is nothing more than a rustling leaf."[605] But God himself prepares us through grace and spirit to lift up our heart "so that it remembers God's mercy and lets go of its thoughts of wrath and turns from God the judge to God the Father."[606] This alternation between anxiety over sin and certainty of forgiveness encompasses our whole life. It is strange, "this life of repentance and confession." We go on living faithfully, possessing the Holy Spirit and yet confessing ourselves to be totally sinful. Only a Christian can lead such a life. Strange too that a person who hears confession can proclaim absolution with divine authority![607]

In CA 12 Melanchthon refers to this life of confession and forgiveness by the term "conversion," *conversio*.[608] The term does not occur anywhere else in the confessional development, not even in Melanchthon's *Visitation Articles*, where one might most likely expect the term in connection with the doctrine of repentance. For Luther, conversion occurs through the Word of God. As word of absolution, it requires and effects faith. It calls us out of our unbelief and false faith, destroys wrong ties, and lets us turn to God. Conversion is therefore a work of the faith that the Spirit has induced. The decisive shift in course is not accomplished by our human will's affirming the forgiveness of sin; rather the Spirit working in the Word carries through the change and opens ear and heart, so that God's inviting call is heard.[609]

Here we have the foundation of an evangelical doctrine of repentance that excludes synergism from the start. But by CA 12, Melanchthon has already

604. *WA* 32:166.1ff., 19:217.20–21; *LW* 19:66. "God takes on a glowering mien. It seems that his anger is not appeased by the death and penalty to which Jonah is willing to submit, and that He cannot avenge himself fiercely enough on him" (*WA* 19:218.28ff.; *LW* 19:67). Human burdens are so great that they "outweigh the entire world" (*WA* 19:222.28–29; *LW* 19:71).

605. *WA* 19:226.12ff.; *LW* 19:75.

606. *WA* 19:229.29ff.; *LW* 19:79.

607. *WA* 19:514.8–9, 515.5–6, 521.5, 520.5.

608. ". . . [they] can receive forgiveness of sins whenever they are converted. . . ."

609. "That conversion, through the word of grace, enlightens hearts about God, so that we may abandon our righteousness, self-reliance, and inclinations which turn us away from God and are all idolatries. It is the gospel, however, that converts us to God" (*WA* 31.2:397.27ff.). Cp. ibid., 367.26–27.

deserted this basis; his later development—and therefore the development of his students—took another course. At this point the confrontation between the Augustana and the Luther texts from the same period leads to a dilemma in doctrine and practice that Protestantism has never completely overcome.

We encounter the roots of this difference in Luther's work *On the Bound Will*, which defends the evangelical doctrine of confession against Erasmus.[610] Out of an interest in educating the common people, Erasmus opposed freedom of confession and the abandonment of works of satisfaction; he blamed the decline of sacramental practice on these deficiencies. That was an opportunity for Luther to confirm anew his message of the freedom of a Christian in regard to repentance and confession. It is characteristic that when the humanist encountered Melanchthon's highly pedagogical doctrine of repentance in the *Instructions for the Visitors*, he gave it special praise; the rapprochement with his former disciple that took place at the end of the 1520s is to be understood from this perspective.

Luther's rejection of free will and his praise of freedom that is based on forgiveness—his whole opposition to Erasmus and his repeated distancing of himself from Melanchthon—are grounded in his understanding of repentance and confession; one must make a "fine, full" confession of sins: "Whatever in me and in my powers is outside grace is sin and is condemned." And tied to that is the miracle of forgiveness: "That is the nature of all sin; as soon as it is recognized, it is forgivable and remains absolutely a closed case. Where there is no confession, there is no forgiveness."[611]

But the confession of sin and the comfort of forgiveness happen only where Christ is present. The personal testamentary confession that Luther made before his students on August 22, 1528,[612] thus brings together all the soteriological and christological elements of the Augustana:

> I have often told you and tell you again, and when I am dead remember: all devilish doctors start from above and preach a God separate from Christ, as we once did in the universities. If you want to be secure against death, sin, etc., do not let them persuade you that there is a God other than the one who is sent [*qui est missus*]. Begin your wisdom and your knowledge with Christ and say, "I know no other God than the one who is in Christ," and where another is pointed out, shut your eyes.

29. USE OF THE SACRAMENTS (CA 13)

In his Confession of 1528, Luther made the three sacraments—the sacrament of penance had its own place—dependent on the activity of the Spirit.

610. *WA* 18:624.3ff., 627.24ff. (= *BoA* 3:114.29ff., 118.15ff.); *LW* 33:48, 54.
611. *WA* 28:12.17–18, 13.20ff.
612. *WA* 28:101.1ff. The connection with Luther's *Confession Concerning Christ's Supper*, completed about two months earlier, is obvious.

The discussion is placed within the Trinitarian context. The sacraments thus become "means and methods" of God's saving activity, part of that event which permeates Christendom in the power of the gospel. The proper use of the sacraments thus consists in congregations' and individual Christians' letting that event happen to them. Although it begins outwardly in Word and Sacrament, it becomes an inward event through faith.[613]

Even the definition of the sacraments that is developed in CA 13 offers instructions on how the Christian should make proper, faithful use of an outward, institutional procedure. Melanchthon does this by tying outward and inward together through the concept of signs. The outward signs testify to God's gracious will, expressed in the promises that accompany them. They also make those promises available to faith. There is an explicit rejection of a merely external procedure in which people bind themselves to one another by an external confession and profession (*professio*). What Luther saw as an intrinsic bond between Spirit and sacrament that produces direct effects, Melanchthon describes as the inward correspondence between sign and thing signified that is grasped in the sacramental event by faith—an idea which involves two steps and which is found throughout Melanchthon's work.

The gradual development of the text of CA 13 gives us a good opportunity to watch the unfolding of this theory of signs. In Schwab. 8, the umbilical cord to Luther's Confession of 1528 is not completely severed. The article still has some ties to Luther. The external signs correspond to the oral word. In Luther, however, they have significance only as bearers of the word; in Schwab. 8, they play an independent mediating role.

Article 12 of Na looks more closely at this role. In doing so, it already uses the phrase we have learned from CA 13: the sign is not merely there as an outward identification of the Christian—as the Zwinglians maintained—but it also gives evidence of God's saving will. Moreover, its use strengthens Christian faith in the promise. There is thus clearly a difference between the external sign and the spiritual event for which the sacrament is really intended. Article Nb 13 and the German version of CA 13 reinforce this spiritual bond; the sacraments require faith and strengthen it when they are received in faith. The external character of the sign recedes even further here, and also in the Latin version of CA 13; the distance between outside and inside thus increases as the editing of the article moves forward.

In this development we must also include Luther's statements about the sacraments in general from the period around 1530. They are not especially numerous, nor are they particularly emphasized. In fact, only careful analysis will distinguish them from Melanchthon's concept of signs. They represent

613. See above, pp. 389ff. See also *WA* 26:506.4ff. (= *BoA* 3:511.30ff.); *LW* 37:366.

an echo of the allegorical perspective that is particularly evident in Luther's Old Testament exegesis and that constitutes a frequent component of his preaching activity. Similar instances can be found in Augustine. In the first years, Luther's understanding of signs is closely related to the Augustinian one.

The development can be illustrated by some examples from Luther's expositions of the prophets from these years. Israel's exodus from Egypt and all the miracles accompanying it are signs for baptism and the Lord's Supper and remind us of the saving events of the New Testament. Certain striking signs like Noah's ark, the passage through the Red Sea, and the tablets of the law "signify" the New Testament sacraments and thereby reflect certain experiences of faith, such as the dying of the old man in baptism. Their New Testament counterpart is foot washing, which depicts the other side of the process, cleansing from sin.[614]

For Luther, baptism retains this signifying character "through all ages" (*per omnia saecula*). Submerging and bringing up out of the water signify death and life. But it is precisely at this point that a deepening of the concept that had begun in the mid-1520s becomes apparent. The sign does not take place in the realm of images while the real spiritual event is concentrated in the realm of actuality. Baptism is not a sign that points away from itself. In it the true God who created heaven and earth reaches out to humanity. We do not just perform an external rite; during the external action, God acts through his Word, and baptism is valid only because of this Word.[615]

A similar thing happens in the case of circumcision. It was widely seen as a "type" of baptism, merely a predecessor pointing the way. For Luther it was historically limited to the era of Moses and was replaced by the coming of Christ, just as every major figure of the Old Covenant—Abel, Noah, Abraham, David—had his own special sign that particularly touched people and spoke to them in their day. They were in part foolish signs (particularly circumcision), signs of God's foolishness (*vult stultificare*), signs of a passing covenant; our baptism, however, is a sign of everlasting grace![616]

Marriage is not a sacrament but a sign of one, a sign of the joy that fills the hearts of bride and groom, especially at the beginning of their married state.[617] As an earthly sign of the bond between two people it suggests the bond between the believing soul and Christ. Thus, during the decisive 1520s one can observe a development in Luther's concept of signs which leads ever closer to the crucial sentence of CA 13: "Sacraments . . . are signs and

614. *WA* 13:331.17ff., 607.11ff., 432.19; *LW* 18:258, 20:68, 19:121; *WA* 15:507.7ff.
615. *WA* 16:178.8–9, 179.8, 275.5ff., 304.6, 30.2:111.16; *LW* 46:165 (against a spiritualizing escapism).
616. *WA* 27:1.6ff., 2.26ff.
617. *WA* 15:419.22ff.

testimonies of the will of God toward us." Notice here the two-stage relationship of sign and thing signified.

By the end of the 1520s, however, Luther is already well on the way to
overcoming that relationship. In fact, that had happened in principle and
with undeniable clarity as early as 1519 in "A Sermon on Preparing to Die."[618]
Here the sign does not refer to a different, absent object; it incarnates the
dying and risen Christ: "It points to Christ and his image." The sacraments
embody God's promise as a sure sign of his grace, namely, "that Christ's life
overcame my death in his death, that his obedience blotted out my sin in his
suffering, that his love destroyed my hell in his forsakenness. This sign and
promise of my salvation will not lie to me or deceive me. It is God who has
said it."[619]

Thus the sign is not an empty word that points to some other sort of
activity and is fulfilled by it. Granted, it is an "external word of God, spoken
by a priest," but at the same time it is "a visible sign of divine intent, to which
we should cling with a staunch faith." There "your God, Christ himself,
deals, speaks, and works with you through the priest. What happens is not
human work or words." The sacraments are a "sign and testimony." "Christ's
life has taken your death, his obedience your sin, his love your hell, upon
themselves and overcome them." In the words of the sacraments, God speaks,
as does Christ himself, communicating divine life in the Word. "Moreover,
through the same sacraments you are included and made one with the saints,
so that they die with you in Christ, bear sin, and vanquish hell."[620]

As a pledge, the sacramental Word is not a promise of heavenly blessings to
be fulfilled sometime, somewhere; it is—in the literal sense—communication
of the divine-human life given by the Crucified and Risen One. His image is
not just a devotional picture that is modeled for me at a certain distance; it is
"built in." The communicants all become one body and members of Christ,
helping the individual to conquer sin, death, and hell; "in that hour the work
of love and the communion of saints are earnestly and mightily active."[621]
Such a common life in Christ and in the communion of saints begins in the
Sacrament. There "the priest gave me the holy body of Christ, which is a sign
and promise of the communion of all angels and saints that they love me,
provide and pray for me, suffer and die with me, bear my sin, and overcome
hell." "The divine sign does not deceive me."[622] The divine sign is not simply
the word of a priest, not just a biblical word of promise, but a Word that
imparts salvation.

618. *WA* 2:esp. 692–95 (= *BoA* 1:168–71); *LW* 42:107–12.
619. *WA* 2:693.7–13 (= *BoA* 1:169.16–23); *LW* 42:109
620. *WA* 2:692.28–38 (= *BoA* 1:168.40–169.10); *LW* 42:108–9.
621. *WA* 2:695.20–24 (= *BoA* 1:171.30–34); *LW* 42:112.
622. *WA* 2:694.22–27 (= *BoA* 1:170.31–35); *LW* 42:111.

As such, the sign is to be accepted in faith; otherwise the miracle of communion with Christ will not take place: "Faith must be present for a firm reliance and cheerful venturing on such signs and promises of God." One must cling to the divine sign "with a staunch faith as to a good staff . . . or a lantern by which one is to find one's way." In the Sacrament, the believer finds "a sign and a promise from God with which he can exercise and strengthen his belief that he has been called into Christ's image and to his benefits."[623]

Christ's image is *the* sign toward which faith is directed.[624] The sacraments bear witness to Christ; therefore they are "sure and appointed signs," tested by the faithful. Thus we can practice our faith on them. We should therefore learn "what the sacraments are, what purpose they serve, and how they are to be used."

In his sermon from 1519, Luther also gives instructions on how we are to use the sacraments. The contrast with the rule set up by CA 13 is obvious. Luther is not content with the insight conferred by the sign as the means for awakening and strengthening faith. It is the signs that show and act; they promise "Christ . . . with all his blessing, which he himself is." They destroy sin, death, and hell; "that happens in us through Christ if we use the sacraments properly." In the perils of death we are sustained by the sign. "It points to Christ and his image. . . . God promised and in his sacraments he gave me a sure sign of his grace."[625]

The sign in the sacrament is the Christ who is present and active in the believer. This insight was not just an expression of the young Luther in his early sermon, or in the message of the "joyous exchange," from 1520; it accompanied him through the years of the conflict over the sacraments. We found it in his expositions of the doctrine of justification and ultimately in his teaching on the Lord's Supper.[626] His statement in a sermon of April 7, 1527, comes out of the context of the struggle over the Lord's Supper: "We have one sacrament that completes them all; it is Christ and him crucified, . . ."[627] In the sacraments we are not dealing with signs that signify something else; we have to do with Christ himself, who became man, was crucified, and rose again. "The whole Christ is in the flesh. We grasp no other God than the one who is in that man, who came down to us." "That God and man are one person—this is the mighty work and wonder of God, which makes all reason

623. *WA* 2:693.30–31, 692.38–693.2, 694.18–19 (= *BoA* 1:169.40–170.1, 169.9–12, 170.26–27); *LW* 42:110, 108–9.

624. On the following, see *WA* 2:694.33ff. (= *BoA* 1:171.3ff.); *LW* 42:111.

625. *WA* 2:695.7–10, 693.7–9 (= *BoA* 1:171.16–19, 169.16–19); *LW* 42:111, 109.

626. In *The Babylonian Captivity* (*WA* 6:511.34ff. [= *BoA* 1:442.30ff.]; *LW* 36:35), Luther established the link between Christology and the doctrine of the Sacrament once and for all: "Thus, what is true in regard to Christ is also true in regard to the Sacrament."

627. *WA* 25:411.13ff.

foolish and to which alone faith must cling." This faith lives from the sacraments, and the sacraments maintain it: "There stands the common article of our faith, that Christ's flesh is full of divinity, full of eternal good, life, and salvation, and he who takes a bite of it takes to himself therewith eternal good, life, full salvation, and all that is in this flesh."[628]

628. *WA* 20:727.5–6, 23:141.33, 143.1, 251.20–23; *LW* 37:62, 63, 129–30.

POSTSCRIPT

At the end of a long life sustained by gratitude and respect for Martin Luther, I want to subscribe to the confession that he made at the end of the introduction to the *Confession Concerning Christ's Supper* (*BoA* 345.10–11).

Luther wishes "to confess all articles of my faith against this and all other new heresies so that they will not be able to boast now or after my death that Luther was on their side, as they have already done in some writings."

The articles themselves come from the time between Saint Martin's Day of 1529 (ibid., 353.22–23) and early the following summer. They contain theological statements of prime importance.

One who has traveled a long way with Luther has to thank many people who were guides and companions along the way. Above all, my thanks are due to my beloved colleague and successor, Gerhard Müller, along with his assistants and collaborators. Among them I mention particularly my student, Dr. Hans-Ulrich Hofmann, who has provided student readers with an indispensable introduction to both parts of this work through his index of the sources cited.

Erlangen, Christmas 1977   W. Maurer

INDEXES

INDEX OF BIBLE REFERENCES

See also Index of Persons and Places, esp. Luther, Martin; and Melanchthon, Philipp.

INDEX OF CONFESSIONS AND SOURCES

INDEX OF PERSONS AND PLACES

INDEX OF SUBJECTS

See also Index of Confessions and Sources, esp. the relevant articles of the Augsburg Confession.